Grammar in Action

Studies in Language and Social Interaction (SLSI)
ISSN 1879-3983

Studies in Language and Social Interaction is a series which continues the tradition of *Studies in Discourse and Grammar*, but with a new focus. It aims to provide a forum for research on grammar, understood broadly, in its natural home environment, spoken interaction. The assumption underlying the series is that the study of language as it is actually used in social interaction provides the foundation for understanding how the patterns and regularities we think of as grammar emerge from everyday communicative needs. The editors welcome language-related research from a range of different methodological traditions, including conversation analysis, interactional linguistics, and discourse-functional linguistics.

For an overview of all books published in this series, please see
benjamins.com/catalog/slsi

Editors

Sandra A. Thompson
University of California, Santa Barbara, USA

Elizabeth Couper-Kuhlen
University of Helsinki, Finland

Editorial Board

Peter Auer
University of Freiburg, Germany

Galina Bolden
Rutgers University, USA

Arnulf Deppermann
Institut für Deutsche Sprache, Germany

Paul Drew
University of York, UK

Barbara A. Fox
University of Colorado, USA

Makoto Hayashi
Nagoya University, Japan

Marja-Liisa Helasvuo
University of Turku, Finland

K.K. Luke
Nanyang Technological University, Singapore

Volume 37

Grammar in Action. Building comprehensive grammars of talk-in-interaction
Edited by Jakob Steensig, Maria Jørgensen, Jan Lindström, Nicholas Mikkelsen,
Karita Suomalainen and Søren Sandager Sørensen

Grammar in Action

Building comprehensive grammars
of talk-in-interaction

Edited by

Jakob Steensig
Aarhus University

Maria Jørgensen
Aarhus University

Jan Lindström
University of Helsinki

Nicholas Mikkelsen
Aarhus University

Karita Suomalainen
Åbo Akademi University

Søren Sandager Sørensen
University of Agder

John Benjamins Publishing Company
Amsterdam / Philadelphia

The paper used in this publication meets the minimum requirements of the American National Standard for Information Sciences – Permanence of Paper for Printed Library Materials, ANSI z39.48-1984.

DOI 10.1075/slsi.37

Cataloging-in-Publication Data available from Library of Congress:
LCCN 2025003925 (PRINT) / 2025003926 (E-BOOK)

ISBN 978 90 272 2008 0 (HB)
ISBN 978 90 272 4489 5 (E-BOOK)

© 2025 – John Benjamins B.V.
No part of this book may be reproduced in any form, by print, photoprint, microfilm, or any other means, without written permission from the publisher.

John Benjamins Publishing Company · https://benjamins.com

Table of contents

CHAPTER 1. Grammar in action: Social interaction as a basis for a comprehensive grammar?   1
Jakob Steensig, Maria Jørgensen, Jan Lindström, Nicholas Mikkelsen, Karita Suomalainen & Søren Sandager Sørensen

SECTION 1. **From Action to Grammar**

CHAPTER 2. On granularity in grammar and action   26
Barbara A. Fox & Chase Wesley Raymond

CHAPTER 3. 'Idea-Suggestions' in an interactional grammar: Sequential organization and grammatical formats   47
Elizabeth Couper-Kuhlen & Sandra A. Thompson

CHAPTER 4. Grammatical formats of requests for immediate actions: Observations on Danish talk-in-interaction   78
Jakob Steensig

CHAPTER 5. Structurally 'incomplete' social action formats in the grammar of talk-in-interaction? The case of deontic infinitives in spoken German   116
Alexandra Gubina

CHAPTER 6. Responses to specifying WH-questions, and their place in a comprehensive grammar of interactional Danish   155
Maria Jørgensen

CHAPTER 7. Parenthesis in storytelling in Danish talk-in-interaction   192
Nicholas Mikkelsen

SECTION 2. **From Grammar to Action**

CHAPTER 8. The use of past tense formats in German talk-in-interaction   226
Sophia Fiedler

CHAPTER 9. Second-person singular imperatives in Finnish everyday conversations: Multifunctionality and routinization of grammatical formats   264
Karita Suomalainen

CHAPTER 10. Copula variation in Danish and the intertwined
nature of grammar 301
Søren Sandager Sørensen

CHAPTER 11. An interactional grammar of insubordination:
The case of French *si* 'if'-clauses 332
Simona Pekarek Doehler & Anne-Sylvie Horlacher

CHAPTER 12. Action formation, projection, and participation framework:
Pseudoclefts in Swedish talk-in-interaction 366
Sofie Henricson & Jan Lindström

CHAPTER 13. Other-extensions in Italian: A case *of* and *for*
Collaborative Grammar 392
Virginia Calabria

CHAPTER 14. Discussion: Where are we now and what are the next steps
toward an Interactional Grammar? 421
Jakob Steensig, Maria Jørgensen, Jan Lindström,
Karita Suomalainen & Søren Sandager Sørensen

Index 439

CHAPTER 1

Grammar in action

Social interaction as a basis for a comprehensive grammar?

Jakob Steensig[1], Maria Jørgensen[1], Jan Lindström[2],
Nicholas Mikkelsen[1], Karita Suomalainen[3]
& Søren Sandager Sørensen[4]
[1] Aarhus University | [2] University of Helsinki | [3] Åbo Akademi University
| [4] University of Agder

In this chapter, we introduce the background for the studies in this volume.
We review the treatment of grammar in Conversation Analysis and
Interactional Linguistics and introduce the basic concepts in this analytical
approach. We then discuss how interactional perspectives may relate to
grammar writing, with examples from previous research and implications
for future studies. We conclude this introduction with an overview of the
chapters.

Keywords: grammar, action, talk-in-interaction, social action format,
Interactional Linguistics, Conversation Analysis, language description,
methodology, embodied conduct, emergence

This volume investigates how analyses of actions in social interaction may contribute to grammar writing and, ultimately, addresses establishing comprehensive grammars of talk-in-interaction. The authors are interactional linguists and conversation analysts who study grammatical phenomena in interactional data in Danish, English, Finnish, French, German, Italian, and Swedish. Unlike earlier studies in Interactional Linguistics (IL) and Conversation Analysis (CA), the authors do not limit themselves to describing and analyzing such phenomena, they also discuss how their descriptions and analyses may be included in a comprehensive grammar of talk-in-interaction, and they make concrete suggestions about the organization of such grammars.

The title of the volume, *Grammar in Action*, reflects the attempt by all authors in the book to link grammatical formats to social actions in interaction. The first

https://doi.org/10.1075/slsi.37.01ste
© 2025 John Benjamins Publishing Company

part of the volume, *From Action to Grammar*, contains chapters that take specific actions as their point of departure and consider the grammatical means by which they are accomplished, and the second part, *From Grammar to Action*, starts with grammatical formats and links these to social actions.

In this introduction, we discuss the premises underlying our attempt to build an Interactional Grammar. We begin by reflecting on what a grammar is and how the chapters in this book relate to other approaches to grammar writing (Section 1). We then introduce the methodological foundations of this volume, CA and IL (Section 2). Subsequently, we outline some important contributions to grammar writing that can be found in these traditions and account for central concepts that have informed the thinking of the authors of this book (Section 3). We conclude the introduction with a discussion on how this volume came into being and give an overview of the chapters (Section 4).

1. What is a grammar?

Grammar as a concept or a goal of analyses has not been in focus in much IL and CA research. And, conversely, grammar writing has not used the methodologies of IL or CA to any larger extent. We will, therefore, in this section clarify what we mean with the concept "grammar" and specify which types of grammars we relate our endeavor to.

1.1 Different types of comprehensive grammars

A grammar (book) is a description of the aspects of a specific language that are considered the grammar of that language, including syntax, morphology, and phonology. Grammar is often understood in contrast to the *lexicon* of a language. The lexicon lists and accounts for the content words of a language, whereas the grammar deals with systematic features that may be used to construct words and link words together. Historically, grammars used to be prescriptive, but there are grammars of many different types, designed for a variety of audiences and purposes. The ones which are relevant for this volume are grammars that are *descriptive* and *comprehensive*. The term "descriptive" stands in contrast to prescriptive grammars, of, e.g., a grammar for a standard, written language. By "comprehensive", we mean grammars that account for most aspects of the structures of the language (Rice 2006), such as phonology, morphology, parts of speech, syntax, and possibly also the meaning and use of these structures.

The languages that are analyzed in this book all have long traditions for written language, and several comprehensive reference grammars exist for these languages. The individual chapters of the book will refer to the most relevant ones for the languages analyzed in the chapters. In almost all cases, these grammars are based on written language, in some cases supplemented with examples from spoken language. The grammars often exhibit a "written language bias", privileging structures and insights from idealized monologic and atemporal language use (Linell 2005). Some grammars make systematic use of language corpora, mostly from written sources, others use introspection, possibly combined with (focused) searches in written, and sometimes also spoken, sources.

A different tradition for grammar writing is found in what is sometimes referred to as "descriptive grammars", often of "undescribed or lesser described languages" (Ameka, Dench & Evans 2006b). When describing a language without a written tradition, the grammarian needs to document the language in the process of writing the grammar (besides learning it to some extent). This means attending to and collecting spoken data. The descriptive grammar tradition uses elicitation techniques with informants who speak the language, in order to discover patterns and confirm or disconfirm hypotheses about the structures of the language. Word lists and narratives are collected as well, and all these data are used to construct grammatical descriptions and often also as documentation, both for the reliability of the grammar and for future use (Evans & Dench 2006). However, only in rare cases (see below) do such grammars focus on interactional patterns. Excerpts are usually presented as if they were said by one speaker, that is, isolated from the interactional context.

The grammars that are envisaged or suggested in this book differ, in a number of ways, from both the reference grammars based on written language and the descriptive grammars based on spoken language. The authors of the chapters in this book are already speakers of the languages they analyze, so they use their insights as competent interactants in their interpretations and analyses; they do not have to collect word lists or do elicitations to understand the basic patterns of the language. The data corpora used for the chapters in this book are collections of recordings of people interacting in their daily lives. The data have not been collected specifically for the purpose of grammar writing but are instances of language use in naturally occurring interactions (Mondada 2013). This means that there may be grammatical formats in the language that are not represented in the data, but also that formats occur that the researcher would not think of eliciting. The fact that all data used in this book are interactional has consequences for the analytic procedures: the reactions from other interactants to a focus utterance give a window into participants' own understanding of what the utterance does, and this "next turn proof procedure" (Sacks, Schegloff & Jefferson 1974: 729) becomes an important basis for the analysis of the grammatical formats that are considered (more on the methodologies of IL and CA below).

1.2 Towards an interactional grammar

The chapters in this book all exemplify and document how the analysis of interaction may broaden and challenge perspectives of other grammar traditions. In order to give a taste of some of the features that the interactional perspective provides for grammar writing and to introduce the reader to the use of data excerpts, we will show two brief examples here.

In Excerpts (1)–(2), we encounter the phrases *di non buttar via il cibo* 'not to throw the food away' (in Italian), and *ikk så hurtig* 'not so fast' (in Danish), both produced by single speakers without being part of a clause or other larger structure in that speaker's turn. These are, thus, phrasal utterances that function as stand-alone items. A grammar of talk-in-interaction should be able to account for such structures, both their internal formats and the contexts of their use. Any grammar of Italian and Danish would categorize the words according to their parts of speech and their morphological properties, and they would account for the types and structures of the phrases. The more extensive grammars may, additionally, categorize such structures as 'non-clausal sentences' or the like (see also Steensig this volume). But, in addition to this, an interactional grammar explains the systematic properties that make it possible to understand what the phrasal utterances are doing when used in an interaction context.

Excerpts (1) and (2) exemplify this with (simplified) excerpts from the chapters of the book. The transcription conventions are the ones designed by Gail Jefferson (Jefferson 2004; Hepburn & Bolden 2012). Embodied actions are transcribed using Mondada's (2018; 2019) conventions. Focus lines have been provided with Leipzig Glossing (Comrie, Haspelmath & Bickel 2015) for additional linguistic clarity. These conventions are used throughout the volume unless otherwise indicated in the chapters.

In Excerpt (1), in Italian, from Calabria's chapter (this volume), ANG's infinitival phrase in line 4 is designed to be an extension of GIO's turn in lines 1–3, by reusing the structure *di* 'to' + infinitive, found in lines 1 and 2, fitting the argument structure of *chiedere* 'to ask' in line 1.

Excerpt 1. *di non buttar* **'not to throw'** (Mi13PRO2-42 18:38-18:51), **from Calabria, this volume, Excerpt (1)**

```
01 GIO: >io gli chiedo< di mettere a posto il tavolo,
        I ask them to tidy the table,
02       di non sbriciolare per terra, e di non rovesciare
         not to drop crumbs on the floor, and not to spill
03       l'aqua.
         the water.
```

Chapter 1. Grammar in action 5

```
04 ANG: di non buttar    via il      cibo.
        to not throw.INF away DEF.ART.M food(M)
        not to throw the food away.
05 GIO: e di non- (.)
        and not to-
```

ANG's extension uses an argument structure that would be described in a section on syntax in most grammars, but, given that the grammar we envisage describes language as it is used in interaction, the grammar will also have to explain how this structure can be used to construct collaborative constructions. Calabria (this volume) points to this as the Collaborative Grammar aspect of the grammar.

Excerpt (2) is in Danish, from Steensig's chapter (this volume). Here, the adverb phrase *ikk så hurtig* 'not so fast' (line 7) comes in a context where Sisse (SIS) is guiding Lina (LIN), who is trying to find something on Sisse's smartphone.

Excerpt 2. *ikk så hurtig* **'not so fast' (AULing: haarfarvning_1), from Steensig, this volume, Excerpt (6)**

```
04      %(2.1)
   lin  %1. thumb is moving on phone screen-->
05 SIS: >prøv lige  å  vent<.
        >try LIGE and wait<. ((wait a moment))
06      (.)
07 SIS: ikk så hurtig_
        not so fast
        not so fast_
08      (0.6)%
   lin     -->%
09 SIS: *n:*% det der (.) opslag=
        *n:* that (.) posting=
   lin      %lifts 1. thumb from phone-->>
```

Sisse first directs Lina to wait using an imperative format in *prøv lige å vent* 'wait a moment' (line 5). This does not result in Lina stopping her movements, and in line 7, Sisse pursues a reaction with the adverb phrase *ikk så hurtig* 'not so fast', which Lina then responds to by lifting her thumb from the phone (line 9). The reason why this adverb phrase is understood as performing an action on its own, and not being a continuation of the imperative or any other utterance, is that it is a reaction to the physical movements the co-participant is doing (line 4 and onwards) and to the non-reaction following the directive in line 5. Steensig (this volume) calls the format a "phrasal action-guiding request" and points to the need of describing both its internal structure and the interactional context in which it occurs.

Excerpts (1) and (2) illustrate formal properties of talk-in-interaction that are different from non-interactional language use: Coherent utterances may be produced by more than one speaker, and people can produce phrasal and lexical utterances that have their own independent function and meaning. They also point to the importance of including the interaction context in the categorization and explanations of these formal properties, and, potentially, also the necessity to include a description of nonverbal features in grammatical descriptions. This is just one example of features that the interactional context makes it necessary to consider. The comprehensive grammars of talk-in-interaction that we envisage in this volume aim at including such features in systematic ways into the grammar. As far as we know, no comprehensive grammar has yet done this consistently. However, certain grammars and other linguistic descriptions have covered some distance towards this goal, and we will consider some of those in what follows.

1.3   Inspiration from earlier grammars and other linguistic research

Some parts of descriptive grammar writing (Ameka, Dench & Evans 2006a) have come some way towards what we are trying to do in this volume. As mentioned above, talk-in-interaction may be used as one source of information about the grammar of the investigated languages. To various extents, they attempt to incorporate interactional structures. Ameka (1991), on Ewe, contains a part focusing on phenomena like routines for addressing and greeting people and interjections, which have some interactional and sequential aspects. Mihas (2017) is a work that accompanies a reference grammar (Mihas 2015), on Alto Perené, and focuses on the "conversational structures" with parts dedicated to epistemics, repair, turn-taking and nonverbal resources like gaze and gesture. Rüsch (2020), on Acholi, and Sicoli (2020), on Zapotec, also focus on interactional resources and structures like repair and nonverbal resources in a specific language, mainly from an anthropological perspective.

There are also a few comprehensive grammars that are based on corpus analysis and, to some extent, also account for interactional patterns. *The Longman Grammar of Spoken and Written English* (Biber & Quirk 2012) contains a chapter on "The Grammar of Conversation" (pp. 1031–1120), which treats structures and formats that are specific to conversational language. These are, however, treated apart from the rest of the grammar, and this differs from what we aim for with this volume: a grammar that truly integrates the formats and functions of talk-in-interaction in a structural account.

The grammar that comes the closest to our aim is *The Comprehensive Grammar of Finnish* (*Iso suomen kielioppi*, Hakulinen et al. 2004). It includes thorough accounts of structures in talk-in-interaction, with examples taken from interactional data in Finnish. These are integrated in parts of the overall grammar, but not consistently, and the grammar also considers written language. This means that the account of the interactional features becomes a supplement to the overall description of the grammar of Finnish. The grammar we are aiming for takes talk-in-interaction as its exclusive basis and considers the entire grammar of that language mode.

The Danish project *samtalegrammatik.dk* (DanTIN 2024) is an attempt to create a grammar that is based solely on a corpus of naturally occurring interactions. It is a web-based grammar sharing the aims of the chapters in this volume, and the work with this grammar has been the point of departure of several authors in this volume (see Section 4.1 on how the volume came into being). However, this grammar is under construction and, therefore, far from comprehensive at this point in time.

2. The methodological foundations of the volume

The methodological foundations of this volume are Conversation Analysis (CA) and Interactional Linguistics (IL). Both entail detailed, moment-by-moment sequential analysis of interaction, considering the participants' verbal and embodied behavior in the situated, material environment.

Conversation Analysis strives to describe everyday social interaction as an orderly phenomenon, analyzing recordings and transcriptions of naturally occurring interaction to uncover how interactants produce social meaning. At its core, CA assumes that there is "order at all points" (Sacks 1984: 22): since interactants need to work together to reach their goals in interaction, they organize and format their actions in sedimented, recognizable ways, displaying to each other their understanding of what is going on in the interaction. This public display allows analysts to reconstruct the meaning-making tools and principles employed by the interactants. Using an emic, radically empirical approach and a rigorous methodology, involving close transcription of data, observations of potentially relevant phenomena, compilations of instances of such phenomena, and a thorough analysis of the environment of the phenomenon, conversation analysts have uncovered key organizing principles of interaction, such as the mechanics of turn-taking (Sacks et al. 1974) and sequence organization (Schegloff 2007). Additionally, a large number of sedimented uses of specific linguistic and embodied structures which interactants use to carry out recognizable social actions (e.g., Levinson 2013) have been uncovered. These practices, or *social action formats* (Fox 2007), are language-specific, though many social actions as such have been shown to be relevant across languages, in some cases employing similar resources.

CA has never had any particular interest in language at heart (Couper-Kuhlen & Selting 2018: 6), although attention to the usefulness of linguistic resources in organizing interaction has been noticed since the beginning (Sacks et al. 1974).

Interactional linguistics (IL), on the other hand, focuses specifically on how linguistic resources are used in conversational interaction. The term originated in the early 2000s (Couper-Kuhlen & Selting 2001; Selting & Couper-Kuhlen 2000, 2001) as a cover term for separate approaches to research on, among other things, grammar in interaction (Ford, Fox & Thompson 1996; Ochs, Schegloff & Thompson 1996; Thompson, Fox & Couper-Kuhlen 2015) and the prosody and phonetics of conversation (Couper-Kuhlen & Selting 1996; French & Local 1983; Local, Kelly & Wells 1986; Ogden 2021). The main premise of IL is that "linguistic categories are designed for service in the organization of social interaction and must be described and explained accordingly" (Couper-Kuhlen & Selting 2018:14–15). For many interactional linguistic researchers, this is done using CA-informed analyses of particular linguistic structures.

3. Contributions from Conversation Analysis and Interactional Linguistics to grammar writing

Right from its inception, Interactional Linguistics (IL) has focused on linguistic phenomena that may be called grammatical. We will first review some of the sources that have inspired us in this volume and then present some of the foundational concepts concerning grammar and analysis of grammatical issues that have been discussed within IL.

3.1 Interactional Linguistic contributions to grammar writing

The first more substantial linguistic work to deal with questions related to the use of grammar in interaction was the aptly named collected volume *Grammar and Interaction*, edited by Ochs, Schegloff and Thompson (1996). The contributors of the volume approach grammar as "organizations of practices — which underlie the organization of social life" (Ochs, Schegloff & Thompson 1996:2). They argue against the view in which grammar and its order was understood as a self-enclosed organization and encourage rethinking "what sort of thing grammar might be thought to be and how it might be configured" (Ochs, Schegloff & Thompson 1996:28). The papers in the volume explore the relationship between turn-construction and syntax, the creation of interactional units in conversation, the role of grammar in repair practices, the use of specific grammatical formats in particular type of activities, the use of grammar in projection of the turn and its ending, and the use of a specific grammatical category, particles, as part of different social actions. Another collected volume with great influence is *Studies in Interactional Linguistics*, edited by Couper-Kuhlen and Selting (2001), which, with its 20 chapters, shows the large body of work that was done within interactional linguistics in only a few years across several countries and languages.

One of the topics that has received remarkable attention is syntactic structuring from the viewpoint of language use and the emergence of syntactic relations in talk-in-interaction. Helasvuo (2001) studies the emergence of syntactic units in Finnish conversations, focusing on the clause core as the locus of syntactic structuring. Further, she shows that in spoken discourse, there are syntactic structures that cannot be found in grammars based on written language; an example of such a structure is a free syntactic unit, the free NP. Tao's (1996) study on Mandarin conversation challenges some basic syntactic notions developed from sentence-level data, showing that Mandarin spoken discourse syntax consists of structures that do not support dominant ideas present in the study of syntax. Syntactic structures typical for spoken discourse are also in focus in the follow-up volume *Syntax and Lexis in Conversation: Studies on the use of linguistic resources in talk-in-interaction*, edited by Hakulinen and Selting (2005). The edited volumes by Laury and Suzuki (2011) and Maschler et al. (2020) both deal with complex syntax from an emergent point of view and from a cross-linguistic perspective; the former focuses on clausal subordination and interclausal relations, the latter on the on-line emergence of clause-combining patterns as well as their routinization and sedimentation.

The role and relevance of traditionally accepted linguistic units for the analysis of naturally occurring talk have been questioned in interactional linguistic work. The edited volumes *Units of Talk − Units of Action* (Szczepek Reed & Raymond 2013) and *Usage-based and Typological Approaches to Linguistic Units* (Ono, Laury & Suzuki 2021) study the nature of units in actual usage in a range of languages, suggesting that an emergent and interactional view provides a better foundation for understanding the patterns and regularities of everyday language use. It has also been suggested that formulaicity is a central feature of everyday grammar, which has led to explorations of so-called fixed expressions as basic utterance-building resources for interaction (Laury & Ono 2020). Some studies have also paid special attention to the prosodic-phonetic chunking of language (see, e.g., Tao 1996 and Barth-Weingarten 2016 on intonation units).

Some collected volumes and special issues have addressed phenomena that come to the fore when language is studied in the here-and-now of social interaction. For example, the volume *Temporality in Interaction* (Deppermann & Günthner 2015) focuses on the aspect of time and projection in turn and action construction, and the special issue *Turn continuation in a cross-linguistic perspective* (Couper-Kuhlen & Ono 2007) presents important definitional work on increments to turns. Turning a bit more towards semantics and pragmatics, the volume *The Morality of Knowledge in Conversation* (Stivers, Mondada & Steensig 2011) elaborates on matters of epistemics and how epistemics affects turn design and sequential progressivity. Further, the collection *The Grammar-Body Interface in Social Interaction* (Pekarek Doehler, Keevallik & Li 2022) explores multimodal aspects of turn construction, focusing on the interplay of language structure and embodied acts.

The relationship between turn-construction and grammar has been explored in some languages in rather extensive ways. Steensig (2001) is an account of turn-construction methods in Danish, linking turn-taking to grammar and prosody. Lindström (2008) takes a similar perspective on Swedish, adding an interactional approach to parts of speech. Both aim to develop models that could be used to build an "interactional grammar" in respective languages. Recently, Steensig et al. (2023) have continued working on the grammar of Danish talk-in-interaction and explored the possibilities of developing a comprehensive grammar of talk-in-interaction for a specific language based on descriptions of social actions. Focusing on specific sequential locations, Thompson, Fox and Couper-Kuhlen (2015), identify and account for different formal categories of responding turn types in American English conversation.

Finally, there are a number of volumes that focus on either a specific grammatical category or a grammatical element, such as subordination (Laury & Suzuki 2011), imperatives (Sorjonen, Raevaara & Couper-Kuhlen 2017) or certain particles (Heritage & Sorjonen 2018; Betz et al. 2021), exploring what the category looks like from the point of view of talk-in-interaction.

The volumes mentioned above build on analyses of interactional data from a wide range of languages. However, they rarely perform explicit comparison between languages, and they do not attempt to reach any kind of typological representativity. The approach of those volumes, as well as of the present one (see Section 4.1 below), has been to invite researchers with expertise on the interactional study of specific areas to write about the languages they happen to study. A series of studies originated at the Max Planck Institute for Psycholinguistics in Nijmegen, The Netherlands, have taken a more typological approach. Based on research in CA and IL, they have coded and compared interactional data from a range of languages, including lesser described ones. The focus has been on interactional structures – such as turn-taking (Stivers et al. 2009), repair (Dingemanse & Enfield 2015), and person reference (Enfield & Stivers 2007) –, specific formats, such as interjections (Dingemanse, Torreira & Enfield 2013; Dingemanse 2024), as well as on actions and sequences of actions, e.g., questions and answers (Enfield, Stivers & Levinson 2010), and request and recruitment sequences (Floyd, Rossi & Enfield 2020).

These studies have expanded the linguistic horizon of IL, and they have raised central questions about the universality and language specificity of particular interactional phenomena: Do certain interjections have universal commonalities (such as *huh*, and more?), are turn-taking norms universal, can the 'same' actions be found and compared across languages? This volume does not venture into such comparisons. Our approach has been to clarify, as precisely as possible, how grammatical phenomena are linked to interaction and to explore how this can be reflected in comprehensive grammars. This is relevant to typological studies in a different way: If patterns of talk-in-interaction are to be compared between languages, it is beneficial to know how they function inside the languages that are to be compared.

3.2 Central concepts in Interactional Linguistics concerning grammar

As shown above, IL has made extensive contributions to the study of grammar by expanding our idea of what belongs to grammar and how it can be investigated. Studies within IL focus on how linguistic resources are used to create meaning and perform actions in interaction in a real-time perspective. In this view, grammar is connected to *action formation*, which Schegloff described in the following way: "how are the resources of the language, the body, the environment of the interaction, and position in the interaction fashioned into conformations designed to be, and to be recognized by recipients as, particular actions" (Schegloff 2007:xiv). Another conversational procedure that grammar is also closely linked to is *turn construction*, as grammatical formats are produced in turns-at-talk in real time. This fact is important to understand both in action formation (Levinson 2013) and the interface between grammar and interaction (Sacks, et al. 1974; Schegloff 1996). While these perspectives permeate all CA and IL research on grammatical features, researchers use quite different terms and perspectives to label and describe the entities in focus. We will briefly account for our understanding of the most important of these concepts, many of which are used in this volume. By doing this, we hope to contribute to the clarification of concepts and the terminology used.

One of the key concepts that links together grammatical patterns and social action is the term *social action format*, coined by Fox (originally in Fox 2000, quoted in Fox 2007). She describes these formats as "grammatical formats for sequentially-specific actions" (Fox 2007:304), using the difference between the formats for questioning and answering as examples of this fundamental position-sensitive nature of linguistic forms (see Schegloff 2007; Thompson et al. 2015). Steensig et al. (2023) attempt to formalize the social action formats, defining a social action format as "a limited and predictable string of words with specific prosodic properties and accompanying embodiment", which "occupies a specific sequential position" and "is used for performing a specific social action" (p.121).

This formalization is further used to build grammatical models, which are named after the actions they perform, and which include both an "external" syntax (see Anward & Nordberg 2005), reflecting, across speakers, the sequential context in which the format occurs, and an "internal" syntax, describing the order and shape of elements within the turn's format itself.

Such a holistic view of grammatical formats has some affinities with analytic attempts in other usage-based language models, notably Construction Grammar, which considers constructions "intricate patterns containing several layers of information" (Fried & Östman 2004:19). These layers can deal with syntax, semantics, and pragmatics, including aspects of prosody, sequence organization, and discourse patterns. The notion of *construction* has in this view a theoretical status, referring to an abstracted pattern of regularities that can be found in users' instantiations of constructions, which are termed *constructs*. That is, a construction is a blueprint that speakers orient to and target in somewhat varied ways in real language use. This dialectic relation between particular instantiations and analytically necessary abstractions made out of them is clearly of interest for interactional linguistics and has led to some attempts to combine interactional and constructional analyses of patterns of interaction that meet patterns of grammar (see, e.g., Günthner & Imo 2006; Lindström 2025) and even to suggest a new, interactionally informed approach called Interactional Construction Grammar (Imo 2015). At the same time, there does not appear to be a consensus on how (abstract) constructions should be represented in more interaction-oriented Construction Grammar accounts, which shows that this side of the Construction Grammar tradition is still rather underdeveloped.

A more radical usage-based approach is advocated in explorations of grammar as an *emergent* phenomenon, emphasizing the relevance of real language instantiations and questioning the existence of a finite state grammar. Emergent grammar is, as Hopper (2011) puts it, constantly being negotiated and epiphenomenal to real language use and "consists not of sentences generated by rules, but of the linear on-line assembly of familiar fragments" (see also Hopper 1987; Auer & Pfänder 2011). In this view, grammatical structures do not exist in advance of the communicative setting but are instead seen as fluid and spontaneous products of interaction: they are elaborated in and by communication, in response to local interactional contingencies (Hopper 2011; Pekarek Doehler et al. 2020). This view of "grammar" and "grammatical structures" is very close to the view of IL; according to Couper-Kuhlen and Selting (2018:14–15), the most important premise of interactional linguistic research is that linguistic categories and structures are designed for service in the organization of social interaction. Similarly to emergent grammar, IL considers grammatical formats that occur in talk-in-interaction temporal and locally adaptive, interactionally achieved, and actively produced and reproduced in real time. Recently, the viewpoints of emergent grammar and IL have been brought together especially in the study of formulaic language in which the focus has been the emergence of so-called *fixed expressions*, prefabricated functional and structural units with which speakers operate to navigate interaction (see, e.g., Laury & Ono 2020).

Focusing on the emergent nature of grammar makes it relevant to treat grammatical formats as an online phenomenon. Auer (2005, 2009) has developed the notion of *online syntax* to describe the real-time emergence of syntactic structures in spoken interaction. Online syntax highlights the temporal aspect of spoken interaction: syntax is seen as dialogically emerging in time. The term *projection* describes the ability of an individual action or part of it to foreshadow another (Schegloff 1996; Goodwin 2002; Auer 2005); when the term is applied to syntactic structures, it refers to the ways in which the speaker creates expectations in the listener about how the syntactic pattern in a turn-constructional unit will unfold (Auer 2009: 4). Auer (2005: 14) argues that "syntax is a formal(ized) way of human language to make projection in time possible".

In online syntax, syntactic patterns are seen as emergent units of interaction: their temporal trajectory is defined by the interplay of projecting and projection-fulfilling phases (Auer 2009, 2023). One element in a speaker's turn opens up a multitude of possible continuations, but as the syntactical pattern unfolds, the array of projectable continuations will be more and more limited. Towards the closure of the so-called syntactic gestalt produced by the speaker, the final components will often become entirely predictable and recognized as unit-final elements by the recipient (Auer 2009: 4). These elements may, however, be expanded after a syntactic completion point (see, e.g., Ono & Couper-Kuhlen 2007 on increments). Projection at the linguistic level is also crucial for turn-taking, as it enables the prediction of possible turn completion points (Auer 2009: 4).

Finally, the notion of *action* is central to this volume and to many of the concepts we have discussed above. But what is an action? How can actions be categorized and delimited? The original approach in CA has been to refrain from making *a priori* definitions of actions: actions and their categorization need to be understood as the local accomplishments of language users, and the status of an utterance as performing a specific action is something that can be challenged and negotiated in interaction (Schegloff 1984). This view opens up to discovering actions that may not have a name in a culture but are still treated as specific actions by interactants, as shown in Pomerantz (1980) on "telling my side" or Schegloff (1996) on "confirming allusions". A different stance in IL has been to take broader categories as a point of departure, either building on what is treated in the next turn as the main job of an utterance (Levinson 2013) or building on the tendency to use similar linguistic formats for building specific actions (Couper-Kuhlen 2014).

The question of action formation and action ascription has recently been discussed thoroughly within CA and IL (for a recent overview, see Deppermann & Haugh 2022) and we aim not to enter into this discussion here. The policy of the present volume has been that authors use their own definitions or approaches and that they try to be as explicit about this as possible. Fox and Raymond (this volume) expands on how action can be understood when using the concept for grammar writing.

4. This volume

4.1 How the volume came into being

The primary idea behind this volume is rooted in the *Grammar in Everyday Life* research project, which ran from 2019 to 2023, funded by the Independent Research Fund Denmark. The main goal of this project was to test the possibility that thorough descriptions of social actions in interaction could be used as a basis for creating a grammar (see Steensig et al. 2023). In connection with this project, an international research workshop, *From Action to Grammar*, was held in Aarhus, Denmark, on August 18–19, 2022 (hybrid online). The participants were asked to present research on interactional phenomena with a focus on actions and grammar. The workshop participants were invited because they were doing grammar-relevant research in the realm of interaction studies, and we believed that a focus on grammar writing could be developed from their work. This turned out to be the case, and the present volume is the result of this work. The idea of this volume arose at the workshop, and after the presentations at the workshop, participants wrote first drafts for their chapters in the volume. In the revision process, authors were encouraged to make the grammar-writing perspective as explicit as possible. The result is, in our opinion, that the volume represents an important step towards making interactional linguistic research relevant for grammar writing and explorations of grammar.

The downside of how the volume came into being is that the languages represented are far from being typologically diverse. All languages are major European (and North American) languages, and the only language families represented are Indo-European and Finno-Ugric. This means that there are many grammatical phenomena of importance to languages of the world that are not represented. We still think that this is a good beginning, and we hope that the volume can inspire researchers working with other languages to focus more on the links between action, interaction, and grammar.

4.2 The chapters of the volume

The volume is divided into two sections. The first section is called "From Action to Grammar". It contains six chapters that all take a social action as their point of departure, in most cases by focusing on one specific action type and the different ways this action can be performed. The chapters in the second section, "From Grammar to Action", start with specific grammatical formats and relate them to the social actions they perform. This dual perspective, from action to grammar and from grammar to action, is recognized as offering adequate and complementary starting points for interactional linguistic queries (Couper-Kuhlen and Selting 2018). In all chapters, the authors discuss the implications of their findings for the structure and logic of a comprehensive grammar on the language they describe.

Fox and Raymond's chapter is a programmatic one, discussing what it means that actions in interaction can be described with different levels of detail, or granularity. They review earlier studies on three interactional phenomena in English and show how follow-up studies have revealed order at increasingly finer levels of granularity. Based on this, they claim that it will always be possible to find finer levels of granularity, which then poses a problem for grammar writing. A grammar will need "to make decisions on inclusion/exclusion criteria for the grammar in as systematic and defensible of ways as possible" (Fox & Raymond this volume: 40), while at the same time recognizing that other — and finer — levels of detail can be described. Without claiming to have found a final solution to this problem, Fox and Raymond exemplify how an extensive use of hyperlinks between different parts of the grammar, and to other grammars and descriptions, may be one way of dealing with this complexity.

Couper-Kuhlen and Thompson's chapter analyzes a specific subtype of Suggestions, "Idea-Suggestions", in American English, arguing that they are implemented by "social action formats" in the sense of Fox (2007). Apart from accounting for the syntactic and sequential aspects of this action, Couper-Kuhlen and Thompson present discovery procedures and criteria for finding, naming and delimiting social actions. They further discuss how to describe Idea-Suggestions in an Interactional Grammar of American English. They outline two possible paths for mapping the relationship between formats and actions, reflecting the two sections of the current book. The "onomasiological" one starts with the action in its home environment, and from there, it proceeds to describing the recurrent formats for doing the action. The other path, the "semasiological" one, starts with the formats and links them to all the actions that make use of those formats. The choice of either of these paths should be based on the target audience, and some considerations for this are suggested.

The third chapter by Jakob Steensig analyzes three formats — embodied-only formats, phrasal formats, and modal verb formats — for requesting immediate action in Danish. As was the case with the Idea-Suggestions in Couper-Kuhlen and Thompson's chapter, it is argued that the formats in this chapter are "social action formats" (Fox 2007) that should be described in a comprehensive grammar of Danish talk-in-interaction. The grammar in question is *samtalegrammatik.dk* (DanTIN 2024), which is being constructed as a webpage as the chapter is written. The chapter limits itself to discussing how each of the three formats should be represented in the formats part of the grammar. Steensig proposes that embodied features should be included and described in the grammar. He further shows how *external*, or inter-unit, syntactic descriptions of the analyzed formats might be presented systematically, and he discusses and challenges the relevance of a number of concepts and categorizations from grammars that are not based on analyses of interaction.

Alexandra Gubina's chapter focuses on a particular social action format in German talk-in-interaction, deontic infinitives, which is used to implement a specific directive action, that of implementing instructions, based on normative rules. One main point is that "structurally incomplete" formats, which can be shown to perform social actions, have been largely neglected or at least down-played in earlier grammars, and that they deserve proper treatment in a grammar of talk-in-interaction. In Gubina's collection of deontic infinitives, almost all of them are used to perform instructions. After reviewing the rare exceptions to this, the chapter takes us through the different sequential contexts, in which the action of instructing based on a normative rule can be evoked and discusses the affordances of the specific grammatical construction, the deontic infinitive, compared to other formats for doing similar actions. Based on the analyses, Gubina argues that a comprehensive grammar must include not only lexical, morpho-syntactic, and sequential aspects, but also multimodal features of the environment, agency, as well as epistemic and deontic positions. She further highlights the practical use for the teaching of German as a second language of a grammar that describes the sequential logic of a format, rather than operating with general notions of politeness.

Maria Jørgensen's chapter reviews the consequences for grammar writing of her insights into the difference between phrasal and clausal responses to specifying *wh*-questions in Danish talk-in-interaction (Jørgensen 2024), according to which phrasal responses display sequential embeddedness and clausal responses index sequential detachment. The main part of the chapter presents models and implications for a position-sensitive grammar of the two response formats. It compares traditional topological clause models with more format-sensitive models for the internal syntax of the formats, and it proposes real-time sensitive models of the external syntax of the formats. The chapter also discusses how the social actions of *wh*-questions and their responses should be presented in the grammar, and it views some implications of this for a presentation of questions and responses more generally. In the concluding discussion, Jørgensen suggests that grammatical parasitism and minimality can be linked to specific social actions and sequential positions more generally.

The last chapter in the section "From Action to Grammar" by Nicholas Mikkelsen focuses on the adjustments that storytellers make to accommodate the reactions or lack of reactions on the part of recipients, specifically the parenthetical insertions into an otherwise projected continuation of the story. Mikkelsen analyzes two types of calibration that the parentheses are used for creating: early turn recalibration, where the focus is on establishing an understanding of the characters and the scene of the story, and late turn recalibration, aimed at ensuring recipients' affiliation with the conclusion of the story. The fact that the recalibrations are fundamentally sensitive to the negotiation of participation highlights the need for a "collaborative grammar", something which is also discussed by Calabria (this volume). Mikkelsen further details where and how this perspective and the descriptions of the parentheses in storytelling might fit into the structure of the earlier mentioned *samtalegrammatik.dk* grammar (DanTIN 2024).

The first chapter in the second section, "From Grammar to Action", by Sophia Fiedler, is about the use of past tense formats in German. German can express past tense with two different morphological means, a preterite form, as in 'I saw', and a present perfect form, as in 'I have seen', both translatable as 'I saw'. The difference between these two forms has earlier been described as mainly regional, or as a difference between modalities (written versus spoken). Fiedler examines the use of the two forms in first and third person of the verbs *meinen* 'to mean', *glauben* 'to believe' and *finden* 'to find' in a large corpus of German talk-in-interaction. Fiedler is able to show that the choice between the two past tenses, as well as the choice of using a past tense in the first place, is tied to the actions performed and, consequently, to the meaning-in-context of the verbs. She summarizes this by proposing a list of "constructions" and discusses how these findings can be included in a grammar of talk-in-interaction. She suggests and exemplifies different descriptions for different target groups of such a grammar.

The second chapter in this section by Karita Suomalainen analyzes the interactional use of seven verbs in the imperative in Finnish. She demonstrates how these verbs can be used in directive actions but are just as much used in fixed expressions and as particles, in which cases they are parts of other social actions, e.g., informings, storytellings, news deliveries, and assessments. When used in these contexts, the imperative verbs do not require compliance, they rather "recruit the recipient(s) in discursive tasks" (Suomalainen this volume: 296), preparing them for alignment and inviting them for "mutual sense making" (Suomalainen this volume: 296). Suomalainen argues that a grammar should pay full attention also to the non-directive uses of imperatives, and she presents a framework for a description of imperatives in a grammar that unites the types of uses and the social actions in a systematic way. She further argues that these insights can be used in the grammars of other languages than Finnish and exemplifies how these descriptions can be useful for second language teaching.

The third chapter in this section by Søren Sandager Sørensen is also about specific verb forms, this time in Danish. The chapter investigates variation in copula clauses, that is, clauses in which the verb *er* — 'to be' in the present tense — is used to tie together an item and a quality. The focus is on cases where the verb is audible, and sometimes stressed, and similar clauses where the verb is not pronounced. Sørensen explores the relationship between actions, specifically assessments, and the different versions of the verb, and finds that the choice of a particular version has action and turn-construction implications. The results are related to larger aspects of the grammar, and suggestions are made for how these can be included in the *samtalegrammatik.dk* grammar (DanTIN 2024).

In their chapter, Simona Pekarek Doehler and Anne-Sylvie Horlacher investigate a larger structure, *si* 'if'-clauses, in French talk-in-interaction. These can occur as subordinate clauses with a main clause expressing the "consequent" of the *si*-clause. But in interaction, *si*-clauses are also found as incrementally added expansions; in co-constructed turn-constructional units; as free-standing, "insubordinate", clauses, with embodied completions; and in formulaic, particle-like uses. The analysis presents some of the conditions for the different versions of *si*-clauses and which social actions they perform, or contribute to performing. The types of *si*-clauses are described as being on a continuum of (in)subordination, and the authors argue that, and show how, the position in sequences, the temporal unfolding, the action accomplishment, and the co-occurring bodily and vocal conduct can and must be part of grammatical description of *si*-clauses.

Sofie Henricson and Jan Lindström also consider larger grammatical formats in their chapter on pseudocleft constructions in Swedish talk-in-interaction. An (English) example of a pseudocleft construction could be *what I don't like is her nasal voice*, in which the first, or preliminary, part, *what I don't like*, is a relative clause without a head, followed by the verb 'to be' (here in the present tense, *is*) and a second part, a noun phrase, *her nasal voice*. Henricson and Lindström take us through the structural variations of pseudoclefts when used in interaction and argue that such variations should be described in the grammar. Earlier accounts of pseudoclefts have focused on their information-structural functions, in that they can be seen as a way of placing new or contrasting information in the final part of the construction. The authors extend the analysis to cover projection, both within the format and beyond, and they show how pseudoclefts are used in directive-commissive and evaluative social actions, in discursive transitions, and in claiming and negotiating epistemic positioning. Henricson and Lindström argue that a grammatical description of pseudoclefts should include turn design, action formation, sequence organization, and participation framework, and they outline a format for such a description that includes functional characteristics and interactional impact.

The last chapter in the volume is by Virginia Calabria, who examines other-extensions in Italian talk-in-interaction. The focus is on instances in multi-person interaction where one speaker reaches a point of possible completion and another speaker extends that turn, in grammatically and actionally fitted ways. Calabria shows how the extensions can be used for providing additional information, demonstrating understanding, and for reframing the implications of prior talk. She also points out how micro-grammatical, actional, prosodic, and embodied aspects are oriented to in the production and treatment of other-extensions. Calabria argues that other-extensions and other co-constructions require a "collaborative grammar". Such a grammar sees talking collaboratively as a pervasive aspect of interaction, and it breaks with a monologic tradition in grammar writing that deals with linguistic structures as finite products spoken by one speaker. She also points to places within a comprehensive grammar where the collaborative aspect could be highlighted and explained.

In the final discussion, the editors try to spell out the take-away lessons for grammar writing that the chapters of the volume have provided. We consider both the future perspectives and the unsolved problems in writing grammars on the basis of analyses of interaction. We hope that the final discussion — as well as the volume as a whole — will inspire and contribute to a more focused discussion on the relationship between grammar and action. Finally, we wish that this volume will not only give inspiration but also practical help for researchers who are trying to build "interactional grammars".

Acknowledgments

The editors wish to thank two anonymous reviewers for insightful and inspirational comments in their reviews of the proposal for this volume. We are grateful to all authors for their reviews of chapters by other authors and for the great work they have put into revising and developing their own chapters. We are especially grateful to the series editors for helping us in the process and for providing crucial and precise comments and suggestions to the chapters of the volume. We also wish to thank the publishers for their patience and assistance. The responsibility for the present chapter and for the concrete editorial tasks lies with us alone.

References

Ameka, Felix. K. 1991. *Ewe: Its grammatical constructions and illocutionary devices* (PhD dissertation). Australian National University.

Ameka, Felix K., Alan Dench, and Nicholas Evans (eds). 2006a. *Catching Language: The Standing Challenge of Grammar Writing*. Berlin/New York: Mouton de Gruyter..

Ameka, Felix K., Alan Dench, and Nicholas Evans (eds). 2006b. "Preface." In *Catching Language: The Standing Challenge of Grammar Writing*, ed. by Felix K. Ameka, Alan Dench, and Nicholas Evans. Berlin/New York: Mouton de Gruyter.

Anward, Jan, and Bengt Nordberg. 2005. "Indledning [Introduction]." In *Samtal och Grammatik: Studier i Svenskt Samtalsspråk [Conversation and Grammar: Studies in Swedish Conversational Language]*, ed. by Jan Anward, and Bengt Nordberg, 5–9. Lund: Studentlitteratur.

Auer, Peter. 2005. "Projection in interaction and projection in grammar." *Text* 25 (1): 7–36

Auer, Peter. 2009. "Online-syntax: Thoughts on the Temporality of Spoken Language." *Language Sciences* 31 (1): 1–13.

Auer, Peter. 2023. "Online syntax." In *Encyclopedia of Terminology for Conversation Analysis and Interactional Linguistics*, ed. by Alexandra Gubina, Elliott M. Hoey, and Chase Wesley Raymond International Society for Conversation Analysis (ISCA).

Auer, Peter, and Stefan Pfänder (eds). 2011. *Constructions: Emerging and Emergent*. Berlin: de Gruyter.

Barth-Weingarten, Dagmar. 2016. *Intonation Units Revisited. Cesuras in Talk-in-Interaction*. Amsterdam: John Benjamins.

Betz, Emma, Lorenza Mondada, Arnulf Deppermann, and Marja-Leena Sorjonen (eds). 2021. *OKAY across Languages: Toward a Comparative Approach to Its Use in Talk-in-Interaction*. Amsterdam: John Benjamins.

Biber, Douglas, and Randolph Quirk (eds). 2012. *Longman Grammar of Spoken and Written English*. 10th impression. Harlow: Longman.

Comrie, Bernard, Martin Haspelmath, and Balthasar Bickel. 2015. *The Leipzig glossing rules: Conventions for interlinear morpheme-by-morpheme glosses*. https://www.eva.mpg.de/lingua/pdf/Glossing-Rules.pdf

Couper-Kuhlen, Elizabeth. 2014. "What Does Grammar Tell Us about Action?" *Pragmatics* 24 (3): 623–47.

Couper-Kuhlen, Elizabeth, and Margret Selting (eds). 1996. *Prosody in Conversation: Interactional Studies*. Cambridge: Cambridge University Press.

Couper-Kuhlen, Elizabeth, and Margret Selting. 2001. "Introducing Interactional Linguistics." In *Studies in Interactional Linguistics*, ed. by Margret Selting, and Elisabeth Couper-Kuhlen, 1–22. Amsterdam: John Benjamins.

Couper-Kuhlen, Elizabeth, and Marget Selting. 2018. *Interactional Linguistics: Studying Language in Social Interaction*. Cambridge: Cambridge University Press.

Couper-Kuhlen, Elizabeth & Tsuyoshi Ono (eds.). 2017. Turn continuation in a cross-linguistic perspective. *Journal of Pragmatics* 17(4).

DanTIN. 2024. "Samtalegrammatik.dk." 2024. https://samtalegrammatik.dk/.

Chapter 1. Grammar in action 21

Deppermann, Arnulf, and Susanne Günthner (eds). 2015. *Temporality in Interaction.* Amsterdam: John Benjamins.

Deppermann, Arnulf, and Michael Haugh (eds). 2022. *Action Ascription in Interaction.* Cambridge University Press.

Dingemanse, Mark. 2024. "Interjections at the Heart of Language." *Annual Review of Linguistics* 10 (1): 257–77.

Dingemanse, Mark, and N. J. Enfield. 2015. "Other-Initiated Repair across Languages: Towards a Typology of Conversational Structures." *Open Linguistics* 1 (1).

Dingemanse, Mark, Fransisco Torreira, and N. J. Enfield. 2013. "Is 'Huh?' A Universal Word?: Conversational Infrastructure and the Convergent Evolution of Linguistic Items." *PLOS ONE* 8 (11): 1–10.

Enfield, N. J., and Tanya Stivers (eds). 2007. *Person Reference in Interaction: Linguistic, Cultural and Social Perspectives.* Cambridge: Cambridge University Press.

Enfield, N. J., Tanya Stivers, and Stephen C. Levinson. 2010. "Question–Response Sequences in Conversation across Ten Languages: An Introduction." *Journal of Pragmatics* 42 (10): 2615–19.

Evans, Nicholas, and Alan Dench. 2006. "Introduction: Catching Language." In *Catching Language: The Standing Challenge of Grammar Writing*, edited by Felix K. Ameka, Alan Dench, and Nicholas Evans, 1–39. Benjamins.

Floyd, Simeon, Giovanni Rossi, and N. J. Enfield (eds). 2020. *Getting Others to Do Things: A Pragmatic Typology of Recruitments.* Berlin: Language Science Press.

Ford, Cecilia E., Barbara A. Fox, and Sandra A. Thompson. 1996. "Practices in the Construction of Turns: The 'TCU' Revisited." *Pragmatics* 6 (3): 427–54.

Fox, Barbara. A. 2000. *Micro-syntax in English Conversation.* Paper presented at the conference *Interactional Linguistics*, Spa, Belgium.

Fox, Barbara A. 2007. "Principles Shaping Grammatical Practices: An Exploration." *Discourse Studies* 9 (3): 299–318.

French, Peter, and John Local. 1983. "Turn Competitive Incomings." *Journal of Pragmatics* 7 (1): 17–38.

Fried, Mirjam, and Jan-Ola Östman. 2004. "Construction Grammar: A Thumbnail Sketch." In *Construction Grammar in a Cross-Language Perspective*, ed. by Mirjam Fried and Jan-Ola Östman, 11–86. Amsterdam: John Benjamins.

Goodwin, Charles. 2002. "Time in Action." *Current Anthropology* 43 (S4): 19–35.

Günthner, Susanne, and Wolfgang Imo. 2006. "Konstruktionen in der Interaktion [Constructions in the interaction]." In *Konstruktionen in der Interaktion*, ed. by Susanne Günthner, and Wolfgang Imo, 1–22. Berlin: De Gruyter.

Hakulinen, Auli, Maria Vilkuna, Riitta Korhonen, Vesa Koivisto, Tarja Riitta Heinonen, and Irja Alho (eds). 2004. *Iso suomen kielioppi [Comprehensive Finnish Grammar].* Helsinki: Suomalaisen Kirjallisuuden Seura.

Hakulinen, Auli, and Margret Selting (eds). 2005. *Syntax and Lexis in Conversation: Studies on the Use of Linguistic Resources in Talk-in-Interaction.* Amsterdam: John Benjamins.

Helasvuo, Marja-Liisa. 2001. *Syntax in the Making: The Emergence of Syntactic Units in Finnish Conversation.* Amsterdam: John Benjamins.

Hepburn, Alexa, and Galina B. Bolden. 2012. "The Conversation Analytic Approach to Transcription." In *The Handbook of Conversation Analysis*, ed. by Jack Sidnell and Tanya Stivers, 57–76. Oxford: Wiley Blackwell.

Heritage, John, and Marja-Leena Sorjonen (eds). 2018. *Between Turn and Sequence: Turn-Initial Particles across Languages*. Amsterdam: John Benjamins.

Hopper, Paul. 1987. "Emergent Grammar." In *Proceedings of the Thirteenth Annual Meeting of the Berkeley Linguistics Society*, ed. by Jon Aske, Natasha Beery, Laura Michaelis, and Hana Filip, 139–57. Berkeley, CA: Berkeley Linguistics Society.

Hopper, Paul. 2011. "Emergent Grammar and Temporality in Interactional Linguistics." In *Constructions: Emerging and Emergent*, ed. by Peter Auer, and Stefan Pfänder, 22–44. Berlin: De Gruyter.

Imo, Wolfgang. 2015. "Interactional Construction Grammar." *Linguistics Vanguard* 1 (1): 69–77.

Jefferson, Gail. 2004. "Glossary of Transcript Symbols with an Introduction." In *Conversation Analysis: Studies from the First Generation*, ed. by Gene H. Lerner, 13–23. Amsterdam: John Benjamins.

Jørgensen, Maria. 2024. "A Question of Embeddedness: On Clausal and Phrasal Responses to Specifying WH-Questions in Danish Talk-in-Interaction." *Research on Language and Social Interaction* 57 (3): 323–344.

Laury, Ritva, and Tsuyoshi Ono (eds). 2020. *Fixed Expressions: Building Language Structure and Social Action*. Amsterdam: John Benjamins. https://benjamins.com/catalog/pbns.315.

Laury, Ritva, and Ryoko Suzuki (eds). 2011. *Subordination in Conversation: A Cross-Linguistic Perspective*. Amsterdam: John Benjamins.

Levinson, Stephen C. 2013. "Action Formation and Ascription." In *The Handbook of Conversation Analysis*, ed. by Jack Sidnell, and Tanya Stivers, 103–130. Oxford, U.K.: Wiley-Blackwell.

Lindström, Jan. 2008. *Tur och ordning: Introduktion till svensk samtalsgrammatik [Turn and Order: Introduction to Swedish Grammar for Conversation]*. Stockholm: Norstedts akademiska förlag.

Lindström, Jan. 2025. "Constructions in Spoken Interaction." In *The Cambridge Handbook of Construction Grammar*, ed. by Mirjam Fried, and Kiki Nikiforidou, 309–334. Cambridge, U.K.: Cambridge University Press.

Linell, Per. 2005. *The Written Language Bias in Linguistics: Its Nature, Origins, and Transformations*. Routledge.

Local, John, John Kelly, and Bill Wells. 1986. "Towards a Phonology of Conversation: Turn-Taking in Tyneside English." *Journal of Linguistics* 22 (2): 411–37.

Maschler, Yael, Simona Pekarek Doehler, Jan Lindström, and Leelo Keevallik (eds.). 2020. *Emergent Syntax for Conversation*. Amsterdam: John Benjamins.

Mihas, Elena. 2015. *A Grammar of Alto Perené (Arawak). A Grammar of Alto Perené (Arawak)*. Berlin: De Gruyter Mouton.

Mihas, Elena. 2017. *Conversational structures of Alto Perené (Arawak) of Peru*. Amsterdam: John Benjamins.

Mondada, Lorenza. 2013. "The Conversation Analytic Approach to Data Collection." In *The Handbook of Conversation Analysis*, ed. by Jack Sidnell and Tanya Stivers, 32–56. Oxford, U.K.: Wiley-Blackwell.

Mondada, Lorenza. 2018. "Multiple Temporalities of Language and Body in Interaction: Challenges for Transcribing Multimodality." *Research on Language and Social Interaction* 51 (1): 85–106.

Mondada, Lorenza. 2019. "Conventions for Multimodal Transcription." https://www.lorenzamondada.net/multimodal-transcription.

Ochs, Elinor, Emanuel A. Schegloff, and Sandra A. Thompson (eds.). 1996. *Interaction and Grammar*. Cambridge: Cambridge University Press.

Ogden, Richard. 2021. "The Phonetics of Talk in Interaction." In *The Cambridge Handbook of Phonetics*, ed. by Jane Setter and Rachael-Anne Knight, 657–681. Cambridge: Cambridge University Press.

Ono, Tsuyoshi, and Elizabeth Couper-Kuhlen. 2007. "Increments in Cross-Linguistic Perspective: Introductory Remarks." *Pragmatics* 17 (4): 505–512.

Ono, Tsuyoshi, Ritva Laury, and Ryoko Suzuki (eds). 2021. *Usage-Based and Typological Approaches to Linguistic Units*. Amsterdam: John Benjamins.

Pekarek Doehler, Simona, Yael Maschler, Leelo Keevallik, and Jan Lindström. 2020. "Complex Syntax-in-Interaction: Emergent and Emerging Clause-Combining Patterns for Organizing Social Actions." In *Emergent Syntax for Conversation: Clausal Patterns and the Organization of Action*, ed. by Jan Lindström, Yael Maschler, Simona Pekarek Doehler, and Leelo Keevallik, 1–22. Amsterdam: John Benjamins.

Pekarek Doehler, Simona, Leelo Keevallik, and Xiaoting Li. 2022. "Editorial: The Grammar-Body Interface in Social Interaction." *Frontiers in Psychology* 13 (April).

Pomerantz, Anita. 1980. "Telling My Side: 'Limited Access' as a Fishing Device." *Sociological Inquiry* 50 (3–4): 186–98.

Rice, Keren. 2006. "A Typology of Good Grammars." *Studies in Language* 30 (2): 385–415.

Rüsch, Maren. 2020. *A Conversational Analysis of Acholi: Structure and Socio-Pragmatics of a Nilotic Language of Uganda*. Leiden: Brill.

Sacks, Harvey. 1984. "Notes on Methodology." In *Structures of Social Action: Studies in Conversation Analysis*, ed. by John Heritage, and J. Maxwell Atkinson, 2–27. Cambridge: Cambridge University Press.

Sacks, Harvey, Emanuel A. Schegloff, and Gail Jefferson. 1974. "A Simplest Systematics for the Organization of Turn-Taking for Conversation." *Language* 50 (4): 696–735.

Schegloff, Emanuel A. 1984. "On Some Questions and Ambiguities in Conversation." In *Structures of Social Action: Studies in Conversation Analysis*, ed. by J. Maxwell Atkinson, and John Heritage, 28–52. Cambridge: Cambridge University Press.

Schegloff, Emanuel A. 1996. "Confirming Allusions: Toward an Empirical Account of Action." *American Journal of Sociology* 102 (1): 161–216.

Schegloff, Emanuel A. 2007. *Sequence Organization in Interaction: A Primer in Conversation Analysis*. Cambridge University Press.

Selting, Margret, and Elizabeth Couper-Kuhlen. 2000. "Argumente für die Entwicklung einer 'interaktionalen Linguistik [Arguments for the Development of an 'Interactional Linguistics']." *Gesprächsforschung* (1): 76–95.

Selting, Margret, and Elizabeth Couper-Kuhlen (eds). 2001. *Studies in Interactional Linguistics*. Amsterdam: John Benjamins.

Sicoli, Mark A. 2020. *Saying and doing in Zapotec: Multimodality, resonance, and the language of joint actions*. London: Bloomsbury Academic.

Sorjonen, Marja-Leena, Raevaara, Liisa, and Elizabeth Couper-Kuhlen (eds). 2017. *Imperative Turns at Talk: The Design of Directives in Action*. Amsterdam: John Benjamins.

Steensig, Jakob. 2001. *Sprog i virkeligheden: bidrag til en interaktionel lingvistik [Language in Reality: Contributions to an Interactional Linguistics]*. Aarhus: Aarhus University Press.

Steensig, Jakob, Maria Jørgensen, Nicholas Mikkelsen, Karita Suomalainen, and Søren Sandager Sørensen. 2023. "Toward a Grammar of Danish Talk-in-Interaction: From Action Formation to Grammatical Description." *Research on Language and Social Interaction* 56 (2): 116–140.

Stivers, Tanya, N. J. Enfield, Penelope Brown, Christina Englert, Makoto Hayashi, Trine Heinemann, Gertie Hoymann, Federico Rossano, Jan Peter de Ruiter, Kyung-Eun Yoon and Stephen C. Levinson. 2009. "Universals and Cultural Variation in Turn-Taking in Conversation." *PNAS* 106 (26): 10587–92.

Stivers, Tanya, Lorenza Mondada, and Jakob Steensig (eds). 2011. *Knowledge, Morality and Affiliation in Social Interaction*. Cambridge: Cambridge University Press.

Szczepek Reed, Beatrice, and Geoffrey Raymond (eds). 2013. *Units of Talk — Units of Action*. Amsterdam: John Benjamins.

Tao, Hongyin. 1996. *Units in Mandarin Conversation*. Amsterdam: John Benjamins.

Thompson, Sandra A., Barbara A. Fox, and Elizabeth Couper-Kuhlen. 2015. *Grammar in Everyday Talk: Building Responsive Actions*. Cambridge: Cambridge University Press.

SECTION 1

From Action to Grammar

CHAPTER 2

On granularity in grammar and action

Barbara A. Fox & Chase Wesley Raymond
University of Colorado, Boulder

In this study, we explore the relevance of granularity to the study of grammar-in-interaction, with special reference to the writing of an online grammar (cf. Steensig, et al. 2023). In CA/IL research, it routinely occurs that a form or action is described and analyzed at one level of detail, and then subsequent research reveals that that form/action actually displays meaningful and ordered variation that deserves more focused examination. Here we summarize previous studies which reveal the significance of more granular descriptions, and we discuss our maxim — arising from Sacks' claim that there is 'order at all points' — that the more granular our analytic approaches are, the more granular our understandings of forms and actions will become.

Keywords: grammar, interaction, granularity, morphosyntax, prosody, particles, interactional linguistics, conversation analysis

1. Introduction

In any scientific analysis of a phenomenon which attempts to describe and explain that phenomenon, there must be decisions as to the terms in which the description and explanation will be framed. The set of terms selected in turn shapes the scope of adequacy of the description and explanation being pursued. Importantly, we can notice that over time, as scientific examination of that phenomenon and others develops, the terms of description and analysis may change — becoming more or less granular in nature, specified at broader or finer levels of detail. Such developments in scientific inquiry are a natural result of continued investigation into phenomena.

Within Conversation Analysis (CA) and Interactional Linguistics (IL) (for recent comprehensive overviews, see Clift 2016; Couper-Kuhlen & Selting 2018; Robinson, et al. 2024), we see instances of these very trajectories of development. In this chapter, we draw on concrete examples from the literature to explore the importance of granularity in examinations of linguistic phenomena, especially as

https://doi.org/10.1075/slsi.37.02fox
© 2025 John Benjamins Publishing Company

concerns the interactional and multidimensional functions of grammar. Our goal is to demonstrate that the greater the level of granularity we allow for in our grammatical descriptions, the greater the level of granularity that will emerge in our understandings of social actions. We find, moreover, that this gradually increasing granularity in scientific inquiry is a natural part of the evolution of CA/IL as a field.

In the process of our exploration, we will argue that greater granularity in the description of both form and action is always possible; that is, there is no limit in principle to the level of detail which can be meaningfully described for a given language. If there is "order at all points" (Sacks 1984), then every 'point' through which we go deeper into detail will reveal order, which for us means that we will be able to identify recurrent details of format being used to accomplish recurrent actions in interaction. There is thus no end to the levels of granularity which a grammar must be able to incorporate. With regard to the objectives of the current volume — namely, interrogating how a grammar of a language might be constructed on the basis of interactional findings — the question becomes: How can a comprehensive grammar incorporate infinite granularity of both format and action? This puzzle becomes even more complex if we consider that we cannot know in advance just how granularity will matter for a particular form or action. Before the introduction and evidencing of the concept of "recruitment" (Kendrick & Drew 2016), for example, we could not have known to include it in grammars. Thus not only is granularity limitless, but its precise formulation cannot be known in advance of the research which reveals it. So how can the infinite and unknowable be incorporated into such a grammar? In this study, we seek to examine this question and others that arise in incorporating expanding granularity into a grammar of a language, in particular into the grammar of Danish designed by Steensig and colleagues (Steensig, et al. 2023).

We begin by reviewing a well-studied particle in English interaction — the change-of-state token *oh* (Heritage 1984) — and we discuss how greater granularity has been brought to bear on the examination of this particle over time (Section 2). We then consider clausal grammatical formats and their relationships to action, drawing upon some of our own work to further demonstrate the theoretical significance of granularity. Considering the beginnings of clauses (Section 3), we focus on offers and requests designed with *((do) you) want...* at differing levels of granularity (Curl 2006; Raymond, et al. 2021). Occurring at clausal endings (Section 4), we interrogate the 'X' component of the request formats *can you X* (Fox & Heinemann 2017). In the Discussion (Section 5), we describe some of the implications that this argument has for the writing of grammars, and for CA/IL more broadly, by reconsidering both 'grammar' and 'action' in greater detail, and we close with some concluding thoughts and reflections (Section 6).

2. Granularity in the study of a particle: The case of *oh*

As an initial case in point illustrating greater granularity and specificity over time within CA/IL inquiry, consider the now well-known cluster of studies on the English particle *oh*. In Heritage's (1984) foundational study, all exemplars of *oh* were included in the author's collection, as the crucial category of analysis was the change-of-state token itself: What is this interactional object doing in interaction, and how can we (as analysts) bear witness to that interactional work? Heritage wrote that *oh* is used "to propose that its producer has undergone some kind of change in his or her locally current state of knowledge, information, orientation or awareness" (1984:299), and he demonstrated this by drawing on a range of sequence- and action-types — from question-elicited informings (1984:307–312), to counter-informings (1984:312–315), to other-initiated repair (1984:315–318), and more. The following extract offers two question-answer-*oh* sequences (lines 1–3, 5–9), as Nancy asks about Hyla's new love interest:

Excerpt 1. (HG:II:25) (Heritage 1984:310, modified)[1]
```
01 NAN: Q-> .hhh Dz he 'av 'iz own apa:rt[mint?]
02 HYL: A->                         [.hhhh]Yea:h,=
03 NAN: oh-> =Oh:,
04           (1.0)
05 NAN: Q-> How didju git 'iz number,
06           (.)
07 HYL: A-> I(h) (.) c(h)alled infermation'n San
08      ->  Fr'ncissc(h)[uh!
09 NAN: oh->            [Oh::::.
10           (.)
11 NAN:      Very cleve:r, hh=
```

In this example, Nancy requests information twice (lines 1 and 5), and receives information twice (lines 2 and 7–8), and in third position of each sequence, produces change-of-state *oh*s (lines 3 and 9). In the second case, the *oh* is followed by a further post-completion assessment (line 11) (see Schegloff 2007:118–120, 141–142).

In subsequent studies of *oh*, Heritage concentrated on specific turn, sequential, and action environments — e.g., *oh*-prefaced responses (Heritage 1998, 2002) — where he showed how the generic change-of-state meaning of *oh* can be particularized based on context. In responses to questions, for instance, *oh*-prefaced responses can index that a prior question was inapposite (Heritage 1998). In responses to assessments, *oh*-prefacing can work to "inexplicitly yet insistently" (Heritage 2002:198) index epistemic independence from the prior speaker's initial

---

1. Our preference has been not to alter authors' original transcripts. We have kept the transcript text lines as they were in the original, including cases where they deviate from the conventions used in the present volume.

Chapter 2. Granularity in grammar and action   **29**

assessment (see also 1998: 291–296). Consider the following Excerpt (2), in which Gay is giving Jeremy a German telephone number. After receiving several digits, Jeremy expresses his surprise as to the length of the number and assesses it (line 13), to which Gay issues an *oh*-prefaced, repetitional response (line 14):

Excerpt 2. [Heritage:OI:7:3] (Heritage 2002: 199, modified)
```
01 GAY: So the ↑number is (0.2) oh↓ one oh:↓.
02 JER: Oh one oh↓,
03      (1.0)
04 JER: Yeup,
05 GAY: ↑Four ni:ne,
06      (0.5)
07 JER: Ri:ght?
08 GAY: Sev'n three,u-six o:ne?hh
09      (0.6)
10 JER: Sev'n three: six o:ne?
11      (0.3)
12 GAY: Ei:ght ni:ne,
13 JER: °Gosh° it goe:s (.) goes on'n on
14 GAY: Oh it doe:s Germany doe:s.
```

About this exchange, Heritage writes:

> Here, Gay could have responded with a simple agreement [e.g., *yes*], which [...] would have conveyed that her agreement was grounded in the "here and now" common experience of an interminable telephone number. Instead, her *oh*-prefaced response — *Oh it doe:s* — treats his remark as reviving an earlier observation of the same type that she had made independently of this occasion, and she thereby conveys that, in contrast to Jeremy, she finds it unsurprising. By this means she also manages to indicate that she is an 'old hand' at phoning abroad. (2002: 199)

Gay's turn design — the *oh*-preface followed by a repetition (*it does*, cf. *yes*) — indexes that her own knowledge of the extensiveness of German phone numbers exists independently of Jeremy's having just said so (see Thompson, Fox & Couper-Kuhlen 2015: ch. 4). And as the last line of Heritage's analysis above suggests, such claims, challenges, and defenses of rights and obligations to knowledge can be implicated in the enactment and negotiation of social roles and responsibilities, which Heritage explored in further subsequent collaborative work that included instances of *oh* (Heritage & Raymond 2005; Raymond, Clift & Heritage 2021; Raymond & Heritage 2006; see also Heritage 2018).

Consider now another dimension of granularity that was added to the puzzle of *oh* along the way, initiated by Local's (1992, 1996) explorations of the prosodic composition of *oh*. By focusing on details of the prosodic forms that *oh* can take, Local was able to identify a range of actions accomplished by the particle as a news receipt. He shows that a rising-falling pitch contour, for instance, routinely accomplishes "displays of having been misinformed and displays of forgetfulness", which is often topicalized through "more talk from the same speaker" (1996: 205). An instance of this prosody can be seen in line 51 of Excerpt (3) below, with the precise sort of continuation Local describes in line 53:

Excerpt 3. [NB IV:10:R:21] (Clift & Raymond 2018: 106, modified)
```
49 LOT: Yih'av no idea it's right across the street
50      from the:::El Dorad*o.
51 EMM: .t Oh:: ↑ :: ↓::.
52 LOT: Ye:ah.
53 EMM: Oh not near the Indian W*e:lls.
54      (1.0)
55 LOT: °ihYe::ah:?° (0.2) It's ih-*i-Indian We:lls?
56      uh well it's a:ll Indi[an We [:lls'n P]a:lm=
57 EMM:                        [.hhhh [ Ye*ah. ]
58 LOT: =Desert now they've cha:nged it
59      yihkn[ow tuh P]a:lm De:sert,
60 EMM:      [Yeah:.  ]
```

Such a news-receipt *oh* (line 51) is distinct from terminal-falling *oh*, for example, which Local does not find produced in the same environments (see also Thompson, Fox & Couper-Kuhlen 2015: 64–75).[2] Later prosodic studies by other scholars identified other actions accomplished by particular prosodic manifestations of *oh*, including disappointment (Couper-Kuhlen 2009), surprise (Thompson, Fox & Couper-Kuhlen 2015: 66; Wilkinson & Kitzinger 2006: 154), and other sorts of "cognitive-affective coloring" (Thompson, Fox & Couper-Kuhlen 2015: 66; see, e.g., Freese & Maynard 1998; Maynard & Freese 2012).[3]

For the purposes of the present inquiry regarding granularity, it is essential to highlight that the series of studies of *oh* — focused on different compositional, positional, and action-relevant aspects of its use — do not invalidate Heritage's (1984) original claims regarding the change-of-state work done by *oh*. Instead, by looking in greater detail at the forms and functions of *oh*, Local, Couper-Kuhlen, Freese & Maynard, and Thompson, et al., *inter alia* — in addition to Heritage himself — were able to identify more fine-grained action-types which could all be classified as 'changes of state', but which merited more systematic examination in their own right. The steady stream of research on English *oh* over the years has thus served to further refine and specify the terms of the analysis and thereby enrich our understanding of both form and action, as well as the relationships between the two.

---

2. For a concrete illustration of the analytic implications of misrepresenting phonetic detail, using this same extract, see Clift and Raymond (2018: 105–107). See also Jefferson (1985) and the discussion in Section 5 here.

3. See also work on *ohs* that are combined with other elements — e.g., *oh+okay* (Couper-Kuhlen 2021), *oh that's right* (Küttner 2018).

3. Granularity in the study of clause beginnings: The case of *((do) you) want...*

Having considered granularity in the examination of a particle, let us now transition to the theoretical relevance of granularity in the study of clausal formats. We'll begin, in this section, with clause beginnings, using offers and requests designed with *((do) you) want...* as a concrete illustration; we'll explore clause endings in the next section.

In her influential study on the syntax of offers, Curl (2006) examined offers formatted with *do you want...* (as in Excerpt (4)), distinguishing them from those formatted with other designs (e.g., conditional *if* or assertions, as in Excerpt (5)).

Excerpt 4. [NB:IV:10R:41–42] (Curl 2006:1267, modified)
```
01 EMM: [.hh].hhh]h ALRIGHT HONEY WELL .hh good-
02      I:'m SO gladje hhadda wunnerf'l ti:me.h=
03 LOT: =Well listen (.) e-uh: do you want me uh
04      come dow'n getchu tu[hmorrow or]a n y t h]ing?
05 EMM:                     [n:N o : : ] dea:r.  ]
06 EMM: No[:  I'm] fine]
07 LOT: [to the]sto::]re or any[thi[:ng?
08 EMM:                         [.hh[I:'VE got
09      everything bought dea:r:
```

Excerpt 5. [NB:IV:4R:4–5] (Curl 2006, pg. 1271, modified)
```
01 EMM: W'l anyway tha:t's a'dea:l so I don't know
02      what to do about Ba:rb'ra .hhhhh (0.2) c'z
03      you see she was: depe[nding on:=
04 (L):                      [(Yeh)
05 EMM: =him takin'er in tuh the L A deeple s:-
06      depot Sunday so [he says]
07 LOT:                 [I:'ll  ] take'er in: Sunday,
```

On the basis of her collection of cases, Curl argued that:

> Offers which are educed (i.e., brought out or developed from a condition of latent or merely potential existence) from prior talk by the proposed recipient are always produced with the *do you want me to X* syntactic construction; offers which are directly responsive to prior talk about some particular trouble or problem are done with a variety of constructions, but never in the *do you want* format.
>
> (2006:1259)

The verb *want* turned out to be crucial to Curl's analysis: "One reason for avoiding (as well as using) the [*do you want*] construction to make an offer is the way in which it foregrounds the putative recipient of the offer as an agent — one who 'wants' something from the other" (2006:1274, emphasis in original). This contrasts with other offer formats — e.g., *I'll pick her up* — which do not express the recipient's 'wants' in the grammar of the turn. In the context of Curl's study, then, *want*-formatted offers became a unified subset of cases within the analysis, as participants were shown to orient to such offers as being (not) normatively positioned at particular points within conversation compared to other offer designs.

In a subsequent study, Raymond, et al. (2021) looked more closely at the *want* verb phrases used in offers (and requests). The authors noticed that sometimes speakers produced a canonically interrogative format (i.e., *do you want…*), while on other occasions more minimal formats were used (i.e., *you want…, wanna…*). The question then became: Do participants orient to these different formats in different ways with regard to social action? That is, is there evidence that participants orient to this level of granularity in the morphosyntactic design of offers in context?

Examining the cases in their collection, Raymond, et al. (2021) propose a cline with regard to both (i) the degree of minimization of the morphosyntactic format, and (ii) speakers' stances toward the likelihood of recipient acceptance (see also Zinken & Deppermann 2017 on imperatives). We will illustrate the Raymond et al. paper's argument with cases taken from the counter of a leather and shoe repair shop (Fox & Heinemann 2015, 2016, 2017; see also Fox, Mondada & Sorjonen 2023).

Raymond, et al. argue that speakers position the *do you want…?* format in contexts in which there is no (or sometimes contrary) evidence (verbal, vocal, embodied, artifactual) in the interaction that recipients are disposed toward accepting the offer; this enacts a relatively neutral or agnostic stance with regard to possible acceptance. A case-in-point is found in Excerpt (6). The customer requests one (and only one) service (lines 5–6), and the shoetender offers another, distinct service (line 13).

Excerpt 6. [Shoe Shop 10–13–2013] (Raymond, et al. 2021: 60–61)
```
01 SHO: how are you::,
02      (0.6)
03 CUS: good!
04      (.)
05 CUS: (hey) I wanted to find out (1.2) if (you can) sew:-
06      this back onto here?
07      (0.2)
08 SHO: mm hm:,=
09 CUS: =.hh
10      (0.3)
11 CUS: u:m,
12      (1.3)
13 SHO: and do you want to replace these elastics as well?
14      (1.9)
15 SHO: they aren't really- (0.3) func[tioning as elastics
16 CUS:                               [yeah,h
17 SHO: anymore,
18      (.)
19 CUS: yeah, that's for sure
20      (4.0)
21 CUS: alright
```

The authors argue that the *do you want...?* format is well-fitted to this offer for a distinct service, as the shoetender has little to no interactional evidence as to the customer's disposition toward accepting this particular offer.

In contrast, the more minimal *you want...?* and *want...?* formats are recurrently positioned in sequential contexts in which there *is* evidence that recipients are disposed to accept the offer; these formats display increasingly stronger stances of expectation for acceptance. Relative to the *you want...?* format, the *want...?* format appears in contexts in which recipients have demonstrated a particularly strong or explicit disposition toward acceptance, and is regularly produced and understood as seeking (re)confirmation of acceptance. This is what occurs in case (7) below, also taken from the shoeshop. After reviewing the material that would be used for a repair to a customer's shoes, and an aside in which the customer apologizes for their dirtiness (Heritage, Raymond & Drew 2019), an acceptance or rejection of the proposed service is due from the customer (Fox & Heinemann 2017). In that slot, the customer produces a prosodically enthusiastic ↑*yea:h,* (line 28), thereby quite explicitly agreeing to what's been proposed. It is in response to this that one of the shoetenders seeks reconfirmation with a quickly articulated >*wanna do it?*< (line 30), the minimal format indexing his stance that acceptance is very likely.

Excerpt 7. [Shoe Shop 1–18–2014, 123230e] (Raymond, et al. 2021: 65–68)
```
13 SH2: and we'd put somethin' like this on.
14      (1.5) ((C inspects the material))
15 CUS: .pt °okay:,°
16      (0.5)
17 CUS: and that, will they still- mthey'll-
18      (0.3) .hh (0.7) yeah ('n) they're so comfortable.
19      (1.3)
20 CUS: I'm sorry they're dirty I just (0.7)
21      hhh (0.5) have trouble not wearing them,
22      (0.4)
23 SH2: right.
24      (0.4)
25 SH2: I [hear ya
26 CUS:   [u:m
27      (0.5)
28 CUS: ↑yea:h,
29      (0.4)
30 SH2: >wanna do it?<
31      (.)
32 CUS: ↓let's do it,
33      (.)
34 SH2: mkay,
```

Compare Excerpts (6) and (7), above, with (8), below. Here the offer occurs in a context where the shoetender and the customer are in agreement both with regard to what the problem is (i.e., broken laces in shoes) as well as what the solution is (i.e., putting on appropriate new laces) (lines 9–16). The shoetender thus infers that the customer may be disposed toward accepting an offer to put the laces on the shoes: He has more sequential evidence of the recipient's disposition toward acceptance than in (6), but not as much as in (7); the *you want...?* format indexes this intermediary stance.

Excerpt 8. [Shoe Shop 5–30–2015, 123517]
```
01 SHO: hi how we doin,=
02 CUS: =hi good, how are you.
03      (0.2)
04 SHO: fantastic.
05      (0.2)
06 CUS: awesome
07      (0.9)
08 SHO: what can I do for ya.
09      (1.3)
10 CUS: busted.
11      (0.5)
12 SHO: uh! laces,
13      (0.3)
14 CUS: yeah. so I went and got these from REI,
15      and I'm pretty sure (   ) these are the
16      only ones I saw
17 SHO: yeah, looks good.
18 SHO: you want 'em on (the shoes)
19 CUS: yeah
20 SHO: yeah
21 CUS: yeah
22 SHO: okay, cool
```

In contrast to Curl (2006), who collected multiple formats of offers, then, Raymond, et al. (2021) focused only on those designed with *want*. In this way, Raymond, et al. removed one of the dimensions of complexity and variation (i.e., other syntactic formats), while introducing others in line with the aims and scope of the new inquiry (i.e., greater granularity of *want* verb phrase itself, as well as comparing institutional [shoeshop and medical] and mundane interaction). And as they looked with greater granularity at the morphosyntax of offers, they identified finer modulations of action.

Notwithstanding the three-way categorization offered by Raymond, et al., further granularity might be explored. For example, the lines between *do you want...?* and *you want...?* can become blurred with a pronunciation closer to *d'you wanna...*; it is a matter for future research to explore the potential interactional significance of such distinctions.[4]

---

4. For another example of prosodic fuzziness and its potential relevance to action, see Barth-Weingarten, Küttner and Raymond (2021), and González Temer and Ogden (2021).

4. Granularity in the study of clause endings: The case of *The Problem with 'X'*

In the previous section we examined granularity before the main verb *want*; in this section we shift our focus to explore morphosyntactic granularity after the main verb, in the segment of the turn that is often notated as 'X' in the CA/IL literature on formats. Here we discuss a study by Fox and Heinemann (2017) which provides evidence that participants orient to subtle distinctions in the X component of certain types of turns.

Fox and Heinemann (2017) analyze requesting turns at the shoe repair shop, as we saw in the examples in the previous section. While customers in this setting employ a variety of syntactic designs for making their requests for service, the 2017 study focuses on two recurrent formats: *can you X* and *I wonder if X*. In previous studies of requesting formats (e.g., Curl & Drew 2008), scholars had focused on the main verb and its subject (here, *can you*, or *I wonder*), glossing the rest of the turn as 'X'. Fox and Heinemann (2017) ask the question: Could small variations in the X component also shape the action of the turn in demonstrable and interactionally consequential ways?

For the purposes of the present discussion, here we will review Fox and Heinemann's findings for *can you X*. With regard to this format, the authors examine three variations in the X component:

i.   when the X is a direct object NP, or an object of a preposition (e.g., *can you run a circular seam around it*);
ii. when the X is a deictic direct object (e.g., *can you fix this*); and
iii. when the X is an indefinite, unspecific formulation of a trouble spot on the item brought in for repair (e.g., *can you do something about this*).

In these three subtypes, the authors argue in favor of a gradation in the specificity of the requested repair, from most specific to least specific; they moreover demonstrate that these different levels of specificity have consequences for the unfolding requesting sequence.

Consider Excerpt (9), in which the customer asks *can you (find) new soles for this?*, holding up the shoes with soles facing the staff person (line 6).[5] After a beat of silence, the staff person nods, confirming that they can do the requested work, subsequently verbally confirming with *yeah* (lines 7–8).

---

5. See Mondada (2024) for multimodal transcription conventions.

Excerpt 9. [Shoe Shop 2-7-2015] (Fox & Heinemann 2017:36)

```
01      ɔ (1.2)            ɔ (0.3)      ɔ (1.0)      ɔ
   cus  ɔplaces bag on counterɔreleases bagɔsteps backɔ
02      (1.4) ɔ (3.0)
   cus         ɔ steps to counter, unties one bag
03      ∇ (0.3)#
   sho  ∇shifts gaze to bag
04 SHO: ɔ*(   )         gɑːt.* ɔ ((sniff))
   cus  ɔbrings shoe out of bagɔ
05      (.)
06 CUS: can you guys (find) newɔ #soles for this? ɔ
   cus                   ɔpresents sole to Sɔ
07      (0.2) ∇ (.)       ∇
   sho        ∇vertical nods∇
08 SHO: yeah,
09      ɔ (0.5)                 ɔ
   cus  ɔlowers shoe to counterɔ
10 CUS: kay,
11      ɔΛ #(1.5) Λɔ
   sho  Λpicks up shoe, inspects soleΛ
   cus  ɔunties second bagɔ
12 SHO: let's see:,
13 CUS: ɔI had to uːm, sː- (0.3) uːm (0.3) ɔshoe Λgoo,#
   cus  ɔ2nd shoe out of bag, onto counter ɔsole to S
   sho                                      Λgaze
                                            to sole
14 CUS: (0.4) one of 'em,
15      (0.2)
```

We can compare the quick and minimal granting of the request in the above Excerpt (9) with a somewhat more expanded sequence in Excerpt (10) below. Here the customer produces Fox and Heinemann's (2017) second variation of *can you X*, with a deictic direct object: *can you clean these up* (line 11). Although the request is granted quickly at line 12, the sequence is expanded at line 14 with a follow-up question from the staff member: *clean and polish?*; this kind of sequence expansion is typical of the second variation of *can you X* requests.

Excerpt 10. [Shoe Shop 7-29-2015] (Fox & Heinemann 2017:37)

```
10 SHO: #(he's) hard to getΛ up,
   sho  >>Λgaze to dog     Λgaze to shoes, poises pen
   cus  >>>ɔgaze to shoes-->
11 CUS: ɔΛcan you clean these up,
   sho  Λlowers pen
   cus  ɔlifts one shoe, sole facing S
12 SHO: ɔΛmm hm,
   sho  Λpoises pen
   cus  ɔturns shoe, heel facing S
13 CUS: [(   )
14 SHO: [clean ɔΛand polish?
   cus         ɔlowers one shoe to counter
   sho         Λgaze to counter, lowers pen to pad
```

```
15 CUS: yeaΛ:h, ɔΛ
            -->ɔlooks up-->
   sho      Λturns pen upside down and clicks on counterΛ
16       Λ(0.2)
   sho   Λlowers pen to pad
17 CUS: >(specially)< the heels,= ɔand thenΛ um (.)
   cus                        -->ɔgaze to shoes
   sho                                     Λgaze-shoes
18       .tchhh this: (0.2) little (0.1) decorative
19       part here, it looks like the leather split,
```

In the third variation of *can you X*, with an indefinite and unspecific formulation, Fox and Heinemann find staff members responding with a candidate type of repair, which the customer can in turn accept or decline. This is seen in case (11) below, where the customer opens with the request *can you do anything about this?* (line 2). In the course of delivery of the requesting turn, the staff member leans in and inspects the item visually, and then at line 3 offers a candidate repair: *yeah we can reline it*.

Excerpt 11. [Shoe Shop 10–13–2013] (Fox & Heinemann 2017: 38)

```
01       ɔ(0.2)ɔ
   cus   ɔlifts shoeɔ
02 CUS: can you do anyɔΛthing about ɔthi:s?ɔ=
   cus               ɔpoints        ɔtaps shoeɔ
   sho             Λleans in
03 SHO: =yeah ɔwe can reline it,
   cus           ɔputs shoe down
04       ɔ(0.5)
   cus   ɔcontinues to look at shoe-->
05 SHO: put a new leather Λliner inside (it),
   sho                    Λbacking away from counter
06       (2.0)       ɔ (1.0)  ɔ (1.0)  ɔ (1.0)  ɔ (1.0)
   cus -->ɔlooks up ɔdown    ɔup      ɔdown    ɔup>>
07       Λ(2.0) ɔ (1.0)      Λ (1.0)
   sho   Λapproaches counterΛ
   cus           ɔblows out air
   sho                    Λ picks up shoe, inspects>>
08 CUS: how much would that go about
```

Fox and Heinemann (2017) thus show that the specificity of the X component shapes the unfolding requesting sequence in significant ways. A specific NP typically gets a quick and minimal granting response; a deictic NP typically gets a granting response but then with an expansion to clarify details of the repair; and finally, an unspecific NP receives a candidate repair type, which can then be accepted or declined by the customer.

5. Discussion: What is 'grammar', and what is 'action'?

The present volume and the grammar-writing project that gave rise to it (Steensig, et al. 2023) are concerned with *grammar* in *action* in social interaction. In this section, we probe both 'grammar' and 'action' in a bit more detail, with a particular eye toward the writing of the grammar of a language. Here we pull on the threads of each of these concepts in an effort to draw attention to decisions that will need to be made as an interactionally informed grammar is being developed.

5.1 What is 'grammar'?

The studies reviewed in this chapter challenge many traditional notions of 'grammar', which is often taken to refer primarily (or only) to the morphosyntactic features of language. Written grammars of languages frequently embody this perspective, taking as their goal a comprehensive description of, e.g., sentence types in the language in question (declarative, interrogative, and imperative; Sadock & Zwicky 1985). Both the Raymond, et al. (2021) and the Fox and Heinemann (2017) studies cast such received linguistic classifications into doubt, or at least cast them in a new light, through their more-granular approaches — in the first case by blurring the boundaries between such categories, and in the second case by showing that the post-verbal components of clauses can play an important role in their interactional functions. So even with the strictest conceptualization of what is included in 'grammar' — i.e., morphosyntax — an interactionally informed written grammar of a language must be careful to be sensitive to the (in)adequacy of traditional, received linguistic categorizations to describe grammar-in-use. As Sacks put it in his *Lectures*: "The roughest message you might pick out of what I shall say is that in dealing analytically with conversations, you must be at least cautious in the use of what you've been taught about grammar" (1992: 334).

What about prosody? Would prosodic features likewise be included in the written grammar of a language? Here we saw just how much action-relevance can be conveyed prosodically on the change-of-state token *oh* (e.g., Couper-Kuhlen 2009; Freese & Maynard 1998; Heritage 1984, 1998, 2002, 2018; Local 1992, 1996; Thompson, Fox & Couper-Kuhlen 2015; Wilkinson & Kitzinger 2006): How will such variation be handled within the grammar? Moreover, as we described in Section 2, given the multitudinous interactions that prosody has with other features of turn design (e.g., different sorts of turn expansions) — and in the service of social action — such interactions merit serious consideration if a comprehensive, interactionally informed grammar is the goal.

Assuming prosody is included in the grammar, what about other prosodic-phonetic features and practices observable within the language? In the case of

English, ambiguous pronunciations (e.g., Jefferson 1978) and unreleased /t/ consonants (e.g., Local & Walker 2012) are perhaps one order of phonetic practice that can be mobilized in the service of action. But what about more continuous rhythmic patterning, like wobble voice (e.g., Ford & Fox 2010)? Perhaps even further from the traditional core of what is meant by 'grammar' are phenomena like non-phonemic clicks (e.g., Ogden 2013; Wright 2011), sighs (Hoey 2014), and other sounds that exist "on the margins of language" and are yet "at the heart of interaction" (Keevallik & Ogden 2020). And what about laughter, given that transcribing it in detail shows a range of systematicites in both form and function in interaction (e.g., Glenn 2003; Hepburn & Varney 2013; Jefferson 1979, 1985; Jefferson, Sacks & Schegloff 1987)?

Last but not least, given the embodied nature of face-to-face language use, will the body be included in the conceptualization of 'grammar'; and if so, in what ways? While there is debate amongst interactional linguists as to whether bodily conduct does (e.g., Keevallik 2018) or does not (e.g., Couper-Kuhlen 2018) constitute part of grammar, all analysts uniformly agree that embodied phenomena are produced and recognized in the service of action, as part of the semiotic totality of face-to-face social interaction. So the question remains how to account for such phenomena in an interactionally informed grammar of a language?

5.2 What is 'action'?

A parallel set of decisions will need to be made with regard to the category of 'social action', and the level(s) of granularity at which actions will be described and accounted for within the written grammar of a language. On the one hand, we have vernacularly accessible action-types with common names — e.g., request, offer, proposal, suggestion — and these can be formally specified in terms of their characteristics (e.g., Clayman & Heritage 2014; Couper-Kuhlen 2014). However, researchers have also looked more granularly at subtypes of these vernacular actions — e.g., proposals for joint-activities (Thompson, Fox & Raymond 2021) as opposed to other sorts of proposals (e.g., Zinken & Ogiermann 2011) — highlighting these as distinct, identifiable actions in their own right. Then there are actions that appear undiscoverable outside of their sequential placement, but which are nonetheless demonstrably oriented to as specific actions, implemented by particular practices in context — e.g., 'confirming an allusion' (Schegloff 1996).

How is a written grammar to deal with this complex array of different sorts of actions? What will the 'entries' be in the grammar? Just as the jury is still out on what belongs under the umbrella of 'grammar' and what does not, which components of action are more primary vs. which are less so is still an open question. When we notice significant differences in social actions being implemented by variations in syntactic format, do these differences rise to the level of being different actions? Or should they be considered under a heading of "collateral effects" (Sidnell & Enfield 2012) of some sort or another? For example, is *do you want to replace these elastics as well* the same action as *wanna do it* — both 'offers'? Or should the differences between them be understood as subtypes of the same action? While we might be comfortable claiming that *can you run a circular seam around it* and *can you do anything with this* are both 'requests', would there be analytic leverage in treating them as different actions? And even if there is analytic leverage in treating them as different actions, does that indicate that participants orient to them as different actions? On the other end of the granularity spectrum, we might also think about bringing various 'different' actions together under the same rubric — e.g., 'recruitment' (Kendrick & Drew 2016) — to see what analytic traction might be gained from thinking about such actions as constituting 'families' of actions.

Whatever the answers to these questions might be, it is clear that participants are dealing with many layers of detail as they produce and orient to turns, using all of it in the service of action; and so which precise components of that detail will and will not be included in a grammar of the language with regard to the actions that participants constitute and interpret?

Notwithstanding the list-like presentation of the questions in this section, we do not mean to offer them in any sort of pessimistic tone as concerns the grammar-writing project. Indeed, the issue of what exactly should be included under the umbrella of 'grammar' and 'action' is a complex one, with differing opinions within the field. The objective, it seems to us, should not be an attempt to satisfy everyone (because that will be impossible), but rather to make decisions on inclusion/exclusion criteria for the interactional grammar in as systematic and defensible a way as possible.

5.3 How to incorporate granularity into written grammars

As we have suggested, the levels of detail of grammar that will be relevant for our project in CA/IL are both unpredictable and in principle infinite. This theoretical claim is grounded in both Sacks' edict that there is 'order at all points', and in the empirical studies we presented above. We are now in a position to ask: how can such extraordinary flexibility and contingency be incorporated into a written grammar of a language?

We believe that the model being created by Steensig and colleagues represents a promising direction to pursue. The grammar is organized by social action formats (Fox 2007) and by actions, with hyperlinks connecting formats to actions. If every morpheme or component of a social action format is linked by hyperlinks to actions and to further descriptions of that morpheme/component, that seems to us to provide the kind of flexibility we envision being needed to incorporate maximal granularity. Moreover, such a model allows findings from any language to be added to the findings for Danish. For example, if a study is published on *I wonder X* in English, the postulated action would be linked to *I wonder X*. If a future study finds, for example, that *I wonder* + direct interrogative accomplishes a different action than does *I wonder* + indirect question (cf. Fox & Heinemann 2017, then two new hyperlinks can be added to *I wonder X*, one for each of the newly described formats. Something similar could be done from the action side: the new types of request (for example) revealed by an exploration of *I wonder* + direct interrogative could be added as hyperlinks to the descriptions of requests, with links to *I wonder X*, and *I wonder* + direct interrogative. Any future findings on similar formats in Danish, or some other language, could be linked by hyperlink to the relevant descriptions of English.

What we envision is thus massive hyperlinking, the efficacy of which has been demonstrated by Wikipedia. In a Wikipedia model, we can have hierarchy, which can change when new findings require it, as well as simple linking. Hierarchy can be achieved by linking a social action format to what might be a superordinate or subordinate format (or action). To continue with *I wonder X*, for example, *I wonder* + direct interrogative would be linked to *I wonder X* and its descriptions, and *I wonder X* could be linked to a category label such as 'embedded questions', or something similar. If such hierarchical organization is not desired, then such superordinate and subordinate links and labels would not be used.

In addition, if future research discovers that two formats that are currently disaggregated should be combined, that can be easily achieved by removing the links that separate them and putting them together as a single format.

If prosody and bodily movements are deemed to be important in the description of a format, that can be added to the description of that format; in addition, bodily movements and prosodic details can exist as separate networks of links, such that all uses of, for example, palm-up gestures are linked to one another and to the formats and actions they are associated with. For prosody, phenomena such as rise-fall pitch movements, or turn-final rallentando, can be linked to all findings on the format side as well as on the action side.

A massively linked model such as this would also be useful in supporting the experience of researchers from different traditions: a scholar from a more traditional linguistics approach could click on just the links they are interested in (e.g., 'embedded questions'), while a CA/IL scholar might be more interested in accessing information about *I wonder* + direct interrogatives and recent research on this new topic.

We are thus excited by the prospects of the massive hyperlink approach initiated by Steensig and colleagues, and we look forward to continued developments as the project continues to expand.

6. Conclusion

In a brief paper called "On Granularity", published in the *Annual Review of Sociology*, Schegloff (2000) considers in detail the design of the first few lines of a story shared between friends. He concludes by offering the following series of observations concerning the granularity of practices, of social actions, and of the observations analysts make about interactional data:

> [L]et me observe that my noticing all the particulars of the interactional fragment examined above, and my registering of these noticings in the preceding text, themselves embody a level of granularity [...]. On the one hand, the introduction of this order of observation [...] is grounded in the claim — amply supported by prior work — that interaction is co-constructed by its participants at this level of "detail" and finer yet, and that by the deployment of such resources for interaction, determinate social actions are differentially deployed, relationships constituted, etc. On the other hand, the level of granularity at which noticing is done matters not only for the social actors being studied, but for us as investigators as well; so too at what level the observed or noticed world is described. [...] In other words, a concern with granularity is a reflexive one. It is, as Garfinkel used to put it (Garfinkel 1967), both a topic and a feature of inquiry. Knowing how granularity works matters then not just substantively, but methodologically.
>
> (Schegloff 2000: 719)

In the same breath, though, Schegloff goes on to assert that "a better grasp than we have now of granularity will be needed, for we will need to know at what levels of detail actions and practices are orderly and are oriented to in the production of the quotidian life of the society" (2000: 719). How far have we come in achieving this "better grasp" on granularity in the two and a half decades since Schegloff's writing?

As we have continued to explore different dimensions of grammatical practices, and at different levels of granularity, it seems safe to say that researchers have overwhelmingly continued to discover "order at all points" (Sacks 1984) in the production and interpretation of action. That is, that every layer of grammatical detail has its reflection in the unfolding of the action sequence. And as we continuously get a better handle on how grammar is used in interaction — i.e., toward what social-interactional ends — we get a deeper understanding of what actions are and how participants produce and interpret them in context.

Our argument in this chapter has been that the more granularly we explore grammar (e.g., formats), the more granularly we understand social actions. Put another way, if we don't attend to different levels of granularity in our analyses, we won't be able to notice their effects; that is, if we don't allow for a level of granularity to have implications for social action, we won't see those implications — and, consequently, we won't be able to include them in a written grammar of the language. Thus, on the one hand, we must be alert to the possibilities of granularity — in grammar and in action — and use that to guide our inquiries. On the other hand, though, we must likewise recognize that science is produced incrementally; there will always be more levels of granularity to explore, another level deeper to look for systematicities in the formation and ascription of action.

References

Barth-Weingarten, Dagmar, Uwe-A. Küttner, and Chase Wesley Raymond. 2021. "Pivots revisited: Cesuring in Action." *Open Linguistics* 7 (1): 61–637.

Clayman, Steven E., and John Heritage. 2014. "Benefactors and beneficiaries: Benefactive status and stance in the management of offers and requests." In *Requesting in Social Interaction*, ed. by Paul Drew, and Elizabeth Couper-Kuhlen, 55–86. Amsterdam: John Benjamins.

Clift, Rebecca. 2016. *Conversation Analysis.* Cambridge: Cambridge University Press.

Clift, Rebecca, and Chase Wesley Raymond. 2018. "Actions in practice: On details in collections." *Discourse Studies* 20 (1): 90–119.

Couper-Kuhlen, Elizabeth. 2009. "A sequential approach to affect: The case of 'disappointment'." In *Talk in Interaction: Comparative Perspectives*, edited by Markku Haakana, Minna Laakso, and Jan Lindström, 94–123. Helsinki: Suomalaisen Kirjallisuuden Seura (Finnish Literature Society).

Couper-Kuhlen, Elizabeth. 2014. "What does grammar tell us about action?" *Pragmatics* 24 (3): 623–647.

Couper-Kuhlen, Elizabeth. 2018. "Finding a place for body movement in grammar." *Research on Language and Social Interaction* 51: 22–25.

Couper-Kuhlen, Elizabeth. 2021. "OH+OKAY in informing sequences: On fuzzy boundaries in a particle combination." *Open Linguistics* 7 (1): 816–836.

Couper-Kuhlen, Elizabeth, and Margret Selting. 2018. *Interactional Linguistics.* Cambridge: Cambridge University Press.

Curl, Traci S. (2006). "Offers of assistance: Constraints on syntactic design." *Journal of Pragmatics* 38: 1257–1280.

Curl, Traci S., and Paul Drew. 2008. "Contingency and action: A comparison of two forms of requesting." *Research on Language and Social Interaction* 41 (2): 1–25.

Enfield, Nick J. and Jack Sidnell. (2012). "Collateral effects, agency, and systems of language use [Reply to commentators]". *Current Anthropology* 53(3): 327–329.

Ford, Cecilia E., and Barbara A. Fox. 2010. Multiple practices for constructing laughables. In *Prosody in Interaction*, edited by Dagmar Barth-Weingarten, Elisabeth Reber, and Margret Selting, 339–368. Amsterdam: John Benjamins.

Fox, Barbara A. (2007). "Principles Shaping Grammatical Practices: An Exploration." *Discourse Studies* 9 (3): 299–318.

Fox, Barbara A., and Trine Heinemann. 2015. "The alignment of manual and verbal displays in requests for the repair of an object." *Research on Language and Social Interaction* 48 (3): 342–62.

Fox, Barbara A., and Trine Heinemann. 2016. "Rethinking format: An examination of requests." *Language in Society* 45 (4): 499–531.

Fox, Barbara A., and Trine Heinemann. 2017. "Issues in action formation: Requests and the problem with x." *Open Linguistics* 3: 31–64.

Fox, Barbara A., Lorenza Mondada, and Marja-Leena Sorjonen (eds.). 2023. *Encounters at the Counter: The Organization of Shop Interactions*. Cambridge: Cambridge University Press.

Freese, Jeremy, and Douglas W. Maynard. 1998. "Prosodic features of bad news and good news in conversation." *Language in Society* 27: 195–219.

Garfinkel, Harold. 1967. *Studies in Ethnomethodology*. Englewood Cliffs, N.J.: Prentice-Hall.

Glenn, Phillip. 2003. *Laughter in Interaction*. Cambridge: Cambridge University Press.

González Temer, Verónica, and Richard Ogden. 2021. "Non-convergent boundaries and action ascription in multimodal interaction." *Open Linguistics* 7(1): 685–706.

Hepburn, Alexa, and Scott Varney. (2013). "Beyond ((laughter)): Some notes on transcription." In *Studies in Laughter in Interaction*, ed. by Phillip Glenn and Elizabeth Holt, 25–38. London: Bloomsbury.

Heritage, John. 1984. "A change-of-state token and aspects of Its sequential placement." In *Structures of Social Action*, ed. by J. Maxwell Atkinson, and John Heritage, 299–345. Cambridge: Cambridge University Press.

Heritage, John. 1998. "*Oh*-prefaced responses to inquiry." *Language in Society* 27 (3): 291–334.

Heritage, John. (2002). "*Oh*-prefaced responses to assessments: A method of modifying agreement/disagreement." In *The Language of Turn and Sequence*, ed. by Cecilia E. Ford, Barbara A. Fox, and Sandra A. Thompson, 196–224. Oxford: Oxford University Press.

Heritage, John. (2018). "The ubiquity of epistemics: A rebuttal to the 'epistemics of epistemics' group." *Discourse Studies* 20 (1): 14–56.

Heritage, John., Chase Wesley Raymond, and Paul Drew. 2019. "Constructing apologies: Reflexive relationships between apologies and offenses." *Journal of Pragmatics* 142: 185–200.

Heritage, John, and Geoffrey Raymond. 2005. "The terms of agreement: Indexing epistemic authority and subordination in assessment sequences." *Social Psychology Quarterly* 68 (1): 15–38.

Hoey, Elliott. 2014. "Sighing in interaction: Somatic, semiotic, and social." *Research on Language and Social Interaction* 47 (2): 175–200.

Jefferson, Gail. 1978. "What's In a 'Nyem'?" *Sociology* 12 (1): 135–139.

Jefferson, Gail 1979. "A Technique for Inviting Laughter and its Subsequent Acceptance/Declination." In *Everyday Language: Studies in Ethnomethodology*, ed. by George Psathas, 79–96. New York: Irvington Publishers.

Chapter 2. Granularity in grammar and action **45**

Jefferson, Gail. 1985. "An Exercise in the Transcription and Analysis of Laughter." In *Handbook of Discourse Analysis Volume* 3, ed. by Teun A. van Dijk, 25–34. New York: Academic Press.

Jefferson, Gail, Harvey Sacks, and Emanuel A. Schegloff. 1987. "Notes on Laughter in the Pursuit of Intimacy." In *Talk and Social Organisation*, edited by Graham Button, and John R. E. Lee, 152–205. Clevedon: Multilingual Matters.

Keevallik, Leelo. 2018. "What does embodied interaction tell us about grammar?" *Research on Language and Social Interaction* 51: 1–21.

Keevallik, Leelo, and Richard Ogden. 2020. "Sounds on the Margins of Language at the Heart of Interaction." *Research on Language and Social Interaction* 53 (1): 1–18.

Kendrick, Kobin H., and Paul Drew. 2016. "Recruitment: Offers, Requests, and the Organization of Assistance in Interaction." *Research on Language and Social Interaction* 49 (1): 1–19.

Küttner, Uwe-A. 2018. "Investigating inferences in sequences of action: The case of claiming 'just-now' recollection with *oh that's right*." *Open Linguistics* 4 (1): 101–126.

Local, John. 1992. "Conversational phonetics: Some aspects of news receipts in everyday talk." *York Papers in Linguistics* 16: 37–79.

Local, John. 1996. "Conversational phonetics: Some aspects of news receipts in everyday talk." In *Prosody in Conversation*, ed. by Elizabeth Couper-Kuhlen, and Margret Selting, 177–230. Cambridge: Cambridge University Press.

Local, John, and Gareth Walker. 2012. "How phonetic features project more talk." *Journal of the International Phonetic Association* 42 (3): 255–280.

Maynard, Douglas W., and Jeremy Freese. 2012. "Good News, Bad News, and Affect: Practical and Temporal 'Emotion' Work in Everyday Life." In *Emotion in Interaction*, ed. by Anssi Peräkylä, and Marja-Leena Sorjonen, 92–112. Oxford: Oxford University Press.

Mondada, Lorenza. 2024. "Multimodal Transcription Conventions." In *The Cambridge Handbook of Research Methods in Conversation Analysis*, ed. by Jeffrey D. Robinson, Rebecca Clift, Kobin H. Kendrick, and Chase Wesley Raymond. Cambridge: Cambridge University Press.

Ogden, Richard. 2013. "Clicks and percussives in English conversation." *Journal of the International Phonetic Association* 43 (3): 299–320.

Raymond, Chase Wesley, Rebecca Clift, and John Heritage. 2021. "Reference without anaphora: On agency through grammar." *Linguistics: An Interdisciplinary Journal of the Language Sciences* 59 (3): 715–755.

Raymond, Chase Wesley, Jeffrey D. Robinson, Barbara A. Fox, Sandra A. Thompson, and Kristella Montiegl. 2021. "Modulating action through minimization: Syntax in the service of offering and requesting." *Language in Society* 50: 53–91.

Raymond, Geoffrey, and John Heritage. 2006. "The epistemics of social relations: Owning grandchildren." *Language in Society* 35: 677–705.

Robinson, Jeffrey D., Rebecca Clift, Kobin H. Kendrick, and Chase Wesley Raymond. 2024. *The Cambridge Handbook of Methods in Conversation Analysis*. Cambridge: Cambridge University Press.

Sacks, Harvey. 1984. "Notes on Methodology." In *Structures of Social Action*, ed. by J. Maxwell Atkinson, and John Heritage, 21–27. Cambridge: Cambridge University Press.

Sacks, Harvey. 1992. *Lectures on Conversation (2 vols.)*. New York: Blackwell.

Sadock, Jerrold, and Arnold M. Zwicky. 1985. "Speech act distinctions in syntax." In *Language Typology and Syntactic Description*, ed. by Timothy Shopen, 155–96. Cambridge: Cambridge University Press.

Schegloff, Emanuel A. 1996. "Confirming Allusions: Toward an Empirical Account of Action." *American Journal of Sociology* 102 (1): 161–216.

Schegloff, Emanuel A. 2000. "On granularity." *Annual Review of Sociology* 26: 715–20.

Schegloff, Emanuel A. (2007). *Sequence Organization in Interaction: A Primer in Conversation Analysis (Volume 1)*. Cambridge: Cambridge University Press.

Steensig, Jakob, Maria Jørgensen, Nicholas Mikkelsen, Karita Suomalainen, and Søren Sandager Sørensen. 2023. "Toward a grammar of Danish talk-in-interaction: From action formation to grammatical description." *Research on Language and Social Interaction* 56 (2): 116–140.

Thompson, Sandra A., Barbara A. Fox, and Elizabeth Couper-Kuhlen. 2015. *Grammar in Everyday Talk: Building Responsive Actions*. Cambridge: Cambridge University Press.

Thompson, Sandra A., Barbara A. Fox, and Chase Wesley Raymond. 2021. "The Grammar of Proposals for Joint Activities." *Interactional Linguistics* 1 (1): 123–151.

Wilkinson, Sue, and Celia Kitzinger. (2006). "Surprise as an interactional achievement: Reaction tokens in conversation." *Social Psychology Quarterly* 69: 150–182.

Wright, Melissa. 2011. "On clicks in English talk-in-interaction." *Journal of the International Phonetic Association* 41 (2): 207–229.

Zinken, Jörg, and Arnulf Deppermann. 2017. "A cline of visible commitment in the situated design of imperative turns." In *Imperative Turns at Talk: The Design of Directives in Action*, ed. by Marja-Leena Sorjonen, Liisa Raevaara, and Elizabeth Couper-Kuhlen, 27–64. Amsterdam: John Benjamins.

Zinken, Jörg, and Eva Ogiermann. 2011. "How to Propose an Action as Objectively Necessary: The Case of Polish *Trzeba x* ('One Needs to *x*')." *Research on Language and Social Interaction* 44 (3): 263–287.

CHAPTER 3

'Idea-Suggestions' in an interactional grammar
Sequential organization and grammatical formats

Elizabeth Couper-Kuhlen & Sandra A. Thompson
University of Helsinki | University of California Santa Barbara

In this chapter, we explore the grammar of 'Suggestions' and the sequences they engender. 'Suggestion' is used here as a technical term to refer to a speaker forwarding an action to be performed by the recipient that will benefit the recipient. The data suggest several sub-types of Suggestion, the focus here being on the sub-type in which a speaker initiates a sequence by volunteering an idea for something that the other might do to their benefit, which we call 'Idea-Suggestion', or 'I-Suggestion'. We discuss the formats that speakers of American English use to put forth these kinds of Suggestions, and argue that the tentativeness built into the work that I-Suggestions do reveals what participants orient to in the trajectory of the ensuing sequence. A final section explores how our findings might be captured in an interactional grammar of American English.

Keywords: Suggestion, advice, recruitment, Idea-Suggestion, benefit, social action format, *why don't you*, hypothetical conditional

1. Introduction

In this paper we build on distinctions between four types of directive action in English that participants can be shown to orient to in mundane conversation: Request, Offer, Proposal, and Suggestion (Couper-Kuhlen 2014). All four of these action types have in common that they involve one participant trying to get another to do something (Erwin-Tripp 1976). However, they can be distinguished from one another in terms of *agency*, who will carry out the action being advocated, and of *benefaction*, who will benefit from the action in question (cf. also Clayman & Heritage 2014). While with Requests the speaker is advocating that the recipient carry out an action that will benefit the speaker, with Offers the speaker is advocating that they themselves carry out an action that will benefit the recipient. With Proposals the speaker is advocating an action that will be carried out by both speaker and recipient and that will benefit both, whereas with Sugges-

https://doi.org/10.1075/slsi.37.03cur
© 2025 John Benjamins Publishing Company

tions the speaker is advocating that the recipient carry out an action that will benefit the recipient. Requests, Offers, and Proposals as action types have each received a good deal of attention in the recent literature (Curl & Drew 2008; Drew & Couper-Kuhlen 2014; Thompson et al. 2015; Kendrick & Drew 2014; Stivers & Sidnell 2016; Thompson et al. 2021). Suggestions, however, have not been investigated as extensively. With this chapter we attempt to right the balance, and at the same time to show what an interactional grammar account might look like.

Our study is in line with the approach adopted by Steensig et al. (2023) in their work on an interactional grammar for Danish talk-in-interaction. Like them, we assume that the relevancies to be captured in an interactional grammar are those between the social actions that participants can be observed to engage in through talk-in-interaction and the linguistic resources, broadly understood, that they routinely mobilize to implement these actions. Like them, we appeal to the notion of 'social action format' as proposed by Fox (2007) to designate recurrent patterns of action implementation. We start from the assumption that in order to study social action formats empirically, we need to have a clear idea of what counts as the social action in question. One way to do so is to develop 'technical' understandings of related social actions based on what participants orient to in their interactions with one another. With this approach it is possible to establish robust relations between formats and social actions that lend themselves to the writing of interactional grammars.

There appear to be several sub-types of Suggestion, understood as a technical term in the sense of Couper-Kuhlen (2014), i.e., the speaker is advocating that the recipient carry out an action that will benefit the recipient. One type is encountered in contexts of troubles-telling and complaining, when an interlocutor presents something as problematic (Jefferson & Lee 1981) and the recipient responds by giving *advice* (for more on advice-giving see Couper-Kuhlen & Thompson 2022; Heritage & Sefi 1992; Stivers et al. 2017). We will refer to this sub-type here as 'Advice-Suggestion', or 'A-Suggestion' for short. However, there is another sub-type of Suggestion that has little to do with troubles or complaints: it occurs in environments of planning future events (Robinson & Kevoe-Feldman 2016; Heritage & Clayman 2024) or of spontaneously organizing an ongoing activity. It is this sub-type, which we propose to call 'Idea-Suggestion' or 'I-Suggestion', that we wish to focus on here. An investigation of I-Suggestions is particularly significant for building an interactional grammar, because it invites a careful study of the relationship between grammatical formats and social actions. We will return to this relationship in Sections 5 and 6.

Our motivation for adopting the term 'Idea-Suggestion' comes from the fact that participants themselves sometimes refer to this kind of suggestion as "an idea", "a good idea", or "not a bad idea". For instance, in Excerpt (1) Mom is at dinner with her son Wesley, his fiancée Prudence, and her daughter Virginia, and now inquires whether anyone would like more iced tea:

Excerpt 1. "More ice" (Virginia_6:39), face-to-face, informal interaction
```
16 MOM: =.hhh whooh! it is so hot tonight.
17      would somebody like some more iced tea.
18      (0.8)
19 WES: uh(b)- (0.4) I('ll) take more ice.
20      (1.3)
21 MOM: .hhhh well,
22      (2.0)
23 MOM: let me: get up and go get some.
24 VIR: whynchya get it yourself. ((addressed to Wesley))
25      (.)
26 PRU: ehhh!
27 MOM: that's a good idea,
```

Mom's rather pointed response to Wesley's request for more ice (line 19), something that was not originally on offer, is formulated as offering to 'get up and go get some' (although she is already moving about) (line 23). Virginia now challenges this move by suggesting that Wesley get the ice himself (line 24). In line 27, Mom seconds Virginia's suggestion by calling it 'a good idea'.

2. Data and procedure

Our data consist of transcribed recordings of naturally occurring informal everyday conversations in American English. All are either audio recordings of telephone calls or video recordings of face-to-face interactions, thus ensuring that we have roughly comparable access to the bodily-visual behavior of the participants as the participants themselves did. The data come from a variety of sources, including our private corpora, which are indicated with each extract, and which total approximately 30 hours of conversation.

For this chapter on Idea-Suggestions, we collected all sequences in which a speaker proposes that a recipient do something in the immediate or remote future that will be to the recipient's benefit, exhaustively where possible and otherwise to a saturation point. We consider this collection, totaling 75 such sequences, to be representative of I-suggestions in mundane American English conversation. Cases involving advice-giving, i.e., in which the recipient has been complaining, engaging in troubles talk, or has specifically requested advice, were excluded. (We will return to similarities and differences between Idea-Suggestions and Advice-Suggestions in Section 4.) For the extracts selected as examples here, we have aimed to preserve or convert to a modified Jeffersonian transcription (Jefferson 2004) with orthography normalized for readability.

3. Features of Idea-Suggestion sequences

3.1 Preliminaries to I-Suggestions

As a directive type of action, Suggestions can be delicate: a participant can be perceived as presumptuous if they attempt to manage a recipient's future by advocating that the recipient undertake some action, even if in their estimation it would be in the recipient's interest. In part perhaps to prevent such an impression arising, speakers of I-Suggestions may anticipate in a preliminary move that what they are about to put forward is just an 'idea', with that term implying that it is not an injunction, but only a tentative thought that might or might not be welcome or feasible in practice.

When I-Suggestions are projected in a pre-sequence (Schegloff 1980, 2007), a preliminary turn is used to announce an upcoming I-Suggestion either explicitly, e.g., 'here's an idea', or implicitly, e.g., 'I'll tell you what' (Terasaki 2004). This provides an opportunity for recipients to either align with or block what is projected to come next. For the most part, recipients signal acquiescence by simply letting the opportunity pass or agreeing with 'okay'. For instance, in the following excerpt from a telephone conversation between Mark and JoAnn, the two have been talking about when JoAnn might come and visit Mark:

Excerpt 2. "Call me 1" (SF 1: 4), telephone, informal interaction
```
01 JOA: =can I come on the weekend?
02 MAR: .hhh ya:h?
03      (0.4)
04 JOA: oka:y,?
05 MAR: .hhh (          ), .t .hh how about Saturday.
06 JOA: (      fu:n.)
07 MAR: .hhhh okay I'll tell you what JoAnn,
08      (0.4)
09 MAR: .khhhhh(w) (0.2) why: don:'t
10      if I don't see you and I probably will before
11      Saturday;
12      (0.8)
13 MAR: .t .khhhhh uh:m why don'tchu call me Saturday
14      morning.
15 JOA: u-w'l I'll probably call you Thursday.
```

In line 5, in response to JoAnn's request in line 1 to come on the weekend, Mark proposes Saturday. JoAnn's response is unclear, but Mark's turn in line 7 reveals that he takes it as affirmative. He now projects an upcoming suggestion by saying *I'll tell you what*, appending JoAnn's name in an appeal (Clayman 2013). Note that JoAnn does not respond in the ensuing 0.4-sec. pause, implying that she has no objection to Mark's making a suggestion. Then, in line 9, Mark begins to formulate an I-Suggestion with *why don't*, repairing it, after an interspersed compound conditional, to a full-blown I-Suggestion in lines 13–14: *why don't you call me Saturday morning*. This suggestion would benefit JoAnn, as it is she who has expressed an interest in visiting Mark (line 1). Following Mark's suggestion, JoAnn responds by agreeing to call, but on Thursday rather than Saturday (line 15).

A little later in the same call, another I-Suggestion sequence ensues. Mark is just giving JoAnn his phone number:

Excerpt 3. "Call me 2" (SF 1), telephone, informal interaction
```
01 MAR: o:kay, it's four nine eight,
02 JOA: mm hm, hh .hh
03 MAR: three eight,
04 JOA: mm hm,
05 MAR: oh three.
06 JOA: (okay.)
07 MAR: yeh.
08 JOA: got it.
09 MAR: .hhhhh oka::y now here's the plan.
10 JOA: okay.
11 MAR: pk .hhhhhh uh:m if I don't see you?
12      (0.7)
13 MAR: .hhh why don'tche call me sometime before noon
14      Saturday.
15 JOA: okay.
16 MAR: okay?
17 JOA: mm-hm.
```

In line 9, Mark announces his upcoming Idea-Suggestion with another pre-, *here's the plan*, to which JoAnn acquiesces by saying *okay* (line 10). Mark reiterates his suggestion that if he doesn't see her beforehand she should call him, now with a more precise time line: *why don't you call me sometime before noon Saturday* (lines 13–14). JoAnn agrees to this plan in next turn (line 15).

3.2 Formats for I-Suggestions

In the previous sections, we encountered several instantiations of one of our most frequent Idea-Suggestion formats: *why don't you...* We note that fully one-third of our collection involves the use of *why don't you* (=WDY). In our recent work on advice-giving (Couper-Kuhlen & Thompson 2022, Thompson & Couper-Kuhlen 2020), we also found WDY to be a frequent format, underlining one striking similarity between I-Suggestions and A-Suggestions in American English. In Section 4 we return to further similarities and to differences between these two action sub-types.

There are, however, other recurrent formats for I-Suggestions in our data. Here are our top five, in order of their frequency in our collection. All of these formats contain *you* referring to the recipient, reflecting the fact that Suggestions advocate something that the recipient might do in the future.

- Fixed expression *why don't you*: *why don't you...*
- Obligation & necessity modals: *you should/ought to/you'll have to/you'd better...*
- Hypothetical conditionals: *if you V(-ed)*
- Ability & possibility modals: *you can/could...*
- Constructions with *want to*: *(maybe) you wanna...*

90% of our collection involves one of these five format types. We will examine each of these in the following, paying particular attention to their distinct interactional affordances.

3.2.1 'Why don't you' (WDY) formats

Despite their interrogative form, WDY formats are not doing questioning when they are used to make I-Suggestions. Nor, despite their negative form, are they suggesting that the recipient *not* undertake the action named. In Excerpt (3), Mark's *why don't you call me some time before noon on Saturday* is not asking JoAnn to account for an intention not to call him on Saturday morning. One indication that this WDY is a formulaic expression, not to be understood in its literal sense, is provided by JoAnn's answer in Excerpt (3): *okay* in line 14 is not a possible answer to a genuine *why* question. Instead this *okay* shows that JoAnn has interpreted Mark's prior turn as an arrangement-making suggestion that will facilitate their getting together on the weekend, and with it she acquiesces in the proposed arrangement. Further evidence can be seen in the fact that *why don't you* is articulated in a reduced form, represented in the transcript of Excerpt (3) as *why don'tche* and in Excerpt (1) as *whynchya*, or /ˈwaɪn-tʃə/ (Thompson & Couper-Kuhlen 2020).

WDY formats can come across as relatively presumptuous when used to make I-Suggestions. This may be because in other contexts they imply that there is no good reason for the recipient *not* to undertake the action being advocated (Couper-Kuhlen & Thompson 2022; Thompson & Couper-Kuhlen 2020). In fact, for this reason a WDY format is sometimes avoided in making an Idea-Suggestion. This is arguably what happens in the following telephone call between Mom and her daughter Sally (Chris is Sally's partner):

Excerpt 4. "Tennis lessons" (Call Friend engn 6899), telephone, informal interaction
```
01 MOM: what's Chris up to today.
02      (0.6)
03 SAL: ((click))he's [playing tennis.=right no:w;
04 MOM:              [yeh
05      oh is he.
06 SAL: yea:h
07      (0.4)
08 MOM: .hhh ih ↑why don'tch-
09      (0.3)
```

```
10       ↑have you decided about taking tennis lessons?
11       (1.2)
12 SAL: hh ihhh no::[hhh hhh hhh hhh
13 MOM:             [↓have you ↑thou:ght about taking
14       tennis lessons.
15 SAL: ↑no:: ≈hhh hhh hhh hhh hhh
16 MOM: becau::se?
17 SAL: hhh ihhh
18       ihhh u::h:
19       (0.4)
20       ↑I don't know
21       I guess I ju? (0.4) don't like it enou:gh.
22       (1.4)
23 MOM: °okay,°
24       (1.3)
25 MOM: ihhh ↑I mean you don't have to=
26       =I wouldn't suggest you play with him; initially
27       anyway.
28 SAL: no I ca:n't.
29       (1.5)
30       I tri:ed that once already
```

Upon hearing that Chris is out playing tennis, Mom launches a turn in a high-pitched voice beginning with *why don'tch-* (line 8) but suddenly breaks off before formulating the action she wishes to advocate. From what transpires, we can surmise that Mom was about to say 'take tennis lessons' (cf. lines 10 and 13) and that what she is aiming for is a suggestion about what Sally should do (this becomes obvious when she says in lines 26–27 that she is *not* suggesting Sally play tennis with Chris right away, leaving unstated what she *is* suggesting). However, in line 10, instead of *advocating* that Sally take tennis lessons, Mom opts in favor of *inquiring* whether Sally has decided to do so. Her self-repair suggests that a WDY format recommending the action in question is judged to be less appropriate in the given context than an interrogative form inquiring whether that action will take place. Indeed, the latter format assigns autonomy over the future to Sally by framing tennis lessons as Sally's decision, not Mom's recommendation.

We can conclude that a WDY format puts forth an I-Suggestion purely from the speaker's perspective: by presenting the action to be advocated as the speaker's recommendation irrespective of any wish or desire on the part of the recipient, it deprives the recipient of autonomy. It only indirectly allows for the possibility of circumstances or conditions that might prevent the recipient from carrying out the action. Essentially it treats the recommended action as the obvious thing to do, so obvious that there is no alternative.[1]

---

1. It may not be a coincidence that in our data, WDY formats that are used for suggestions are often preceded by pre-s, that is, after the recipient's willingness to hear a suggestion has gone on record. This observation, however, requires further research to be substantiated.

3.2.2 *Formats with obligation and necessity modals*

Idea-Suggestions can also be implemented with modal auxiliaries such as *should, ought to, 'll have to* or *'d better*: we subsume these under the label of obligation and necessity because of their modal semantics (see also Quirk et al. 1985: 221).[2] When used to make Idea-Suggestions, obligation and necessity modals occur in declarative statements with main verbs formulating the action and *you* subjects referring to the recipient.

For instance, in the following excerpt Wendy, who is currently in Brooklyn, has telephoned her friend Chris, who is working in Madrid. They are discussing Wendy's plans to visit her mother in Florida for Christmas. The allusive reference (Ewing 2018) in line 1 is presumably to a travel agent:

Excerpt 5. "You should come" (Call Home 6071_283.236), telephone, informal interaction

```
01 WEN: ↑today I called-
02      (0.4) °hh
03      ↑do you know it's the same price:
04      for me to go to Spai:n,
05      as it is to go to Florida?
06 CHR: re:ally?
07 WEN: .hh it's five hundred and seventy dollars.=
08 CHR: [(it's that) cheap? ]
09 WEN: [=it's a hundred dol]lars more.
10 CHR: .hh you should co:::me.((sung))
11 WEN: I'd like to come but when: (.) are you going to
12      Morocco:.
13      (0.2)
14 CHR: from the twenty-eighth to the third.
15      (0.4)
16 WEN: aw (hhow luck)
17      (0.6) .hh
18      cuz I don't think I can ^ge:t there;=
19      =until the (.) the twenty-ninth.
20      I don't think I can ^le::ave until the
21      twenty-ninth.
```

Wendy's announcement that travelling to Spain is roughly the same price as travelling to Florida prompts Chris to make a spontaneous suggestion that she should join him in Spain: *you should co:::me* (line 9). In this context, the implication is that if the price is so cheap (cf. line 8), Wendy has an obligation to choose Spain over Florida.

---

2. We use this designation, 'Modal Auxiliaries,' as a convenient way to group the cases in question. Clearly, categories and terms from non-interactional grammars should be used advisedly in interactional grammars. They are most meaningful if internal evidence for them can also be found in the data (cf. Ford et al. 2013).

Chapter 3. Idea-Suggestions in an interactional grammar   55

Clearly, for one participant to state categorically that a recipient has an obligation to do something is presumptuous, even if it is judged to be for their own benefit (which Chris is implying would be the case). This may be why Chris adds a jocular overlay to the word *come* in line 10, producing it in a sung voice that carries an element of non-seriousness. Wendy's response, however, shows that she takes Chris' suggestion seriously, and a lengthy sequence of negotiation ensues over how the two can coordinate their plans to get together in Spain.

On other occasions, speakers making Idea-Suggestions attenuate the categorical nature of a *you should* format by adding a mark of uncertainty, e. g., 'maybe' or 'I guess'. This is what happens in the following excerpt from a telephone conversation between two erstwhile friends, Bob and Mark. Bob is planning a party for later that week, which Mark has found out about via the grapevine. Bob explains that he thought Mark would 'pick up' the information and know that he was invited, but Mark insists that no one mentioned it to him. The two agree that communication between them isn't "quite what it should be" (data not shown here). Now Mark asks who else will be at the party, to which Bob responds "the old crew", "the old social clique", and continues:

Excerpt 6. "Make a few phone calls" (SF2_683.49), telephone, informal interaction

```
01 BOB: wonder if Ted'n Patty know about it.
02      (0.4)
03 MAR: [.hhhhh
04 BOB: [(            )
05      (0.4)
06 MAR: .hhh[hhhh
07 BOB:     [_(_)_.
08 MAR: .hhh well I don't⁷ (.) I doubt that they do:,
09      (0.4)
10 BOB: ye[:ah.
11 MAR:   [I mean who is going to tell them.
12 BOB: I guess::: maybe that's up to us.
13 MAR: well maybe you should uh make a few ↑phone
14      calls.
15 BOB: yeah maybe I shou:ld. uh
16      (0.3)
```

When Mark observes that Ted and Patty probably don't know about Bob's upcoming party (line 8) and asks rhetorically *who is going to tell them* (line 11), Bob declares that the responsibility may lie with Mark and himself (*that's up to us*, line 12). But Mark now makes a different suggestion, namely that Bob be the one to let his invitees know about the party: *well maybe you should uh make a few phone calls* (lines 13–14), a suggestion that is designed to benefit Mark, since it is in Mark's interest that his friends not be excluded from his party.

The choice of a *you should* format is perhaps not surprising in this context, given what has transpired so far between Bob and Mark. Rather than advancing an idea spontaneously with a WDY format, i.e., 'whyncha make a few phone calls', Mark opts to foreground Bob's moral obligation with *you should*. But he attenuates the effect of his assertion by prefacing it with a mark of uncertainty, *maybe*, which – not coincidentally – resonates with Bob's prior *maybe that's up to us* (line 12). Interestingly, Bob picks up *maybe* in his response: *yeah maybe I should* (line 15). Thus, both participants in this sequence acknowledge that Bob has an obligation but they downplay it by qualifying it as tentative.

In approximately half of the cases in our collection speakers use either WDY formats or assertions with obligation or necessity modals (optionally attenuated with *maybe* or *I guess*) — both relatively presumptuous formats — for making Idea-Suggestions. In the other half, however, they opt for less presuming formats. It is to these we turn now.

3.2.3 *Hypothetical conditional formats*

In these formats, speakers incorporate the naming of the action they are advocating into a hypothetical conditional clause beginning with *if you*. The tense of the following verb may be either present or past. In the latter case, it is said to be 'backshifted' (Quirk et al. 1985:1091), which is generally considered to be indicative of a more remote possibility. The conditional clause is often left freestanding, with an unexpressed consequent clause.[3] Both of these features, backshifting and a freestanding conditional clause, are present in the I-Suggestion that Mom makes to her daughter Sally in the follow-up to their exchange in Excerpt (4), presented here as Excerpt (7):

Excerpt 7. "Beginner's group" (Call Friend engn 6899), telephone, informal interaction

```
25 MOM: ihhh ↑I mean you don't have to=
26       =I wouldn't suggest you play with him; initially
27       anyway.
28 SAL: no I ca:n't.
29       (1.5)
30       I tri:ed that once already.
31       (0.4)
32 MOM: ↑well but I mean if you pla:yed- (0.4)
33       you know with a b- (0.4) beginning grou:p,=
34       =beginner's grou:p,
```

---

3. This format has long been noted to have evolved as a vehicle for a range of directive actions, particularly requests, in a variety of languages (see, e.g., Günthner 2000, Laury 2012, Lindström et al. 2016, Maschler et al. 2020, Pekarek Doehler & Horlacher this volume); Excerpt (7) illustrates its use for doing I-Suggestions as well.

Chapter 3. Idea-Suggestions in an interactional grammar   57

```
35 SAL: yea:h_
36      (0.5)
37 SAL: ((fumbling with phone))
38      (0.6)
39 MOM: ↑because you're y:ou're you:'re uh (0.4)
40      u:h a good a:thlete,
41      (1.5)
42      you're aggre:ssi:ve,
43      (1.0)
44      ihhh and I think if if you developed some
45      proficiency with it;=
46      =you would like it.
47      (3.4)
48 MOM: ↑thi:nk?
49      (0.6)
50 SAL: ↑I probably wou:ld,
51      but the one thing that I (.) do not li:ke;
52      ↑mo:st about it is:- (0.4)
53      it's generally a (0.3) spri:ng summer type of
54      spo:rt;
55      (1.2)
56 SAL: and it's very aerobic;=
57      =and I ca:n't sta:nd running around out in the
58      heat like tha:t.
```

Mom's I-Suggestion that Sally should play tennis with a beginner's group is embedded in a hypothetical conditional clause: *if you played...* (lines 32–34). Note that the conditional clause has no accompanying consequent clause. Both the repaired phrase *beginning group* and its repair *beginner's group* are produced with final rising pitch, which treats the turn-constructional unit as possibly complete, and mobilizes a response to it (Stivers & Rossano 2010): cf. Section 3.3 below. Sally comes in without delay, albeit with a non-committal *yea:h* (line 35). After a lapse in which Sally can be heard to fumble with her phone (lines 36–38), Mom now proceeds to provide accounts for her I-Suggestion, citing Sally's athletic constitution and combative character (lines 39–40 and 42), which she implies predestine her to be successful at something that would bring her pleasure if she engaged in it (lines 44–46). Note the use of the conditional auxiliary 'would' here, which – in contrast to the predictive auxiliary 'will' – underlines the more remote nature of the consequent following a backshifted protasis.

How does a hypothetical conditional format for implementing an I-Suggestion compare with WDY formats and modal-auxiliary assertions? To begin with, it treats the action being advocated not as the speaker's recommendation ('I recommend you do X') nor as the recipient's obligation ('you are obligated to do X'), but as a remote possibility in a hypothetical world ('suppose you did X'). With a hypothetical conditional format, the action is removed from the real world into an alternative world full of contingencies and thus appears more remote and

58 Elizabeth Couper-Kuhlen & Sandra A. Thompson

less likely. A speaker who uses the hypothetical format to implement a suggestion makes this remoteness explicit by choosing backshifted forms.

3.2.4 *Formats with ability and possibility modals*

I-Suggestions can also be made with assertions that involve ability and possibility modal verbs, e.g., *can* or *could*, and that have *you*-subjects referring to the recipient. The action to be advocated is presented as a possibility, often because it is known to be within the recipient's ability or capability. Here is an instance where such a format is deployed: Roberta, who is American, is describing to a friend how she plans to raise her young daughter bilingually with her Dutch husband.

Excerpt 8. "Speak French" (Call Friend engn 4984), telephone, informal interaction

```
01 ROB: what do you think of that plan.
02 LIZ: I think that's a great pla:n.
03 ROB: °you know° I thi:nk I ? (0.3)[it's
04 LIZ:                            [cause she's gonna
05      be more inclined to speak English,=
06      =she's going to speak it [at school,
07 ROB:                          [anyway (.)
08      yea:[h.
09 LIZ:     [she's gonna hear it on [tee_vee:
10 ROB:                             [yeah
11      °yeah°
12      (0.3)
13 LIZ: you kno:w,
14      and you could als:o=
15      =↑they [↑Ro:b;
16 ROB:        [((clears throat))
17 LIZ: [you could ] spe:ak Fre:nch to her!=
18 ROB: [((coughs))]
19 LIZ: =maybe she'll [be ftr]i:lingual. hhh  hhh
20 ROB:               [ri:ght.]
21 LIZ: °hhh hhh hhh hhh hhh hhh°
22 ROB: oh: we've got enough [on our [plate as it  is]
23 LIZ:                      [hhh   [.hhh   heh  heh]
24 ROB: fri:ght no:w! .hhhhh
25      [but uh::
26 LIZ: [fI'm just teasing you.
```

Having explained why she approves of Roberta's plan in lines 4–6 and 9, Liz suddenly breaks off to advance a new idea. The break is announced with a high-pitched *hey Rob* (line 15), somewhat reminiscent of the I-Suggestion preliminary *I'll tell you what JoAnn* that we encountered in Extract (2). Liz now moves to present her I-Suggestion in an animated voice: *you could speak French to her!* (line 17), followed immediately by a possible incentive for doing so, *maybe she'll be trilingual* (line 19). The implication is that this would be beneficial to both

Chapter 3. Idea-Suggestions in an interactional grammar **59**

Roberta and her daughter. Liz's smile voice in this TCU together with her subsequent voiceless laughter (line 21) imply that her suggestion may not be wholly serious; this is later confirmed when she describes it as *teasing* (line 26). However, the format she employs is a genuine one encountered elsewhere for implementing I-Suggestions.

An I-Suggestion made with an ability or possibility modal format is distinct from one delivered with an obligation or necessity modal. Although both are used to make assertions about the action being advocated, formats with *should* or *ought to* treat this action as morally compelling, while those with *can* or *could* merely present it as a possibility.

3.2.5 *Formats with 'you want to'*

I-Suggestions made with these formats are intriguing because they are formulated as assertions that couch the action the speaker is advocating as something the recipient 'wants', although *prima facie* the speaker has no epistemic access to the other's wishes or desires.[4] Often these formats are accompanied by a mark of speaker uncertainty, e.g., *maybe you wanna...*, or tentativeness, e.g., *you may/ might wanna...*, allowing for the eventuality that the action may not correspond to the other's desires. For instance, in the following telephone conversation two erstwhile friends, Ava and Bee, are negotiating over how they might get together the next day. Bee used to go to the same school that Ava still attends.

Excerpt 9. "Come down to school" (Two Girls_834.00), telephone, informal interaction
```
15 AVA: lemme give you a call about ten thi:rty.
16 BEE: ˚hh yeah.
17 AVA: [alri:ght?]
18 BEE: [I'll  soo] what's-
19 BEE: yeah. [˚see what's going O:N˚.            ]
20 AVA:       [maybe you wanna come down to school=]
21       =see what the new place looks like;
22       (0.5)
23 BEE: ↑yeh may:be.
24       (n)a::[h,   but  I  hadn'-]
25 AVA:        [↑you can  come into] a cla:ss with m[e.
26 BEE:                                             [I
27       haven't thought about that la(h)tely hh huh
28       eh-[huh!
```

In lines 20–21 Ava suggests that Bee come with her to see their old school, which has undergone some renovation in the meantime. She presents this as something

---

4. We have no clear cases of interrogative forms of *want to*, e.g., *do you wanna...*, being used as suggestions in the technical sense employed here. (For *do you wanna* as a request, see Raymond et al., 2021).

Bee might 'want' to do, tempering the assertion of Bee's desire with *maybe*. In this case the action is not treated as the speaker's recommendation, nor as the recipient's obligation, but rather as the recipient's wish. In contrast to a WDY format, which takes the speaker's perspective, a *you want to* format refers to the recipient's interests: it is in this sense other-oriented.

On occasion, *you want to* formats are embedded in conditional constructions. This is what we find happening in another exchange between Ava and Bee; this one takes place immediately prior to the one in Excerpt (9). Ava has just said she will call Bee the next day around 2:00 or 3:00 in the afternoon.

Excerpt 10. "**Leave about eleven**" (**Two Girls_818.95**), telephone, informal interaction

```
01 BEE: I-I might go to the city in the mo:rning
02      any[way;
03 AVA:    [it depends on how (tough the)=
04      =so ↑what time are you leaving for the city;
05 BEE: oh:: probably about: te[n=
06                              [((ringing sound in
                                 background))
07 BEE: =ten-thirty eleven, er-[n-d-ih-] °hh           ]
08 AVA:                        [o h   ] if you wanna] leave
09      about eleven
10      [I'll walk down with [you.] °cuz I hafto go] to school°
11      [((ringing sound in b[ackg]round))           ]           ]
12 BEE                       [i t ]  d e p e n: d s]how I ro:]ll
13      outta bed tom(h)orr(h)ow![.hh  ]
14 AVA:                          [well ] let'[s see-eh-so ]
15 BEE:                                      [how I fee:l.]
16      hh
```

Bee's announcement that she might go to 'the city' the next morning (the two are currently on Long Island) prompts Ava to inquire when she will be leaving (line 4). Bee's reply is vague, *probably about ten=ten-thirty eleven* (lines 5 and 7), whereupon Ava now launches an I-Suggestion advocating that Bee leave at eleven, presenting this as something Bee possibly 'wants' to do. It is implied that this action will benefit Bee, on the assumption that she desires it. The suggestion is embedded in an 'open' conditional construction (Quirk et al. 1985):[5] *if you wanna leave about eleven I'll walk down with you* (lines 8–10), which asserts that the consequent will ensue (Ava will join Bee) provided that the condition holds (Bee leaves at eleven). In this case then, the action which Ava is advocating, leaving at eleven, is turned into a contingency upon which another, putatively desirable

---

5. "Open conditions" are neutral: they leave unresolved the question of the fulfillment or non-fulfillment of the condition, ..." (p.1091).

Chapter 3. Idea-Suggestions in an interactional grammar   **61**

event depends. And it is a contingency that acknowledges Bee's wishes with *you want to*. However, whether the condition will be realized or not is left open.

To summarize: We have reviewed five recurrent formats for implementing I-Suggestions:

i.   Fixed expression *why don't you* ('I recommend that you...')
ii.   Modals of obligation and necessity ('you have the obligation to...')
iii. Hypothetical conditionals ('if you...')
iv.   Modals of ability and possibility ('it is possible for you to...')
v.   Constructions with *want to* ('maybe you wanna...')

With all these formats, the speaker is advocating that the recipient undertake some action in the immediate or remote future that will be to their benefit. Yet they have different affordances and quite distinct syntactic and interactional profiles. Syntactically, they include negative interrogative (i), declarative (ii), (iv), and (v), and conditional (iii) forms. Yet the interrogative form in (i) does not function as a question nor does the conditional form in (iii) specify a condition for another event that is contingent upon it. Instead, the syntactic forms used to make I-Suggestions – interrogative, declarative, conditional — all function indirectly as appeals to the recipient to do something. Significantly, the one syntactic form that is *dedicated* to making an appeal, namely the imperative, is missing from this list. We return to the implications of this observation in Section 4.

The five I-Suggestion formats differ not only syntactically but also in the amount of *autonomy* attributed to the recipient in determining the future. For example, with *why don't you...* the recipient has less autonomy than with *(maybe) you wanna....* The formats also differ with respect to how much *compulsion* is attributed to the action being advocated: with *why don't you...* the action is more compelling than with *if you V-ed....* Finally, they differ with respect to how much speaker *certainty* is on display. With *why don't you...* the speaker comes across as most certain: this format does not lend itself to attenuation, while the other formats can and often do have an added 'maybe' or 'I guess'.

3.3   Responses to I-Suggestions

As first pair-parts, I-Suggestions open up an opportunity space for responding – either verbally or non-verbally – in a subsequent turn. The examples discussed above illustrate some of the response options that recipients have. We review them in the following.

One option is to *endorse* what has been suggested: this can entail committing to carry out the action recommended, as in this extract from Excerpt (3), renumbered here as Excerpt (11):

Excerpt 11. (from Excerpt (3) "Call me 2", SF 1), telephone, informal interaction

```
11 MAR: pk .hhhhhh uh:m if I don't see you?
12      (0.7)
13 MAR: .hhh why don'tche call me sometime before noon
14      Saturday.
15 JOA: okay.
16 MAR: okay?
17 JOA: mm-hm.
18 MAR: .hhhh and then if I do see you then we can make
19      .hh arrangements.
20 JOA: okay.
21 MAR: okay?
22 JOA: sou:nds like a pla:n.
23 MAR: yeh. ( ) .hhhhhh okay we:ll um,
((talk continues on another topic))
```

Recall from Excerpt (3) that Mark and JoAnn are working out a time to get together. Finalizing their arrangements, in lines 13–14 Mark suggests that JoAnn call him before noon on Saturday if they don't see each other beforehand. JoAnn's response in line 15 commits to doing this, whereupon Mark spells out the alternative plan if they do meet before Saturday. JoAnn fully endorses this suggestion too (line 20).

In endorsing an Idea-Suggestion a recipient can, however, refrain from committing to carrying out the action in question, but simply *agree* with the speaker's assertion that they indeed have an obligation, as we saw in Excerpt (6) (renumbered here as Excerpt (12)):

Excerpt 12. (from Excerpt (6) "Make a few phone calls", SF2_683.49), telephone, informal interaction

```
11 MAR:   [I mean who is going to tell them.
12 BOB: I guess::: maybe that's up to us.
13 MAR: well maybe you should uh make a few ↑phone
14      calls.
15 BOB: yeah maybe I shou:ld. uh
16      (0.3)
```

When Mark suggests that Bob be the one to let his invitees know about the party: *well maybe you should uh make a few phone calls* (lines 13–14), Bob's *yeah maybe I should. uh* in line 15 endorses the suggestion by making public that he agrees he should make those phone calls without, however, committing to doing so.

A recipient can also endorse a suggestion by affirming that they *have the ability* to carry it out, as illustrated in Excerpt (13). In this phone call Jeff has just announced to Mom that he'll be home for Christmas; Mom has expressed pleasure at hearing this (data not shown):

Chapter 3. Idea-Suggestions in an interactional grammar **63**

Excerpt 13. "Home for Christmas" (CH 5888_1636.33), telephone, informal interaction

```
01 MOM: except if you could wait until June the weather'd
02      be nicer,
03      (0.7)
04 JEF: well (.) I can do,
05      (0.2)
06 JEF: I can do that,
```

In line 1, Mom adds the suggestion that Jeff wait until June for better weather. Jeff's responses in lines 4 and 6 endorse Mom's suggestion by asserting that he *can do that*, but he does not explicitly commit to doing so. In subsequent talk (not shown here), Mom presents the advantages of her suggestion, but at the same time acknowledges that it would mean a delay of six months before they see each other, whereupon Jeff concurs and lets the suggestion drop.

Finally, a recipient can endorse a suggestion by claiming *a potential desire* to carry out the action in question, as shown in Excerpt (14):

Excerpt 14. (from Excerpt (9) "Come down to school", Two Girls_834.00), telephone, informal interaction

```
20 AVA:     [maybe you wanna come down to school=]
21      =see what the new place looks like;
22      (0.5)
23 BEE: ↑yeh may:be.
24      (n)a::[h,   but I  hadn'-]
25 AVA:        [↑you can come into] a cla:ss with m[e.
```

In line 23, Bee agrees with Ava's suggestion that she might want to visit her old school and thus initially endorses it. However, she then continues with a possible objection, which is broken off before completion (line 24).

While in Excerpt (11), then, the recipient commits to carrying out the suggested action, in Excerpts (12)–(14), recipients instead only agree with their interlocutor that the action is a potential obligation (Excerpt (12)), a possibility (Excerpt (13)), or a potential desire of theirs (Excerpt (14)). Nevertheless, in all these cases the responses can be said to endorse the Idea-Suggestion as a bona fide suggestion.

Alternatively, a recipient can *reject* the I-Suggestion, for instance, by presenting obstacles that preclude carrying out the action. This is what we see happening in the following conversation: Anthony has called his girlfriend Ellen, who is currently on a year abroad in Paris. In this excerpt he announces that a mutual friend Gabe will soon be nearby:

Excerpt 15. "Go see him" (Call Home 6265_915.717), telephone, informal interaction

```
01 ANT: so Gabe's gonna be in England.
02      (0.6)
```

```
03 ELL: ^oh ^really.
04 ANT: yeah. heh
05      (0.4)
06 ELL: ↑oh that's wonderful.>
07 ANT: next semester.
08      (0.5)
09 ANT: >whyncha go see him.<
10      (0.9)
11 ELL: I'm gonna- I'm not gonna be arou::nd;
12 ANT: aww:
13      (0.6)
14 ANT: sa:d.
15      (0.5)
16 ELL: ehhhh .hhhhh
```

Anthony follows up his announcement about Gabe with the I-Suggestion that Ellen should go see him in England (line 9), implying that this would be a source of pleasure for Ellen and thus benefit her. But Ellen's response — after a delay — is to report circumstances that imply she will be unable to do so: *I'm gonna- I'm not gonna be around* (line 11) (cf. Drew 1984). That is, Ellen rejects Anthony's suggestion not because of an unwillingness but because of an inability to carry out the action due to circumstances.[6] Anthony treats this as a disappointment (lines 12, 14).

A third response option is for the recipient to simply *acknowledge* the suggestion without either endorsing or rejecting it. This is what happens in Excerpt (7), renumbered here as Excerpt (16):

Excerpt 16. (from Excerpt (7) "Beginner's group", Call Friend engn 6899), telephone, informal interaction

```
32 MOM: ↑well but I mean if you pla:yed- (0.4)
33      you know with a b- (0.4) beginning grou:p,=
34      =beginner's grou:p,
35 SAL: yea:h_
36      (0.5)
37 SAL: ((fumbling with phone))
38      (0.6)
```

---

6. In this sense the response in Excerpt (15) resonates with the one given in Excerpt (5), where Wendy expresses a desire to visit Chris in Spain but anticipates that circumstances may prevent her from doing so:[From Excerpt (5) "You should come" (Call Home 6071_283.236), telephone, informal interaction]

```
11 WEN: I'd like to come but when: (.) are you going to
12      Morocco:.
13      (0.2)
14 CHR: from the twenty-eighth to the third.
15      (0.4)
16 WEN: aw (hhow luck)
17      (0.6) .hh
18      cuz I don't think I can ^ge:t there;=
19      =until the (.) the twenty-ninth.
20      I don't think I can ^le::ave until the twenty-ninth.
```

Here, Sally's non-committal *yeah* indicates that she is aligned as a recipient of Mom's I-Suggestion but it does not convey either endorsement or rejection of what Mom is advocating. In fact, as the ensuing pauses and phone fumbling indicate, Sally is not prepared to do either at the moment. In subsequent talk it emerges that Sally is on the fence: she admits that she might enjoy playing in a beginner's group but confesses that she doesn't like running around in hot weather (see lines 50–58 of Excerpt (7)). A freestanding *yeah* response to an I-Suggestion thus simply acknowledges receipt of the prior turn. Because of its inherent positivity, the token may seem to imply agreement, but in responding this way the recipient is effectively neither endorsing nor rejecting what has been suggested.

Finally, recipients can respond *non-verbally* to I-Suggestions: this is especially common when the I-Suggestion is delivered in the context of organizing ongoing activities. Consider again Excerpt (1), now with a notation of participants' bodily behavior, renumbered as Excerpt (17):

Excerpt 17. (=Excerpt (1) "More ice", Virginia_6:39), face to face, informal interaction
```
16 MOM: =.hhh *whooh! it is so hot tonight.*
   mom        *pushes chair back, gets up from table*
17      *would somebody like some more iced tea.*
   mom  *moves to sideboard, picks up pitcher of tea*
18      (0.8)
19 WES: *uh(b)- (0.4) I('ll) take more ice.*
   mom  *returns to table*
20      (1.3)
21 MOM: *.hhhh well,*
   mom  *pours tea in her glass*
22      (2.0)
23 MOM: *let me: get up and go get some.*
   mom  *turns, moves towards sideboard with pitcher*
24 VIR: *+whynchya get it yourself.+* ((addressed to Wesley))
   vir  +gazes at Wesley+
   mom  *stops, turns to pour tea into Wesley's glass*
25      (.)
26 PRU: ehhh!
27 MOM: *that's a good idea,*
   mom  *puts pitcher on table, returns to her seat*
((9 lines of laughter and jocularity))
36 WES: f^excuse me.
   wes  *stands up and moves into the kitchen
```

Virginia's I-Suggestion that Wesley get more ice himself (line 24) is seconded by Mom, who calls this *a good idea* (line 27) and proceeds to sit down again. After a profusion of laughter and further jocularity, Wesley now moves to carry out the recommended action by excusing himself from the table and heading into the kitchen to get the ice himself (line 36). I-Suggestions can thus be taken up non-verbally if they concern the organization of an ongoing activity.

Strikingly, it is non-committal agreeing with the speaker's assertion, acknowledging with *yeah,* and non-verbal or no verbal uptake that predominate among the I-Suggestion responses in our collection.[7] This finding holds across all five formats. That is, regardless of whether the speaker takes a relatively presuming stance with, e.g., *why don't you...* or a much more tentative stance with, e.g., *if you V-ed...* towards the action being advocated, the recipient is more likely to agree with the speaker's assertion (as in Excerpts (12), (13), and (14)), acknowledge the suggestion with *yeah* (as in Excerpt (16)), or respond non-verbally (as in Excerpt (17)), than to verbally commit to the suggestion or reject it. This type of responsive behavior is characteristic of I-Suggestions. In fact, it appears to be one of the several features that distinguish I-Suggestions from A-Suggestions, to which we turn now.

4. Idea-Suggestions vs. Advice-Suggestions

I-Suggestions and A-Suggestions have in common that with both action sub-types, the speaker recommends an action that the recipient should carry out that is judged to be to the recipient's benefit. Yet they have different home environments: unsolicited A-Suggestions ensue in the context of prior complaints or troubles telling, while solicited A-Suggestions arise in the context of requests for advice. I-Suggestions, by contrast, are spontaneous, occurring in the context of planning future events (arrangement-making) or of organizing ongoing activities.

These two sub-types of Suggestion differ not only with respect to home environment. I-Suggestions, as we have seen, have dedicated preliminaries, e.g., *I'll tell you what, here's an idea, here's the plan.* However, we have not encountered any dedicated pre-s for A-Suggestions.

As for the formats that are recurrently used to implement the two action sub-types, there are some commonalities but also clear differences. Our study of Advice-Suggestions revealed five common formats for advice-giving in everyday American English conversation (Couper-Kuhlen & Thompson 2022), in order of frequency:

(a) *Do ... !/Don't ...!*   e.g., *well wash them ou::t /*
                               don't stay down there all by yourself

---

7. Non-verbal uptake as in Excerpt (1) is encountered in face-to-face interaction with I-Suggestions that concern ongoing activities; lack of verbal uptake can be encountered in both telephone and face-to-face conversation if the suggestion concerns an action in the more remote future.

(b)	*Why don't you...?*	e.g., *why don't you stay dow::n*
(c)	*I'd/I would/I wouldn't*	e.g., *I::'d leave o:ff the mea:t*
(d)	*You should/ought to....*	e.g., *you should make stencils*
(e)	*You can/could...*	e.g., *you could go down every Saturday*

Three of these formats, (b) *Why don't you...*, (d) *You should/ought to...,*, and (e) *You can/could...*, are also attested with I-Suggestions, as we have seen, and in the same order of frequency. This underscores the commonality between Idea-Suggestions and Advice-Suggestions and serves as an additional justification for grouping them together as types of Suggestion.

Importantly, however, there are differences: Format (c), *I'd/I would/I wouldn't....,* was not found at all for I-Suggestions; that is, the *I'd X* format seems to be reserved for giving advice. Format (a), *Do...!,* was not among the five most frequent ones attested for making I-Suggestions; it is used only under special conditions.[8] Finally, the I-Suggestion formats *if you V-ed* and *(maybe) you wanna...* were not attested at all for giving advice. These facts point to I-Suggestions as a distinct sub-type of Suggestion with its own characteristic means of implementation, including the 'weakest', least imposing formats and excluding the 'strongest', most presumptuous one, the imperative.

This comparison of formats is revealing. The imperative format for giving advice was described as displaying a maximum of deontic strength: it expects immediate compliance and allows the recipient no autonomy in deciding how to remedy their problem. Displays of this amount of deontic strength are lacking with I-Suggestions. In fact, one of the hallmarks of an I-Suggestion is precisely that it is 'just an idea', a thought that might not be practicable. On the other hand, the hypothetical and other-oriented formats are lacking with A-Suggestions. Idea-Suggestions thus encompass formats that allow for recipient autonomy, while Advice-Suggestions encompass formats that are maximally compulsive.[9]

The fact that these clusters of properties distinguishing I-Suggestions from A-Suggestions are not simply an analyst's 'binning' exercise (Enfield & Sidnell 2017a, Sidnell 2017) can be seen in the differentiated way in which recipients orient to them in next turn, treating what they take to be I-Suggestions as more tentative, more weakly 'imposing' on them than A-Suggestions, and responding (or not) accordingly.

---

8. One of these conditions appears to be the use of an overt subject *you* with the imperative, as in *you think about it*. More research is needed to determine under what conditions this happens

9. This is not to deny that suggestions can be made with a degree of compulsion nor that advice can be given tentatively.

With A-Suggestions, according to our (2022) findings, deontically strong formats tended to encounter resistance, with the recipient rejecting either the content of the advice (e.g., *that's not therapeutic*) or the role of advisee (e.g., *that's what I'm doing right now*). But with I-Suggestions, resistance and rejection are the least frequent response types. Instead, a *yeah* agreement or acknowledgement is one of the most frequent response types in I-Suggestion sequences.[10] Moreover, the lack of verbal uptake altogether, frequently encountered with I-Suggestions, was not observed at all with A-Suggestions. Thus, the opportunity space following I-Suggestions, despite some overlap, is nevertheless distinct from that following A-Suggestions.

In sum, there are significant differences with respect to home environments, preliminary sequences, recurrent formats, and most frequent response types between A-Suggestions and I-Suggestions. For this reason, we argue that I-Suggestions should be treated as a sub-type distinct from A-Suggestions within the overarching category of Suggestion.[11]

5. Idea-Suggestions in an interactional grammar

What are the implications of these findings for an interactional grammar? We assume that an interactional grammar — as distinct from other kinds of descriptive grammar — aims to capture the ways in which linguistic resources are deployed systematically for the implementation of social actions in interaction. While most descriptive grammars to date are focused on decontextualized examples for generalizations and exemplification, an interactional grammar provides a radical new orientation to the relationship between linguistic resources and social actions.

We see two possible paths in mapping this relationship. One path is onomasiological: it starts from the actions that participants are known to implement in social interaction and considers what linguistic resources in a given language can be mobilized to implement these actions. The other path is semasiological: it starts from a language's resources and shows how specific forms are mobilized by interactants for the implementation of particular social actions. Both paths are

---

10. In advice-giving sequences, a *yeah* response was attested only with the deontically weak formats, *I'd ...* and *you can/could....*

11. Evidence from Japanese conversation further supports a distinction between A-Suggestions and I-Suggestions: it has been reported, for instance, that *tara doo desu ka* 'why don't you X' does not occur as a format for offering advice in troubles and complaint environments, but appears only when participants are "suggesting new approaches in situations where [a] problem or complaint is absent" (Hatsuda 2024).

data-driven, the data being provided by situated language use. In the following we do not choose between these paths; instead, we will sketch what each path might look like for Idea-Suggestions in an interactional grammar of American English.

5.1 Idea-Suggestions: From action to grammar

Going from action to grammar, an action entry under the heading 'Idea-Suggestion' would ideally start with a clear example of this action as attested in naturally occurring everyday talk-in-interaction. It would characterize the action and describe its home environment. Moreover, since actions do not occur in isolation in social interaction, it would also show possible lead-ups, or preliminaries, to Idea-Suggestions, such as those documented in Excerpts (2) and (3) above, and it would show which options are relevant in the 'response opportunity space' following Idea-Suggestions, as discussed in Section 4 above. Treating Idea-Suggestions not in isolation but as engendering sequences is, we argue, a hallmark of an interactional approach to social action. In grammatical terms, it corresponds to encompassing *outer syntax*, i.e., relations of an utterance to its sequential context, as much as *inner* syntax, relations between its component parts (Steensig et al. 2023).

Having presented the sequential embedding of I-Suggestions, the next part of the action entry would present recurrent formats for implementing this action and address their most significant grammatical features as well as the affordances associated with each format. As our analysis has shown, for I-Suggestions these formats would include:

i. The use of a negative interrogative frame with *why* as a fixed expression (*why don't you...*)
ii. The use of a modal auxiliary denoting obligation or necessity (*you should/ ought to...*)
iii. The use of a hypothetical conditional construction, with optional freestanding protasis, with or without tense backshifting (*if you V(-ed)*)
iv. The use of a modal auxiliary denoting ability or possibility (*you can/could...*)
v. The use of an auxiliary-like expression referring to desire (*you want to...*)

For all of these formats an interactional grammar would need to specify that instantiations implementing I-Suggestions are obligatorily built with an explicit *you*-subject referring to the recipient and a formulation of the action being advocated, and that they optionally allow the addition of a mark of tentativeness or uncertainty ('maybe', 'I guess'), with this being most likely for (v) and least likely for (i).

Ideally, the action entry should include attested examples illustrating each of these formats in their context of occurrence, including possible sequential lead-ups and subsequent responses.

A major issue in moving from action to grammar is the question of how and whether to account for the work that participants do in interaction in terms of types and, possibly, sub-types of social actions (see, e.g., Deppermann & Haugh 2022, Fox & Raymond this volume, Schegloff 1988, Sidnell & Enfield 2014). As Enfield and Sidnell (2017a, 2017b) argue, one does not need to be able to label a prior action in order to be able to respond to it. But Deppermann and Haugh (2022) maintain that "while ascriptions of action can vary in their degree of granularity, the interactional reality of action types for response generation, and thus for members, is strongly supported by observable regularities and expectancies concerning sequential organization". Our study has appealed to observed "regularities and expectancies" of sequential organization in arguing for the interactional reality of Idea-Suggestions.

5.2 Idea-Suggestions: From grammar to action

For the path leading from grammar to action, we assume that an interactional grammar would focus on recurrent patterns for implementing actions. We could envisage a hypertext link from an attested I-Suggestion instantiation (e.g., see our Excerpts (1)–(3) and (5)–(10), (13), and (15)) to a grammar entry for the format, which would in turn be linked to an action entry 'Idea-Suggestion'. In all likelihood, the grammar entry in question would also have a link to other action entries. For example, in the case of the I-Suggestion *why don'tchu call me Saturday morning* from Excerpt (2) above, the form *why don'tchu* would be linked to an entry for this fixed expression (Thompson & Couper-Kuhlen 2020), which in turn would link to the action entry 'Idea-Suggestion'. Other actions, such as, e.g., Advice-Suggestions, would also have a link to the same grammar entry. The linkage of multiple actions to one format in the grammar would be a way to capture "collateral effects" as described by Sidnell & Enfield (2012).[12] Such effects help explain why a *why don't you...* format is sometimes avoided in making I-Suggestions, as in Excerpt (4) above: this format is also frequently used to give unsolicited advice with an A-Suggestion, where it connotes that the recommended action is an obvious solution that the recipient should have thought of themselves.

---

12. "Because each language's strategy draws on lexicogrammatical resources that are used for other functions as well, this introduces 'collateral effects' on how the action is done" (Sidnell & Enfield 2012: 313).

It may thus be considered overly presumptuous by participants wishing to make an Idea-Suggestion.

We assume that the entry for *why don't you...* would also be linked to related formats such as *why don't we...*, which has been shown to function as a means for making a proposal for joint activities (Thompson et al. 2021) and to *why don't I...*, which is used for making offers (Couper-Kuhlen 2014).[13]

Further grammatical features of the I-Suggestion formats that would merit linkage to an 'Idea-Suggestion' entry include:

- the modal auxiliary *should* as in *you should come* (Excerpt (5)), which, in declarative form and together with *you*, would also have a link to an action entry for Advice-Suggestions (Couper-Kuhlen & Thompson 2022).
- the modal auxiliary *could* as in *you could speak French to her* (Excerpt (8)), which, in declarative form and together with *you*, would also have a link to an action entry for Advice-Suggestions (Couper-Kuhlen & Thompson 2022).
- the freestanding hypothetical *if*-conditional as in *if you played in a beginner's group* (Excerpt (7)), which, together with *you* and (optional) tense backshifting, would also have a link to other directive-action entries such as ones for requests for action (Ford 1997) and offers of assistance (Curl 2006).
- the auxiliary-like *want to*, in declarative form and together with *you*, as in *maybe you wanna come down to school see what the new place looks like* (Excerpt (9)). This format would also be linked to the related interrogative format *want to* with *you*-subject (*do you wanna...*), which would have a link to action entries for offers and requests (Raymond et al. 2021).

Conceivably, recurrent linguistic features of preliminaries to I-Suggestions could also be linked to the action entry 'Idea-Suggestion', under a sub-entry 'Preliminary to Idea-Suggestion'. One candidate might be, for instance, the use of *what* as in *I'll tell you what* (Excerpt (2)). This form would presumably also have a link to an action entry for announcements, specifically preliminaries to announcements as in 'guess what' (Terasaki 2004).

We believe that either of the two paths sketched out here could be usefully followed, depending on the specific purpose to which the interactional grammar is put.

---

13. The linkage of related formats might be thought of in analogy to the model for derivational morphology presented in Bybee (1998: 423).

6. Discussion

As we have seen, the study of the grammatical features of Suggestions can be discussed very profitably in the framework of an interactional grammar. And yet, for either of these two paths, we might ask, "But where is the interaction?" It is true that we have argued for a sequential approach that captures possible responses to Idea-Suggestions within the action entry: see Section 5.1 above. But where in such a grammar would we discuss the ways in which participants orient to, and engage with, sequences of sequences? What happens when an Idea-Suggestion is not taken up immediately or appropriately and the speaker pursues a response? To take a case in point, consider what ensues in the interaction between Ava and Bee (Excerpt (9) above) after Ava suggests that Bee should come down to Ava's school with her the next day:

Excerpt 18. "Come down to school" (Two Girls_834.00), telephone, informal interaction

```
15  AVA:    lemme give you a call about ten thi:rty.
16  BEE:    .hh yeah.
17  AVA:    [alri:ght?]
18  BEE:    [I'll  see] what's-
19  BEE:    yeah. [°see   what's   going o:n.°        ]
20  AVA:          [maybe you wanna come down to school=]
21          =see what the new place looks like;
22          (0.5)
23  BEE:    ↑yeh may:be.>
24          (n)a::[h,  but I hadn'-  ]
25  AVA:          [↑you can come into] a cla:ss with m[e.
26  BEE:                                               [I
27          haven't thought about that la(h)tely hh huh
28          eh-[huh!
29  AVA:       [why donch[a.=
30  BEE:                 [°hh
31  AVA:    =[°I mean you won't have to do any]thing,°
32  BEE:     [↑you    know    I    wu-u-u    ]
33  BEE:    I wonder if Do:nna went back to school,
34          i'z [I was curious to know]
((7 lines omitted in which Ava explains why she has a class on Friday, when most
others have off))
42          (0.7)
43  AVA:    tch! but if you wanna uh:m (0.2) come in and see.
44  BEE:    tch! I wouldn't know where to look for her(hh)
45          hnhh-hnh[h!.hh
46  AVA:            [well ↑you know,
47          you know (.) come along with me,
((talk continues on the subject of Ava's class the next day))
```

Bee's initially positive response to Ava's I-Suggestion, *↑yeh may:be* (line 23), is followed by a lengthened *(n)aa::h*, perhaps indicating that she is now tending more

Chapter 3. Idea-Suggestions in an interactional grammar **73**

towards rejection. This may be what prompts Ava to come in in overlap with a further I-Suggestion ↑*you can come into a cla:ss with me* (line 25), to serve as an incentive for Bee to take up her original suggestion. But Bee again avoids committing by reporting that she hasn't thought about attending class recently, trailing off into laughter (lines 26–28). Now Ava becomes insistent with a more compelling *why doncha* (line 29), immediately followed by another incentive *I mean you won't have to do anything*, designed to overcome Bee's reluctance. That is, what we observe happening here is Ava making a succession of I-Suggestions, in part reiterated, in order to persuade Bee to agree to her original suggestion. Particularly revealing in this sequence of sequences is that, beginning with *maybe you wanna...* (line 20), successive sequences use more compelling formats.

Thereafter, following a short interlude in which Ava veers off on a topical tangent, she returns to her original I-Suggestion and another sequence of sequences ensues, beginning with a weakly compelling *if you wanna come in and see* (line 43) and, following Bee's dismissive report that she wouldn't know where to look for Donna, culminating in a strongly compulsive form *come along with me* (line 47), In fact, the compulsion associated with this imperative form conveys such a strong investment on Ava's part in getting Bee to join her the next day that it can be interpreted as self-interest — making this action more akin to requesting.

At least two aspects of the interaction shown in Excerpt (18) would be difficult to capture in an interactional grammar. First, sequences of sequences, here specifically successive Idea-Suggestion sequences, in their contingent, moment-by-moment unfolding: Under what circumstances do they arise? How are they implemented on successive iterations? What is the effect of different format choices? Second, the morphing of I-Suggestion actions and action sequences into related actions such as requesting, proposing, offering, and the like: Under what circumstances does such morphing happen? What determines which direction it takes? For these and other such questions we will need to await further research for answers, and arguably an interactional grammar will need a third dimension in order to capture them, one defined by what Enfield calls "enchronic time", which asks "How does the behavior fit in a contingent sequence of moves?" (2013: 31).

Attentive readers will have noticed that prosodic and embodied aspects of I-Suggestion sequences do not figure in the two paths outlined here. This is not because we underestimate the importance of prosody and the body for the conduct of conversation, but rather because it is difficult to make generalizations about them at the level of grammatical action format. On occasion, a grammatical format does have a predictable prosodic-phonetic shape, as we have argued is the case for the fixed expression *why don't you...* (Thompson & Couper-Kuhlen 2020). However, we have not encountered this degree of prosodic-phonetic predictability with other Suggestion formats. How to incorporate prosody and embodiment as two crucial dimensions of social interaction in an interactional grammar thus remains a challenge.

7. Conclusion

In the last couple of decades, Interactional Linguistics has uncovered numerous relationships between social actions and what has been traditionally thought of as 'grammar'. Steensig et al. (2023) have outlined a number of considerations in building an interactional grammar. With this study we hope to have contributed to this endeavor. While there are serious challenges in the construction of such a grammar, it is already clear from research delving into the relationship between linguistic regularities and the organization of social interaction that only such an approach will be relevant. As we have seen, the implications for grammar writing will differ depending on whether one takes an onomasiological or a semasiological path. In the former case, an inventory of social actions must be assembled for which linguistic formats are known to be deployed; in the latter case, a language-specific inventory of linguistic and embodied formats must be established and their multifarious links to social actions determined. We suggest that the applications for the two sorts of interactional grammar that result will likewise differ depending on which path has been followed. A grammar that moves from social action to linguistic-embodied format is likely to be relevant especially for researchers in communication and intermediate and advanced language learners, while a grammar that moves from linguistic-embodied format to action is more likely to be of interest to interactional linguists and those interested in grammaticalization and pragmaticalization. In either case, we believe that since grammar has consistently been shown to emerge from social interaction, every effort should continue to be made to understand the nature of this process.

References

Bybee, Joan 1998. "The Emergent Lexicon." *CLS 34: The Panels*, 421–435. University of Chicago: Chicago Linguistic Society.

Clayman, Steven E. 2013. "Agency in Response: The Role of Prefatory Address Terms." *Journal of Pragmatics* 57:290–302.

Clayman, Steven E., and John Heritage. 2014. "Benefactors and Beneficiaries: Benefactive Status and Stance in the Management of Offers and Requests." In *Requesting in Social Interaction*, ed. by Paul Drew, and Elizabeth Couper-Kuhlen, 55–86. Amsterdam: John Benjamins.

Couper-Kuhlen, Elizabeth. 2014. "What does Grammar Tell us about Action?" *Pragmatics* 24 (3):623–647.

Couper-Kuhlen, Elizabeth, and Sandra A. Thompson. 2022. "Action Ascription and Deonticity in Everyday Advice-giving Sequences." In *Action Ascription in Interaction*, ed. by Arnulf Deppermann, and Michael Haugh, 183–207. Cambridge: Cambridge University Press.

Curl, Traci S. 2006. "Offers of Assistance: Constraints on Syntactic Design." *Journal of Pragmatics* 38:1257–1280.

Curl, Traci S., and Paul Drew. 2008. "Contingency and Action: A Comparison of Two Forms of Requesting." *Research on Language and Social Interaction* 41 (2):129–153.

Deppermann, Arnulf, and Michael Haugh. 2022. "Action Ascription: Interaction in Context." In *Action Ascription in Interaction*, ed. by Arnulf Deppermann, and Michael Haugh, 1–27. Cambridge: Cambridge University Press.

Drew, Paul. 1984. "Speakers' Reportings in Invitation Sequences." In *Structures of Social Action. Studies in Conversation Analysis*, ed. by J. Maxwell Atkinson, and John Heritage, 129–151. Cambridge: Cambridge University Press.

Drew, Paul, and Elizabeth Couper-Kuhlen (eds). 2014. *Requesting in Social Interaction*. Amsterdam: John Benjamins.

Enfield, Nick J. 2013. *Relationship Thinking. Agency, Enchrony and Human Sociality*. New York: Oxford University Press.

Enfield, Nick J., and Jack Sidnell. 2017a. "On the Concept of Action in the Study of Interaction." *Discourse Studies* 19 (5):515–535.

Enfield, Nick J., and Jack Sidnell. 2017b. *The Concept of Action*. Cambridge: Cambridge University Press.

Ervin-Tripp, Susan. 1976. "'Is Sybil there?' The Structure of Some American English Directives." *Language in Society* 5 (1):25–66.

Ewing, Michael C. 2018. "Investigating Indonesian conversation: Approach and rationale." *Wacana* 19 (2):342–374.

Ford, Cecilia E. 1997. "Speaking Conditionally: Some Contexts for *If*-clauses in Conversation." In *On Conditionals Again*, ed. by Angeliki Athanasiadou, and René Dirven, 387–413. Amsterdam: John Benjamins.

Ford, Cecilia E., Barbara A. Fox, and Sandra A. Thompson. 2013. "Units and/or action trajectories? The language of grammatical categories and the language of social action." In *Units of Talk – Units of Action*, ed. by Beatrice Szczepek Reed, and Geoffrey Raymond, 13–56. Amsterdam: Benjamins.

Fox, Barbara A. 2007. "Principles Shaping Grammatical Practices: An Exploration." *Discourse Studies* 9 (3):299–318.

Günthner, Susanne. 2000. "From Concessive Connector to Discourse Marker: The Use of 'obwohl' in Everyday German Interaction." In *Cause – Condition – Concession – Contrast*, ed. by Bernd Kortmann, and Elizabeth Couper-Kuhlen, 439–468. Berlin: Mouton de Gruyter.

Hatsuda, Ayana. 2024. "Japanese *tara doo desu ka*: A Canonical Advice Form. Or is it?" Paper presented at IIEMCA, Seoul.

Heritage, John, and Steven E. Clayman. 2024. "Making Arrangements: A Sketch of a 'Big Package'." *Research on Language and Social Interaction* 57 (3):279–300.

Heritage, John, and Sue Sefi. 1992. "Dilemmas of Advice: Aspects of the Delivery and Reception of Advice in Interactions between Health Visitors and First-time Mothers." In *Talk at work. Interaction in institutional settings*, ed. by Paul Drew, and John Heritage, 359–417. Cambridge: Cambridge University Press.

Jefferson, Gail. 2004. "Glossary of Transcript Symbols with an Introduction." In *Conversation Analysis: Studies from the First Generation*, ed. by Gene H. Lerner, 13–31. Amsterdam: John Benjamins.

Jefferson, Gail, and John R. E. Lee. 1981. "The rejection of Advice: Managing the Problematic Convergence of a 'Troubles-telling' and a 'Service Encounter'." *Journal of Pragmatics* 5:399–422.

Kendrick, Kobin H., and Paul Drew. 2014. "The Putative Preference for Offers over Requests." In *Requesting in Social Interaction*, ed. by Paul Drew, and Elizabeth Couper-Kuhlen, 87–113. Amsterdam: John Benjamins.

Laury, Ritva. 2012. "Syntactically Non-integrated Finnish *jos* 'if' Conditional Clauses as Directives." *Discourse Processes* 49:213–242.

Lindström, Jan, Camilla Lindholm, and Ritva Laury. 2016. "The Interactional Emergence of Conditional Clauses as Directives: Constructions, Trajectories and Sequences of Action." *Language Sciences* 58:8–21.

Maschler, Yael, Simona Pekarek Doehler, Jan Lindström, and Leelo Keevallik (eds). 2020. *Emergent Syntax for Conversation: Clausal Patterns and the Organization of Action*. Amsterdam/Philadelphia: John Benjamins.

Quirk, Randolph, Sidney Greenbaum, Geoffrey Leech, and Jan Svartvik. 1985. *A Comprehensive Grammar of the English Language*. London: Longman.

Raymond, Chase W., Jeffrey D. Robinson, Barbara A. Fox, Sandra A. Thompson, and Kristella Montiegal. 2021. "Modulating Action through Minimization: Syntax in the Service of Offering and Requesting." *Language in Society* 50 (1):53–91.

Robinson, Jeffrey D., and Heidi Kevoe-Feldman. 2016. "The Accountability of Proposing (vs. Soliciting Proposals of) Arrangements." In *Accountability in Social Interaction*, ed by Jeffrey D. Robinson, 264–293. New York: Oxford University Press.

Schegloff, Emanuel A. 1980. "Preliminaries to Preliminaries: 'Can I Ask You a Question?'". *Sociological Inquiry* 50:104–152.

Schegloff, Emanuel A. 1988. "Description in the Social Sciences I: Talk-in-Interaction." *Papers in Pragmatics* 2 (1):1–24.

Schegloff, Emanuel A. 2007. *Sequence Organization in Interaction: A Primer in Conversation Analysis*. Cambridge: Cambridge University Press.

Sidnell, Jack. 2017. "Action in interaction is conduct under a description". *Language in Society* 46 (3):313–337.

Sidnell, Jack, and Nick J. Enfield. 2012. "Language Diversity and Social Action: A Third Locus of Linguistic Relativity." *Current Anthropology* 53(3):302–333.

Sidnell, Jack, and Nick J. Enfield. 2014. "The Ontology of Action, in Interaction." In *The Cambridge Handbook of Linguistic Anthropology*, ed. by Nick J. Enfield, Paul Kockelman, and Jack Sidnell, 423–446. Cambridge: Cambridge University Press.

Steensig, Jakob, Maria Jørgensen, Nikolas Mikkelsen, Karita Suomalainen, and Søren Sandager Sørensen. 2023. "Towards a Grammar of Danish Talk-in-interaction: From Action Formation to Grammatical Description." *Research on Language and Social Interaction* 56(2):116–140.

Stivers, Tanya, and Makoto Hayashi. 2010. "Transformative Answers: One Way to Resist a Question's Constraints." *Language in Society* 39:1–25.

Stivers, Tanya, John Heritage, Rebecca K. Barnes, Rose McCabe, Laura Thompson, and Merran Toerien. 2017. "Treatment Recommendations as Actions." *Health Communication* 33(11):1335–1344.

Stivers, Tanya, and Federico Rossano. 2010. "Mobilizing Response." *Research on Language and Social Interaction* 43(1):3–31.

Stivers, Tanya, and Jack Sidnell. 2016. "Proposals for Activity Collaboration." *Research on Language and Social Interaction* 49(2):148–166.

Terasaki, Alene K. 2004. "Pre-announcement Sequences in Conversation." In *Conversation Analysis: Studies from the First Generation*, ed. by G. H. Lerner, 171–223. Amsterdam: John Benjamins.

Thompson, Sandra A., and Elizabeth Couper-Kuhlen. 2020. "English 'why don't you X' as a Formulaic Expression." In *Fixed Expressions. Building Language Structure and Social Action*, ed. by Ritva Laury, and Tsuyoshi Ono, 99–131. Amsterdam: John Benjamins.

Thompson, Sandra A., Barbara A. Fox, and Elizabeth Couper-Kuhlen. (2015). *Grammar in Everyday Talk: Building Responsive Actions*. Cambridge: Cambridge University Press.

Thompson, Sandra A., Barbara A. Fox, and Chase W. Raymond. 2021. "The Grammar of Proposals for Joint Activities." *Interactional Linguistics* 1(1):123–151.

CHAPTER 4

Grammatical formats of requests for immediate actions
Observations on Danish talk-in-interaction

Jakob Steensig
Aarhus University

This chapter investigates three social action formats for requesting immediate action in Danish talk-in-interaction: embodied-only formats, phrasal formats, and modal verb formats. The analyses of the use of these formats serve as a basis for discussing how entries in a comprehensive grammar of Danish talk-in-interaction should be organized and written. This is related to an ongoing project to develop such a grammar (DanTIN 2024). I focus on the consequences of the analyses for concrete entries in the grammar, and for the use of concepts such as multimodality, ellipsis, interrogativity, and sequentiality in the grammar. I argue that some nonverbal formats must be included in the grammar, and I suggest how this can be done. I also argue that sequence organization must be part of a syntactic description, and that the centrality of some traditional syntactic concepts must be reconceptualized.

Keywords: requests, social action formats, embodied formats, phrasal formats, modal verb formats, syntax, parts of speech

1. Introduction

This section of the volume takes social action as the point of departure for writing concrete sections and entries in a grammar. In this chapter, I do this by analyzing requests for immediate action in Danish talk-in-interaction. I focus on three main formats: embodied-only formats, phrasal formats, and modal verb formats. On the basis of analyses of these formats, I discuss how entries in a grammar of Danish talk-in-interaction could be written in a way that does justice to these formats.

https://doi.org/10.1075/slsi.37.04ste
© 2025 John Benjamins Publishing Company

1.1 Social action formats

I use the concept of *social action formats* (Fox 2007) as the basic unit of description for this analysis. Social action formats are recurrent grammatical patterns for "sequentially specific actions" (Fox 2007:304). This definition sums up what is important to a grammar that aims to be true to how actions are carried out in social interactions: Social action formats are recurrent, that is, they must be recognizable to participants, they are grammatical (see below and in the introduction, Steensig et al. this volume, for a discussion of what can be considered grammatical), they are based on action formation (Levinson 2013), and they situate the actions in their sequential context. The last point is pertinent to my view of grammar, as it also entails an external, or sequential, syntax: Social action formats have an internal order of elements, which is what is traditionally described by syntax, but they also occur with an external syntax (Anward & Nordberg 2005; Auer 2005), in which the formats occupy a slot in a sequence of actions. In other words, grammar is "position sensitive" (Schegloff 1996b; Thompson, Fox & Couper-Kuhlen 2015). Therefore, this chapter will distinguish between the *intra-unit syntax* (the internal syntax) of the social action formats and their *inter-unit syntax* (the external or sequential structure they occur in) when considering the units that perform the immediate requests.

1.2 The grammar

The grammar that my analyses will be used for is not just an imaginative grammar. It is actually being written. The grammar in question is the *samtalegrammatik.dk* (DanTIN 2024), which is an online grammar of Danish talk-in-interaction. This grammar is based on the study of recordings of everyday interactions in Danish, and it aims to be comprehensive and include chapters about phonology, morphology, parts of speech, syntactic structures, and so on. Its target audience comprises language and interaction researchers and students, teachers and students of Danish as a first or second language, and others with an interest in the Danish language and talk-in-interaction.

The *samtalegrammatik.dk* grammar is divided into three main sections. The first one, called *The Building Blocks of Talk-in-interaction*, is the part that most resembles a traditional grammar. It describes the formats and structures of the language as they occur in the data. The second section is *Interactional Phenomena*, which is a list of documented local practices. The third one is called *Social Actions*. It is a systematic account of social actions and the logic of their use; it contains a subsection on *Requests* and, under this, a description and definition of *Requests for Immediate Action*. The *Interactional Phenomena* and *Social Actions* sections will be informed by the analyses of social action formats such as the ones in this chapter, but this chapter will focus on entries to *The Building Blocks of Talk-in-interaction*, as this is where the core grammatical descriptions are presented.

1.3 Requests and grammar

Requests have been investigated extensively in conversation analysis and interactional linguistics (Drew & Couper-Kuhlen 2014b; Curl & Drew 2008; Kendrick & Drew 2016; e.g., M-L. Sorjonen & Raevaara 2014; Heinemann 2006; Gubina 2021; Rossi 2012; Lindström 2005). This research will not be reviewed here; only the distinctions and terminology that matter to this chapter will be mentioned.

My definition of requests takes its point of departure in the one used by Drew and Couper-Kuhlen (2014a): A request is an attempt by a requester to get the recipient of the request to do something that benefits the requester. In Excerpt (1), this is clear in the wording of the request turn. It comes from a recording of four people playing card games.

Excerpt 1. *se din hånd* 'see your hand' (AULing: Board-game-coffee1)

```
01      €(0.6)                          €
   sve  €puts card down on table€

02 SVE: jeg ve' €   gerne se      din€     hånd_
        I   will.PRS PTC   see.INF your.SG.C hand(C)
        I would like to see your hand_
   sve          .......€points tow. MAR----€,,,,,,,,,,

03      &(1.1)          &(0.2)
   mar  &looks down     &moves hand-->>
```

In line 2, Svend (SVE) makes a move in the game, and asks to see Margrete's (MAR) "hand" (the cards she is holding in her hand), after which Margrete starts to move her hands to comply with the request. In this case, the action targeted by the request benefits the requester (Svend), but this is not always the case in my data. Excerpt (2) contains an action that I have treated as a request, even though it does not benefit only the requester. The excerpt comes from a recording of a coffee break in a secondhand store. One of the camera crew, Dina (DIN), has walked away to get some coffee, and is off-camera when the extract begins. The person making the request (lines 4–5) is Elise (ELI), who is behind the camera and not visible. On camera, a microphone is seen hanging on the wall, attached to an electric cable, and this position of the microphone is what the request addresses.

Chapter 4. Grammatical formats of requests   81

Excerpt 2. *klips' mikrofonen* 'clip the mic' (AULing: genbrugs3)

```
01 ELI: Dina,
02      (0.2)
03 DIN: ja:,=
        yes,=
```

```
04 ELI: =ka du      ikk lige klips'  mikrofonen
         can you.SG not PTC  clip.INF microphone.DEF.C
        =can't you attach/clip the microphone
```

```
06 ELI: lidt       længere hen,
         a.little long.COMP over.DYN
         a little further over,
```

```
07      (0.6)
```

After a summons–answer sequence (lines 1–3), Elise (the requester) asks Dina (the recipient) to move the microphone. In this case, however, the beneficiary of the targeted action is not merely the requester. The recording is a project in which both participants are involved, and correctly positioning the microphone benefits both parties. Therefore, I have added an "at least" to the "benefit of the requester" to my definition. In many cases in my corpus, the beneficiary's status is left open, or requested actions occur in global projects to which both parties have committed (Gubina 2021), and/or may be seen as bilateral (Heinemann & Steensig 2017; Rossi 2012). I use the term *project* "to refer to a series of actions or moves coherently articulated to achieve an interactional outcome" (Rossi 2012: 430), and I call them *global* as soon as they can be seen as consisting of more than one local project (Gubina 2021: 278).

Local contingencies — that is, whether there are foreseeable obstructions to carrying out the targeted actions — and entitlement — that is, if the speakers claim that they have the right to make the request — have been shown to be important in the choice of request format (Curl & Drew 2008; Heinemann 2006). In the requests I consider here, the requesters generally present themselves as entitled to make their requests, and only rarely do they orient to contingencies (Curl & Drew 2008), but these aspects will be addressed when they apply.

In my search for possible requests in the data, I did not exclude requests of the more "instructing" kind. One difference between a request proper and an instruction is that a person making an "instructing" request has a higher epistemic status than the recipient (Couper-Kuhlen & Thompson this volume; Heritage 2012; Heritage & Raymond 2005). In cases where this matters to the design of the format, the epistemic aspects will be included in the analysis.

Another perspective on request sequences has been proposed by Kendrick and Drew (2016): Requests often occur as *recruitments* of assistance, and this may be relevant to the choice of specific format (or action). I will consider embodied (and other) recruitments, but in this investigation, I will focus on requests as the focal point. The reason the recruitment terminology has not been chosen as a point of departure is that it does not fit all the social actions covered, and that the intended readers of the grammar may find it easier to relate to a description of formats for making requests, than to resources for recruiting assistance.

1.4   Chapter overview

After introducing the data and my focus, I analyze three main formats. After the analysis of each format, I discuss the implications for the grammar of the analysis of that particular format. In these discussions, I present grammatical models and consider choices of terminology. In the concluding discussion, I sum up the consequences of my analysis for the writing of a grammar, and I suggest points that should be addressed in grammars of talk-in-interaction that take their point of departure in analyses of social action.

2.   Data and focus

I identified all instances of apparent requests in 60 hours of video-recorded face-to-face interactions. The recordings belong to two corpora, the publicly available *samtalebank* (Wagner et al. 2024) and the *AULing* collection of conversational data from Aarhus University, Denmark (DanTIN 2023). Both corpora comprise recordings of people interacting in their everyday lives. No sociolinguistic or other criteria were used when selecting participants or settings. The corpora are opportunity samples, that is, recordings of people who were willing to be recorded in their everyday lives. This means that the settings, participant identities, number of participants, duration, camera perspective, and so on are incidental. Most of the recordings have two, three, or four participants, and more women than men or other genders are included. All this means that the frequency and availability of specific formats and specific social actions do not reflect statistical trends in the Danish population. Certain formats and actions are less well-represented here than they would be in a larger or more representative corpus, and, similarly, some formats and actions may be overrepresented in our data. This is a basic, general condition of descriptive grammars that use real-life data, and it is not in any way detrimental. The choice of actions and formats is necessarily informed by what occurs in the data, but the formats are recognizable to me as an analyst and competent language user, and we can also see that participants recognize the formats and the actions they perform.

All participants in the recordings have given their informed consent, and the data collection and storage are consistent with the European General Data Protection Rules ("General Data Protection Regulation (GDPR) — Official Legal Text," n.d.). All information that might lead to the identification of participants has been anonymized.

All in all, I identified 540 instances of requests. When I reviewed the immediate surroundings and the reactions to the requests, I interpreted 470 instances as requests for immediate action. I started by categorizing these according to their syntactic format, using traditional categories. Table 1 shows my distribution of formats into these categories.

Table 1. All instances of requests for immediate action according to syntactic formats

Format	Number	Percentage of all instances
1. Embodied-only, e.g., pointing at an object	8	1.7
2. Phrasal, e.g., *lidt op* 'a little upwards'	147	31.3
3. Imperative, e.g., *gi mig den* 'give me that'	112	23.8
4. Modal verb interrogative, self-referencing, e.g., *må jeg se* 'may I see'	41	8.7
5. Modal verb declarative, self-referencing, e.g., *jeg ve' gerne ha* 'I would like'	52	11.1
6. Modal verb interrogative, other-referencing, e.g., *ka du vippe dit øre lidt ned* 'can you tilt down your ear a little'	26	5.5
7. Modal verb declarative, other-referencing, e.g., *du ska spille et kort nu* 'you must play a card now'	17	3.6
8. Non-modal declarative, self-referencing, e.g., *så tar jeg lige det så* 'then I just take that then'	12	2.6
9. Non-modal declarative, other-referencing, e.g., *du starter* 'you start'	10	2.1
10. Non-modal interrogative, other-referencing, e.g., *har I en skål* 'do you.PL have a bowl'	19	4.0
11. Other (mixed, 3rd person and passive formats, undetermined)	26	5.5
TOTAL	**470**	**99.9**

This chapter focuses on the embodied-only, the phrasal, and some of the modal verb formats (#4–6 in Table 1). As we will see below, they represent challenges to a grammatical description. This, and not their relative frequency, is the main reason for including them in this chapter.

I have made close, single-case analyses of instances of all the social action formats, and, on the basis of this, I have extracted the social action format features that seemed relevant to the types of social action that I review in this chapter. Some of the examinations of particular formats were made as regular "collection studies" (Schegloff 1996a; Sidnell 2012), and they are published elsewhere (Heinemann & Steensig in prep; Steensig, n.d.; in preparation); others were analyzed specifically for this chapter.

3. Analyses of three formats and their implications for grammar writing

Each of the three analytic sections below will have a section at the end considering their implications for the grammar. In those sections, I will address the formats' inter-unit and intra-unit syntax and discuss the relevance of grammatical terms and models for describing the formats in the grammar.

3.1 Embodied-only requests

Of the 470 instances of requests for immediate action in the data, eight are made exclusively through nonverbal, embodied means. I will argue that these requests are social action formats, and that this alone makes it reasonable to consider their place in a comprehensive grammar.

In the following, I will analyze one of the eight instances that presents features typical of all the instances in the data, in order to extract the features that may be relevant to the grammar.

3.1.1 *Embodied-only requests as social action formats*

Excerpt (3) presents features that are recurrent in this social action format. Two friends (Lau and Kim) are eating together; they are seated on either side of a table. They are discussing how speed-dating works, while Lau is serving Kim from a large dish of food that sits in the middle of the table between them. A water dispenser sits beside Lau's chair, out of Kim's reach (see Figure 1).

Figure 1. The table arrangement during Excerpt (1)

Chapter 4. Grammatical formats of requests **85**

In my analysis of Excerpt (3), the focus is on the embodied actions, which are not coordinated with the verbal actions. To avoid making the transcript too complex, I have included only the English translations of the conversation (even though it was carried out in Danish).

Excerpt 3. 'filling glass' (AULing: drengespiseraftensmad)

```
01 KIM: &consider this you have to meet five new  per&sons
    lau &puts food on kim's plate with big    spoon---&

02 KIM: o*:[:r* [ten new &persons_=·hhh    &

03 LAU:    [  hm[:_
    lau                     &lets go of spoon&

04    (0.7)

05 KIM: &and then it's just=it's like a little            &
    lau &picks up something on table, puts it on food dish&

06 LAU: find &something new to talk €#about=
    lau      &moves hand to mouth-->
    kim                         € ....... €#grabs glass,
                                  lifts it-->
                                   #fig.2

07 LAU: =[all the t&ime.€

08 KIM: [%yes_
    lau       -->&licks fingers-->
    kim   %looks twd water dispenser-->
    kim             -->€

09 KIM: €I %don't want to& about the sa%me_€=
    kim €#tilts glass twd LAU-------------€
    kim -->%looks at glass------------%looks twd LAU-->
    lau             -->&looks twd KIM-->
        #fig.3

10 LAU: =€m=th[heh heh%                          €

11 KIM:     [(   )
    kim €glass in upright position, lh grabs glass€
    kim          -->%looks at glass-->

12 KIM: €fo&rty times_
    kim €hands glass twd LAU w. lh-->
    lau    &reaches twd KIM and glass w lh-->

13    #(0.2)€&
    kim   -->€
    lau   -->&
        #fig.4

14 LAU: &m:.
    lau &takes glass w lh-->

15    (0.2)&
    lau   -->&
```

```
16 LAU:  &one could use (it/a little)here. I think.
    lau  &moves glass to rh, puts it under water tap of dispenser and fills glass w
         water-->
17       (9.0)& ((they keep talking))
    lau    -->&
18       &(2.5) ((more talk))&
    lau  &hands glass to  KIM-&
19       €(1.1) ((more talk))€
    kim  €takes  glass--------€
```

Figure 2. Kim lifts glass   **Figure 3.** Kim tilts glass   **Figure 4.** Kim hands glass to Lau

The food is served simultaneously with a discussion of speed-dating. The request occurs in line 12, when Kim hands his glass to Lau (Figure 4). Lau starts to move his hand forward immediately after this, and the glass changes hands during lines 12–13. Then Lau fills the glass with water and hands it back to Kim, who takes it and puts it on the table, without any other orientation to that action (line 19). After the glass-filling sequence is complete, Lau pours water into his own glass (not shown), thus indicating that he sees the filling of Kim's glass as a completed action, and as a part of a sequence of actions that belong together.

The glass-filling sequence comes right after Lau has finished serving both of them food from a dish of food. After both their glasses have been filled with water, Kim proceeds to serve himself some salad from a salad bowl (not shown). In keeping with Gubina's ideas (2021), I see the overall sequence of serving food and drinks as the global project, and the separate events, such as filling a glass, as local projects within the global one. However, there is no automaticity to the order of events, so the request for water has to be arranged in a way that fits the overall trajectory and the recipient's local actions.

We can see that Kim times his request for water so it fits with Lau finishing serving the food. During lines 8–9, Lau licks his fingers after having put down the serving spoon and picked up something from the table. At this point, Kim has picked up his glass and tilted it towards Lau (lines 6–9, Figures 2 and 3), while looking at the glass. This may be seen as a summons (Schegloff 1968) that attracts Lau's attention to the glass as a relevant object. Lau looks at Kim in line 9, which may be seen as a response to the summons. At the point when this happens, Kim proffers his glass and begins to hand it to Lau (lines 11–13, Figure 4). This makes it possible for Lau to react immediately, to take the glass and perform the requested action (lines 14–18). Thus, there are two steps in Kim's embodied actions: First, he manipulates an object in a way that attracts Lau's attention, and then he moves it in a way that is understood as a request for the immediate action of taking the glass and filling it with water. The summons–answer sequence becomes a pre-sequence to the request sequence, which consists of a request, compliance, and a receipt.

All the instances of embodied-only requests in my corpus are bounded sequences, limited by other actions and local projects before and after the request sequences. They all take place in global projects, within which the targeted action benefits the requester, but is also a contribution to the global project. All the embodied-only request sequences consist of a requesting action and a response that treats the first action as a request. In all instances but two, the response consists of the immediate, embodied performance of the targeted action; in the last two instances, the request is rejected. If we look closer at the physical circumstances, we can see that the targeted action involves an object that is visible to the parties, but that is under the recipient's control. Although the embodied request presents the object in question as relevant to the course of events, it still relies on the recipient's ability to recognize the relationship between the object and a relevant action.

The preparatory move of getting the recipient's attention is common to all instances of embodied-only requests. In Excerpt (3), the two steps are separate; in other cases, there is no pre-sequence: Either the movement that attracts attention continues into the requesting action, without awaiting a response to the summons, or the movement that attracts attention and the request occur as one action. There is no verbal or nonverbal receipt by the requester in any of my cases. This may be coincidental. In some instances, the request sequence is followed by an assessment of the requested object.

The fact that the requests are complied with immediately (or, in two cases, rejected with an account) indicates that we are dealing with recognizable requests here, not just "weaker" types of requests on the "recruitment continuum" (Kendrick & Drew 2016: 11).

3.1.2 *Embodied-only formats in the comprehensive grammar*

There is a consensus that embodied actions are an integral part of what participants orient to during talk-in-interaction, whenever they can see and/or physically interact with one another (Nevile 2015). But are they part of the *grammar*? Keevallik (2018) argues that embodied actions that fill slots in verbal formats are indeed integral to the grammar, whereas Couper-Kuhlen (2018) argues that the fact that embodied actions may fill syntactic slots is not sufficient to treat embodied actions as grammatical. Body movements "do not create syntactic projections (...) they lack conventionalization (...) they are depictions, which operate in a fundamentally different way from descriptions," and "they are not wholly linear" (Couper-Kuhlen 2018:23). My take has been explorative: What happens to our view of grammar if we seriously consider that (some) embodied actions should indeed be described in the grammar? And where and how should they be described?

The embodied-only request formats have a specific position in a sequence, a recognizable shape, and there are systematic, alternative ways of executing an action. The sequential positions in which these formats occur may be filled with verbal formats that perform similar actions. So, the embodied-only requests belong to a list of possible options, in which both verbal and embodied formats may occur. If the grammar is to provide an instruction on which formats to choose from to execute specific actions, it would be strange not to include the embodied-only ones.

The obvious position of a description of embodied formats in the *Building Blocks* section of the grammar is in a special section for embodied expressions. It should contain all the embodied expressions that occur systematically in social action formats. In Excerpt (3), the tilting of the glass drew the recipient's attention to the object that the action was to be carried out on. In other cases, it is pointing, a head movement, or touching an object. Moving the glass towards the recipient in Excerpt (3) was the gesture that indexed the targeted action. In other cases, the requester reaches for the targeted object, or points at it, in which cases the pointing both draws attention to, and indexes, the targeted action. The embodied expressions section of the grammar would also include embodied formats that are used systematically to carry out other social actions, which would mean that physical expressions such as nodding, shaking the head, gaze, manipulation of objects, posture shifts, and so on would have to be included. The section might be organized according to the main body part — or object — used, which would yield subsections on the use of the hands, fingers, eyes, upper body, face, and so on (more about this in Steensig in prep.).

If we treat attracting attention and requesting as two separate actions — which may or may not be merged — a model of the inter-unit, or sequential, syntax may be proposed. Figure 5 presents an attempt to do so, in a way that makes the inter-unit syntax for this social action format comparable to the formats that will be examined later in this chapter.

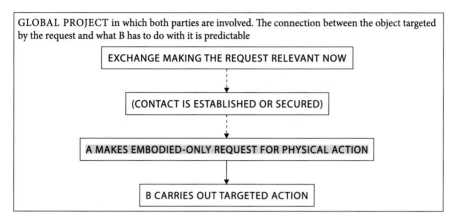

Figure 5. Inter-unit syntax of embodied-only requests.

The dotted arrow before the embodied-only request indicates that this action is not made conditionally relevant by what precedes it; other things may be done, but the context makes it possible to recognize what is being requested. The unbroken arrows indicate that the response to the request is a projectable, necessary, subsequent action.

3.2 Phrasal or subsentential requests

My data indicate that people sometimes make requests in an "item-only" format (Kuroshima 2010), or another type of phrasal format. This fact may present a challenge to grammars that are based on the concept of the clause as the basic utterance format. In this section, I will examine two types of phrasal request formats: "item-only requests" and "phrasal action-guiding requests."

3.2.1 *Item-only requests*

"Item-only" requests (Kuroshima 2010) are requests made by mentioning the requested item only. In my data, these requests are noun phrases or single nouns. These requests come almost exclusively from two contexts: an encounter in a convenience store, and recordings of people playing card games. Excerpt (4) is from a recording of three people playing the card game, *Fisk* 'Fish', in which the players take turns asking for cards. If the player addressed has the requested card, they must give it to the requester; if they do not, they say *fisk*, and the requester must pick up a card from the table ("fishing"). We enter just after the game has started. Charlie (CHA) has taken the first turn by addressing Bine (BIN), and using a modal interrogative format, >*må jeg< be om alle dine ↑tiere* 'may I ask for/request all your ↑tens'. It turns out that Bine has tens in her hand, and she gives them to Charlie, who then asks whether that means that he can continue (line 1).

Excerpt 4. *alle dine niere* 'all your nines' (AULing: kollegiespil)

```
01 CHA: €·hhh må jeg så €igen eller hva_
         ·hhh may I then again or what_
    cha €looks down-----€looks up tow BIN and ARN-->

02      (0.5)

03 BIN: m:hm[: [:   :  :

04 AND:    [°j[am'  :  m :  :  °]=
              °well:::°=

05 CHA:       [hva ska vi sige_ ]
               what should we say_

06 AND: =m:: €må du vel.
        =you m:may I suppose.
    cha     €looks at cards in his hands-->>

07      (0.3)

08 BIN: ja det går jeg [ud=SPØRG om]
        yes I assume=ASK about

09 CHA:              [°*ja:*° ok]ay.
                      °*yeah:*° okay.

10      (.)

11 CHA: Arne &alle dine    n:iere.          &
        NAME all.PL your.PL nine.PL
        Arne all your n:ines.
    arn      &looks at cards in his hands&

12      &(1.9)                             &
    arn &takes card from hand and slides it twd CHA&

13 ARN: °°(    [   )°°

14 CHA:        [ja nu kører det.
                yes now it's running.
```

In line 1, Charlie asks whether this means that he is allowed to make another request. He receives hesitant answers from his two fellow players in lines 3 and 4, and pursues an answer in line 5 by asking, *hva ska vi sige_* 'what should we say_'. Apparently, Charlie hears Arne's (ARN) beginning of line 6 as a confirmation, as he starts to examine the cards in his hands. Both Arne and Bine give more elaborate confirmations in lines 6 and 8, and Charlie acknowledges this in line 9. After this, he summons Arne, and immediately issues a phrasal request (line 11), *alle dine n:iere.* 'all your n:ines.' After the summons in line 11, Arne looks at the cards in his hands, and immediately after the phrasal request, he slides a card across the table to Charlie, thus complying with his request. In line 14, Charlie reports and celebrates his success. After this sequence, all the subsequent requests for cards (not shown) have the format of line 11: a summons (if necessary) and a phrasal, item-only request, with the same structure, with or without the word *alle* 'all'. The responses consist of compliance, as in Excerpt (4), or the game-warranted rejection (saying *fisk* 'fish', forcing the requester to pick up a card). This may or may not be followed by comments from either party, which evaluate the success or failure of the move. Only when the game is resumed, either because a new game has begun, or because the participants have been doing other things, do we find clausal requests. Thus, when the game is going on, phrasal item-only requests seem designed to be subsequent moves in a series of moves.

Phrasal requests are frequent in service encounters. The corpus contains two recordings of exchanges in a convenience store. Excerpt (5) exemplifies the use of an item-only request in this setting. The excerpt begins as the customer (CUS) approaches the counter, behind which the seller (SEL) is standing. The customer is standing at the left of the frame, and until line 15, only a small part of her body and hands may be seen.

Excerpt 5. *ti marlbo' light* 'ten Marlboro lights' (AULing: Kiosk2B)

```
01 CUS: hej_
        hi_
02 SEL: hej,
        hi,
03      Ω(0.4)
   sel  Ωlooks twd where CUS is standing-->
04 CUS: ti    marlbo'  light,Ω
        ten   NAME.OF.BRAND
        ten   Marlboro lights,
   sel                     -->Ω
05      Ω(0.2)
   sel  Ωturns around-->
06 SEL: °ja    tak°_Ω
        °yes   thank you_°
   sel          -->Ω
07      Ω(0.9)
   sel  Ωgrabs cigarette packet with lh in cupboard behind him-->
08 SEL: ellers  ↑andet_
        anything ↑else_
09      (0.3)
10 CUS: nejΩ tak,
        no   thanks,
   sel  -->Ωmoves cigarette packet over desk-->>
```

After the initial greetings, the customer mentions the brand and the size of the packet of cigarettes that she wishes to buy in line 4, *ti marlbo' light*, 'ten Marlboro lights'. The seller acknowledges this (line 6), and turns to take down the requested item, which he scans and pushes across the counter towards the customer (lines 7–10). This shows that the seller treats the mention of the product as a request for him to sell it (see also Sorjonen & Raevaara 2014). The request is immediately followed by an embodied, complying action, in this case accompanied by verbal appreciation (line 6). The exchange runs smoothly, as this is an expected next move in this institutional framework.

The foregoing request is made with a noun phrase, *ti marlbo' light*, 'ten Marlboro lights'. Noun phrases are traditionally defined as phrases that have a noun or a pronoun as their core, or "head" (Christensen & Christensen 2014: 164; Rijkhoff 2002: 19; Hansen & Heltoft 2011: 518ff). Here, the head noun is the compound "Marlboro lights," with the number "ten" as a quantifying modifier. In other cases, in the data related to the convenience store, the noun phrases are modified by demonstratives, as in *den is der* 'that ice cream there'.

As item-only requests are almost exclusively found in the convenience store and card game data, these settings may be considered their "base environment" (Sacks 1992, 1: 8–11). The contexts of use of these phrasal formats resemble those of the embodied-only formats. They occur in global projects to which both parties have committed, the requested actions are relevant next steps in those projects, there is a low degree of contingency, the discourse identities (Zimmerman 1998) of requester and recipient are established, and the requested actions are carried out immediately and physically. The difference between the contexts of item-only and embodied-only formats is that the exact requested object or the exact targeted action is less predictable in the case of the item-only requests, compared to the embodied ones. The requesters have specific knowledge about what is requested, that the recipients do not have, so the exact item needs to be mentioned, in order for the recipients to carry out the targeted actions.

3.2.2 *Phrasal action-guiding requests*

A different type of phrasal request occurs in situations where one party is engaged in a physical activity that the other party is following closely. There are only five instances of this in my data, mainly because there are few situations with this kind of activity. Excerpt (6) shows two instances of this format. It comes from a recording made in the home of one of the participants, in which Sisse (SIS) is dyeing Lina's (LIN) hair. When we enter, the participants have been discussing someone, and Sisse, who has her hands full, has asked Lina to take Sisse's phone and take a look "in the group" (a Facebook group), in order to see something that this person has posted. Lina is holding Sisse's phone and is trying to find where this thing is written. She is using her thumbs to navigate on the phone.

Chapter 4. Grammatical formats of requests 93

Excerpt 6. *ikk så hurtig* 'not so fast' (AULing: haarfarvning_1)

```
01 LIN: °hvor: °er det° han 'ar skrevet %det_°
        °where °is it° that he has written it_°
    lin                                    %r. thumb up-->
02      (.)%Ω(0.3)
    lin --->%
    sis     Ωbends fwd, looking at phone-->>
03 SIS: ·pth inde unde:r ø:h.
        ·pth in unde:r u:h.
04      %(2.1)
    lin %1. thumb is moving on phone screen-->
05 SIS: >prøv      lige     å    vent<.
        try.IMP    PTC      IFM  wait.INF
        >try LIGE and wait<. ((wait a moment))
06      (.)
07 SIS: ikk så hurtig_
        not so fast
        not so fast_
08      (0.6)%
    lin    --->%
09 SIS: *n:*% det der (.) opslag=
        *n:* that (.) posting=
    lin      %lifts 1. thumb from phone
10 SIS: =↓nej_=
        =↓no_=
11 SIS: %lidt      op.
        a.little   up.DYN
        a little upwards.
    lin %1. thumb moves on screen-->
12      (0.7)
13 SIS: det der opslag.%
        that posting.
    lin              --->%
14      %(0.2)
    lin %lifts 1. thumb from phone-->>
```

After asking where the place in question is (line 1), Lina starts to navigate the phone with Sisse watching her movements closely (lines 2–14). Sisse starts telling Lina where to look, but hesitates (line 3), and Lina keeps moving her thumb (line 4). In line 5, Sisse uses an imperative format, *>prøv lige å vent<. '((wait a moment.))'*, to pause Lina's actions on the phone. Apparently, this does not work, and in line 7, she asks Lina to slow down, using the phrasal format, *ikk så hurtig_* 'not so fast_'. This is more successful: Lina lifts her thumb from the phone (line 8), and in line 9, Sisse indicates (temporary) success, *det der (.) opslag* 'that (.) posting'. But in line 10, Sisse indicates that Lina has not yet found the exact spot with a ↓*nej_* '↓no_', immediately followed by another phrasal request, *lidt op* 'a little upwards ((up a bit))', to direct Lina's movements. Apparently, Lina's movements are now in the correct direction, as in line 13, Sisse indicates that Lina has now found the desired post. After this, Lina opens the post, which makes it possible for the participants to read and discuss it (not shown).

I categorized the actions in lines 7 and 11 in Excerpt (6) as requests, based on the broad search criteria mentioned in the Section 1.3 above: They are attempts to get the recipient of the request to do something that (also) benefits the requester. As was the case with both embodied-only and the item-only requests, here, participants are engaged in an already-established, common project. But here, the request aims to change something related to the recipient's physical actions, and the requester claims to know and be able to guide the recipient in the right direction. I have chosen the term "action-guiding" to describe them, inspired by Borchmann (2024), who analyzes what he calls "discourse initial action-guiding subsententials" in the practical activities of "gliding, cycling, football, cross country mountain bike training, climbing, archery training and slaughtering of game" in Danish (Borchmann 2024:5). The actions and the formats also resemble the instruction formats ("phrasal instructions") described for Swedish personal training settings by Huhtamäki et al. (2019).

Phrasal action-guiding requests consist of an adverb phrase, which may contain a manner adverb modified to indicate some kind of change, as in *ikk så hurtig_* 'not so fast_' (Excerpt (6), line 7), or a place adverb in the "dynamic" form, which may also be modified to indicate degree, as in *lidt op.* 'a little upwards.' (line 11).[1] They may also consist of prepositional phrases, such as *bare te' næste* 'just to the next ((item))', when a speaker is guiding another speaker who is using a computer to go to the next point of an online form they are filling out together.

3.2.3 *Phrasal requests in the comprehensive grammar*

A comprehensive grammar should account for both the internal structure of the social action formats and for their position in larger structures, and this is what I will do here for the two phrasal request formats of this section. We will start by looking at the inter-unit syntax of the two formats, which is displayed in Figures 6 and 7.

---

1. Danish has a series of place adverbs that have two forms, a static one, indicating location only, and a dynamic one (DYN in the glossing line), indicating a movement to that location.

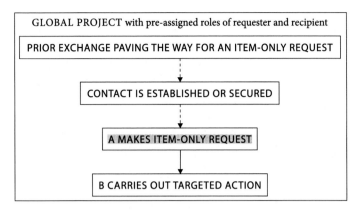

Figure 6. Inter-unit syntax of item-only requests.

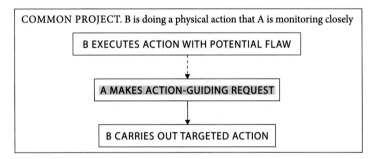

Figure 7. Inter-unit syntax of action-guiding requests.

The environments in which the two types of phrasal requests occur are quite different. The inter-unit syntax of the item-only requests (Figure 6) is very much like that of the embodied-only requests: Both occur in global projects in which the parties participate in pre-assigned roles. And both happen at a point when the previous interaction has made it reasonable and predictable to make the request then and there. The difference is that the targeted object is directly accessible to both parties in the embodied-only requests, whereas in the item-only requests, the request-recipient does not know beforehand what will be requested, so the requester needs to specify it to get it.

The action-guiding phrasal requests are part of a local, common project, which may be integrated into a global project, as was the case with the action-guiding request mentioned above, as one party filled out an online form on a computer while the other party watched. But the common project may also be more locally established, as was the case in Excerpt (6) above, in which the need to check something on a phone came up as a side activity. What the action-guiding requests have in common is that the requester is, or claims to be, an authority on how the action that the recipient is doing should be done.

The relationship between the action preceding the request and the request sequence is looser in Figure 7, compared to Figure 6. Whereas both (all) parties were aligned with respect to the immediate relevance of an item-only request, only one party (called A in Figure 7) can see that there may be a problem that calls for an action-guiding request. In syntactic terms, the action-guiding requests are more like free adverbials in a clause, that is, constituents that are not as strongly projected as syntactic objects, for instance. However, once the action-guiding request has been issued, the projection of a complying action is strong.

The internal, or intra-unit, structures of the two phrasal formats are also different, although both are phrasal. All the grammars and analyses that treat formats such as the ones in this section take the "non-clausalness" of the formats as their point of departure. Both Huhtamäki et al. (2019) and Borchmann (2024) compare them to clausal formats, but recognize them as formats of their own, designed to be used in the circumstances they describe. The *Longman Grammar of Spoken and Written English* lists the "non-clausal units" that its authors found in their corpus of conversational English, among them "condensed directives," of which they give examples that resemble both the item-only and the action-guiding ones, without describing them further (Biber et al. 1999: 1101f). *The Comprehensive Finnish Grammar* provides examples of phrasal formats that function as requests, along with other non-clausal units that function as free-standing units (and actions) in spoken Finnish (Hakulinen et al. 2004: §864). The *Grammar of the Danish Language* recognizes phrasal formats as *sætningsemner* 'clause/sentence prospects,' defined as "a predication without a finite verb" (Hansen & Heltoft 2011: 1623).[2] Their examples resemble the action-guiding formats in this section, and in the works of Huhtamäki et al. (2019) and Borchmann (2024).

The internal structure of the item-only requests is that of a normal Danish noun phrase (Hansen & Heltoft 2011: 518). In Table 2, I have used the relevant slots in a noun phrase to insert the words of the formats that I have found in the item-only requests.

It is quite possible that a recipient may be able to recognize that an item-only request is being made already on the occurrence of the first word(s) of these formats, when they occur in their base environments.

When it comes to the internal structure of the action-guiding formats, *The Grammar of the Danish Language* contains an elaborate model, or "topology" of the "predications without a verb" (Hansen & Heltoft 2011: 1625f), that builds on a main clause model, without a verb. Borchmann provides a more basic model

---

2. Translated from Danish, "en prædikation uden et finit verbum."

Chapter 4. Grammatical formats of requests   97

Table 2. The internal structure of item-only request formats

Determiner	General quantifier	Possessive	Quantifier	Descriptors	Head	Post-specification
			syv 'seven'	*grønne* 'green'	*kings* ((brand of cigarettes)) 'Kings'	
den 'that'					*is* 'ice cream'	*der* 'there'
	alle 'all'	*dine* 'your'			*n:iere* 'nines'	

of his action-guiding formats (Borchmann 2024: 16). Table 3 is inspired by these models and shows the internal positions of elements in the action-guiding formats in my data.

Table 3. Internal structure of action-guiding formats[3]

Negator	Modifier	Change indicator
	lidt 'a little'	*op* 'upwards'
ikk 'not'		*så hurtig* 'so fast'
	bare 'just'	*te' næste* 'to the next one'

The models in the literature contain an extra slot at the end of the phrase for the "indication of circumstance" (Borchmann 2024: 16f) or "free adverbials" (Hansen & Heltoft 2011: 1625), which may be prepositional phrases or adverbs that indicate circumstances, such as, *nu* 'now', or *sammen* 'together'. I do not happen to have instances of this in my data, but I am convinced they may be found, and, if so, a slot should be added for this in Table 3.

Some grammars see phrasal requests as elliptical versions of clausal formats (e.g., Diderichsen 1962: 153), which "reconstruct" a full clause, of which the phrase could be a constituent. An argument for an "ellipsis analysis" could be made on empirical grounds: The item-only formats alternate with clausal ones in the same recordings. Thus, customers in the convenience store data sometimes say, for

---

3. The *så* 'so' in the second row may be seen as a modifier. I have chosen to put it in the change indicator cell because it is what makes it possible to see this as an indication of change.

instance, *jeg ska ha en lyner.* literally, 'I would like a "lyner" (a special type of lottery ticket)', rather than just *en lyner* 'a "lyner"'. I have not made a full analysis of the clausal formats in the convenience store data, but we know from studies of convenience store interactions that the use of clausal formats to request goods may be coordinated with the participants' physical positions and movements (Sorjonen & Raevaara 2014). In Section 2.2.1, above, we saw that a new round of a card game may be initiated with a full clause, so that rather than just requesting *alle dine tiere* 'all your tens', Charles says >*må jeg< be om alle dine* ↑ *tiere* 'may I ask for/request all your ↑ tens'. However, the clausal and the phrasal formats are used in different phases of the game; the clausal ones only when initiating or resuming a game, the phrasal ones for all subsequent requests for cards. So, regarding the phrasal formats as elliptical would overlook the point that these formats have a specific interactional function when they occur as free-standing requests in their sequential environment. And it is the sequential environment that is the relevant structure in which the formats have a specific position. They may be seen as constituents of the inter-unit syntax.

Given that the difference between phrasal and clausal formats matters (see also Jørgensen, this volume), it makes sense to have a separate section on phrasal formats in the grammar. We saw that the noun phrases used in the item-only requests were describable by using the traditional categories of the internal structures of noun phrases. With the action-guiding requests, which used an adverbial phrasal format, the situation may be different. The categories used to describe the various parts of the internal structure may be describable in ways that better reflect what the phrases are used for than is the case in traditional grammars. Furthermore, it is possible that various adverb phrases should be distinguished in the grammar, according to the jobs they do in the inter- and/or intra-unit grammar, and to their internal structure.

3.3 Modal verb request formats

The modal verb request formats are relevant to grammar writing not only because they occur quite frequently (see Section 2 above), but also because they are clausal. Thus, their grammatical description will highlight syntactical questions related to the clause, which any grammar will need to address.

As was the case with my description of other request formats above, I will first analyze various formats, and then I will discuss the implications of this analysis for the grammar. Among the clausal request formats, the ones with modal verbs are, by far, the most frequent in the data. Tables 4 and 5 illustrate the basic grammatical structure of modal verb requests.

Chapter 4. Grammatical formats of requests 99

Table 4. Basic format of declarative modal verb request

Modal format			Targeted action		
jeg	ve'	gerne	se	din	hånd_
I	will.PRS	PTC	see.INF	your.SG.C	hand(c)
SUBJECT	MODAL VERB	PARTICLE	MAIN VERB		OBJECT
*I would like to see your hand_*					

Table 5. Basic format of interrogative modal verb request

Modal format		Targeted action			
ka	du	vippe	dit	øre	lidt ned_
can.PRS	you.SG	tilt.INF	your.SG	ear	a.little down.DYN
MODAL VERB	SUBJ.	MAIN VERB		OBJECT	ADVERBIAL
*can you tilt down your ear a little_*					

The modal verb in Table 4 is *ve'* 'will', and in Table 5, *ka* 'can'. Both are in the present tense, which is almost always the case in my data. In Table 4, the subject pronoun *jeg* 'I' comes before the modal verb, indicating that the clause is declarative, whereas in Table 5, the syntactic subject, *du* 'you' comes after the verb, indicating the interrogative mood. Modal verb request formats often contain discourse particles that help mark the requests' pragmatic and sequential functions (in Table 4, it is *gerne*; more on this particle below). These particles follow the subject and modal verb. A description of the targeted action follows these. In most cases, this description consists of a main verb in the infinitive form and the complements (objects and adverbials) projected by the verb.[4] Prosodically, there is no stress on the subject and the verb; there may be on discourse particles, and then there is always stress on words in the description of the targeted action, according to the pattern described below.

Tables 4 and 5 further illustrate two main distinctions in modal verb requests: (1) between declaratively formatted ones (Table 4) and interrogatively formatted ones (Table 5), and (2) between self-referencing formats (Table 4, with *jeg* 'I') and other-referencing formats (Table 5, with *du* 'you').

In Section 2.3.1, I will analyze the self-referencing formats and compare declarative (as in Table 4) and interrogative types (with the modal verb *må* 'may, be allowed to'), and in Section 2.3.2, I will focus on the other-referencing, inter-

---

4. The only exceptions are two cases in which the clause is left incomplete.

rogative formats (as in Table 5), where I will compare formats with the modal verbs *ve'* 'will' and *ka* 'can'.[5]

3.3.1 *Self-referencing modal verb request formats*

Excerpt (7) shows the format from Table 4 in its context of use. Four people are sitting around a table, playing a game in which one of the rules is that a player may ask to see another player's cards. When we enter, the participants are eating pizza while playing, and they are all quite occupied with eating, wiping their hands, and so on. Margrete (MAR) has made her move in the game by taking up a card and saying *safe*, which passes the move to Svend (SVE).

Excerpt 7. *jeg ve' gerne se* 'I would like to see' (AULing: board-game-coffee2:)

```
01      Ω(2.2)                                           Ω
   sve  Ωreaches to the middle of table, picks up a cardΩ
02 TOR: >du ska ikk bare Ωsafe=
        >you shouldn't just "safe"=
   sve                 -->Ωlooks at card-->
03 TOR: =du ska< ʃangribe &ham, ʃ
        =you have to attack him,<
   tor           ʃpoints twd SVEʃ
   liv                 &looks twd SVE-->
04 MAR: hm.
05      (0.7)
06 MAR: Ω°okay.°
   sve  Ωpicks up a card lying in front of him-->
07      (0.8)Ω(1.8)
   sve  -->Ωlooks at card and up,puts down card,
             looks twd LIV-->
08 MAR: ·hnffh ((snorts))&
   liv                 -->&
09      &(0.7)     &Ω(1.0)        Ω
   liv  &looks down&looks twd sve-->
   sve             Ωpoints twd livΩ
10 SVE: Ωjeg ve'     gerne se     din        hånd_Ω
        I   will.PRS PTC  see.INF your.SG.C  hand(C)
        I would like to see your hand_
   sve  Ωputs down card on the middle of  table---Ω
11      Ω(0.3)
   sve  Ωreaches twd liv-->
```

---

5. Modal verb request formats also exist with other modal verbs, among them *gider* 'be bothered', *ska* 'must, be supposed to'. The grammar must be able to account for the use of formats with these verbs. An analysis of this is beyond the scope of this chapter.

```
12     &(1.2)Ω                                    &
  liv  &looks down,takes card, hands it twd sve&
  sve     -->Ω

13     &Ω(0.8)                        Ω    &
  liv  &lets go of  card,  sits back&
  sve  Ωtakes card, sits backΩ

14     Ω(0.8)
  sve  Ωlooks at card-->

15 SVE: ·pthh m%:↑m:_              %
  sve          %moves head up-down%

16     Ω(1.5)                  Ω&(0.2)
  sve  Ωhands card to livΩ
  liv                         &takes card-->>
```

In line 1, Svend picks up a card. Tor comments on Margrete's move (lines 2–3), which Margrete acknowledges (lines 4 and 6). This is followed by a 2.6 second silence (line 7), during which Svend picks up another card, looks at it, puts it down again, and starts to look at Liv. In line 9, Svend points at Liv, and in line 10, he begins the request sequence by saying *jeg ve' gerne se din hånd_*, 'I would like to see your hand'. He then immediately reaches towards Liv. Liv takes the card she has in front of her, and hands it to Svend, who takes it, looks at it, and hands it back again (lines 11–16). Before Svend hands back the card, he registers what he has seen with *m:↑m:_* (line 15), then Liv takes back the card, and the game proceeds to the next move (not shown). The request format is *jeg ve' gerne* 'I would like'. The literal meaning of the particle *gerne* is 'voluntarily' or 'willingly', but I have chosen a more idiomatic translation, 'would like'.[6] *Gerne* co-occurs with *ve'* in almost all instances of the modal format *jeg ve'* ('I will').[7]

The modal verb request format in Excerpt (7) is used to execute the next move in the game, but unlike the item-only request in Excerpt (4), which was made as a next move of a series, this comes after participants have had an unrelated exchange and are not focusing on the game.

Self-referencing *interrogatives* are also used to request immediate actions. The format *må jeg* 'may I' occurs in much the same environment as the declarative, self-referencing *jeg ve' gerne*, 'I would like to'. Excerpt (8) comes from earlier in the same recording as Excerpt (7). Svend (SVE) has been dealing cards to begin a new round of the game. At the same time, the participants have been discussing bad losers and bad winners; Margrete's (MAR) turn in lines 1–2 is part of that discussion.

---

6. The particle *gerne* resembles the German particle, *gern*, both in format and use.

7. Another particle that occurs in this position is *godt* (literally, 'well'). There are subtle differences between the two, on which I will not elaborate here (but see Hansen & Heltoft 2011: 1088–1091; Widahl 2023).

Excerpt 8. *må jeg se* 'may I see' (AULing: board-game-coffee1)

```
01 MAR: %jeg ka bedreΩ           %li når de: smålige
        I like it better when they're petty minded
   sve  %looks at cards in his lh%looks twd TOR-->
   sve               Ωlifts rh, index finger raised-->
02 MAR: når de taber end når de vinder.
        when they lose than when they win.
03      Ω(0.7)        Ω
   sve  Ωpoints vigorously at TOR and puts down
        hand on tableΩ
04 SVE: tor:_
05      (.)
06 SVE: Ω>må   jeg< se    din€       hånd.Ω
        may.PRS I   see.INF your.SG.C hand(C)
        >may I< see your hand.
   sve  Ωputs   down  card on table--------Ω
   tor                €looks at card in his hands-->
07      (0.3)€Ω(1.4)
   tor    -->€ puts card quickly up tw SVE's face-->
   sve       Ωmoves hand twd tor, changes direction
             and lifts hand to hold on to tor's card-->
08 SVE: aↄhaΩ€::.        Ω                      €
   sve  -->Ωlets go of cardΩ
   tor  -->€drags card back to himself and looks at it€
09      (1.0)
```

In lines 1–2, we can see Svend (SVE) preparing for what he then does in lines 3–4, when he selects and summons Tor by pointing forcefully at him and saying his name. He then makes the request, >*må jeg< se din hånd.* '>may I< see your hand.' (line 6). Tor looks down and quickly moves his card towards Svend (line 7), who grabs it, looks at it, makes a change-of-state exclamation *a↑ha::.* (line 8) and releases the card. In this case, the request to 'see the hand' is made as a first move in a round of the game.

With both formats, the requests are made without any orientation to possible contingencies, and the recipients comply immediately, after which the handing-over of cards happens smoothly and quickly, usually accompanied by a receipt that recognizes and potentially assesses the information on the card, as in Excerpts (7) and (8). The sequence is an institutionally warranted one, as the action is part of the game rules. Most of the instances of *jeg ve' gerne* 'I would like' in the data come from people playing games and asking for something that is consistent with the game rules, or, in the convenience store data, from customers using the format to request items. The *må jeg* 'may I' format is mainly found in the game data, where it is followed by the main verb, *se* 'see' or *be om* 'ask for'. In the game data, both formats contrast with phrasal formats in the way that the modal

Chapter 4. Grammatical formats of requests 103

verb formats are used to begin or restart (a round of) the game. In the convenience store data, the potential differences between the phrasal item-only requests and the modal verb requests are less clear.

In the settings described here, there is no difference between the declarative formats with *jeg ve' gerne* 'I would like to' and the interrogative *må jeg* 'may I'. However, this is only true of requests for immediate actions. The format with *må jeg* 'may I' is also used to request permission for a remote action or service, but in this chapter the focus is on requests for immediate actions, and in this capacity, the two formats are directing the same actions and occurring under similar conditions.

In this case, an analysis that starts with the literal meaning of the modal verbs does not tell us much about their use in social action formats. Taken literally, *jeg ve' gerne* 'I would like to' expresses volition, and *må jeg* 'may I' asks for permission, but in the instances in the data, this difference does not seem to matter to these formats; neither does the fact that one format is declarative and the other is interrogative. There is a difference in collocations, though: When used to request an object, *jeg ve' gerne* 'I would like to' is only used with the main verb *ha* 'have', whereas *må jeg* 'may I' collocates with *få* 'get'.

3.3.2 *Other-referencing modal verb request formats*

The two most frequently used other-referencing request formats are both interrogative. These are the ones that begin with *ka du* 'can you' and *ve' du* 'will you'.[8] I do not have enough instances to examine the difference between the positive and negative formats. Instead, I will consider the general use of *ve' du* 'will you' and *ka du* 'can you'. In my corpus, there are 12 instances with *ka du* and 8 with *ve' du*.

Excerpt (9) shows a typical use of *ka du* 'can you', here co-occurring with the negation, *ikk* 'not' and the modal particle, *lige*. On some occasions, the particle *lige* may be translated as 'just', in other cases it is left untranslated (see below for a further explanation). The excerpt is from a recording of three elderly ladies having coffee and cake in the back room of a secondhand store where they do volunteer work. When the extract starts, one of the ladies is serving a customer and not present; the two remaining participants, Carina and Birte, are sitting by the coffee table, and they do not take part in the exchange. One of the camera crew, Dina (DIN), has gone to get herself a cup of coffee, and is off camera when the excerpt

---

8. The written forms of the two modal verbs in the present tense are *vil* and *kan*. In the requests recorded in my data, they are consistently pronounced *ve'* and *ka*. In other contexts, the final consonant may be pronounced, which is why I have chosen to write them in a way that is orthographically deviant. This makes it possible to see whether different pronunciations correlate with specific social action formats. This will not be examined further here.

104 Jakob Steensig

begins. The person making the request is Elise (ELI), who is behind the camera and not visible.

Excerpt 9. *klips' mikrofonen* 'clip the mic' (AULing: genbrugs3)

```
01      (5.7)
02 ELI: Dina,
03      (0.2)
04 DIN: jaɪ,=
        yes,=
05 ELI: =ka du     ikk lige klips'  mikrofonen
        can you.SG not PTC  clip.INF microphone-DEF.C
        =can't you attach/clip the mic
06 ELI: lidt      længere hen,
        a.little long.COMP over.DYN
        a little further over,
07      (0.6)
08 ELI: ble'et lidt (i skærmen)(    )
        remained a bit (in the monitor) (    )
09      (1.9)
10 ELI: %(d'n ka/bare) næsten ikk nå mere_
           (it can/just) almost not reach anymore_
    din  %puts coffee cup on table-->
11       &(0.7)%                           &
    din  &looks twd cable, fastened on wall behind her&
    din     -->%
12       %(0.6)                    %
    din  %lets go of cup, turns twd cable%
13       %(1.4)    %
    din  %moves rh to microphone that hangs on cable
         on the wall%
14 ELI: %bare (lige lidt) måske lidt den anden retning så,
           just (LIGE a little) perhaps a little the other direction then
    din  %holds rh on mic-->
15 ELI: (det:/ja) okay.
        (it's/yes) okay.
16       (0.2)
17 ELI: hvis det var,%
        if it were,
    din           -->%
18       %(0.5)                           %
    din  %takes microphone off cable, moves off camera%
19       %(6.5)                      %
    din  %shades on the wall of DIN handling mic%
20       %(0.6)
    din  %rh handles microphone cable-->>
```

Chapter 4. Grammatical formats of requests   105

On camera, we can see the wall behind the scene, on which a cable with the microphone is hanging, apparently attached with a clip or a clamp. In line 2, Elise summons Dina, Dina accepts the summons (line 4), and Elise then asks Dina to move the microphone (lines 5–6). She adds an account in lines 8–10, and as she is finishing this, Dina puts down her cup, moves towards the microphone and starts to move it, while Elise comments on how the microphone should be placed (lines 12–18). After this exchange, Dina sits down by the table and takes part in an interaction between Carina and Birte (not shown).

Elise finds a moment when Dina is unoccupied to make her requests. However, Dina is holding a cup of coffee, and she is getting ready to sit down and drink it. Dina will have to stop this in order to carry out the requested action. The global project is the recording, and the request initiates a local project in the service of that global project, but in contrast to what was the case with the self-referencing request formats, the targeted action is not something that both parties see as an obvious next move. It is the requester who has discovered a potential obstacle to the global project, so she has the necessary knowledge. However, it is the recipient who is able to execute the targeted action, as she is closer to the cable (and perhaps also because Elise is operating the camera).

Excerpt (10) is a quite similar instance, this time with the format *ve' du* 'will you'. It comes from a recording of a family dinner. Around a table are three children, Anne, Charly and Eline, as well as the mother, Ditte, and the father, Bjarke. When the excerpt begins, Eline is telling about somebody at her school. Our focus is on Eline, Ditte, and Anne.

Excerpt 10. *ta et stykke papir* 'take a piece of paper' (AULing: aftensmad_og_ loegn)

```
01 ELI: han ve' ikk §jeg hedder E€line?
        he doesn't know my name is Eline?
    eli              §wipes rh against her shirt-->
    dit                        €looks twd ELI-->
02 DIT: det ved han ikk_€§
        he doesn't know that_
    dit              -->€
    eli              -->§
03      §(1.0)      §
    eli §shakes head§
04 ELI: (men) [(            )]
        (but)  ( )
05 BJA:      [&du har fået ketchup på][næsen_&
             you have gotten ketchup on your nose_
06 CHA:                        [(sej_)
    bja       &looks intensely twd CHA--------&
07      $(.)
    ann $looks twd CHA-->
```

```
08 BJA: eller o̱ss har du €blo̱dtud °(der)°.
         or else you have a bloody nose °(there)°.
     dit                      €looks twd ANN-->

09       (0.5)

10 DIT: %Anne  ve'    du   ikk €lige        €ta
        NAME   will.PRS you.SG not PTC        take.INF
        Anne won't you LIGE take
     dit %points twd ANN and/or tissue-holder-->
     dit                     -->€looks twd ELI€looks twd ANN-->

11 DIT: et $stykke   pa%pir   te' Eline_
        a.N piece(N) paper(N) to  NAME
        a piece of paper ((tissue)) for Eline_
     dit              -->%lowers hand-->
     ann   -->$looks down-->

12 DIT: hun si̱dder lige: å €%tørrer      €$fingre    af_
        she sit.PRS PTC  and  wipe.PRS    finger.PL off
        she is sitting and wiping her fingers_
     dit              -->€looks twd ELI€looks ahead-->
     dit              -->%small point twd ELI-->
     ann                      -->$looks at her
                                 rh-->

13       (1.0)€&$(1.0)      €
     dit    -->€looks twd ANN€
     bja        &looks twd ANN-->
     ann      -->$ takes tissue, dries own hands-->

14 ANN: €·hnfhh% ((snorts))
     dit €looks down and in front of her-->>
     dit    -->%uses hand to pour drink in her glass-->>

15       (1.0)&$(4.0)        $
     bja    -->&
     ann    -->$puts own tissue down, tears off two
               tissue pieces from tissue holder, hands one
               piece to ELI$
```

In line 1, while telling her story, Eline smears some food onto her shirt, which Ditte, the mother, sees. The interaction goes on, in two dyads, one between Ditte and Eline, and one between Bjarne and Charly (lines 1–8). On line 8, Ditte starts to look at the older sister, Anne, and on lines 10–11, Ditte asks Anne to get Eline a piece of paper towel. She adds an account (line 12), after which Anne takes a tissue, wipes her hands, and then takes another tissue and hands it to Eline, as requested.

The local sequence is similar to what we saw in Excerpt (9). The requester summons the recipient, and then asks her to carry out an action that will force her to momentarily stop what she is doing; in Excerpt (9), it was Dina's coffee drinking, and here it is Eline's eating. This may be one reason that the formats include the particles *ikk* 'not' and *lige*. The negation, *ikk* 'not', may frame the targeted action as routine or 'no problem' (Heinemann 2006), and *lige* may serve to frame the targeted action as a sub-project in a larger project (Heinemann & Steensig 2017), and/or as something trivial, harmless, and insignificant (Levisen & Waters 2015). In other requests with *ka du* 'can you' or *ve' du* 'will you', the targeted actions are presented as actions the recipients can do as part of what they are already doing. But in all cases with these formats, only the requester sees and has access to the problem that the targeted action is supposed to resolve.

The literal meaning of the two modal verbs used in this format is not the same: *ve'* focuses on willingness, *ka* on ability. This difference has consequences in Heinemann's (2006) analysis, and it may also be oriented to in other contexts, for example, in responses to requests for remote (not immediate) actions (Steensig & Heinemann 2014).[9] It is less clear whether this semantic difference in the literal meaning of the modal verbs matters in my corpus, so I will treat them as part of the same social action format.

3.3.3 *Modal verb request formats in the Comprehensive Grammar*

If we approach the grammar of the self-oriented and the other-oriented modal verb request formats from the point of view of their positions in the inter-unit syntax, we can see that they occur in quite different sequential — and inter-unit syntactical — contexts. Figures 8 and 9 are models of the inter-unit syntax of these two types of request.

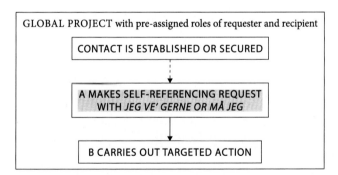

Figure 8. Inter-unit syntax of modal verb requests with *jeg ve' gerne* 'I would like' and *må jeg* 'may I'.

---

9. In other contexts, the verb *ville* 'to want, to be willing to', of which *ve'/vil* 'will' is the present tense form, may indicate future action. This is not the case when *ve'* is used in requests. We have not detected any instances of requests with *ve'* being about the future, either in requests for immediate action, or in requests for remote action. In the cases of responses to remote actions, we found the format *det vil jeg godt* 'I will certainly do that', which may focus on willingness, but not on the fact that it will happen in the future (Steensig & Heinemann 2014).

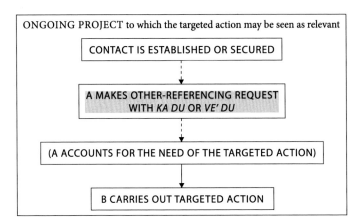

Figure 9. Inter-unit syntax of modal verb requests with *ka du* 'can you' and *ve' du* 'will you'.

As may be seen in Figures 8 and 9, the main difference between the two formats is the environment in which the two types of modal verb requests occur. Self-referencing formats are used when the parties are already taking part in a global project that demands that their roles as requester and recipient are given in that context. In the case of other-referencing requests, it is only in retrospect, with the formulation of the request, that the targeted action may be seen as relevant to an ongoing project. This may also be one reason why these requests are often followed by the requester accounting for why they make a request. This is consistent with what is described by Larsen (2013), who found that self-referencing formats were by far the most frequent in her corpus of requests for an ambulance in Danish emergency calls. In these circumstances, the global project and the roles of requester and recipient are given at the outset. In Heinemann's (2006) study of home help recipients' requests to carers, almost all requests are other-referencing, which reflects the fact that the actions targeted by the requests are parts of what home help carers are expected to do, but they are not obvious next moves in the ongoing projects.

If we compare the self-referencing modal verb formats with the item-only formats from Section 2.2.1 above, we can see that they occur in similar situations, when it comes to the global project and the pre-assigned roles. The difference lies in whether or not the prior exchange makes this request relevant at that point in time (calling for a phrasal item-only format) or whether this is not the case, which is when the self-referencing modal verb formats are used. The latter indicate that this is a new round, a new (sub)exchange, or a return to the global project. This may at least partly explain the different conditions for the use of a phrasal versus a clausal format.

The requests in this section are clauses with a number of common patterns in their inner structures. They all have at their core a description of the targeted action, which consists of a main verb and potential complements, as shown in Table 6.

Table 6. The order of elements in the description of the targeted action in modal verb requests

Excerpt	Main verb	Projected item(s)	Other items
Table 5	*vippe*	*dit øre lidt ned_*	
	tilt	down your ear a little_	
9	*klips'*	*mikrofonen lidt længere hen,*	
	attach	the microphone a little further over	
7, 8	*se*	*din hånd.*	
	see	your hand	
10	*ta*	*et stykke papir*	*te' Eline_*
	take	a piece of paper ((tissue))	for Eline_

The description of the targeted action may also consist of a main verb only, as in *må jeg se* 'may I see' (from game data), in which case it is obvious from the context what the requester is asking to see. Whether a complement is called for and what kind of complement it will be, is projectable from the type of verb and the stress pattern. If the main verb is unstressed, it often projects an object plus an adverbial, as in Table 5, *dit øre* 'your ear' [object] plus *lidt ned_* 'literally, a little down' [adverbial] or in Excerpt (9), *mikrofonen* 'the microphone' [object] *lidt længere hen* 'a little further over' [adverbial], or just an adverbial (with stress). If the main verb is stressed, the projected item is typically a noun phrase that acts as a syntactic object, or nothing, if the main verb is intransitive or the object is already established in the prior interaction.

There are two different orders of the subject and verb in the modal verb formats, reflecting the difference between declarative and interrogative formats. This is shown in Tables 7 and 8.

Table 7. The order of elements in declarative modal verb formats

Excerpt	Subject	Modal verb	Particles	Targeted action
7	*jeg*	*ve'*	*gerne*	*se din hånd_*
	I	will	PTC	see your hand_

Table 8. The order of elements in interrogative modal verb formats

Excerpt	Modal verb	Subject	Particles	Targeted action
Table 5	*ka*	*du*		*vippe dit øre lidt ned_*
	can	you		tilt down your ear a little down_
8	*må*	*jeg*		*se din hånd.*
	may	I		see your hand.
9	*ka*	*du*	*ikk lige*	*klips' mikrofonen lidt længere hen,*
	can	you	not PTC	attach the microphone a little further over,
10	*ve'*	*du*	*ikk lige*	*ta et stykke papir te' Eline_*
	will	you	not PTC	take a piece of paper for Eline_

When the subject comes first (Table 7), the format is declarative, while the ones with the modal verb first (Table 8) are interrogative. The tables further show that the subjects and modal verbs are never stressed in these formats. The first stress comes on either the particles or the relevant parts of the description of the targeted action. This stress pattern is an integral part of the modal verb request formats.

There are basic grammatical differences between self- and other-referencing requests. The self-referencing requests use main verbs that describe the targeted action, as seen from the requester's point of view, whereas the other-referencing requests have main verbs that describe what the recipient should do. So, for instance, if the targeted action is to show something to the requester, the main verb is *se* 'see' in recipient-referencing requests and *vise mig* 'show me' in other-referencing ones. This correspondence is projectable from the occurrence of the syntactic subject, and it should be explained in the grammar.

The interrogative format shown in Table 8 is a yes/no interrogative (see, e.g., Raymond 2003; Steensig & Heinemann 2013). However, when it used to request immediate actions, no "yes" (or "no") response is required. Most often, the targeted action is just carried out by the recipient, possibly with an accompanying comment, and only occasionally with a "yes". So, the term "yes/no interrogative" may be an insufficient label for these formats. Above, we also saw that the difference between interrogative and declarative formats did not seem to matter when they were used for self-referencing requests. However, the term "interrogative" does reflect a structural difference on a more abstract level. The ordering of subject and verb creates a difference (between "interrogative" and "declarative" structures), which does matter for other social action formats and possibly also for an action's degree of response mobilization (Stivers & Rossano 2010). The fact that the distinction between interrogative and declarative may matter for some social action formats, but not for all, raises important questions about their degree of abstractness or granularity (see also Fox & Raymond this volume; Steensig et al. 2023).

A description of modal verb formats used as requests should occur in the syntax of the grammar, perhaps under a special heading for clauses with modal verbs. It should include the inter-unit syntax, of which the modal verb requests are "constituents," and a description of the internal structure of the formats. It would be important to describe the difference between self- and other-referencing formats, the (non)role of declarative versus interrogative syntax, and the stress patterns that seem inherent to all modal verb formats. Furthermore, the collocations between self- and other-referencing formats and certain main verbs should be outlined. Links should be made between this syntactic description and more thorough descriptions of stress patterns, verbal morphology, interrogative and declarative clauses, and modal verbs in other places in the grammar.

4.   Discussion and conclusion

The main implications of the foregoing analyses and discussion are the following ones.

1.   The grammar must include a section on *Embodied actions*, which deals systematically with the formal aspects of the embodied actions that are either actions in themselves (as was the case here) or contribute decisively to actions carried out with verbal means. It remains an open question whether the social action format of the embodied-only requests is language-specific, or whether it belongs in a more general, and possibly cross-linguistic, action description. However, we cannot examine putative "universals" without having descriptions of the formats in the language-specific grammars.

2.   Phrases that present independent actions are not elliptical. They deserve treatment as units in their own right. This does not mean that such phrasal requests do not rely on the prior context, but it is important to note that they fill a slot as constituents of the inter-unit syntax (see Figures 6 and 7).

3.   The grammar must contain both an intra-unit syntax and an inter-unit one. Ideally, the description of formats must contain an account of both syntagmatic and paradigmatic distribution. The former refers to the position of an item in real-time production, whereas the latter refers to what could come instead of the produced item.

4.   Traditional syntactic clause aspects, such as the difference between interrogative and declarative clauses, or the general topology (i.e., ordering of elements) of clauses may matter to some formats, but not necessarily to all.

5. Meaning potential matters and must have a place in the grammar.
   a. The internal structure of phrases, that is, those that occur as social action formats on their own, may need to be described with functional labels that pertain to what the phrases do (as in Table 3 above).
   b. The meaning potential of modal verbs is specific to request formats. This must be part of the description of these verbs.
   c. The choice of action verbs used to describe the targeted actions in the request formats is dependent on the self- versus other-referencing character of the modal formats. This should have a place in the description of verbs in the grammar.

The attempt to go from descriptions of social action formats to grammatical descriptions and categories, which has been done in this chapter, has been instructive. It has indicated the need for new categories and types of descriptions that are not like the ones used in more traditional grammars. Moreover, having to put interactional findings into grammatical categories helped me see things that had otherwise escaped my analytical eye. There were things I discovered mainly because I was forced to look at the structural aspects of the formats: the difference between a summoning and a requesting action in embodied-only requests, the difference between item-only and action-guiding phrases, and the fact that the interrogative *må jeg* 'may I' and declarative *jeg ve' gerne/godt* 'I would like to' formats are used in the same sequential environments. I considered prosodic aspects to only a limited degree, and when I did, I looked only at the distribution of stress. I do believe that prosody is an essential aspect of grammar — words are never said without prosody — but I was unable to generalize about the use of prosody, beyond my comments about stress distribution.

The focus on one specific action type, requests for immediate actions, indicates the need to reconsider various parts of the grammar. I see this as an important contribution to grammar writing, but it must be supplemented by a systematic consideration of the formal categories, or the building blocks, of the grammar.

Acknowledgements

This study was developed within the research project *Grammar in Everyday Life* (GEL), supported by the *Independent Research Fund Denmark (grant number 9037–00072B)*. The initial collaboration with the editors and the authors of this book was also supported by this grant, for which I am very grateful. Virginia Calabria acted as a very insightful reviewer of an earlier draft, and Michaela Scioscia did a thorough language check on the last version of the chapter. The insights reflected herein were developed in close collaboration with the editors of the book, and with the GEL and DanTIN research groups. Any errors or shortcomings in this final version are solely my responsibility.

References

Anward, Jan, and Bengt Nordberg. 2005. "Indledning [Introduction]." In *Samtal och grammatik: Studier i svenskt samtalsspråk* [Conversation and grammar: Studies in Swedish conversational language], 5–9. Lund: Studentlitteratur.

Auer, Peter. 2005. "Projection in Interaction and Projection in Grammar." *Text — Interdisciplinary Journal for the Study of Discourse* 25 (1): 7–36.

Biber, Douglas, Stig Johansson, Geoffrey Leech, Susan Conrad, and Edward Finegan. 1999. *Longman Grammar of Spoken and Written English*. Harlow: Longman.

Borchmann, Simon. 2024. "A Little Less Conversation — On the Completeness of Discourse-Initial Action-Guiding Subsententials." *Language Sciences* 103 (May):101628.

Christensen, Lisa Holm, and Robert Zola Christensen. 2014. *Dansk grammatik* [Danish grammar]. Odense: Syddansk Universitetsforlag.

Couper-Kuhlen, Elizabeth. 2018. "Finding a Place for Body Movement in Grammar." *Research on Language and Social Interaction* 51 (1): 22–25.

Curl, Traci S., and Paul Drew. 2008. "Contingency and Action: A Comparison of Two Forms of Requesting." *Research on Language and Social Interaction* 41 (2): 129–53.

DanTIN. 2023. "Data." https://samtalegrammatik.dk/en/about-samtalegrammatikdk/our-method/data.

DanTIN. 2024. "Samtalegrammatik.dk." 2024. https://samtalegrammatik.dk/.

Diderichsen, Paul. 1962. *Elementær Dansk Grammatik* [Elementary Danish Grammar]. Copenhagen: Gyldendal.

Drew, Paul, and Elizabeth Couper-Kuhlen. 2014a. "Requesting: From Speech Act to Recruitment." In *Requesting in Social Interaction*, ed. by Paul Drew and Elizabeth Couper-Kuhlen, 1–34. Studies in Language and Social Interaction. Amsterdam: John Benjamins.

Drew, Paul, and Elizabeth Couper-Kuhlen, eds. 2014b. *Requesting in Social Interaction*. Amsterdam: John Benjamins.

Fox, Barbara A. 2007. "Principles Shaping Grammatical Practices: An Exploration." *Discourse Studies* 9 (3): 299–318.

"General Data Protection Regulation (GDPR) — Official Legal Text." n.d. General Data Protection Regulation (GDPR). Accessed March 14, 2023. https://gdpr-info.eu/.

Gubina, Alexandra. 2021. "Availability, Grammar, and Action Formation: On Simple and Modal Interrogative Request Formats in Spoken German." *Gesprächsforschung – Online-Zeitschrift Zur Verbalen Interaktion* 2021 (22): 272–303.

Hakulinen, Auli, Maria Vilkuna, Riitta Korhonen, Vesa Koivisto, Tarja Riitta Heinonen, and Irja Alho 2004. *Iso suomen kielioppi* [Comprehensive grammar of Finnish]. Suomalaisen Kirjallisuuden Seuran toimituksia 950. Helsinki: Finnish Literature Society.

Hansen, Erik, and Lars Heltoft. 2011. *Grammatik over Det Danske Sprog* [Grammar of the Danish Language]. København: Det Danske Sprog- og Litteraturselskab.

Heinemann, Trine. 2006. "'Will You or Can't You?': Displaying Entitlement in Interrogative Requests." *Journal of Pragmatics* 38 (7): 1081–1104.

Heinemann, Trine, and Jakob Steensig. 2017. "Three Imperative Action Formats in Danish Talk-in-Interaction." In *Imperative Turns at Talk: The Design of Directives in Action*, ed. by Liisa Raevaara, Marja-Leena Sorjonen, and Elizabeth Couper-Kuhlen, 139–73. Amsterdam: John Benjamins.

Heinemann, Trine, and Jakob Steensig. in prep. "Seeing It Our Way versus Seeing It My Way. Two Formats for Directing Attention to an Object in Danish Talk-in-Interaction."

Heritage, John. 2012. "Epistemics in Action: Action Formation and Territories of Knowledge." *Research on Language and Social Interaction* 45 (1): 1–29.

Heritage, John, and Geoffrey Raymond. 2005. "The Terms of Agreement: Indexing Epistemic Authority and Subordination in Assessment Sequences." *Social Psychology Quarterly* 68 (1): 15–38.

Huhtamäki, Martina, Inga-Lill Grahn, Jan Lindström, Jenny Nilsson, Catrin Norrby, and Camilla Wide. 2019. "Frasformade instruktioner med uppföljningar under personlig träning [Phrasal instructions with follow up actions in personal training]." *Språk och stil* 29: 9–40.

Keevallik, Leelo. 2018. "What Does Embodied Interaction Tell Us About Grammar?" *Research on Language and Social Interaction* 51 (1): 1–21.

Kendrick, Kobin H., and Paul Drew. 2016. "Recruitment: Offers, Requests, and the Organization of Assistance in Interaction." *Research on Language and Social Interaction* 49 (1): 1–19.

Kuroshima, Satomi. 2010. "Another Look at the Service Encounter: Progressivity, Intersubjectivity, and Trust in a Japanese Sushi Restaurant." *Journal of Pragmatics* 42 (3): 856–69.

Larsen, Tine. 2013. "Dispatching Emergency Assistance: Callers' Claims of Entitlement and Call Takers' Decisions." *Research on Language and Social Interaction* 46 (3): 205–30.

Levinson, Stephen C. 2013. "Action Formation and Ascription." In *The Handbook of Conversation Analysis*, ed. by Jack Sidnell and Tanya Stivers, 103–30. Oxford, U.K.: Wiley-Blackwell.

Levisen, Carsten, and Sophia Waters. 2015. "Lige, a Danish 'Magic Word'? An Ethnopragmatic Analysis." *International Journal of Language and Culture* 2 (2): 244–68.

Lindström, Anna. 2005. "Language as Social Action: A Study of How Senior Citizens Request Assistance with Practical Tasks in the Swedish Home Help Service." In *Syntax and Lexis in Conversation: Studies on the Use of Linguistic Resources in Talk-in-Interaction*, ed. by Auli Hakulinen and Margret Selting, 209–30. Amsterdam: John Benjamins.

Nevile, Maurice. 2015. "The Embodied Turn in Research on Language and Social Interaction." *Research on Language and Social Interaction* 48 (2).

Raymond, Geoffrey. 2003. "Grammar and Social Organization: Yes/No Interrogatives and the Structure of Responding." *American Sociological Review* 68 (6): 939–67.

Rijkhoff, Jan. 2002. *The Noun Phrase*. Oxford: Oxford University Press.

Rossi, Giovanni. 2012. "Bilateral and Unilateral Requests: The Use of Imperatives and Mi X? Interrogatives in Italian." *Discourse Processes* 49 (5): 426–58.

Sacks, Harvey. 1992. *Lectures on Conversation*. Edited by Gail Jefferson. Vol. 1. Oxford: Basil Blackwell.

Schegloff, Emanuel A. 1968. "Sequencing in Conversational Openings." *American Anthropologist* 70 (6): 1075–95.

Schegloff, Emanuel A. 1996a. "Confirming Allusions: Toward an Empirical Account of Action." *American Journal of Sociology* 102 (1): 161–216.

Schegloff, Emanuel A. 1996b. "Turn Organization: One Intersection of Grammar and Interaction." In *Interaction and Grammar*, ed. by Emanuel A. Schegloff, Elinor Ochs, and Sandra Thompson, 52–133. Cambridge: Cambridge University Press.

Sidnell, Jack. 2012. "Basic Conversation Analytic Methods." In *The Handbook of Conversation Analysis*, ed. by Jack Sidnell and Tanya Stivers, 77–99. Oxford, U.K.: Wiley-Blackwell.

Sorjonen, Marja-Leena, and Liisa Raevaara. 2014. "On the Grammatical Form of Requests at the Convenience Store: Requesting as Embodied Action." In *Requesting in Social Interaction*, ed. by Paul Drew and Elizabeth Couper-Kuhlen, 243–68. Studies in Language. Amsterdam: John Benjamins.

Steensig, Jakob. in prep. "Embodied Actions in a Comprehensive Grammar of Talk-in-Interaction."

Steensig, Jakob. n.d. "How Do You Say 'Please' in Danish? Clausal Formats for Making Requests for Immediate Actions."

Steensig, Jakob. in preparation. "The Problematic Convergence of Formats for Doing Offers, Proposals and Suggestions."

Steensig, Jakob, and Trine Heinemann. 2013. "'When 'Yes' Is Not Enough — as an Answer to a Yes/No Question." In *Units of Talk — Units of Action*, ed. by Beatrice Szczepek Reed and Geoffrey Raymond, 207–42. Amsterdam: John Benjamins.

Steensig, Jakob, and Trine Heinemann. 2014. "The Social and Moral Work of Modal Constructions in Granting Remote Requests." In *Requesting in Social Interaction*, ed. by Paul Drew and Elizabeth Couper-Kuhlen, 145–70. Studies in Language and Social Interaction 26. Amsterdam: John Benjamins.

Steensig, Jakob, Maria Jørgensen, Nicholas Mikkelsen, Karita Suomalainen, and Søren Sandager Sørensen. 2023. "Towards a Grammar of Danish Talk-in-Interaction: From Action ForMation to Grammatical Description." *Research on Language and Social Interaction* 56 (2): 116–140.

Stivers, Tanya, and Federico Rossano. 2010. "Mobilizing Response." *Research on Language and Social Interaction* 43 (1): 3–31.

Thompson, Sandra A., Barbara A. Fox, and Elizabeth Couper-Kuhlen. 2015. *Grammar in Everyday Talk: Building Responsive Actions*. Cambridge: Cambridge University Press.

Wagner, Johannes, Lone Laursen, Patrizia Paggio, Frans Gregersen, and Peter Henrichsen. 2024. "Samtalebank." https://samtale.talkbank.org.

Widahl, Alexandra Caroline Bødker. 2023. "A Conversation Analytic Investigation of the Use of the Danish Modal Particles Godt and Gerne in Natural-Occurring Danish Conversations." Aarhus: Unpublished MA thesis, Department of Linguistics, Cognitive Science and Semiotics.

Zimmerman, Don H. 1998. "Identity, Context and Interaction." In *Identities in Talk*, ed. by Charles Antaki and Sue Widdicombe, 87–106. London: SAGE.

CHAPTER 5

Structurally 'incomplete' social action formats in the grammar of talk-in-interaction?

The case of deontic infinitives in spoken German

Alexandra Gubina
Leibniz Institute for the German Language (IDS)

The chapter focuses on deontic infinitives, i.e., free infinitives not governed by a matrix clause or an auxiliary; such clauses have not been treated in German reference grammars because they are considered syntactically incomplete. This chapter shows that in contrast to similar practices for requests, directives, and instructions (Gubina & Deppermann frthc.), deontic infinitives implement instructions of a normatively proper procedure or rule, which, in most cases, applies both now *and* each time this procedure is accomplished. The chapter discusses which features (e.g., sequence and activity context, distribution of agency, epistemic and deontic positionings, etc.) should be included in reference grammars of talk-in-interaction and in current curricula of German as Foreign/Second Language. The chapter concludes by discussing possible challenges for creating a comprehensive grammar of spoken language.

Keywords: social action format, deontic infinitive, rule, instruction, request, agency, epistemics, embodiment, German as Foreign/Second Language, Interactional Linguistics

1. Introduction

When creating a comprehensive grammar of talk-in-interaction in a particular language, i.e., "a publication containing the necessary information about the patterns people use systematically to make sense in talk-in-interaction" (Steensig et al. 2023: 116), the most important question — and indeed the most difficult one — is what grammar actually *is* in the context of talk-in-interaction. Normative linguistic approaches, such as formal, structural, or functional grammar, treat

https://doi.org/10.1075/slsi.37.05gub
© 2025 John Benjamins Publishing Company

Chapter 5. Deontic infinitives in spoken German   117

grammar as an abstract and static system of rules. In contrast, more interactional approaches, like Conversation Analysis (hereafter: CA) and Interactional Linguistics (hereafter: IL), view grammar "as an adaptive and emergent set of resources by which participants accomplish actions in mutually recognizable ways" (Pekarek Doehler 2018: 3; see also Hopper 2011; Selting & Couper-Kuhlen 2001: 260f.; Schegloff 1996). This situated and context-sensitive understanding of grammar-*for*-interaction (Pekarek Doehler 2018) typically encompasses "regular patterns at the level of sounds, words, and larger units such as phrases, clauses, and sentences" (Thompson & Couper-Kuhlen 2005: 482). Recent research has shown that yet other resources such as prosody (Couper-Kuhlen & Selting 1996; Imo & Lanwer 2020) or bodily movements (Keevallik 2018; but see Couper-Kuhlen 2018) could be seen as part of a grammatical description as well.

Despite these recent findings, grammars of spoken language (which are not numerous) often do not address many recurrent interactional practices because they are treated as ungrammatical or marginal (Fries 1987; see Zifonun, Hoffmann, & Strecker 1997). The current chapter focuses on one such construction in German, namely *deontic infinitives* (Deppermann 2006: chap. 2; Deppermann 2007), which up to now have not been included in standard grammars of written or spoken German. Deontic infinitives are free infinitives (Fries 1983, 1987), i.e., they are not governed by a matrix clause or an auxiliary. Consider the following excerpt from an interaction between two sisters — Pauline (PAU) and Tamara (TAM) — who are renovating Pauline's room (see Excerpt (12) for the full transcript and analysis of this case):

Excerpt 1. *stehen bleiben* 'to stand still' (FOLK_E_00217_SE_01_T_02), face-to-face, informal interaction, room renovation[1]

```
13 PAU: *stell HIN,*
         put down
    pau *points at the place where TAM is standing*
14      *(.) LUMpen;
         rag
    pau *points at place on the floor without the film-->
15      +(.) du bist da (.) hier is des WEGgerutscht;
         you are there- here it is where it slipped away
    tam +continues carrying the ladder-->
16      (.) un du hast es nich ich*
         and you did not it I
    pau                    -->*
```

---

1. In this chapter, all deontic infinitives will be translated into English as *to*-infinitives because English infinitives without *to* have the same form as imperatives and might thus be ambiguous.

```
17       *<<ff>ble+ib STEHN>?
                 stand still
   pau  *points at the place where TAM is standing-->
   tam       -->+

18     (0.6)*

   pau  -->*

19 PAU: <<ff>*NICH DURCHlaufen*>. (.)
                 NEG   walk_through.INF
                 not to walk through
   pau       *points at place on the floor without film*

20 PAU: <<f>*STEhenbleiben*>;=
                 stand_still.INF
                 to stand still
   pau       *points at the place where TAM is standing*

21 PAU: =<<f>*L[EIter   +hin]stellen>.=
                 ladder     put_down.INF
                 to put down the ladder
   pau       *points at the place where TAM is standing-->
   tam                   +puts down the ladder-->

22 PAU: =<<f>jet[z ]>.
                 now
```

In lines 19–21, Pauline produces three deontic infinitives that are characterized by the following grammatical features: In contrast to other infinitive constructions in German, deontic infinitives are used without the particle *zu* 'to'. Furthermore, they usually lack subjects, while other arguments precede the infinitive (Deppermann 2006, 2007). Finally, they are sometimes treated as elliptical constructions of utterances with modal verbs, like '[you can/should/must/have to] not eat too much', or '[can/may/should I] try?', although it is not always possible (and also not necessary) to reconstruct a precise full-fledged utterance this way (Weinrich 1993:280–281; cf. Fries 1983; Zinken 2020:294–295 for Polish). The crucial feature of deontic infinitives in German is that only constructions that are not syntactically parasitic on prior talk are treated as deontic infinitives.[2]

The idea for this study originated from another study on different practices for accomplishing requests, directives, and instructions in spoken German (Gubina & Deppermann frthc.; see also Gubina 2021). The data showed that although deontic infinitives are systematically used for getting the Other to do some practical action, they are doing something different than imperatives or interrogatives — the two practices that have mostly been associated with prototyp-

---

2. Although the deontic infinitives in Excerpt (1) can be seen as relying on an available requesting pattern activated through the imperative form at line 17, it is not a recurrent feature in the use of deontic infinitives in German. Furthermore, similar cases that occur after or in response to modal verb constructions are not treated as deontic infinitives (cf. line 4 in Excerpt (9)).

Chapter 5. Deontic infinitives in spoken German **119**

ical requests (see Steensig, this volume). In this chapter, I will demonstrate that and how in using deontic infinitives, speakers invoke a generally valid normative procedure or rule for how something is to be done.

In what follows, I will first provide a brief theoretical overview of deontic infinitives and similar social action formats that, from a normative perspective, can be considered grammatically or structurally 'incomplete' (Section 2). After presenting the data and methods and delimiting the phenomenon (Sections 3 and 4 respectively), the study will provide a detailed sequential analysis of the use of deontic infinitives in German talk-in-interaction (Section 5). In particular, it will show that deontic infinitives implement instructions for a normatively proper procedure or rule that typically applies each time this procedure is accomplished. In addition, it will describe how deontic infinitives afford this use and how they fit the interactional environments in which they typically occur. Section 6 will summarize the results and discuss the practical implications of this study for creating a comprehensive grammar of talk-in-interaction. Specifically, it will discuss which interactional features (such as the distribution of agency, epistemic positioning of the participants, and their bodily involvement in the ongoing practical activity) should be included in the description of grammar. Moreover, Section 6 will show the practical benefits of the current study and of including the features mentioned above in the grammar of talk-in-interaction for current curricula of German as a Foreign Language. Finally, it will discuss possible challenges for creating a comprehensive grammar of spoken language.

2. Theoretical background: Deontic infinitives and other structurally 'incomplete' units in talk-in-interaction

In general, one can differentiate between at least two types of units in talk-in-interaction that could be seen as 'incomplete' from a normative perspective:[3]

i. interactionally 'incomplete' or unfinished units (e.g., Ford & Thompson 1996; Selting 2001), and
ii. structurally 'incomplete' grammatical units (e.g., Deppermann 2020).

In the first case, TCUs (turn-constructional units) are abandoned or cut-off before a (TRP) is recognizably reached. Examples in question are cut-offs in case of self-repair initiation (Fox, Hayashi & Jasperson 1996; Fox, Maschler & Uhmann 2010; Pfeiffer 2015), cut-offs resulting from overlap and interruption (Schegloff 1987) or,

---

3. It is important to note that these two types of units are not mutually exclusive and can overlap.

e.g., designedly incomplete turns used to assess (e.g., Aldrup et al. 2021) and, in pedagogic contexts, to invite students to complete the turn in a correct way (e.g., Fox 1993; Hazel & Mortensen 2019; Koshik 2002; Persson 2017).

In contrast, in the case of structural 'incompleteness', elements that are considered obligatory according to normative grammar are omitted. In line with this perspective, a grammatically complete and well-formed utterance should usually (but not always!) contain (i) a finite verb, (ii) a subject (with, e.g., imperatives being an exception) as well as (iii) other arguments that fill obligatory slots in the valence frame of the main verb (Ágel & Fischer 2015; Tesnière 1959). Contrary to this perspective, talk-in-interaction is often characterized by *lean syntax*, i.e., "argument realizations which are "reduced" from the point of view of the full realization of argument frames, which are said to be associated with verbs in the (mental) lexicon" (Deppermann 2020:256). Such 'lean' syntactic structures are not only treated by interactants as unproblematic but also accomplish systematic interactional tasks and regularly occur in specific interactional contexts. Phenomena in question are, e.g., different types of responsive actions, like phrases or partial repeats in response to questions (Fox & Thompson 2010; Jørgensen, this volume; Sorjonen 1996; Stivers 2005; Thompson, Fox & Couper-Kuhlen 2015) or 'telescoping' in response to requests (Fox & Heinemann 2019), different types of increments (Auer 2007; Couper-Kuhlen & Ono 2007; Ford, Fox & Thompson 2002), collaborative completions (Bolden, Hepburn & Potter 2019; Hayashi 1999; Lerner 1991, 2004), and non-overt reference expressions, or so-called 'zero' anaphora in languages like Chinese, Japanese, Korean, and Thai (e.g., Oh 2007; see also Couper-Kuhlen & Selting 2018: 411–412, chap. F, 15–16).

While most of these structures in one way or another build on the prior sequential context, structurally 'incomplete' grammatical structures (like *if*-clauses; see Couper-Kuhlen & Thompson, this volume; Pekarek Doehler & Horlacher, this volume) can also be found in first actions. For example, actions such as instructions or complaints are sometimes produced with grammatically incomplete structures that can be completed with nonverbal actions, bodily-visual displays, or vocalizations (e.g., Keevallik 2013, 2014, 2015; Skogmyr Marian 2021; Steensig, this volume). Raymond et al. (2021) explore the use of *do you want...?*, *you want...?* and *want...?* for accomplishing requests and offers in American English. They demonstrate that the complexity of syntactic design depends on the disposition for, or expectation of, a preferred response, i.e., more minimal forms — *you want...?* and *want...?* — treat the recipient as being more disposed towards producing a preferred response (i.e., compliance after requests and acceptance after offers; see also Fox & Raymond, this volume). Deppermann and Gubina (2021) analyze full and minimal structures in the formats *darf ich...?* 'may I...?' and *kann ich...?* 'can I...?'. They show that more minimal forms are usually used

(i) when the mutual visual salience of referents is secured and (ii) when actions addressed with the formats are indexed as highly expectable. Moreover, minimal forms can mobilize a bodily adjustment from a recipient whose physical presence might prevent the speaker from doing something they are entitled to do (e.g., asking someone to move out of your way when you want to leave the bus). Minimal forms have also been explored in the recent research on requests: In particular, different studies have demonstrated that minimal phrasal verbless request forms are mostly used when "the action requested is projectable to some degree, but some element of it isn't" (Rossi 2015: 54; see also Mondada 2011, 2014; Sorjonen & Raevaara 2014; Urbanik 2021).

Deontic infinitives constitute a grammatical format that, at least from a traditional grammar view, might be seen as structurally incomplete. However, they are of a different type of 'incompleteness' than the cases discussed so far, in which the 'lean', or 'incomplete' version is the appropriate grammatical form in the sense of *positionally-sensitive grammar* (Schegloff 1996), since what is 'omitted' is plainly available from the context. However, with deontic infinitives, the 'incompleteness' is not (only) a positional phenomenon. Prototypically, deontic infinitives are found in written manuals, traffic signs (like *Einfahrt freihalten!* 'Keep driveway clear'), or recipes, as in Excerpt (2) from a cooking interaction. Here, Saskia (SAS), Roman (ROM), and Lisa (LIS) are baking a cake from a cake mix. In lines 4 and 5, Roman reads the recipe aloud, in particular, the part about stirring the ingredients (see Figure 1):

Excerpt 2. *kurz verrühren* 'to stir briefly' (FOLK_E_00372_SE_01_T_01), face-to-face, informal interaction, backing a cake

```
01      (2.6)
02 SAS: so drei Eier,=ne?
        so three eggs right
03      (0.4)
04 ROM: *auf nä#chst niedr  niedrigster stufe kurz     verRÜHren;
        on  next    low-  lowest     level briefly stir.INF
        to stir briefly at the next lowest level
   rom  *starts reading aloud from the pack-->
   fig        #1
```

Figure 1. Roman reads the recipe aloud

```
05 ROM: (.) dann auf HÖ*CHster stufe;=
             then at the highest level
     rom            -->*
06        =also DOCH niedrigste.
             so PTC/(it IS) the lowest
07        (3.4)
```

The only interactional study on deontic infinitives in social interaction was conducted by Deppermann (2006, 2007). Using constructional grammar and interactional approaches, he demonstrated that deontic infinitives can be used for different kinds of *directive-commissive actions* (Couper-Kuhlen 2014), such as requests, instructions, recommendations, proposals, etc. Which action is being accomplished depends on the degree of obligation embodied through the deontic infinitive and the agent of the addressed action. Moreover, he shows that deontic infinitives — in contrast to modal verb constructions — allow for more freedom of interpretation by the recipient due to the absence of deontic modality encoding and can, thus, appear less face-threatening. However, his analysis does not include what Deppermann refers to as *empractical* deontic infinitives, i.e., infinitives that concern ongoing practical activity. Thus, he calls for further research on deontic infinitives in empractical settings and from a multimodal perspective, which is exactly what the current chapter will focus on.

In line with the study by Deppermann (2006, 2007), the current chapter will demonstrate that, although deontic infinitives have been treated as 'grammatically incomplete' in normative approaches, they are interactionally *complete* practices: Specifically, they constitute prosodically complete TCUs that accomplish a precise action in their own right and with their own sequential implications, which indicates their praxeological autonomy, and they are systematically treated as complete by the recipients.

3.   Data and methods

This study draws on approx. 80 hours of video-recorded data from mundane and institutional contexts selected from the Research and Teaching Corpus of Spoken German (FOLK-corpus, Version 2.20 with approx. 220 hours of video-recorded data and 347 hours of audio-recorded data; Schmidt 2016). The settings include participants involved in joint activities, like having breakfast/lunch/dinner together, cooking together, renovating a room, or a bath, driving somewhere, and playing board games, as well as different institutional settings, like driving lessons, emergency drills, physiotherapy, riding lessons, etc. Such an extensive corpus, encompassing a wide range of settings, participation frameworks, and speaker groups, offers the opportunity to illustrate certain general distribution patterns and to provide a robust analysis of how a certain practice is used across *various* interactional types. This is crucial for the development of a *comprehensive* reference grammar of talk-in-interaction. Nevertheless, it is important to note that different interactional settings are not equally represented in the sub-corpus used for the current study (e.g., the number of service encounters is still relatively small). Similarly, some speaker groups are more prevalent than others (e.g., younger participants predominate in the sub-corpus). Another challenge lies in the comparability of the settings and participation frameworks (e.g., family breakfast vs. driving lesson). Future research should explore whether these factors can truly influence the representativity of the corpus and the analytical results developed based on the data.

One part of the collection used for this chapter was taken from a study on different linguistic practices that German speakers employ to get recipients to accomplish a specific practical action in mundane talk-in-interaction, including cases of requests, directives, and instructions (Gubina & Deppermann frthc.).[4] In each video, all cases of possible requests, instructions, and directives were collected. In the data set created, only the first 10 contiguously occurring cases per interaction were included. This initial data set allowed us to identify the most frequent social action formats that are used for implementing the actions mentioned above. The third most frequent, systematically occurring practice in our data set were deontic infinitives. For this chapter, the collection of deontic infinitives was expanded with cases of deontic infinitives implementing other actions than the ones mentioned above and also with cases of deontic infinitives from institutional contexts.

All in all, the data yielded 169 cases of deontic infinitives from about 80 hours of video-recorded data, which implies that the phenomenon is not extremely frequent in German talk-in-interaction but is also not too rare. After extensive sequential and multimodal case analyses, the collection was coded according to different formal and analytical variables that were identified as relevant while analyzing the data, such as negation markers, full verb, direct object, indirect object, prepositional phrase, adverb, suspension marker, transition marker, type of requested action, etc.

---

4. In contrast to requests and directives, instructions not only aim at getting others to do something, but additionally have a function of knowledge transfer (see, e.g., Ehmer et al. 2021; Ehmer & Brône 2021; Lindwall, Lymer & Greiffenhagen 2015; see Craven & Potter 2010; Curl & Drew 2008; Drew & Couper-Kuhlen 2014; Ehmer et al. 2021; Rossi 2012, 2015; Zinken 2016: chap. 2 for further discussion of similarities and distinctions between these and related action categories).

The current study draws on the methodological frameworks of multimodal Conversation Analysis (Sidnell & Stivers 2012; Robinson et al. 2024) and Interactional Linguistics (Couper-Kuhlen & Selting 2018). All the excerpts were transcribed according to GAT2 transcription conventions (see Couper-Kuhlen & Barth-Weingarten 2011; Selting et al. 2009), with additional annotation of embodied conduct according to Mondada's transcription conventions (Mondada 2024). All names appearing in the transcripts have been anonymized. Written informed consent for scientific use of the data was obtained from all research participants.

4. Delimiting the phenomenon

While the original goal of this chapter was to show a spectrum of different social actions accomplished with deontic infinitives, the analysis of the collection yielded unexpected results: Only 6 cases out of 169 cases were *not* used for requesting a specific practical action or instructing the Other about what (not) to do. These 6 cases included 2 announcements, 2 offers, one proffer of advice, and one request for permission. An example of one of these cases is Excerpt (3) from a baking interaction.

Here, Charlene (CHA) is baking cupcakes, while her mother Rahel (RAH) is sitting behind her, watching her during the whole interaction. Before the extract begins, Charlene starts pouring the caramel sauce into the topping cream for the cupcakes. At the beginning of the extract, Rahel points out that it would have been better if Charlene had flipped the bottle with the sauce upside down before (line 1). In line 2, she checks whether the sauce is coming out well. Still, even while producing her turn, she displays her orientation to a positive answer by producing a turn-final candidate answer *jo* 'yes' (line 2):

Excerpt 3. *mal probieren* 'to try' (FOLK_E_00331_SE_01_T_03), face-to-face, informal interaction, baking

```
01 RAH: vielleicht hättst die ma aufn KOPF stellen müssen;=
        perhaps you should have flipped it upside down
    cha >>pours the caramel sauce into cupcakes cream-->
02      =oder geht alles RAUS?=↓jo.
        or is everything coming out yes
03      (0.4)
04 CHA: <<p>geht eigentlich GUT rAus>;
            (it) is going out well
05      (0.5)
06 RAH: ((sniffs)) !OH!;
                    oh
07      (0.5)
```

Chapter 5. Deontic infinitives in spoken German 125

```
08 RAH: ((schniffs))*mmm:::#;
                    mmm
    cha           -->*takes caramel sauce from the bottle
        with her finger-->
    fig                        #2
```

Figure 2. Charlene is about to try the caramel sauce

```
09 CHA: mal proBIeren?
        PTC  try.INF
        PTC  to try
10 RAH: ((sniffs)) *(.) oh;*
                        oh
    cha           -->*puts finger with sauce into her mouth*
11      (1.0)
12 CHA: ↑mhh::;=
        hm
13      =o[h       W]OW.
         oh         wow
14 RAH:   [<<l>oh>.];
            oh
15 RAH: oh des RIESCHT auch.=
        oh it smells also
16      =des riecht bis hierHER; (.)
        it smells until here
```

After Charlene confirms (line 4), Rahel produces an emotional change-of-state token *oh* (line 6; Golato 2012) and an enactment of gustatory pleasure (line 8; Wiggins 2002). Meanwhile, Charlene takes caramel out of the bottle with her finger. In line 9, Charlene initiates a deontic infinitive that concerns her own upcoming action, namely tasting the caramel sauce, which is already projectable from her prior embodied conduct (see Figure 2). In this case, Charlene's turn can thus be interpreted as an announcement, or a kind of *online commentary* (e.g., Heritage & Stivers 1999), whereby the speaker makes publicly available her upcoming action. Such cases differ from the majority of cases in my collection since the deontic infinitive in Excerpt (3) neither invites nor requests any practical action from the addressee. Since such cases constitute less than 5% of the whole collection and are in addition quite heterogeneous, they will not be part of the analysis presented in Section 5.

Furthermore, cases of fixed expressions that take the form of deontic infinitives were also excluded from the current analysis and were not part of the collection. One example of such expressions is the format *mal gucken/schauen* ('let's see/we will see'), which in a stand-alone position is used for 'non-committal' answers to questions, suggestions, proposals, etc., as shown in Excerpt (4). Here, Isabella (ISA) and Ferdinand (FER) are driving together in a car. In line 2, Isabella asks Ferdinand if he 'actually' (*eigentlich*) 'also' (*noch ma*) wants to organize a housewarming party with his friends. In response, Ferdinand produces a marked out-breath and *ma gucken* ('we will see', line 4):

Excerpt 4. *ma gucken* 'we will see' (FOLK_E_00301_SE_01_T_02), face-to-face, informal interaction, driving

```
01     (0.9)
02 ISA: wolltest du eigentlich noch ma ne EINweihungsfeier mit deinen jungs machen?
        did you actually also want PTC to organize a housewarming party with your
        guys?
03     (0.4)
04 FER: h° ma GUCken,
        PTC see.INF
        we'll see
05     (0.6)
06 FER: und jetz die nÄchsten wochenenden ham wir halt auch überhaupt keine ZEIT;
        and now in the next weekends we also have PTC absolutely no time
07     (1.1)
```

With the deontic infinitive in line 4, Ferdinand produces a non-answer (Stivers 2022: chap. 3): It displays a low degree of commitment towards the future course of action suggested by Isabella in line 2. The dispreferred nature of this answer is also reflected in the marked out-breath and the account in line 6, which formulates a circumstance that makes the suggested course of action (i.e., organizing a housewarming party) especially difficult, if not impossible. If we compare the deontic infinitive in Excerpt (4) and those in Excerpt (1), it becomes apparent that although both structures can be called deontic infinitives, *ma(l) gucken/schauen* is a social action format that is *not* used for requests, directives, or instructions.[5]

---

5. The reduction of the modal particle *mal* (=ma) in line 4 in Excerpt (4) can also be seen as a sign of formulaicity (see Günthner 2017; Proske 2017).

Chapter 5. Deontic infinitives in spoken German **127**

For this reason, such cases were excluded from the current chapter. The question, however, remains whether such uses should be included in the comprehensive analysis of deontic infinitives in general. The issues of granularity of the format description will be addressed in Section 6 (see also Fox & Raymond, this volume). After all the cases mentioned above were excluded, the final collection used for the current study comprised 163 cases of deontic infinitives.

5. Analysis

This section will show that deontic infinitives are used for 3 action types: instructing the proper procedure for next steps within an activity (Section 5.1), corrective instructions (Section 5.2), and changing tack after failed compliance with prior requests (Section 5.3). Section 5.4 will demonstrate how the linguistic form of deontic infinitives allows for indeterminacy concerning action formation and degree of obligation.

5.1 Instructions for next steps within an activity

The first regular use of deontic infinitives in my data is instructions concerning the next steps within an activity that the recipient is already involved in, as in Excerpt (5). Here, the patient (PAT) is lying on his stomach on the couch with his right leg bent to the side (see Figure 3). The therapist (THE) holds the patient's right leg and presses it from above:

Excerpt 5. *und locker lassen* 'and to relax' (FOLK_E_00360_SE_01_T_01), face-to-face, institutional/medical/pedagogical interaction, physiotherapy

```
01      (1.0)
   the-g >>holds and presses the patient's right leg-->
   pat   >>lies with his right leg bent-->
02 THE: jaWOLL;#
        exactly
   fig          #3
```

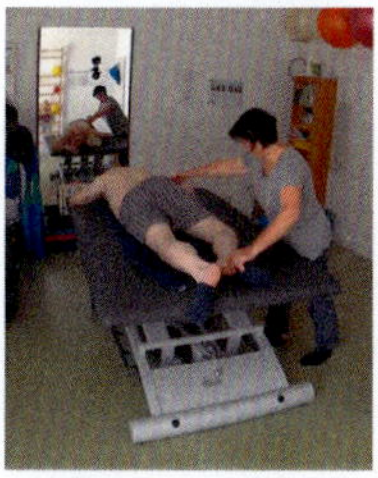

Figure 3. The therapist presses the patient's right leg, while he bends it

```
03       (0.8)
04 THE:  geNAU;=
         exactly
05       =dA    BLEIben;
         there stay.INF
         to stay there
06       (1.3)
07 THE:  und NOCH en bissel bleiben;=
         and more a bit      stay.INF
         to stay there a bit more
08       =SEHR gut-=
         very well
09       =SEHR gut-=
         very well
10       =sehr GUT-=
         very well
11       =sehr GUT-
         very well
12       (1.2)
13 THE:  ↑U::ND ↓LOCker lassen.*
         and      loose  let.INF
         and to relax
     the-g                    -->*
14       (3.0)§(1.0)
     the-b      §walks towards the patient's left leg-->>
15 THE:  rEchtes    bE%in en  bissel AUSstrecken,=%
         right.N.SG leg  a   bit    stretch_out.INF
         to stretch out the right leg a bit
     pat            -->%stretches out the right  leg%
16       =*und das      LINke  jetzt* mal %so maximal  ANbeugen?
         and  the.N.SG  left.SG now   PTC  so maximally bend.INF
         and now PTC to bend the left one to the maximum
     the-g ->*takes the right leg and moves it to the left*
     pat                                -->%bends the left leg-->>
17       (4.4)
```

In this example, we get a series of steps that the therapist tells the patient to do: to stay in the position in which he is lying right now (lines 5 and 7), to relax (line 13), to stretch out the right leg (line 15), and to bend the left leg to its maximum (line 16). All these steps concern the activity — the exercise — that the patient is already visibly involved in. These deontic infinitives differ in their syntactic complexity: The deontic infinitives in lines 5, 7, and 13 are produced with minimal syntax (either a deictic expression *da* 'there' in line 5 or no arguments at all in lines 7 and 13), since they belong to the part of the exercise that the patient is already doing. In contrast, further instructions (lines 15–16) are produced with a more elaborate

Chapter 5. Deontic infinitives in spoken German **129**

argument structure: Although the exercise remains the same, the patient should change legs, which has not become salient/accessible to the patient through the prior context yet. In lines 5, 7, and 13, it is difficult to see the patient's understanding of the prior turns because the deontic infinitives either request remaining in the same position (lines 5–7) or relaxing the muscles, which is sometimes also hard to observe.[6] In contrast, it is clear that the patient orients to the therapist's deontic infinitives in lines 15 and 16 as making an immediate compliance relevant because he starts complying immediately, even before the therapist has completed each instruction. What is important is that in this whole sequence, the therapist not only gets the patient to accomplish some bodily actions here-and-now, but also formulates a normative procedure for the exercise, i.e., how this exercise is to be accomplished (in the future), as can be seen from the wider context of this fragment. Finally, the very fact that deontic infinitives occur within a series of instructions is important because it contributes to the sense that these instruct a proper procedure.

The instructional and normative properties of deontic infinitives can be observed especially well in Excerpt (6). Amelie (AME) and Christoph (CHR) are cooking together. After Amelie has poured the water out of a pot of pasta, Christoph formulates the next step in the joint project with a deontic infinitive request *dann kurz ABtrocknen lassen?* ('then let (them) dry briefly', line 3):

Excerpt 6. *abtrocknen lassen* 'to let dry' (FOLK_E_00332_SE_01_T_01_727), face-to-face, informal interaction, cooking

```
01      (8.7)
02 AME: ((laughs))
03 CHR: (.) *dann kurz ABtrocknen lassen?
            then PTC   dry.INF      let.INF
            then to let (it) dry briefly
    ame >>pours the pasta into the colander*brings the pot back to the stove-->
04      (0.6)
05 AME: JAha,
        yes
06      (.) ich WEIß,
            I    know
07      (0.9)
08 AME: hab schon mal n*udeln geKOCHT. ((giggles, 1 sec))
        (I) have already cooked pasta before
    ame                 -->*walks back to sink and shakes the
        colander with pasta-->>
09      (2.1)
```

---

6. In addition, the degree of pressure in the therapist's touching practices, its continuous or discontinuous nature, duration, etc. might also be crucial for the analysis, although they may escape the analyst's visual access.

As in the previous case, the deontic infinitive is used for introducing a new step within the activity that Amelie is involved in, namely cooking and draining the pasta. The deontic infinitive in line 3 occurs without the object (*pasta*) as it is salient to both participants. Amelie's response, consisting of a response particle *jaha* 'yes' (line 5), *ich weiß* 'I know' (line 6, see Mikesell et al. 2017, Zeschel 2017), and a statement that she has cooked pasta before (line 8), displays her understanding of Christoph's turn in line 3 not just as a request, but also as an explanation of a normative procedure for draining pasta. With her response, she thus pushes back against Christoph positioning her as an unknowledgeable, or [K-], participant (Heritage 2012; see also Gubina & Deppermann frthc.). At the same time, her response confirms the validity of Christoph's instruction as a normative step to be taken when cooking pasta.

Excerpts (5) and (6) demonstrate that deontic infinitives can be used for producing instructions for the next steps within an activity that the recipients are already involved in and are also responsible for, which allows for the minimal syntactic structure. In Excerpt (6), the referent (i.e., the pasta) is already the focus of Amelie's current activity, which is why it is salient and visually accessible for both participants. When the referent is accessible, but cannot be identified unambiguously, deontic infinitives are produced with objects (see Excerpt (5), lines 15 and 16).

Still, the question remains how deontic infinitives afford being taken up as instructive information and what the difference is between deontic infinitives and other practices, e.g., imperatives that seem to be able to occur in similar sequential environments for implementing similar actions (see Excerpt (5)). So far, we have seen that deontic infinitives have a strong instructional potential and position the Other as [K-] by formulating a requested action as a rule, or a normative procedure for how a specific task (like an exercise in physiotherapy or a specific task while cooking) is done. Yet, I argue that this is just one piece of the puzzle: What deontic infinitives do in comparison to, e.g., imperatives (see Gubina & Deppermann frthc.), is that in formulating an action in an impersonal way (i.e., without specifying explicitly the agent or the addressee), they allow their producers to position themselves as an *animator*, i.e., the producer of the instruction, but not as its *author* (Goffman 1981), while the 'authorship' is ascribed to external rules and norms. Furthermore, by not specifying the agent, or the addressee, deontic infinitives frame the instructed information as a general rule that concerns *everyone*, not just the recipient. Finally, since deontic infinitives do not express tense/aspect and are thus unmarked for time, they are naturally fitted to 'timeless rules' "that transcend[...] the local circumstances" and "[are] applicable in the future" (Rossi 2020: 174; see also Deppermann 2006, 2007; Parry 2013; Raevaara 2017; Zinken 2016: 117–130).

Thus, these examples demonstrate that in order to describe the interactional work accomplished by deontic infinitives, it would not suffice to talk only about their syntactic structure. Instead, other contextual factors such as the distribution of agency and the participants' epistemic and deontic positioning should also be included in the grammatical description of this practice. But what is even more important for such a description is to work out the differences between deontic infinitives and other practices that can occur in similar positions and accomplish similar actions (like imperatives).

5.2 Corrective instructions

Deontic infinitives are also used for initiating corrective instructions. The recipient's action can be treated as problematic or faulty according to different normative rules, e.g., game rules or etiquette, as in Excerpt (7). In lines 2–6, Anne (ANN) complains that it is unfair that her sister Maja will get new inline skates with no achievement in return, while Anne herself is supposed to abstain from eating hazelnut cream for a week. Anne's turn is rather difficult to hear, because she is still chewing her bread while talking:

Excerpt 7. *fertich kauen* 'to finish chewing'
(FOLK_E_00355_SE_01_T_01_DF_01), face-to-face, informal interaction, family breakfast

```
01 ANN: <<chewing> aber dis dann BLÖD.=
                    but this is unfair

02      =weil dann (.) weil dann bekomm die maja AUFF neue,=
        because then because then Maja also gets new ones

03      =und iff bekomm NEUe,=
        and I get new ones

04      =und mUss dafür was MACHen,=
        and I have to do something in return

05      =und sie muff NIX dafür machen.>=
        and she doesn't have to do something in return

06 CHR: =so.=und jetz hab ich nIx verSTANden.
        so and now I have not understood anything

07      (0.5)

08 CHR: *ah *hah hah erstmal*  FERtich  kauen.=
                    first.PTC  complete chew.INF
                    first to finish chewing
   ann  *...*smiling, visibly swallowing*

09 ANN: =ALso.
        so

10 ANN: (.) °h is dann aber BLÖD.=
        (it) is unfair then however
```

In response to Anne's complaint (lines 1–5), her mother Christina (CHR) complains that she did not 'understand anything' (line 6). The extreme case formulation *nix* ('nothing', line 6; Pomerantz 1986; Whitehead 2015) is clearly overdone with respect to Anne's lengthy turn. Instead of initiating repair directly, Christina uses the statement about Anne's unintelligibility to account for her ensuing corrective request *erstmal fertig kauen* ('first to finish chewing', line 8). The deontic infinitive here is used for a local, corrective instruction for a next action that is treated as a prerequisite for adequately redoing the recipient's prior action (i.e., formulating her complaint), which means having finished chewing before producing an action. In doing so, Christina seems to be invoking her category membership, or identity as *mother,* and reminding her daughter of a more general rule of eating etiquette and normative rules for talking effectively, which is why the instruction can also be seen as a pedagogical one. As in prior cases, in using a deontic infinitive, Christina positions her daughter as [K-] concerning the rules described above. Furthermore, as we can see in the transcript, Anne is already starting to adjust her conduct in a relevant way at the beginning of line 8, i.e., she visibly starts preparing to swallow. Thus, Christina's deontic infinitive at line 8 is not entirely here-and-now-relevant but can (also) be heard as 'proper conduct in general'.

Corrective instructions with deontic infinitives can also concern other types of normative rules, like driving rules as in Excerpt (8). The student (STU) has been driving on a two-way narrow road. During a pause in line 1, another car approaching the student's car becomes visible (see Figure 4) and the student starts slowing down his car. The instructor (INS) confirms the initiated course of action with *ganz genau* ('exactly'), by which he claims epistemic authority (Oloff 2017) and assesses the student's initiated procedure as correct. In doing so, he orients to the situation that has emerged as a training, or exam situation, in which the normative procedure for handling such situations on the road is being evoked:

Excerpt 8. *nicht stehenbleiben* 'not to stop' (FOLK_E_00168_SE_01_T_01), face-to-face, institutional/pedagogical interaction, practical driving lesson

```
01      (2.0)*(1.4)
    aut      *slows down-->
02 INS: ((smacks)) GANZ genau.
                   exactly
03 INS: (.) SCHAL+ten,
            to shift (the gear)
    stu            +puts right hand onto the gearshift-->
04      (0.4)*
    aut    -->*
```

```
05 INS: +NICHT s#tEhenbleiben?
             NEG    stop.INF
             not to stop
     stu  +shifts the gears-->
     fig           #4
```

Figure 4. Another car approaches the student's car on a narrow road

```
06      (0.3)
07 INS: SPIElen,+
          play.INF
          to move slowly
     stu          -->+
08      (3.1)
09 INS: ((smacks)) °h die nächste straße (.) LINKS.
                   the next street to the left
```

After confirming the correctness of the student's embodied actions, the teacher formulates the next relevant step in this activity and tells the student to shift gears, which is also formulated with a deontic infinitive (line 3; see Section 5.1). The student moves his hand toward the gearshift during the teacher's instruction in line 3. However, while the student is moving his hand towards the gear stick, the car almost stops. This is exactly when the teacher formulates two corrective instructions with deontic infinitives, namely *nicht stehen bleiben* ('not to stop', line 5), after which the car continues moving, and *spielen* ('to move slowly', line 7). In contrast to Excerpt (7), the corrective instruction in this case not only contains the formulation of what *is* to be done (i.e., moving slowly) but also an explicit formulation of what is *not* to be done (i.e., stopping the car) each time a similar situation occurs in the future. Like in all prior cases, the producer of the deontic infinitives positions himself as the one having epistemic access to the procedural knowledge.

Instructions with deontic infinitives can also be produced 'preemptively' (in a broader sense), i.e., as a sort of 'laying down ground rules' *before* any relevant problematic behavior takes place. An example is Excerpt (9), where two sisters — Pauline (PAU) and Tamara (TAM) — are renovating Pauline's room (see Excerpt (1)). Before the excerpt begins, Pauline and Tamara talk about moving a wooden dresser. The problem is that it is too heavy to push and move around the room. For that, the sisters decide to put rags underneath to make it easier to move the dresser. In line 2, Pauline asks Tamara for her preferences concerning the division of labor, i.e., if she wants to lift the dresser or push rags underneath. Tamara chooses to push the rags underneath the dresser (line 4) and reaches out for the rags even before fully completing her turn (see Figure 5). Before proceeding to the actual practical task, Tamara produces a deontic infinitive and asks Pauline not to let the dresser fall onto her hand (line 7):

Excerpt 9. *nicht fallen lassen* 'not to let fall' (FOLK_E_00217_SE_01_T_04), **face-to-face, informal interaction, room renovation**

```
01        (1.1)
02 PAU:   ä:h willst du ANheben+ oder DRUNterschieben,
          uh do you want to lift or to push underneath
   pau-b  >>approaches the dresser+
   tam-b  >>approaches the dresser-->
03        (0.2)
04 TAM:   DRUNter*%schieben.%#
          push underneath
   tam-h        *reaches out for rags-->
   pau-h        %hands out the rags to TAM%
   fig                          #5
```

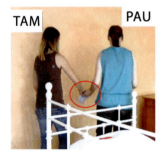

Figure 5. Tamara takes rags from Pauline

```
05        (0.2)
06 PAU:   <<p>gut.*
          good
   tam-h      -->*
07 TAM:   +°h <<whining> aber NICH auf meine meine HAND fallen [lassen>; ]
                        but  NEG  on   my.F.ACC    hand fall.INF let.INF
                        but not to let fall onto my hand
   pau-b  +approaches the dresser-->
08 PAU:                                                        [+nein&,= ]
                                                                no
   pau-b                                                       -->+
   tam-b                                                              -->&
```

09		=MACH ich nicht. *I (will) not do (it)*
10		(1.0)
11	PAU:	fangen wa HINten an. *let us start behind*
12		(1.0)

As in previous cases, the deontic infinitive is produced to accomplish a request that concerns the ongoing activity in which both participants are involved. However, the deontic infinitive in this case differs from prior cases in several respects: First, the deontic infinitive is related to a *future* course of action of the recipient. More specifically, what it makes relevant next is not getting something done, but rather being cautious while accomplishing the task to which the recipient previously committed. This is also reflected in the prosodic design of the turn: The deontic infinitive is produced with a 'whining' tone of voice, which indexes the speaker's orientation towards the action of letting the dresser fall onto her hands as undesirable and problematic. In this use, actions formulated with deontic infinitives usually concern something that happens accidentally, without the Other's intention to do so (e.g., falling down from the table or the ladder while repairing something on the ceiling, or letting some object fall and break).[7] Finally, such cases of deontic infinitives are often followed by explicit formulations of commitment: In this case, Pauline produces a negative response token *nein* ('no', line 8) and then explicitly commits to not doing this (line 9).

Excerpt (9) raises the question about the granularity of action (see Fox & Raymond, this volume). As the analysis shows, although Excerpt (9) can be treated as a special case of corrective instructions, there are also good sequential and interactional arguments for treating deontic infinitives that 'lay down the ground rules' before the occurrence of problematic behavior as special cases or uses that are distinct from other types of instructions. These utterances exhibit special behavior in terms of their position within the sequence and/or activity, their occurrence before any problematic behavior takes place or is even projectable, the accidental nature of the addressed undesirable events, as well as the explicit formulations of commitment we see in response.

This section has shown that deontic infinitives can be used for corrective instructions when the recipients' previously initiated actions are treated as problematic or faulty according to normative rules, although it is important to note that corrective instructions designed with deontic infinitives typically concern minor alterations (in contrast to declarative corrective requests, cf. Gubina &

---

7. This feature, however, is *not* a constitutive feature of *all* deontic infinitives in my collection, but rather concerns specifically cases like Excerpt (9).

Deppermann frthc.). Deontic infinitives can formulate either the correct procedure (Excerpt (7)) and/or negate the (potentially) wrong procedure already initiated by the recipient (Excerpts (8) and (9)). Moreover, Excerpt (9) also demonstrated that deontic infinitives can be used for preemptive corrective requests that aim at preventing a certain action and asking the recipient to be careful while accomplishing a certain practical action. Finally, Excerpts (7)–(9) also demonstrate that by producing deontic infinitives, speakers position recipients as not having epistemic access to normative rules concerning culturally obvious procedures such as for talking while eating (Excerpt (7)), straining pasta (Excerpt (8)), or dropping large pieces of furniture onto others (Excerpt (9)). Such constructions thus treat the recipients as in some ways culturally inept with regard to the basic rules of society.

5.3   Changing tack after failed compliance with prior requests

Finally, deontic infinitives are regularly used after recipients have verbally or nonverbally failed to comply with the prior directives(s) of the speaker. Consider Excerpt (10) from the same renovating interaction as Excerpt (9). Here, the sisters are painting walls. Before the extract begins, Pauline (PAU) tells Tamara (TAM) to give her the ladder because she needs to paint the walls on the top and Tamara will not be able to do that since it is too high for her. Tamara starts carrying the ladder from behind a wardrobe (see Figure 6). However, Pauline stops her (lines 2–3) because the plastic sheet on the floor is gone (lines 4–5) and thus the floor can get dirty. In line 9, she produces another suspension marker *warte* ('wait', see Keisanen, Rauniomaa & Haddington 2014) and tells her that first of all they need a rag (line 10). In line 13, she tells Tamara to put down the ladder. However, despite this request, Tamara continues walking backwards in line 15. In line 17, Pauline formulates a corrective request with an imperative. After Tamara stops, Pauline formulates a series of instructions designed as deontic infinitives, namely *nicht durchlaufen* ('not to walk through', line 19), *stehen bleiben* ('to stand still', line 20) and *leiter hinstellen* ('to put down the ladder', line 21):

Excerpt 10. *nicht durchlaufen* 'not to walk through'
(FOLK_E_00217_SE_01_T_02), informal interaction face-to-face, room renovation

```
01 PAU: KLAPPT alles-=
        everything works
    tam >>carries out the ladder from behind the wardrobe->
02      =oh HALT?*#
        oh stop
    tam       -->*
    fig          #6
```

Chapter 5. Deontic infinitives in spoken German   137

Figure 6. Tamara carries the ladder from behind the wardrobe

```
03       (.) bleib STEhen,
             stand still
04       (.) hier is die FOlie weg.=
             here is the film away
05       =un hier is auch schon far-
             and here is also already pain-
06       (.) was is_n hier pasSIERT,
             what PTC happened here
07       (0.3)
08 PAU: genau des was ich MEIne;=
             that's exactly what I mean
09       =*WARte,=
             wait
    pau  *points at the place on the floor where the film is gone-->
10       =jetz brauch ma erst_n LUMpen;
             now we need PTC first of all a rag
11 TAM: ((moans))
12       (0.4)*
    pau       -->*
13 PAU: *stell HIN,*
             put  down
    pau  *points at the place where TAM is standing*
14       *(.) LUMpen;
             rag
    pau  *points at place on the floor without the film-->
15       +(.) du bist da (.) hier is des WEGgerutscht;
             you are there- here it is where it slipped away
    tam  +continues walking backwards and carrying the ladder-->
16       (.) un du hast es nich ich*
             and you did not it I
    pau                       -->*
17       *<<ff>ble+ib STEHN>?
             stand still
    pau  *points at the place where TAM is standing-->
    tam         -->+
18       (0.6)*
    pau       -->*
```

138   Alexandra Gubina

```
19 PAU: <<ff>*NICH DURCHlaufen*>. (.)
              NEG walk_through.INF
              not to walk through
     pau      *points at place on the floor without film*
20 PAU: <<f>*STEhenbleiben*>;=
              stand_still.INF
              to stand still
     pau      *points at the place where TAM is standing *
21 PAU: =<<f>*L[EIter +hin]stellen>.=
              ladder    put_down.INF
              to put down the ladder
     pau      *points at the place where TAM is standing-->
     tam                +puts down the ladder-->
22 TAM:          [(de)    ]
                  (th)
23 PAU: =<<f>jet[z      ]>.
             now
24 TAM:          [<<p>hm ] Aua>-
                      hm    ouch
25      (0.4)
26 TAM: <<p>ja>-
             yes
27      (0.6)+*
     tam     -->+
     pau     -->*
```

Although lines 19–21 can be seen as corrective instructions, as we saw in Section 5.2, Pauline's instructions with deontic infinitives are produced after Tamara visibly fails to comply with Pauline's first requests to stand still (line 3) and to put down the ladder (line 13). This is a more specific context in which requests with deontic infinitives can occur than the one described in Section 5.2 because there is a difference in accountability between doing something wrong after having been told *not* to do so and doing something wrong *without* having been told anything yet. Pauline produces deontic infinitives in a very loud voice and additionally expands the series of requests in lines 19–21 with an incremental *jetzt* ('now', line 23), which highlights the urgency of compliance.[8] Moreover, she accompanies her series of requests with pointing gestures and holds the pointing gesture directed to where the ladder is to be put down until Tamara complies and finally puts down the ladder. Thus, Pauline additionally employs bodily resources to increase the relevance and urgency of compliance. Before putting down the ladder, Tamara produces a vocalization *aua* (line 24), which in this case can be seen as displaying Tamara's orientation to her wrong actions before.

---

8. It is important to note that the degree of urgency and pressure that is put on the recipient in this particular case seems to have something to do with possible negative consequences for Pauline (and especially her floor) in case of Tamara's failed compliance.

Chapter 5. Deontic infinitives in spoken German **139**

In using deontic infinitives for these second instructions, Pauline seems to orient to Tamara's embodied action as displaying that Tamara failed to hear/notice/correctly understand Pauline's first request, which is why Pauline needs to sound the alarm. Moreover, the deontic infinitives formulate a precise procedure consisting of concrete steps for what is to be done by Tamara. Furthermore, the initial imperative requests in lines 3 and 13 are designed ambiguously: For instance, in line 13, while Pauline produces the imperative request *stell hin* ('put down'), she points to where Tamara is standing. However, in the very next moment, she starts pointing at the place on the floor without the film (line 14), which in this position might also be understood as a *new* place where Tamara is supposed to put down the ladder. Furthermore, this second imperative request comes a few moments after the original imperative request was produced (*bleib stehen* 'stand still', line 3). Thus, the temporal distance between these two requests could also contribute to Tamara's understanding of *stell hin* ('put down') with the ambiguous pointing gesture (lines 13–14) as presenting a *new* solution or launching a *new* course of action that 'cancels' the relevance of the prior request to stand still (line 3). Thus, in producing a deontic infinitive, Pauline can be seen as changing tack from merely requesting to instructing what is to be done, when, and in which order, in light of Tamara's failure to understand/hear/notice her prior requests.

However, deontic infinitives after prior requests do not necessarily put as much pressure on the recipient as in Excerpt (10). The next case from a physiotherapy session will demonstrate this. Here, the patient is supposed to be doing stretching. In lines 2–4, the therapist asks the patient if she notices how her buttocks tense when she stretches herself out, which gets rejected by the patient (line 6). In line 9, the therapist asks the patient to push herself out properly. However, we can observe no visible changes in the patient's bodily position. In line 11, the therapist produces a modified version of her prior request, which is now designed as a deontic infinitive — *nach unten rausschieben* ('to push out downwards'):

Excerpt 11. *rausschieben* 'push out' (FOLK_E_00343_SE_01_T_01), face-to-face, **institutional/medical/pedagogical interaction, physiotherapy**

```
01    (0.2)
02 THE: MERken se,
        do you notice
03      (.) dass die pobacken (.) ANspannen,=
            that the buttocks tense
04      =wenn se sich (0.25) LANGmachen?
            when you stretch yourself
05      (0.2)
```

```
06 PAT: hm: NEE die ha bis jetz *NICH gemacht.
        hm no I haven't done this until now
    pat                             *moves legs up and down-->
07      (0.6)
08 PAT: die HÄNde*; [h°   ]
        the hands
    pat        -->*
09 THE:            [schie]ben sich ma RAUS richtig.
                   push yourself out properly
10      (0.4)
11 THE: *nach   Unten RAUSschieben.
        towards below push_out.INF
        to push out downwards
    pat *moves legs up and down-->
12      (0.7)*
    pat    -->*
13 CLI: *ich SCHIEB mich. (.)
        I am pushing myself
    the *walks towards the patient's feet-->
14 THE: hm(.)↑HM?
15      (0.3)
16 PAT: aber meine *pobacken würden (.) dann würd ich
        würd_s [ANders geh]n;
        but my buttocks would        then would
        it would go differently
    the           -->*takes the patient's feet into her
        hands-->>
17 THE:        [<<f>ja>?  ]
                 yes
18 PAT: dann würd ich nach Oben [kommen.  ]
        then I would come upwards
19 THE:                        [dann KOMM]T der po auch
        hoch;
        then the buttocks also come upwards
20      (0.2)
```

In contrast to Excerpt (10), the deontic infinitive here is not produced in a marked way, neither prosodically nor in terms of visible, embodied means. Nevertheless, as in Excerpt (10), the deontic infinitive is used for reformulating an initial request with which the recipient failed to comply. In addition, the deontic infinitive also specifies what is meant by 'pushing oneself out properly' (line 9) by virtue of adding *nach unten* ('downwards'), which could be hearable as additional help. The imperative in line 9 is quite vague (due to lack of the direction and the adverb *richtig* 'properly'), while what is specified by the infinitive is grounded in the procedural norms, i.e., they consist of details of an action performance to which the speaker has access and thus the right to supervise the fulfilment of the procedure.

Chapter 5. Deontic infinitives in spoken German **141**

In response, the patient treats the therapist's instruction as unnecessary by stating that she is indeed pushing herself (line 13). After a minimal acknowledgment token (line 14), the therapist walks toward the patient's feet and takes them into her hands. In the meantime, the patient says that if she pushed herself out, her buttocks would come upwards, which might be seen as an account for her 'too little' or 'barely visible' attempt to stretch herself out (line 16 and 18). In response to this account, the therapist states that that is exactly what is supposed to happen with her buttocks if she stretches herself out properly (line 19).

This section demonstrated how speakers can use deontic infinitives to coordinate procedural steps that the recipient is not following. Furthermore, both Excerpts (10) and (11) highlight the informational aspect of deontic infinitives, namely changing tack from requests to alert/alarm (Excerpt (10)) or instructive information (Excerpt (11)). In constructing their requests with deontic infinitives without any concrete explicitly stated addressee, speakers frame the action as a *general rule* or *procedure* not *authored* by the speakers themselves (Goffman 1981). Nevertheless, speakers can still claim deontic authority for supervising the recipients when the latter fail to comply or have trouble complying with the prior request.

5.4 Ambiguity of deontic stance and degree of obligation in deontic infinitives

So far, we have looked at cases in which both the speakers and recipients orient to the deontic infinitive as making immediate compliance relevant next. However, since deontic infinitives can express different degrees of obligation, it can sometimes come to a negotiation of the deontic stance expressed by the format (see also Deppermann 2006, 2007), as Excerpt (12) will demonstrate.

In this case, Mariola (MAR), her friend Lisa (LIS) and Lisa's family — father Bartosz (BAR) and mother Zusanna (ZUS) — are going to another town to have lunch together. Mariola is driving the car down the federal road, while Lisa is watching her the whole time since Mariola is a novice driver. At the beginning of the extract, Zusanna tells Mariola what is missing in her car (e.g., a hand cream, lines 1–12). Meanwhile, the car passes the traffic sign indicating the maximum permitted speed of 120 kilometers per hour. After that, Lisa looks twice into the side mirror (see Figure 7) and onto the speedometer. In line 13, Lisa tells Mariola to move over a bit, namely to the right lane. In line 17, Mariola produces a request for confirmation to check her understanding of what Lisa meant by *rüber* ('over'). After a confirmation from Bartosz from behind, Lisa produces a deontic infinitive *un bissle gas geben* ('and to speed up a bit', line 20). Afterwards, she initiates an account in line 21 by producing a factual declarative (Rossi 2018) *hier is hundertzwanzig* ('it's 120 here'):

Excerpt 12. *gas geben* 'to speed up' (FOLK_E_00291_SE_01_T_02), face-to-face, informal interaction, driving

```
01 ZUS: h° mariola wa[s dir im] Auto FEHLT,
             NAME what is missing in your car
02 LIS:              [mann,   ]
                      God
03 BAR: (.) äh [(ja)]
             uh (yes)
04 ZUS:        [äh si]nd ja diese äh HILFsmittel wie bei mir.
                uh are PTC these uh tools/aids like I have
05         °h die HAutcreme; ((lacht))
             the hand cream ((laughs))
06 MAR: °h ja?
             yes
07 ZUS: °h (.) die gAnzen dinge die ich im AUto hab.=
                 all the things that I have in the car
08         =weil ich wollte jetz *eine HANDcreme nehmen*,
             because I wanted now to take a hand cream
    lis                          *gaze into the right-side
             mirror*
09         (.) °h und die GIBT_s *jetz #nicht;
                 and there is no (cream)
    lis                          *gaze into the right-side mirror-->
    fig                          #7
```

Figure 7. Lisa gazes into the right-side mirror

```
10      (0.3)
11 ZUS: °h*
    lis -->*
12 BAR: *MACHT nichts;*
         it's okay
    lis *gazes at the speedometer*
13 LIS: [etwas  RÜ]ber;
         a bit over (there)
14 ZUS: [na   ja,=]
         well
15 MAR: [ähm     ]
         uhm
```

Chapter 5. Deontic infinitives in spoken German **143**

```
16 ZUS: äh da[s is nich]
        uhm it's not

17 MAR:    [ja    HI]ER?
            yes    here

18      (0.3)

19 BAR: [ja-]
         yes

20 LIS: [un ] bissle GAS geben;=
        and  a.bit  gas give.INF
        and to speed up a bit

21      =hier is hundertZWANzig.
         it's 120 here

22      (0.3)

23 LIS: °h

24      (0.3)

25 LIS: ((laughs))

26      (0.3)

27 MAR: ich DARF [doch auch !HUNDERT! f]ahrn
        I may/am allowed PTC to drive also 100

28 LIS:          [kannst es ma aus     ]
                  can you it out

29 MAR: bei hundertzwa[nzi::g;           ]
        if it's 120

30 LIS:              [ja,=aber du kannst] es auch ma AUSnutzen;=
                      yes but you can also PTC exploit it

31 LIS: =musst auch Üben wenn du ANGST vor der autobahn hast.
        (you) must also practice if you are afraid of highway
```

Interestingly, in this case both Lisa's TCUs — the deontic infinitive in line 20 and the factual declarative in line 21 — seem to be ambiguous in terms of deontic modality, or, at least, the degree of pressure on Mariola. In lines 27–28, Mariola says that she *may* also drive 100 if the speed limit is 120. The focal accent is on the modal verb *darf* 'may': In designing her turn this way, she highlights that her actions are not wrong and thus not in need of correction. Moreover, she constructs her turn with a modal particle *doch*, which indicates that the proposition should actually be known to recipient, but the recipient did not attend to this knowledge while producing her prior action (Lütten 1979; Pittner 2007). In doing so, the prior speaker's action is treated as inapposite because its proposition contradicts knowledge shared between the participants. In reacting this way to Lisa's turn in lines 20–21, Mariola treats Lisa's turn in line 20 as a proper thing to do. In response, Lisa produces a concessive response: After agreeing with Mariola, she adds that Mariola *can* exploit it to practice if she is afraid of highway driving (it turns out later that Mariola is indeed afraid of highways, not shown). In this way, Lisa frames her turn merely as a helpful or cooperative *suggestion* for Mariola in light of her fear of highways and not an *instruction* of what Mariola is supposed to do. What Excerpt (12) demonstrates is that deontic infinitives — by virtue of their design features — allow ambiguity concerning the degree of obligation and deontic stance embodied by the format, i.e., whether the recipient *must* do a certain action, *should* do a certain action, or *may* or *can* do it (see also Deppermann 2006, 2007).

6. Conclusion and discussion

6.1 Summary and practical implications of the results of the current study

This chapter has examined different recurrent uses of deontic infinitives in German talk-in-interaction. It has shown that most deontic infinitives are used for accomplishing requests and for formulating them as a rule or a normative procedure for doing something "that transcends the local circumstances and is applicable in the future" (Rossi 2020: 174; see also Deppermann 2006, 2007; Parry 2013; Raevaara 2017; Zinken 2016: 117–130). Additionally, we have seen that deontic infinitives are always used for producing requests concerning the participants' already launched line of action, i.e., concerning a local task or project that the recipients are already involved in. This also allows for the use of such a minimal linguistic structure with *lean* syntactic features (Deppermann 2020).

The study has demonstrated that the rule or the normative procedure of a specific task, project, or course of action can be evoked in different sequential contexts, namely (i) in explanatory contexts, i.e., when a certain procedure is being explained (Section 5.1), (ii) in contexts in which recipients (can) act against normative rules (Section 5.2) or (iii) in the face of previously failed compliance (Section 5.3). What all these examples have in common is that the speaker — although positioned only as an animator and not an author of the instruction — is the one who claims the right to require (and supervise) the following of the rule either because of their institutional role or their activity-specific role. Thus, the characteristic of the deontic modality is based on the reference to rules and norms as the sources of *authorship* for instructing, whereas imperatives frame speakers *both* as authors *and* animators of the produced actions (see also Gubina & Deppermann frthc.). Moreover, Section 5.4 highlighted the affordances (Hutchby 2001) of the linguistic form of deontic infinitives, i.e., how their indeterminacy in terms of the expressed deontic modality affords ambiguity of deontic stance and degree of obligation as well as ambiguity of actions accomplished with the practice.

The results of the study highlight the features that are relevant for describing a social action format comprehensively. As the analysis demonstrates, these include not only formal linguistic, i.e., lexical and morpho-syntactic, features but also the description of sequential / activity context, and multimodal features of the environment; the distribution of agency and epistemic access; as well as the deontic positioning of the participants. While it is still part of an ongoing debate whether bodily actions belong to grammar or not (Couper-Kuhlen 2018; Keevallik 2018), the current study shows that the participants' embodied conduct in the form of their already ongoing visible physical *involvement* in a certain task, their visible embodied *failure to comply*, their nonverbal *compliances,* etc. *must* be part of a comprehensive grammar of talk-in-interaction — at least, as part of the description of contexts in which a specific social action format is used.[9]

Moreover, the results of the study have clear practical implications, as they can contribute to further development of current curricula of German as a Foreign and Second Language. Typically, textbooks in German as a Foreign and Second Language still operate with concepts like 'more/less/extremely/etc. polite' requests or directives and label some formats as polite and others as impolite on a politeness scale. However, it is unclear how the degree of politeness expressed by particular request formats is estimated in such cases. Furthermore, none of the cases of deontic infinitives (or imperatives) presented in the current chapter have been treated as impolite or rude by the participants. Instead, the current study has demonstrated that in employing specific grammatical practices in similar sequential positions for implementing similar actions, participants orient to a number of other interactional features, such as sequential and activity context, epistemic and deontic positioning of the participants, agency, and participation roles invoked by the use of particular formats, to name just a few. All these features are important for understanding how a given practice is actually used in a language, which is why it is crucial to convey this to language learners. In addition, formats like deontic infinitives and phrasal formats are usually treated as 'incomplete' or 'ungrammatical', which is why they are usually not included in language teaching curricula for German. Yet, this study has demonstrated that formats like deontic infinitives constitute a frequent, routinized, context-sensitive practice for accomplishing specific social actions in German talk-in-interaction, one that is also treated as such a practice by other 'competent members'. Thus, my results offer solid argu-

---

9. For this study, a very schematic description of the participants' embodied conduct would suffice, i.e., it does not require an exact description of all embodied actions by the participants and how these actions are accomplished physically. However, it is important to highlight that this concerns only this particular study, and that precise description of participants' physical actions can be a crucial part of grammatical description of other interactional phenomena.

ments for including deontic infinitives — as well as similar constructions that have been typically treated as incomplete (see Section 2) — not only in reference grammars of spoken German, but also in the curricula of German as a Foreign and Second Language.

6.2 Some (possible) challenges and considerations for creating a comprehensive grammar

Along with practical implications, the current study brings to light possible challenges and considerations for creating a comprehensive grammar of talk-in-interaction. A *comprehensive* grammar of talk-in-interaction presupposes that the description of a social action format and its functional spectrum will be ideally full or complete. However, it is important to communicate to the audience of such a grammar that providing a comprehensive account of the whole functional spectrum of a specific interactional phenomenon — even if we take a social action format approach (Steensig et al. 2023) — might sometimes be an *incremental*, or a *stepwise* process and that entries in such a grammar might need to be updated as new research comes up. This is also in line with the standard approach within Conversation Analysis and Interactional Linguistics, i.e., it may very often take time until a grammatical structure, or a social action format, is described in various contexts, settings, sequential positions, and thus functions (see, e.g., an overview of research on the English change-of-state *oh* in Fox & Raymond, this volume).

Moreover, the incremental process of writing comprehensive entries on phenomena in talk-in-interaction may depend on the limitations of our data sets, since we can only work with settings that are available to us. As discussed in Section 2, access to a large volume of data from a wide range of interaction types and speaker groups allows for a more robust and nuanced investigation of (relatively) common phenomena than with small corpora from a limited number of interactional settings. Furthermore, large corpora can provide us with the possibility of presenting some general distribution patterns. Still, while the patterns described in this paper are similar in both mundane and institutional settings, there are surely phenomena that function differently in different types of settings and participation frameworks. This is linked to another problem: Section 4 showed that there are other uses than requests or instructions in my collection, although the number of such cases in this study did not allow for their further analysis. A small number of cases does not always have to be problematic because there can be systematic and routinized practices that are still very rare. Yet, it is not clear whether this number of cases has something to do with my own data set or whether it really tells us something about the actual use of deontic infinitives in social interaction, i.e., whether this can be seen as an argument for a strong association between deontic infinitives and directive actions like requests or instructions. Furthermore, while for this study I excluded cases of deontic infinitives that accomplish very specific actions (like *mal gucken/schauen*, see Excerpt (4)), it would still be important for future research to analyze these social action formats in more detail and check whether it is still possible to identify a core meaning that is present across all uses of deontic infinitives.

Finally, the study has hopefully demonstrated that in order to describe the interactional work accomplished by one practice, it is often necessary to compare it with other practices that can be used for implementing actions within the same social action category in similar sequential environments (see also Couper-Kuhlen & Selting 2018:24 on discriminability as one type of evidence). However, the question arises concerning how this can be represented and, more importantly, implemented in a reference grammar. Thus, the challenge is to demonstrate all the (sometimes subtle) differences within social action categories and across them, because in all these cases it is important to take into account at least position and composition (Schegloff 1993:121), but sometimes other factors as well (e.g., embodiment, materiality, and the like). Another related challenge for the analysis of social action formats in general and for writing a comprehensive grammar of talk-in-interaction specifically is the indeterminacy and often lack of clear boundaries between these different action categories (e.g., such as requests or instructions). Still, we could think about all these actions being related to each other, for instance, in terms of family resemblances and what such actions make relevant next, which would be just one overlapping similarity among all these granular action types (see Wittgenstein 1953; Rosch 1978; Raymond 2019). This might allow us to show that there are more prototypical cases of requests (or other actions like instructions) and cases that are similar to requests, but that are additionally doing something else and do not need to be "equally good members" (Rosch 1987:153) of the category of request-like actions.[10]

Acknowledgments

I am grateful to Emma Betz, Arnulf Deppermann, Barbara Fox, Anne-Sylvie Horlacher, Silke Reineke, Pawel Urbanik, and Jörg Zinken for their valuable and helpful input on earlier drafts, which significantly improved the final version of this chapter. I would also like to extend a special thanks to the editors of this volume, especially Jakob Steensig, for coordinating my contribution and offering insightful guidance. I would also like to thank the participants of the

---

10. See also a similar solution within the project 'Grammar of Danish Talk in Interaction': <https://samtalegrammatik.dk/en/the-grammar/functions/actions/directive-actions-and-responses>.

workshop *From Action to Grammar* for their helpful feedback on my talk that the current chapter partially builds on. All remaining errors are my own.

References

Aldrup, Marit, Küttner, Uwe-A., Lechler, Constanze, and Reinhardt, Susanne (2021). "Suspended assessments in German talk-in-interaction." In *Prosodie und Multimodalität / Prosody and Multimodality*, ed. by Maxi Kupetz, and Friederike Kern, 31–66. Heidelberg: Winter Verlag.

Ágel, Vilmos, and Klaus Fischer. 2015. "Dependency Grammar and Valency Theory." In *The Oxford Handbook of Linguistic Analysis*, ed. by Bernd Heine, and Heiko Narrog, 225–257. Oxford: Oxford University Press.

Auer, Peter. 2007. "Why Are Increments Such Elusive Objects?" *Pragmatics* 17 (4): 647–658

Bolden, Galina B., Alexa Hepburn, and Jonathan Potter 2019. "Subversive Completions: Turn-Taking Resources for Commandeering the Recipient's Action in Progress." *Research on Language and Social Interaction* 52 (2): 144–158.

Couper-Kuhlen, Elizabeth. 2014. "What Does Grammar Tell Us About Action?" *Pragmatics. Quarterly Publication of the International Pragmatics Association (IPrA)* 24 (3): 623–647.

Couper-Kuhlen, Elizabeth. 2018. "Finding a Place for Body Movement in Grammar." *Research on Language and Social Interaction* 51 (1): 22–25.

Couper-Kuhlen, Elizabeth, and Dagmar Barth-Weingarten. 2011. "A System for Transcribing Talk-in-Interaction: GAT 2. Translated and adapted for English." *Gesprächsforschung — Online-Zeitschrift zur verbalen Interaktion* 12: 1–51.

Couper-Kuhlen, Elizabeth, and Tsuyoshi Ono. 2007. "'Incrementing' in Conversation. A Comparison of Practices in English, German and Japanese." *Pragmatics. Quarterly Publication of the International Pragmatics Association (IPrA)* 17 (4): 513–552.

Couper-Kuhlen Elizabeth, and Margret Selting (eds). 1996. *Prosody in Conversation*. Cambridge: Cambridge University Press.

Couper-Kuhlen Elizabeth, and Margret Selting (eds). 2018. *Interactional Linguistics: Studying Language in Social Interaction*. Cambridge: Cambridge University Press.

Craven, Alexandra, and Jonathan Potter. 2010. "Directives: Entitlement and Contingency in Action." *Discourse Studies* 12 (4): 419–442.

Curl, Traci S., and Paul Drew. 2008. "Contingency and Action: A Comparison of Two Forms of Requesting." *Research on Language and Social Interaction* 41 (2): 129–153.

Deppermann, Arnulf. 2006. "Deontische Infinitivkonstruktionen: Syntax, Semantik, Pragmatik und interaktionale Verwendung [Deontic Infinitive Constructions: Syntax, Pragmatics and Interactional Use]." In *Konstruktionen in der Interaktion* [Constructions in the Interaction], ed. by Susanne Günthner, and Wolfgang Imo, 239–262. Berlin/New York: de Gruyter.

Deppermann, Arnulf. 2007. *Grammatik und Semantik aus gesprächsanalytischer Sicht* [Grammar and Semantics from a Conversation-Analytic Perspective]. Berlin/New York: de Gruyter.

Deppermann, Arnulf. 2020. "Lean Syntax: How Argument Structure is Adapted to Its Interactive, Material, and Temporal Ecology." *Linguistische Berichte* 263: 255–294.

Deppermann, Arnulf, and Alexandra Gubina. 2021. "When the Body Belies the Words: Embodied Agency with *darf/kann ich?* ("May/Can I?") in German." *Frontiers in Communication* 6.

Drew, Paul, and Elizabeth Couper-Kuhlen. 2014. "Requesting: From Speech Act to Recruitment." In *Requesting in Social Interaction*, ed. by Paul Drew, and Elizabeth Couper-Kuhlen, 1–34. Amsterdam/Philadelphia, John Benjamins.

Ehmer, Oliver, and Geert Brône. 2021. "Instructing Embodied Knowledge: Multimodal Approaches to Interactive Practices for Knowledge Constitution." *Linguistics Vanguard* 7 (s4): 20210012.

Ehmer, Oliver, Florence Oloff, Henrike Helmer, and Silke Reineke (eds). 2021. ""How to Get Things Done" — Aufforderungen und Instruktionen in der multimodalen Interaktion. Einführung in das Themenheft [Requests and Instructions in Multimodal Interaction. Introduction to the Special Issue]." *Gesprächsforschung: Themenheft "How to get things done" — Aufforderungen und Instruktionen in der multimodalen Interaktion* 22: 670–690.

Ford, Cecilia E., and Sandra A. Thompson. 1996. "Interactional Units in Conversation: Syntactic, Intonational, and Pragmatic Resources for the Management of Turns". In *Interaction and Grammar*, ed. by Elinor Ochs, Emanuel A. Schegloff, and Sandra A. Thompson, 134–84. Cambridge: Cambridge University Press.

Ford, Cecilia E., Barbara A. Fox, and Sandra A. Thompson. 2002. "Constituency and the Grammar of Turn Increments." In *The Language of Turn and Sequence*, ed. by Cecilia E. Ford, Barbara A. Fox, and Sandra A. Thompson, 14–38. New York: Oxford University Press.

Fox, Barbara A. 1993. *The Human Tutorial Dialogue Project*. New Jersey: Lawrence Erlbaum.

Fox, Barbara A., and Sandra A. Thompson. 2010. "Responses to *wh*-Questions in English Conversation." *Research on Language and Social Interaction* 43 (2): 133–156.

Fox, Barbara, and Trine Heinemann. 2019. "Telescoping Responses to Requests: Unpacking Progressivity." *Discourse Studies* 21 (1): 38–66.

Fox, Barbara A., Makoto Hayashi, and Robert Jasperson. 1996. "Resources and Repair: A Cross-Linguistic Study of the Syntactic Organization of Repair." In *Interaction and Grammar*, ed. by Elinor Ochs, Emanuel A. Schegloff, and Sandra A. Thompson, 185–237. Cambridge: Cambridge University Press.

Fox, Barbara A., Yael Maschler, and Susanne Uhmann. 2010. "A Cross-Linguistic Study of Self-Repair: Evidence from English, German, and Hebrew." *Journal of Pragmatics* 42 (9): 2487–2505.

Fries, Norbert. 1983. *Syntaktische und semantische Studien zum frei verwendeten Infinitiv und zu verwandten Erscheinungen im Deutschen* [Syntactic and Semantic Studies on the Freely Used Infinitive and Related Phenomena in German]. Tübingen: Narr.

Fries, Norbert. 1987. "Zu einer Randgrammatik des Deutschen [On a Peripheral Grammar of German]." In *Satzmodus zwischen Grammatik und Pragmatik* [Sentence Mood Between Grammar and Pragmatics], ed. by Jörg Meibauer, 75–95. Tübingen: Niemeyer.

Goffman, Erving. 1981. "Footing." In *Forms of Talk*, ed. by Erving Goffman, 124–159. Philadelphia: University of Pennsylvania Press.

Golato, Andrea. 2012. "German *oh*: Marking an Emotional Change of State." *Research on Language & Social Interaction* 45 (3): 245–268.

Gubina, Alexandra. 2021. "Availability, Grammar, and Action Formation. On Simple and Modal Interrogative Request Formats in Spoken German." *Gesprächsforschung — Online-Zeitschrift zur verbalen Interaktion* 22: 272–303.

Gubina, Alexandra, and Arnulf Deppermann. frthc. "Action formation of Requests in German: Interactional and Pragmatic Factors Affecting the Choice of Linguistic Formats."

Günthner, Susanne. 2017. "Diskursmarker in der Interaktion — Formen und Funktionen univerbierter *guck mal-* und *weißt du-*Konstruktionen [Discourse Markers in Interaction — Forms and Functions of Univertized *guck mal-* 'Look' and *weißt du-* 'You Know' Constructions]." In *Diskursmarker im Deutschen. Reflexionen und Analysen* [Discourse Markers in German. Reflections and Analyses], ed. by Hardarik Blühdorn, Arnulf Deppermann, Henrike Helmer, and Thomas Spranz-Fogasy, 103–130. Göttingen: Verlag für Gesprächsforschung.

Hayashi, Makoto. 1999. "Where Grammar and Interaction Meet: A Study of Co-Participant Completion in Japanese Conversation." *Human Studies* 22: 475–499.

Hazel, Spencer, and Kristian Mortensen. 2019. "Designedly Incomplete Objects as Elicitation Tools in Classroom Interaction." In *Objects, Bodies and Work Practice*, ed. by Dennis Day, and Johannes Wagner, 216–249. Bristol, United Kingdom: Multilingual Matters.

Heritage, John. 2012. "Epistemics in Action: Action Formation and Territories of Knowledge." *Research on Language & Social Interaction* 45 (1): 1–29.

Heritage, John, and Tanya Stivers. 1999. "Online Commentary in Acute Medical Visits: A Method of Shaping Patient Expectations." *Social Science & Medicine* 49 (11): 1501–1517.

Hopper, Paul J. 2011. "Emergent Grammar and Temporality in Interactional Linguistics." In *Constructions*, ed. by Peter Auer, and Stefan Pfänder, 22–44. Berlin/Boston: de Gruyter.

Hutchby, Ian. 2001. "Technologies, Texts, and Affordances." *Sociology* 35 (2): 441–456.

Imo, Wolfgang, and J. Philipp Lanwer (eds.). 2020. *Prosodie und Konstruktionsgrammatik* [Prosody and Construction Grammar]. Berlin/Boston: De Gruyter.

Keevallik, Leelo. 2013. "The Interdependence of Bodily Demonstrations and Clausal Syntax." *Research on Language and Social Interaction* 46 (1): 1–21.

Keevallik, Leelo. 2014. "Turn Organization and Bodily-Vocal Demonstrations." *Journal of Pragmatics* 65: 103–120.

Keevallik, Leelo. 2015. "Coordinating the Temporalities of Talk and Dance." In *Temporality in Interaction*, ed. by Arnulf Deppermann, and Susanne Günthner, 309–336. Amsterdam/Philadelphia, John Benjamins.

Keevallik, Leelo. 2018. "What Does Embodied Interaction Tell Us about Grammar?" *Research on Language and Social Interaction* 51 (1): 1–21.

Keisanen, Tiina, Mirka Rauniomaa, and Pentti Haddington. 2014. "Suspending Action: From Simultaneous to Consecutive Ordering of Multiple Courses of Action." In *Multiactivity in Social Interaction*, ed. by Pentti Haddington, Maurice Nevile, Lorenza Mondada, and Tiina Keisanen, 109–136. Amsterdam: John Benjamins.

Koshik, Irene. 2002. "Designedly Incomplete Utterances: A Pedagogical Practice for Eliciting Knowledge Displays in Error Correction Sequences." *Research on Language and Social Interaction* 35 (3): 277–309.

Lerner, Gene H. 1991. "On the Syntax of Sentences-in-Progress." *Language in Society* 20 (3): 441–458.

Lerner, Gene H. 2004. "On the Place of Linguistic Resources in The Organization of Talk-in-Interaction: Grammar as Action in Prompting a Speaker to Elaborate." *Research on Language and Social Interaction* 37 (2): 151–185.

Lindwall, Oskar, Gustav Lymer, and Christian Greiffenhagen. 2015. "The Sequential Analysis of Instruction." In *The Handbook of Classroom Discourse and Interaction*, ed. by Numa Markee, 142–157. Hoboken, NJ: Wiley.

Lütten, Jutta. 1979. "Die Rolle der Partikeln *doch, eben* und *ja* als Konsensus-Konstitutiva in gesprochener Sprache [The Role of the Particles *doch, eben*, and *ja* as Consensus Constituents in Spoken Language]." In *Die Partikeln der deutschen Sprache* [The Particles of the German Language], ed. by Harald Weydt, 30–38. Berlin: De Gruyter.

Mikesell, Lisa, Galina B. Bolden, Jenny Mandelbaum, Jeffrey D. Robinson, Tanya Romaniuk, Alexa Bolaños-Carpio, Darcey Searles, Wan Wei, Stephen M. DiDomenico, and Beth Angell. 2017. "At the Intersection of Epistemics and Action: Responding with 'I know'." *Research on Language and Social Interaction* 50 (3): 268–285.

Mondada, Lorenza. 2011. "The Organization of Concurrent Courses of Action in Surgical Demonstrations." In *Embodied Interaction: Language and Body in the Material World*, ed. by Jürgen Streeck, Charles Goodwin, and Curtis LeBaron, 207–226. Cambridge: Cambridge University Press.

Mondada, Lorenza. 2014. "Instructions in the Operating Room: How the Surgeon Directs Their Assistant's Hands." *Discourse Studies* 16 (2): 131–61.

Mondada, Lorenza. 2024. "Appendix II: Multimodal Transcription Conventions." In *The Cambridge Handbook of Methods in Conversation Analysis*, ed. by Jeffrey D. Robinson, Rebecca Clift, Kobin H. Kendrick, and Chase W. Raymond. Cambridge: Cambridge University Press.

Oh, Sun-Young. 2007. The Interactional Meanings of Quasi-Pronouns in Korean Conversation. In *Person Reference in Interaction*, ed. by Nick J. Enfield, and Tanya Stivers, 203–225. Cambridge: Cambridge University Press.

Oloff, Florence. 2017. "*Genau* als redebeitragsinterne, responsive, sequenzschließende oder sequenzstrukturierende Bestätigungspartikel im Gespräch [*Genau* as Speech-Internal, Responsive, Sequence-Closing, or Sequence-Structuring Confirmation Particles in Conversation]." In *Diskursmarker im Deutschen. Reflexionen und Analysen* [Discourse Markers in German. Reflections and Analyses], ed. by Hardarik Blühdorn, Arnulf Deppermann, Henrike Helmer, and Thomas Spranz-Fogasy, 207–232. Göttingen: Verlag für Gesprächsforschung.

Parry, Ruth. 2013. "Giving Reasons for Doing Something Now or at Some Other Time." *Research on Language & Social Interaction* 46 (2): 105–124.

Pekarek Doehler, Simona. 2018. "Elaborations on L2 Interactional Competence: The Development of L2 Grammar-For-Interaction." *Classroom Discourse* 9 (1): 3–24.

Persson, Rasmus. 2017. "Fill-in-the-Blank Questions in Interaction: Incomplete Utterances as a Resource for Doing Inquiries." *Research on Language and Social Interaction* 50 (3): 227–248.

Pfeiffer, Martin. 2015. *Selbstreparaturen im Deutschen* [Self-repair in German]. Berlin: de Gryuter.

Pittner, Karin. 2007. "Common Ground in Interaction: The Functions of Medial *doch*." In *Lexical Markers of Common Grounds*, ed. by Anita Fetzer, and Kerstin Fischer, 67–87. Boston: Elsevier.

Pomerantz, Anita. 1986. "Extreme Case Formulations: A Way of Legitimizing Claims." *Human Studies* 9: 219–229.

Proske, Nadine. 2017. "Zur Funktion und Klassifikation gesprächsorganisatorischer Imperative [On the Function and Classification of Conversational Organizational Imperatives]." In *Diskursmarker im Deutschen. Reflexionen und Analysen* [Discourse Markers in German. Reflections and Analyses], ed. by Hardarik Blühdorn, Arnulf Deppermann, Henrike Helmer, and Thomas Spranz-Fogasy, 73–102. Göttingen: Verlag für Gesprächsforschung.

Raevaara, Liisa. 2017. "Adjusting the Design of Directives to the Activity Environment: Imperatives in Finnish Cooking Club Interaction." In *Imperative Turns at Talk: The Design of Directives in Action*, ed. by Marja-Leena Sorjonen, Liisa Raevaara, and Elizabeth Couper-Kuhlen, 381–410. Amsterdam: John Benjamins.

Raymond, Chase W. 2019. "Intersubjectivity, Normativity, and Grammar." *Social Psychology Quarterly* 82 (2): 182–204.

Raymond, Chase W., Jeffrey D. Robinson, Barbara A. Fox, Sandra A. Thompson, and Kristella Montiegel. 2021. "Modulating Action through Minimization: Syntax in the Service of Offering and Requesting." *Language in Society* 50 (1): 53–91.

Robinson, Jeffrey D., Rebecca Clift, Kobin H. Kendrick, and Chase W. Raymond (eds). 2024. *The Cambridge Handbook of Methods in Conversation Analysis*. Cambridge: Cambridge University Press.

Rosch, Eleanor. 1978. "Principles of Categorization." In *Cognition and Categorization*, ed. by Eleanor Rosch, and Barbara B. Lloyd, 27–48. Killsdale, NJ: Lawrence Erlbaum.

Rosch, Eleanor. 1987. "Wittgenstein and Categorization Research in Cognitive Psychology." In *Meaning and the Growth of Understanding*, ed. by Michael Chapman, and Roger A. Dixon, 151–166. Berlin: Springer.

Rossi, Giovanni. 2012. "Bilateral and Unilateral Requests: The Use of Imperatives and *mi X?* Interrogatives in Italian." *Discourse Processes* 49 (5): 426–458.

Rossi, Giovanni. 2015. *The Request System in Italian Interaction*. [PhD dissertation]. Nijmegen: Radboud University.

Rossi, Giovanni. 2018. "Composite Social Actions: The Case of Factual Declaratives in Everyday Interaction." *Research on Language and Social Interaction* 51 (4): 379–397.

Rossi, Giovanni. 2020. "The Recruitment System in Italian." In *Getting Others to Do Things. A Pragmatic Typology of Recruitments*, ed. by Simeon Floyd, Giovanni Rossi, and Nick J. Enfield, 147–201. Berlin: Language Science Press.

Schegloff, Emanuel A. 1987. "Recycled Turn Beginnings: A Precise Repair Mechanism in Conversation's Turn-Taking Organization." In *Talk and Social Organisation*, ed. by Graham Button, and John R. E. Lee, 70–85. Clevedon, England: Multilingual Matters.

Schegloff, Emanuel A. 1993. "Reflections on Quantification in the Study of Conversation." *Research on Language and Social Interaction* 26 (1): 99–128.

Schegloff, Emanuel A. 1996. "Turn Organization: One Intersection of Grammar and Interaction." In *Interaction and Grammar*, ed. by Elinor Ochs, Emanuel A. Schegloff, and Sandra Thompson, 52–133. Cambridge, Cambridge University Press.

Chapter 5. Deontic infinitives in spoken German **153**

Schmidt, Thomas. 2016. "Good Practices in the Compilation of FOLK, the Research and Teaching Corpus of Spoken German." *International Journal of Corpus Linguistics* 21 (3): 396–418.

Selting, Margret. 2001. "Fragments of Units as Deviant Cases of Unit-Production in Conversational Talk." In *Studies in Interactional Linguistics*, ed. by Margret Selting, and Elizabeth Couper-Kuhlen, 229–258. Amsterdam: Benjamins.

Selting, Margret, Peter Auer, Dagmar Barth-Weingarten, Jörg Bergmann, Pia Bergmann, Karin Birkner, Elizabeth Couper-Kuhlen, Arnulf Deppermann, Peter Gilles, Susanne Günthner, Martin Hartung, Friederike Kern, Christine Mertzlufft, Christian Meyer, Miriam Morek, Frank Oberzaucher, Jörg Peters, Uta Quasthoff, Wilfried Schütte, Anja Stukenbrock, Susanne Uhmann. 2009. "Gesprächsanalytisches Transkriptionssystem 2 (GAT 2) [Conversation Analytic Transcription System 2 (GAT 2)]." *Gesprächsforschung* 10: 353–402.

Selting, Margret, and Elizabeth Couper-Kuhlen. 2001. "Forschungsprogramm „Interaktionale Linguistik" [Research program "Interactional Linguistics"]." *Linguistische Berichte* 187: 257–287.

Sidnell, Jack, and Tanya Stivers (eds). 2012. *The Handbook of Conversation Analysis*. John Wiley & Sons.

Skogmyr Marian, Klara. 2021. "Assessing without Words: Verbally Incomplete Utterances in Complaints." *Frontiers in Psychology*, 12: 689443.

Sorjonen, Marja-Leena. 1996. "On Repeats and Responses in Finnish Conversation." In *Interaction and Grammar*, ed. by Elinor Ochs, Emanuel A. Schegloff, and Sandra Thompson, 277–327. Cambridge: Cambridge University Press.

Sorjonen, Marja-Leena, and Liisa Raevaara. 2014. "On the Grammatical Form of Requests at the Convenience Store: Requesting as Embodied Action." In *Requesting in Social Interaction*, ed. by Paul Drew and Elizabeth Couper-Kuhlen, 243–268. Amsterdam/Philadelphia: John Benjamins.

Steensig, Jakob, Maria Jørgensen, Nicholas Mikkelsen, Karita Suomalainen, and Søren Sandager Sørensen. 2023. "Toward a Grammar of Danish Talk-in-Interaction: From Action Formation to Grammatical Description." *Research on Language and Social Interaction* 56 (2): 116–140.

Stivers, Tanya. 2005. "Modified Repeats: One Method for Asserting Primary Rights from Second Position." *Research on Language and Social Interaction* 38 (2): 131–158.

Stivers, Tanya. 2022. *The Book of Answers*. Oxford: Oxford University Press.

Tesnière, Lucien. 1959. *Éléments de syntaxe structural* [Elements of Structural Syntax]. Paris: Klincksieck.

Thompson, Sandra A., and Elizabeth Couper-Kuhlen. 2005. "The Clause as a Locus of Grammar and Interaction." *Discourse Studies* 7 (4–5): 481–505.

Thompson, Sandra A., Barbara A. Fox, and Elizabeth Couper-Kuhlen. 2015. *Grammar in Everyday Talk: Building Responsive Actions*. Cambridge: Cambridge University Press.

Urbanik, Pawel. 2021. Directives in the Construction Site: Grammatical Design and Work Phases in Second Language Interactions with Crane Operators. *Journal of Pragmatics* 178: 43–67.

Weinrich, Harald. 1993. *Textgrammatik der deutschen Sprache* [Text Grammar of the German Language]. Mannheim: Dudenverlag.

Whitehead, Kevin A. 2015. "Extreme-Case Formulations." In *The International Encyclopedia of Language and Social Interaction*, ed. by Karen Tracy, Cornelia Ilie, and Todd Sandel.

Wiggins, Sally. 2002. "Talking with Your Mouth Full: Gustatory *mmms* and the Embodiment of Pleasure." *Research on Language and Social Interaction* 35 (3): 311–336.

Wittgenstein, Ludwig. 1953. *Philosophical Investigations*. Oxford: Blackwell.

Zeschel, Arne. 2017. "*Denken* und *wissen* im gesprochenen Deutsch [*Think* and *know* in Spoken German]." In *Bewegungsverben und mentale Verben im gesprochenen Deutsch* [Motion Verbs and Mental Verbs in Spoken German], ed. by Arnulf Deppermann, Nadine Proske, and Arne Zeschel, 249–335. Tübingen: Narr.

Zifonun, Gisela, Ludger Hoffmann, and Bruno Strecker. 1997. *Grammatik der deutschen Sprache* [Grammar of German Language]. Berlin/New York: de Gruyter.

Zinken, Jörg. 2016. *Requesting Responsibility: The Morality of Grammar in Polish and English Family Interaction*. Oxford: Oxford University Press.

Zinken, Jörg. 2020. "Recruiting Assistance and Collaboration in Polish." In *Getting Others to Do Things. A Pragmatic Typology of Recruitments*, ed. by Simeon Floyd, Giovanni Rossi, and Nick J. Enfield, 281–324. Berlin: Language Science Press.

CHAPTER 6

Responses to specifying WH-questions, and their place in a comprehensive grammar of interactional Danish

Maria Jørgensen
Aarhus University

This chapter examines how interactional analyses of response formats to specifying, information-seeking WH-questions in Danish may inform a comprehensive grammar of Danish talk-in-interaction. Based on analyses in Jørgensen's work (2024), phrasal responses are shown to index sequential embeddedness and treat questions as part of an ongoing trajectory, whereas clausal responses are shown to treat questions as initiating new sequences and trajectories. This chapter analyzes how these descriptions could inform an interactional, comprehensive grammar. I find that it would be useful to include some traditional, grammatical concepts to account for the formats and their differences. However, adopting a more locally specific and positionally sensitive perspective is even more useful. Furthermore, this perspective can be used as a tool for discovering levels of organization at finer levels of granularity.

Keywords: questions, responses, phrases, clauses, syntax, social action formats, inter-unit syntax, intra-unit syntax, sequential embeddedness

1. Introduction

Questions and their responses are inherently interactional phenomena. In both traditional grammars and in interactional research, questions are understood as requests for affirmation, confirmation (Sorjonen 2001), or information, to be delivered as answers by some other interactant. However, the description of question and response formats in traditional grammars can be relatively limited. For example, in Hansen and Heltoft's (2011: 601) authoritative grammar of Danish, the authors recognize that responses to information-seeking questions (i.e., WH-questions) may be either phrasal or clausal. However, they only acknowledge this indirectly, making no comment on a possible functional difference between the

https://doi.org/10.1075/slsi.37.06jor
© 2025 John Benjamins Publishing Company

formats or any potential difference in the contexts they occur in. Meanwhile, we know from interactional research that the grammatical format of both questions and answers may vary, depending on interactional motivations, and that speakers' choice of one alternative over the other is not coincidental (e.g., Enfield et al. 2019; Fox & Thompson 2010; Hakulinen 2001; Heritage & Raymond 2005; Keevallik 2010; Raymond 2003; Sorjonen 2001; Stivers 2018; Stivers & Hayashi 2010).

Thus, questions and their responses make a good starting point for investigating how to build a comprehensive grammar that takes interaction seriously. They are interactional phenomena that are best studied in their natural setting, and an interactional comprehensive grammar would have to account for the systematic, interactionally motivated variations in their form. In this chapter, I explore some of the ways in which this could be done in such a grammar. As an example, I focus on two different response formats for answering specifying information questions (that is, questions that request limited, specific pieces of information; Fox & Thompson 2010) in Danish-talk-in-interaction, namely phrasal and clausal responses. As I demonstrate in another work (Jørgensen 2024), and as I will also demonstrate in this chapter, the two formats have different sequential home environments in which they are aligning, unproblematic responses – phrasal responses are usually found in expansion sequences, whereas clausal responses are found in base sequences. They also differ in how they position themselves in relation to the preceding question: Speakers use phrasal responses as parts of ongoing courses of action, whereas clausal responses are used to orient to questions as starting a new sequence and trajectory, where the information is not yet in the common ground (Clark 1996). An interactional grammar should account for these regularities. Thus, in this chapter, I try to answer the following research questions:

How can an interactional analysis of two practices for responding to specifying questions in Danish inform a comprehensive grammar of Danish that takes interaction seriously? What would such a grammar need to include, to be able to adequately account for the two practices and the systematicities in their distribution?

To answer the foregoing questions, I will first present a condensed version of my main analytical findings on phrasal and clausal responses (see Jørgensen 2024 for more detail). Then, in the chapter's main section (Section 4), I discuss and analyze what a comprehensive grammar of Danish would have to include to adequately account for the regularities of the two response formats. In this section, I draw inspiration from Steensig et al. (2023), who compare traditional grammatical analyses with an alternative, interactional approach, and DanTIN (2021), who propose an alternate view of syntax. I base the structure of the section on the structure of Samtalegrammatik.dk (2024a), an online, in-progress grammar of

Danish talk-in-interaction that approaches descriptions of interactional practices from two perspectives: Social Actions on the one hand, and Building Blocks, that is, linguistic and other formal resources, on the other. I will return to Samtalegrammatik.dk in Section 5.

I have three main goals for this chapter. First, I aim to contribute to research in Interactional Linguistics (e.g., Couper-Kuhlen & Selting 2018a) by testing and analyzing various ways of systematizing interactional observations into a grammatical framework. Second, I aim to contribute to a discussion of how linguists could better work with naturally occurring interaction in grammar writing. Thus, my intended readers include both interactional linguists and descriptive linguists who may not have an interactionalist background, but who are interested in working with naturally occurring interaction. Finally, the chapter is meant as a concrete step in developing the online grammar, Samtalegrammatik.dk, by discussing what should specifically be included in various parts of the grammar, by testing grammatical frameworks, and by raising various questions and concerns for future research.

The chapter is structured as follows. In Section 2, I present my data and method. In Section 3, I present an interactional analysis of the response formats in question. I use four examples to present the formats' interactional motivations and sequential home environments, including one case where a response occurs outside of its home environment "for cause." This section is a condensed version of some of my other work (Jørgensen 2024). In Section 4, I analyze how my results could be treated in a comprehensive grammar. In Section 5, I discuss the results of the previous section, and finally, I present my conclusion in Section 6.

Before I move on to my data and method, I will clarify some key terms that I use in this chapter, including the concept of *specifying questions*.

1.1   Terminology

In this chapter, I focus on responses to *specifying WH-questions* (Fox & Thompson 2010; Thompson, Fox & Couper-Kuhlen 2015), that is, questions seeking specific, limited pieces of information, rather than longer stretches of talk (i.e., *telling questions*, ibid.). In their seminal article on this matter, Fox and Thompson (2010) show that, in American English, speakers make an interactionally motivated distinction between two response formats when responding to specifying information questions. Phrasal responses (e.g., "Ten miles," as a response to the question "How far up the canyon are you?") are found to be the most common, and are simple answers, whereas clausal responses (e.g., "We came home at one thirty" as a response to "What time did we get home?") are found to be less common, and orient to something problematic in the question or sequence (ibid.; Thompson, Fox & Couper-Kuhlen 2015). As I mentioned above, speakers of Danish differentiate between the same types of formats: phrasal and clausal responses. But the interactional motivation behind the choice of response format in specifying questions in Danish talk-in-interaction seems to be different. I will return to this in Section 3.

In this chapter, *phrasal responses* are to be understood as responsive turns that deliver some requested information as a single phrase — that is, as a unit smaller than a clause. This unit may consist of a single lexeme, but it may also be a head with dependents such as determiners, adjectival modifiers, and relative clauses (Christensen & Christensen 2009:164). By *clausal response*, I mean responses that deliver some requested information in a clausal format, that is, a unit that contains at least a subject and a verb (i.e., a *nexus*; Heltoft 2013; see also Section 4.1.1.). Clausal responses may also contain other constituents, and they may be multi-clausal.

I use the term *question* in an interactional sense rather than a syntactic one — if a turn requests information, I treat it as a question. The term *interrogative* is instead used exclusively to describe turns designed with interrogative word order.

2. Data and method

The analyses in this chapter are based on my collection of 98 instances of responses to specifying WH-questions, found in 18 video-recorded conversations (7 hours and 45 minutes total) of naturally occurring Danish talk-in-interaction (see also Jørgensen 2024). Since I define questions in a interactional sense (as requests for information), the collection includes instances of other-initiated repair in cases where the repair provides additional, specific information. The collection does not include responses to open-class repair initiations (Dingemanse & Enfield 2015; Drew 1997) or those involving trouble with hearing. My data are from two interactional corpora: AULing (Samtalegrammatik.dk 2024b), hosted by Linguistics, Aarhus University, Denmark, and the publicly accessible Samtale-Bank (MacWhinney & Wagner 2010). The collection was analyzed applying Conversation Analysis (CA; Sidnell & Stivers 2013) and Interactional Linguistics (IL; Couper-Kuhlen & Selting 2018a). As mentioned above, four representative cases from the collection will be presented in Section 3.

In Section 4, I analyze and discuss how my observations may be treated in a systematic, grammatical way. I use a comparative approach in this analysis, which was inspired by Steensig et al.'s (2023) work. I test and assess the usefulness of various concepts, models, and terms used in traditional approaches to grammar, and compare them to alternative approaches that take interaction as its point of departure. I also attempt to analyze the various response formats using inter-/intra-unit syntax analysis (DanTIN 2021) and social action format models (Steensig et al. 2023; see also Fox 2007).

All excerpts presented in this chapter follow Hepburn and Bolden's (2013) transcription conventions, with the addition of the semicolon to indicate slightly falling final intonation. Embodied actions are transcribed using Mondada's (2018) conventions. Focus lines have been provided with Leipzig Glossing (Comrie, Haspelmath & Bickel 2015) for additional linguistic clarity.

3. Responses to specifying WH-questions in Danish

This section will present analyses of responses to specifying questions in Danish talk-in-interaction (see also Jørgensen 2024). Table 1 is an overview of the responses in the collection the analyses are based on.

Table 1. Overview of collection (adapted from Jørgensen 2024:326)

	Phrasal	Clausal	TOTAL
Requested information	39	35	74
No-access response	1	7	8
Unrelated responses	0	16	16
TOTAL	40	58	98

No-access responses are responses such as *Jeg ved det ikke* 'I don't know', whereas "unrelated responses" (Thompson et al. 2015) are clausal responses that do not reuse any lexical material from the question.

Fox and Thompson (2010) find phrasal responses to be the most common in their data. However, in the Danish data, clausal responses are the most common. This is an early indication that the interactional motivation behind the two response formats is different in Danish than in English. Even if we disregard no-access and unrelated clausal responses, the number of clausal responses is almost equal to the number of phrasal responses.[1] As I will argue in the following sections, the motivation instead has to do with the sequential embeddedness (Fox 2007) vs. independence of the question-response pair. Phrasal responses index — and treat their question as showing — a high degree of embeddedness in an ongoing sequence and trajectory, whereas clausal responses treat their questions

---

1. Note that in Fox & Thompson's data (2010), no-access and unrelated clausal responses are not disregarded. For this reason, they were included in the collection this chapter is based on. However, since both these response types perform fundamentally different kinds of actions than specifying responses, they are not addressed in greater detail in this analysis (cf. Jørgensen 2024).

as independent of previous talk by indexing that independence. Simultaneously, phrasal responses orient to a degree of common ground (Clark 1996) between the participants, whereas clausal responses orient to a lack of common ground. This echoes similar findings from Interactional Linguistic research. "Less minimal forms" (e.g., Thompson et al. 2015) have been shown, through analyses of practices in various languages, to index a higher degree of independence from previous talk, whereas "more minimal forms" typically orient to a higher degree of sequential embeddedness (Fox 2007), reliance on, and connection to previous talk (see, e.g., Fox 1987; Keevallik 2010; Schegloff 1996b; Raymond, Robinson et al. 2021).

One type of evidence for the claims I make in this chapter is distributional. Phrasal responses tend to occur in expansion sequences and big packages, whereas clausal responses tend to occur in base sequences. These sequences may be said to be the home environments of the response types.

In the next two subsections, I present some key examples of both response formats.

3.1 Phrasal responses that index sequential embeddedness

In Danish, speakers use phrasal responses to index sequential embeddedness. They display their understanding of the preceding question as part of a larger, ongoing sequence and course of action, and they position their response in this course of action. Consider the following excerpt, where teenagers Astrid and Britt gossip about an ex-boyfriend of Britt's. Astrid has just told Britt a story about an ex-boyfriend of hers. In line 1, Britt launches the potential beginning of a second story, informing Astrid that she once had a boyfriend who was missing part of his finger. After some initial laughter, Astrid starts to ask follow-up questions, including about the boyfriend's name (not shown). It turns out Astrid knows him.

Excerpt 1. *finger* 'Finger' (AULing_SofaSladder_05:20), face-to-face, informal

```
01 BRI: jeg havde engang en kæreste der havde mis:tet noget
        I once had a boyfriend who had lost some
02 BRI: af sin finger;
        of his finger;
((15 lines omitted, including naming the ex-boyfriend.))
18 AST: >ER DET< HAM:,
        is it him,
19 BRI: £JEh:::£ [HA HA
        yes
20 AST:         [£↑har han ↑det?£
                has he that?
```

Chapter 6. Responses to specifying WH-questions in Danish 161

```
21 BRI: £ja£ (.) .↑HU:[:::
          yes
22 AST:               [hh
23 BRI: hh %.hu=
   ast    %gaze>own fingers-->
24 AST: =.he: hvilken   ↑E::n$:.
              which-C    one-C
        .he: which one.
   bri                       $..-->
25      (0.2)
26 BRI: °£d%$en  h:er;£°
          this-C here
          this (one) here;
   ast    %gaze>BRI's hands-->
   bri    ....$L index on R index-->>
27 AST: %NEJ:?
         NO:?
   ast %gaze>BRI, wide eyes, clutches hands at chest-->>
```

In lines 18 and 20, Astrid produces two requests for confirmation, displays her recognition of Britt's ex, and treats the information in line 1 as surprising and counter to her expectations (Jørgensen 2021; Steensig et al. 2023). The question in line 20 repeats Britt's original informing as a proform-question — that is, a request for confirmation (Sorjonen 2001), formulated in pro-terms (Jørgensen 2021) — but uses the verb *har* 'has' in the present tense, thus treating the ongoing trajectory more like a news telling. With this repeat, Astrid makes more talk about the initial informing relevant, and in line 24 she asks a specifying question in a phrasal format (*hvilken en* 'which one') while looking at her hands, fingers spread out. Britt immediately starts raising her right hand to point at the index finger of her left hand (line 24), and as she touches the finger, she responds phrasally, *den her* 'this (one) here' in line 26. Astrid receipts this information with a loud *NEJ* 'no' (line 27), appropriately displaying shock and surprise, and orienting to the appropriateness of a phrasal response. She then continues to ask follow-up questions (not shown), and further expands on the information.

Astrid's specifying question in line 24 is highly embedded in the current sequence. It is part of a series of follow-up questions, each of which requests information about something previously established, and collaboratively builds the story or news-telling sequence underway. Grammatically, the question relies on the referents established by the initial informing and uses a locally subsequent anaphoric *en* 'one' to reference the word *finger* 'finger' (cf. Schegloff 1996b; Fox 1987) and thus treat the information in line 1 as in the common ground (Clark 1996).

Britt's response in line 26 is also phrasal, and, like Astrid's phrasal question, relies on the original informing and the trajectory it has launched. With her minimal phrasal response, she treats the question as something that requires only a small operation for the sequence to continue. Britt thus aligns herself with the sequential embeddedness of the question and shows her understanding of it as asked in the service of an ongoing course of action. Additionally, she orients to a certain degree of information as already established. Thus, the phrasal response works like a tying mechanism (Sacks 1992: 159). Both question and response may further be said to be grammatically parasitic (Raymond, Robinson et al. 2021) on previous utterances: Their phrasal form is afforded by the constituents having been established.

Excerpt (1) represents a typical sequential environment of phrasal responses in the collection this analysis is based on: They mostly occur in expansion sequences (Schegloff 2007) or as responses to follow-up questions in collaboratively built "big packages" (Couper-Kuhlen & Selting 2018b), such as stories or news-tellings.

Phrasal responses' capacity to index sequential embeddedness and imply a degree of shared, established information seems to have certain epistemic implications: They allow participants to appeal to common ground outside the immediate sequence, as in Excerpt (2) below. In this excerpt, three elderly women are talking about a successful couple they know. Eva suggests that the husband's large income is the reason the couple have done well for themselves (omitted). Lis counters this by suggesting that the wife is the breadwinner (lines 1–2), then accounts for this. She orients to Kirsten as being in the know, with the shared knowledge particle *jo* in line 3 (cf. Heinemann, Lindström & Steensig 2011), but then looks at Eva (line 3) and instead directs the utterance at her, re-designing her account as news (line 6). Eva receipts it as such with a nod and raised eyebrows (lines 9–11). After the account is completed (omitted), Eva produces a final confirmation token (line 18), after which Kirsten opens an expansion sequence by asking for the wife's job title with a specifying question (line 19).

Excerpt 2. *revisor* 'Accountant' (TalkBank_OmFodbold_01:56), face to face, informal

```
01 LIS: jeg tror nok snarere det hende
        I do rather think it's her
    lis  >>gaze>KIR-->

02 LIS: der slæver pengene hjem_
        who drags the money home_

03 LIS: hu[n er] jo:$::;=
        she is JO;
    lis            $gaze>EVA-->

04 KIR: [ja:;]
         yes;

05 KIR: =ja- hun [ha- har også;]
         yes she ha- has also;
```

Chapter 6. Responses to specifying WH-questions in Danish **163**

```
06 LIS:        [hun er revi:s][or;]
                she is an acco:untant;

07 KIR:                       [ja_]
                               yes_

08    (0.2)

09 KIR: ¤hun ø:::h
         she u:::h
   eva ¤nod, raise eyebrows, close eyes-->

10 LIS: å  hun¤
        and she
   eva       -->¤

11 LIS: [har-  tager den e:ne] uddannelse efter den anden
        has-   takes one education after the other

12 KIR: [har også en god løn;]
        has also a good wage;

((5 lines omitted))

18 EVA: #aerh#_

        yeah_

19 KIR: ¤hva $e:rt        hun er.
        what COP.PRS=it-N she  COP.PRS
        what is it she is. (i.e. what does she do)
   kir ¤turns head, gaze>LIS, furrowed brow-->
   lis     -->$gaze>KIR-->>

20 LIS: revi:sor¤;
        accountant;
   kir -->¤eyebrow raise, turns head, gaze>forward>>

21 KIR: .hhh revi:[so:   ]r.=
        .hhh accountant.

22 LIS:           [°°ja°°]
                   yes

23 KIR: =ja det rigtigt.
        yes that's right.
```

The format of Kirsten's question (*hva er:t hun er* 'what is it she is/does' rather than *hva er hun* 'what is she') is routinely used to mark requested information as known, but forgotten (Hamann & Nielsen 2022) — Kirsten is specifically asking for repair because of a problem of remembering. She has indeed shown her independent knowledge of the wife's wage (lines 4, 5, 7, 9, 12). This has happened in overlapping speech, independently of Lis's account, and the question's format suggests that Kirsten has not heard Lis mention the wife's occupation.[2] She is not asking for auditive repair but is instead trying to remember the job title.

Kirsten's question is part of a larger sequence, trajectory, and course of action: She opens the post-expansion to solve her memory issue, which will allow for satisfactory sequence closure — thus, we may see the question as part of an ongoing course of action. Lis orients to it as such, responding immediately and minimally with all that is needed for the trajectory to reach a satisfactory conclusion, her phrasal response aligning with Kirsten's question. In receipt of this, Kirsten unfurrows her brow (line 20), nods while turning away, and registers the information as now remembered with a repeat (line 19; cf. Nissen, 2015). With her final *ja det rigtigt* 'yes that's right', Kirsten orients to the information as already known, and her receipts thus treat Lis's response as both acceptable and as specifically repairing her remembrance issue.

Apart from showing a response in its sequential home environment, Excerpt (2) thus additionally shows participant orientation to an epistemic dimension. It seems that the dependence of phrasal responses on previous talk allows them to appeal to common ground that is beyond the immediate sequence.

To summarize, phrasal responses in Danish index sequential embeddedness, and they appeal to knowledge in the common ground. They orient to their questions as part of ongoing courses of action, and as requests for only minimal operations in the service of a given course of action.

In the next section, I will present an example of a clausal response in its typical home environment, and also a case where it occurs outside its home environment, but does so "for cause" — i.e., a deviant case.

3.2 Clausal responses that index independence

Where phrasal responses orient to, and index, embeddedness in an ongoing sequence, clausal responses orient to the question as independent of previous talk, and index that same independence themselves. Clausal responses in Danish typically occur in base sequences (Schegloff 2007), and often respond to questions that act as topic proffers. This is the case in Excerpt (3) below. Preben and Thomas are colleagues, and are drinking beer in Preben's living room. In line 5, Preben launches a new topic, and uses a specifying WH-question as a topic proffer.

---

2. Close inspection of the video data suggests that the *ja* 'yes' in line 7 extends Kirsten's agreement from lines 4 and 5. It seems to be produced as part of Kirsten's independent knowledge-assertion project, rather than as a response to line 6.

Chapter 6. Responses to specifying WH-questions in Danish   165

Excerpt 3. *Nørre Snede* 'Nørre Snede' (TalkBank_Preben&Thomas _29:50), face to face, informal

```
01 PRE: >hheh<.

02      (0.5)

03 PRE: °.h:$¤rgnh sådn er det.°
            .h:rngh that's how it is.
        pre      $grabs lighter
        tho         ¤reaches for bottle-->

04      (.) $ (.) ¤ (0.9) ¤ (2.5) $ ¤ (.)
        pre      $lights cig.         $puts lighter down
        tho         -->¤grabs ¤sips      ¤lowers bottle-->

05 PRE: hvor bo:r    du    ¤egentlig henne?
        where live-PRS you.SG actually at
        where do you live by the way?
        tho                  -->¤bottle hits table

06      (.)

07 THO: .mgh jeg bor       ude  i  nørre snede.
            I    live-PRS out  in north snede
        .mhg I live out in TOWN-NAME1.

08      (0.9)

09 PRE: ↓n:ørre [snede.
        TOWN-NAME1.

10 THO:         [#ø:hm#
                 uhm

11      (0.3)

12 THO: jeg ved ikk om du ved nør:- nørre sundby;
        I don't know if you know nør:- TOWN-NAME2;

13      (0.4)

14 PRE: nå::: ↑jo=nørre snede;
        oh    yeah TOWN-NAME1;
```

Preben's question (line 5) requests specific information, such as a town name or an address. Thomas delivers this information in a full clausal format (line 7), and does so immediately (after swallowing a sip of beer, the sound of which can be heard at the beginning of the turn).

Preben's topic-proffering question follows observable moves towards topic and sequence closure (lines 1 and 3), as well as a lapse (line 4), and thus may be seen as starting a new base sequence. Additionally, it is designed with the adverb *egentlig* 'actually, by the way', which functions as a misplacement marker (cf. Clift 2001). This marks the question's independence from preceding talk, hearable as not just a request for specific information, but also as a topic proffer that initiates a new course of action and requests information about which the participants share no common ground (Clark 1996). Thus, two aspects are relevant for Thomas to orient to in his response: delivering the requested information, and accepting or rejecting the topic proffering — and, if he accepts, to orient to the question as presenting a new, expandable topic.

Thomas's clausal response is immediate. As a second action, it grammatically relies on the previous turn by recycling the subject and verb, adjusted for deixis. However, compared to a phrasal response, it does constitute a "less grammatically parasitic format" (Raymond, Robinson et al. 2021) — this turn does not depend on previous talk to be interpretable. Delivering his response in a clausal format gives Thomas's response some independence. This allows him to show agency in accepting the new topic proposed by Preben — a topic on which he is the epistemic authority (Heritage & Raymond 2005, Heritage 2012), and on which the two share no common ground yet. At the same time, Thomas is able to deliver the information that was requested. His clausal response thus allows him to orient not only to the information request, but also to the fact that the question launches a new trajectory, which Thomas accepts as a relevant topic that can be further developed. Indeed, once Preben's initial trouble (line 9) locating the town Thomas lives in is resolved, Thomas goes on to talk more about the town and what it is like to live there (not shown), and he continues to orient to the question as a topic proffer.

Although both phrasal and clausal responses are mostly found in their sequential home environments — that is, clausal responses in base sequences where new trajectories and courses of action are launched, and phrasal responses in sequence expansions where trajectories are ongoing — both response types are sometimes found outside of these environments. However, when we analyze such deviant cases, we see that the response formats retain the interactional implications of their home environments. They occur outside their environment "for cause," and speakers use them as resources to achieve particular effects or address various issues. For example, a phrasal response in a base sequence may be seen to appeal to shared knowledge and recontextualize previous talk, perhaps even to hint that the response to the question asked in a base sequence should have been obvious (Jørgensen 2024). Clausal responses may instead be used to claim epistemic authority. Both formats may also be used to manage trajectories of talk, as illustrated in the following deviant case.

Twenty-something friends Lina and Sisse have dyed Lina's hair, and are now waiting for it to dry. They are scrolling through social media on their phones while chatting. Sisse finds a picture of a chocolate cake and shows it to Lina, then declares that she could eat some cake right now (line 1). This prompts Lina, at whose home they are, to tell Sisse that she has some cake in the freezer.

Chapter 6. Responses to specifying WH-questions in Danish **167**

Excerpt 4. *kage* 'Cake' (AULing_haarfarvning2_07:45), face to face, informal

```
01 SIS: E::J: fuck jeg ku godt spise kage_
        PRT fuck I could eat some cake_

02      (0.3)

03 LIN: <jeg har en kage i fryseren;>
        I have a cake in the freezer;

04 SIS: hva  forn        e:n;
        what for=ART-C   one-C
        which one/kind;

05      (0.2)

06 LIN: de:t bare en     helt  >almindelig< chokoladekage_=
        it=is just ART-C wholly ordinary    chocolate-cake
        it's just a totally ordinary chocolate cake_

07 LIN: =aå de:t bare sån en helt tynd en
        ou it's just like a totally thin one

08 LIN: å så: det meningen der ska smørcreme udenom;
        and then buttercream is meant to go around it;

09      (0.2)

10 LIN: men du ka ikk ha smørcreme #ka du.#
        but you don't like buttercream do you.

11 SIS: #jo:#:,
        yes,

12 LIN: ka du;
        do you;
```

Sisse treats Lina's informing in line 3 as a potential offer and launches an insert sequence meant to determine what kind of cake it is, so she can decide whether or not to accept the offer. The question is a specifying, phrasal question that uses a common construction, *hva forn en* 'what for a one' (Hansen & Steensig 2018). Although not all questions that receive phrasal responses in my collection are themselves phrasal, practically all phrasal-format questions receive phrasal responses. The example above presents the only phrasal question in the collection that receives a clausal response, namely Lina's eventual response in line 6. As a clausal response to a question in an insert sequence, and as a clausal response to a phrasal question, this constitutes a deviant case. However, it seems to appear here for cause.

Lina suddenly remembers that there is a condition that may undermine her offer: The cake needs to be covered in buttercream to be appealing (line 8). However, as far as she knows, Sisse does not like buttercream (line 10). There is thus an issue concerning the premise of the offer, as the cake in the freezer may not appeal to Sisse in the first place. Lina must address this issue to avoid the moral transgression (Stivers, Mondada & Steensig 2011) of forgetting or ignoring what she may be supposed to know about Sisse and her tastes.

Lina's response is clausal — that is, a less minimal, more grammatically independent format. By indexing a higher degree of independence, Lina shows that she is "breaking the frame of the ongoing trajectory" (Jørgensen 2024:340) and launching an account of why the offer may be inappropriate (lines 7–10). The additional clause-expanding (Thompson et al. 2015) constituents, *bare* 'just' and *almindelig* 'ordinary', help Lina to address the issue by downgrading the cake as it is (i.e., without buttercream).[3] The constituents seem tied to her argument that buttercream is needed, and that therefore, the cake is not suitable for Sisse, as she immediately latches her account to the question. An additional argument for this appears in lines 11–12. Sisse disconfirms Lina's assumption of her preferences with a *jo* 'yes2' (used to disaffirm/disconfirm negatively framed questions; Heinemann 2015), effectively saying that she *does* like buttercream. Lina then asks for a confirmation with a proform-question (Jørgensen 2021), *kan du*, showing that Sisse's non-issue with buttercream was counter to her expectations (see also Jørgensen in prep.).

To summarize, clausal responses usually occur in base sequences, where they treat their questions as launching new trajectories, and also index this independence by implying a lack of established common ground between the interactants. They are useful for delivering requested information and orienting to the launch of a new sequence and trajectory, typically a topic on which the answerer is an authority.

Both phrasal and clausal responses to specifying questions have particular home environments in which they are common, unproblematic, and aligning. However, their distribution is not deterministic, and in cases where the response types occur outside of their home environment, they carry the same implications as they do in their home environments. Thus, they may be used as resources to manage epistemic issues or address the trajectory of talk, for example, to pave the way for accounts or other new directions.

4. How do the analyses inform a comprehensive grammar of Danish?

In this section, I examine how the above-mentioned analyses and the collection on which they are based could inform a reference grammar that takes interaction seriously. What would such a grammar have to capture and codify (Evans & Dench 2006:1) to adequately account for the orderliness of the two response

---

3. These minor changes do not make the response a non-phrase-in-clause (Fox & Thompson 2010) or unrelated causal response (Thompson et al. 2015). The response still delivers the requested information.

practices analyzed in the section above — and how should this orderliness be represented? Although many insights could be drawn from the analyses and the collection behind them, this chapter will focus on the fact that the two response practices have different grammatical formats (phrasal vs. clausal), that they occur in different sequential environments (base sequences vs. expansion sequences; Schegloff 2007), and that they orient to different aspects in the interaction (sequential embeddedness or independence; common ground or lack thereof; Clark 1996).

To examine this, I use the framework of the in-progress grammar of Danish talk-in-interaction, Samtalegrammatik.dk (2024a; see also Section 1). In the next sections, I first examine how the analyses may inform the Building Blocks section of the grammar, in which various linguistic, prosodic, and embodied resources are described. Then I examine how the analyses may inform the grammar's Social Actions section, in which social actions are described in abstract terms.

4.1 The impact of the analyses on the Building Blocks section of the grammar of Danish

Since interactants make a systematic, interactionally motivated distinction between phrases and clauses, an interactional reference grammar of Danish should include descriptions and definitions of both these unit types. Furthermore, the two response formats have a strong tendency to occur in different sequential environments. Our grammar needs to account for this positional sensitivity (Schegloff 1996a).

In Sections 4.1.1 and 4.1.2, I first explore various possible ways to describe phrases and clauses as units, both abstractly and as they occur in interaction. I discuss and analyze how traditional grammatical approaches can and cannot contribute to such descriptions. In Section 4.2, I argue that an expanded view of syntax (DanTIN 2021; Steensig et al. 2023) can synthesize the organization of elements on a turn-level and on a sequential level. Here, I also present an example of a detailed analysis in this framework, which demonstrates the possibilities of this approach, and which serves as a tool for discovery.

4.1.1 Defining phrases and clauses: Abstract models

In my analyses, participants make an interactionally motivated, abstract distinction between phrases as one category, and clauses as another. Longer phrases seem to work in the same way as shorter phrases, and shorter clauses seem to work in the same way as longer clauses (cf. Jørgensen 2024). Thus, distinguishing between phrases and clauses on an abstract level seems relevant to interaction, and warrants a description of both unit types in our interactional reference grammar of Danish.

We might want to look to traditional grammatical accounts of Danish to get an idea of how we might define these units. Traditional accounts define phrases as non-clausal units that consist of a head and possibly one or more dependent elements (e.g., Christensen & Christensen 2009:164), whereas clauses are usually defined as units that contain at least a *nexus* (Jespersen 1937; Heltoft 2013) — that is, both a subject and a verb — and possibly other constituents (e.g., Christensen & Christensen 2009:198 ff.). Elements of both phrases and clauses are described as predictably organized: In noun phrases, for example, determiners, numerals, and adjectival modifiers precede the head (in that order), whereas modifiers such as prepositional phrases and relative clauses follow (Christensen & Christensen 2009:166). In clauses, the predictable order of elements is typically demonstrated by the so-called topological field model (Christensen & Christensen 2009; Diderichsen 1946). Table 2 shows how clausal responses to WH-questions, taken from the analyses in Section 3 and from my broader collection, fit into this model.[4]

The front field in the model may contain all nominal and adverbial constituents. If the grammatical subject occurs in this field, the subject slot after the finite verb is left unoccupied; if another constituent occurs in the front field, the subject will instead occur in the subject slot. In the last example, I have conflated the front field and the finite verb field because the copula verb *er* 'be.PRS' has been reduced to a lengthening of the pronoun *det* 'it'. This copula reduction, and sometimes also copula drop, is a widespread grammatical feature of Danish talk-in-interaction; it is treated in depth by Sørensen (this volume).

Table 2 below shows that clausal structures from interactional Danish fit into the topological model. We may wish to include such models in our grammar, since they accurately and consistently predict the possible order of elements in our interactional data. The fixed order of elements is also something to which speakers orient when projecting possible turn progression and completion (DanTIN 2021), which makes it important to include in the grammar.

The concept of *nexus* — most commonly used to describe the connection between subject and verb, and the idea that what this connection creates, that is, a clause, is more than the sum of its parts — has been part of the Danish grammatical tradition since it was introduced by Otto Jespersen (1937), and it has generally been found useful for defining various structures, most importantly clauses (Heltoft 2013). The analyses in this chapter suggest that *nexus* may also be a useful concept for an interactional comprehensive grammar.

---

4. See Puggaard (2019) and Steensig et al. (2023) for similar proposals and results.

Chapter 6. Responses to specifying WH-questions in Danish   171

Table 2. Examples of clausal responses in the topological field model

Conjunction field	Front field	Nexus field					Content field	
Conjunctionals	Nominals and adverbials	Finite verb	Subject	Central adverbs	Infinite verb(s)	Nominals		Adverbials
	jeg *I*	har *have*	–		været *been*			der i ni måneder nu_ *there for nine months now*
.mgh	jeg *I*	bor *live*	–					ude i nørre snede. *out in TOWN NAME*
	hun *she*	↑filmer *is filming*	–			øs; *us*		
jam *yes_ but*	han *he*	har *has*	–	jo *PRT*				i: tusindvis; *thousands*
	det *that*	har *have*	Vi *we*	li:ge *just*	gjort_ *done*			
	de:t *it's*		–	bare *just*		en helt >almindelig< chokoladekage_ *a totally ordinary chocolate cake*		

4.1.2   *Defining phrases and clauses as they occur in interaction*

As I argued above, some abstract structures and terms may be useful and relevant when defining phrases and clauses. However, the grammatical description may also be done in a way that comes closer to the way phrasal and clausal responses actually behave in interaction.

The two response formats examined in this chapter are paradigmatic alternatives: Both unit types may constitute complete turns. As mentioned in the analysis, one potential explanation for this correlation between "more minimal" forms (Thompson et al. 2015) and sequential embeddedness, on the one hand, and "less minimal forms" (ibid.) and sequential independence, on the other, is grammatical parasitism (Raymond, Robinson et al. 2021): the grammatical dependence of a turn on previous talk. The definition of phrases and clauses in our reference grammar must explicitly state that phrases may constitute fully-fledged turns-at-talk and that these are grammatically more parasitic on previous turns, relying on what has been established and leaving "[previous constituents] intact" by not expressing them, as Hakulinen and Sorjonen (2009:127) suggest for verb repeat second assessments in Finnish. Clauses should be defined as more grammatically independent, though clauses in second position, such as the responses presented in this chapter, will often recycle material from previous turns (adjusted for deixis).

It is an empirical question for the grammar to what degree the principle of parasitism may be observed in other types of practices (see Thompson et al. 2015:271). If a general principle that is found throughout practices in Danish is that more parasitic turns achieve a closer connection to previous talk whereas less parasitic turns achieve greater independence, we may wish to write a separate grammar entry on parasitism, and perhaps one that addresses how different actions in paradigmatic relationships may occur on a "cline of minimality" (Raymond, Robinson et al. 2021).

Describing phrasal turns-at-talk as more parasitic is a good alternative to describing them as "elliptical," which is often done in traditional grammars. Seeing phrases as ellipses implies that they are constituents of a partly omitted clause whose other elements may be inferred from the context, which implies that they "correspond," on some level, to an expanded variant of the proposition (Thompson et al. 2015:298). However, our two response formats are equally valid and complete alternatives with different interactional motivations, which an elliptical view would overlook.

4.1.3 Inter- and intra-unit syntax: Product syntax models

So far, I have been concerned with what the grammar should include in its definition of phrases and clauses. As mentioned above, the abstract models for ordering elements in phrases and clauses are useful for discussing projection, and since speakers in the analyses of our response formats differentiate on an abstract level between phrases and clauses, it seems useful to be able to describe them on that level. However, there are things that the abstract models do not capture. First, the models are atemporal and non-sequential, which means that they cannot address the fact that the two response formats systematically occur in different sequential environments. This positional sensitivity (Schegloff 1996a) needs to be addressed in a comprehensive, interactional grammar. Secondly, the models are, by definition, neither local nor specific. Although their abstractness is useful in some respects, it is inadequate in other ways. Social action formats — that is, particular formats that accomplish particular actions in particular sequential positions (Fox

2007) — are local and specific (e.g., Fox & Heinemann 2017), and we would want a grammar to capture this. It might be particularly important to consider this in the case of phrasal questions and responses: on what, exactly, are they parasitic, and how? This is an important aspect of what makes them index embeddedness, and it might be more systematic than one might think at first glance.

For our grammar to adequately address the positional sensitivity of the two practices, we would need it to consider temporality and sequential context. For this, the concepts of *inter-* and *intra-unit syntax* may be useful. This approach, proposed by the Samtalegrammatik.dk research group (see DanTIN 2021), is inspired by Auer (2005, 2014), Anward (2015), and Anward and Nordberg (2005), and considers syntax along two different axes: one sequential or inter-unit, and one TCU-based or intra-unit. It suggests that participants use their understanding of valency, dependency, and topology, and their understanding of courses of action and knowledge of specific social action formats (Fox 2007), including their typical sequential positions (DanTIN 2021:1), to project the specific action that is underway at any given moment, which allows them to supply relevant next actions at an appropriate time.

DanTIN (2021) differentiates between the "process syntax" and the "product syntax" of particular social actions. The process syntax concerns how interactants look for relevant nexts and is informed by our understanding of projection in interaction (e.g., Sacks, Schegloff and Jefferson 1974; Auer 2005; see also Hopper 2011). Each new element produced in an utterance gradually, and in real time, changes projectability, and thus limits what action interactants may ascribe to an utterance among a limited selection of potentially relevant nexts, finally narrowing it down to a projectable action. The product syntax is instead a model that displays the general pattern of particular social action formats that interactants rely on when they recognize actions in utterances and sequences. The analyses in Section 3 reveal that there should be at least two separate product syntax models to represent the different inter-unit syntax of the response practices as they behave in their home environments. For example, they could look like Figure 1.

The model in Figure 1 should be read as follows: At any point in a conversation, but often after sequence and/or topic closings, or following practices that normatively indicate these things, it is possible (but not mandatory) for speakers to open a new potential trajectory in a base sequence (F_b– first pair part of base sequence; cf. Schegloff 2007) with a specifying question, for example, in the form of a topic proffer (cf. Section 3 and Jørgensen 2024). In this case, speakers normatively respond in a clausal format, completing the base sequence (S_b — second pair part of base sequence). In contrast, a model for phrasal responses could be schematized as in Figure 2.

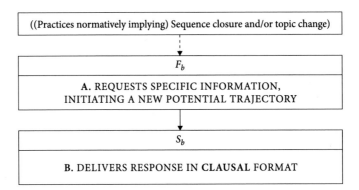

Figure 1. Inter-unit product syntax for clausal responses to specifying WH-questions

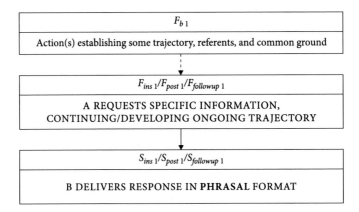

Figure 2. Inter-unit product syntax for phrasal responses to specifying WH-questions

The figure should be read as follows: Following actions that establish a course of action and common ground — for example in the form of particular referents — speakers may (but do not necessarily) ask a specifying question that continues the unfolding of the ongoing trajectory. They can, for example, do this by asking follow-up questions to help develop a story, or by opening insert- or post-expansion sequences requesting repair (cf. Section 3 and Jørgensen 2024). If such a question is asked, responses will normatively be delivered in a phrasal format, which completes the expansion or follow-up-question sequence.

Thus, by considering syntax as ordering of elements along both an in-utterance (intra-unit) and a sequential (inter-unit) axis, we are better able to capture one of the systematicities of phrasal and clausal responses, as well as differentiate between them. Relying on these syntactic patterns may be what allows the responses to be used as resources when they occur outside their home environments.

4.1.4 *Inter- and intra-unit syntax: Social action format models*

Although the two models presented above capture key intra-unit differences between the two response formats, they are not locally specific. For example, they do not show where the lexical material of the responses comes from (e.g., if it is reused from previous talk). However, inter- and intra-unit syntactic analysis may also be used to develop social action format models (Steensig et al. 2023; see also Fox 2007) of particular practices. These models combine insights from both inter- and intra-unit syntactic analysis, to provide a positionally sensitive, local, and specific overview of particular practices. These models supplement both the information in the product syntax models above, and the information in the topological field model. Analyzing practices in terms of their social action formats in this way may even be used to reveal systematicities at finer levels of granularity (Schegloff 2000; see also Fox and Raymond this volume). In this section, I will demonstrate this analytical approach and its potential, by using the phrasal specifying question and its phrasal response in Excerpt (1) from Section 3 as my starting point. I will go through the process syntax first — that is, the ongoing projectability of each turn. For both the question and the response, I start with the inter-unit syntax (i.e., the sequential order), then move to the intra-unit syntax (i.e., order of elements in the turn). I then examine how we can use this way of working with syntax to discover more details at finer levels of granularity, and finally, I propose a social action format model in two steps.

Let us first consider the inter-unit syntax of the specifying question in line 20 of Excerpt (1) (repeated as a detail below as Excerpt (5)). It is a first action in an adjacency pair, but more broadly, it comes at an interesting point in the trajectory. Astrid has started to ask follow-up questions, each of which takes a locally subsequent format (Schegloff 1996b). Their formats show that the talk is part of an ongoing trajectory and is developing something previously established. Furthermore, Astrid has taken on the role of an excited follow-up questioner, an almost interviewer-like role, as the one who drives the trajectory forward. More follow-up questions from her would be likely and relevant next actions. Finally, it is worth noting that the second follow-up question in the series, a proform-question (Jørgensen 2021; Steensig et al. 2023) in line 20, uses a pro-term repeat (*det* 'that') of the original informing in line 1, with the verb now in the present tense, treating it more like news.

Excerpt 5. *finger* 'Finger' — detail 1 (AULing_SofaSladder_05:20), face-to-face, informal

```
01 BRI: jeg havde engang en kæreste der havde mis:tet noget
        I once had a boyfriend who had lost some
02 BRI: af sin finger;
        of his finger;
((17 lines omitted, including naming the ex-boyfriend.))
```

```
20 AST:      [£↑har han ↑det?£
               has he   that?
21 BRI: £ja£ (.) .↑HU:[:::
         yes
22 AST:             [hh
23 BRI: hh %.hu=
     ast    %gaze>own fingers-->
24 AST: =.he: hvilken ↑E::n$:.
         .he: which one.
     bri                 $..-->
```

As described in Section 3, the proform-question (Jørgensen 2021) in line 20 allows Astrid to reestablish the ongoing trajectory of Britt's original informing, which makes talk on its specifics relevant. All in all, a follow-up question aimed at unfolding something in the original informing is a highly relevant next action. We note, moreover, that the two questions establish not just a pattern of Astrid asking questions, but also a rhythmic pattern of questions with two strongly stressed syllables.

Let us now consider the intra-unit syntax, that is, the syntactic configuration of the turn and the real-time projectability of its components. At line 24, after an initial inbreath, which signals that she will indeed be the next person to speak, Astrid produces a high-pitched, stressed question word, ↑*hvilken* 'which', which sharply narrows the number of possible actions underway. Combined with Astrid's looking at her fingers, the action underway may only be the beginning of a specifying question. The content of the question — which finger was affected — is highly projectable at this point: The question immediately follows the proform reintroduction of the line 1 informing; *hvilken* asks for an identification of a specific kind or instance in a category in the common gender (-*n*), and Astrid looks at her fingers — also a common-gender word. Britt is indeed able to recognize this as a complete question very quickly, and she starts the embodied part of a response before the last element of the question is even finished. This last element is a loud, stressed proterm ↑↑*E::n* 'one (common gender)', which asks Britt to identify the affected finger. As mentioned, Britt immediately recognizes this as a completed question.

The phrasal format of the question seems afforded by various aspects of the question's inter-unit syntax, that is, its integration into the ongoing big package sequence and course of action (Astrid asking follow-up questions), the projectability of a follow-up question about the informing as a relevant next, and the continuation of the questions' rhythmic pattern. The clear projectability of its intra-unit components' content seems to contribute as well, as described above. Britt's quick reaction to it is possible because of these elements. Additionally, she may recognize the question as being implemented with a sedimented social action format (Fox 2007), which further aids her process of action ascription (cf. DanTIN 2021; Steensig et al. 2023). Indeed, if we examine all phrasal questions in the collection (11 in total), we find the following common features:

1. All are sequentially embedded in an ongoing trajectory;
2. All are preceded by (full or proform copies of) informings in this trajectory; these informings may occur immediately before the question, or be slightly removed by insert sequences or silences, for example.

All the questions request either

3. More information about an already-present constituent in the informing (often subject or object)

or

4. Information about things that could have been additional constituents of the informing.[5]

Our current example has the first three features. So does the question in Excerpt (4), Section 3.2. Two additional questions in my collection, shown as Excerpts (6) and (7) below, also have the first three features in the list. In Excerpt (6), two female students are working on a paper. The women look at their laptops and papers while eating cake, and do not look at each other, which accounts for the lapses (lines 2, 4, 6, 9 and 11).

Excerpt 6. *stadier* 'Stages' [AULing_StudiegruppeLIN2011_13:46], face-to-face, **informal**

```
01 YRS: m: egentlig var det en ret god en hun ha:vde der;
        but actually it was a pretty good one she had there;
02      (1.9)
03 YRS: altså >det var jo sån< ret overskueligt.
        PRT it was PRT like pretty clear.
04      (0.6)
05 SØS: >hvilken< en;
        which-c   one-C
        which one;
06      (0.7)
07 YRS: den hvor hun: taget de fem: stadier på;=
        the one where she's added the five stages;[6]
```

---

5. See Jørgensen (2023).

6. From the information accessible in the data, it seems that the students' professor has presented them with a table or illustration of a psychological model, then added another model onto that illustration (she has "added the [model of] five stages [to another model]") to more clearly illustrate the interplay between the factors the two models represent.

```
08 SØS: =.mkt
09      (2.2)
10 SØS: nå:: ja ↑billedet;
        oh yes the picture;
11      (0.8)
12 YRS: jah=m hva kalder m::- tabel_
        yes=but what do you call- table_
```

Yrsa announces that something a professor of theirs used in a lecture was "pretty good" (line 1), which implies that it could be useful for their paper. The referent is unclear, and Søs asks for repair of the constituent with the specifying question *hvilken en* 'which one' (line 5) in an insert sequence. Her use of *hvilken* 'which' treats the constituent as part of some category, although it is a vague one. Yrsa offers repair in line 7, which is still vague. Søs then offers a candidate understanding, "the picture," marked with *nå ja*, showing now-realization. Yrsa confirms this tentatively, and offers the more precise referent, *tabel* 'table'.

Excerpt (7), from Astrid and Britt's conversation on a sofa at their school (cf. Excerpt (1)), has Britt informing Astrid that she has potato chips and soda in her bag (lines 1–2 and 4).

Excerpt 7. *chips* 'Chips' (AULing_SofaSladder_ 07:32), face-to-face, informal

```
01 BRI: og jeg har chips >inde i min<
        and I have chips inside my
02      taske [>som ligger< lige derin]de;=
        bag which lies right in there;
03 AST:       [.MT=A:e:j::;            ]
              PRT
04 BRI: =og £co::laf;
         and cola;
05 AST: å:rh hvilken chips_
        PRT  which-C potato.chip.C
        PRT which [kind of] chips_
06 BRI: >°ghrn°<=m: de de::r;=
                   those there;
07      =hva hedder de. ((word search))
        what are they called.
```

Astrid's drawn-out *aej* (line 3) shows appreciation of the chips, and possibly regret that the chips are out of reach in an adjacent room (cf. line 2). Astrid's show of interest possibly treats Britt's informing as an offer. Britt then adds an increment to her informing, *og cola* 'and cola' (line 4). Astrid, however, continues to orient to the chips and asks for specification of the type in an insert sequence (*hvilken chips* 'which (kind of) chips', line 5). To show that she is targeting the constituent *chips*, and not the recently added *cola*, she repeats it as a full lexical copy.

The questions in Excerpts (6) and (7) function similarly to the questions in Excerpts (1) and (4). Sequentially, all appear in an insert sequence. Functionally, each asks that a constituent in a preceding informing be specified in greater detail or selected as a specific instance of some category to which it belongs (of all the fingers, which specific one was affected?). Linguistically, they are structured in a very similar way, as illustrated in Table 3.

Table 3. Intra-unit structure, specifying questions that seek an instance of a specific category

Excerpt	Question word	(Pro-term) copy of informing constituent selected for further detail
Finger, ex. 1	hvilken	↑E::n:.
[AULing_SS_05:43]	which-c	one-c
	which	*One*
Kage, ex. 4	hva forn	e:n;
[AULing_HF2_07:48]	what for=ART.C	one-c
	which	*one/kind*
Stadier, ex. 6	hvilken	en;
[AULing_SGLIN_11-13:46]	which-c	one-c
	which	*one*
Chips, ex. 7	hvilken	chips_
[AULing_SS_07:35]	which-c	potato.chip.c
	which	*chips*

With the foregoing information, we can construct a social action format model (Steensig et al. 2023) for specifying questions that target constituents of a previous, sequentially embedded informing, and combine our inter- and intra-unit insights as in Figure 3.

Examining turns in terms of inter- and intra-unit syntax may reveal systematicities at finer levels of granularity and make us aware that specifying questions may have various specific social action formats on which speakers rely in action formation and ascription. Furthermore, using this perspective and the model above to present the acquired insights supplements the abstract unit models discussed in Section 4.1.1 by presenting a more local, specific, and positionally sensitive perspective: We see the relevance of the format's lexical material, systematicities in what constitutes the turn, and when this particular format occurs. Furthermore, we can show how these questions are afforded by an informing embedded in the same trajectory, as well as how they are embedded in this trajectory in terms of grammar, sequence, action, and prosody.

Let us now turn to the specifying response that follows in Excerpt (1), shown here as Excerpt (8), to examine its inter- and intra-unit syntax. This will allow for an expansion of the social action format model in Figure 3, eventually giving us a comprehensive picture of the practice.

Excerpt 8. *finger* 'Finger' – detail 2 (AULing_SofaSladder_05:20), face-to-face, informal

```
24 AST: =.he: hvilken ↑E::n$:.
             which-c  one-c
        .he: which one.
    bri                    $...-->

25      (0.2)

26 BRI: °£d%$en h:er;£°
         it-C here
         this (one) here;
    ast     %gaze>BRI's hands-->
    bri     ....$L index on R index-->>
```

On the inter-unit syntax level, a response that provides the requested information is the conditionally relevant next action. It may also be relevant for Britt to show an orientation to the question as part of an ongoing trajectory. We might expect this response to take a phrasal (or, perhaps, a purely embodied) format, considering this position in the course of action, and the phrasal format of the question.

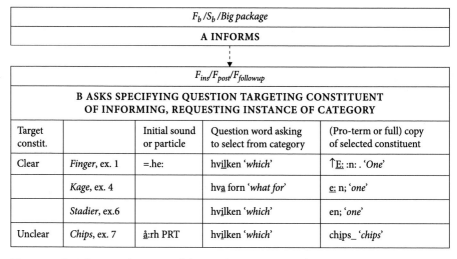

Figure 3. Social action format model, specifying questions that seek a specific instance of some category of things

Chapter 6. Responses to specifying WH-questions in Danish   **181**

On the intra-unit syntax level, Britt starts the embodied part of her response, a finger point, during Astrid's question. The motion continues for 0.2 seconds, during which Astrid continues to look at her fingers. Britt then begins a verbal turn, and her right index finger lands on her left one at the same time as the stress on the first verbal element, a demonstrative pronoun. This utterance is immediately hearable as a phrase, thanks to the stress it carries. Had a verb been the next element, the stress would have been less pronounced. The pronoun matches the common gender of the previous utterance's referent (*en,* referring to *finger*). In conjunction with the pointing, it is immediately clear that Britt is delivering the requested response in a phrasal format. However, Britt adds one more element, a location-specifying adverb (*her* 'here'). Astrid then reacts with ritualized disbelief.

Comparing the response in Excerpt (8) to the responses in the four other cases I examined in this section (cf. Table 3 and Figure 3 above), its additional specification beyond a simple pronoun, such as a location adverb, can be seen as part of the response's social action format. In the *Chips* example (Excerpt (7), with detail repeated as Excerpt (9) below), Astrid requests a specification of the kind of chips in Britt's bag. Although Britt launches a word search in line 6, she initiates her response in the same way as in Excerpt (8). A demonstrative pronoun that matches the question phrase's head, *chips,* is followed by a location specifying adverb, *der* 'there'.

Excerpt 9. *chips* 'Chips' — detail (AULing_SofaSladder_ 07:32), face-to-face, informal

```
05 AST: å:rh hvilken chips_
        PRT which (kind of) chips_

06 BRI: >°ghrn°<=m:  de      de::r;=
                     those   there
                     those   there;

07      =hva hedder de.
        what are they called.
```

In this case, the location specifying *der* 'there' is abstract, contextualizing the chips as being of a type known by both Astrid and Britt (Pedersen 2014).

In the *Stadier* example (Excerpt (6) above, with detail repeated as Excerpt (10) below), Yrsa's response in line 7 also starts with a demonstrative pronoun that matches the question phrase's head. This time, it is not followed by a location-specifying adverb, but instead by a subordinate clause that provides a specifying description.

Excerpt 10. *stadier* 'Stages' – detail [AULing_StudiegruppeLIN2011_13:46], face-to-face, informal

```
05 SØS: >hvilken< en;
          which one;
06       (0.7)
07 YRS: den hvor hun:    taget    de fem: stadier på;=
         it-C where she=has take-PRTC DEF five stage-PL on
         the one where she's added the five stages;
```

The response in our final case (Excerpt (4)) is a deviant case and will not be considered further here.

All three non-deviant responses provide a location or description of the constituent singled out by the question. They do so in a similar linguistic format. Table 4 shows this intra-unit structure of the responses with some preliminary headlines.

Table 4. Intra-unit structure, embedded specific responses providing localization or description of a selected constituent

Excerpt	Dem. pron. matching question	Localizer or specifying description	Potential further spec.
Finger, ex. 8 [AULing_SS_05:43]	°ɛden this-C *this (one)*	h:er;ɛ° here *here*	>>point>>
Chips, ex. 9 [AULing_SS_07:35]	de those *those (ones)*	de:r; there *there*	[word search launch]
Stadier, ex. 10 [AULing_SGLIN11-13:46]	den it-C *the one*	hvor hun: taget de where she=has take-PRTC DEF.PL fem: stadier på;= five stage-PL on *where she's added five stages;*	

With the information presented in Table 4, we may update our previous social action model to now include both questions and responses (see Figure 4), excluding, however, our deviant case. As in Figure 3, the dotted arrow indicates that the next action can, but does not have to, occur, whereas the unbroken arrow indicates the next action that will normatively occur.

As I hope to have shown in this section, adopting a temporal, sequential view of syntax allows not only for the determination of more precise social action formats than a more traditional view does, but also for the presentation of their sequential positions and online calibration in real time. The syntax approach functions as a tool for further exploring data, and as a model for hypothesizing about other structures and possibilities to be tested empirically.

To accurately describe projectability in real time, we do need the more traditional grammatical insights into topology, for example (cf. Steensig et al. 2023). However, a comprehensive grammar of interactional Danish should emphasize that using the abstract, traditional approach alone is not enough to describe the order of units in Danish talk-in-interaction.

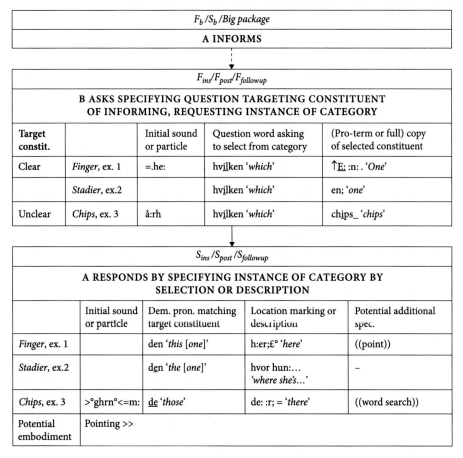

Figure 4. Social action format model, embedded specifying responses giving an instance of a specific category

4.2 How do the analyses inform the Social Actions section of the grammar?

Now that we have considered several ways in which our analyses of practices may inform the Building Blocks part of a grammar of interactional Danish — and conversely, how interaction-focused approaches could deepen our understanding of the practices — let us now turn to the Social Actions section of the grammar and determine what it should include to account for the two practices.

4.2.1 Social Actions: Questions in general and WH-questions in particular

We might assume that a general section on questions in the Social Actions part of the comprehensive grammar would clarify certain fundamental points, such as the fact that speakers ask questions from a position of less knowledge than the potential answerer (e.g., Heritage & Raymond 2005), and that the conditional relevance between questions and answers is quite strong; there are social consequences to not answering questions. Furthermore, we might want this part of the grammar to provide a functional, action-based definition of "question", such as the one adopted in this chapter, as there is no one-to-one correlation between form and function (see Section 1.1.). As shown in this chapter, non-clausal utterances can perform questioning actions. So can declarative utterances (e.g., Seuren & Huiskes 2017). At the same time, interrogative utterances may perform other actions than questioning. Instead, we may define questions as actions that request affirmation, confirmation (Sorjonen 2001), or information. In addition to this, we would have to make it clear that questions are often vehicles for other actions (Schegloff 2007), meaning they will often perform more than just a questioning action.

The analyses presented in this chapter demonstrate that a sub-section on WH-questions in a comprehensive grammar of interactional Danish would need to clarify that this is a diverse category that comprises at least two major question types: telling and specifying questions.[7] Both these subtypes of WH-questions would need an abstract entry that describes their features (requests for tellings and requests for specific information), and, as discussed in this chapter, even more subtypes within these two general categories, in the form of local and specific social action formats (Fox 2007), may be identifiable (e.g., specifying question that requests a specific instance of some category).

---

7. Although the analysis in this chapter documents only specifying questions, several telling questions were found during the collection stages.

4.2.2 Social actions: Responses to WH-questions

Responses to questions, and in particular WH-questions, are surprisingly neglected in traditional grammars. As mentioned in the introduction, Hansen and Heltoft (2011: 601) say only that responses to WH-questions "fill out the frame posed by the question," and only indirectly acknowledge that they can take more than one format. They do not discuss the fact that these formats could have different interactional motivations and consequences.

Generally, in an interactional grammar of Danish, answers to questions should be described in terms of their conditional relevance, the response speaker's epistemic authority and K+ stance (Heritage & Raymond 2005), the type of information they convey, the actions they can perform (e.g., repair; Jørgensen 2023; 2024), and a general overview of what they can orient to. For instance, the prosody of yes/no responses in Danish may make them hearable as affiliative or non-affiliative (Sørensen 2021), and responses to specifying WH-questions index sequential embeddedness or non-embeddedness through the form they take, and treat their questions as displaying the same embeddedness or non-embeddedness.

Apart from a more general section on responses, we might want a more specific section on responses to content questions. This section should clarify that there are different categories of responses to content questions, such as telling and specifying responses. Under the heading of specifying responses, it should be noted that a piece of specific information is the conditionally relevant second pair part of specifying questions, and also that specifying responses are sensitive to their sequential context. Additionally, we might wish to mention the fact that responses can show an orientation to epistemics, potential issues in the interaction (e.g., moral issues), and the relative embeddedness of the response in the ongoing trajectory.

5. Discussion

Above, I have presented my analyses of two response practices, and analyses and explorations of ways that these practices could inform an interactionally focused, comprehensive grammar of Danish.

One question that could be investigated is how generalizable the observations made in this chapter are, both to other practices in Danish and to practices in other languages. The practice descriptions themselves are of course language specific. They say nothing about how responses to specifying questions might work in other languages — and indeed, they seem to work differently from Danish in American English (Fox & Thompson 2010; Thompson et al. 2015). However, some of the observations made in this chapter about the grammatical organization and interactional logic of the two practices may be relevant to explore further in terms of potential generalizability. For example, it might be interesting for a comprehensive grammar of interactional Danish to explore the apparent correlations among grammatical parasitism, common ground, sequential embeddedness, more minimal forms, and actions that connect to previous talk on the one hand, and, on the other, grammatical and sequential independence, newness, less minimal forms, and actions that detach from previous talk. If generalizations could be made, for example, that clauses in general tend to orient to something new, whereas phrases orient to something ongoing, across practices, that would be a significant step for the grammar.

Results from interactional studies of practices in other languages support the idea that the correlations just mentioned are important to explore further. In several languages, there seems to be a "cline of minimality" (Raymond, Clift & Heritage 2021), where the more semantically heavy, less minimal forms are locally initial, assert agency, and imply that nothing has been established, whereas the more minimal forms do the opposite. Some examples are verb vs. particle responses to yes/no questions in Estonian (Keevallik 2010), the use of full referents rather than pronouns in locally subsequent sequential positions in English (Fox 1987; Schegloff 1996b; Raymond, Clift & Heritage 2021), and the various offer formats, *wanna*, *you wanna*, and *do you wanna*, in English (Raymond, Robinson et al. 2021; see also Fox & Raymond this volume). Although these formats perform different actions than the questions and responses considered in this chapter, they present very similar interactional motivations and mechanisms. This should inspire more investigation into minimality vs. maximality as resources in a broader IL sense, and it should be something writers of reference grammars should keep an eye out for.

It is an open question where exactly a description of a "cline of minimality" would belong in a grammar. It is connected to forms, both in an intra-unit, TCU sense, and in an inter-unit, sequential sense. However, it is also connected to functions and the actions performed. We might have to address it in various ways throughout the grammar and collect all the insights into something that was not description of practices, abstract description of form, or abstract description of function. This highlights the interconnectedness of position, action, and action design.

6.   Conclusion

In this chapter, I have examined how an interactional analysis of specific practices in Danish may inform a prospective grammar of interactional Danish.

I have presented two response practices, namely, phrasal and clausal responses to specifying WH-questions. Phrasal responses are shown to index embeddedness in an ongoing sequence or trajectory, and imply a certain amount of shared information as common ground. Clausal responses are shown to orient to the non-embeddedness of the question that occasions them, instead indexing independence and implying that a new trajectory is beginning, and that, as yet, there is no common ground. Each response has particular sequential home environments but may occur "for cause" outside of these environments. I presented one such deviant case (Excerpt (4)).

I have also attempted to answer my research questions, namely, how can an interactional analysis of two practices for responding to specifying questions in Danish inform a comprehensive grammar of Danish that takes interaction seriously, and what would such a grammar need to include to adequately account for the two practices and the regularities in their distribution? I have used Samtalegrammatik.dk as a model, and focused on what it would have to include in its Building Blocks section and its Social Actions section, with a particular focus on syntax. Some traditional concepts, such as the topological field model and the concept of nexus, could be included in the grammar, since they help account for some regularities. However, they cannot account for all the regularities we find, most notably because they are atemporal, non-local, and non-specific. By showcasing analyses of questions and responses that consider both the inter-unit and the intra-unit syntax, I show how such an expanded approach to syntax may add the dimensions that are missing from traditional approaches, and how it may yield precise and differentiating descriptions of the two different social action formats. Additionally, I show how the approach may be used as a tool for making new discoveries.

The analyses and discussions in Section 4 provide ample points of departure for future research, among the more interesting of which are cross-linguistic examinations of the role of grammatical minimality vs. maximality in the design of social actions. Throughout languages and practices, there seem to be general tendencies that, if explored further, could contribute information not only to interactional grammars, but also to a deeper theoretical understanding of language in interaction.

Acknowledgements

I would like to thank Marja-Leena Sorjonen for invaluable advice, comments, and support in the initial development of this study. I am also very grateful to my colleagues in the DanTIN research group for their comments, critiques, and suggestions. The study was conducted as part of the research project *Grammar in Everyday Life* (GEL), supported by the *Independent Research Fund Denmark (grant number 9037–00072B)*.

References

Anward, Jan. 2015. *Doing Language*. Linköping: Linköpings Universitet

Anward, Jan, and Bengt Nordberg. 2005. "Indledning [Introduction]." In *Samtal och grammatik: Studier i svenskt samtalsspråk* [Conversation and Grammar: Studies in Swedish Conversational Language], ed. by Jan Anward, and Bengt Nordberg, 5–9. Lund: Studentlitteratur.

Auer, Peter. 2005. "Projection in Interaction and Projection in Grammar." *Text* 25 (1): 7–36.

Auer, Peter. 2014. "Syntactic Structures and their Symbiotic Guest: Notes on Analepsis from the Perspective of Online Syntax." *Pragmatics* 24 (3): 533–560.

Christensen, Robert Z., and Lisa H. Christensen. 2009. *Dansk Grammatik* [Danish Grammar]. 2nd edition. Odense: Syddansk Universitetsforlag.

Clark, Herbert H. 1996. *Using language*. Cambridge: Cambridge University Press.

Clift, Rebecca. 2001. "Meaning in Interaction: The Case of Actually." *Language* 77 (2): 245–291.

Comrie, Bernard, Martin Haspelmath, and Balthasar Bickel. 2015. *The Leipzig Glossing Rules: Conventions for interlinear morpheme-by-morpheme glosses*. https://www.eva.mpg.de/lingua/pdf/Glossing-Rules.pdf.

Couper-Kuhlen, Elizabeth, and Margret Selting. 2018a. *Interactional Linguistics: Studying Language in Social Interaction*. Cambridge: Cambridge University Press.

Couper-Kuhlen, Elizabeth, and Margret Selting. 2018b. "Online Chapter D: A 'Big Package': Storytelling." In *Interactional Linguistics: Studying Language in Social Interaction*, by Elizabeth Couper-Kuhlen, and Margret Selting. Cambridge: Cambridge University Press

DanTIN. 2021. "Syntax in Danish Interaction." In *Samtalegrammatik.dk*. https://samtalegrammatik.dk/gel/syntax-in-danish-talk-in-interaction

Diderichsen, Paul. 1946. *Elementær Dansk Grammatik*. København

Dingemanse, Mark, and N.J. Enfield. 2015. "Other-initiated repair across languages: Towards a typology of conversational structures." *Open Linguistics* 1, 95–118.

Drew, Paul. 1997. "'Open' Class Repair Initiators in Response to Sequential Sources of Troubles in Conversation." *Journal of Pragmatics* 28 (1): 69–101.

Enfield, N.J., Tanya Stivers, Penelope Brown, Cristina Englert, Katariina Harjunpää, Makoto Hayashi, Trine Heinemann, Gertie Hoymann, Tiina Keisanen, Mirka Rauniomaa, Chase Wesley Raymond, Federico Rossano, Kyung-Eun Yoon, Inge Zwitserlood, and Stephen C. Levinson. 2019. "Polar answers." *Journal of Linguistics* 55(2): 277–303.

Evans, Nicholas, and Alan Dench. 2006. "Introduction: Catching language." In *Catching Language: The Standing Challenge of Grammar Writing*, ed. by Felix N. Ameka, Alan Dench, and Nicholas Evans, 1–39. Berlin: Mouton De Gruyter.

Fox, Barbara A. 1987. *Discourse Structure and Anaphora: Written and Conversational English.* Cambridge: Cambridge University Press.

Fox, Barbara A. 2007. "Principles Shaping Grammatical Practices: An Exploration." *Discourse Studies* 9 (3): 299–318.

Fox, Barbara A., and Tine Heinemann. 2017. "Issues in Action Formation: Requests and the Problem with x." *Open Linguistics*, 3 (1): 31–64.

Fox, Barbara A., and Sandra A. Thompson. 2010. "Responses to Wh-Questions in English Conversation." *Research on Language & Social Interaction* 43 (2): 133–56.

Hakulinen, Auli. 2001. "Minimal and non-minimal answers to yes-no questions." *Pragmatics* 11 (1): 1–15.

Hakulinen, Auli, and Marja-Leena Sorjonen. 2009. "Designing Utterances for Verb Repeat Responses to Assessments." In *Talk in Interaction: Comparative Dimensions*, ed. by Markku Haakana, Minna Laakso, and Jan Lindström, 124–151. Helsinki: Finnish Literature Society.

Hamann, Magnus G. T., and Jørgen F. Nielsen. 2022. Social and Moral Relevance of Memory: Knowing and Remembering in Conversations with a Person with Traumatic Brain Injury. *Journal of Interactional Research in Communication Disorders* 12 (1): 54–76.

Hansen, Carsten, and Jakob Steensig. 2018. "Ord i samtaler — findes de? [Words in interaction — do they exist?]." *Nordiske Studier i Leksikografi* 14: 113–119.

Hansen, Erik, and Lars Heltoft. 2011. *Grammatik over det Danske Sprog* [Grammar of the Danish Language]. Odense: Syddansk Universitetsforlag.

Heinemann, Trine. (2015). Negation in interaction, in Danish conversation. *Skrifter om Samtalegrammatik* 2 (12). https://samtalegrammatik.dk/fileadmin/samtalegrammatik/sos /2/Heinemann_2015_Negation_in_interaction_in_Danish_conversation.pdf

Heinemann, Trine, Anna Lindström, and Jakob Steensig. 2011. "Addressing Epistemic Incongruence in Question–Answer Sequences through the Use of Epistemic Adverbs." *The Morality of Knowledge in Conversation*, ed. by Tanya Stivers, Lorenza Mondada, and Jakob Steensig, 107–130. Cambridge: Cambridge University Press.

Heltoft, Lars. 2013. "Om neksusbegrebets nødvendighed [On the Necessity of the Concept of Nexus]." *Ny Forskning i Grammatik* 20: 109–126.

Hepburn, Alexa, and Galina Bolden. 2013. "The Conversation Analytic Approach to Transcription." In *The Handbook of Conversation Analysis*, ed. by Jack Sidnell, and Tanya Stivers, 57–76. Hoboken, NJ: Wiley-Blackwell.

Heritage, John. 2012. "Epistemics in action: action formation and territories of knowledge." *Research on Language and Social Interaction* 45(1): 1–29.

Heritage, John, and Geoffrey Raymond. 2005. "The Terms of Agreement: Indexing Epistemic Authority and Subordination in Assessment Sequences." *Social Psychology Quarterly* 68 (1): 15–38.

Hopper. Paul J. 2011. "Emergent Grammar and Temporality in Interactional Linguistics." In *Constructions: Emerging and Emergent*, ed. by Peter Auer, and Stefan Pfänder, 22–44. Berlin: De Gruyter.

Jespersen, Otto. 1937. *Analytic Syntax*. Copenhagen: Einar Munksgaard.

Jørgensen, Maria. (In prep.) "Flagging knowledge discrepancies with proform-questions in Danish talk-in-interaction." Aarhus: Department of Linguistics, Cognitive Science and Semiotics, Aarhus University

Jørgensen, Maria. 2021. "Er *har du det* et reelt spørgsmål — og hvilken forskel gør 'det'? En interaktionel analyse [Is *har du det* a real question and what difference does 'that' make? An interactional analysis]." In *18. Møde om Udforskningen af Dansk Sprog*, ed. by Yonathan Goldshtein, Inger. S. Hansen, and Tina. T. Hougaard, 337–358. Aarhus: Aarhus University.

Jørgensen, Maria. 2023. "Question words and phrasal questions in Danish." *Unpublished working manuscript*. Aarhus: Department of Linguistics, Cognitive Science and Semiotics, Aarhus University.

Jørgensen, Maria. 2024. "A Question of Embeddedness: On Clausal and Phrasal Responses to Specifying WH-Questions in Danish Talk-in-Interaction." *Research on Language and Social Interaction* 57 (3): 323–44.

Keevallik, Leelo. 2010. "Minimal Answers to Yes/No Questions in the Service of Sequence Organization." *Discourse Studies* 12 (3): 283–309.

MacWhinney, Brian, and Johannes Wagner. 2010. "Transcribing, searching and data sharing: The CLAN software and the TalkBank data repository." *Gesprächsforschung* 11: 154–173.

Mondada, Lorenza. 2018. "Multiple Temporalities of Language and Body in Interaction: Challenges for Transcribing Multimodality." *Research on Language and Social Interaction* 51 (1): 85–106.

Nissen, Annette. 2015. "Intonationens betydning for gentagelsers interaktionelle funktion [The Intonation's Significance for Repeats' Interactional Function]." *Skrifter om Samtalegrammatik* 2 (10).

Pedersen, Henriette F. 2014. Om konstruktionen *sån en N* i danske samtaler. [On the construction *sån en N* in Danish conversations]. *Skrifter om Samtalegrammatik* 1 (1).

Puggaard, Rasmus. 2019. "Flexibility of Frequent Clause Openers in Talk-in-Interaction: *Det* 'it, that' and *så* 'then' in the Prefield in Danish." *Nordic Journal of Linguistics* 42 (3): 291–327.

Raymond, Chase W., Rebecca Clift, and John Heritage. 2021. "Reference without Anaphora: On Agency through Grammar." *Linguistics* 59 (3): 715–755.

Raymond, Chase. W., Jeffrey D. Robinson, Barbara A. Fox, Sandra A. Thompson, and Kristella Montiegel. 2021. "Modulating Action through Minimization: Syntax in the Service of Offering and Requesting." *Language in Society* 50: 53–91.

Raymond, Geoffrey. 2003. "Grammar and Social Organization: Yes–No Interrogatives and the Structure of Responding." *American Sociological Review* 68: 939–967.

Sacks, Harvey. 1992. *Lectures on Conversation I–II*. Malden, MA: Blackwell.

Sacks, Harvey, Emanuel A. Schegloff, and Gail Jefferson. 1974. "A Simplest Systematics for the Organization of Turn-Taking for Conversation". *Language* 50 (4): 696–735.

Samtalegrammatik.dk. 2024a. "Front page." In *Samtalegrammatik.dk*. https://samtalegrammatik.dk/en

Samtalegrammatik.dk. 2024b. "Data." In *Samtalegrammatik.dk* https://samtalegrammatik.dk/om-samtalegrammatikdk/vores-metode/data.

Schegloff, Emmanuel. A. 1996a. "Turn Organization: One Intersection of Grammar and Interaction." In *Interaction and Grammar*, ed. by Elinor Ochs, Emmanuel A. Schegloff, and Sandra A. Thompson, 52–133. Cambridge: Cambridge University Press.

Schegloff, Emmanuel. A. 1996b. "Some Practices for Referring to Persons in Talk-in-Interaction: A Partial Sketch of a Systematics." In *Studies in anaphora*, ed. by Barbara A. Fox, 437–485. Amsterdam: John Benjamins.

Schegloff, Emmanuel. A. 2000. "On Granularity." *Annual Review of Sociology* 26: 715–20.

Schegloff, Emmanuel. A. 2007. *Sequence Organization in Interaction*. Cambridge: Cambridge University Press.

Seuren, Lucas M., and Mike Huiskes. 2017. "Confirmation or Elaboration: What Do Yes/No Declaratives Want?," *Research on Language and Social Interaction* 50 (2), 188–205.

Sidnell, Jack, and Tanya Stivers (eds). 2013. *The Handbook of Conversation Analysis*. Hoboken, NJ: Wiley-Blackwell.

Sorjonen, Marja-Leena. 2001 "Simple Answers to Polar Questions: The Case of Finnish." In *Studies in Interactional Linguistics*, ed. by Margret Selting and Elizabeth Couper-Kuhlen, 405–31. Amsterdam: J. Benjamins.

Stivers, Tanya. 2018. "How We Manage Social Relationships Through Answers to Questions: The Case of Interjections". *Discourse Processes* 56 (3): 191–209.

Stivers, Tanya, and Makoto Hayashi. 2010. "Transformative Answers: One Way to Resist a Question's Constraints." *Language in Society* 39 (1): 1–25.

Stivers, Tanya, Lorenza Mondada, and Jakob Steensig. 2011. "Knowledge, Morality and Affiliation in Social Interaction." In *The Morality of Knowledge in Conversation*, ed. by Tanya Stivers, Lorenza Mondada, and Jakob Steensig, 3–26. Cambridge: Cambridge University Press.

Steensig, Jakob, Maria Jørgensen, Nicholas Mikkelsen, Karita Suomalainen, and Søren S. Sørensen. 2023. "Toward a Grammar of Danish Talk-in-Interaction: From Action Formation to Grammatical Description." *Research on Language and Social Interaction* 56 (2): 116–140.

Sørensen, Søren S. 2021. "Affiliating in Second Position: Response Tokens with Rising Pitch in Danish." *Research on Language and Social Interaction* 54 (1): 101–125.

Thompson, Sandra. A., Barbara A. Fox, and Elizabeth Couper-Kuhlen. 2015. *Grammar in Everyday Talk: Building Responsive Actions*. Cambridge: Cambridge University Press.

CHAPTER 7

Parenthesis in storytelling
in Danish talk-in-interaction

Nicholas Mikkelsen
Aarhus University

This chapter investigates two types of parentheses in storytelling in Danish talk-in-interaction. The first type is used as a way of making early-turn recalibrations to the unfolding talk and deals with issues regarding the recipients' displays of knowing or understanding referents before commencing the story proper. The second type of parenthesis does late-turn recalibration and deals with setting up the climax of the story. This can be a response to recipients not displaying participation (e.g., not looking at the speaker) or not showing affiliation with the already suggested mode of the story. Finally, the chapter discusses the various resources on which parentheses in storytelling can draw (e.g., syntactic projection, particles, and embodied actions) in relation to how they might be described within a grammar of talk-in-interaction.

Keywords: participation, multimodality, grammar, storytelling

1. Introduction

This chapter contributes to conversation analysis and interactional linguistics by investigating two types of parenthesis in storytelling in Danish talk-in-interaction. During storytelling, as in other multiunit turns, speakers will often temporarily abandon their projected course of talk and then return to it following a short parenthesis or temporary digression. I find these kinds of parenthesis to be an important contribution to the negotiation of participation between speaker (storyteller) and co-participants, and thus worthy of further investigation as part of the project 'Grammar in everyday life: how people negotiate participation in Danish everyday interaction.' 'Participation' here refers to the various different kinds of co-participation on which interlocutors can draw to contribute during the production of a stretch of talk. Participation as described in this way is somewhat akin to Calabria's work on *Collaborative Grammar* (this volume) but does

https://doi.org/10.1075/slsi.37.07mik
© 2025 John Benjamins Publishing Company

not necessarily deal with co-construction of linguistic units in the same fashion. In this context, I find storytelling to be an arena where the negotiation of participation is important to the bigger project. The right to tell a story is a negotiable matter in the first place, requiring co-participants to act as listeners to the story before the story can commence; and at the other end of the story, the teller will in most cases end the story in a conclusion or punchline that also requires participation before participants can move on to assessing the story. However, storytelling also involves actions at a more granular level, whereby participants are, for instance, invited to display their recognition of characters or locations. These actions may be positioned neatly along the trajectory of talk already projected at the beginning of the story, but stories may also be constructed in a more ad hoc fashion, one chunk of talk at a time. In such cases, the negotiation of participation is more prevalent throughout the story. Likewise, even in the most streamlined of multiunit turns, local circumstances may arise that make parentheses or other deviations from the main trajectory relevant. An investigation of the use of parentheses may therefore add to the existing literature on storytelling by further detailing how such larger structures are organized at the microlevel. Insights into parentheses may also help us to understand how speakers and their co-participants negotiate participation during storytelling.

Thus, this chapter will attempt to analyze storytelling both from the perspective of the speaker and from that of their co-participant(s). This has not previously been described in Danish talk-in-interaction. One aim of the chapter is therefore to discuss how a description of the phenomenon of parenthesis may add to the grammar of Danish talk-in-interaction that we are working on building at *samtalegrammatik.dk* (Steensig et al. 2013; Steensig et al. 2023). That grammar is organized into two main parts. One, *The Building Blocks of Talk-in-interaction*, is organized in similar fashion to traditional reference grammars, describing sounds, morphemes, parts of speech, syntax, and larger discourse units, but also including a part on embodied and non-lexical expressions as well as repetitions. The other part of the grammar, *Social Actions*, describes the various social actions for which these building blocks are used in talk-in-interaction.

The methodological approach of the chapter is rooted in our work published in Steensig et al. (2023). Part of our task in contributing to the general body of work on interactional linguistics is not just to analyze and describe isolated phenomena, but also to compile them in a coherent grammar of talk-in-interaction. In this regard, our approach calls for stronger consistency across descriptions of phenomena in order to allow them to be collected in a coherent body of work. In Steensig et al. (2023), we suggest an approach that builds in part on social action formats (cf. Fox 2007), but also draws on more structuralist approaches to language description (Diderichsen 1946). Core to our approach is position sensitivity, in the sense that any contribution to a conversation is shaped by what comes before it and, in turn, shapes what follows it (C. Goodwin 2018; Schegloff 1984; 2007). In a similar fashion, we are concerned with *social action formats*, which are recurring resources used for carrying out actions in specific contexts. These resources are not restricted to what we might traditionally describe as linguistic resources, but also include embodied conduct such as gaze, gesture, and, more generally, positioning of participants' bodies in relation to one another. Likewise, facial expressions and prosodic packaging of utterances also play an important role. As such, *social action formats* are defined by the convergence of a range of resources used for carrying out actions in specific social contexts. On the other hand, while structuralist approaches to language description are not concerned with the same sensitivity toward context, they do provide some important insights, for instance, with regards to projection and turn-construction (Steensig et al. 2023: 136).

The following section will provide some context for the current study by relating it to already existing research on similar topics. This will be followed by an analysis of six excerpts from conversations during which speakers make a parenthesis in their ongoing multiunit turn. Finally, I will sum up my findings and discuss how these might fit into our grammar of Danish talk-in-interaction.

2. Previous research

Here I will outline some of the previous research done on parentheses and related phenomena in order to position my findings in relation to the broader field of conversation analysis and interactional linguistics. In general, as a speaker talks, their contributions follow a projected trajectory. As speakers add to their ongoing talk, they also limit what can come next until, at some point, an end to the ongoing turn is clearly projected. However, while producing a turn of talk, it is not uncommon for speakers to momentarily deviate from the projected trajectory of their turn. Such deviations can also be initiated by another participant than the current speaker, but this is not the focus of the current paper. In the literature, such departures from the current trajectory and the subsequent resumptions have been dealt with in different ways and for different purposes. As such, they are often referred to by different names for different analytical intents. Here, I will be using the term *parenthesis* (cf. Duvallon & Routarinne 2005; C. Goodwin 1984). In a similar vein Lerner writes about *parenthetical inserts* (1991) and Mazeland writes about *parenthetical sequences* (2007; 2012).

Important to this topic is also Jefferson's analysis of side sequences (1972). In her paper, though, these often appear to be more akin to repair sequences —

specifically, other-initiated repair (Schegloff, Jefferson, & Sacks 1977: 367). On the other hand, Jefferson made an important contribution describing these sequences sequentially in relation to the surrounding talk. Specifically, she describes these sequences as beginning with an ongoing sequence, followed by a side sequence and subsequently by a return to the ongoing sequence (Jefferson 1972: 316). Of importance is also how interactants move from the side sequence back to the ongoing sequence. Jefferson distinguishes between "resumption," which she uses to indicate the speaker encountering some problem in making this transition, and "continuation", which indicates the absence of any problems in doing so (1972: 319). This sequential perspective is similar to the notion of frame constructions as pursued by Stoltenburg (2003: 10–16) and Duvallon and Rotarinne (2005: 46). Here, a frame construction is temporarily abandoned by a parenthesis before being resumed.

Other studies use the term "aside" to describe departures from a projected trajectory by the speaker or a recipient. However, what this concept covers is more elusive. In some contexts, it merely refers to any party making an irrelevant contribution to the ongoing talk (Kent 2012: 726; Kjærbeck & Asmuß 2005: 15); in other contexts, asides are described more in line with side sequences (cf. Jefferson 1972) in that they are dealing with some trouble in the unfolding turn, such as understanding a referent (Heinemann 2015: 342) or improper participation during classroom interaction (MacBeth 2011: 448).

Another aspect of the literature to which this paper will contribute is that of recalibration. In the context of parenthesis, I find this term to be apt for describing the kind of action carried out by the parenthesis. In conversation analytic literature, recalibration is sometimes used to describe slight adjustments to be made to gestures (Eskildsen 2021: 248; Matoesian 2010: 554). M.H. Goodwin and Cekaite (2013) employ the term in the context of directives in parent–child interaction. Here, for instance, a parent stooping down to their child is seen as a "spatial recalibration of her [the parent's, ed.] directive" (M. H. Goodwin & Cekaite 2013: 132): that is, the context for the action is recalibrated through the repositioning of the body. In somewhat similar fashion, Heinemann and Wagner (2015) describe how the context for reported speech and thought can be recalibrated at different stages of the production of the report. This allows for further context to be added before the report is produced, or for the order of elements in a report to be changed. Heinemann and Wagner also point out that these kinds of recalibrations are a form of parenthesis (Heinemann & Wagner 2015: 727). I will return to this point during the analysis in the following sections.

This chapter is also concerned with the role of embodiment in relation to grammar, a question explored by other contributions to this volume, such as those by Calabria, Steensig, Pekarek Doehler & Horlacher. My position on the role of embodiment in relation to grammar is that embodied resources are intertwined with the strictly linguistic resources employed by participants in talk-in-interaction. Some examples outside of this volume include work on nodding, which can be used for carrying out various actions (Aoki 2011; C. Goodwin & Goodwin 1992; Oshima 2014; Stivers 2008). Gaze, for instance, can be used for turn retention (Kendon 1967: 42), pursuit of response (Stivers & Rossano 2010), and selection of recipients (C. Goodwin 1979: 99). Likewise, recipients' embodied behavior is routinely monitored by the speaker (M. H. Goodwin 1980: 313), and speakers in turn orient toward this when designing their own turns (e.g., C. Goodwin 1979: 106; C. Goodwin & Goodwin 2004: 230). In this volume, Steensig describes how gestures are used for making requests in Danish talk-in-interaction. Similarly, Pekarek Doehler & Horlacher (this volume) demonstrate how embodied actions such as touching the hair may take the place of a main clause.

All of the papers and chapters cited above demonstrate, in one way or another, that disentangling embodied conduct from what we traditionally understand as linguistics is a rather complicated matter. Rather than pursuing such an ambition, embodied resources as described in this chapter and the works cited above *should* have a place in a grammar of talk-in-interaction, that is, in the descriptive work. In this chapter, I will thus discuss how this can be organized within the larger framework of a grammar of talk-in-interaction.

3.   Data

The data for this chapter come from a collection of stories in everyday Danish talk-in-interaction. From working with this initial collection, I developed an interest in how participants construct the core of the story — that is, the parts of the story that fall between the story preface and its conclusion and subsequent assessment. This interest led me to build a subcollection of excerpts in which the speaker digresses from the previously projected trajectory of talk. In total, this subcollection consists of 45 examples taken from 15 different recordings of everyday interaction in Danish, amounting to a total of 6 hours and 10 minutes of recordings. Some recordings are taken from the freely available corpus *Samtalebank* (MacWhinney & Wagner 2010), while others are taken from the corpus *AULing,* hosted in the Department of Linguistics at Aarhus University. All participants in the data have provided informed consent, and information in the data that might make participants identifiable has been anonymized. Data collection and storage are in accordance with the European General Data Protection Rules ("General Data Protection Regulation (GDPR) — Official Legal Text," n.d.). Of the 15 conversations, two are phone conversations (amounting to 14 minutes in total), while the rest are video recordings of face-to-face interaction. Most of the recordings are of people engaged in talk while seated around a table (8 in total); one is a recording of interaction between customers and a shop assistant in a kiosk. Three recordings are from a hair salon, while one is from a domestic setting in which a woman is assisting her friend in dying her hair.

I find the amount of data and the variety of settings sufficient to make some generalizations about how parentheses in storytelling are constructed in Danish talk-in-interaction, as well as to highlight the various resources employed in their construction. The range of data also helps to illustrate how parenthesis is a quite situated practice, responding to local contingencies.

The excerpts have been transcribed using Jefferson's conventions (2004). In addition, I have adapted the underscore from Hepburn and Bolden's conventions for showing level unit-final intonation (2012:62). Multimodal transcription has been done using Mondada's conventions (2018).

4. Analysis

This part of the paper is organized in two parts, one dealing with what I will call early-turn recalibration and the other with what I will refer to as late-turn recalibration. Early-turn recalibration refers to instances where a parenthesis occurs early in the production of a multiunit turn. In the context of telling a story, this is the place where the teller sets up the characters of the story and the setting in which the story takes place. The kind of actions involved at this stage of a multiunit turn also has implications for the kind of participation required from the co-participants. In setting up the characters and location of a story, for instance, displays of recognition or understanding may be a relevant way of participating (Enfield 2012; Sacks & Schegloff 1979). Later in the turn, in what I will term late-turn recalibration, other kinds of participation will become relevant. As the end of the turn draws closer, speaker transition may ultimately become relevant, which in turn will make the availability of co-participants as speakers relevant. By the end of a multiunit turn, co-participants may also be required to take part in, for instance, assessments (of a story) or to affiliate with the punchline of a story. In this way, speakers can perform some recalibration of their unfolding turn to ensure that co-participants demonstrate an affiliation matching the mode of the story or, in other instances, that co-participants are simply available to participate in the conclusion of the turn at all (e.g., by gazing at the speaker rather than interacting with food or other objects in a manner that might inhibit their participation).

198 Nicholas Mikkelsen

4.1 Early-turn recalibration

In the excerpt below, Anne and Beate have been discussing a party that Beate attended over the weekend. Due to some miscommunication between the two women, Anne did not attend the party. In line 1, Beate begins a story directly following Anne's account of what she did instead. Of interest here is the parenthesis from line 2 to 4.

Excerpt 1. *lidt nederen* 'a little downer' (Samtalebank | anne_og_beate | 5:01)

```
01 BEA: *nå* † men hvis det kan trøste dig
        oh but if it can be of comfort to you
   bea     †smiles with teeth--->>
02 BEA: så var de også sån lidt
        they were also a little like
03 BEA: ø::h
        u::h
04 BEA: i- +ikk mikkel selvfølgelig
        n- not Mikkel obviously
   bea     +looks and points at AN--->
05 BEA: men ¤de der    ¤ hans venner    §der
        but 3.PL there    3.GEN friend.PL there
        but his friends you know
   bea     ¤rh finger ¤
            up and down
   ann                        .........§nods--->
06      (.) +
   bea  --->+looks down--->
07 ANN: hm §¤
   ann  --->§
   bea      ¤rh flat
08      (0.4)
09 BEA: ↑li::+dt ↓nederen_ +
        a little downer
   bea  ---->+looks at AN +looks down
```

In line 1, an upcoming assessment, most likely in the form of an adjective, is projected. In Danish, *sån lidt* 'a little like' is routinely followed by an adjective; in the context, this is presented as a consoling fact for Anne's not having joined the party. This points to the upcoming assessment as being negative in some sense. The *de* 'they' of line 1 refers to the people present at the party that Anne did not attend; however, at the point where the negatively loaded assessing word is due, Beate recalibrates the referent by first excluding their common acquaintance Mikkel from the *de* 'they': *ø::h i- ikk mikkel selvfølgelig* 'u::h n- not Mikkel of course.' With the word *selvfølgelig* 'of course,' Beate frames the exemption of Mikkel as self-evident, strongly inviting agreement on the part of Anne.

At *ikk* 'not,' Beate also repositions herself. Having previously looked down, she now looks at Anne and also makes a pointing gesture. In this way, the shift to the parenthesis is not just verbally constructed, but also embodied. Next, Beate reiterates that 'they' refers exclusively to Mikkel's friends: *men de der hans venner der* 'but his friends you know.' The format *de der X der* 'those there X there' is routinely employed in Danish talk-in-interaction to establish referents and to invite a response (Mikkelsen & Zachariassen 2021: 400, 410). The *de der* is also accentuated by Beate moving her right-hand index finger up and down in a flicking motion.

The verbal and embodied resources employed by Beate in lines 4 and 5 invite participation in the form of a display of recognition of the referents being introduced. Anne's nodding in overlap with Beate's talk in line 5 matches Beate's turn and constitutes a fitting response to it. Immediately following Anne's nodding, Beate looks down, indicating turn retention (Kendon 1967: 42). While Beate has thus disengaged the mutual gaze that was held during the parenthesis, Anne further provides a *hm* (line 7) before Beate continues with the projected assessment ↑*li::dt* ↓*nederen* 'a little downer.' In resuming her main line of talk, Beate also reuses *lidt* 'a little' from line 1. After the assessments, Beate further expands her turn into a story about Mikkel's friends.

To sum up: In the excerpt above, Beate initiates further talk about the party she attended in such a way as to set up a negative assessment of the people present. However, she makes an on-the-fly recalibration of her turn by specifying who the assessment applies to, thus re-establishing the referent. In carrying out this recalibration, Beate makes use of a range of resources that show departure from the previously projected assessing action by using a hesitation marker (line 3), repositioning the body (line 4), and gesturing (lines 4–5). A grammar of talk-in-interaction must be able to account for how an assessing action is projected, as well as the resources employed in deviating from the projection. Likewise, during the recalibration, Beate makes use of resources inviting a specific kind of participation from her interlocutor — that is, the word *selvfølgelig* ('obviously,' line 4), the format *de der X der* 'those there X there' (line 5), and her turning her gaze away from Anne in such a way as to retain the turn (line 6). During Beate's turn, Anne responds with *hm* and by nodding. A grammar of talk-in-interaction must also be able to account for how the co-participant's responses are designed and positioned in relation to Beate's talk.

Excerpt (2) below illustrates a parenthesis at a similar point in a multiunit turn. Here, Anni, Benedikte, Cathrine, and Dicte are seated at a table, talking about various aspects of their everyday lives. Prior to the beginning of Excerpt (2), Benedikte has initiated talk about an ongoing competition taking place in town. However, it quickly becomes apparent that Anni and Cathrine at least have no knowledge of the competition. Through a request for an explanation (not shown),

Anni has clearly demonstrated this to be the case. This has some implications for how Benedikte designs her subsequent turn. On the one hand, the fact that Anni quite explicitly requests an explanation allows for Benedikte to carry out this larger project uncontested. On the other hand, she will also have to redesign her original turn to accommodate the fact that Anni possesses no knowledge about the reported event. Thus, the explanation is carefully designed in a way that orients to the co-participants' lack of knowledge (C. Goodwin 1979:104; Heritage & Raymond 2005:24).

Excerpt 2. *sidde inde i en ford* 'sit inside a Ford' (AULing | kc | 13:24)

```
01 BEN: det sån e- et øh::m:::.
        it's such a- a uh::m:::

02 BEN: en konkur↑rence
        a competition

03      (0.7)

04 BEN: der blevet $lavet,
        that's been made
ben                    $looks at A--->

05 BEN: ·hh hvor øh: ↑fire personer;
        ·hh where uh: four persons

06      (0.2)

07 BEN: der ikk kender $hinanden ·hh
        who don't know each other·hh
ben                --->$looks at C--->

08      (0.2)

09 BEN: €de blevet €valgt $    ud  på €en eller anden måde_
        3.PL be.PTCP select.PTCP out on one or     other way
        they've been selected in some way
ben €raises hands, palms out
ben              €lowers hands, palms down
ben                  ---->$looks at A--->
ben                              €raises hands,
                                 palms out--->

10 BEN: det ved      jeg ikk hvordan_
        that know.PRS 1.SG not how
        I don't know how

11      (.)

12 BEN: men så skal €de sidde inde i sån $en€ løh:_
        but then they're gonna sit in such a uh:
ben         ---->€lowers hands slightly,
                  palms facing each other€
ben                           ---->$looks straight
                                   ahead---->
ben                               €raises
                                  hands--->
```

Chapter 7. Parenthesis in storytelling **201**

```
13 BEN: en ↑bil$    ↓en    $€ford_
        a car a Ford
   ben          $looks at A$looks at D--->>
   ben                  ---->€lowers hands slightly--->>
14      (.)
15 DIC: hm hm [hh
```

In lines 1–2, Benedikte presents the event as being a competition: *det sån e- et øh::m::::. en konkur↑rence* 'it's such a- a uh::m::: a competition.' The construction *sån en N* is commonly used to invite recognition (Pedersen 2014); in this instance, however, the co-participants do not respond.

Following a 0.7 second pause, Benedikte continues with a relative clause: *der blevet lavet* 'that's been made.' While this might seem somewhat redundant in terms of the progression of the explanation, it also glosses over the question of who is behind the competition, treating it as a trivial matter.

In line 5, Benedikte introduces the participants of the competition: *·hh hvor øh: ↑fire personer* '·hh where uh: four persons.' The adverb *hvor* 'where' points back to *en konkur↑rence* 'a competition' in line 2. Line 5 could have been followed by a verb phrase describing some action to be carried out by the participants, but instead it is followed by a relative clause further specifying the persons: *der ikk kender hinanden* 'who don't know each other.' During line 7, Benedikte also shifts her gaze from Anni to Cathrine. However, at this point, none of the co-participants have made any displays of understanding or recognition in relation to her explanation.

From lines 4 through 7, Benedikte has expanded upon the competition, dealing with the people involved in it through the grammatically fitted subordinate clauses in these lines. These clauses, in other words, are not designed as departures from the unfolding turn, but rather are nested within the space of what can projectably come next. Following line 7, a verb phrase attributing some action to the *↑fire personer* 'four persons' in line 5 could again have been expected. However, line 7 is instead followed by a short pause and then *de blevet valgt ud på en eller anden måde* 'they've been selected in some way' in line 9. There is room for discussion as to whether this should be considered a new main clause or another subordinate clause that is part of the *hvor* construction beginning in line 5, such that *de* 'they' is then a pronominal copy of *fire personer der ikk kender hinanden* 'four persons who don't know each other.' I find, though, that several factors contribute to an understanding of line 9 as a new unit. In part, the pauses between the *hvor* utterance in line 5 and the subsequent lines obscures the connection between the individual units from lines 5 through 9. Likewise, the emphasis on *de* 'they' in line 9 makes it hearable as an independent unit serving to highlight the selection of participants, as opposed to, for instance, further elaborating on their not knowing each other beforehand. In this regard, the delivery of line 9 is not designed so as to build directly upon the talk immediately preceding it (i.e., line 7). Thus, in the context of Benedikte's explanation of the competition, line 9 is a parenthesis that disengages from the projected trajectory at a point where none of the co-participants have provided any displays of understanding or recognition.

Through line 9, Benedikte works to position herself with regard to access to knowledge about the competition, but also to demonstrate what kind of knowledge is relevant to the progression of the explanation and what kind is not. With the reported manner of selection (*på en eller anden måde* 'in some way or another'), she positions herself as not knowing the exact method by which participants have been selected, but at the same time, this type of knowledge is presented as irrelevant to her current project. This is also underlined by Benedikte's use of her hands already at the beginning of line 9. Kendon calls this kind of gesture Vertical Palm Open Hand Prone Gesture (2004: 251) and states that it is often associated with the suspension of an ongoing action (Kendon 2004: 255). Across our data, this displaying of the palms by speakers is often used at points where they are displaying some uncertainty, yet at the same time treating it as insignificant to the current project. In that sense, the action performed by line 9 is already projected at the very beginning; from the speech alone, however, the action is not clear until after *på* ('on'), as Benedikte could likely also have said something like *de er blevet valgt ud på baggrund af NP* ('they've been selected based on NP'), where the noun phrase would refer to some quality determining their selection.

The following line (line 10) makes explicit that Benedikte is unaware of the exact manner in which the participants were selected. After a brief pause, she resumes her talk with the resumption marker *men* ('but') in line 12 marking the end of the parenthesis. In the following two lines, she describes the actions that participants in the competition are required to carry out.

The excerpt above is an example of an incrementally constructed explanation, whereby Benedikte first explains the general nature of the reported event, then moves on to matters about who is involved. The parenthesis comes at a point where her co-participants have not made any clear displays of recognition. In this regard, it deals pre-emptively with potential trouble regarding the selection of participants for the competition, before the speaker returns to the main line of the explanation by describing the actions that participants must carry out. In other words, such parentheses can be used by speakers to demonstrate how parts of a multiunit turn fit together and how they are relevant to the overall project. At this early stage in her turn, Benedikte deals with the participants of the competition first, before she moves on to address the actions they performed as part of the competition.

A grammar of talk-in-interaction must be able to account for the resources used to invite responses from the co-participants, but it must also account for how non-response at this point further shapes the trajectory of talk. While grammars of Danish do include descriptions of main-clause and relative-clause word order, a grammar of talk-in-interaction must also be able to account for how the different syntactic structures are used to organize the emergent talk and how they contribute to inviting or negotiating participation at specific points. A grammar must also be able to account for how specific gestures are used to assist or to carry out certain actions by themselves in the interaction. In the case of Excerpt (2) above, Benedikte makes use of a gesture in line 9 which can also be observed in other parts of our data. This warrants further investigation, as it could potentially deserve its own entry in the grammar.

In Excerpt (3) below, three women (Kirsten, Lis, and Ann) are drinking coffee and talking about various matters related to their everyday lives. In line 1, Lis initiates talk about having given her grandchildren a DVD of a Christmas TV series.

Excerpt 3. *jul i gammelby* 'Christmas in Old Town' (Samtalebank | omfodbold | 6:36)

```
01 LIS: ·hf:: så-  ·h- i går der;
        then yesterday there

02     (0.5)

03 LIS: da havde vi ø::hm_
        then had we u::hm

04     (0.7)

05 LIS: der gav vi $unger$ne_
        there gave we the kids
   lis            $looks at KIR
   lis                 $looks at ANN--->

06     (0.2)

07 LIS: *ø:::h*_
        u:::h

08     (0.5)

09 LIS: camille $og marco_
        Camille and Marco
   lis      ---->$looks straight ahead

10 LIS: ·hhh en $de ve $de_
        ·hhh a DVD
   lis           $looks at KIR
   lis                 $looks at ANN

11 LIS: *ø:h* $me' ø:$hm jul i ↑gammelby;
        u:h with u:hm Christmas in Old Town
   lis        $looks straight ahead
   lis                 $looks at ANN

12 ANN: [$nå:::] ja.
        o:::h yes

13 KIR: [$ uha ]_
        ooh
   lis $looks at KIR
```

14 LIS: $ja jeg havde ↑set ↓den var i handlen_
yes I had seen it was on sale
lis $looks at ANN

15 ANN: $ja_
yes
lis $looks straight ahead--->

16   (0.5)

17 LIS: brug€$sen
coop.DEF.C
the co-op
lis   €raises hands
lis ---->$looks down

18 LIS: €det var $så i brug$sens $katalog
it be.PST then in coop.DEF.C.GEN catalogue
it was then in the co-op's catalogue
lis €moves hands apart
lis $looks straight ahead
lis $looks at KIR
lis $looks at ANN--->

19 LIS: jeg havde set€ [det.   €
I had seen it
lis   €lowers hands€

20 ANN: [ja_
yes

21    $(0.5)
lis $looks straight ahead--->

22 LIS: å::h tænkte den må du *ha ikkos*;
a::nd thought that must you have right

23 LIS: *jeg tænkte der var*_
I thought there were

24   (0.3)

25 LIS: det var $ikk første de$cember endnu_=
it was not December first yet
lis   ---->$looks at ANN $opens eyes wide,
                looks straight ahead

26 LIS: =men $så var den jo ↑udsolgt.
but then it was sold out
lis $looks at ANN, eyes open wide

27 ANN: n$å::: nå.$
o:::h oh
lis $closes eyes
lis $looks at KIR--->

28 KIR: er det rig[tigt]_
is it true

29 LIS: [ja:-]$
yes
lis   ---->$looks into space between
          KIR and ANN--->>

The mention of the title of the TV series receives some relatively animated responses from her co-participants (lines 12–13). Following this response, Lis expands her turn into what is recognizably a story, detailing the circumstances of the acquisition of the DVD. While looking at Ann, she continues by stating that she had seen it on sale (line 14). The DVD is portrayed, that is, as being available for general purchase or available at some yet unspecified location. Here, Ann responds with a *ja* 'yes,' prompting continuation by Lis.

In the following lines, though, Lis does some work to recalibrate the context regarding where she had seen the DVD on sale. Already in line 16, she disengages her gaze from Ann to look straight ahead. Then, following a short pause, continues with *brugsen* 'the co-op'[1] while simultaneously looking down. Line 17 here comes off as parenthetical to her line 14, as it is not grammatically fitted. She could, for instance, have provided a prepositional phrase such as *i brugsen* 'at the co-op,' which could have been heard as further expanding line 14 (i.e., it was on sale at the co-op). The word *brugsen* 'the co-op' alone, on the other hand, is designed as disjunct to the previous talk. She also looks down during line 17 before continuing: *det var så i brugsens katalog jeg havde set det* 'it was then in the co-op's catalogue I had seen it.' During *brugsens katalog* 'the co-op's catalogue,' she also looks first at Kirsten and then at Ann; in overlap with *det* 'it,' Ann responds with a *ja* 'yes.'

What lines 17–19 do in this instance is recalibrate the context for the setup of the story. While the DVD is at first presented as being generally available, it is then recalibrated as only available through the co-op. On the one hand, this has local consequences for how the context of the story is presented to the co-participants at this point. Through this parenthesis, in other words, Lis sets the co-op as the scene of the story before going on to report her own thoughts on having seen the DVD in the catalogue (lines 22–24). On the other hand, it has implications with regard to line 26, where the fact that the DVD was sold out is portrayed with a clearly emotive stance (her wide-open eyes and animated intonation on *udsolgt* 'sold out'). From being a story about the general availability of the DVD, in other words, it is now recast as being about the DVD's availability only at this specific chain of supermarkets where, unfortunately, it turned out to be out of stock.

In producing this parenthesis to her unfolding story, Lis makes use of various resources for which a grammar of talk-in-interaction must also be able to account. These include gaze management, by first breaking the mutual gaze with her co-participant, then re-establishing it at the point of returning to her main line of talk. Likewise, when Lis engages in the parenthesis, she does so in a manner that

---

1. The word *brugsen* may be considered a noun referring to a grocery store, or it could be a proper name referring to a chain of supermarkets under the company Coop Danmark.

is not grammatically fitted to her immediately preceding talk. Finally, the parenthesis is also outlined by the raising and lowering of her hands. A grammar of talk-in-interaction must be able to account for how such resources are employed in relation to turn design.

What the previous three excerpts have shown is speakers making recalibrations to projects early in a multiunit turn. These are typically instances related to establishing some referent *before* turning to the narrative itself, where a sequence of actions carried out by the actors of the story is reported. In Excerpt (1), the story is initiated with a negative assessment of the characters involved, but adjustments are made as to who the negative assessment specifically applies to. In this way, the speaker deals with potential trouble with regard to negatively assessing a common acquaintance between the interactants. Excerpt (2) also pre-emptively deals with trouble during storytelling. At a point where the co-participants have not responded to the speaker's explanation, she provides a parenthesis admitting to not knowing certain aspects of the characters of the explanation, while at the same time treating this as unimportant to her overall project. She then proceeds to provide an account of the actions the characters must carry out as part of the competition she is explaining. In Excerpt (3), Lis makes recalibrations with regard to where she has seen a DVD on sale before continuing by relating how she found out it was out of stock.

In these three excerpts, the tellers make adjustments to their referents before commencing the narrative proper, that is, detailing a series of events. On the one hand, they deal with the immediate context of the incrementally unfolding project by showing consideration for their co-participants' understanding and participation; on the other hand, though, even these early recalibrations might impact the projected completion of the project and might invite co-participants to align themselves in a certain way even at this early point in the project. Both Excerpts (1) and (3) deal with here-and-now matters related to the unfolding turn, but also point to the conclusion of the turn. For instance, beyond trying to establish who the story is about at the outset, the parenthesis in Excerpt (1) also has implications for the conclusion of the story Beate is telling. Likewise, in Excerpt (3), Lis's specification as to where the DVD in question was available is relevant to setting up the fact that it was out of stock. In this way, early-turn recalibrations also have more general implications for the unfolding of a turn. Thus, we find that projection (Sacks, Schegloff, and Jefferson 1974; Steensig et al. 2023) is an important driver not just at the utterance level, but also as part of larger constructions such as the telling of a story. In this regard, I argue that projection of the conditions for finishing a story is also inherently grammatical.

4.2 Late-turn recalibration

While early-turn recalibration deals with matters related to situating a story, such as establishing characters and the scene of the story, late-turn recalibration can work to ensure the co-participants' affiliation with the conclusion of the story.

Excerpt (4) below is taken from a recording from a hairdressing salon. Here, Dale is having her hair cut by Christine while they discuss various topics relevant to their lives. In the excerpt below, Dale relates a story about a prank her boyfriend pulled on her at some point.

Excerpt 4. *Milano* 'Milano' (AULing | klipto | 23:26)

```
01 DAL: h- haj
        h- PRT
02 DAL: det var så ↑ledt ↓på et tidspunkt
        it was so mean at one point
03 DAL: så £hh he£
        then hh he
04      (.)
05 DAL: så æh kom han ↑op ↓om aftenen_
        then uh he came up in the evening
06 DAL: å så var han sån lidt æhm;
        and then he was a bit like uhm
07 DAL: så spurgt (jeg) ↑hva: nå hva ↓ska du lave i morgen,
        then (I) asked what PRT what are you doing tomorrow
08 DAL: så: æ- sagde han
        the:n u- he said
09 DAL: nejm jeg ska ned å snakke med et ↑FIRma;
        no but I'm going down to talk with a company
10      (0.2)
11 DAL: £hf::£
12 CHR: okay_
        okay
13 DAL: sådn ↑nå: hva: det for et firma;
        like PRT what kind of company is that
14      (0.6)
15 DAL: å   det var   lige efter
        and it  be.PST just after
        and it was just after
16 DAL: jeg havde   fået   å vide
        1.SG have.PST get.PTCP to know.INF
        I had been told
17 DAL: jeg havde   fået   job oppe i grønland.
        1.SG have.PST get.PTCP job up   in Greenland
        I had gotten the job in Greenland
```

```
18 CHR: ((giggles))
19 CHR: [£ja ja£
         yes yes
20 DAL: [hf:=
21 DAL: =[så sagde han øhm
          then he said
22 CHR: [£ethi£
23 DAL: namen øh
         but uh
24 DAL: ej men jeg ville egentlig ikk sige noget
         PRT but I would really rather not say anything
25 BIR: ((laughs))
26 CHR: ((laughs))
27 DAL: å så er jeg sådan hvad mener du
         and then I am like what do you mean
28 DAL: ej men jeg ville først sige noget
         PRT but I would first say something
29 DAL: når det er sikkert
         when it is certain
30 BIR: ej for helvede
         PRT hell
```

In lines 1 and 2, Dale initiates a story by providing an assessment, *det var så ↑ledt ↓på et tidspunkt* 'it was so mean at one point.' This hints at an eventual conclusion to the story. In the following lines, she starts laying out a sequence of events organized with *så* 'then' and *å så* 'and then' as well as some reported speech in lines 7 to 9. What is relevant here, though, is that she also provides hints of the mode of the story — that it is, ultimately, a funny story (Jefferson 1978: 228; Larsen 2015; Sacks 1974: 341). This happens in line 3, where she provides some laugh tokens and again with her snickering in line 11. In that regard, she displays a stance toward the story. However, Christine's response in line 12 is not hearable as affiliating with the stance projected by the laugh tokens and snickering. Rather, it can be heard as a matter-of-fact display of understanding which functions as a continuer (Knudsen 2015: 18). In line 13, Dale adds a further report of her own speech or stance, but this does not receive any response from Christine. Line 13 still follows the trajectory already projected by how the story has unfolded so far.

However, line 15 is marked as a parenthesis to the story. The parenthetical aspect of lines 15 and 16 is in part marked by the initial *å* 'and,' which marks it as adding information to the story, rather than advancing the sequence of events in the manner of *så* 'then' and *å så* 'and then' used previously. The following *det var lige efter* 'it was just after' corroborates this, as it adds further details about the timing of the reported events in relation to other developments in Dale's life by referring to an event that took place before the story thus far. In this way, lines

15 to 17 provide a temporal break from the previously projected trajectory. This earlier event, as Dale further elaborates, is her accepting a job offer in Greenland. Through her insertion of this additional context, Dale hints more strongly at the eventual punchline of the story (not shown). What Dale has already hinted at, at this point, is how her boyfriend has tricked her into thinking that he has been in talks with a company not based in Greenland, thereby jeopardizing their moving to Greenland together as initially planned.

This is clearly picked up by Christine as she giggles in line 18 and provides a smiley-voiced £*ja ja£* 'yes yes' in line 19. Thereby, she affiliates with the mode of the story as originally suggested by Dale's lines 3 and 11. Following this, Dale returns to the main line of the story with *så sagde han* 'then he said', which is followed by further reported speech.

To sum up: This excerpt sees the teller of the story orienting to a lack of affiliation from the co-participant by inserting a parenthesis into her telling. This is designed in a fashion that indicates the mood of the story more strongly and thereby works to request affiliation from her co-participant, which is, in turn, provided. Following this, Dale resumes the main line of the story. A grammar should account for how a story is initiated and subsequently organized (note the early assessment and the following use of resources like the words *så* and *å så*); however, a grammar should also be able to account for how laugh tokens invite certain types of participation on the part of co-participants, and how other tokens may be employed to temporarily halt the progression of the unfolding talk.

Affiliating with the mode of a story is one way in which recipients can participate in the telling of a story. Another facet of participation relates to how recipients position themselves with their bodies, for instance, in relation to gaze. In much of our data, mutually present participants are engaged in additional shared activities beyond *just talking*. Often, this involves some form of eating or drinking, but it might also be something else — like cutting the hair in the previous excerpt. As co-participants during talk may engage in and disengage from these other activities, adapting the ongoing talk to accommodate these other activities is an important aspect of everyday talk-in-interaction. In the excerpt below, Sisse and Lina are talking about how Lina acquired a poster at their local co-op. Near the conclusion of Lina's telling, she recalibrates her turn to deal with Sisse's temporary disengagement from participating in the storytelling.

Excerpt 5. *madpyramiden* 'the food pyramid' (AULing | Haarfarvning_2 | 00:40)

```
01 SIS: har i fået madpyramiden fra coop=
        have you got the food pyramid from Coop

02 SIS: =den er virkelig sød synes jeg;$
        it is really cute I think
   lin                  .............$looks left--->
```

```
03     (0.6)

04 LIN: hva for noget_
        what

05 SIS: madpyramiden [fra coop_
        the food pyramid from Coop

06 LIN:               [jaer
                       yeah

07 SIS: koster den noget.$
        does it cost anything
   lin        ---->......$looks at SIS--->

08 LIN: M:: den er gr+atis=
        M:: it is free
   sis                +looks at LIN

09 LIN: =du ka bare hente den i brug+sen;
         you can just pick it up at the co-op
   sis                            +looks straight ahead

10     (0.8)+$(2.2)+
   sis      +looks down
   lin  ---->$looks down and turns head to look left
   sis              +looks straight ahead--->

11 LIN: jeg var bare dernede en dag å $hente ø:hm_
        I was just down there one day to pick up u:hm
   lin                                $looks down and
                                      turns head right--->

12     (0.2)

13 LIN: grønne af+faldspo$ser_
        green garbage bags
   sis      ---->+looks at LIN--->
   lin             ---->$looks at SIS--->

14     (0.7)

15 SIS: [ka man hente det gratis dernede;
        can you pick that up for free down there

16 LIN: [(              )

17     (0.3)

18 LIN: ja ja dem henter vi bare nede i brugsen.
        yes yes we just pick those up down at the co-op

19     (0.4)$
   lin  ---->$closes eyes

20 LIN: øhm$::;
        uhm::
   lin     $looks right

21     (0.2)$
   lin        $looks at SIS--->

22 LIN: å så +spurgte § hun;
        and then she asked
   sis  ---->+looks down--->
   sis                §reaches for cup--->
```

Chapter 7. Parenthesis in storytelling 211

```
23    (0.5)
24 LIN: jeg §havde   $egentlig  godt§ set
        1.SG  have.PST  actually   good  see.PTCP
        I had actually already seen
   sis  ---->§moves cup tow face
   lin          ---->$looks straight ahead
   sis                        §drinks from cup
25 LIN: en    reklame me'  at   æ§h:
        art.C ad       with that  uh:
        an ad that uh:
   sis                        §puts cup down
26 LIN: ·h [de  havde   $fået     (+sånnogen)
        ·h 2.PL have.pst get.PTCP  (such)
        ·h they had got (such)
   lin                 $looks at SIS
   sis                     ---->+looks at LIN
27 LIN: p- pyra+§mider_
        p- pyramid.PL
        p- pyramids
   sis        +looks at coffee pot--->
   sis         §reach for coffee pot--->
28 SIS:  [m:_
          m:
29 LIN: $·hh $
   lin  $closes eyes
   lin       $looks down--->
30 LIN: å s sagde hun bare;
        and then she just said
31 LIN: om jeg ville §ha en plakat me'_
        if I would like to have a poster too
   sis            ---->§pours coffee--->
32 LIN: å  ja$ det  ville jeg gerne_
        and yes I would like that
   lin  ---->$looks at SIS
33    $(0.2)
   lin  $closes eyes and turns head left
34 LIN: for jeg $synes egentlig den er mega fin,
        cause I actually think it is mega nice
   lin         $opens eyes and looks left--->>
35    (0.4)
36 SIS: den er +mega s§ød.
        it is mega cute
   sis        +looks straight ahead--->>
   sis  .........---->§puts coffee pot down
37 LIN: m:: _
        m::
38    (0.5)
```

At the beginning of the excerpt, Sisse asks a couple of questions about a poster she has noticed in the room. Following Lina's answer to Sisse's question in line 7, there is a pause during which both participants reorient their gaze before Lina begins a story about how she acquired the poster in line 11: *jeg var bare dernede en dag å hente ø:hm* 'I was just down there one day to pick up u:hm.' Having looked in the direction of the poster, Lina looks down at *hente* 'pick up' and turns her head to look at Sisse while adding *grønne affaldsposer* 'green garbage bags.' This occasions a side sequence where Sisse asks about the distribution of the garbage bags. Following a hesitation marker (line 20), Lina returns to the story, redirecting her gaze toward Sisse before continuing in line 22: *å så spurgte hun* 'and then she asked.' From the context, *hun* 'she' most likely refers to an employee at the co-op. However, rather than Lina providing a report of what she said, a pause of 0.5 seconds ensues before Lina provides a parenthesis to the story in lines 24–27: *jeg havde egentlig godt set en reklame me' at æh:·h de havde fået (sånnogen) p- pyramider* 'I had actually already seen an ad that uh:.h they had got (such) p- pyramids.' In overlap with *de* 'they,' Sisse provides a continuer, as the ad mentioned is projectably about the poster. At the beginning of the parenthesis, Lina looks away from Sisse, but looks back at her at *fået* 'got', and mutual gaze between the two participants is established at *sånnogen* 'such.' In lines 29–30, Lina returns to her story with a slight rephrasing of line 22, this time providing a report of what the co-op employee said before continuing by assessing the poster.

Of importance here is what might occasion a parenthesis at this point in Lina's story (i.e., lines 24–27). In retrospect, Lina is likely setting up the punchline of her story already in line 22 — at least the repeat in line 30 has the added *bare* 'just' used as an intensifier. This is of importance to our understanding of line 22, as Lina, during this line of talk, is repositioning herself in a way that is important to her role as recipient of a potential upcoming conclusion to the story. Here, she reaches for her cup (line 22), and starts to move it toward her face and then to drink (line 24). That she is about to drink is already recognizable from line 22. Drinking naturally hinders her ability to respond verbally to the ongoing talk — in this case, Lina's approaching assessment. These circumstances make a suspension of the conclusion to the story relevant. Lina solves the emerging problem by adding further context to her story about the acquisition of the poster. While Sisse is pouring coffee during Lina's resumption of the story, she is able to respond verbally, which she does by taking part in assessing the poster at the end of the story in line 36.

Excerpt (5) is illustrative of how the participation between interactants shapes the trajectory of the emerging talk. In this regard, a grammar should also be able to account for how recipients of a story (or of other turns) position themselves, and how this may affect the unfolding turn produced by a speaker. Likewise, a grammar should be able to account for the resources utilized by the speaker in dealing with such situations as those in Excerpt (5) (see also C. Goodwin 1979: 106).

Another example of late-turn recalibration is Excerpt (6) below, taken from the same conversation between Sisse and Lina as Excerpt (5). Here, Sisse has provided a rather lengthy story about some troubles she had while getting her hair colored. Having already assessed parts of the story, she continues by expanding the story, beginning in line 1 below:

Excerpt 6a. *vænnet mig te' det* 'gotten used to it' (AULing | Haarfarvning2 | 20:37)

```
01 SIS: å +så kom jeg hjem;
        and then I got home
    sis    +looks straight ahead
02      (0.5)+
    sis        +looks left
03 SIS: å    bare fordi_
        also just because
        also just because
04 SIS: det +var   en   +rigtig fri§sørsalon.
        it   be.PST ART.C real   hairdressing salon
        it was a real hairdressing salon
    sis  --->+looks down
    sis              +looks at LIN--->
    sis                        §nods twice
05 LIN: m:[:,
06 SIS:    [as du  §ved;+
            PRT 2.SG know.PRS
            PRT you know
    sis            §nods
    sis            ---->+looks left
07 SIS: det noget     andet [hvis +man er     på sko:le_
        it  something else.N if    one be.PRS on school
        it's something else if you are at school
    sis                          +looks at LIN--->
08 LIN:                     [det var ikk oppe på sko:len.
                             it wasn't up at the school
09 SIS: §N[EJ_
          no
    sis  §shakes head
10 LIN:   ['aer $
           yeah
    lin   ---->$looks down at cup--->
11 SIS: ·hh+hh
    sis  -->+looks straight ahead--->
12 SIS: åh jeg €kom $hjem_
        and I came home
    lin        €drinks from cup--->
    lin        ---->$looks at SIS--->
```

Sisse returns to the story with *å så kom jeg hjem* 'and then I came home' in line 1 while looking straight ahead. This line projects an expansion of the story in the following lines. However, in line 3, she adds some more context to her unfolding turn: *å bare fordi det var en rigtig frisørsalon* 'also just because it was a real hairdressing salon.'

With the stress on *å* 'and' in line 3 this is hearable early on as a justification, to which Lina responds with an *m::* in line 5. This *m::* does not demonstrate understanding, but rather works as a continuer. Lines 3 and 4, though, seem to have some specific implications beyond simply reporting the location of the hair coloring, underlined in part by how it is framed as 'a real hairdressing salon.' Thus, Sisse continues to elaborate on what is implied by line 4: *as du ved det noget andet hvis man er på sko:le* 'PRT you know it's something else if you are at school.' The initial particle *as* (<altså>) indicates a departure from the previously projected trajectory (Heinemann & Steensig 2018), while the subsequent *du ved* 'you know' invokes shared knowledge between the participants (Asmuß 2011: 209).

In overlap, in line 8 Lina provides an interpretation (*det var ikk oppe på sko:len* 'it wasn't up at the school'), thereby demonstrating understanding. Sisse agrees with *NEJ* 'no' in line 9, while Lina, in overlap, also provides an agreeing response token (*'aer* 'yeah'). At the same time, Lina repositions her body and starts to drink from her cup from lines 10 through 12, while resuming the story by, in line 12, essentially repeating line 1: *åh jeg kom hjem* 'and I came home.'

With this recalibration of her stance, she has provided justification for her own and her boyfriend's stance at the time toward her experiences at the hairdresser. This stance is provided in the following lines:

Excerpt 6b. *vænnet mig te' det* 'gotten used to it' (AULing | Haarfarvning2 | 20:45)

```
13 SIS: å jeg var sån lidt_
        and was like a little

14 SIS: å: da mathias +kom ned å (betal€te mig)_
        and when Mathias came down and (paid me)
   sis            ---->+looks down at cup--->
   lin                       ---->€puts cup down

15 SIS: da var han å sån he§lt;
        then he was also totally
   sis                    §lifts cup while frowning

16      (0.9)§
   sis      §stops frowning,
            still lifting cup tw mouth--->

17      (1.0)

18 SIS: det +[synes han *heller ikk+ det var okay*.
        he didn't think that was okay either
   sis ---->+closes eyes, turns head tw LIN
   sis                       +looks at LIN
```

```
19 LIN:        [aer
                yeah

20 LIN: +ej  §
         PRT
    sis +looks straight ahead--->
    sis ---->§drinks from cup--->

21     (0.7)$
    lin ---->$looks left

22     (0.9)§ $
    sis       §puts cup down
    lin         $looks down--->

23     (0.6)+
    sis ---->+looks down--->

24     (0.6)

25 LIN: fuck hvor nederen_ $
         fuck how downer
    lin                 ---->$looks at SIS--->
```

The reported stance in the excerpt above is another way of making an assessment in the here-and-now (i.e., in Sisse's current conversation with Lina). In this regard, the parenthesis in lines 4 through 7 also comes at a point of transition from evaluating one aspect of Sisse's story in the talk prior to Excerpt (6a) to continuing the story (line 1), then moving on to assess another aspect of the story: Sisse's stance on the experience after returning home. With the parenthesis in lines 3 through 7 in Excerpt (6a), Sisse provides justification that works to set up the assessment in the form of the reported stance in lines 13–18. Following the report, Lina responds with an evaluative particle *ej* (cf. Tholstrup 2014); after a pause where Sisse drinks from her cup, she further adds an assessment (*fuck hvor nederen* 'fuck how downer') agreeing with Sisse's reported stance.

As stated above, Sisse and Lina find themselves at a stage in the story where the telling has in fact been concluded and subsequently evaluated. However, Sisse continues to expand the story in a way that prompts her to repeatedly recalibrate her contributions to fit the current context. This is also the case as Sisse continues in the excerpt below:

Excerpt 6c. *vænnet mig te' det* 'gotten used to it' (AULing | Haarfarvning2 | 20:58)
((lines 26–31 omitted))

```
32     (0.5)+
    sis ---->+looks into mirror--->>

33     (0.5)

34 SIS: men nu=
         but  now

35 SIS: =§as nu når jeg lige har
         PRT now when 1.SG just have.PRS
         PRT now when I have
    sis  §runs her lh fingers through her hair--->
```

36 SIS: **vænnet   mig   te' det;**
     accustom.PTCP 1.SG.OBL to it.N
     gotten used to it

37 SIS: **så synes jeg faktisk_**
     then I actually think

38 SIS: **altså jeg synes [det fint;**
     PRT I think [it's fine

39 LIN: **[jeg synes faktisk det pænt.§**
                          I actually also think it's nice

     sis   ---->§

40 LIN: **å §man [lægger ikk mærke §te'-**
     and you [don't become aware of-
     sis ..§runs rh fingers   §
            through hair

41 SIS: **[jaer**
            yeah

Following a few lines of some interim talk (omitted), Sisse looks into the table mirror in front of her and continues with *men nu* 'but now' in line 34. This *men nu* indicates that what follows is somehow in opposition to the stance previously reported — that is, it is projected that she has now changed her stance either regarding her hair or her experience at the hairdresser. It is also implied that her current stance is more positive. However, rather than immediately providing a display of the stance she is currently holding, she instead provides a parenthesis that adds further context to the nu: *as nu når jeg lige har vænnet mig te' det* 'PRT now when I have just gotten used to it.' As with the previous excerpts, the particle *as* flags the utterance as a departure from the progressivity of her turn, while the rest of the turn adds more context, detailing the stage between the stance she previously reported and the one projected by *men nu* in line 34. Likewise, her running her fingers through her hair helps Sisse to disambiguate that the change in stance concerns how her hair looks — not the experience at the hairdresser.

The parenthesis here comes at a point where both women in their prior talk have provided some rather strong negative assessments of Sisse's reported experiences. Before she can provide an assessment taking an opposite stance, Sisse recalibrates the context for the assessment by providing a parenthesis that justifies her current stance. In the following lines, Lina too engages in positively evaluating Sisse's hair. Previous excerpts have all illustrated speakers deviating from the projected trajectory of a story, but in Excerpt (6), the motivation for such a digression is slightly different, as the main issue here is not the co-participant's understanding of a sequence of events reported in the story or understanding references to persons or places. Rather, the issue is one of affiliating with the speaker's stance toward what is being told. Here, the particle *altså* is used to indicate a departure from progressivity, while *du ved* 'you know' evokes shared knowledge on part of the co-participant. In this regard, a grammar of talk-in-interaction should not only account for how stories are organized but should also be able to account for the resources employed by speakers in setting up the punchline of a story. Likewise, it should be able to account for the resources used by recipients to display participation in a manner that affiliates with the mode of the story.

Based on Excerpts (1) to (6) above, we have seen how parentheses are found at places of transition between the different parts of a story. When I speak of transition in this context, I do not take it to mean that the transition of the turn between speakers is relevant at these points. Rather, the transition is between different parts of the story that require different kinds of participation from the co-participants in interaction. In other words, establishing the characters and setting of a story requires the recipients to conduct themselves in a different manner than they would during the telling proper. Likewise, ensuring that the co-participants are positioned to participate in a preferred manner at the conclusion of the story is also important to speakers before they can transition into the final part of the story. While for much of the time these kinds of transitions between parts of the story are worked out rather seamlessly between participants, the excerpts above exemplify instances where more interactional work is required for the story to progress. The excerpts demonstrate ways in which stories are not just finished packages that a speaker performs for an audience, but interactional entities that require different kinds of participation at different stages. At the same time, speakers constantly monitor the co-participants in the interaction and make adjustments to the story accordingly.

Through these excerpts, I have also shown how participants employ various resources that are used more broadly across contexts. Heinemann and Steensig (2018), for instance, have described the use of *altså* as a turn-initial particle in various contexts used to justify a departure from the previously projected trajectory. In support of their findings, Excerpt (6) above also shows how it is used within a story for some of the same ends described in their paper — namely, specification, explanation, and elaboration (Heinemann & Steensig 2018: 446).

5.   Discussion

When telling a story, speakers are tasked with keeping it coherent and indicating how each part is relevant (or not) to the whole. But, as has been demonstrated by the excerpts analyzed above, stories often do not follow neatly along a projected trajectory from beginning to end. In these cases, parentheses in the stories are used to make on-the-fly adjustments in ways that may impact the suggested mode of the story or suggested stance toward it at the point of completion.

This chapter has dealt with two different ways in which tellers of a story may diverge from the projected trajectory: early-turn and late-turn recalibration. These kinds of parentheses in the emerging talk differ in that each kind deals with issues that are relevant to different parts of the story. Early-turn recalibration, on the one hand, deals with establishing referents, while late-turn recalibration is concerned with setting up the climax of the story by ensuring affiliation with the mode of the story, or ensuring that the co-participant is able to participate by acting as recipient to the punchline and the subsequent assessment of the story.

In this manner, these kinds of recalibrations also show at a more granular level how stories are organized, thereby adding to the existing literature on the topic. The positioning of the parentheses within the stories shows an orientation to transitions between different parts of the story. In addition, it should also be considered how parentheses and the resources employed in their construction can be organized in a grammar of talk-in-interaction. Within the framework of our grammar of Danish talk-in-interaction, the current chapter can further qualify our description of stories as a type of discourse unit. From a social action perspective, parenthesis in storytelling can add to the part of the grammar that deals with openings and closings, in that the speaker establishes a digression to the ongoing talk while at the end of the parenthesis resuming the main line of the talk. Likewise, parenthesis during storytelling is a general resource for negotiating participation and can thus contribute to the part of the grammar that deals with expressions of participation.

Again, at a more granular level, it should be pointed out that parentheses in storytelling draw on a number of different resources that we may describe either in isolation or as component parts that make up an identifiable social action. In the following, I will briefly sum up the main resources used, with an emphasis on the embodied resources, and discuss how they fit into the larger framework of a grammar.

While somewhat different in nature, both types of parenthesis make use of some of the same resources. These include speakers gazing away from the co-participant and re-establishing mutual gaze at the end of the parenthesis, as in Excerpts (1), (3), (5), and (6). Gaze management plays an important role in outlining actions (Rossano 2012: 319). A grammar of talk-in-interaction must therefore also contain an entry on how this resource is employed. In a similar fashion, the gaze of a story recipient is also an important part of how a story is constructed (C. Goodwin 1981: 86–88), as was also noted in relation to Excerpt (5). In this regard, we must consider gaze management to be a central building block of everyday talk-in-interaction, but also to be a resource that is drawn upon in carrying out actions such as requests for participation and response mobilization (cf. Stivers & Rossano 2010).

The excerpts above also demonstrate various uses of hesitation markers, such as *øh* 'uh'. In Excerpts (2) and (5), hesitation is used in the context of word search, but in Excerpt (1) it marks the beginning of the parenthesis. Both uses are in line with previous research on the matter (Brøcker et al. 2012: 33–34).

In our grammar, the particle *altså* already has an entry, based on Heinemann & Steensig (2018). From the perspective of a traditional grammar, it is described as a turn-initial particle; from a social action perspective, *altså* can be part of a question requesting either confirmation or information, but it can also initiate repair. With the above analysis in mind, we can expand our understanding of *altså* to encompass deviations from a projected trajectory more broadly — for instance, in the context of storytelling.

Another important aspect of our analyses is how the embodied resources might fit into our grammar. Under our entry for building blocks of talk-in-interaction, we have already reserved a section for describing embodied and non-lexical expressions. Gaze, based on the analysis above, can be described from both a speaker and a recipient perspective. From a speaker perspective, gaze can be described in terms of gazing at the recipient, gazing away, or alternating between gazing at various participants. From the recipient perspective, gaze can be described in terms of either looking at the speaker or looking away. Other perspectives beyond the analysis at hand could include looking at objects in the immediate environment, or participants jointly looking at such objects. From a social action perspective, on the other hand, gaze is instrumental in expressing participation. The recipient gazing at the storyteller is essential to the storytelling activity, as demonstrated also by the analysis of Excerpt (5). The gaze of the teller is important in managing turn-taking and is, in general, an important feature of turn design (cf. Stivers & Rossano 2010). As such, it is an important aspect of how participation is negotiated during talk-in-interaction.

The excerpts above also show the use of specific gestures. While the analysis at hand is insufficient to make any generalizations about the use of these specific gestures, our grammar is designed to include entries on gestures as well. The form of these gestures can already be described as a building block of language. And while some gestures, such as pointing, may be linked to specific social actions — in this case, speaker selection or requesting — it may be harder to point to some specific action carried out by other gestures like those in Excerpts (2) and (3), even when they are part of carrying out a social action. Rather, they converge with other resources in carrying out social actions. This, arguably, poses a challenge for writers of grammars. In my analysis of Excerpt (3), for instance, I argued that Lis uses her raising and lowering of her hands to outline the parenthesis, but it might prove difficult to describe this gesture in terms of social actions without taking into account the other resources Lis employs in constructing the parenthesis.

Further research into gestures in Danish talk-in-interaction might be able to better account for the use of specific gestures. However, a grammar of talk-in-interaction should also be able to account for how multiple resources can be employed in carrying out one action. This is in line with how Stivers and Rossano describe the use of several different resources for pursuing response (2010), or how Ford and Thompson describe interactants' reliance on a combination of syntax, pragmatics and intonation in determining transition relevance places in conversation (1996). This approach is also congruent with how research on gestures treats the combination of talk and gesture as *ensembles* (Kendon 2004:108), or a broader combination of multimodal resources as *complex multimodal gestalts* (Mondada 2014a; 2014b; 2016; 2018).

In constructing parentheses to ongoing multiunit turns, interactants rely on multiple resources for digressing from the previously projected trajectory and for returning to the main line of talk following the parenthesis. For the most part, these resources can be described as building blocks of talk-in-interaction that are used to carry out specific social actions. However, a grammar of talk-in-interaction must also be attentive to how individual resources are combined into social actions. Isolating a single resource for the purpose of determining which specific social action it performs might prove difficult. It is at this point that we as analysts and writers of grammars might draw the line concerning what should be granted an entry into the grammar and what should not.

Acknowledgements

This study was developed within the research project *Grammar in Everyday Life* (GEL), supported by the *Independent Research Fund Denmark (grant number 9037–00072B)*.

References

Aoki, Hiromi. 2011. "Some Functions of Speaker Head Nods." In *Embodied Interaction: Language and the Body in the Material World*, ed. by Charles Goodwin, Jürgen Streeck, and Curtis LeBaron, 93–105. Cambridge: Cambridge University Press.

Asmuß, Birte. 2011. "Proposing Shared Knowledge as a Means of Pursuing Agreement." In *The Morality of Knowledge in Conversation*, ed. by Tanya Stivers, Lorenza Mondada, and Jakob Steensig, 207–34. Cambridge: Cambridge University Press.

Brøcker, Karen Kiil, Magnus Glenvad Tind Hamann, Maria Jørgensen, Simon Bjerring Lange, Nicholas Hedegaard Mikkelsen, and Jakob Steensig. 2012. "Samtalesprogets grammatik. Fire fænomener og nogle metodiske overvejelser [The grammar of talk-in-interaction. Four phenomena and some methodological considerations]." *NyS, Nydanske Sprogstudier* 42:10–40.

Diderichsen, Paul. 1946. *Elementær Dansk Grammatik* [Elementary Danish grammar]. Copenhagen: Gyldendal.

Duvallon, Outi, and Sara Routarinne. 2005. "Parenthesis as a Resource in the Grammar of Conversation." In *Syntax and Lexis in Conversation: Studies on the Use of Linguistic Resources in Talkin-Interaction*, ed. by Auli Hakulinen, and Margret Selting, 45–74. Amsterdam / Philadelphia: John Benjamins.

Enfield, Nick J. 2012. "Reference in Conversation." In *The Handbook of Conversation Analysis*, ed. by Jack Sidnell, and Tanya Stivers, 433–454. Oxford, U.K.: Wiley-Blackwell. http://10.1002/9781118325001.ch21.

Eskildsen, Søren Wind. 2021. "Embodiment, Semantics and Social Action: The Case of Object-Transfer in L2 Classroom Interaction." *Frontiers in Communication* 6.

Ford, Cecilia E., and Sandra A. Thompson. 1996. "Interactional Units in Conversation: Syntactic, Intonational, and Pragmatic Resources for the Management of Turns." In *Interaction and Grammar*, ed. by Emanuel A. Schegloff, Elinor Ochs, and Sandra A. Thompson, 134–84. Cambridge: Cambridge University Press.

Fox, Barbara A. 2007. "Principles Shaping Grammatical Practices: An Exploration." *Discourse Studies* 9 (3): 299–318.

"General Data Protection Regulation (GDPR) — Official Legal Text." n.d. General Data Protection Regulation (GDPR). Accessed March 14, 2023. https://gdpr-info.eu/

Goodwin, Charles. 1979. "The Interactive Construction of a Sentence in Natural Conversation." In *Everyday Language: Studies in Ethnomethodology*, ed. by George Psathas, 97–121. New York: Irvington Publishers.

Goodwin, Charles. 1981. *Conversational Organization: Interaction between Speakers and Hearers*. London: Academic Press.

Goodwin, Charles. 1984. "Notes on Story Structure and the Organization of Participation." In *Structures of Social Action: Studies in Conversation Analysis*, ed. by J. Maxwell Atkinson, and John Heritage, 225–46. London: Cambridge University Press.

Goodwin, Charles. 2018. *Co-Operative Action. Learning in Doing: Social, Cognitive and Computational Perspectives*. New York, NY: Cambridge University Press.

Goodwin, Charles, and Marjorie H. Goodwin. 2004. "Participation." In *A Companion to Linguistic Anthropology*, ed. by Alessandro Duranti, 222–44. Oxford: Blackwell.

Goodwin, Charles, and Marjorie Harness Goodwin. 1992. "Assessments and the Construction of Context." In *Rethinking Context: Language as an Interactive Phenomenon*, ed. by Alessandro Duranti, and Charles Goodwin, 147–90. Cambridge: Cambridge University Press.

Goodwin, Marjorie Harness. 1980. "Processes of Mutual Monitoring Implicated in the Production of Description Sequences." *Sociological Inquiry* 50 (3–4): 303–17.

Goodwin, Marjorie Harness, and Asta Cekaite. 2013. "Calibration in Directive/Response Sequences in Family Interaction." *Journal of Pragmatics* 46 (1): 122–38.

Heinemann, Trine. 2015. "Negation in Interaction, in Danish Conversation." *Skrifter Om Samtalegrammatik* 2 (12): 1–452.

Heinemann, Trine, and Jakob Steensig. 2018. "Justifying Departures from Progressivity: The Danish Turn-Initial Particle Altså." In *Between Turn and Sequence: Turn-Initial Particles Across Languages*, ed. by John Heritage, and Marja-Leena Sorjonen, 445–76. Amsterdam / Philadelphia: John Benjamins.

Heinemann, Trine, and Johannes Wagner. 2015. "Recalibrating the Context for Reported Speech and Thought." *Text & Talk* 35 (6): 707–29.

Hepburn, Alexa, and Galina B. Bolden. 2012. "The Conversation Analytic Approach to Transcription." In *The Handbook of Conversation Analysis*, ed. by Jack Sidnell, and Tanya Stivers, 57–76. Oxford, U.K.: Wiley-Blackwell.

Heritage, John, and Geoffrey Raymond. 2005. "The Terms of Agreement: Indexing Epistemic Authority and Subordination in Talkin-Interaction." *Social Psychology Quarterly* 68 (1): 15–38.

Jefferson, Gail. 1972. "Side Sequences." In *Studies in Social Interaction*, ed. by David Sudnow, 294–338. New York: Free Press.

Jefferson, Gail. 1978. "Sequential Aspects of Story Telling in Conversation." In *Studies in the Organization of Conversational Interaction*, ed. by Jim Schenkein, 213–48. New York: Academic Press.

Jefferson, Gail. 2004. "Glossary of Transcript Symbols with an Introduction." In *Conversation Analysis: Studies from the First Generation*, ed. by Gene H. Lerner, 13–31. Amsterdam / Philadelphia: John Benjamins Publishing Company.

Kendon, Adam. 1967. "Some Functions of Gaze-Direction in Social Interaction." *Acta Psychologica* 26:22–63.

Kendon, Adam. 2004. *Gesture: Visible Action as Utterance.* Cambridge: Cambridge University Press.

Kent, Alexandra. 2012. "Compliance, Resistance and Incipient Compliance When Responding to Directives." *Discourse Studies* 14 (6): 711–30.

Kjærbeck, Susanne, and Birte Asmuß. 2005. "Negotiating Meaning in Narratives: An Investigation of the Interactional Construction of the Punchline and the Post Punchline Sequence." *Narrative Inquiry* 15 (1): 1–24.

Knudsen, Anette Dahl. 2015. "'O(↑)Kay(?), ↑Ohkay' – En Prosodiafhængig Ytringspartikel? ['O(↑)Kay(?), ↑Ohkay' – a prosody dependent utterance particle]" *Skrifter Om Samtalegrammatik* 2 (1).

Larsen, Tine. 2015. "Leksikalsk Genanvendelse: En Ressource Til Synliggørelse Af Historiers Afslutning [Lexical reuse for indication of the end of a story]." *Skrifter Om Samtalegrammatik* 2 (11): 1–29.

Lerner, Gene H. 1991. "On the Syntax of Sentences-in-Progress*." *Language in Society* 20 (3): 441–58.

MacBeth, Douglas. 2011. "Understanding Understanding as an Intructional Matter." *Journal of Pragmatics* 43 (2): 438–51.

MacWhinney, Brian, and Johannes Wagner. 2010. "Transcribing, Searching and Data Sharing: The CLAN Software and the TalkBank Data Repository." *Gesprächsforschung: Online-Zeitschrift Zur Verbalen Interaktion* 11:154–73.

Matoesian, Gregory M. 2010. "Multimodality and Forensic Linguistics: Multimodal Aspects of Victim's Narrative in Direct Examination." In *The Routledge Handbook of Forensic Linguistics*, ed. by Malcolm Coulthard, and Alison Johnson, 541–57. New York, NY: Routledge.

Mazeland, Harrie. 2007. "Parenthetical Sequences." *Journal of Pragmatics* 39 (10): 1816–69.

Mazeland, Harrie. 2012. "Grammar in Conversation." In *The Handbook of Conversation Analysis*, ed. by Jack Sidnell, and Tanya Stivers, 475–91. Oxford, U.K.: Wiley-Blackwell.

Mikkelsen, Nicholas, and Ditte Zachariassen. 2021. "'Ikkå' er altså mere end at kræve svar, ikkå! [Ikkå is more than a request for response, ikkå!]" In *18. Møde om Udforskningen af Dansk Sprog*, ed. by Yonatan Goldshtein, Inger Schoonderbeek Hansen, and Tina Thode Hougaard, 397–417. Aarhus: NORDISK, Institut for Kommunikation og Kultur, Aarhus Universitet.

Mondada, Lorenza. 2014a. "Pointing, Talk, and the Bodies: Reference and Joint Attention as Embodied Interactional Achievements." In *From Gesture in Conversation to Visible Action as Utterance: Essays in Honor of Adam Kendon*, ed. by Mandana Seyfeddinipur, and Marianne Gullberg, 95–124. Amsterdam / Philadelphia: John Benjamins.

Mondada, Lorenza. 2014b. "The Local Constitution of Multimodal Resources for Social Interaction." *Journal of Pragmatics* 65:137–56.

Mondada, Lorenza. 2016. "Challenges of Multimodality: Language and the Body in Social Interaction." *Journal of Sociolinguistics* 20 (3): 336–66.

Mondada, Lorenza. 2018. "Multiple Temporalities of Language and Body in Interaction: Challenges for Transcribing Multimodality." *Research on Language and Social Interaction* 51 (1): 85–106.

Oshima, Sae. 2014. "Consensus through Professionalized Head Nods: The Role of Nodding in Service Encounters in Japan." *Journal of Business Communication* 51 (1): 31–57.

Pedersen, Henriette Folkmann. 2014. "Om Konstruktionen Sån En N i Danske Samtaler [On the construcion *sån en N* 'such an N' in Danish conversations]." *Skrifter Om Samtalegrammatik* 1 (1): 1–23.

Rossano, Federico. 2012. "Gaze in Conversation." In *The Handbook of Conversation Analysis*, ed. by Jack Sidnell, and Tanya Stivers, 308–29. Oxford, U.K.: Wiley-Blackwell.

Sacks, Harvey. 1974. "An Analysis of the Course of a Joke's Telling in Conversation." In *Explorations in the Ethnography of Speaking*, ed. by Joel Sherzer, and Richard Bauman, 337–53. London: Cambridge University Press.

Sacks, Harvey, and Emanuel A. Schegloff. 1979. "Two Preferences in the Organization of Reference to Persons in Conversation and Their Interaction." In *Everyday Language: Studies in Ethnomethodology*, ed. by George Psathas, 15–21. New York, NY: Irvington Press.

Sacks, Harvey, Emanuel A. Schegloff, and Gail Jefferson. 1974. "A Simplest Systematics for the Organization of Turn-Taking for Conversation." *Language* 50 (4): 696–735.

Schegloff, Emanuel A. 1984. "On Some Questions and Ambiguities in Conversation." In *Structures of Social Action: Studies in Conversation Analysis*, ed. by J. Maxwell Atkinson, and John Heritage, 28–52. Cambridge, U.K.: Cambridge University Press.

Schegloff, Emanuel A. 2007. *Sequence Organization in Interaction: Volume 1: A Primer in Conversation Analysis*. Cambridge: Cambridge University Press.

Schegloff, Emanuel A., Gail Jefferson, and Harvey Sacks. 1977. "The Preference for Self-Correction in the Organization of Repair in Conversation." *Language* 53 (2): 361–82.

Steensig, Jakob, Karen Kiil Brøcker, Caroline Grønkjær, Magnus G. T. Hamann, Rasmus P. Hansen, Maria Jørgensen, Mathias Høyer Kragelund, et al.. 2013. "The DanTIN Project — Creating a Platform for Describing the Grammar of Danish Talkin-Interaction." In *New Perspectives on Speech in Action. Proceedings of the 2nd SJUSK Conference on Contemporary Speech Habits*, ed. by Jan Heegård, and Peter Juel Henrichsen. Frederiksberg: Samfundslitteratur.

Steensig, Jakob, Maria Jørgensen, Nicholas Mikkelsen, Karita Suomalainen, and Søren Sandager Sørensen. 2023. "Toward a Grammar of Danish Talkin-Interaction: From Action Formation to Grammatical Description." *Research on Language and Social Interaction* 56 (2): 116–140.

Stivers, Tanya. 2008. "Stance, Alignment, and Affiliation During Storytelling: When Nodding Is a Token of Affiliation." *Research on Language and Social Interaction* 41 (1): 31–57.

Stivers, Tanya, and Federico Rossano. 2010. "Mobilizing Response." *Research on Language & Social Interaction* 43 (1): 3–31.

Stoltenburg, Benjamin. 2003. "Parenthesen Im Gesprochenen Deutsch." *InList*. InList — Interaction and Linguistic Structures, 2003.

Tholstrup, Emilie. 2014. "'Ej Hvor Fint' — En Undersøgelse Af Den Danske Interjektion Ej [*Ej how nice — investigation of the Danish interjection ej*]." *Skrifter Om Samtalegrammatik* 1 (3): 1–15.

SECTION 2

From Grammar to Action

CHAPTER 8

The use of past tense formats in German talk-in-interaction

Sophia Fiedler
Université de Neuchâtel

The present chapter investigates three frequent German verbs, *finden* 'to find', *glauben* 'to believe', and *meinen* 'to mean' in first and third person preterite and present perfect. Prior research on past tense distribution primarily identifies regional variation as a driving force (Fischer 2018) or treats preterite and present perfect as 'interchangeable' (Helbig & Buscha 2001). I test these assumptions by investigating a large corpus of German talk-in-interaction. My findings show that speakers use lexico-syntactic constructions consisting of past tense formats and specific grammatical components to implement distinct actions. Identifying these paste tense constructions, I demonstrate that tense is not only a 'traditional' grammatical category but also crucial for implementing social actions, thus constituting an indispensable part of a grammar for talk-in-interaction.

Keywords: past tense, social action format, preterite, present perfect, German, cognitive verbs, variation, assessments, reported speech

1. Introduction

Past tense is a basic grammatical category in German that speakers need to interact and that language learners acquire in order to formulate complex sequences in talk-in-interaction. As a crucial morpho-syntactic tool, tense in general allows speakers to create temporal structures between past, present, and future in relation to the moment of speaking. As such, tense is a crucial part of action formation, providing speakers with the possibility to express whether something has happened, is happening at the moment, or will happen in the near future.

Even though past tense plays an important part in temporally structuring actions in everyday talk, it has barely been the focus of interaction research. Most research on past tense in German is based on written data or language atlases (see Fischer 2018 for a recent account). As a consequence, prescriptive grammars —

https://doi.org/10.1075/slsi.37.08fie
© 2025 John Benjamins Publishing Company

at least for German — present rules that were neither established on the basis of actual language use nor verified with unelicited oral data. Consequently, we do not know much about how speakers use past tense in naturally occurring talk in general (but see Leonhard 2022), and specifically about how the two most frequent past tenses, preterite and present perfect, are distributed in German talk-in-interaction.

The present chapter is a first step in remedying this. It goes beyond the description of past tense as a category expressing temporal and/or aspectual meaning. It investigates purportedly 'interchangeable' forms for reference to past time in German by verifying whether this assumption of 'interchangeability' is actually borne out in interactional data. To do so, I focus on three frequently used verbs (see Auer 1998) in first- and third person singular that have been mostly investigated in their (first-person singular) present tense under the semantic category of *verba sentiendi*, namely *finden* 'to find', *glauben* 'to believe', and *meinen* 'to mean'.[1] *Verba sentiendi* are verbs that are semantically defined through their common feature of designating "processes of sensory perception, belief, opinion, thinking, feeling" (Bußmann 2008: 774, my translation). However, *finden, meinen,* and *glauben* are not only used as *verba sentiendi*. The three verbs have multiple meanings: *Finden* also designates the event of discovering something; *meinen* can be used to introduce reported speech; *glauben* can refer to subscribing to a belief system, for instance of a religion.

In the course of this chapter I describe two components that contribute to the distinction in the use of these verbs as either *verba sentiendi* or as reflecting one of the meanings listed above: (i) the choice of past tense format (preterite or present perfect) and (ii) the grammatical components (e.g., a complement clause or an adjective) that the respective format occurs with. In contrast to prior findings (see Section 2), the uses that I determine for first- and third-person singular are independent of the speakers' region of origin.

---

1. *Denken* 'to think' has already been investigated by Fiedler (2024), who shows a systematic difference between different past forms according to action formation; while the analytic past form is used for affective and epistemic stance-taking, the synthetic past form is almost exclusively used for affective stance-taking.

2. Past tense in German

In German, there are two different morphological means for referring to past time: a synthetic form, the so-called *Präteritum* ('preterite', e.g., *ich sah*, lit. 'I saw') and an analytic form, the so-called *Perfekt* ('present perfect', e.g., *ich habe gesehen*, lit. 'I have seen'). Morphologically, the preterite and present perfect are formed as shown in Table 1:

Table 1. Morphological construction of German synthetic and analytic past tense

Infinitive	Synthetic past form	Analytic past form	
meinen	ich mein-te	ich hab-e	ge-mein-t
'to mean'	1SG mean-PST.1SG	1SG have-AUX.1SG	PTCP-mean-CIRC
	I meant	*I have meant*	
glauben	ich glaub-te	ich hab-e	ge-glaub-t
'to believe'	1SG believe-PST.1SG	1SG have-AUX.1SG	PTCP-believe-CIRC
	I believed	*I have believed*	
finden	ich fand	ich hab-e	ge-fund-en
'to find'	1SG PST\find.1SG	1SG have-AUX.1SG	PTCP-find-CIRC
	I found	*I have found*	

Meinen and *glauben* are considered 'regular' because they do not change their root vowel in their preterite forms. *Finden*, in contrast, is categorized as 'irregular' because it changes its root vowel in preterite and in present perfect.

How the two past tenses are distributed in spoken and/or written German is a widely discussed linguistic question. In many languages, three categories are decisive for the distribution of past forms: tense (Comrie 1985), aspect, and *Aktionsart* (Vendler 1957, 1967).[2] Whether German tense distribution is sensitive to aspect or *Aktionsart* is a debate that goes beyond the scope of this paper, but an insightful discussion of the issue can be found in Leonhard (2022).

For German specifically, prior research has identified and discussed diverse factors that seem to influence the distribution of preterite and present perfect:

---

2. Even though most of the literature agrees that German tense distribution is not ruled by aspect, there have been explanations that do include aspect as a possibility of distribution (Streitberg 2009 [1891]) or that consider tense and aspect as interwoven categories in German (Eisenberg 1994; Goedsche 1934; Klein 2000).

Chapter 8. The use of past tense formats 229

- regional effects (Fischer 2018, 2021; Rowley 1983; Schirmunski 1962; Sütterlin 1924; Trost 1980): The loss of the use of preterite forms, the so-called *Präteritumschwund* is more pronounced in the South of Germany than in the North (Fischer 2018).
- semantics of the verb (*Aktionsart*) (Ballweg 1988; Ehrich & Vater 1989; Harweg 1975; Reichenbach 1947): State and activity verbs, for instance, tend to occur more often in preterite (Fischer 2021; Leonhard 2022) than accomplishment and achievement verbs.
- historical eclipse of preterite: Late Middle High German already exhibits the use of the present perfect as a kind of 'general past' (Fischer 2018: 264ff; see also Dentler 1997; Zeman 2010: 218) that can express perfective and imperfective meaning (see also Dal 1960; Dentler 1997; Klein 1974; Lindgren 1963).
- 'written past' (preterite) vs. 'spoken past' (present perfect): Most prescriptive grammars state that preterite is the past tense for written, formal, and/or narrative discourse, while the present perfect should be used in less formal, spoken language (see also Fischer 2018: 213; Zeman 2010).
- discourse structure (foreground vs. background): Hopper (1979) argues that speakers may foreground and background actions within narratives through aspect and tense (see also Fischer 2018: 191; Leonhard 2022: 245–262 on present perfect and double perfect; Zeman 2013).[3]

The most widespread and accepted explanation is a distribution according to geographical regions. In her meta-study of a large number of linguistic atlases and individual papers, Fischer (2018) confirms that there is a relation between the distribution of tense and regional dialects: While in the South of Germany (e.g., in Bavarian or Alemannic), preterite has almost completely disappeared, northern regions (e.g., Mecklenburg-Western Pomerania) still make ample use of the synthetic past tense. In some regions of transition in the middle of Germany, the variety of verbs that are still used in preterite is simply more restricted, or even reduced to *sein* 'to be' (Fischer 2021: 334). It is important to note, given the interactional background of the present chapter, that this sociolinguistically grounded explanation emerges from an analysis of written data and language atlases, which often provide maps with patchy information coverage.

That said, when past tense format choice is examined in talk-in-interaction, it emerges that, regardless of region, what matters to speakers is the social action they are engaged in: Speakers of German tend to use the preterite format for one

---

3. Like Hopper (1979), I do not conceptualize this distribution of past forms as a distribution of "ready-made devices 'deployed' in discourse because they happen already to exist" (Hopper 1979: 217). Instead, I see their use as "deriving" (Hopper 1979: 217) from interaction in line with Hopper's subsequently developed notion of *emergent grammar* (see Section 4).

type of action and the present perfect format for another. To give but one brief example: In my corpus of first- and third-person singular occurrences of *finden*, *meinen*, and *glauben*, the preterite format of *meinen* ($n=80$) is almost equally distributed between introducing reported speech ($n=34$) and repairing a prior turn ($n = 38$). The present perfect format of *meinen*, however, is barely used for repair ($n=3$). Instead, 83.6% ($n=46$) of the 55 occurrences introduce reported speech.[4] This distribution of past tense formats according to action formation can be schematically illustrated as follows:[5]

Verb + past-tense [(i)] implements ($\rightarrow$) Action[(i)]
Verb + past tense [(ii)] $\rightarrow$ Action[(ii)]

Since my analysis also shows that these past tense formats are tightly linked to the grammatical components with which they co-occur, this first schema will be further developed in the course of this chapter.

My empirical analysis suggests that the distribution of preterite and present perfect formats, at least concerning frequently used verbs like *finden*, *meinen*, and *glauben*, is interactionally motivated. Since the preterite and present perfect format of each of the three verbs is recurrently used to accomplish distinct actions in first and third person singular, I conceptualize these respective past tense forms of *finden*, *meinen*, and *glauben* as *social action formats* (Fox 2007, Schegloff 1996; for a discussion, see Gubina 2022: 67–69). Social action formats are recurrent grammatical patterns that speakers repeatedly use for implementing specific actions, thus making them recognizable for interlocutors.

Understanding past tense in interaction as a grammatical phenomenon that emerges from and is shaped by interaction, my analysis also provides evidence that both past tense formats recurrently co-occur with the same grammatical components, thus forming lexico-syntactic constructions for implementing recognizable actions.

---

4. In comparison to the high number of present tense forms of *meinen* in first-person singular ($n=2770$) due to the latter's use as discourse marker (Günthner & Imo 2003), the number of past tense, i.e., preterite and present perfect formats in first-person singular ($n=135$) is relatively low.

5. See Deppermann (2006) and Imo (2014) on the possible schematization of constructions in spoken language and for a detailed discussion; see Günthner (2011) on *N be that*-constructions in spoken German for a concrete application of Construction Grammar.

3. Data and methodology

My corpus comprises the whole *Forschungs- und Lehrkorpus* (FOLK) from the Leibniz-Institute for the German Language. This corpus consists of 682 video- and audio-recordings, totaling 336 hours and 3 minutes of mundane talk (as of August 2023), including institutional, public, and everyday settings. The recordings were made between 2003 and 2021 and are not restricted to specific regions in Germany. In other words, FOLK includes recordings of speakers from regions where preterite is still supposed to be commonly used (e.g., Western Westphalian, Mosel Franconian, and Ripuarian) and regions where preterite is supposed to have completely disappeared (e.g., Swabian, Bavarian, and Alemannic) (for an overview, see Fischer 2018:33). Because the present chapter does not seek to uncover sociolinguistic variation, it will be left to future studies to find out if and how preterite is used in specific spoken dialects.

In line with the goal of building a grammar-for-interaction, the methodology that the present chapter applies is *Interactional Linguistics* (Couper-Kuhlen & Selting 2018). That means that I understand grammar as one of multiple — also bodily — resources that speakers exploit to accomplish social actions. The analysis of conversational turns and sequences allows me to show that speakers use both past tense formats, preterite and present perfect, in a systematic way that is related to the action that speakers implement, such as repairing or assessing.

To investigate *finden* 'to find', *meinen* 'to mean', and *glauben* 'to believe', I first searched the FOLK-corpus for all occurrences of the three verbs in singular form. Assuming that the past forms of the three verbs function similarly to their present tense equivalents (i.e., with the tendency to form patterns overwhelmingly in first and/or third-person singular), and for frequency reasons more generally, I decided to only include first- and third-person singular forms (see also Tables 2, 3, 7, and 10).

Table 2. Frequency of verbs in present and past tense

Verb	Person	Preterite (synthetic past form)	Present perfect (analytic past form)
finden 'to find'	1SG	638	135
	3SG	51	87
meinen 'to mean'	1SG	80	55
	3SG	287	252
glauben 'to believe'	1SG	1	14
	3SG	1	10

After the determination of all occurrences, all instances were first classified according to other grammatical components related to their function; for instance, whether the verbs co-occur with a complement clause (with or without complementizer), an adjective, and/or a noun phrase. In a second step, after refining the basic linguistic transcripts according to the Jeffersonian transcription conventions (Jefferson 2004a), the actions that speakers accomplish with *finden*, *meinen*, or *glauben* together with these components were analyzed, for instance, *ich fand* 'I found' together with the noun phrase *feta* 'feta' and the adjective *ekelhaft* 'disgusting' forming an assessment, like in Excerpt (1):

Excerpt 1. *ekelhaft* 'disgusting' (FOLK_E_00300_SE_01_T_01_c1903), face-to-face, informal interaction

```
01 EDW: [und dann] hatt ich plötzlich, (.)
         and then suddenly I had

02       irgendwann,
         at some point

03       ich fand       feta immer total   ekelhaft,=
         1SG PST\find.1SG feta always totally disgusting
         I   found       feta always totally disgusting

04       =und dann war ich in südafrika und da,
         and then I was in south africa and there

((4 lines of side sequence omitted))

09 EDW: >un ich dachte irgendwann<,
         and I thought at some point

10       (0.34)

11 EDW: oah ich hätte jetz bock auf [feta.
         oah I am really craving       feta
```

The analysis of grammatical components brought to light that all three verbs bear several meanings. On the one hand, they are used as so-called *verba sentiendi*, in other words, they refer to perceptional or mental processes or feelings (see above for a definition). On the other hand, *finden* and *meinen* have more 'concrete' meanings: *Finden* can also refer to the event of discovering something; *Meinen* can, of course, be used as a synonym to 'wanting to say something' or 'having something in mind', but it is also used as quotative introducing a reported stretch of talk. Only *glauben* always refers to a mental process.

To analyze the accomplished action, I considered the overall activity in which a speaker is involved, the immediate adjacent turns, and, if relevant, the sequential position. Due to the large amount of data, a systematic determination of the sequential position was not possible. First results suggest, however, that future studies should investigate this line of research further.

4. An interactional approach to past tense

The investigation of past tense in talk-in-interaction has thus far focused on individual verbs. In most studies, these verbs occur in one specific past tense, forming a formulaic pattern that speakers routinely use to accomplish an action. For English, Kärkkäinen (2012) shows that *I thought* is recurrently used as a format for taking a stance. Speakers either employ *I thought* to introduce an explicit epistemic or evaluative stance, an affective stance, or a change of state (Heinemann & Koivisto 2016). This latter function has already been described by Jefferson (2004b), who investigates the format *at first I thought x but then I realized y* — a study based on previous findings by Sacks (1992). Smith and Seuren (2022) show that English *I thought that X* and Dutch *ik dacht dat X* can be a practice for uncovering troubles in understanding: When speakers realize their own misunderstanding, they first "[index] a change-of-state and then [explicate] their misapprehension" with *I thought that X* and *ik dacht dat X*. Finnish *mä ajattelin että* 'I thought that' has been shown to frame the speakers' stance, but also to introduce his or her personal plans or possible joint projects with interlocutors (Laury, Helasvuo & Rauma 2020). Investigating a diachronic data set, Laury et al. (2020) are able to show that, over time, not only did *mä ajattelin että* become more and more fixed, it also occurred with a greater variety of complements in the recent data set. Their results suggest that past tense formats, in combination with certain grammatical components, can be used to implement specific social actions — a result that is in line with the findings of the present chapter.

Similar to English *I thought*, German *ich dachte/ich habe gedacht* 'I (have) thought' is used for epistemic and affective stance-taking in everyday talk (Deppermann & Reineke 2017). In contrast to Kärkkäinen (2012) and Jefferson (2004b), Deppermann and Reineke (2017) include synthetic and analytic past forms of *denken* 'to think'. The authors' decision to treat both past forms as interchangeable is understandable, since prior results on tense distribution in German suggest that geography primarily determines speaker's past tense use. Fiedler (2024), investigating a smaller data set of the same corpus as Deppermann and Reineke (2017), shows, however, that there is a tendency for a distribution of *ich dachte* 'I thought' and *ich habe gedacht* 'I have thought' according to action formation: While the synthetic past form constitutes a homogenous practice for taking an affective stance, the analytic past form is used equally for both affective and epistemic stance-taking.

Fiedler's (2024) results suggest that an investigation of past tense use in everyday talk-in-interaction may open new perspectives on how grammar and action formation are intertwined. Such a grammar-in-use of past tenses goes beyond an explanation along traditional lines of grammar, which are usually based on aspect and *Aktionsart*. Investigating past tense in its actual use in everyday talk allows a perspective on a grammatical matter that has so far not been analyzed, namely as a possible resource for action formation. The results that emerge from the qualitative, data-driven analysis may help us, in retrospect, to revisit — or confirm — the relevance of aspect and *Aktionsart* concerning the concrete use of *verba sentiendi* in preterite and present perfect.

Concretely, an interactional approach can contribute to a grammar-for-interaction in the following ways:

i. While it is necessary to maintain the actual distinction of past tenses between preterite and present perfect and also that their distribution is in some way patterned, the interactional approach allows us to test the mechanisms of distribution posited in prior research (geography, aspect, semantics, or narrative structuration, see Section 2) for talk-in-interaction. Investigating the sequences in which speakers use both past tenses of the same verb and the actions that they most frequently carry out with them, enables me to approach past tense from a new perspective that focuses on action formation (Levinson 2013).

ii. While a geographical distribution of past tenses cannot — and should not — be neglected, the present chapter challenges the stable character of this distributional factor, which has not been verified either with recent or interaction data. I suggest that it is necessary to verify distributional rules with oral and recent data. The results of such an investigation may reveal that there are different levels of granularity (see Fox & Raymond, this volume), from geographical factors to the semantics of the verb to social actions, that may also motivate the distribution of preterite and present perfect.

iii. An interactional approach allows me to study past tense use as an emergent phenomenon (Hopper 1987, 2011). This includes the idea that, through the recurrent use of a specific past form of a verb, patterns may form which allow speakers to routinely accomplish the same action in everyday talk (see also Suomalainen, this volume). For the use of past tense, none of the above-mentioned distributional rules would play a role. Instead, as usage-based studies also show, the frequent use of a certain past form may have led to a linguistic routine that speakers deploy for a specific action (for such an example in French talk-in-interaction, the quotative *j'étais là* 'I was there', see Fiedler 2024).

iv. For language learners, understanding language use through the actions that are accomplished by recurrently deploying the same linguistic structure may enhance interactional competence (Hall & Pekarek Doehler 2011). Thinking even further, after the analyses of a larger amount of data, some rules from grammars and grammar books for learners may need to be adjusted according to the idea of a *grammar-for-interaction* in second language acquisition (Pekarek Doehler 2018: 3).

5. Past tense formats in German: Constructions with preterite and present perfect to implement social actions

In first-person singular present tense, *finden, meinen* and *glauben* have been shown to grammaticalize into discourse markers or epistemic parentheticals when they are used as cognitive verbs (Auer & Lindström 2016; Günthner & Imo 2003; Imo 2007a). The following interactional linguistic analysis evidences that such grammaticalization processes — concerning frequency, degree of semantic bleaching, or change of grammatical category (e.g., the change from a matrix clause to a discourse marker for *ich glaube* 'I believe', Imo 2012) — do not exist to the same degree for past tense forms. In the following three sections, I analyze *finden, meinen*, and *glauben* in first- and third-person singular preterite and present perfect in talk-in-interaction. The data excerpts that I provide for each past tense format illustrate the lexico-syntactic constructions that I identified in my corpus. The quantitative distribution of these constructions precedes my empirical analysis in each section — as it did in the entire research process and analysis of my data — thus providing first evidence for the actual use of past tense constructions in everyday talk.

5.1 *Finden* 'to find'

The past tense formats that I investigated for *finden* are first-person singular (*ich fand / ich habe gefunden* 'I (have) found') and third-person singular (*er/sie/es/man fand / hat gefunden* 'he/she/it/one found / has found'). These formats occur with different frequencies, as Table 3 shows:

Table 3. Frequency of *finden* in 1st and 3rd person past tense

Form	Number of occurrences
ich fand	638
er/sie/es/man fand	51
ich habe gefunden	135
er/sie/es/man hat gefunden	87

The numbers evidence that, in first-person singular, the synthetic past form is more than four times more frequent than the analytic past form, while the third-person singular does not show such a large difference in number. The qualitative analysis of all occurrences reveals that this difference in number is due to the fact that first person singular preterite is recurrently used as a social action format for assessing something ($n = 576$). When doing so, it primarily occurs in the syntactic combinations shown in Table 4:

Table 4. Syntactic configurations of *ich fand*

ich fand	Number of occurrences[a]
+ complementizer + complement clause	4
+ complement clause without complementizer	20
+ noun phrase + adjective	515

a. Another 37 cases are part of an assessing-activity, but cannot be attributed to either of the collocative elements because of the speakers' self-repair after *ich fand*, which makes a categorization difficult. 11 cases are single-unit turns of the type *find ich auch* (lit. 'find I too', idiom. 'I think so too') functioning as second pair parts through which speakers confirm a prior assessment. In 2 instances, *ich fand* is combined with a noun phrase. 32 cases occur as parentheticals. The remaining 16 cases are either non-audible or interrupted.

Assessments with *ich fand* are primarily done with the pattern [*ich fand* + noun prase + adjective].[6] In the rare cases in which *ich fand* is combined with a noun phrase (NP) and without an adjective (*n* = 2), speakers use *ich fand* in the sense of 'finding an object'.

Excerpt (2) illustrates the most frequent lexico-syntactic pattern [*ich fand* + noun prase + adjective] as well as the combination of [*ich fand* + complement clause without complementizer].

Excerpt 2. *das buch* 'the book' (FOLK_E_00392_SE_01_SE_01_T_01_c797), face-to-face, informal interaction

```
01 CAR: knapp unter zweihundert seiten glaub ich was bei
        just under two hundred pages I think what for

02      mir noch übrig bleiben aber .h [ä ]hm,
        me is still left ((to read)) but uhm

03 REG:                                [ah,]
                                        oh

04 CAR: also [ich ] fand        des   liest
        PTC  1SG    PST\find.1SG 3SG.M read.PRS.3SG
        so   I      found       it    reads

05 REG:      [okee]
             okay

06 CAR: sich    richtig schnell,=
        REFL.3SG real    quick
                 really fast

07      =des reif,
        this ((booktitle))

08      ich hab (0.37) mir          hat          _s (0.79)
        1SG have.PRS.3SG me-1SG.DAT have-AUX.3SG 3SG
        I   have         I
```

6. For reasons of readability, I use *ich fand* as placeholder for both word orders subject-verb and verb-subject.

09	gefallen	des	buch
	please.PTCP	the	book
	liked it (the/that) book		

10	ich	fand	_s [gut,]
	1SG	PST\find.1SG 3SG	good
	I found		*it good*

11 REG: [okay.]
                                      okay

In this excerpt, Carola and Regine talk about books they have to read for their studies. Regine complains about the workload. At line 2, Carola positively assesses one of the books that she is reading at the moment by saying that one can read it rather quickly. The assessment is formatted as a complement clause, introduced by *ich fand* 'I found' (lines 4, 6, and 7) with the book title added as right dislocation. In line with previous literature on *verba sentiendi*, no complementizer links the matrix clause *ich fand* with the complement clause. Consequently, the verb of the complement clause is in second position, thus making the assessment, *das liest sich richtig schnell des reif* 'it reads itself really fast this reif', as the rhematic part of the utterance, which has been associated with higher pragmatic relevance (Auer 1998). Sequentially speaking, this assessment forms the main argument for why Regina, who previously raised doubts about the length of the book (not in transcript), should read the book herself. After a second positive assessment about the book in general (lines 8 and 9), Carola closes her turn with a final, short assessment at line 10. This time, *ich fand* is combined with an *s* — which can either be a reduced form of the demonstrative (*das* 'that') or of the object pronoun *es* 'it' — and an assessing adjective, *gut* 'good'. Such short assessments have been shown to be a recurrent practice to close especially longer turns (Goodwin 1986: 215). Indeed, in my corpus, [*ich fand* + noun phrase + ADJ] recurrently does terminal work. In a random sample of 100 occurrences of [*ich fand* + ADJ], the pattern remains brief and closes the speaker's turn in 36 cases (= 36%).

Third-person singular *fand* is less frequent than first-person singular (see Table 3). 49 out of 51 third-person singular cases are used to assess something. 48 of these occurrences are combinations with the pattern [noun phrase + adjective]; only one is combined with a complement clause (with complementizer). The remaining two cases are abandoned after *fand*.

Overall, third-person *fand* is used, similar to first-person *fand*, in assessments. Excerpt (3) illustrates such a case. Here, the speaker reports about a third party's assessment. Four roommates (one of whom, LAU, is Italian) are having dinner together. Prior to this excerpt, Nina told a story about how, when she was in Italy on holiday with four (female) friends, two Italian men invited them twice for drinks.

238 Sophia Fiedler

Excerpt 3. *in italien* 'in italy' (FOLK_E_00055_SE_01_T_02_c608), face-to-face conversation, informal interaction

```
01 LAU: aber in italien      ist äh (0.61) [normal. ]
        but  in italy ((it)) is  uh            normal

02 NIN:                                    [ä (.) ja]
                                            uh    yes

03 URS: ä (.) .h ((laughs))
        uh

04 LAU: ja is ganz nor [ja ]
        yes ((it))'s totally nor yes

05 AME:                [ech]t (.) dass d_f frauen
                        really     that t w women

06      einge[laden,  ]
        are invited

07 NIN:      [(war eh)] .h genau wir waren alle
             was anyway   exactly we were all

08      so total erstaunt,
        so totally surprised

09      und und sie  fand          _s (.) normal.
        and and 3SG.F find.PST.3SG 3SG     normal
        and and she  found          it     normal

10 URS: ((laughs)) .h super, ((laughs))
                      great

11 AME: ((laughs))

12 NIN: ((laughs))
```

At lines 1 and 4, Laura, the Italian roommate, responds to the story by framing the event as normal for Italy. First, Amelie utters an incredulous request for confirmation (lines 5 and 6). At lines 7 and 8, Nina affiliates with Amelie's display of surprise with a comparison: While she and her friends were just as surprised as Amelie is now, Laura *fand_s normal* 'found it normal'. This re-telling of Laura's stance implies that she must have heard the story before and that she must have responded in a way similar to what she does at lines 1 and 4.

In contrast to Excerpt (2), Nina does not use *fand* to evaluate a matter herself but to make someone else's evaluation available to all present interlocutors. The report of Laura's evaluation constitutes the punchline of Nina's turn and closes her turn. All three interlocutors respond to the punchline with laughter, thus affiliating with the amusing character of Nina's utterance.

The analytic past form is, like the synthetic past form, more frequent in first-person singular ($n = 135$) than in third-person singular ($n = 87$). Let me first analyze the first person present perfect formats before presenting third-person formats. First-person present perfect is typically used with a noun phrase only ($n = 100$). 6.7% ($n = 9$) of all occurrences take a prepositional phrase, for instance *des hab ich dann bei ((bookstore name)) gefunden* 'I found that at ((bookstore name))'.[7] In combination with these two grammatical components, *hab gefunden* does not refer to a mental process but to the event of discovering something.

All grammatical components that co-occur with first-person *gefunden* 'found' are shown in Table 5:

Table 5. Syntactic configurations of *ich habe gefunden*

ich habe gefunden	Frequency
+ noun phrase	74.1%
+ prepositional phrase	6.7%
+ noun phrase + adjective	12.6%
+ complementizer + main clause	0.7%
+ main clause	3.0%

All 22 cases combined with [NP + ADJ] ($n = 17$) or a complement clause ($n = 5$ including $n = 1$ with complementizer) are assessments. Out of these 22 cases, 6 have the function of closing a sequence (27.3%), which is a slightly lower relative frequency than in the random sample of *ich fand* + NP + ADJ (see end of Excerpt (2)).

Excerpt (4) illustrates the most common use of *ich habe gefunden* 'I have found': its occurrence with a noun phrase. In this lexico-syntactic configuration, speakers do not use the verb in a cognitive sense but as a verb that conveys the action of finding an object, in this case money.

Excerpt 4. *ein euro* 'a euro' (FOLK_E_00024_SE_01_T_01_c196), face-to-face conversation, informal interaction

```
01 SUS: [na ich hab gemerkt d]ass ich dann noch
         ((well)) I realized    that I  then still

02      drei euro fünfzig hatte,=
        had three euros fifty ((left))

03      =wir waren ewig im parkhaus,
        we'd been in the parking garage forever

04      un dann sin mer zum parkhaus,
        and then we went to the parking garage

05      und ich hatte zu wenig geld.
        and I had too little money

06      ich so geil.
        I was like great

07 ANN: ((laughter))
```

---

7. Two other instances occur in proverb-like formulations like *ich habe meinen weg gefunden* 'I found my way' and another forms a single-unit turn. In another two instances, the remaining turn elements are not audible.

```
08 SUS: weißt_e so
        you know like
09      (0.3)
10 SUS: viertel vor zehn,
        quarter to ten
11      .hh hab          ich zum    glück
            have-AUX.1SG   1SG for.DAT luck
            luckily I found
12      noch        _n          euro gefunden,
        still       one/DET.INDF euro PTCP-find.CIRC
        another euro
13      dann hatt_s genau gereicht, ((laughs))
        then it was just enough
14      in der tasche,
        in my purse
```

The turn with *gefunden* is embedded into a longer telling sequence that starts prior to this excerpt. Susanne describes a situation where she didn't have enough coins to pay for parking (lines 1 to 5). After taking a negative stance toward these events (line 6) and a temporal embedding of her description (line 10), Susanne presents the twist of her telling, namely that she unexpectedly discovered an additional euro (lines 11 and 12) in her purse (line 14).

In third-person singular, the use of *gefunden* is similar to first-person singular. The exact frequencies are shown in Table 6:

Table 6. Syntactic configurations of *er/sie/es/man hat gefunden*

er/sie/es/man hat gefunden	Frequency[a]
+ NP	59.8%
Passive construction[b]	21.8%
+ NP + ADJ	3.4%
+ complement clause without complementizer	3.4%

a. 6 further occurrences are fixed expressions where *finden* is part of expressions like *Anwendung finden* 'to be applied' or *Eingang in eine Sammlung finden* 'to become part of a collection'. One further occurrence takes an infinitive, one occurs as a single-unit turn and two cases are not audible.
b. For instance, *bis jetzt wurde nichts gefunden* 'until now, nothing has been found' (FOLK_E_00446_SE_01)

Excerpt (5) illustrates its main use in talk-in-interaction, namely for reporting the event of finding something, just like in first-person singular. Helen tells a story to exemplify the difficult parking situation in some cities.

Chapter 8. The use of past tense formats **241**

Excerpt 5. *in zweiter reihe* 'in second row' (FOLK_E_00305_SE_01_T_01_c594),
face-to-face conversation, informal interaction

```
01 HEL: .h in kassel meine freundin die kam
             in kassel ((= name of city)) my friend

02       die kam also ma spät nach hause,
         so she came home late once

03       .h die hat da net in zweiter reihe geparkt,
             she did not park there in second row

04       sondern in vierter oder fünfter ja,=
         but       in fourth  or   fifth   right

05       =wei die ha- da standen fünf autos nebennander.
         because they ha there were five cars ((parked))
         next to each other

06       (0.41)

07 XEN: hm.

08 HEL: es war ne (.) relativ    große straße,
         it was a      relatively large street

09       (0.2)

10 HEL: un  wei   die einfach nix      anderes
         and because 3SG PTC       nothing else
         and because she just didn't

11       gefunden    hat       ge,
         PTCP-find-CIRC have-AUX.3SG PTC
         find anything else right?

12       (0.71)
```

Like in Excerpt (4), the speaker uses *gefunden* for the concrete action of finding something; only here, the noun phrase is not a concrete object, but an abstract entity, namely *nix anderes* 'anything else' (line 10). Helen tells a story about a friend who had difficulties finding a parking spot in her street when coming home late in the evening (lines 1 to 8). That lack of acceptable alternatives for parking (lines 10 and 11) thereby represents the ultimate argument to justify parking in fifth row and serves as an account.

The comparison of first and third-person preterite *fand* and first and third-person present perfect *gefunden* shows, on a quantitative and qualitative level, that the different past formats occur in specific lexico-syntactic patterns. While the preterite almost exclusively occurs as *verbum sentiendi* that speakers use for assessments in combination with either noun phrases and adjectives or complement clauses, the present perfect serves to report the concrete action of finding an object (occurring as noun phrase), mostly within tellings.

The analysis of past tense formats of *finden* brought to light that much depends on what other grammatical components (i.e., complement clause, adjective, ...) a past tense format is combined with. It is these recurrent patterns [past tense format + grammatical component] that form turn-constructional units (Sacks, Schegloff & Jefferson 1974) and allow speakers to accomplish actions. As such, these patterns seem to be best conceptualized as *constructions*. For *finden*, the most frequent constructions could be schematized as follows:

/*finden* + NP + ADJ ('consider s.th. to be [quality]')/ + preterite →[8] assessment
/*finden* + complement clause ('consider s.th. to be [quality]')/+ preterite → assessment
/*finden* + NP ('discover s.th.')/ + present perfect → report of an event

The results of my qualitative analysis emphasize that it is neither the past tense nor the grammatical components *alone* that are associated with a certain meaning. The present perfect format, for instance, when combined with [NP + ADJ] or a complement clause, also implements assessments, but this pattern is rare. To assess something, speakers seem to prefer the preterite format with either of these two grammatical components. This result evidences that it is the combination of past tense format and syntactic configuration that constitutes a construction, which then allows speakers to routinely implement a specific action.

5.2 *Meinen* 'to mean'

With *meinen*, I also investigate first-person singular (*ich meinte / ich habe gemeint* 'I (have) meant') and third-person singular (*er/sie/es/man meinte / hat gemeint* 'he/she/it/one meant / has meant'). Table 7 gives an overview of all occurrences:

Table 7. Frequency of *meinen* in 1st and 3rd person past tense

Form	Number of occurrences
ich meinte	84
er/sie/es/man meinte	290
ich habe gemeint	53
er/sie/es/man hat gemeint	234

Meinen is the only verb among the three investigated that is more frequent in third than in first-person singular past tense. Nevertheless, both third and first-person past tense co-occur with similar grammatical constituents, namely either with complement clauses (primarily main clauses) or with a noun phrase (primarily pronouns like *mich* 'me' or *das* 'that'). Depending on its past tense format

---

8. As introduced in Section 2, the arrow represents 'to implement' and refers to the action specified afterward.

Chapter 8. The use of past tense formats   **243**

and on the grammatical constituents that *meinen* combines with, the following constructions can be identified:

/*meinen* + NP ('having something else in mind')/ + preterite → self-repair
/*meinen* + complement clause/ + preterite *or* present perfect → reporting speech

In this section, I first treat first and third person preterite before analyzing first and third person *er/sie/es/man hat gemeint.* For *ich meinte,* I identified the following actions in my corpus:

Table 8. Actions accomplished with *ich meinte*

Action	Frequency
Introducing reported speech	47.6%
Self-repair of a misunderstanding	36.9%
Confirmation in second position	12%
Non-audible cases	3.5%

    Again, the combination of the past tense format *ich meinte* with other grammatical components constitutes a TCU that speakers use to accomplish an action.[9] I will focus on the most recurrent combinations, with either a noun phrase (for self-repair) or a complement clause (for introducing reported speech).

    Excerpt (6) illustrates the most frequent use of *ich meinte* as a quotative. Lukas and Erika are talking about a non-present third party and her assumptions regarding homosexual men.

Excerpt 6. *mach mal halblang* 'give me a break'
(FOLK_E_00042_SE_01_T_02_c413), face-to-face conversation, informal interaction

```
01 LUK: [nich je]der also sie meinte halt, .h
        not everyone (well/so) what she meant was
02 ERI: [hm_hm, ]
03      (0.22)
04 LUK: dass schwule (0.43) alle männer anmachen würden.
        that gay (men)  would hit on all men
05      (0.26)
06 LUK: [ja und da]nn meinte    ich
        yes and then mean-PST.1SG 1SG
        yeah and then I said
07 ERI: [hm_hm    ]
```

---

9. For reasons of readability, I use *ich meinte* as placeholder for both word orders, subject-verb and verb-subject.

```
08 LUK: dann mach mal HALBlang ja,
        QUOTE
        then give me a break will you?
09 LUK: ich penn ja jetzt mit dem auch in nem zimmer, (.)
        QUOTE
        I now sleep PART with him in one room, too
10      ja,
        QUOTE
        yeah
11      .h und nur weil ich en mann bin (.) heißt des
        QUOTE
        and just because I'm a guy doesn't
12      ja noch lange nich (0.32) dass der mich anbaggert.
        QUOTE
        automatically mean that he's gonna hit on me
```

At line 1, Lukas introduces the third party's assumption, introduced with *sie meinte*. This is one of the rare instances of indirect reported speech with *meinen* where the complementizer *dass* 'that' introduces the quote (line 4). Lukas' reported response is introduced with *und dann meinte ich* 'and then I said' (line 6). The quote itself scolds the third party, first with *mach mal halblang* 'give me a break' (line 8) and then with a more elaborate account (lines 9–12). The reported exchange is prosodically staged (Yule & Mathis 1992) and conveys to a certain degree the speaker's annoyance about the woman's attitude.

The second most frequent practice with *ich meinte* is its use for self-repair. Excerpt (7) illustrates this use. Alma and Marius are talking about the *Harry Potter* fantasy book series. At line 11, Alma responds to Marius' prior utterance that at some point, one could think that the characters Harry and Hermione would date (not in transcript):

Excerpt 7. *mädchen* 'girls' (FOLK_E_00288_SE_01_T_02_c1101), face-to-face conversation, informal interaction.

```
01 ALM: aber harry kommt auch mit andern lung-
        but harry also  dates   other loy
02      jungs zusammen,
        boys
03      (0.21)
04 ALM: ähm, [((laughs))
        uhm
05 MAR:      [((laughs))
06 ALM: .h mädchen meinte     [ich. h.]
        girls     mean-PST.1SG 1SG
        girls     I meant
07 MAR:                       [.h     ]
```

Chapter 8. The use of past tense formats   **245**

In her response, Alma falsely uses *jungs* 'boys' instead of *mädchen* 'girls', as her self-repair at line 6 shows and clarifies. The repaired item precedes the *meinte ich*-format, which marks *mädchen* post-hoc as the word intended here. Marius' and Alma's laughter at lines 4 and 5 orients towards the amusing character of Alma's slip of the tongue and already projects the upcoming self-repair.

Third-person singular *meinte* is used similarly to first-person singular. The frequencies differ, however, as shown in Table 9:

Table 9. Actions accomplished with *er/sie/man meinte*

Action	Frequency
Introducing reported speech	93.1%
Self-repair of a misunderstanding	3.1%
Confirmation in second position	0.3%
Synonymous use to 'wanting to say something'	0.6%
Non-audible cases	2.8%

These quantitative results demonstrate that, in my corpus, third-person *meinte* is primarily used to introduce reported speech, while other actions are only marginally implemented.[10] In my corpus, third-person *meinte* introducing reported speech is overall more frequent than first-person *meinte* with the same function. Recurrently, a third party's reported speech is introduced with third-person *meinte*, while the narrator's reported speech is introduced with *(und) ich so* ('(and) I like'). Excerpt (8) evidences this.

Excerpt 8. *de de er name* 'GDR name' (FOLK_E_00208_SE_01_T_02_c308), face-to-face conversation, informal interaction

```
01 IDA: .h [un des w]ar letztens so lustig mit svetlana
             and it was so funny the other day with svetlana
02 KAT:     [.h    ]
03      (0.21)
04 IDA: [°h ((click))  (.)  ähm    ]
        uhm
05 UTE: [gibs mir no_mal die lätta,]
        will you pass me the lätta ((=name of margarine))
        again
06      (0.5)
07 IDA: da    meinte       sie (0.78)
        there mean-PST.3SG 3SG
        so    she said
```

10. There are 2 cases where *meinte* in third-person singular is used in the sense of 'wanting to say something' and 8 non-audible occurrences.

08	((click)) .h mensch wie heißt
	QUOTE
	man what's the name of

09	denn die freundin von dem einen freund
	QUOTE
	PART the friend of that one friend

10	den wir haben,=
	QUOTE
	that we have ((in common))

11	=und wir sin beide nich auf den namen gekommen,
	and we both couldn't come up with the name

12	und sie meinte ey des is so_n typischer
	and 3SG mean-PST.3SG QUOTE
	and she said (man) it's like a typical

13	de de er name?
	QUOTE
	GDR name

14	(2.28)

15 IDA:	un ich so na ja so (.) gudrun?
	und I'm like well like gudrun?

16	und so nee nee (.) unsere elterngeneration,
	and like no no our parents' generation

17	ich so hanna
	I'm like hanna

18	un dann hab ich echt richtig geraten.
	and then I actually guessed right

19	(un) war so wirklich hanna des war so .h
	(and) ((it)) was like really hanna that was like

Ida introduces her telling with a pre (line 1), thus situating the upcoming dialogue with regards to time (*letztens* 'the other day') and participating parties (*svetlana*). After some hesitation (lines 3, 4, and 6), Ida utters the first pair part of a reported dialogue, introduced with *da meinte sie* 'so she said' (line 7). She reports how her friend Svetlana was searching for the name of a mutual acquaintance (lines 8–10). The reported stretch of talk is staged as a word search with a pause, a click, an inbreath, and an initial interjection (*mensch* 'man') preceding the reported question. After framing the word search as unsuccessful (line 11), Ida reports Svetlana's continuation: a hint about the name she is looking for (lines 12 and 13). Again, the third party's speech is introduced with *sie meinte*. At line 15, Ida then reports suggesting a candidate (*gudrun*). This suggestion is introduced with another quotative, *und ich so* 'and I'm like' (Golato 2000). The subsequent reported stretches of her own past talk are both introduced with variants of this same quotative: *ich so* 'I'm like' and *und war so* 'and was like' (lines 15 and 17).

This excerpt demonstrates that speakers may alternate between quotatives depending on the reported party, which may be one explanation for the higher number of *meinte* in third-person singular.

The present perfect tense of *meinen* shows a similar distribution between first- and third-person singular concerning action formation (see Table 10).

Table 10. Actions accomplished with *ich habe gemeint* and *er/sie/man hat gemeint*

Format	Action	Frequency
ich habe gemeint (*n* = 53)	Introducing reported speech	81.1%
	Self-repair	11.3%
	Confirmation in second position	5.7%[a]
er/sie/man hat gemeint (*n* = 243)	Introducing reported speech	89.3%
	Other-repair	3.7%
	Display of a discrepant assumption, e.g., *man hat früher mal gemeint, dass* ('one (has) thought in those days that')	1.2%
	'Wanting to say something'	1.2%[b]

a. The remaining instance has the meaning of 'wanting/intending to say something' (*was hab ich mit x gemeint* 'what did I want to say with x').
b. The remaining two instances are one confirmation in second position and one non-audible occurrence.

Because of the parallel use for quoting speech in both past tenses, I do not provide individual examples for each form. Instead, I present two excerpts in order to illustrate a syntactic specificity that distinguishes present perfect first- and third-person singular quotatives that introduce reported speech.

Comparing first and third-person singular *meinen* in present perfect tense, one syntactic difference is striking: If the quotatives are followed by syntactically complete clauses (i.e., not by interjections like *ah* or *oh mann* 'oh man', as may be the case with reported speech), they tend to introduce two distinct syntactic formats. In first-person singular, 81.4% (*n* = 35) of the 43 cases of *ich habe gemeint* introduce a quote with main clause syntax (no complementizer, verb in second position). Only one of those 35 instances contains deictic shifts, which demonstrates a higher syntactic dependence on the introducing quotative.[11] One addi-

---

11. In German linguistics, two formats are distinguished through different technical terms: dependent main clause syntax (no complementizer, verb in second position and no deictic shifts), for instance *Er hat gesagt: du musst um fünf zuhause sein* 'He said: you have be home at five' (invented example) and independent subordinate clause syntax (no complementizer, verb in second position but deictic shifts, possibility of subjunctive mood), for instance *Er hat gesagt,*

tional case is followed by a subordinate clause with the complementizer *dass* 'that'.[12] That means that *ich habe gemeint* primarily introduces complement clauses (i.e., the quote) that are syntactically independent from the introducing main clause (i.e., the quotative). This syntactic configuration indicates a high pragmatic independence of the quote proper, which bears the main content of the entire quoting unit.

The distribution of clause-combining types is different for third-person present perfect: 34.2% ($n = 83$) of all occurrences introduce a main clause with deictic shifts, 26% ($n = 63$) introduce a main clause without deictic shifts, and 6.2% ($n = 15$) a subordinate clause. This result demonstrates that in third-person present perfect quotes are syntactically more dependent on the quotative than in first-person.[13] One reason for this distribution may be that deictic shifts allow the narrating speaker to remain present while quoting — something that may be useful when quoting a third party in order to clearly distinguish between reported and reporting person. A comparison of third-person present perfect and third-person preterite shows that preterite *meinte* tends to introduce syntactically more independent structures (44.8% of main clauses without deictic shifts and 13.7% of non-clausal structures compared to 26% and 2.8% respectively with present perfect *hat gemeint*).

The syntactic differences between the quotes (main clause without deictic shifts vs. with deictic shifts) seems to also be related to distinct actions that speakers accomplish with the quote. The next two excerpts illustrate this contrast by comparing first and third-person present perfect tense.

Excerpt 9. *hat mir nicht gefallen* 'didn't like it' (FOLK_E_00048_SE_01_T_02_c941), face-to-face conversation, informal interaction

```
01 MIA: .h und dann bin ich zurückgekommen,
            and then I came back
02      und die lena gleich,=
        and lena immediately
03      =<<imitating lena> und wie war_s?>
                          and how was it?
04      (0.3)
```

---

ich muss/müsse um fünf zuhause sein 'He said I have/had to be home at five' (invented example). Since the reader may not be familiar with this terminology, I chose a more transparent terminology (main clause syntax without or with deictic shifts) and simply refer here to Imo (2007a) for a detailed explanation.

12. The remaining 7 cases are not definable with regards to their syntactic format other than that they are not linked to the quotative with a complementizer.

13. Additionally, 56 occurrences do not contain enough information concerning deictic shifts, but they occur without a linking complementizer.

Chapter 8. The use of past tense formats **249**

```
05 MIA: ich hab        gemeint      so,
         1SG have-AUX.1SG PTCP-mean-CIRC like
         I    have          said          like
06       nee hat [mir nich ge↑↑fa]llen, ((laughs))
         QUOTE
         no   didn't like it
07 LAR:         [((laughs))      ]
08       ((laughs)) oh gott zum glück.
                    oh god fortunately
```

Mia reports a dialogue between her and an (absent) friend, Lena, about student cities that Mia has been visiting. At lines 1 and 2, Mia first reports Lena's question; at line 5, her response, introduced by *ich hab gemeint so* 'I have meant like'. The introduced quote is preceded by the response cry (Goffman 1981) *nee* 'no', which "[indexes] directly the state of the transmitter" (Goffman 1981: 116), and a clause that fulfills the criteria of a main clause with the verb in first position and no complementizer.[14] In line with Hopper's (1979) explanations on fore- and backgrounding, the adjacency pair follows a certain temporality. The prosodically staged character of the quote with a high pitch movement on *gefallen* 'pleased' emphasizes its pragmatic independence: The speaker seems to attribute a higher relevance to the content of the quote than to the introducing quotative – the quote is, so to say, foregrounded. Larissa's response at line 8 supports this. She affiliates with Mia's quote by displaying her relief about Mia not liking the city in question.

Using a main clause format without deictic shifts as in Excerpt (9) allows the speaker to move the quote to the foreground of the telling while enabling her interlocutors to experience the reported scene in the most direct way possible through a reenactment (Sidnell 2006; see also Golato 2000). This is different when using a main clause *with* deictic shifts as quote, as Excerpt (10) demonstrates. In this case, the quote is backgrounded. Amelie and Pablo talk about the ex-boyfriend of a mutual friend:

Excerpt 10. *sie soll abnehm* 'she should lose weight' (FOLK_E_00047_SE_01_T_02_ c145), face-to-face conversation, informal interaction

```
01 AME: [der hat mit] ihr vor einem jahr schluss gemacht,=
         he broke up with her a year ago
02       =aber sie leidet da immer noch drunter.
         but   she is still suffering   from it
03 PAB: ja.
         yes
```

---

14. Usually, the verb would be in second position. Here, the speaker does not use a subject – a recurrent practice in tellings (Günthner 2006).

```
04 AME: .hh (.) hm (.) hat          sie gemeint
                     have-AUX.3SG 3SG PTCP-mean-CIRC
              hm      she           has said

05       er hätte gesagt (.) immer,
         he'd have said     always

06       ja sie wär zu dick.
         PART she'd be too fat

07       (0.72)

08 AME: und sie soll abnehm,
        and she should lose weight
```

At line 1, Amelie initiates a telling that informs Pablo about some details of the third party's state of mind. In contrast to Excerpt (9), the reported speech at lines 5 to 8 introduces a third party's speech and is not part of a reported dialogue. Instead, the reported stretch of talk, introduced by *hat sie gemeint* (lit. 'has she meant') serves as an account for Amelie's assertion that this third party is still suffering from the separation (line 2). The quote is not prosodically animated like it is in Excerpt (9). One reason for the non-animated rendering of the speech may be that the quote simply delivers additional information to support the legitimacy of Amelie's gossip by using the original speaker's utterance as an information source. The syntactic format matches this purpose: Compared to Excerpt (9), the original speaker remains 'present' during the quote through the personal pronoun *sie* 'she' (lines 6 and 8), which has not been deictically shifted to second-person singular. Another sign for the higher degree of embeddedness of the quote are that *hätte* 'would have' and *wär* 'would be' are in subjunctive mood and that the imperative at line 8 is reformulated to a *soll* 'should'-construction (Radtke 2015: 99). These changes in mood demonstrate that the introducing quotative in past tense influences the morpho-syntax of the complement clause, thus increasing its syntactic dependence. In comparison, in Excerpt (9), neither tense nor mood of the verb format *hat gefallen* 'has pleased/appealed' is modified, even though the quotative is the same as in Excerpt (10) with respect to tense and its main clause-format.

In contrast to preterite tense, in which both first and third-person singular *meinte* introduce staged quotes (Excerpt (9)), it seems to be specific to third-person singular present perfect tense to project non-staged quotes, which are more backgrounded than the ones introduced with preterite. Such non-staged quotes help speakers enhance the legitimacy of their account by presenting the information as coming from an authentic witness, allowing co-participants to re-experience a past scene.

My analysis of *meinen* in preterite and present perfect demonstrates that, at least in third-person singular, both past tense formats are closely related to action

Chapter 8. The use of past tense formats   251

formation since each past tense format is preferably used to accomplish a specific action. Accounting is primarily done with the present perfect format, providing atemporal background information. This function seems to be tied to a specific clause-combining format, namely a main clause without deictic shifts. Preterite is mostly used to report speech in its sequentiality, with the integration of turn-taking that is reported as if it followed the original temporality of events.

In a grammar of talk-in-interaction, *meinen* would need to be introduced in relation to the actions it accomplishes, as well as, in the case of third-person present perfect, with its syntactic features. It may be sensible to categorize *meinen* in past tense as a device to (1) introduce reported speech and (2) repair prior assumptions. These social actions strongly differ from the use of *meinen* in present tense where it is mostly used as a discourse marker (Günthner & Imo 2003; Imo 2007b). In third-person present perfect, the use of two syntactic formats that vary in their degree of syntactic integration emerged from the data. Both are used to quote prior speech. However, each syntactic clause-combining format is associated with distinct actions.

The different constructions that are formed with past tense *meinen* thus need to be further specified. In addition to the constructions presented at the beginning of this section, third person singular present perfect can be schematized as follows:

/*meinen* (3rd p. sg.) + main clause without deictic shifts ('quoting someone')/ + present perfect → Foregrounded actions (oriented towards progressivity of events)
/*meinen* (3rd p. sg.) + main clause with deictic shifts/subjunctive mood ('quoting someone')/ + present perfect → Backgrounded actions (accounting/explaining)

Preterite *meinte* also has this syntactic distinction. It is, however, striking that the percentage of main clauses without deictic shifts is higher with *meinte*: 44.8% compared to 29.0% with present perfect, while the percentage of main clauses with deictic shifts is more similar (33.0% with the preterite format compared to 38.2% with present perfect format).

5.3   *Glauben* 'to believe'

I also analyzed the past tense forms of first-person singular (*ich glaubte / ich habe geglaubt* 'I (have) believed') and third-person singular (*er/sie/es/man glaubte / hat geglaubt* 'he/she/it/one believed / has believed') for *glauben*. The following table gives a quantitative overview:

It is notable that the number of occurrences strongly varies between preterite and present perfect: Whereas each preterite format only occurs once in the whole

Table 11. Occurrences of *glauben* in 1st and 3rd person past tense in the corpus

Form	Number of occurrences
ich glaubte	1
er/sie/es/man glaubte	1
ich habe geglaubt	14
er/sie/es/man hat geglaubt	10

corpus, present perfect formats do occur, even though they are relatively rare compared to *meinen* and *finden*. The two instances of *glaubte* ('believed') occur in a guided tour and a biographic interview. The formal character of these two speech contexts may be the reason why the preterite is used *at all* in my corpus.

The grammatical formats that *glauben* introduces in its present perfect format vary, as Tables 12 and 13 illustrate:[15]

Table 12. Syntactic configurations of *ich habe geglaubt*

ich habe geglaubt	Number of occurrences
+ complementizer + complement clause	2
+ complement clause	2
+ noun phrase (accusative)	3
+ noun phrase (dative)	4
+ 2 noun phrases (dative and accusative)	1
+ prepositional phrase	2

Table 13. Syntactic configurations of *er/sie/es/man hat geglaubt*

er/sie/es/man hat geglaubt	Number of occurrences
+ complementizer + complement clause	2
+ noun phrase (accusative)	3
+ 2 noun phrases (dative and accusative)	2
+ prepositional phrase	3

Even though collapsing first and third-person present perfect formats to identify possible constructions due to the overall low frequency of occurrences, no distinct constructions could be determined in my corpus. All four grammatical combinations that occur — [*glauben* + NP(acc)], [*glauben* (+ *dass*) + complement

---

15. Prepositional phrases occur as *an etwas/jemanden glauben* 'to believe in someone/something'; noun phrases in the accusative case are *etwas glauben* 'to believe something'; in the dative case they figure as *jemandem glauben* 'to believe someone'.

Chapter 8. The use of past tense formats   253

clause], [*glauben* + NP(dat)], and [*glauben* + prepositional phrase] — are used by speakers to display a change of epistemic state. In other words, *glauben* refers to a certain level of knowledge that has been revised. In most cases, the revised epistemic state remains implied or inferable while the prior state is made available to others through *glauben* in the present perfect format. This use of *glauben* has been documented by Jefferson (2004b) for the English verb *to think* in the pattern *at first I thought but then I realized*: "Asserting the wrong 'first thought' reaffirms, in the face of some actuality, *the in-principle correctness of the ordinary alternative*. In effect it is proposing that the wrong 'first thought' should have been right." (Jefferson 2004b:140, original emphasis; on German *ich dachte* 'I thought' with a similar function, see Deppermann & Reineke 2017). Excerpt (11) illustrates this epistemic use of *ich habe geglaubt*. For reasons of clarity, I chose one of the rarer cases where the revised epistemic state is repeated by a coparticipant and does not remain implied.

A family of six is talking about a specific building that seems to have a new tenant. Prior to this excerpt, one family member was talking about the two apartments in the building that were now rented *von einer dame* 'by a lady' (not in transcript). After a slight topic change towards the outside architecture of the building, Gabriele returns to the original topic of the rental of the building and utters her 'first thought':

Excerpt 11. *drei wohnungen* 'three apartments' (FOLK_E_00201_SE_01_T_01_c678), face-to-face conversation, informal interview

```
01 GAB: ja  ich hab          immer  geglaubt
        yes 1SG have-AUX.1SG always PTCP-believe-CIRC
        well I have always thought
02      das wären                drei  wohnungen.
        3SG be.SBJV2             three apartments
        there'd be three apartments
02      (0.31)
03 SEB: nein zwei.
        no   two
04 GAB: °zwei.°
        two
05      (1.2)
```

The complement clause introduced by *ich hab immer geglaubt* 'I have always thought' allows the speaker to inform her interlocutors about a former epistemic state where she has been less knowledgeable than she is now. Even though Gabriele's turn about her former epistemic state clarifies that this state has since been revised, Sebastian responds to her turn with *nein* ('no') and the correct number of apartments, *zwei* ('two'). This response is ratified by Gisela through a repetition in lower volume (line 4). The fact that Gisela utters her first thought despite the prior discussion about the correct number of apartments in the building may indicate, in line with Jefferson's (2004b) findings, "that the wrong 'first thought' should have been right" (Jefferson 2004b: 140) or that there are at least grounds to think so.

In my data, when speakers indicate their change of state with *glauben*, they only do so with the present perfect format. This is true even for speakers, including the one from Excerpt (11), who come from regions (e.g., the Westphalian language region) where, according to Fischer (2018: 33), preterite is still used and could also be used to display this change of state. However, the quasi non-existence of *glauben* in preterite demonstrates that, at least in the investigated data set, speakers do not use the preterite format *glaubte* to do so.

The overall low number of past tense of *glauben* is striking, considering the high frequency of present tense *ich glaube* (see Imo 2012). My results suggest that, in this specific case, a grammar of talk-in-interaction would necessitate a separate treatment of present and past forms of *glauben* in order to reflect their actual use. While the present tense would need to be presented — in its default use — as an epistemic parenthetical, a fixed expression (Laury & Ono 2020) or discourse marker, the past forms would need to be introduced differently. It should for instance be indicated, especially for language learners, that the preterite format is not used in talk-in-interaction unless the discourse context is institutional or formal (i.e., a guided tour). The present perfect format, regardless of its grammatic combinational patterns, is used to indicate an epistemic change of state: Speakers present their 'first thoughts' to "[reaffirm] [...] *the in-principle correctness of the ordinary alternative*" (Jefferson 2004b: 140, original emphasis).

6. Discussion

The present chapter started with the observation that present and past tense formats of *finden, meinen*, and *glauben* are not necessarily comparable concerning their number of occurrences, their grammatical format, and concerning the social actions that they implement. Investigating specifically the two past tense formats preterite and present perfect, the chapter shows that the past tense formats of *finden, meinen*, and *glauben* occur as specific constructions that speakers use to build turn-constructional units and implement distinct actions. My main findings can be summarized as follows:[16]

---

16. If not indicated otherwise, all constructions occur in 1st person singular.

1. *Finden*
   - */finden* + NP + ADJ ('consider s.th. to be [quality]')/ + preterite →
     assessment
   - */finden* + complement clause ('consider s.th. to be [quality]')/+ preterite
     → assessment
   - */finden* + NP ('discover s.th.')/ + present perfect → report of an event

2. *Meinen*
   - */meinen* + NP ('having something else in mind')/ + preterite → self-repair
   - */meinen* + complement clause/ + preterite *or* present perfect → reporting
     speech
     - */meinen* (3rd p. sg.) + main clause without deictic shifts ('quoting
       someone')/ + present perfect → Foregrounded actions (oriented
       towards progressivity of events)
     - */meinen* (3rd p. sg.) + main clause with deictic shifts/subjunctive
       mood ('quoting someone')/+ present perfect → Backgrounded
       actions (accounting/explaining)

3. *Glauben*
   - */glauben* + NP(acc) *or* NP(dat) *or* complement clause *or* prepositional
     phrase/ + present perfect → change of state

Due to an initial quantitative analysis of a relatively large corpus of German everyday talk, I was able to determine the largest groups of constructions in their interplay of past tense format and grammatical components relatively quickly. Even though the subsequent qualitative analysis was necessary for a more fine-grained actional analysis, it was the quantitative approach and the large number of cases that enabled the initial broad findings of the present chapter. Such a quantitative approach to the data may not agree with the emic perspective of Conversation Analysis and Interactional Linguistics and the principle of determining phenomena through 'unmotivated looking'. However, to build a grammar-for-interaction that aims at including frequently used patterns in everyday talk, it may be helpful to implement quantitative methodologies to determine such linguistic patterns relatively quickly (for a discussion, see Skogmyr Marian et al. 2023). An initial quantitative analysis of grammatical units can be a fruitful procedure to detect units that speakers exploit on a regular basis to implement actions. This said, an additional qualitative analysis remains indispensable to identify these social actions and build collections that are not based on formal characteristic alone but on praxeological grounds, thus allowing the determination of form-function pairings.

My findings also point to the importance of collecting meta-data from recorded speakers, such as the region of origin or age. Because the FOLK-corpus includes meta-information on most of the recorded speakers, I was able to demonstrate that speaker origin does not seem to be enough information to explain current past tense use in German talk-in-interaction.

Altogether, the analysis of mundane talk has brought to light different interactional and grammatical aspects that are relevant for a comprehensive grammar of talk-in-interaction and thus for linguists as well as for language learners:

The social actions that speakers accomplish with past tense formats of the investigated verbs differ between present perfect and preterite. Despite their lower frequency compared to their present tense use, past tense formats of *finden*, *meinen*, and *glauben* seem to have a routinized use similar to their present tense formats in that they recurrently accomplish, in combination with specific grammatical components, specific actions. This challenges so-called traditional, structualist grammars in favor of a social action approach (for such a comparison, see also Steensig et al. 2023), while raising an important question concerning past tense distribution: Is the distribution motivated by semantic criteria, especially by the *Aktionsart* of the verbs, as has been suggested by previous research? Or do specific past tense forms become part of social action formats (Fox 2007) due to their routine use for the accomplishment of the same action?

The first explanation would mean a 'solidification' of grammatical features, here tense-marking or a specific *Aktionsart*, over time without considering interactional contexts — a procedure that previous research has adopted without reaching clear results. An explanation through social action formats would mean a loss in grammatical information (namely, the past tense marking) in favor of action formation. That means that the temporal dimension of the marked tense may be of less importance than the action that the verb implements when occurring in its past tense format. In line with similar results for English (Kärkkäinen 2012), Finnish (Laury et al. 2020), and French (Fiedler 2024), this explanation could shed new light on tense 'distribution', namely one according to interactional purposes.

As a consequence, I suggest that a grammar-for-interaction needs to include some information about present perfect and preterite forms that are recurrently used for the same social action in everyday talk (see Steensig et al. 2023 for a similar approach). For example, *finden* in first- or third-person preterite tends to be used to evaluate something in patterns like [*fand* (1st/3rd person) + NP (accusative) + ADJ]. But if one wants to talk about having found a (searched-for) object, interactional data suggest that the present perfect is the unmarked tense to use in first- and third-person singular. Such an explanation would need to be accompanied by the clear statement that these guidelines result from data of everyday talk and therefore only apply to spoken interaction.

The applicability to spoken language is best evidenced by my findings on *glauben*: In spoken language, the verb is barely used in past tense, especially not in preterite — a finding that a grammar-for-interaction would need to include and contextualize. For instance, it could be suggested that in order to indicate a 'first thought', the unmarked linguistic pattern would either be *glauben* in its present perfect format or, according to prior literature, *denken* in its preterite or present perfect format (Deppermann & Reineke 2017: 349–369).

Grammatical 'rules' concerning this finding can be easily described without using technical terms concerning (morpho-)syntactic categories like 'main clause syntax' or 'deictic shifts', for instance: *Meinen* in first- and third-person singular preterite and present perfect is commonly used to introduce reported speech. Especially with preterite tense, the reported speech is not introduced with *dass* ('that'), which is why the verb in the following clause is in second position. In preterite tense, *meinen* can also introduce reported speech without a verb, for example exclamations.

The respective past tense formats occur in what I called 'constructions' in my analyses, i.e., past tense formats in combination with specific grammatical components. These constructions are used to implement specific social actions. This finding is closely intertwined with the first finding on action formation. A grammar-for-interaction would need to include information on the routinized use of such patterns for some past tense formats. In other words, a description of past tense use would need to mention that *finden*, when evaluating something, mainly occurs in preterite and combines most frequently with a noun phrase and an adjective. To express discovering an object, *finden* is used in present perfect and combines with a noun phrase only.

Concerning *meinen*, it may be useful to highlight that the preterite form is preferably used in third-person singular. In this format, *meinte* usually introduces a clause (in 77.8% of all occurrences in my corpus) without complementizer. This clause-combining format is tied to two action formats: Main clauses without deictic shifts, the syntactically more independent format, reenact someone else's speech in order to allow interlocutors to re-experience a past event, while main clauses with deictic shifts and/or in subjunctive mood are used for backgrounding information, for example accounts.

Compared to findings regarding the actions that speakers accomplish with the respective past tense format, these findings on clause-combining require more technical knowledge of syntax, especially of language-specific clause-combining formats. As a consequence, this second point may be reserved for a linguistic public instead of language learners.

In contrast to previous findings on the geographical distribution of past tense in German, my findings show that the variety of German a speaker grew up learning may not be decisive for the use or non-use of preterite. One possible explanation for this result could be that, with the progressive loss of dialects and increasing mobility of speakers (see, e.g., Jeszenszky, Steiner & Leemann 2022), past tense distribution according to regions loses its impact. People are no longer influenced only by their immediate surrounding social network, but also by media and online exchanges, and therefore by speakers from all over Germany. Additional contacts with language learners of German may enhance the loss of dialectal forms (for findings on the Alemannic dialect, see Leonhard 2022).

7. Conclusion

The present chapter investigated three frequently used verbs, *finden* 'to find', *meinen* 'to mean', and *glauben* 'to believe', in first- and third-person past tense in German talk-in-interaction. The combined quantitative and qualitative analysis of over 300 hours of everyday talk allowed me to show that these three verbs are used distinctively in present perfect and preterite tense. Both *finden* and *meinen* tend to form grammatical patterns that are past tense-specific. Moreover, speakers use the two verbs in present perfect or preterite for distinct social actions. In the case of *glauben*, past tense is barely used in spoken language.

These findings add a new dimension to our understanding of past tense distribution in German. In spoken language, the past tense forms of the three verbs seem to be tied to action formation. This correlation is probably independent of the speakers' origin — a result that only the investigation of actual talk-in-interaction has been able to reveal.

Including these findings into a grammar-for-interaction has two distinct potential benefits: For language learners, the clearest tendencies concerning action formation should be formulated as a distributional rule that specifically applies to spoken language. For a public of linguists, syntactic findings about the grammatical combinational patterns should be included in order to evidence the implications that the investigation of everyday talk may have on grammar-writing for a language. Such an approach would also testify to the necessity to regularly update grammatical rules according to their actual use instead of reproducing them without checking if these rules (still) apply.

Acknowledgement

The present study was carried out with the generous support of the Swiss National Science Foundation, grant no. 100012_178819, project *The emergent grammar of clause-combining in social interaction*.

References

Auer, Peter. 1998. "Zwischen Parataxe und Hypotaxe: 'Abhängige Hauptsätze' im gesprochenen und geschriebenen Deutsch. [Between Parataxes and Hypotaxes: 'Dependent Main Clauses' in Spoken German]." *InLiSt* 2: 1–32.

Auer, Peter, and Jan Lindström. 2016. "Left/Right Asymmetries and the Grammar of Pre- vs. Post-Positioning in German and Swedish Talk-in-Interaction." *Language Sciences* 56: 68–92.

Ballweg, Joachim. 1988. "Präsensperfekt und Präteritum im Deutschen. [Present Perfect and Preterite in German]." In *Temporalsemantik: Beiträge zur Linguistik der Zeitreferenz*, ed. by Veronika Ehrich, and Heinz Vater, 81–95. Tübingen: Niemeyer.

Bußmann, Hadumod. 2008. *Lexikon der Sprachwissenschaft*. [Handbook of Linguistics]. Stuttgart: Körner.

Comrie, Bernard. 1985. *Tense*. Cambridge: Cambridge University Press.

Couper-Kuhlen, Elizabeth, and Margret Selting. 2018. *Interactional Linguistics: Studying Language in Social Interaction*. Cambridge: Cambridge University Press.

Dal, Ingerid. 1960. "Zur Frage des süddeutschen Präteritumschwundes. [On the Question of Southern German Preterite Decline]." In *Indogermanica: Festschrift für Wolfgang Krause*, ed. by Hans Hartmann, and Hans Neumann, 1–7. Heidelberg: Carl Winter.

Dentler, Sigrid. 1997. *Zur Perfekterneuerung im Mittelhochdeutschen: Die Erweiterung des zeitreferentiellen Funktionsbereichs von Perfektfügungen*. [On the Renewal of Perfect Tense in Middle High German: The Expansion of the Time-referential Function of Perfective Inflections]. Göteborg: Acta Universitatis Gothoburgensis.

Deppermann, Arnulf. 2006. "*Construction Grammar* — Eine Grammatik für die Interaktion? [*Construction Grammar* — A Grammar for Interaction?]." In *Grammatik und Interaktion*, ed. by Arnulf Deppermann, Reinhard Fiehler, and Thomas Spranz-Fogasy, 43–65. Radolfzell: Verlag für Gesprächsforschung.

Deppermann, Arnulf, and Silke Reineke. 2017. "Epistemische Praktiken und ihre feinen Unterschiede: Verwendungen von *ich dachte* in gesprochener Sprache. [Practices of Indexing Discrepant Assumptions with German *ich dachte* 'I thought' in Talk-in-Interaction]." In *Verben im interaktiven Kontext. Bewegungsverben und mentale Verben im gesprochenen Deutsch*, ed. by Arnulf Deppermann, Nadine Proske, and Arne Zeschel, 337–375. Tübingen: Narr Franke Attempo.

Ehrich, Veronika, and Heinz Vater. 1989. "Das Perfekt im Dänischen und im Deutschen. [Perfect Tense in Danish and German]." In *Tempus — Aspekt — Modus: Die lexikalischen und grammatischen Formen in den germanischen Sprachen*, ed. by Werner Abraham, and Theo Janssen, 103–132. Tübingen: Niemeyer.

Eisenberg, Peter. 1994. *Grundrisse der deutschen Grammatik*. [Fundamentals of German Grammar]. Stuttgart/Weimar: Metzler.

Fiedler, Sophia. 2024. *Direct Reported Thought in French and German: An Interactional and Multimodal Analysis*. Radolfzell: Verlag für Gesprächsforschung.

Fischer, Hanna. 2018. *Präteritumschwund im Deutschen. Dokumentation und Erklärung eines Verdrängungsprozesses*. [Preterite Loss in German: Documentation and Explanation of a Displacement Process]. Berlin/Boston: de Gruyter.

Fischer, Hanna. 2021. "Präteritumschwund im Deutschen. Neue Erkenntnisse zu einem alten Rätsel. [Preterite Loss in German. New Insights into an old riddle]." *Beiträge zur Geschichte der deutschen Sprache und Literatur*, 143 (3): 331–363.

Fox, Barbara. 2007. "Principles Shaping Grammatical Practices: An Exploration." *Discourse Studies* 9 (3): 299–318.

Goedsche, C. Rudolf. 1934. "Verbal Aspect in German." *The Journal of English and Germanic Philology* 33 (4): 506–519.

Goffman, Erving. 1981. *Forms of Talk*. Philadelphia: University of Pennsylvania Press.

Golato, Andrea. 2000. "An Innovative German Quotative for Reporting on Embodied Actions: *Und ich so/und er so* 'and I'm like/and he's like'." *Journal of Pragmatics* 32: 29–54.

Goodwin, Charles. 1986. "Between and Within: Alternative Sequential Treatments of Continuers and Assessments." *Human Studies* 9 (2/3): 205–217.

Gubina, Alexandra. 2022. *Grammatik des Handelns in der sozialen Interaktion: Eine interaktionslinguistische, multimodale Untersuchung der Handlungskonstitution und -zuschreibung mit Modalverbformaten im gesprochenen Deutsch*. [Grammar of Action in Social Interaction: An Interactional, Multimodal Investigation of the Constitution and Attribution of Action with Modal Verb Formats in Spoken German]. Radolfzell: Verlag für Gesprächsforschung.

Günthner, Susanne. 2006. "Grammatische Analysen der kommunikativen Praxis — 'Dichte Konstruktionen' in der Interaktion. [Grammatical Analyses of Communicative Practices — 'Dense Constructions' in Interaction]." In *Grammatik und Interaktion*, ed. by Arnulf Deppermann, Reinhard Fiehler, and Thomas Spranz-Fogasy, 95–122. Radolfzell: Verlag für Gesprächsforschung.

Günthner, Susanne. 2011. "N Be That-Constructions in Everyday German Conversation: A Reanalysis of 'die Sache ist/das Ding ist' ('the Thing Is')-Clauses as *Projector Phrases*." In *Subordination in Conversation: A Cross-Linguistic Perspective*, ed. by Ritva Laury, and Ryoko Suzuki, 11–36. Amsterdam/Philadelphia: John Benjamins.

Günthner, Susanne, and Wolfgang Imo. 2003. "Die Reanalyse von Matrixsätzen als Diskursmarker: *ich mein*-Konstruktionen im gesprochenen Deutsch. [The Reanalysis of Matrix Clauses as Discourse Marker: *ich mein* 'I mean'-Constructions in Spoken German]." *InLiSt* 37: 1–31.

Hall, Joan K., and Simona Pekarek Doehler. 2011. "Introduction: Interactional Competence and Development." In *L2 Interactional Competence and Development*, ed. by Joan Kelly Hall, John Hellermann, and Simona Pekarek Doehler, 206–243. Clevedon: Multilingual Matters.

Harweg, Roland. 1975. "Perfekt und Präteritum im gesprochenen Neuhochdeutsch. Zugleich ein Beitrag zur Theorie des nichtliterarischen Erzählens. [Present Perfect and Preterite in Spoken New High German. At the Same Time a Contribution to the Theory of Non-literary Narration]." *Orbis* 24: 130–183.

Heinemann, Trine, and Aino Koivisto (eds). 2016. "Indicating a Change-of-state in Interaction: Cross-linguistic Explorations." [Special Issue]. *Journal of Pragmatics* 104: 83–88.

Helbig, Gerhard, and Joachim Buscha. 2001. *Deutsche Grammatik: Ein Handbuch für den Ausländerunterricht.* [German Grammar: A Handbook for Teaching Foreigners]. Berlin/München: Langenscheidt.

Hopper, Paul. 1979. "Aspect and Foregrounding in Discourse." In *Discourse and Syntax*, ed. by Talmy Givón, 213–241. New York: Academic Press.

Hopper, Paul. 1987. "Emergent Grammar." In *Proceedings of the Thirteenth Annual Meeting of the Berkeley Linguistics Society*, ed. by Jon Aske, Natasha Beery, Laura Michaelis, and Hana Filip, 139–157. Berkeley, California: Berkely Linguistics Society.

Hopper, Paul. 2011. "Emergent Grammar and Temporality in Interactional Linguistics." In *Constructions: Emerging and Emergent*, ed. by Peter Auer, and Stefan Pfänder, 22–44. Berlin/New York: de Gruyter.

Imo, Wolfgang. 2007a. *Construction Grammar und Gesprochene-Sprache-Forschung: Konstruktionen mit zehn matrixsatzfähigen Verben im gesprochenen Deutsch.* [Construction Grammar and the Investigation of Spoken Language: Constructions with Ten Complement-Taking Predicates in Spoken German]. Tübingen: Niemeyer.

Imo, Wolfgang. 2007b. "Zur Anwendung der *Construction Grammar* auf die gesprochene Sprache – der Fall 'ich mein(e)'. [On the Application of Construction Grammar to Spoken Language – The Case of *ich meine* 'I mean']." In *Zugänge zur Grammatik der gesprochenen Sprache*, ed. by Vilmos Ágel, and Mathilde Hennig, 3–34. Tübingen: Niemeyer.

Imo, Wolfgang. 2012. "'Da hat des kleine glaub irgendwas angestellt' – ein construct ohne construction? ['The little one has *glaub* 'I think' been up to something' – a construct without construction?]." In *Konstruktionen in der Interaktion*, ed. by Susanne Günthner, and Wolfgang Imo, 263–290. Berlin/Boston: de Gruyter.

Imo, Wolfgang. 2014. "Was ist (k)eine Konstruktion? [What is (not) a construction?]." In *Handbuch Satz, Äußerung, Schema*, ed. by Christa Dürscheid, and Jan Georg Schneider, 551–576. Berlin/New York: de Gruyter.

Jefferson, Gail. 2004a. "Glossary of Transcript Symbols with an Introduction." In *Conversation Analysis: Studies from the First Generation*, ed. by Gene H. Lerner, 13–31. Amsterdam/Philadelphia: John Benjamins.

Jefferson, Gail. 2004b. "At First I Thought': A Normalizing Device for Extraordinary Events." In *Conversation Analysis: Studies from the First Generation*, ed. by Gene H. Lerner, 131–167. Amsterdam/Philadelphia: John Benjamins.

Jeszenszky, Péter, Carina Steiner, and Adrian Leemann. 2022. "Effects of Mobility on Dialect Change: Introducing the Linguistic Mobility Index." *PLOS ONE*: 1–30.

Kärkkäinen, Elise. 2012. "*I Thought It Was Very Interesting*: Conversational Formats for Taking a Stance." *Journal of Pragmatics* 44 (15): 2194–2210.

Klein, Horst. 1974. *Tempus, Aspekt, Aktionsart.* [Tense, Aspect, Aktionsart]. Tübingen: Niemeyer.

Klein, Wolfgang. 2000. "An Analysis of the German Perfect." *Language* 76: 358–382.

Laury, Ritva, Marja-Liisa Helasvuo, and Janica Rauma. 2020. "When an Expression Becomes Fixed: *Mä ajattelin että* 'I Thought That' in Spoken Finnish." In *Fixed Expressions: Building Language Structure and Social Action*, ed. by Ritva Laury, and Tsuyoshi Ono, 133–166. Amsterdam/Philadelphia: John Benjamins.

Laury, Ritva, and Tsuyoshi Ono (eds). 2020. *Fixed Expressions. Building Language Structure and Social Action*. Amsterdam/Philadelphia: John Benjamins.

Leonhard, Jens. 2022. *Die Vergangenheitstempora im Alemannischen Deutschlands: Eine korpusbasierte quantitative und qualitative Untersuchung*. [Past Tenses in Alemannic of Germany: A Corpus-Based Quantitative and Qualitative Study]. Berlin/Boston: de Gruyter.

Levinson, Steven C. 2013. "Action Formation and Ascription." In *The Handbook of Conversation Analysis*, ed. by Jack Sidnell, and Tanya Stivers, 103–132. Malden, MA: Blackwell.

Lindgren, Kaj B. 1963. "Über Präteritum und Konjunktiv im Oberdeutschen. [On Preterite and Subjunctive in Upper German]." *Neuphilologische Mitteilungen* 64: 264–283.

Pekarek Doehler, Simona. 2018. "Elaborations on L2 Interactional Competence: The Development of L2 Grammar-for-interaction." *Classroom Discourse* 9 (1): 3–24.

Radtke, Petra. 2015. "Tempus- und Modusgebrauch in der indirekten Rede: diachrone und synchrone Aspekte." [The Use of Tense and Mood in Indirect Speech: Diachronic and Synchronic Aspects]. In *Pragmatische Syntax*, ed. by Frank Liedtke, and Franz Hundsnurscher, 97–114. Tübingen: Niemeyer.

Reichenbach, Hans. 1947. *Elements of Symbolic Logic*. New York: Macmillan.

Rowley, Anthony. 1983. "Das Präteritum in den heutigen deutschen Dialekten. [The Preterite in Today's German Dialects]." *Zeitschrift Für Dialektologie Und Linguistik* 50 (2): 161–182.

Sacks, Harvey. 1992. *Lectures on Conversation (Vols. 1–2)*. Oxford: Blackwell.

Sacks, Harvey, Emanuel A. Schegloff, and Gail Jefferson. 1974. "A Simplest Systematics for the Organization of Turn-Taking for Conversation." *Language* 4: 696–735.

Schegloff, Emanuel A. 1996. "Turn Organization: One Intersection of Grammar and Interaction." In *Interaction and Grammar*, ed. by Elinor Ochs, Emanuel A. Schegloff, and Sandra A. Thompson, 52–133. Cambridge: Cambridge University Press.

Schirmunski, Viktor. 1962. *Deutsche Mundartkunde: Vergleichende Laut- und Formenlehre der deutschen Mundarten*. [German Dialect Studies: Comparative Sound and Form Theory of the German Dialects]. Berlin: Akademie-Verlag.

Sidnell, Jack. 2006. "Coordinating Gesture, Talk, and Gaze in Reenactments." *Research on Language and Social Interaction* 39 (4): 377–409.

Skogmyr Marian, Klara, Melissa Juillet, Fanny Forsberg Lundell, and Simona Pekarek Doehler. 2023. "Combining Longitudinal CA and Automatic Extraction Methods in SLA: Opportunities and Challenges." *ASLA Studies in Applied Linguistics* 30 (4): 376–402.

Smith, Michael S., and Lucas M. Seuren. 2022. "Re-apprehending Misapprehensions: A Practice for Disclosing Troubles in Understanding in Talk-in-interaction." *Journal of Pragmatics* 193: 43–58.

Sütterlin, Ludwig. 1924. *Neuhochdeutsche Grammatik: Erste Hälfte. Lautverhältnisse. Wortbiegung*. [New High German Grammar: First Half. Phonetics. Word Inflection]. München: Beck.

Steensig, Jakob, Maria Jørgensen, Nicholas Mikkelsen, Karita Suomalainen, and Søren Sandager Sørensen. 2023. "Towards a Grammar of Danish Talk-in-Interaction. From Action Formation to Grammatical Description." *Research on Language and Social Interaction* 56 (2): 116–140.

Streitberg, Wilhelm. 2009 [1891]. "Perfective und imperfective Actionsart im Germanischen. [Perfective and Imperfective Aktionsart in Germanic]." *Beiträge zur Geschichte der deutschen Sprache und Literatur* 15: 70–177.

Trost, Pavel. 1980. "Präteritumsverfall und Präteritumschwund im Deutschen. [Preterite Decline and Preterite Loss in German]." *Zeitschrift für Dialektologie und Linguistik* 47 (2): 184–188.

Vendler, Zeno. 1957. "Verbs and Times." *Philosophical Review* 66: 143–160.

Vendler, Zeno. 1967. *Linguistics in Philosophy*. Ithaka/New York: Cornell University Press.

Yule, George, and Terrie Mathis. 1992. "The Role of Staging and Constructed Dialogue in Establishing Speaker's Topic." *Linguistics* 30: 199–215.

Zeman, Sonja. 2010. *Tempus und 'Mündlichkeit' im Mittelhochdeutschen: Zur Interdependenz grammatischer Perspektivensetzung und 'Historischer Mündlichkeit' im mittelhochdeutschen Tempussystem.* [Tense and 'Orality' in Middle High German: On the Interdependence of Grammatical Perspective Setting and 'Historical Orality' in the Middle High German Tense System]. Berlin/New York: de Gruyter.

Zeman, Sonja. 2013. "Vergangenheit als Gegenwart? Zur Diachronie des 'Historischen Präsens'. [Past as Present? On the Diachrony of the 'Historical Present']." *Jahrbuch für Germanistische Sprachgeschichte* 4 (1): 236–256.

CHAPTER 9

Second-person singular imperatives in Finnish everyday conversations
Multifunctionality and routinization of grammatical formats

Karita Suomalainen
Åbo Akademi University

The chapter discusses different ways in which second-person singular imperatives are used in Finnish conversations and how this multifunctionality should be described in a grammar of Finnish talk-in-interaction. In traditional grammar writing, the description of imperatives has focused on their use in directive actions. The chapter shows that in spoken interaction, second-person singular imperatives have a wider range of functions: they can also be used in actions that are not primarily directive, e.g., storytellings, assessments, news deliveries, and informings. In such use, they function as sedimented formulae with fixed local tasks and recurrent collocative elements. The chapter suggests that formulaicity and routinization of grammatical formats play an important role in everyday language use, which should be reflected in grammar writing.

Keywords: Finnish, everyday conversation, fixed expression, formulaicity, imperative, routinization, second-person singular, social action format

1. Introduction

This chapter approaches the multifunctionality of grammatical forms in interaction by studying different ways in which second-person singular imperatives are used in Finnish everyday conversations (e.g., *arvaa* 'guess.2SG.IMP', *kato* 'look.2SG.IMP', or *kuule* 'hear.2SG.IMP'). In traditional grammar writing, the use of imperatives is typically associated with directives (e.g., the comprehensive Finnish grammar *Iso suomen kielioppi* by Hakulinen et al. 2004; Lauranto 2014 for Finnish). However, interactionally oriented linguistic studies have noted that imperative forms can also be employed in non-directive actions, as routinized for-

https://doi.org/10.1075/slsi.37.09suo
© 2025 John Benjamins Publishing Company

Chapter 9. Second-person singular imperatives in Finnish **265**

mulae in specific sequential contexts, or even as discourse markers or particles (e.g., Hakulinen & Seppänen 1992; Hakulinen, Keevallik & Lindström 2003; Keevallik 2001, 2003; Auer 2017; Siitonen, Rauniomaa & Keisanen 2019). Consider Excerpts (1) and (2), which both contain the expression *oota*, the second person imperative form of the verb *o(d)ottaa* 'to wait'. In both excerpts, *oota* is used to suspend something but the sequential position and the performed action in the excerpts differ. In Excerpt (1), *oota* expresses a prototypical request, initiating a directive sequence and concretely asking the recipient to wait for the speaker to come along, while in Excerpt (2), *oota* is a routinized formula, occurring as a part of word-search and forming a parenthetical that indexes an intrapersonal thinking process.[1]

Excerpt 1. *oota miuta* 'wait for me' (SG151, Arkisyn), face-to-face

```
01 MIA: oota        miuta.
        wait.2SG.IMP 1SGPRO.PART
        wait for me.
02      (.)
03 MIA: £et hävii(h) v(h)iälä(h).£
        don't you go yet.
```

Excerpt 2. *Travemünde* (SG108, Arkisyn), face-to-face

```
01 TAR: onks Travemünd- mut mikä on Travemünde Lyypekin (.)
        is Travemünd- but what is Travemünde- Lübeck's
02      >ootas        nyt< (.) ku- (.)
        wait.2SG.IMP.CLT now       because-
        wait now (.) because- (.)
03      mikä sijaitsee missä.
        which is located where.
```

In traditional grammar writing, the description of imperatives has focused on their use as "deontic directives" or "commands" (e.g., Aikhenvald 2010; cf. Excerpt (1)), while other ways of using imperatives have been treated as "non-canonical", secondary, or even trivial, despite their frequency in spoken interaction (cf. Linell 2005:3). From the perspective of interactional grammar, they should have their secondary status removed.

The present chapter aims at developing the grammatical description of Finnish imperatives by acknowledging and describing the variation of use of second-person singular forms in spoken interaction, showing that different uses are deployed systematically for the implementation of social action. The chapter further suggests that different ways of using second-person singular imperatives form a continuum from directive to more routinized uses, occurring in actions

---

1. The focus lines have been glossed according to the Leipzig Glossing Rules.

that are not (primarily) directive. This is referred to as *multifunctionality* of the second-person singular imperative form. In this chapter, grammar is treated as an emergent, situated and context-sensitive phenomenon designed for service in the organization of social interaction (see Hopper 2011; Couper-Kuhlen & Selting 2018). By exploring the different recurrent social actions in which second-person singular imperatives are used, the chapter contributes to the understanding of second-person imperative forms as *social action formats*, i.e., grammatical formats which occupy a specific sequential position and perform a sequentially specific action – or at least occur as a part of such (Fox 2007; Steensig et al. 2023).

2. Background

In the comprehensive grammar of Finnish, *Iso suomen kielioppi* by Hakulinen et al. (2004), the imperative is described mainly from three perspectives: (1) a morphological perspective, as mood alongside the indicative, conditional and potential (ibid.§ 115–118); (2) a syntactical perspective, as a modal clause type (*directive clause*, in Finnish *käskylause*, lit. 'command clause', or *imperatiivilause* 'imperative clause') alongside the declarative, interrogative and exclamative clauses (ibid.§ 886–890); and (3) in connection with directivity as a linguistic phenomenon (ibid.§ 1645–1658). It is, however, acknowledged that imperative forms can also have non-directive uses (ibid.§ 1658), but the description of these uses is very limited compared to the directive use. In addition, the comprehensive grammar of Finnish treats certain second-person imperative forms alongside particles, that is, as *particle-ized* expressions; this is the case for *kato* 'look.2SG.IMP' and *kuule* 'hear.2SG.IMP' (ibid.§ 792).

As in many other languages, the second-person singular imperative forms in Finnish do not have a distinctive morphological marking; the second-person singular imperative is formed from the vowel stem of the verb (e.g., *laula-a* sing-INF 'to sing'; *laula* sing.IMP 'sing'), and the negative imperative, or the prohibitive, is formed with a special negation verb form, *älä*, that can also be followed by a main verb which is in the same form as in the positive imperative (e.g., *älä laula* 'do not sing'; Hakulinen et al. 2004: § 118). There is no subject when using second-person singular imperative forms (Vilkuna 2000: 128), but a term of address, for example a name or a second-person singular pronoun, might occur (e.g., **Annika** *kato nyt tänne* 'Annika, look here now'). While imperative forms exist for all persons other than the first-person singular, the second-person singular form has been shown to be the most common imperative form in Finnish everyday conversational data: in Lauranto's (2013: 178) data of imperative clauses in conversational Finnish, second-person singular imperative forms cover 67.9% of all the impera-

Chapter 9. Second-person singular imperatives in Finnish **267**

tive forms. Similarly, in the data in the present study from the Arkisyn database of conversational Finnish, 83% ($N = 950$) of all the imperative forms are in second-person singular. Typologically, the second-person singular is the most basic of imperative forms in terms of its frequency and formation (Aikhenvald 2010: 339).

Syntactically, imperatives are described as building blocks for directive clauses; these clauses do not have a subject and they normally have a verb-initial word order (Hakulinen et al. 2004: § 889). According to Hakulinen et al. (ibid.), the "speech function" of directive clauses is to urge or request somebody to do something. Forsberg (2019), who has studied an affective imperative construction that she calls *Reproachful Imperative* (in Finnish, *paheksuntaimperatiivi*), criticizes the view in which clauses with a finite verb in the imperative mood are equated with directives. According to Forsberg (ibid.: 6), the concept of *imperative clauses* is based on the idea that a certain schematic clausal unit would consistently establish certain pragmatic meanings. Forsberg points out that in some uses, the directiveness of an imperative form can also remain in the background while other aspects, such as affectivity, are foregrounded. As an example, she provides the reproachful imperative construction with which the speaker may display a negative stance towards the action performed by the addressee (e.g., mother's utterance to her children *repikää nyt se mun hame siinä* 'go on, just tear my skirt there').

The connection between imperatives and directiveness has also been addressed in the study of talk-in-interaction. An edited volume by Sorjonen, Raevaara and Couper-Kuhlen (2017) studies *imperative turns at talk*, paying attention to the design features of these turns as well as their position in the ongoing sequence. In the chapters of the volume, imperative turns are shown to do different work depending on their linguistic composition, sequential position, and temporal embeddedness across different, often embodied activities and settings. Despite the wide interactional focus, the chapters in the volume mostly focus on the use of the imperative in *directive situations* (Sorjonen et al. 2017: 11), leaving the use of the imperative as a particle-like expression or a discourse marker outside the scope of the volume. This type of use is, however, mentioned in the epilogue of the book, in which Auer (2017) discusses the grammaticization and routinization processes of imperative forms. According to him, these processes are "based on the immediacy part of the core function of imperatives" (ibid.: 414), which suggests that it is relevant to study — and describe — both literal and more grammaticized uses of imperatives juxtaposed. This is also the aim of this chapter.

3. Distribution of second-person singular imperative forms in the data

The data for this study come from the Arkisyn corpus of conversational Finnish (see Arkisyn in References), a morphosyntactically annotated database of Finnish everyday conversations. It includes altogether approximately 30 hours of conversations, consisting of 22 face-to-face conversations (26 hours and 25 minutes) and 4 telephone conversations (3 hours and 14 minutes). The data have been recorded during a period ranging from the 1990s to the present day, and they have been transcribed at the Universities of Helsinki and Turku. The data have been morphosyntactically annotated at the University of Turku.

For the purposes of this study, I examined the 15 most common second-person singular imperative (2SG.IMP) verb forms in the Arkisyn corpus. Since the data are morphosyntactically coded, these 2SG.IMP forms could be extracted with the help of the corpus search tool. Table 1 presents the distribution of the 2SG.IMP occurrences among different verbs in the data:

Table 1. Distribution of verbs most commonly used in 2SG.IMP form in the Arkisyn corpus

Verb			N of 2SG.IMP forms
1.	*katsoa*	'to look'	527
2.	*kuulla*	'to hear'	115
3.	*ei (älä)*	negative verb; prohibitive	112
4.	*ajatella*	'to think'	55
5.	*ottaa*	'to take'	55
6.	*odottaa*	'to wait'	41
7.	*näyttää*	'to show'	37
8.	*sanoa*	'to say'	36
9.	*tulla*	'to come'	34
10.	*antaa*	'to give'	28
11.	*laittaa*	'to put; to set'	24
12.	*mennä*	'to go'	19
13.	*arvata*	'to guess'	17
14.	*kertoa*	'to tell'	13
15.	*pistää*	'to put; to stick'	13
			1126

Based on Table 1, I created separate sub-collections of 2SG.IMP forms for each verb and analyzed the ways in which imperative forms were used in turns-at-talk (cf. Sorjonen et al. 2017). The analysis was done using the conversation analytic method, and special attention was given to the type of social action the form was used in and the types of responses it received. The analysis showed that uses of imperative forms could be placed on an actional continuum. At one end of the continuum, there are the 2SG.IMP forms used in directive actions, as an attempt to get an interlocutor to do something in the immediate context of the interaction; these actions make either compliance or non-compliance the relevant next action (Goodwin 2006: 517; Sorjonen et al. 2017: 16; Couper-Kuhlen & Selting 2018: 254). At the other end of the continuum, there are 2SG.IMP forms that occur in actions that are not (primarily) directive (e.g., storytelling, assessing, informing); in these cases, 2SG.IMP forms are best understood as particle-like expressions that may have a multitude of interactional functions. In the middle of the continuum are the cases that fall in between the two extremes. I elaborate on this continuum in Section 5.

The 2SG.IMP forms located at the "directive action" end of the continuum are typically addressed to one specific recipient, and the meaning of the verb is the prototypical meaning given in the dictionary of standard Finnish compiled in the Institute for the Languages of Finland, *Kielitoimiston sanakirja* (e.g., for *katsoa*, 'to direct one's gaze towards something').[2] Regarding the 2SG.IMP forms located at the particle-like end of the continuum, it is not always clear whether they are addressed to one specific recipient, nor does their meaning always correspond to the prototypical meaning given in the dictionary. They do not make compliance or non-compliance to the action the verb denotes as the relevant next action; rather than directing someone to do something in the language-external world, they are used for directing the discourse, or the recipient in the discourse. The cases that fall between the two extremes are typically routinized, formulaic expressions that are used in sequentially and action-wise specific, even limited contexts, and accompanied by recurrent linguistic elements such as conjunctions or particles of various types. They come close to what Laury and Ono (2020) call *fixed* or *semi-fixed expressions*: prefabricated, formulaic items which have idiomatic and non-compositional meanings but are nevertheless associated with different degrees of fixedness, and which serve specific pragmatic and interactional functions tied to and arising from specific sequential contexts. I will discuss this in more detail later in this chapter.

---

2. The dictionary contains over 100,000 entries and provides information on the meaning, usage, register and style of Finnish words today, as well as on their inflection and spelling. Access: https://www.kielitoimistonsanakirja.fi (10.2.2025).

Out of the 15 verbs listed in Table 1, the following 7 verbs in the data were, in addition to directive actions, used in actions that were not (primarily) directive: the negative verb *ei* (in its prohibitive form of *älä*) as well as the verbs *katsoa* 'to look', *kuulla* 'to hear', *ajatella* 'to think', *odottaa* 'to wait', *sanoa* 'to say', and *arvata* 'to guess'. The 2SG.IMP forms of these verbs (*N* = 903) form the collection on which the analysis of this chapter is founded; their distribution is listed in Table 2.

Table 2. Distribution of the 2SG.IMP verb forms occurring in both directive and non-directive actions

Verb		N of 2SG.IMP forms
kat(s)o	'look'	527
kuule	'hear'	115
älä/elä	prohibitive	112
a(j)attele	'think'	55
o(d)ota	'wait'	41
sano	'say'	36
arvaa	'guess'	17
		903

The next section presents in detail the different ways the imperative forms of the verbs listed in Table 2 are used in the Arkisyn corpus of conversational Finnish.

4. Analysis: Use of second-person singular imperative forms

In this section, I provide a description of the use of 2SG.IMP forms in the Arkisyn corpus of conversational Finnish. I will focus on the verbs that most commonly occur in 2SG.IMP form in the data and that are used both in directive and other than (primarily) directive actions (see Table 2 in Section 3). This section is divided into subsections that analyze the imperative forms of each verb individually (Sections 4.1–4.7). The order of subsections follows the frequency of the imperative forms in the data. In each subsection, I will present examples of different uses of the imperative form of the verb in question. These subsections are to be understood as a suggestion of the core content to be included in the grammar entry or entries dealing with imperatives, were it to appear in a usage-based, comprehensive grammar of Finnish. At the end of this section (4.8), I will sum up the results of the analysis before moving on to reflecting on the implications the analysis presented here has on grammar writing in Section 5.

4.1 *Kat(s)o* 'look.2SG.IMP'

The verb *katsoa* 'to look' ($N=527$) is the most common 2SG.IMP form in the data. It occurs most of the time in the reduced form of *kato*, in both directive and non-directive actions. The different ways of using *kat(s)o* have been previously addressed by Hakulinen and Seppänen (1992), who have analyzed the expression's particle-like use in everyday conversation data, and by Siitonen, Rauniomaa and Keisanen (2019, 2021), who have studied actions that include the use of *kat(s)o* in nature-related activities.

In directive actions, *kat(s)o* functions as the finite verb and behaves syntactically like transitive verbs, that is, having the potential of having an object (Hakulinen & Seppänen 1992: 530–531). Action-wise, directive *kat(s)o* turns are used to guide the recipient's (visual) attention. According to Siitonen et al. (2021: 5–14), the directive *kato* actions in nature-related activities are produced (1) as noticings, to initiate a new course of action by directing the recipient's gaze to a target that the speaker treats as newsworthy; (2) as showings, to initiate an evaluative course of action by directing the recipient's gaze and to align with the speaker's stance toward the target; or (3) as prompts, to contribute to an ongoing course of action by directing the recipient to do something relevant to or with the target.

Excerpt (3) demonstrates the use of *kat(s)o* in directive actions. In such use, the imperative form is clearly a verb form used to address the one, specific recipient, making compliance the relevant next action. The excerpt is taken from a conversation between four friends: Teppo, Ville, Tuomas and Heikki. The participants are spending time at Teppo's place. Teppo has a cat that Ville is playing with prior to the excerpt. In the beginning of the excerpt (line 1), Teppo's cat scratches Ville, who makes a sound of surprise, indicating that it hurt. Teppo reacts to the situation and accounts for the cat's behavior. The 2SG.IMP form (*kato*) occurs in connection with Teppo's account (line 6). [3]

---

3. The imperative verb forms are not glossed or translated in the English translations in the excerpts. This is due to the fact that in the actions that are not primarily directive, the literal translation of the verb does not always catch the lexical meaning of the expression.

Excerpt 3. *iha naarmuil* 'all covered with scratches' (SG444, Arkisyn), face-to-face
((Ville is playing with Teppo's cat))

```
01 VIL: <noh.:
          PTC

02      (0.2)

03 TEP: joo se rupee leikkii £noih,£
          yeah it starts to play £like that£,

04 VIL: @↑a:u::.@
          @auuuch.@

05      (.)

06 TEP: £mhy hyh£ (0.2).hh *no £kato *ny,£
                            PTC  kato  now
          £he he£ (0.2)  .hh  well KATO now£
    tep                              *shows VIL his arms
    vil                              *looks at tep's arms
    hei                              *looks at tep's arms

07 TEP: *tullu vähä lei[kittyy sen kanssa,
          I've been playing with him a little.
    vil *looks at tep's arms

08 TUO:              [khhheh heh
                      ((laughter))

09 HEI:              [he he heh
                      ((laughter))

10 VIL: hheh heh heh heh heh .hhh he he .hee
          ((laughter))

11 TEP: °o_ _vittu° iha, (.) iha naarmuil,
          it's fucking all, (.). all covered with
          scratches,
```

In the excerpt, the turn with *kato* is preceded by Ville's demonstration of being hurt (lines 1, 4) and Teppo's account (line 3) in which he indicates that the demonstrated behavior is typical for his cat. Teppo then further demonstrates this by showing his wounded arms to Ville while producing the turn with *katsoa*.2SG.IMP (*no* **kato** *nyt* 'well look now', line 6). Action-wise, the imperative form here is directing the recipient's gaze and general attention, which is highlighted by the embodied conduct: Teppo's showing of his arms. Following Siitonen et al. (2021), the action in which *kato* occurs is to be understood as a showing. Syntactically, *kato* functions as a finite verb that could have an object, but in this case, the object is presented multimodally, by Teppo's embodied conduct. As to the next-turn proof procedure, the directiveness of the action is confirmed by the recipients' responses: immediately after the imperative has been produced, two of the other participants, Ville and Heikki, turn to look at Teppo's arms. Based on the preceding turns, Teppo's imperative can be interpreted as directly addressed to Ville, but the multiparty conversation context makes it relevant for others to comply also.

Chapter 9. Second-person singular imperatives in Finnish **273**

As a particle-like element in actions that are not primarily directive, *kat(s)o* typically functions as an explanatory element, highlighting something central regarding the ongoing interaction. This has also been demonstrated in studies by Hakulinen and Seppänen (1992) and Siitonen et al. (2019). It often occurs in turns that present a new or contrastive point of view in relation to the preceding turns. Thus, the particle-like use does have some of the same semantic properties as the non-particle use: both guide the recipient to pay attention to something new, to something that was not in the center of attention earlier (see also Hakulinen & Seppänen 1992:536; Siitonen et al. 2019:539). In the particle-like use, *kat(s)o* does not behave like a transitive verb, nor does it function as a finite verb, meaning there is another verb occupying this syntactic position in the utterance (see Seppänen & Hakulinen 1992:532). Like (other) particles, it may occupy a multitude of turn-constructional positions (cf. Hakulinen & Seppänen 1992:532–535).

Excerpt (4) demonstrates the use of *kat(s)o* as a particle-like element. It comes from the same conversation as Excerpt (3). Here too, the participants are discussing Teppo's cat. The cat is looking out of the window, and one of the participants, Heikki, comments on this, evaluating the cat's action as 'funny' (line 1). This leads to Teppo sharing a personal experience related to the cat's behavior.

Excerpt 4. *kissa päivystää* 'a cat is looking out' (SG444, Arkisyn), face-to-face

```
01 HEI: £on kyl hau[ska näköst] ku kissa päivystää
        £it does look funny when a cat is looking out
02 TUO:            [(- -)      ]
03 HEI: ikkunast tollee [tuijottaa£, ]
        the window like that staring£,
04 TEP:                 [mhjoo mhy hy] ↑mä o- aina aina
                        yeah heh, I am- always always
05      (- - ) ku mä tuun kotii >mä aattele et< jo- k-
        (- -) when I come home I think that if- w-
06      millo se ois ikinä kattelee sillon ku mä
        when would he ever be looking when I
07      tuun £mut ei se ikinä oo£,
        come £but he never is£,
08      (0.8)
09 TEP: no ne kyl tukk- tykkää katella tost [noi,
        well they do like to look from there,
10 HEI:                                     [mmh,
                                             mm,
11      (0.4)
12 VIL: sä et     vaan kato huomaa      sitä    ku
        2SG NEG.2SG PTC   kato notice.CONNEG DEM.PART when
        you just don't KATO notice it/him when
```

13	se tuijottaa [sua ɛtuol[ta (ni)ɛ]
	DEM stare.3SG 2SG.PART DEM.ABL PTC
	he stares at you from there
14 HEI:	[no nɪi[:] °joo°,
	well, yeah, yep,

Teppo's personal experience deals with the fact that when he comes home, he wishes that the cat would look at him, but the cat never does (lines 4–7). As nobody responds to this (pause in line 8), Teppo produces a general statement concerning his cat's behavior, which is received by Heikki's acknowledging *mmh* response (line 10). After a short pause (line 11), Ville produces a delayed response to Teppo's utterance, and it is in this turn that *katsoa*.2SG.IMP occurs (line 12). On his turn (lines 12–13), Ville introduces a new point of view related to Teppo's utterance: the cat might be looking at Teppo, but Teppo just does not notice it. Heikki reacts to Ville's turn by aligning laughter (line 14), while Teppo goes on to initiate a new sequence (not shown here).

In comparison to *kato* in Excerpt (3), *kato* in Excerpt (4) is both interactionally and syntactically quite different. Sequentially, *kato* in Excerpt (4) comes in a (delayed) response to Ville's turn (lines 4–6), occurring in a second position turn, while in Excerpt (3), Teppo's *kato* turn was used as a first pair part in a request. As regards the syntactic composition of the turn, *kato* in Excerpt (4) occurs as an insert between the negative verb *et* 'NEG.2SG' and the main verb *huomaa* 'notice.CONNEG' which form the finite verb in the clausal unit; in Excerpt (3), *kato* was the finite verb. As regards the action context in Excerpt (4), Ville does not try to get Teppo to carry out an embodied action, as opposed to Excerpt (3): the turn in which Ville's *kato* occurs is not a request of 'looking', nor do the other participants treat it as such. Instead, in Excerpt (4), Ville playfully provides an explanation tying back to Teppo's earlier telling of personal experience, presenting him with a new perspective, which also makes relevant next a set of alternative responses. In Excerpt (4), *kato* contributes to the explanative function of the action, and invites the addressee to 'perceive', 'see', 'observe', or to 'grasp' something.

4.2   *Kuule* 'hear.2SG.IMP'

The second most common imperative form in the Arkisyn database is *kuule*, formed with the verb *kuulla* 'to hear' (*N* = 115). *Kuule* is not used in a literal, concrete way in any of these cases, meaning it is not intended to guide the recipient to hear something auditory.[4]

---

4. Instead, the guidance of recipients' auditory attention is typically done with the verb *kuunnella* 'to listen' (*kuuntele* 'listen.2SG.IMP'). In the Arkisyn database, *kuuntele* is only used in directive actions; there are no occurrences of it used in a particle-like manner. Thus, in Finnish,

The particle-like way of using *kuule* has been previously studied by Hakulinen, Keevallik and Lindström (2003). They compared the Finnish *kuule* to similar expressions in Estonian (*kule*) and Swedish (*hördu*). According to them, the particle-like *kuule* can be used both in first-position and second-position turns, with slightly different interactional functions.

In first-position turns, the particle-like *kuule* may occur in the beginning, in the middle or at the end of the turn (Hakulinen et al. 2003: 204–210), similar to *kat(s)o* presented in the previous subsection. In the beginning of the turn, *kuule* is used as a projecting item, typically occurring in the beginning of a TCU (Hakulinen et al. 2003: 204). The Arkisyn data also contains utterances where *kuule* is used as a preliminary element, a preface that prepares the recipient for the upcoming action. Excerpt (5) demonstrates this kind of use. It is taken from a multiparty conversation in which the participants are trying to label old pictures. Before the excerpt, one of the participants, Maija, has told a story about how she once found an old telegram that a famous Finnish composer Jean Sibelius had addressed to a fellow musician, cellist Ossian Fohström. *Kuule* (line 6) occurs after Maija has finished the story and Hanna starts to share the information she is reading about Ossian Fohström's siblings:

Excerpt 5. *Ossian Fohström* (SG435, Arkisyn), face-to-face

```
01 ILM: siis kenelle se oli osotettu; se[:,  ]
        who was it addressed to; that (telegram),

02 MAI:                               [Fo: ]hst-
                                       to Fohst-

03     Ossian Fohströ[mille.]
       to Ossian Fohström.

04 ILM:               [ Ossi]an Fohströmi[lle.]
                       to Ossian Fohström.

05 MAI:                               [joo;]
                                       yeah;

06 HAN: no kuule tässä tuota mä luen
        PTC kuule here  PTC   1SG read.1SG
        well KUULE I'm reading

07     Ossian Fo:h>strömistä< .hh
       name    name.ELA
       about  Ossian Fohström .hh

08     yksi sisaruksii oli Alma Fohström
       one of his siblings was Alma Fohström
```

---

kuule may very well incorporate the meaning of 'listen.2SG.IMP' when used as a discourse marker or a particle.

09   [aika]nsa kuuluisimpia laulajatta[ria? .mhh mth]
        one of the most famous female singers of her time?
10 ILM: [joo?]
        yeah?
11 MAI: [just (.) joo.]
                                okay (.) yeah.

In Excerpt (5), *kuule* occurs as a part of Hanna's informing (see Maynard 1997; Thompson, Fox & Couper-Kuhlen 2015) concerning a character in Maija's story; it builds on the preceding turn, but also initiates some form of topic transition. In its context of use, *kuule* is preceded by the particle *no*, which is typical in transitions that guide the ongoing project. According to Vepsäläinen (2019), the particle *no* implies that the turn or TCU it is prefacing is relevant to the larger actional project. Also, *kuule* has been shown to occur in different types of transitions (Hakulinen et al. 2003). The transition context may make its use relevant in this excerpt as well.

Hanna starts her informing by introducing the source of information (*no kuule tässä tuota mä luen Ossian Fo:h>strömistä* 'no kuule here umm I am reading about Ossian Fohström'), after which the new information comes. In this context, *kuule* addresses the recipients, attracting their attention and signaling that something relevant is about to come. Interestingly, *kuule* is in second-person singular even if it is a question of a multiparty conversation. Looking at the responses, we can see that both Ilmari and Maija place themselves in the role of the recipient and orient to Hanna's turn by producing minimal responses (line 10: *joo?* and line 11: *just (.) joo.*).

In Excerpt (5), the speaker uses *kuule* in an epistemically asymmetrical situation: to share information that she has but that the other participants do not necessarily have. A certain epistemic asymmetry seems to be a more general feature of *kuule*, in other turn-constructional positions also. Consider Excerpt (6), in which *kuule* is used in turn- and TCU-medial position. In the excerpt, hairdresser (H) and customer (C) are discussing galoshes (*kalossit*). The excerpt is preceded by the customer's story concerning a girl who was using plastic bags to protect her shoes from the rain. The hairdresser is commenting on the story by producing an evaluation of a better way to protect one's shoes, namely using galoshes. After the customer's aligning *nii* response (see Sorjonen 2001), the hairdresser produces an informing that contains the particle-like *kuule* (line 3). She states that galoshes are (still) being sold. *Kuule* presents the provided information as somewhat surprising (cf. Hakulinen et al. 2003 on the use of *kuule* in transitions in epistemic relations), at the same time indicating that the recipient did perhaps not know this fact, or that it might not be common knowledge.

Chapter 9. Second-person singular imperatives in Finnish   277

Excerpt 6. *kalossit* 'galoshes' (SG108, Arkisyn), face-to-face

```
01 H: .hh se pitäs hommata nämä: ↑kalos[sit. hh heh]
      .hh (one) should get these galoshes. hh heh
02 C:                                  [nii.    ]
                                        yeah.
03 H: .hh niitä     muuten on    kuule myynnissä.(.)
          DEM.PL.PART PTC    be.3SG kuule sale.INE
      .hh they are, for that matter, being KUULE sold.
```

The epistemic asymmetry that *kuule* indexes might also be used for humorous purposes, as in Excerpt (7) in which *kuule* occurs as a part of reported speech. Prior to the excerpt, the mother, Elli, who works as a teacher in middle school, has told her family a story about a boy in her class for whom his friends had organized a blind date. The boy did not want to go on the date, and Elli tried to encourage him to go:

Excerpt 7. *elinikäinen ihmissuhde* 'a lifelong relationship' (SG441, Arkisyn), face-to-face

```
01 ELL: mä s'noi et @no älä nyt suhtaudu noin
        I said that @don't be so preconceiving
02      ennakkoluulosesti et siitä voi kuule alkaa vaikka
        preconceiving it could KUULE even become
03      £elinikäinen ihmissuhde£@, he
        a lifelong relationship@, he
```

In Excerpt (7), *kuule* occurs in Elli's reported speech. She was trying (humorously) to argue for why the boy should go on the blind date; he might find a partner for life. By using *kuule*, Elli is playfully indicating that there is an aspect that the boy has not realized yet.

4.3 *Älä* 'NEG.2SG.IMP'

The third most common 2SG.IMP form in the data is the negative imperative *älä* (*N*=112; sometimes in the dialectal form of *elä*). In initiating directive action, *älä* is used to forbid somebody to do something, making it a prohibitive. In directives, it can occur alone, normally in the context where the forbidden action is multimodally available for the participants, or then together with another verb that specifies the forbidden action (e.g., *älä huuda* 'do not yell').

Excerpt (8) demonstrates the use of *älä* as a part of directive action. Prior to the excerpt, Siiri has told her friend Missu that she has become engaged. She then asks Missu not to tell anybody else about it yet (line 1), with which Missu complies (line 3):

Excerpt 8. *älä kerro vielä muille* 'don't tell anyone yet' (SG113, Arkisyn), telephone

```
01 SII: >↑älä   kerro v-,<   ↑älä    kerro       vielä muille,
        älä    tell.CONNEG   älä    tell.CONNEG yet   other.PL.ALL
        ÄLÄ (don't) tell y-, ÄLÄ (don't) tell anyone yet,

02       mää kerron itten_ni,=
         I will tell them myself,

03 MIS: =juu en kerro.
         yeah no I won't tell.
```

While *älä* in Excerpt (8) occurs in a first-position turn, there are also cases in which *älä* is used in a second-position turn (cf. Keevallik 2017). In such cases, the directive meaning of the imperative form is still present, but the turns in which *älä* occurs are affective or evaluative in nature (cf. Hakulinen et al. 2004: § 1723). Consider Excerpt (9), which is from a multiparty conversation. In the excerpt, Jere is telling the others how he plays computer games for several hours, "just like that" (lines 1–2). Sari responds to Jere's self-generalizing account (see Visapää 2021) by producing an *älä* turn (line 3):

Excerpt 9. *noihi peleihi* 'those games' (SG121, Arkisyn), face-to-face

```
01 JER: mie taas kyl jää jumettaa noihi peleihi iha keppaa
        I get stuck on those games, just stagnating

02       ain monta tuntii [iha tost vaa, ]
         always many hours, just like that,

03 SAR:                   [no  <älä>  nyt] <liio>ttele,
                          PTC  älä   PTC  exaggerate.CONNEG
                          ÄLÄ (don't) exaggerate,

04 JER: ↑no em mie liiottele pätkääkää,
        I'm not exaggerating at all,
```

Sari's turn *no <älä> nyt <liiot>tele,* 'don't exaggerate' can be interpreted as a critical evaluation of Jere's turn, accusing Jere of exaggerating the time he spends playing computer games; the affective stance is further shown by Sari's use of the particle *nyt* which is typical in reactive contexts (Hakulinen 1998).

Second-position *älä* turns can also be rather fixed in their linguistic form, as is the case with the collocation *älä viitti* or *älä viitsi*, in which *älä* is accompanied by the verb *viitsiä* 'to bother'. In this collocation, *viitsiä* is not used in a concrete way, but instead, the expression is used to indicate participational resistance or non-collaboration: the speaker does not want to hear or see more from the previous speaker's side, or then wants to show disalignment with the ongoing line of talk. This is the case in Excerpt (10), taken from the same discussion as Excerpt (9). Sari uses *älä viitti* (line 3) to indicate that she thinks Jere's and Tero's (playful) idea of buying rally cars is absurd and that she is not interested in hearing any more about the matter. Her stance is further shown by the turn-initial particle chain *höpö höpö*, which is used to indicate that something is nonsense, and the turn-

Chapter 9. Second-person singular imperatives in Finnish **279**

final, self-referential comment *mie en jaksa* 'I can't take it', which further underscores her stance:

Excerpt 10. *ralliautot* 'rally cars' (SG121, Arkisyn), face-to-face

```
01 JER: ostetaaks ralliautot,=
        should we buy rally cars,

02 TER: =↓ostetaa,
        let's do it,

03 SAR: höpö höpö, [älä viitti mie en      jaksa,]
        PTC  PTC     älä bother 1SG NEG.1SG take.it.CONNEG
        nonsense, ÄLÄ (stop it) I've had enough,

04 JER:              [minuu kiehtos iha hulluna  ]
                      it would fascinate me like crazy

05      ajaa rallii>
        to drive rally
```

A rather fixed collocation in the data is also *älä ny(t)*, in which *älä* occurs with the particle *ny(t)* (cf. Excerpt (9)), but without the main verb. In the comprehensive grammar of Finnish, Hakulinen et al. (2004: § 1712) call such cases "reactive phrases". Such collocations occur in second position in the data in this study also. They are reactive to the preceding turn and can be approached as a practice for topicalizing something in another participant's just-prior turn. *Älä ny(t)* cases express an ambiguous stance in a humorous way, and they can be used to indicate that there is also an alternative point of view to the one that was presented in the previous turn. However, whether the current speaker commits to this alternative point of view themselves or merely introduces its existence, is left open.

Consider Excerpt (11) which is from a multiparty conversation. Prior to the excerpt, the participants have been discussing different kinds of wedding presents they have received, and a measuring cup set (*mittasarja*) has been mentioned as an example of a very random present. In the excerpt, Antti tells the other participants how he, too, has once bought a measuring cup set as a present, but as a joke. According to him, this choice of present was motivated by his girlfriend who said that he should buy the measuring cup set because nobody else would think to buy one.

Excerpt 11. *mittasarja* 'a measuring cup set' (SG346, Arkisyn), face-to-face

```
01 ANT: ei vitsi mä osti keh- he hhhh tom
        you know I bought onc- he hhhh that

02      .mittasarjan? .mhhh ninku sillei (.) iha
        measuring cup set .hhh like (.) just (as)

03      läppä >si'te Jossu sano et< (0.4) .hhhhh no jos
        a joke >then Josu said that< (0.4.) .hhhhh well if

04      et sä osta >s'tä ni< (- ei osta kukaa muukaa)
        you don't buy >it then< (nobody else will either)

05      ((everybody laughs))
```

```
06 KER: älä ny?
        älä PTC
07 KER: [(ehkä) kaikkei arv-]
        (maybe) the most dist-
08      [((laughter))      ]
09 KER: kaikkei arvovaltasimmat vieraat osti.
        the most distinguished guests bought one.
```

As a response to Antti's story, Kerttu produces a TCU consisting of *älä ny* (line 6) and then continues to state that perhaps the most distinguished guests did buy that present (lines 7, 9). Kerttu mentioned earlier that she and her partner had received a measuring cup set as a present from her partner's parents and that it was actually useful. By *älä nyt*, Kerttu humorously criticizes the idea that is implicitly present in Antti's turn, i.e., that a measuring cup set would be a useless present. Instead, Kerttu suggests that maybe it was the present given by the most distinguished guests. This is, however, done in a joking manner (note everybody laughing, lines 5 and 8), which indicates that the presented point of view does not necessarily represent that of Kerttu's, even though she is the one voicing it.

All *älä*'s in Excerpts (8)–(11) carry, at least to some extent, the prohibitive meaning associated with the negative imperative, but in Excerpts (9)–(11), *älä* occurs in a second-position turn as a part of an affective response to the previous speaker's turn.

4.4 *A(j)attele* 'think.2SG.IMP'

The data comprise 55 instances of the verb *ajatella*, 'to think', in 2SG.IMP form. In most cases (*N* = 43), the imperative occurs in the reduced form of *aattele*, in which the two first syllables of the verb *ajatella* are merged into one (cf. Laury, Helasvuo & Rauma 2020), but the non-reduced form *ajattele* also occurs.

A(j)attele is rather ambiguous regarding whether it should be understood as a directive or not. In all cases, *a(j)attele* occurs in connection with actions that are not directive: storytelling, assessments, and informings. It is not clear whether it forms a part of these actions or occurs as a stand-alone directive. Based on the interaction, it is difficult to show whether the recipient treats the imperative form as a directive and complies with it, but at least the recipients to whom *a(j)attele* is directed do not produce any obvious signals of "thinking", such as gestures, hesitation markers, or a "thinking face". The distinction between the more concrete and the more particle-like use of *a(j)attele* can perhaps be best defined through the syntactic context. The more concrete cases are typically followed by a direct object NP (e.g., *aattele semmost et* think.2SG.IMP such.PART COMP 'think about such (a situation)') or a clausal object complement initiated with the conjunctions

Chapter 9. Second-person singular imperatives in Finnish   **281**

jos 'if' or *kun* 'when', or the complementizer *että* (e.g., ***aattele et** sil oli semmoset saappaat mis ei ollu vuorii ollenkaa* 'think (imagine) that she had such boots in which there was no lining'). Regarding the more particle-like cases of *a(j)attele*, they are not followed by linguistic content that could be interpreted to stand in an obvious syntactic relation to the imperative form.

Different uses of *a(j)attele* typically occur in similar actional contexts, i.e., in turns where the current speaker describes something from their own point of view and invites the recipient to share this view. This happens most typically in assessments (see Pomerantz 1984). Consider Excerpts (12) and (13). Excerpt (12) is taken from a multiparty conversation, but the turn in question (lines 3–4) is addressed to one specific participant, Tero. The participants are watching television and commenting on the behavior of a woman in a TV program.

Excerpt 12. *ketkuttamas* 'wiggling' (SG121, Arkisyn), face-to-face

```
01 TER: <mitä tuo täti tekee>.
         what is that woman doing.
02      (2.0)
03 MIK: <ei jumalauta.>  Tero aattele nyt ku
         NEG goddammit        name aattele PTC CONJ
         goddammit. Tero AATTELE now that(/when)
04      sie oisit tuol ketkuttamas,
         you were there wiggling,
05 SAR: [eh heh    ] heh
06 JER: [he he he  ]
07 TER: [he he he  ]
```

Excerpt (13) is from a conversation between two people (even if we only see one participant's turns here), and the topic is the alleged corruption of Finnish media, and a Finnish newspaper called *Helsingin Sanomat* (referred to as *Hesari*, line 2) in particular:

Excerpt 13. *Hesari* (SG398, Arkisyn), face-to-face

```
01 KAT: #että#< nyt niinkun muutki: huomaa mitä
         #that#< now like others also notice what
02      mä oon puhunu koko ajan sitä Hesarii et
         I've been saying all the time about Hesari that
03      mua °öllöttää se°.
         I'm disgusted by it.
04      (0.4)
05 KAT: h. ↑ja ajattele ne  ei voineet  #e::
            CONJ ajattele DEM.PL NEG can.PRF.3PL PTC
         h. and AJATTELE they couldn't e-
```

06	Saddami °hi::rt°tämiseen edes <ottaa kantaa.>	
	name hanging.ILL even take.a.stand.INF	
	even take a stand to the hanging of Saddam.	
07	(0.7)	

In Excerpt (12), Tero is first commenting on a woman dancing on the television. Mika responds to it by producing an affective turn, which starts with a TCU consisting of a fixed expletive expression *ei jumalauta* '(no) goddammit' (line 3), expressing Mika's stance on what happens on the television. After this, Mika moves on to address Tero by name, followed by the imperative *aattele*.[5] *Aattele* is followed by the particle *nyt* 'now' and a clausal complement initiated by the conjunction *ku*. In the complement clause, Mika introduces the idea of Tero acting in the same way as the woman on the television. The affectedness of the utterance can be seen in Mika's choice of words: to refer to the kind of dance the woman is doing, he uses the verb *ketkuttaa*, which has the connotation of (unnecessarily) sexual dancing. The other participants respond to Mika's turn by laughing (lines 5, 6, 7), which indicates that they interpret the turn with *aattele* as a humorous assessment concerning the way of dancing they see. Excerpt (12) is followed by Mika's request to change the channel (not shown here).

In Excerpt (13), *ajattele* occurs in Kati's assessment turn (lines 5–6), concerning the way the *Helsingin Sanomat* newspaper (referred to as *Hesari*) reported the hanging of Saddam Hussein. Already in the beginning of the excerpt, Kati states how she has been "disgusted" by *Helsingin Sanomat* (lines 1–3) for a long time, and the turn with *ajattele* is linked to this (note the additive conjunction *ja* in line 5). In this context, *ajattele* functions as a projecting element: it precedes an extreme example of how things are reported in the newspaper in question. *Ajattele* is not syntactically linked to the following content, e.g., with the help of a complementizer, which makes the expression syntactically particle-like, similar to *kato* 'look.2SG.IMP' and *kuule* 'hear.2SG.IMP' discussed earlier in this section. Interestingly, Kati's assessment is not followed by any response by the recipient, and actually, further in the same sequence, the other participant Tarja shows that she does not really affiliate with Kati's stance (not shown here).

It is a more general tendency that the particle-like *a(j)attele* occurs in contexts where the recipient has not previously shown enough, if any, alignment or affiliation with the speaker. In such contexts, the particle-like *a(j)attele* functions as an interpersonal device to invite the recipient even more strongly to recognize the situation from the presented personal point of view and potentially show alignment and affiliation. In all the cases, *a(j)attele* is typically used to mark descrip-

---

5. In many cases in my data, *a(j)attele* could perhaps best be translated into English as 'imagine'.

Chapter 9. Second-person singular imperatives in Finnish   **283**

tions of states of affairs that are surprising or even controversial in relation to what the participants may already know or expect.

4.5   *O(d)ota* 'wait.2SG.IMP'

There are 41 instances of the verb *odottaa* 'to wait' in the 2SG.IMP form. In most cases (*N*=36) the form is realized in the reduced form of *oota*, in some cases accompanied by the clitic *-s* (*oota-s*). The rest of the cases are in the non-reduced form of *odota* (or in its regional variant *orota*), and this form, too, can have the clitic *-s* attached to it. The use of the clitic *-s* in connection with imperatives is typical; in such contexts, the clitic *-s* has been suggested to lend the utterance a flavor of plea and immediacy (Hakulinen et al. 2004: § 838; Stevanovic 2017: 359).

In a study concerning the Estonian second-person imperative form *oota*, Keevallik (2001) describes the use of the expression on a continuum of more literal to more particle-like (or, *particulized*, using Keevallik's terminology). On this continuum, Keevallik differentiates between the following: literal usage; thinking periods and word searches; side sequences and digressions; repair initiatives and clarification requests; topic retrieval and change. Similar ways of using *o(d)ota* can be found in the Finnish data.

In the literal, concrete use, *o(d)ota* occurs as a part of a directive, through which the speaker is asking the recipient to literally wait while something happens outside the ongoing main activity frame. Below is an example of how *o(d)ota* is used to pause, or suspend, the ongoing activity while another side-activity is being initiated. The excerpt is taken from a telephone conversation between two friends, one of which (Vikke) asks the other (Missu) for an address of a mutual friend (line 1). In response, Missu produces a turn with *ootas*, addressed to Vikke (line 2), and starts to look for the friend's address in her apartment. *Ootas* is accompanied by the mitigating adverb *vähä* 'a little', a reference to the time the suspension will take:

Excerpt 14. *ootas vähä* 'wait a little' (SG112, Arkisyn), telephone

```
01 Vikke: voisitsää sanoo mulle Kari:tan, (.) osotteen.
          could you tell me Karita's, (.) address.
02 Missu: .hh juu oota-s vähä;   hhh
               PTC   oota-CLT a.little
          .hh yeah OOTA-S  a little; hhh
03        (1.2) ((clattering sound))
```

Moving on a continuum from the literal towards the particle-like uses, Keevallik (2001: 133) mentions the use of the Estonian *oota* as a "conversational stop sign" that can be used to delay or postpone the ongoing activity, or to signal some kind of digression from it. In my data, such uses can be seen especially when *o(d)ota* is used as a part of word searches, including what Keevallik (2001:127–129) calls *thinking periods* in which the current speaker puts the conversation on hold and signals that an intrapersonal thinking process is going on. In these cases, *o(d)ota* forms a TCU, sometimes even a turn, either on its own or accompanied by (other) particle-like elements, such as expressions *hetki/hetkinen* 'a moment' (cf. Vatanen & Haddington 2024) or *nyt* 'now'. *Hetki(nen)* is typically used in actions such as suspensions and word searches and has the interactional function of halting the ongoing activity (Teeri-Niknammoghadam & Surakka 2023; Vatanen & Haddington 2024). When used as a discourse particle, *nyt* marks the turn it occurs in as reactive (Hakulinen 1998). In word-search contexts, it may also signal that the speaker is departing from the main line of activity (Hakulinen et al. 2004:§823).

Consider Excerpt (15), in which *oota* is used in a word-search context, preceded by *hetkinen* and followed by *nyt*. In the excerpt, Ilmari is trying to recall how old a person he sees in a photograph was at the time the picture was taken. By producing *hetkinen oota nyt* 'wait a moment now' (line 4), he is signaling a word search and pauses the ongoing activity for a short thinking period before finishing the turn (line 7) that he started earlier:

Excerpt 15. *hetkinen* 'a moment' (SG435, Arkisyn), face-to-face

```
01 ILM: tossa vaiheessa nimittäi Pe- ä: Esa-Pekka
        at that point Pe- um Esa-Pekka

02      oli vi- ö[:::  seitsemänkymme-]
        was fi- umm seventy-

03 MAI:          [ (mie::s:::::::::::::]:::)
                   man

04 ILM: hetkinen        [oota nyt;]
        MOMENT           oota PTC
        wait a moment now;

05 MAI:                 [joo  ei o]o Ku-
                         yeah (it) isn't Ku-

06      [ei  oo  kyllä Kulttuurita]lo eikä Akatemia,
        for sure isn't Kulttuuritalo and not Akatemia either

07 ILM: [seitsemänkytäyhdeksän,    ]
         seventy-nine,
```

Vatanen and Haddington (2024), who have studied the linguistic structure of the suspension turns in family interaction, have noted that *oota* 'wait' and *hetki(nen)* 'a moment' are typical elements in suspensions. They suggest that these turns should be treated as fixed expressions: formulaic structures achieving certain, routinized interactional goals. According to Vatanen and Haddington (ibid.25), the more fixed the suspension turn is, the less accountable it makes the pro-

Chapter 9. Second-person singular imperatives in Finnish **285**

ducer of the turn. These notions also seem relevant in relation to the data used in this chapter: The turns with *o(d)ota* are produced as fixed formulae, recurrently accompanied by certain linguistic elements, such as the particles *hetki(nen)* and *nyt*. *O(d)ota* is a routinized way to signal word search, and the producers of the *o(d)ota* turns are not held accountable for the pausing of the conversational activity.

O(d)ota can also be used in the beginning of an other-initiated repair (cf. Keevallik 2001: 133–135 on the Estonian *oota*), in which case it is used to initiate a repair turn that returns to something that was said earlier, typically asking for a clarification that is necessary before the sequentially indicated next action can take place (see Schegloff, Jefferson & Sacks 1977: 379). In these cases, *o(d)ota* is placed in the beginning of a TCU, but unlike in a word search, it does not form a TCU on its own but occurs as a part of a larger unit. It is typically produced quite fast and without any hesitation markers, and often in the reduced form of *oota*. The next excerpt demonstrates this. It is taken from a multiparty conversation among friends. One of the participants, Susa, is telling others what she and her family members have won in a raffle:

Excerpt 16. *stereot* 'stereos' (SG151, Arkisyn), face-to-face

```
01 SUS: ja sit mein äiti viel=tota (.)
        and then in addition, our mother umm (.)

02      voitti eile ne stereot ne on viel sikasiistit
        won yesterday those stereos they are really cool

03      ne on semmoset pienet. (.)
        they are that kind of small ones. (.)

04      >sis< TO[si pienet semmoset-]
        I mean really small the kind of-

05 MII:        [mut saaks saat-, oo]ta
               but do you get you get, OOTA

06      onkse nyt niillä vai saatteks työ ne.
        do they have it now or will you get them.

07 SUS: ei kato ku ↑myöhä ostettii Tuomas osti sillo
        no because we did buy Tuomas bought then

08      ku mie läksin Helsinkii ni Tuomasha osti
        when I left to Helsinki Tuomas bought

09      meille uuet stereot.=
        new stereos for us.

10 MII: =aijaa jaa.
        aha yeah.
```

In the beginning of the excerpt, Susa tells how her mother won a very nice small stereo set in a raffle (lines 1–4). In response, Miia starts to produce the verb *saada* 'get' in second-person form, in overlap with Susa (line 5), probably to ask whether

Susa and her partner will get the stereo set from the mother (cf. line 6). However, Miia then stops and restarts her turn, first producing *oota* (line 5) after which she reformulates her request for clarification concerning the future owner of the stereo set. Miia's turn is followed by Susa's clarification (lines 7–9) and Miia's receipt (line 10).

In Excerpt (16), *oota* on the one hand signals that there is something unclear about the preceding turn, but on the other, functions as a request to halt the interaction. The use of *oota* in initiating other-oriented repair may also be motivated by the fact that Susa does not seem to react to Miia's first repair initiation (*mut saaks saat-* 'but do you get you get-') but instead, keeps on producing overlapping speech; noteworthy regarding this is that right after Miia starts to produce *oota*, Susa stops her turn.

4.6   *Sano* 'say.2SG.IMP'

The Arkisyn data contains 36 occurrences of *sanoa* 'to say' in 2SG.IMP form (*sano*). In most cases, *sano* is used in directive actions, either in the first-position turn, normally in the meaning of 'telling' or 'sharing information' (see Excerpt (17)), or then in second-position turn, in a more literal meaning of giving somebody the permission to talk, for example, in the context of overlapping speech (see Excerpt (18): line 5; see also Pouttu 2010; see Sorjonen 2017 for the use of the modal particle *vaa(n)* 'just' in connection with the imperative). Further, *sano* can also be used in a fixed collocation of *sano terveisiä* 'say hello' (Excerpt (19): lines 1, 2–3; see Auer 2017: 415).

Excerpt 17. *mihi aikaa* 'at what time' (SG355, Arkisyn), face-to-face

```
01 MIK: sano mihi aikaa, mihi aikaa meitin
        SANO (say) at what time, at what time do we

02      täytyy täältä [lähtee,
        have to leave from here,

03 MIR:              [nii,
                      yeah,

04 MIK: ku m'ollaa sev verra,
        because we are so,

05 JOH: jos se lähtee pual kuus ni viideltä,
        if it (the vehicle) leaves half past five then at five,
```

Excerpt 18. *sori* 'sorry' (SG441, Arkisyn), face-to-face

```
01 ELL: oli t[ota.]
        there was umm.

02 IIR:    >[SAAM] MÄ,<
           >can I have,<
```

Chapter 9. Second-person singular imperatives in Finnish **287**

03   (0.8)

04 ELL: hmm,

05 IIR: sori, (.) joo sano vaa.
        sorry   PTC sano PTC
        sorry, (.) yeah just/go ahead and SANO (say).

06 ELL: oli tota,
        there was umm,

Excerpt 19. *terkkuja* 'say hello' (SG112, Arkisyn), face-to-face

01 MIS: ↑juu soitellaan; =sano te[rkkuja Sallalle.]
        yeah let's call again; SANO (say) hello to Salla.

02 VIK: [sanoppa Marikalle]
                             SANO (say) Marika

03   terveis[iä.
        hello.

04 MIS: [joo, mää sano.
               yeah, I will say.

Sano co-occurs often with clitic particles *-pA* (*sano-pa*; Excerpt (19)), *-s* (*sano-s*) or the compound particle *-pAs* (*sano-pas*). As stated in connection with *o(d)ota*, 'wait', *-s* has been suggested to lend the utterance a flavor of plea and immediacy, while *-pA* has been analyzed to mitigate the directive aspect of the expression it is attached to and to draw attention to the speaker's locally and interactionally grounded deontic status (Hakulinen et al. 2004: § 835; Stevanovic 2017). Regarding the *-pAs* combination, Stevanovic (2017: 376) explains that it invokes the globally and institutionally grounded right to determine the agenda of the participants' joint activity, at least in instructional contexts. The data in this chapter suggests that the clitic particles do not always seem to carry such explicit meanings as described by Stevanovic (2017), which could be due to the fact that the imperatives studied here are rather formulaic.

An example of a rather formulaic or idiomatic expression, comprising the imperative *sano*, is a combination of *sano* and the pronoun *muu* 'else' in the partitive case (*muu-ta* 'else-PART') where *sano* may sometimes be accompanied by the clitic particles. This formulaic expression is used to show strong alignment (see Hakulinen et al. 2004: § 1723) and in certain contexts, it could be translated into English as 'indeed'.[6] It has a rather limited context of use: it can only occur in a second-position turn as a response to the previous speaker's assessment. Consider Excerpt (20):

---

6. In Finnish, the same kind of alignment can also be shown by using the negative imperative of the verb *sanoa*: *älä muuta sano* lit. 'do not say anything else' (Hakulinen et al. 2004: § 1723; cf. Section 4.3 on *älä*). However, these kinds of expressions do not occur in the data used here.

288 Karita Suomalainen

Excerpt 20. *radiotekniikka* 'radio technology' (SG435, Arkisyn), face-to-face

```
01 ILM: kuule radiotekniikka [on hie[no,
         KUULE radio technology is fancy,

02 EIJ:                      [ehh ha[ha ha ha ha  ]

03 OUT:                             [£sano£ muuta.]
                                    SANO  else.
```

The data also contain a few cases where *sano* is used rather particle-like, as a part of word-searches. *Sano*-initiated word-searches may be collective in nature, so that the word-search is done mutually among the participants, but it seems that in these situations, *sano* is not really addressed to any of the participants.[7] Rather, it is a formulaic expression indexing that the right word is being sought. In these contexts, it is often accompanied by the particle *ny(t)* 'now', which indexes immediacy. Excerpt (21), taken form a multiparty conversation among friends, exemplifies such use of *sano*. In the excerpt, the participants are discussing the last name of the priest at the confirmation class they attended together some years earlier:

Excerpt 21. *sukunimi* 'last name' (Sapu119, Arkisyn), face-to-face

```
01 JAT:  >mikä se Tommi sukunimi o?<
         what was Tommi's last name?

02       (1.0)

03 MIR:  Tommi-, (.) mikä se o,
         Tommi-, (.) what is it,

04       (0.2)

05 ANN:  ei vitsi.
         gosh.

06 ALI:  ku se tuli, se ei ollus se oli vaan kesän Raumal,
         when he came, he wasn't he was in Rauma just for the summer,

07       sit se muutti.
         then he moved away.

08 MIR:  >sano-s   ny.<
         sano-CLT  PTC
         SANO (say) now.

09 ALI:  ↑kui mä voisi muistaa et se muutti Turkuu,
         how can I remember it as if he moved to Turku,
```

((9 lines omitted in which everybody else but Mirja is discussing the age of the priest))

```
19 MIR:  se oli joku Tommi-, (1.0) ei mitää hajuu.
         it was something like Tommi-, (1.0) no idea.
```

---

7. One option would be to interpret these types of *sano* expressions as self-directed speech. However, as there is no evidence for this in the turns-at-talk, this chapter approaches *sano* expressions in word-searches as formulaic expressions that have become fixed as a result of their recurrent use in these contexts.

Chapter 9. Second-person singular imperatives in Finnish   **289**

In Excerpt (21), the participants are searching for the last name of the priest (*Tommi*) together. In line 3, Mirva initiates a word search by starting to produce the name of the priest. In line 8, she produces the *sanos ny* expression 'lit. say now'. In this context, her *sanos ny* turn could be interpreted to do intersubjective work regarding the ongoing word-search: on the one hand, it shows others that Mirva is busy thinking about the name (and not just not participating by being quiet), but on the other, it also signals that she is in the middle of a word-search, even if the other participant, Alina, has moved on to discuss other matters concerning the priest (lines 6–7). In line 19, Mirva indicates that the word-search has come to an end, but without success. She repeats the first name of the priest but after a pause adds an increment stating that she has no idea of the last name of the priest (*ei mitään hajuu* 'no idea').

4.7   *Arvaa* 'guess.2SG.IMP'

Arvaa, the 2SG.IMP form of *arvata* 'to guess', occurs in the data 17 times. When used in a more directive and literal fashion, it initiates a *pre-announcement* (Terasaki 2004 [1976]; see also Schegloff 2007: 37–39; Levinson 2012: 117). These pre-announcements consist of the imperative form *arvaa* followed by the question word *mitä* 'what.PART', i.e., 'guess what', and they occur as first pairs of pre-sequences, designed to prepare the recipient(s) for an upcoming story, a piece of news, or an announcement. According to Sorjonen (2002: 170), *arvaa mitä* is a canonical way of building up a generic pre-announcement in Finnish conversations. *Arvaa* turns of this type are typically followed by a go-ahead response *no* by the recipient (Sorjonen 2002); in this sense, the recipient does not interpret *arvaa* in a literal way, as a request to guess, but instead recognizes its role as a projective device. Excerpt (22) demonstrates this. It is taken from a telephone conversation between a mother, Irja, and a daughter, Heta. Prior to the excerpt, the previous sequence has just ended, and Heta starts a new sequence with an *arvaa mitä* turn (line 1):

Excerpt 22. *snadi kuli* 'short hair' (SG124, Arkisyn), telephone

```
01 HET: =.hhh ↑arvaa mitä.
              arvaa what.PART
         .hhh ARVAA what.

02 IRJ: ↑noh,
         PTC

03 HET: ↑mul on ihan snadi kuli. .mh mh [mh mh]
         I've got really short hair. mhe mhe mhe

04 IRJ:                                 [a:i. ]
                                         oh.
```

```
05      [no missäs sä,]
        where (did) you,
06 HET: [meikkis kävi  ] parturis.
        I've been to barber's.
```

In the excerpt, the *arvaa mitä* turn forms a first-pair part of a pre-sequence. It projects the telling of a piece of news to come but does not reveal any details of its subject matter. It is followed by Irja's response *noh* (line 2), through which Irja gives a go-ahead to Heta; according to Sorjonen (2002: 170–171), *no* responses in these kinds of contexts offer a second pair part that encourages the speaker to get on with the production of the core action projected by the pre-announcement. Following *noh*, Heta moves on to the projected action and tells the piece of news: she has gotten a new, very short haircut (line 3).

In the data, *arvaa* also occurs as a part of critical assessments, typically at the latter part of a longer sequence. In these contexts, *arvaa* is followed by an interrogative subordinate clause that presents the criticized state-of-affairs. These subordinate clauses are negation-inclining, i.e., based on the preceding context, they project a negatively formulated affiliative utterance as a response. In such contexts, *arvaa* can be seen to engage the recipient and invite them to share the speaker's stance.

Consider Excerpt (23). It is taken from a conversation between two sisters, Jaana and Tuula. They are discussing what it is like to take care of small babies. Jaana has previously told Tuula how one of her friends has twins, and in the excerpt, she goes on to explain what her friend has said about everyday life with infant twins:

Excerpt 23. *vauvaikä* 'infancy' (SG438, Arkisyn), face-to-face

```
01 TUU: [vauvaikä on se,]
        infancy is the,

02 JAA: [ni se että, .hh]hh se ainaki se Saila sano
        the thing is, .hhhh at least Saila said

03      >että kyllä se oli semmosta< hitsin rumbaa
        that it indeed was such a circus

04      että, .hhhm ett #ee# niil oli luojan kiitos
        that, .hhhm that umm thank god it was so

05      kuulemma sie- sillai että:, (.) et ne oli
        apparently the- so that, (.) they were

06      niinkun, .hh eri tah#dissa#, (0.4) että
        like, .hh in different tempo, (0.4) that

07      kerkis aina toisen hoitaa et ne ei huutanu
        (she) had time to take care of one (baby) that they
        didn't cry

08      kumpiki yh#tä aikaa sitte siinä#,=
        both simultaneously there then,
```

Chapter 9. Second-person singular imperatives in Finnish **291**

```
09 TUU: m[m; ]
10 JAA: [mut] se että, .hhhh arvaa kuin paljon
         PTC   DEM COMP       arvaa how  much
         but the thing is, .hhhh ARVAA how much
11       siin (jää)    äidil#le jäi            ai#°kaa°.
         there leave.3SG mother.ALL leave.PST.3SG time.PART
         time is then left for the mother.
12       (0.8)
13 TUU: .hhhh mut se o kuitenki niin pieni aika
         .hhhh but it is after all such a short time
14       ihmise elämässä se, (.) vauva-aika et°tä°,
         in a human's life that,(.) baby period that,
15       (.) .hhhhhh et en mä, (1.0) ↑ei se oo mikään
         (.) .hhhhhh that I don't, (1.0) it's not
16       pahah? (0.8) .phhh °välttämättä°, (1.2) näin mä
         bad? (0.8) .phh necessarily, (1.2) this is how I
17       aattelisi,
         see it,
18       (1.4)
```

In line 9, Tuula produces a minimally aligning *mm* turn (see Kangasharju 1998) to Jaana's telling of her friend's experience, after which Jaana goes on to express her own assessment of the described situation (lines 10–11). Jaana's turn is initiated by *mut se että* utterance that, according to Vatanen, Suomalainen and Laury (2020), projects a gist of a complex telling. This gist is initiated by *arvaa* 'guess', followed by the interrogatively formatted *kuin paljo siin jää äidille aikaah* 'how much time there is left for the mother'. By saying this, Jaana presents her own point of view that taking care of two infants simultaneously does not really leave much (alone) time for the mother. The turn projects a negatively formulated turn as an affiliative response ('not really much time'). However, Tuula does not respond straight away; her response follows after a pause (line 12), which indicates that it may not be preferred. In her response, Tuula disagrees with Jaana (note the contrastive particle *mut* 'but' in the beginning of Tuula's turn). Tuula's turn can be approached as a second assessment, "a responsive utterance which offers an evaluation of the same assessable as the first assessment" (Thompson et al. 2015: 141; see also Pomerantz 1984). In her response, Tuula presents her own, contradicting point of view: she thinks that the time with infants is such a short period in a person's life that she cannot really see it being as difficult as Jaana has claimed it to be (lines 13–17).

Arvaa can also be used in a particle-like way in second-position turns. In these cases, it is followed by linguistic content that cannot really be interpreted as a complement of the verb *arvata*. This is the case in Excerpt (24), in which *arvaa* (line 4) could be interpreted as a syntactically independent turn-initial element projecting an aligning counter-assessment. The excerpt is from a conversation between two friends who are spending an evening at a restaurant.

Excerpt 24. *käsiempesutila* 'hand washing station' (Sapu118, Arkisyn), face-to-face

```
01 JAT: ja vessaki o sellanen ihan niinku NÄIM pieni ja
        and the toilet was like such like THIS small and

02      silti siel on kolme koppii ja käsiempesutila ja
        yet there were three cubicles and a hand washing station and

03      kaikki ovet aukeaa sit niinko si,
        all doors open then like into

04      niinko siihen käsiempesutilaa.
        like into the hand washing station.

05 VAR: arvaa ku   mä     vaihdoin  siin
        arvaa CONJ 1SG    change.1SG there
        ARVAA when I was changing    there

06      laastareitani,
        band.aid.PL.PART.POSS
        my band-aids,

07      (2.0)

08      tämän kassin, (.) tän    laukun   kans.
        DEM.GEN bag.GEN     DEM.GEN purse.GEN with
        with this bag, with this purse.

09 JAT: sitä ei voi laittaa mihinkää.
        you cannot put it anywhere.
```

At the beginning of the excerpt, Jatta criticizes the design and size of the bathroom in the restaurant they are visiting (lines 1–4). In response, Varpu describes how difficult it was to change her band-aids in the bathroom, having her purse with her, too. Varpu's turn contains an aspect of assessment, even if it is rather implicit. The use of *arvaa* plays a central role in signaling assessment: it invites Jatta to imagine the described situation, and since both participants have been to the bathroom, Jatta can be thought to understand the difficulties of the situation, based on this experience, and see that the size and design of the bathroom was the cause for the difficulties. And indeed, following Varpu's turn, Jatta verbalizes the essence of Varpu's implicit assessment (line 9): placing the purse anywhere in the bathroom is impossible.

In Excerpt (24), *arvaa* is followed by the connective *ku(n),* which can be used to initiate a complement cause. *Ku(n)* is typically used to express temporal relations (in the meaning of 'when'), but it can also be used to introduce a cause, reason, or explanation (Herlin 1998). *Arvaa,* however, should get an object complement (cf. Excerpts (22) and (23)), and in Excerpt (24), it is rather questionable whether the following *ku(n)*-clause can be interpreted as an object complement.

Chapter 9. Second-person singular imperatives in Finnish **293**

Hakulinen and Seppänen (1992:536–537) report a similar use of the connective *ku* together with *kato* 'look' and argue that in such contexts, the two form "one conventionalized item". They further hypothesize that this type of usage is "a possible starting point for what may be called a 'process of abstraction'" (ibid.536). In the data used in this chapter, *arvaa* and *ku(n)* seem to form a similar conventionalized item, one that could also be called a *fixed expression*. This item can be used in second-position turns to project a reactive and highly context-dependent assessment which appeals to the recipient's recognition of the presented situation.

4.8 Summary

This section has dealt with the different ways of using the 2SG.IMP forms of the following verbs in Finnish everyday interaction: *katsoa* 'to look', *kuulla* 'to hear', negative verb *ei*, *ajatella* 'to think', *odottaa* 'to wait', *sanoa* 'to say', *arvata* 'to guess'. These verbs can be used not only in directive actions but also in actions where the main function is not primarily directive. The boundary between directive and not primarily directive use is often fuzzy. When the imperatives are used in directive actions they are, like directives in general, used to get the recipient to do something, and the relevant next action is either compliance or non-compliance. When the imperatives are used in actions that are not primarily directive, they are used to orient the recipient to something that is central in regard to the ongoing activity, and in this way, guide the discourse and the participation framework rather than the recipient's actions in the physical world. In such cases, they are used in actions such as storytellings, informings, news deliveries, and assessments and have rather fixed local tasks. For example, the prohibitive *älä* may be used to indicate participational resistance or non-collaboration, *oota* 'wait' to signal a word search, *arvaa* (*mitä*) 'guess (what)' to initiate a pre-sequence, *kato* 'look' to explain a new aspect, and *aattele* 'think, imagine' to invite the recipient to share the current speaker's stance. In such uses, the second-person imperatives may also have recurrent collocative elements, and the meaning of the verb might be rather lexicalized. This supports the idea of approaching such imperatives as *fixed expressions*, some of them even nearing the status of a discourse particle.

Common in all the different uses of 2SG.IMP forms, however, is that they invite recipiency. They point out a place in which recipient participation becomes relevant and thus code the role of the interactional "other" as integral and inherent in the ongoing conversational activity (cf. Suomalainen 2020:26–27). Even the imperatives that are not used in primarily directive actions seem to recruit the recipient(s) in discursive tasks: they prepare the recipients for alignment, especially in contexts where alignment and affiliation cannot be automatically assumed, guide the recipients' attention to something that is central in the produced turn, and invite the recipient(s) to join mutual sense-making.

5. Discussion: Second-person singular imperatives in an interactional grammar

The approach in this chapter is motivated by the idea of an "interactional grammar" that would focus on recurrent linguistic patterns for implementing social actions. This approach makes it relevant to zoom in on a specific morphological form, the second-person singular imperative. The fact that second-person singular imperative forms are multifunctional, i.e., the form with the same morphological resemblance can be used in both directive and non-directive actions, is demonstrated in the analysis in the previous section. Naturally, this raises the question of how the different ways of using 2SG.IMP forms should then be described in an interactional grammar of Finnish — are we dealing with one or several grammatical formats and categories?

The phenomena discussed here are clearly a challenge for a "taxonomic" approach to language. Based on the data, the different uses should be approached as a continuum. A central feature in this continuum is the social action in which the imperative form occurs. In a grammar section pertaining to second-person imperative forms in Finnish, such a continuum could be introduced right at the beginning of section, and the different uses could then be discussed in separate entries that, however, belong in the same section. A visualization of the continuum is presented in Figure 1.

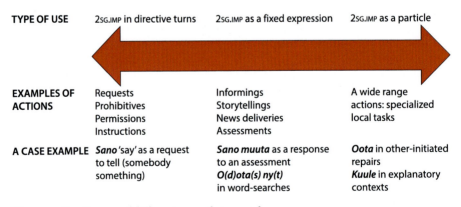

Figure 1. Continuum of different uses of 2SG.IMP forms.

Figure 1 presents the types of use 2SG.IMP forms have, gives examples of the actions in which different uses typically occur, and lists some case examples of different verbs in 2SG.IMP forms. The three types of uses listed at the top part of Figure 1 would form the basis for entries accounting for the use of second-person imperatives in turns-at-talk. The entry "2SG.IMP in directive turns" would focus on the canonical use of imperative forms, but with a focus on social action. Here, the entry could be built on the articles pertaining to Finnish in Sorjonen et al. (2017). While the use of 2SG.IMP in directive turns is not tied to a certain lexeme or action (other than the action being directive), it should be mentioned in connection with the entries "2SG.IMP as a fixed expression" and "2SG.IMP as a particle" that these uses are more lexically specific, i.e., they are tied to certain verbs, and specialized regarding the social actions in which they are used. Lexical specificity means that not all verb paradigms have a 2SG.IMP form used as a fixed expression or particle. Here, it would be relevant to briefly discuss the semantics of the verbs used in fixed expressions, e.g., in additional "fact boxes". In the entry "2SG.IMP as a fixed expression", it would also be important to describe the role of the collocative elements that form the fixed expression together with the imperative form. The entries pertaining to 2SG.IMP forms as fixed expressions or particles would be built on IL and CA research papers on these phenomena. As crystallization or particleization is not only a phenomenon related to second-person singular imperatives, similar entries could be built on other conjugation forms belonging to the verbal person paradigm.

In the above-mentioned suggestion on how the 2SG.IMP forms should be dealt with in an interactional grammar, there is an underlying implication that *formulaicity* and *routinization* of everyday language use and the way they manifest themselves in *fixed expressions* would be taken into account. As Laury and Ono (2020: 2) state, structural approaches in linguistics — which many traditional grammars are built on — have typically seen fixed expressions as a marginal part of human language, even if there are a number of empirical studies which show that fixed expressions are important building blocks in language use in terms of both frequency and the social actions they accomplish. Including fixed expressions as central part of an interactional grammar would also mean taking seriously the idea of grammar as a description of the linguistic categories to which the participants of the interaction actually orient (see Ford, Fox & Thompson 2013).

6. Conclusions

This chapter has discussed the multifunctionality of one grammatical format, second-person singular imperatives, with the aim to broaden the understanding of what interactional work imperatives do in turns-at-talk and to remove the "secondary" status from certain ways of using the second-person imperatives. In everyday interaction, the imperatives are used in a wide range of social actions, all of which should be considered as equal parts of speakers' linguistic repertoire (see Maschler 2012). Special attention has been given to the routinized and formulaic ways of using second-person imperatives, showing that there are similar patterns for interactional routinization among the second-person imperative forms of different verbs. By doing this, the chapter has highlighted the role of fixed expressions as building blocks for social action. While the analysis in this chapter has focused on Finnish second-person singular imperative forms, the phenomenon addressed in this chapter is by no means restricted to Finnish; similar routinized and conventionalized ways of using second-person singular imperative forms can be found across languages (see Auer 2017; see also Aikhenvald 2010).

The chapter has challenged the view that the canonized way of using a linguistic format will always be the most central one. For imperatives, the use in directive actions is highlighted in grammars, but looking at everyday data, other ways of using imperatives appear to be of equal importance. In some datasets, the fixed or particle-like way of using the imperative forms may even be more frequent (e.g., *kato* 'look.2SG.IMP' and *kuule* 'hear.2SG.IMP'). However, more corpus-based research on fixed expressions is needed to fully define their significance across different genres and languages.

Creating an interactional grammar section based on findings presented in this chapter would also resonate with the idea of functional language learning and the recent interest in various construction-based models in the field of study of Finnish as a second language. From a usage-based perspective, "learning grammar" is seen to be a process driven by meaning and schematization, and it also incorporates implicit, formula-based learning (Möttönen & Ahlholm 2018). Different ways of using second-person singular imperatives can be seen as "formulas" that are acquired only through social language use. For a teacher of Finnish as a second language, using grammar entries related to different uses of second-person singular imperatives — as described in this section — as teaching material could also provide a possibility to discuss how the meaning of an expression is local and emerges in and through interaction.

Acknowledgements

This study was supported by the Finnish Academy of Science and Letters, Jutikkala Fund, and by the Ella and Georg Ehrnrooth Foundation. I thank Nobufumi Inaba for the assistance with the Arkisyn corpus search tool and Orli Zewi for the assistance in data collection and coding. I

Chapter 9. Second-person singular imperatives in Finnish **297**

would also like to thank the fellow editors of this volume for their insightful comments on earlier versions of this text; any remaining errors are my own.

References

Aikhenvald, Alexandra. 2010. *Imperatives and Commands*. Oxford: Oxford University Press.

Arkisyn. A morphosyntactically Coded Database of Conversational Finnish. Database compiled at the University of Turku, with material from the Conversation Analysis Archive at the University of Helsinki and the Syntax Archives at the University of Turku. Department of Finnish and Finno-Ugric Languages, University of Turku.

Auer, Peter. 2017. "Epilogue. Imperatives — the Language of Immediate Action." In *Imperative Turns at Talk: The Design of Directives in Action*, ed. by Marja-Leena Sorjonen, Liisa Raevaara, and Elizabeth Couper-Kuhlen, 411–423. Amsterdam: John Benjamins.

Couper-Kuhlen, Elizabeth, and Margret Selting. 2018. *Interactional Linguistics: Studying Language in Social Interaction*. Cambridge: Cambridge University Press.

Ford, Cecilia E., Barbara A. Fox, and Sandra A. Thompson. 2013. "Units and/or Action Trajectories? The Language of Grammatical Categories and the Language of Social Action. In *Units of Talk — Units of Action*, ed. by Beatrice Szczepek Reed, and Geoffrey Raymond, 13–56. Amsterdam: John Benjamins.

Forsberg, Hannele. 2019. "Paheksuntaimperatiivi. Affektinen lausekonstruktio [The reproachful imperative as affective construction]." *Virittäjä* 123 (1): 4–43.

Fox, Barbara. 2007. "Principles Shaping Grammatical Practices: An Exploration." *Discourse Studies* 9 (3): 299–318.

Goodwin, Marjorie Harness. 2006. "Participation, Affect and Trajectory in Family Directive/Response Sequences." *Text and Talk* 26: 513–541.

Hakulinen, Auli. 1998. "The Use of Finnish *nyt* as a Discourse Particle." In *Discourse Markers: Descriptions and Theory*, ed. by Andreas H. Jucker, and Yael Ziv, 83–96. Amsterdam: John Benjamins.

Hakulinen, Auli, and Eeva-Leena Seppänen. 1992. "Finnish *kato*: From Verb to Particle." *Journal of Pragmatics* 18, 527–549.

Hakulinen, Auli, Leelo Keevallik Eriksson, and Jan Lindström. 2003. "*Kuule, kule, hördu* — projicerande praktiker i finska, estniska och svenska samtal [*Kuule, kule, hördu* – practices of projection in Finnish, Estonian and Swedish conversation]." In *Grammatik och samtal. Studier till minne av Mats Eriksson* [Grammar and conversation: Studies in the memory of Mats Eriksson], ed. by Bengt Nordberg, Leelo Keevallik Eriksson, Kerstin Thelander, and Mats Thelander, 199–218. Uppsala: Uppsala universitet.

Hakulinen, Auli, Maria Vilkuna, Riitta Korhonen, Vesa Koivisto, Tarja Riitta Heinonen, and Irja Alho. 2004. *Iso suomen kielioppi* [Comprehensive grammar of Finnish]. Helsinki: Finnish Literature Society. Online version (2008), http://scripta.kotus.fi/visk.

Herlin, Ilona. 1998. *Suomen kun [Finnish kun]*. Helsinki: Finnish Literature Society.

Hopper, Paul. 2011. "Emergent Grammar and Temporality in Interactional Linguistics." In *Constructions: Emerging and Emergent*, ed. by Peter Auer, and Stefan Pfänder, 22–44. Berlin: de Gruyter.

Kangasharju, Helena. 1998. *Alignment in Disagreement: Building Alliances in Multiperson Interaction*. Helsinki: University of Helsinki.

Keevallik, Leelo. 2001. "Tracing Grammaticalization of *oota* 'wait' in Estonian Conversation." In *Papers in Estonian Cognitive Linguistics*, ed. by Ilona Tragel, 119–144. Tartu: University of Tartu.

Keevallik, Leelo. 2003. *From Interaction to Grammar: Estonian Finite Verb Forms in Conversation*. Uppsala: Uppsala University.

Keevallik, Leelo. 2017. "Negotiating Deontic Rights in Second Position Young Adult Daughters' Imperatively Formatted Responses to Mothers' Offers in Estonian." In *Imperative Turns at Talk: The Design of Directives in Action*, ed. by Marja-Leena Sorjonen, Liisa Raevaara, and Elizabeth Couper-Kuhlen, 271–295. Amsterdam: John Benjamins.

Kielitoimiston sanakirja. Institute for the Languages in Finland. Online version, kielitoimistonsanakirja.fi/ (29.5.2023).

Lauranto, Yrjö. 2013. "Suomen kielen imperatiivi — yksi paradigma, kaksi systeemiä [The imperative in Finnish — one paradigm, two systems]." *Virittäjä* 117 (2): 156–200.

Lauranto, Yrjö. 2014. *Imperatiivi, käsky, direktiivi. Arkikeskustelun vaihtokauppakielioppia* [Imperative, command, directive: On interactional syntax in Finnish]. Helsinki: Finnish Literature Society.

Laury, Ritva, Marja-Liisa Helasvuo, and Janica Rauma. 2020. "When an Expression Becomes Fixed: *Mä ajattelin että* 'I thought that' in Spoken Finnish." In *Fixed Expressions: Building Language Structure and Social Action*, ed. by Ritva Laury, and Tsuyoshi Ono, 133–166. Amsterdam: John Benjamins.

Laury, Ritva, and Tsuyoshi Ono (eds). 2020. *Fixed Expressions: Building Language Structure and Social Action*. Amsterdam: John Benjamins.

Levinson, Stephen. 2012. "Action Formation and Ascription." In *The Handbook of Conversation Analysis*, ed. by Jack Sidnell, and Tanya Stivers, 101–130. Chichester: Wiley-Blackwell.

Linell, Per. 2005. *The Written Language Bias in Linguistics: Its Nature, Origins and Transformations*. New York: Routledge.

Maschler, Yael. 2012. "Emergent Projecting Constructions: The Case of Hebrew *yada* ('know')." *Studies in Language* 36 (4): 785–847.

Maynard, Douglas. 1997. "The News Delivery Sequence: Bad News and Good News in Conversational Interaction." *Research on Language & Social Interaction* 30 (2): 93–130.

Möttönen, Tapani, and Maria Ahlholm. 2018. "The Toisto-Method: Speech and Repetition as a Means of Implicit Grammar Learning." *SKY Journal of Linguistics* 31: 71–105.

Pomerantz, Anita. 1984. "Agreeing and Disagreeing with Assessments: Some Features of Preferred/Dispreferred Turn Shapes." In *Structures of Social Action: Studies in Conversation Analysis*, ed. by J. Maxwell Atkinson, and John Heritage, 57–101. Cambridge: Cambridge University Press.

Pouttu, Suvi-Maaria. 2010. *Sanallinen reagoiminen päällekkäispuhuntaan perhekeskustelussa* [Verbal reactions to overlapping speech in family interaction]. Helsinki: University of Helsinki.

Schegloff, Emanuel, Gail Jefferson, and Harvey Sacks. 1977. "The Preference for Self-Correction in the Organization of Repair in Conversation." *Language* 53: 361–382.

Schegloff, Emanuel. 2007. *Sequence Organization in Interaction: A Primer in Conversation Analysis*. Cambridge: Cambridge University Press.

Siitonen, Pauliina, Mirka Rauniomaa, and Tiina Keisanen. 2019. "*Kato. Hulluna puolukoita*: *Kato* vuorovaikutuksen resurssina luontoilussa [*Kato. An insane amount of lingonberries*: *Kato* as an interactional resource in nature-related activities]." *Virittäjä* 123 (4): 518–549.

Siitonen, Pauliina, Mirka Rauniomaa, and Tiina Keisanen. 2021. "Language and the Moving Body: Directive Actions With the Finnish *kato* 'look' in Nature-Related Activities." *Frontiers in Psychology* 12: 661784.

Sorjonen, Marja-Leena. 2001. *Responding in Conversation: A Study of Response Particles in Finnish*. Amsterdam: John Benjamins.

Sorjonen, Marja-Leena. 2002. "Recipient Activities: The Particle "no" as a Go-Ahead Response in Finnish Conversations." In *The Language of Turn and Sequence*, ed. by Cecilia E. Ford, Barbara A. Fox, and Sandra A. Thompson, 165–195. New York: Oxford University Press.

Sorjonen, Marja-Leena. 2017. "Imperatives and Responsiveness in Finnish Conversation." In *Imperative Turns at Talk: The Design of Directives in Action*, ed. by Marja-Leena Sorjonen, Liisa Raevaara, and Elizabeth Couper-Kuhlen, 241–270. Amsterdam: John Benjamins.

Sorjonen, Marja-Leena, Liisa Raevaara, and Elizabeth Couper-Kuhlen (eds). 2017. *Imperative Turns at Talk: The Design of Directives in Action*. Amsterdam: John Benjamins.

Sorjonen, Marja-Leena, Liisa Raevaara, and Elizabeth Couper-Kuhlen 2017. Imperative turns at talk. An introduction. In *Imperative Turns at Talk: The Design of Directives in Action*, ed. by Marja-Leena Sorjonen, Liisa Raevaara, and Elizabeth Couper-Kuhlen, 1–24. Amsterdam: John Benjamins.

Steensig, Jakob, Maria Jørgensen, Nicholas Mikkelsen, Karita Suomalainen, and Søren Sandager Sørensen. 2023. "Toward a Grammar of Danish Talk-in-Interaction: From Action Formation to Grammatical Description." *Research on Language and Social Interaction* 56 (2): 116–140.

Stevanovic, Melisa. 2017. "Managing Compliance in Violin Instruction: The Case of the Finnish Clitic Particles *-pA* and *-pAs* in Imperatives and Hortatives." In *Imperative Turns at Talk: The Design of Directives in Action*, ed. by Marja-Leena Sorjonen, Liisa Raevaara, and Elizabeth Couper-Kuhlen, 357–380. Amsterdam: John Benjamins.

Suomalainen, Karita. 2020. *Kuka sinä on? Tutkimus yksikön 2. persoonan käytöstä ja käytön variaatiosta suomenkielisissä arkikeskusteluissa* [Who is 'you'? On the use of the second person singular in Finnish everyday conversations]. Turku: University of Turku.

Teeri-Niknammoghadam, Krista, and Maija Surakka. 2023. "Hetkinen, mitä tällä tehdään? *Hetkinen*-sana vuorovaikutuksen jäsentäjänä [Uses of the Finnish word *hetkinen* 'moment']." *Puhe ja kieli* 43 (3): 131–146.

Terasaki, Alene Kiku. 2004 [1976]. "Pre-announcement Sequences in Conversation." In *Conversation Analysis: Studies from the First Generation*, ed. by Gene H. Lerner, 171–223. Amsterdam: John Benjamins.

Thompson Sandra A., Barbara Fox, and Elizabeth Couper-Kuhlen. 2015. *Grammar in Everyday Talk: Building Responsive Actions*. Cambridge: Cambridge University Press.

Vatanen, Anna, and Pentti Haddington. 2024. "*Oota pikku hetki*. Lykkäykset avunvärväyssekvensseissä perhevuorovaikutuksessa ['Wait a moment': Suspensions in recruitment sequences in family interaction]." *Virittäjä* 128 (1): 4–34.

Vatanen, Anna, Karita Suomalainen, and Ritva Laury. 2020. "The Finnish Projector Phrase *se että* as a Fixed Expression." In *Fixed Expressions: Building Language Structure and Social Action*, ed. by Ritva Laury, and Tsuyoshi Ono, 167–202. Amsterdam: John Benjamins.

Vepsäläinen, Heidi. 2019. *Suomen no-partikkeli ja kysymyksiin vastaaminen keskustelussa* [The Finnish particle *no* and answering questions in conversation]. Helsinki: University of Helsinki.

Vilkuna, Maria. 2000 [1996]. *Suomen lauseopin perusteet* [Fundamentals of Finnish Syntax]. Second, renewed edition. Kotimaisten kielten tutkimuskeskuksen julkaisuja 90. Helsinki: Edita.

Visapää, Laura. 2021. "Self-Description in Everyday Interaction: Generalizations about Oneself as Accounts of Behavior." *Discourse Studies* 23 (3): 339–364.

CHAPTER 10

Copula variation in Danish and the intertwined nature of grammar

Søren Sandager Sørensen
University of Agder

This chapter explores constructions with the copula verb *er* 'is' in Danish. Practices employing zero copula assessments, stressed copulas and cases where syntax requires overt copula are described. Data are informal Danish interactions.

The constructions are analyzed using Conversation Analysis and Interactional Linguistics. It is found that in reduced or zero copula clauses, the features of the action may depend on the predicate phrase rather than the copula. Stressed *er* marks a turn as asserting or contrasting with something that came before. The syntactic context requiring overt copula may project turn-ending.

The aim is to discuss how the constructions studied are intertwined with other aspects of grammar and how they may fit into an interactional grammar like the Danish project *Samtalegrammatik.dk.*

Keywords: copula, phonology, syntax, assessments, stress, clauses

1. Introduction

Copulas are extremely frequent and do a lot of varied, grammatical work, while being expressed (or not) in various ways. This is also the case in Danish, where especially the significant phonetic variation of the copula verb *er* 'be.PRS' is a widely discussed topic, along with its distribution and purpose. Zero copula clauses, informally known as "copula-drop", are utterances like *det godt* 'it good', where the copula *er* as in *det er godt* 'it is good' is unexpressed. Zero copula clauses occur under certain conditions. The different copula constructions have varying action potential in interaction (J. S. Jensen 2021; Kjær, Brink & Kølbæk 2020; Garly 2019; Kragelund 2015). Note that in Danish, there is no inflection for person, which means that *er* corresponds both to 'is', 'are' and 'am' in English. In Danish, there is inflection for tense, but this study focuses only on present tense.

https://doi.org/10.1075/slsi.37.10sor
© 2025 John Benjamins Publishing Company

Danish copula constructions and forms provide an interesting discussion of the design of a grammar for talk-in-interaction, and how to relate the components or features of complex phenomena to each other. For this reason, I analyze the interactional context of use of different types of copula clauses in Danish, including observations on associated grammatical features. Besides zero copula clauses, I focus on stressed copulas and syntactic conditions that prohibit zero copula clauses. The aim of this chapter is to discuss how to relate such phenomena to various aspects or larger organizations of grammar in a practical manner, such as for a work like Samtalegrammatik.dk, a website devoted to an interactional description of Danish grammar of talk-in-interaction (Steensig et al. 2013).

In Section 2, I review existing research related to the topics investigated here. Section 3 accounts for the method and data in this study. Section 4 contains the analysis, divided into three categories: First I consider copula uses in assessments (4.1), then stressed copulas (4.2) and finally copulas in certain syntactic contexts requiring overt copula (4.3). In Section 5, I discuss copulas in relation to aspects of grammatical organization, and how the practices analyzed fit into grammatical descriptions, e.g., the website Samtalegrammatik.dk. Section 6 is the conclusion.

2. Background

This section summarizes relevant earlier research related to copulas. First, "copula" in general as a linguistic concept is considered (2.1). Then the grammatical features of the Danish copula are described (2.2) and studies on its phonetic and phonological features are treated (2.3). The final subsection (2.4) introduces assessments and the role of copulas in assessments, with particular focus on Danish.

2.1 Copula and its variation

A copula is a linguistic form used to mark a special relationship between elements (a copula relation), where one element provides a description of the other, such as a property being ascribed to the other or the two elements being the same. An example of a copula verb is the English word *be*, which takes a predicate phrase and connects it to a subject, forming a copula clause. For example, in *the researcher is clever*, the copula verb *is* connects a referent, *the researcher*, to the predicate *clever*, so that the property *clever* is being ascribed to *the researcher*. The clause is thus a copula clause. I will refer to the equivalents of *clever* (which can be of many types) as a "predicate phrase" or as having "predicate function" (based on Dik 1980).

However, languages can implement copulas or mark copula clauses in other ways. Some languages have *zero copula clauses*, which means that copula clauses do not contain any element marking the clause as a copula clause, so they only consist of a predicate phrase and a subject juxtaposed. Languages of this type may have zero copula clauses only under certain circumstances, e.g., only in present tense or third person, while other contexts require an overt (i.e., not zero) copula; this is the case, for instance, in Hungarian (Groot 1989). Other languages have no adjectives, but instead express adjective-like properties through verbs, i.e., with morphological marking of tense, person etc. as in the rest of the language. Other languages again have copula particles that do not behave like verbs (Hengeveld 1992).

Dik (1980) proposes a rule of copula support for languages with overt copula in some clauses and zero copula in others. Rather than seeing copula as underlying in zero copula clauses, the copula support rule only inserts a copula element in contexts where a copula can be observed. It may be possible to formulate a copula support system for Danish, but for the current study, negatively defined terms like "zero copula clause" will be employed for practical reasons.

2.2 Copula in Danish grammar

Danish is described as having a copula verb with the infinitive form *være* 'be', present form *er* 'is' and past form *var* 'was'. Importantly, *være* is the main copula verb in Danish: it can ascribe properties both more or less permanent, but can also mean 'exist', including intransitive and locative uses (Hansen & Lund 1983: 58). It is also used as an auxiliary verb to create periphrastic passives and in the construction of the periphrastic perfect tense for intransitive verbs (Hansen & Heltoft 2011: 237), and as a quotation marker, often together with *bare* 'just' and *sån* 'like' (Sommerlund 2021). Not all uses or meanings can be clearly distinguished from the copula function. The copula is extremely frequent and ranks high in frequency lists such as Bergenholtz (1992), based on fiction books, newspapers and magazines, and Thomsen (1972), based on interview conversations.

2.3 Copula in Danish phonetics and phonology

The copula verb in Danish displays significant variation in terms of pronunciation, including a complex system of reduction. The 'dictionary' pronunciation is often given as a diphthong, i.e., [æɐ̯] (e.g., Den Danske Ordbog 2024, whose phonetic transcription system is used in this chapter). The written sequence <er> is often pronounced [ɐ], except in the copula *er* (Basbøll 2005: 70–72). The diphthongal pronunciation is mainly in use when *er* is stressed, and less distinct pronunciations include monophthongs like [æ] and [a] (Schachtenhaufen 2012), which may or may not be stressed. This study focuses only on present tense forms.

The copula can also be "reduced". A reduced copula is realized either as a prolongation of the vowel of a preceding word (also known as *integration* or *contraction*) or is completely absent ("zero-realization"). The word *er* is the most frequently zero-realized word in Danish (Schachtenhaufen 2012). Zero-realization is also known as "copula-drop" (cf. "pro-drop" languages that may leave out pronouns, Payne 1997:170). In the following analysis, I refer to such clauses without a copula as zero copula clauses.

Reduction occurs in certain phonological and syntactic contexts (P. A. Jensen 2012). A construction where a zero copula clause or reduction is possible is a *drop site* (cf. Puggaard 2020). The main phonological criteria are that there is a preceding word ending in a vowel (henceforth *host word*), that *er* is unstressed, and that other words follow *er*. Schachtenhaufen (2012) mentions that host words are mainly monosyllabic function words, especially pronouns, but P. A. Jensen (2012) argues that reduction should not be thought of as restricted to monosyllabic words.

As a verb, *er* is usually positioned as the second constituent in Danish declarative word order. The most frequent host words are then the most frequent words to occur in the initial slot of the clause (Puggaard 2019). *Er* can be initial in interrogative word order, meaning that preceding words are rare and would be conjunctions rather than pronouns or nouns. In a few cases, it is unclear where *er* should be "reconstructed", which means the word order, an important factor in the function of Danish clauses, cannot be clearly determined.

In some contexts, *er* must be stressed, and cannot be reduced to prolongation or zero. Stress placement depends on the syntax of the clause. P. A. Jensen (2012) describes the context of copula reduction as part of the wider system of *unit accentuation* in Danish (from Rischel 1982). Verbs — just by being verbs — attract stress, except in special circumstances. Unit accentuation affects this by treating a verb and its objects, if the object is a bare nominal, as one unit in which only the last part able to take stress will have stress. This is also referred to as incorporation (Petersen 2018:41). P. A. Jensen extends unit accentuation to include copula constructions with not only bare nouns, but also adjectives and other types of predicate phrases. The presence of a predicate phrase makes the copula unstressed and therefore available for reduction.

The syntax can also require that the copula is stressed, for instance, when the predicate phrase is placed before the copula. P. A. Jensen provides examples such as main clauses like *hvor er I* 'where are you (plural)?' and subordinate clauses like *jeg ved ikke hvem du er* 'I don't know who you are'. However, Schachtenhaufen (2012) mentions cases of copula reduction following *hvad* 'what' and *hvor* 'where', without indicating if they are in main clauses. Stress can also be applied for "pragmatic" reasons, e.g., focus or contrast (E. S. Jensen 2012), independent of syntax. The conditions are thus comparable to contractions in English (Labov 1969), but somewhat different from auxiliary absence in Swedish subordinate clauses (Bäckström 2020).

Kragelund (2015) treats variation in copula realization as a continuum with 4 levels: full drop, prolongation, unstressed, and stressed. Puggaard (2020) expects the phonetic difference between the realizations to be gradient rather than categorical.

Variation of *er* is not new. Brink and Lund (1975:140) state that a monophthongal variant existed both stressed and unstressed in the last half of the 1800s, and that *er* assimilated to the quality of the preceding vowel (potentially indistinct from prolongation). The dictionary entry on *være* 'be' in *Ordbog over det Danske Sprog* 'Dictionary of the Danish Language' provides literary examples that likely reflect prolongation, from 1935 and 1939 (*Ordbog over det Danske Sprog* 1954); the dictionary volume containing the entry was published 1954. One of the oldest recordings of Danish — Louise Phister reciting Holberg in 1904 — contains *er* realized as prolongation of the host word.

2.4 Copula in assessments

An assessment is an action that displays an evaluation of a referent. The evaluation can often be described as either positive or negative. Assessments can be organized in two-part sequences, where a first assessment makes it relevant for the next speaker to provide a second assessment of the same referent. First assessments often display a preference for agreeing responses, but not exclusively (Pomerantz 1984). Assessments can be part of conversational closings (Antaki 2002) or occur during tellings (Goodwin 1986), especially when a more involved response is made relevant (Stivers 2008). Assessments can also be part of an assessment activity, where speakers not only perform assessing actions but a range of other actions in the service of talk centered around assessables and opinion sharing (Goodwin & Goodwin 1987).

Copula constructions are common in assessments, where the predicate phrase functions as the assessment term (Goodwin & Goodwin 1987). The assessment term can contribute to a turn's function as an assessment by having a positive or negative meaning, or by denoting something that the speakers consider positive or negative in a given context. This is also the case in Danish, where copula constructions have been noted for being frequent in assessments. Garly (2019:57) describes assessments formats such as the format *det er X* 'it is X' (or *der er* 'there is', or a reduced version) which consists of (1) the pronoun *det* 'it', (2) the copula, and (3) an adjective or noun (cf. Forsskåhl 2008). This format is used both for first and second assessments (Garly 2019:71). Zero copula clauses are not in focus in Garly (2019) but have been the target of other studies. However, note that copula constructions are also frequently used as part of other actions such as informings, reports, news deliveries, noticings, some of which are difficult to distinguish from assessments (Garly 2019), or larger activities such as story-telling or advice-giving, which can include assessments and evaluative stances.

Kragelund (2015) carries out a distribution analysis of different copula clause types in Danish interactional data. Here, it is said that unstressed *er* adds no information, while stressed *er* performs modified repeats (Stivers 2005), and prolongation of the final vowel in a host word does not carry any information but may be part of hesitation like *øh* 'uh'. The study does not specifically attribute an interactional function to zero copula clauses. The current entry on copula reduction in Samtalegrammatik.dk (2024c [2013]) is essentially an abridged version of Kragelund's article and contains examples of assessments, speaker identification, and modified repeats used for agreement.

J. S. Jensen (2021) describes three overall functions of copula clauses: (1) assessments, including cases with zero copula clauses and stressed copula, which may relate to earlier (zero copula) assessments, (2) "confirmations", which could also be called agreements, where special focus is given to the construction *det rigtigt* 'it's true' and varieties thereof that never have overt copula, and (3) "precisionings", a type of agreement that can be realized with both zero copula clauses or prolonged host words and stress, either on the copula or another constituent. Within the last function, the zero copula clause *det det* 'that's that, that's it, it's that', can be used for pre-closing a sequence, while *det er det* 'it is that' with stressed copula is used for modified repeats.

Kjær et al. (2020) mentions that stressed copula is used for two types of modified repeats: confirmation of another speaker's statement (the prototypical type), and confirmation of the speaker's own statement (a type of reassertion). The study further distinguishes "pure assessment" and "underlining assessment". Pure assessment is achieved through unstressed copula after a consonant and through zero copula clauses, while underlining assessment is performed through prolongation of the host word and unstressed copula after a vowel. The unstressed prolonged host word is also described as a possible "doubt indicator" (as in Kragelund 2015), and Kjær et al.'s study also observes that the copula is overt in interrogative and subordinate clauses, which the copula could be part of marking.

The interactional studies on copula in Danish thus identify various practices consisting of copula clauses doing different types of assessments or related actions, but describe them in different, sometimes conflicting ways. This study will not resolve the discrepancies between existing descriptions but will use them for discussing the complexity of relations between grammatical and interactional phenomena and the structure of a grammar accounting for both.

3. Methods and data

This study uses the methods of Conversation Analysis and Interactional Linguistics. It investigates a collection of cases and shows how the cases are understood by the participants in the interaction (Sacks, Schegloff & Jefferson 1974). The study draws on Interactional Linguistics (Couper-Kuhlen & Selting 2018) by considering aspects of linguistic form and asking how the form contributes to interactional function. This study considers aspects of both phonology and syntax.

Since the focus of the chapter is to discuss relations between various areas of grammar, the chapter will analyze a range of constructions and actions, rather than exhaustively treat one or two specific practices. The discussion relates to the goal of the website Samtalegrammatik.dk, which is to create a "comprehensive grammar of Danish talk-in-interaction" (Steensig et al. 2013), by focusing on relations between syntax and phonology as evident in the constructions investigated and how that matters for entries on Samtalegrammatik.dk. Samtalegrammatik.dk is a website with a non-linear structure and multiple hierarchies that function as pathways from more general organizations to smaller ones.

The collection is based on three specific conversations from the AULing corpus (Samtalegrammatik.dk 2024a): a two-person conversation, a three-person conversation and a four-person conversation (recorded 2014 and 2015), totaling a runtime of 49 minutes of video (only the first 2.3 minutes of the three-person conversation were used). Two men participate in the three-person conversation, all others are women. The participants range in age from late teens to mid 20's. All speak Danish and the setting is informal and unstructured. The conversations were chosen because they had sufficiently good audio quality and a manageable length for collecting a high-frequency phenomenon.

In these conversations, I have attempted to identify all cases of *er*, both zero-realized and overt cases. Zero copula clauses were found by carefully listening to the data and identifying potential drop sites where a copula could be expected in consideration of the meaning. Drop sites are clear deviations from the written standard language (where, for instance, a juxtaposed pronoun and adjective phrase is not usually considered acceptable). The resulting collection consists of 222 cases of copula clauses.

It is not always possible to determine clearly for each occurrence whether *er* is fully lacking or whether some "trace" in, e.g., vowel duration or quality may exist (Schachtenhaufen 2012: 138). For this reason, I have not attempted to categorize the instances by their realization. The high range of variation and the gradient nature of realization make the design and implementation of a categorization scheme very demanding, and it is not likely that it would be consistent. It would also not be very informative based on the current data, which are limited in terms of speaker variation and ethnographic information.

Excerpts are transcribed according to Jeffersonian conventions (Jefferson 2004) in the version used in Samtalegrammatik.dk (2024b) with arrows for turn-final intonation contours. In the translation to English, a reduced or zero copula is indicated with *is* in parentheses. Grey highlighting is used to cover the host word, copula, and predicate phrase, which makes the drop site visible even in zero copula clauses.

4. Analysis

In this section, I analyze practices using copula constructions. First, I focus on assessments and how copulas occur in assessment sequences (4.1). Then I consider interactional features of sequences where the copula is stressed (4.2) and cases where the copula must be overt due to the syntactic context (4.3).

It is important to note that assessments are not the only action where copulas occur. Copulas are also often used, among others, in informings, noticings, and news deliveries; and they form part of accounts (incl. accounting for actions other than assessments), tellings, specification of referents, and answers to different types of questions (incl. confirming). Copulas also occur in requests for information and in question tags, which often have interrogative word order and overt copula. Section 4.1 specifically focuses on assessments using a copula construction and their variation, while the other sections should not be thought of as restricted to assessments. However, it turns out that turns with stressed copula (Section 4.2) often relate to assessments or assessment-like descriptions. Action is not the focus of Section 4.3, as the copula clauses in question are often only a small part of the turn as a whole.

4.1 Copula assessments

Most previous research mentions assessment as a very frequent action in which copula clauses are used. In this section, I will try to show how assessing is achieved in constructions with a copula relation and discuss the role of the different constituents in this use.

A very frequent assessment format is the predicative format *det er X* 'it is X, that is X' (Garly 2019), where the copula is very often reduced or not present following the word *det* 'it' (the <t> at the end of the graphic word is never pronounced). *Det er* is usually followed by an assessment term, such as an adjective that can be understood positively or negatively, but it can also be a noun phrase

Chapter 10. Copula variation in Danish **309**

or an adverbial phrase. Other constructions also occur, affecting the grammatical functions of both *det* and what occurs later.

Excerpt (1) shows an instance of the *det (er) X* format without copula. A group of four young women are talking about concert experiences.

Excerpt 1. *koncert* 'concert' (kanin1)

```
01 NEL: det altid sjovest å være til koncert hvis
        it (is) always most fun to be at a concert if

02      man står allerforrest synes jeg\
        one stands fully in front ((of the stage)) I think

03      (0.3)

04 ORK: *jaer*
        yeah

05 LON: *aer* [m det  rigtig nok→ hh
        yeah  b that (is)   true enough

06 NEL:       [virkelig bare sån så langt op foran
               really just like so far up in front

07      du (over)hovedet ka komme\ (.) bum→
        you can get at all              boom
```

In line 1, Nelle is making an assessment by evaluating concert participation close to the stage positively as *sjovest* '(the) most fun'. The turn is initiated with a *det* 'it', a dummy subject for the following infinitive, and it is followed immediately by the temporal adverb *altid* 'always' rather than a copula. The adverb may be contributing to the strength of the assessment. In response, Orkide and Lone agree through **(j)aer** 'yeah', and Lone follows up with *det rigtig nok* 'that's true enough' (line 5). Lone's response also uses the format *det (er) X*, here with *rigtig* 'true, real', which is a format employed specifically for agreeing. The excerpt thus contains two instances, both a first assessment, and a format for agreeing (*det rigtig*), here with an assessment, using zero copula clauses.

In both instances, *det* is the host word occurring before the copula slot. In the first case (line 1), *det* is the very first part of the turn, while in the second case, *aer* 'yeah' takes the place of a turn-initial element. The *m* can be considered turn-initial too but may also be a shortened version of *men* 'but' or reflect the lips being closed and opening as the next sound requires them to be open. *Det* forms the first part of its own turn constructional unit in both cases, however.

In the first instance, in the sentence *det altid sjovest å være til koncert* 'it's always the most fun to be at a concert' (line 1), the word *det* functions as a dummy subject (Danish *foreløbigt subjekt* 'provisional subject', Christensen & Christensen 2014: 181). Thus, *det* does not itself provide any referent, as the referent is specified later with the infinitive phrase *å være til koncert* 'to be at a concert'. The sentence could in principle also have been phrased as *å være til koncert er altid sjovest* 'to be at a concert is always the most fun'. However, heavy constituents like infinitive phrases are very commonly positioned later in clauses with a dummy reference earlier, especially in the spoken language (Christensen & Christensen 2014: 181). In the other instance, *det rigtig nok* 'it's true enough' (line 5), *det* refers to the previous assessment by Nelle. It is different from the previous *det* in that it refers to something preceding and has a 'broad' scope, while the previous *det* is a dummy specified later (Puggaard 2019). This means that the initial placement of *det* cannot be considered a clear projection of what is to come in the ongoing turn, except that generally, something will be referred to, and potentially showcase the possibility that it will be an assessment, though that is not the only action possible.

The assessment is also mainly achieved through adjectives. The first assessment *det altid sjovest* 'it's always the most fun', contains the adjective *sjovest*, superlative form of *sjov* 'fun', a positively loaded term, further modified by *altid* 'always' (which should be interpreted in relation to the *if*-clause). The turn as a whole also ends with the stance marker *synes jeg* 'I think' (line 6), which downgrades the assessment to an individual opinion (cf. English *I think*, Kärkkäinen 2003: 169). Lone's agreement with *det rigtig nok* uses *rigtig* 'true, real' as a description of the previous assessment, framing it as a reasonable description of what can make a concert experience fun, and thereby taking the same perspective and agreeing.

In these two constructions, I cannot come up with good alternatives that are not copula clauses. Possible alternatives matter for the explanation of what the choice of a copula clause construction rather than another format may contribute to the turn. I have the impression that *altid sjovest å være* [...] 'always the most fun to be' could be a turn doing assessment by itself (i.e., without *det*), though the superlative seems uncommon in such use. The construction seems unlikely as a first assessment and more appropriate as a type of formulation of previous talk or move towards sequence closure. While adjectives can be used in assessments by themselves (Garly 2019), I do not think this happens with *rigtig*, but further studies are needed on this topic.

The sequence in focus in Excerpt (1) contains an adjacency pair with two turns that both have *det* as the host word in a copula clause. While they have different grammatical functions, the second turn reuses *det* and thereby ties itself to the turn it responds to.

Excerpt (2) contains more cases of copula clauses with *det*, again a first and second assessment. However, one is used to introduce a quote. Milea is in lines 1–4 telling a story about some people who attempted to secretly photograph a famous person but were revealed by their camera flash.

Chapter 10. Copula variation in Danish   **311**

Excerpt 2. *kæmpe blitz* 'giant flash' (kanin1)

```
01 MIL: man ku sån se de havde prøvet på sån å
         one could like see that they had tried to like

02      skju:le sig men >lige (så var der)< sån
         hide themselves but right (then there was) such a

03      khæmpe blitz i deres hoveder→
         giant flash in their faces

04      det bare sånↃ *ej* så
         it (is) just like EJ then

05      (0.4)

06      opdagede de [det alligevel
         they discovered it anyways

07 ORK:           [det så sjovt når folk
                   it (is) so funny when people

08      ikk *tænker over det*Ↄ
         don't think about it
```

The description of the flash as *khæmpe* 'giant' and *i deres hoveder* 'in their faces' highlights the failure of the attempt at hiding, and the surprise of the situation. After this, Milea adds the utterance *det bare sån* 'it's just like/so'. This zero copula clause frames the upcoming as an assessment of the situation, as part of setting the mood and climax of the story (Kjaerbeck & Asmuß 2005). Here, *det* refers to the situation described in the story. The upcoming talk in line 4 can be considered a quote, as both *sån* and *bare* are frequently used to mark quotation together in copula clauses (Sommerlund 2021). In this situation, the quote reflects what the photographers could say in the situation. This gives listeners more detailed access to the experience and the evaluative properties of a story (Stivers 2008), making affiliation or agreement relevant next actions. The quote consists of the interjection *ej*, also used for assessments (Tholstrup 2014), followed by a statement that the photographers were seen *alligevel* 'anyways', again focusing on the unexpected aspect of the situation.

The response also employs a zero copula clause with *det* as host word. In line 7, before Milea has fully finished, Orkide utters a zero copula clause with *det* as host word, and the predicate phrase *så sjovt* 'so funny' (containing the same adjective as line 1 in Excerpt (1)). In this case, *det* is a dummy subject further specified in the following subordinate clause introduced by *når* 'when'. However, this clause formulates a general version of what has been told in the story, which means that until then the *det* can as well be interpreted as referring back to the situation in the story.

In this case, a zero copula clause is used for an assessment as part of the climax of a telling, and is then responded to with another assessment employing a zero copula clause.

Zero copula clauses following *han* 'he' as subject and host word are found in Excerpt (3). They are very uncommon and the word *han* does not fit the pattern usually described for host words since it is consonant-final. In this conversation, two young women are talking about different people they know. They have just talked about one person very positively before the excerpt, until Astrid asks about another, Liam:

Excerpt 3. *også rar* 'also friendly' (sofasladder)

```
01 AST: åu:: hva så med ↑li:↓am
        oh what then about Liam

02      (1.4)

03 BRI: altså liam han: da oss rar↘
        well Liam he (is) PTC also friendly

04      [he (h)altså d(h)et: h det: ikk det→ .hh
        he w(h)ell i(h)t (is) it (is) not it .hh

05 AST: [h:: ha ha h

06      liam >han er bare< liam liam (han/er) sjov↘
        Liam he is just Liam   Liam (he/is) fun

07 BRI: liam han sjov↘
        Liam he (is) fun

08 AST: .snh

09      (0.8)

10      så der alfred↘ ham ka jeg altså godt bli: lidt
        then there (is) Alfred he can make me a bit
```

Britt starts describing Liam in line 3, after a turn-initial *altså* 'well'. The name is used, but the referent is repeated with the pronoun *han* (Brøcker et al. 2012). A copula is not pronounced, but the prolongation of the final consonant in *han* is clear. Another potentially contributing factor in this context is that the following consonant [d] is also alveolar and thus pronounced the same place as the final consonant of *han*. The predicate phrase is *rar* 'friendly, nice', a positively loaded term about a person. The predicate phrase is also modified with *da* 'surely', suggesting the recipient already knows (Heinemann 2009), and *oss* 'also', saying that he could be assessed the same way as the previously discussed person.

After they both laugh (lines 4–5), Britt utters a prolonged *det:* 'it'. This can be understood either as *det* followed by a copula reduced to prolongation of *det*, or a *det* followed by hesitation. It is followed by a laughter syllable and the zero copula formulation *det: ikk det* 'that's not it' (line 4). The restart after the prolonged *det:* and a laughter syllable suggests that speakers use a pronoun followed by a copula to become the next speaker (cf. Forsskåhl 2008). The laughter has picked up on the much less enthusiastic response about Liam in comparison to the previous person, and *det: ikk det* can be understood to state that the lack of enthusiasm should not be taken as problematic, though it is very implicit. Astrid then says *liam han er bare liam* 'Liam, he's just Liam' (line 6), and instead of using a loaded term or adjective, the name is used both as subject (through a pronominal copy) and predicate phrase. The word *bare* 'just, only' indicates lack of anything special about this person, but the tautology may indicate an implied attitude specific to this person (McGregor 1997: 361), potentially the difference from the previous person already discussed. In the same breath, Astrid produces another utterance, this time describing Liam as *sjov* 'fun'. It is not clear if she is pronouncing *han*, *er*, or both in between the name and adjective, but something occurs there. This assessment shifts from something downgraded or neutral, to something clearly positive. Britt agrees by repeating the assessment with *liam han sjov* 'Liam, he's fun' (line 7) using a clear zero copula construction. After a pause, Astrid mentions another person to discuss. Incidentally, he is introduced with another zero copula clause, here with *så* 'then' as host word (the corresponding form with copula would be *så er der alfred* 'then there's Alfred').

The excerpt thus shows another host word, *han*, occurring in copula clauses. It contains both zero and reduced copula clauses and one with overt *er*. However, there is no obvious difference in function between them that may be due to the realization of copula. The sequence consists of an assessment activity where multiple copula constructions are used one after another, showing that they are used across sequential positions.

In these analyses, we have seen copula clauses performing assessments or being part of assessing. It does not seem that the word *er* or the status of being a copula clause contributes with any distinct meaning to these actions. What the turns do is mostly based on the semantics of the predicate phrase or the referent, in relation to the sequential position. The lack of any clear purpose of the presence of a copula could be part of explaining why the copula is subject to reduction and non-realization. A better understanding of copula clauses could be pursued by contrasting them with freestanding adjectives or studying specific predicates or constructions, such as *det rigtig* 'that's true' or quotative copula constructions. Another direction would be to focus on the subject (cf. Forsskåhl 2008) and its construction or referent, both grammatically (dummy subjects, pronominal copy, other) and the status of the referent as, e.g., newly introduced, or whether it is a person, object or previous statement.

In the construction of turns, copula constructions like these seem to be placed initially in a turn construction unit, but after any turn-initial particles or elements like pronominal copies. There may be other turn construction units before, but a subject in a copula clause seems to start a new unit. This is not a particularly strong projection (many cases of a pronominal subject and a verb form the start of a new unit), but the important aspect is that the turn is not finished at the place where a copula could be realized.

4.2 Stressed *er*

The issue of describing zero copula clauses is that they may be considered "unmarked" in line with the lack of specific meaning added. However, this suggests that contrastive forms may be the meaningful phenomenon to study. In this section, I investigate cases where *er* is stressed, and how stressed *er* may be understood as part of the action of the turn. In all these cases, a zero copula clause is possible (i.e., there is a conventionally acknowledged drop site) but does not happen. It turns out that instances of stressed *er* seem to index a relation to something previous. This section does not aim to focus on assessments. However, turns with stressed *er* may relate to preceding assessments or form part of an assessment activity or other evaluative description.

In Excerpt (4), Milea is talking about her father's behavior after a night of getting drunk.

Excerpt 4. *sidder og synger* 'sitting and singing' (kanin1)

```
01 MIL: >så det (alt)så< bare ham *der sån sidder*↘
        then it (is) (well/then) just him that is sitting
02      (0.4)
03 NEL: [tHhh
04 MIL: [°*å synger*°
         and singing
05      (0.5)
06      °y:° ((mimics weird singing noise))
07      (0.3)
08 ALL: ((laughter))
09 ORK: n(h)e(h)ej↘
        ((a laughed no))
10 MIL: det er bare sånogen ↑lyde↘ å det ikk sån ↑sang
        it is just such sounds     and it (is) not like song
11      det bare sånoget ðe ðe å så↘
        it (is) just such ((makes sounds)) and then
```

Before the excerpt, Milea has set the scene of her father acting a certain way after drinking. In line 1, she describes what one would see when coming across her father in this state, with a zero copula clause *så det altså bare ham der sån sidder å synger* 'then it's just him who is sitting and singing' (lines 1–4). This is followed by her performing weird singing in line 6, framing the father's behavior as odd.

All participants (including Milea) respond with laughter in line 8, and Orkide produces a laughed *nej* 'no', a display of disbelief (Heinemann 2015:126), all having understood the previous as odd and out of the ordinary in a funny or humorous way. Milea follows up with the turn *det er bare sånogen lyde* 'it is just such sounds' (line 10). Here, the copula *er* is stressed. It occurs after *det*, just as other instances do in Excerpts (1), (2) and (3). The *det* refers to the sounds of the father and can be seen as an upgrade or reinforcement of the previous description and the evaluation conveyed through that and the illustrative sounds, by referring back with *sånogen lyde* 'such sounds'. This way, the stressed copula connects back to the copula clause in line 1, indexing that an earlier assessment was made, relating to the same referent. Milea continues elaborating with two copula clauses: *det ikk sån sang* 'it's not like song' seems to remove any possible association with singing, which could otherwise be understood positively, and *det bare sånoget ðe ðe* 'it's just something like ðe ðe' (line 11) is another instance of a quotative copula clause and it mimics the sounds again. They are both zero copula clauses, with a *det* having the same referent as the copula clause with stressed *er*. They both support the reinforcement performed by the stressed copula clause and revise aspects of the original description. In this case, the predicate phrases are not in themselves assessing, but refer back through *sån*, *sånogen* and *sånoget* 'such, like'. In summary, a quotation conveying a certain assessment is delivered, and then, following lack of sufficient uptake, reinforced with a stressed copula clause, which itself is elaborated by further copula clauses (with zero copula) specifying features that listeners may need to understand the evaluation.

Another use of stressed *er* is for contrasting with something in the preceding talk. In Excerpt (5), Lone imagines an interaction that people analyzing the recording could have:

Excerpt 5. *tøvende* 'hesitating' (kanin1)

```
01 LON: ↑jajaↆ så ka folk sidde sån
        oh yeah then people can sit like
02      ej hun er meget sån tøvende i det
        PTC she is very like hesitating in this
03      eller *sånoget*↘ °sån° nej jeg ↑er ikk↘
        or something like no I am not
```

Here, Lone quotes an imagined person analyzing her talk and describing her as very *tøvende* 'hesitating' (line 2). The describing turn is formatted as a copula clause with an overt copula, as copulas are (usually) overt after consonant-final pronouns like *hun* 'she'. Lone adds what she would respond to this description, with *nej jeg er ikk* 'no, I am not' (line 3). This is formatted with a copula clause with stress on the copula, despite the pronoun *jeg* 'I' allowing a zero copula clause.

The response disagrees with or denies the analyst's description by negating it. It has no predicate phrase of its own but refers to the previous one (*meget sån tøvende* 'very, like, hesitating', line 2). In this case, the response with a stressed *er* contrasts with a previous copula clause representing a description by an imagined speaker.

In this section, we have seen how an overt and stressed *er* can be used in contexts where zero copula clauses were possible alternatives. The function seems to be to (re)assert something that indexes or contrasts with earlier statements.

4.3 Syntactically conditioned overt copula

In this section, I consider cases where a copula must be realized for syntactic reasons, sometimes formulated as contexts where zero or reduced copula is prohibited. The conditions for this are complex, but P. A. Jensen (2012) formulates the conditions as cases where the predicate phrase has been placed earlier than the copula. This is possible in subordinate clauses where a conjunction or relative pronoun with predicate function is placed in the conjunctional slot. Since subordinate clauses often use a word order where the conjunctional slot, subject and adverb occur before the verb, the verb is often final in the clause, but not always. This word order is rare in main clauses in spoken language (Sørensen 2023), so the analysis here will be limited to subordinate clauses. It seems that this overt *er* can mark turn-ending.

In Excerpt (6), people are discussing participation in concerts.

Excerpt 6. *højere end jeg er* 'taller than I am' (kanin1)
```
01 NEL: til koncert så går jeg bare ↑op i det↘ så jeg
        at a concert then I am just into it    then I (am)

02      en d*el* af det↘ så det bare sån du ska
        a part of it    then it (is) just like you should

03      fucking ikk stille dig foran mig
        fucking not position yourself in front of me

04      når du: to meter højere end jeg er↘
        when you (are) two meters taller than I am

05      (.)

06      [.ssssss ssss

07 MIL: [ej vi så [emil thorup å thomas ↑skov derinde oss→
        PTC we saw Emil Thorup and Thomas Skov there too

08 LON:           [*jaer stop det*
                  yeah stop it
```

Nelle is talking about her concert participation experience, in which she describes the specific situation of being behind a taller person. This ends with a quote of what she would say to the tall person: *du ska fucking ikk stille dig foran mig når du: to meter højere end jeg er* 'you should fucking not position yourself in front of me when you're two meters taller than I am'. The quote is introduced with a zero copula clause in *så det bare sån* 'then it's just like' (line 2). The quote is a critique by requesting the taller person to stop doing something. It is followed by an exaggerated description of the tall person's height in the subordinate clause *når du: to meter højere end jeg er* 'when you're two meters taller than I am' (line 4). This is itself a reduced copula clause, with *du:* 'you're' as host word, and contains the comparative clause with a stressed copula *end jeg er* 'than I am'. *Jeg* 'I' is a common host word in zero copula clauses. Here, both *er* and *jeg* are stressed, and *er* cannot be left out because of the syntax, since *end* 'than' refers back to *to meter højere* 'two meters taller', acting as the predicate phrase.[1] Both clauses share the same predicate phrase, but the first has a reduced copula while the second has an overt copula.

After a short pause (line 5), Nelle adds an inhaled [s], a sound of frustration. Lone responds to Nelle's activity, producing *jaer stop det* 'yeah, stop it' (line 8) addressed to the taller person in the situation described by Nelle. Lone agrees by animating a request in line with Nelle's. In the meantime, Milea has moved towards a new topic.

In this case, the syntactic formulation — a comparative clause — occurs where a complex activity with multiple clauses ends. It is followed by a pause showing that the speaker, Nelle, is finished. While she does add something, another speaker turns to a different topic, having understood the telling as having reached its end. Nelle's own continuation can be understood as a post-completion stance marker (Schegloff 1996:92) in further pursuit of a response, by reissuing her stance through new material. These factors point to overt *er* as marking the end of the complex turn in lines 1–4.

A case with a different type of subordinate clause is found in Excerpt (7). Here, a word occurs after the copula. The participants have recently started the conversation and talk about being aware of being recorded.

---

1. Comparatives without verbs (often treated as ellipsis) are possible in Danish. The corresponding construction would be *højere end jeg* 'taller than I'. This construction is uncommon in spoken language and somewhat formal. A common variant would be *end mig* 'than me', i.e., with an oblique pronoun in a prepositional phrase rather than a clause (cf. Nguyen & Hartling 2023).

Excerpt 7. *hvor akavet det er* 'how awkward it is' (sofasladder)

```
01 AST: vi ska bare snak↗ (.) det gør vi jo oss ↑nu→
        we just have to talk (.) we PTC also do that now

02      (.)

03 BRI: m ja:ja↘
        oh yes

04      (0.7)

05      men vi snakker jo ikk rigtig om noget→
        but we PTC don't really talk about anything

06      vi snakker kun om hvor akavet det er [å:
        we only talk about how awkward it is (to/and)

07 AST:                                     [jaer↘
                                             yeah
```

Here, they are (and have been) doing meta-talk about talking. In line 5, Britt states that they *snakker jo ikke rigtig om noget* 'are not really talking about anything', and backs this up by saying *vi snakker kun om hvor akavet det er* 'we only talk about how awkward it is'. In this way, her negative statement in line 5 (that they are *not* talking about anything) is followed by a positive statement about what they *are* talking about. This statement is downgraded with *kun* 'only', suggesting that this is not *noget* 'anything, something', and not a proper topic. The topic *hvor akavet det er* 'how awkward it is', as Britt formulates it, refers back to a discussion they have had earlier about how they feel they are not properly contributing to the data. It is a complement clause consisting of the predicate phrase *hvor akavet* 'how awkward' placed initially, with *det* 'it' as subject, referring broadly to their current situation. Since *er* follows both the predicate phrase and subject, it must be present and receive stress. The turn is not fully finished, as Britt afterwards says *å:*, which is ambiguous between being the coordinating conjunction *og* 'and', which would mean she indicates she could make a list or mention other things, and the infinitive marker *at* (Bruun 2018). Technically, but not very likely, *det* could be a dummy subject for an infinitive phrase (as discussed in the analysis of Excerpt (1)), though it can be broad enough to cover both (Puggaard 2019). As seen from many previous cases, *det* is a common host word, but not in this case.

In response, Astrid delivers a *jaer* 'yeah' in line 7. It is overlapped with *å:* in Britt's turn. This suggests that the construction with the stressed *er* is understood as ending or projecting the end of the turn, despite further talk being produced. After the *jaer*, Britt does not continue either, but the two look out the window, also treating the turn as finished.

Both cases suggest that a copula that is overt due to the syntactic context marks the end of a turn. This contrasts with the (zero) copula clauses and stressed cases of *er* which are in the middle of a construction, rather than at a possible end, and seem to be part of initiating a turn construction unit together with the host word.

5. Discussion

This section will describe and discuss the analyzed phenomena in the context of larger grammatical organizations. For this reason, the discussion extends beyond the analyzed phenomena and connects them to other linguistic forms and structures. The final subsection discusses how to handle this in Samtalegrammatik.dk.

5.1 Copula in interaction

This study shows that copulas are used in assessment activities and assessment sequences, both first assessments, second assessments, and other kinds of assessments or actions often related or adjacent to assessing. An assessment with a copula can respond to another assessment with a copula. The copula itself may not contribute any meaning by itself, except by constructing a copula clause with a predicate phrase, whose properties or semantics as an assessment term can then contribute with a positive or negative valency. The vague (or lack of) semantics in the copula may be part of the reason for zero copula clauses — combined with the present tense possibly being the "default" tense since it becomes unmarked in zero copula clauses. One potentially meaningful distinction is that between copula clauses with declarative word order, and those where *er* occurs initially and must be overt. Since the latter are often requests for confirmation, the overt copula may mark the action (Kjær et al. 2020) and not just be overt because of the lack of a host word. Stressed cases also often relate to previous turns, including assessments, but may support them or go against them. This chapter attempts to provide knowledge about the question of how the semantics of a predicate phrase works together with the clause type, and for further studies of attitudinal modification (Rijkhoff 2014; for assessments leaving out the predicate phrase, see Park & Kline 2020; Aldrup et al. 2021).

While the focus has mainly been on action, the structures also matter for turn-taking. Reduced or zero copula clauses seem to occur in the beginning of turn construction units after turn-initial particles, which suggests they project more talk to come (cf. Forsskåhl 2008). However, it is not clear to what extent this may be specific to copula clauses, as it may be the case for many other verbs or combinations of one constituent and a verb. Reduced, zero, and some stressed copula clauses seem to be contrastive with syntactically conditioned overt copulas: the latter are often placed turn-finally and may project the end of a turn, as seen in the timing of the next speaker's turn.

Any further possible details of the meaning or interactional function of overt contra zero copula will need to be described in the context of the word or construction preceding the copula to address the question of why zero copula clauses (mainly) happen after certain words. Other aspects of interaction may also matter for a deeper description of the actions implemented (assessments or other actions), such as bodily conduct and prosodic factors other than stress.

5.2 Copula in the grammar of clause types

Copula clauses are often considered a distinct type of clause: for instance, predicate phrases are said to have a different function than objects, given that they are realized by different types of phrases (e.g., adjectives not being able to function as objects). It is possible that zero copula clauses are in the process of grammaticalizing in Danish. Zero copula clauses could be recognized as a new type of construction, either as a "verbless" (Bondarenko 2021) or "nominal" sentence, such as those known in Arabic and related languages (Zewi 1996) or Hungarian (Groot 1989).

There are sentence or utterance constructions in Danish that qualify as verbless or nominal. The most frequent ones are probably different kinds of freestanding phrases. A relevant specific type is the possessive predicational (vocative) construction. It consists of a second person singular possessive pronoun, *din* 'your', followed by a noun or noun phrase that can include adjectives, such as *din lille idiot* 'you little idiot' (Julien 2016). Though no interactional studies exist of these, they seem to be assessing, and the predicate phrase can contain some of the same material as copula clauses. In contrast to zero copula clauses, they are always verbless and have no counterpart with verbs and do not display the same variation. Possessive predicational constructions may form a separate assessment format, distinct from zero copula clauses, since they only contain second person singular possessive pronouns (and not plural or non-second person forms). The term "nominal sentence" can cover specifically zero copula clauses and possessive predicational constructions.

Other verbless formats are one-word-constructions (excluding freestanding verbs). Freestanding adjectives are relevant in comparison since they are also used for assessments. Some adjectives — such as *godt* 'good' and *virkelig* 'real, really' — may be used so frequently that they have acquired special functions in freestanding use, while some predicate phrases in copula clauses also may have specific action uses that differ from the same phrases in other grammatical functions. How freestanding adjectives differ from copula clauses (and phrasal turns) is still an open question (but see some speculation in the discussion of Excerpt (1)).

This suggests that Danish clause or sentence types, especially regarding copula, should be reconsidered. However, in contexts where a distinction between clausal and phrasal matters for the function of a turn (e.g., Jørgensen 2024), it seems that zero copula constructions count as clausal despite not containing a verb (Jørgensen, this volume).

5.3 Copula in the grammar of stress

When stressed, the copula acquires a specific form that can mark it as distinct from unstressed or zero copula clauses. Speakers use stressed copula clauses to reinforce or contrast a point in relation to something prior in the conversation, while unstressed and zero copula clauses do not necessarily index prior activities. The phonetic difference between stressed and unstressed *er* may be greater than other stress-based vowel differences in Danish (as described in Basbøll 2005), but the many different cases of reduction in Danish (Schachtenhaufen 2023), some of which may relate to stress, have not been studied in enough detail to give a systematic account. Further research in this area is needed.

The interactional effect of stress can relate in different ways to the previous talk, both assertive and contrastive. Stress is generally used for emphasis, which in turn can highlight something already mentioned, or highlight the contrast to something already mentioned. Contrastive or "pragmatic" stress (E. S. Jensen 2012) does not necessarily affect copulas differently from other stressed words. However, the account does not currently explain why stress is placed on the copula verb in contrast to cases of stress on host words or predicate phrases.

The contrastive use of stressed copula in Danish is comparable to the English *do*-construction to index a contrast (Raymond 2017), which is however not formulated with the copula verb *be*. The reinforcing use may be more comparable to modified repeats (Stivers 2005, cf. Kragelund 2015, Kjær et al. 2020 and J. S. Jensen 2021), but not all uses are in second position or reflect the details of the epistemic stance described in Stivers (2005).

Copula clauses also show how stress can be determined by syntax, e.g., in subordinate clauses subject to unit accentuation. Other constructions with copulas are also affected by stress rules. One example consists of exclamative clauses with *hvor* 'how', such as *hvor er det dog livsbekræftende* 'how life-affirming it is!', which can be considered assessing. With declarative word order, these exclamatives place stress on the verb (Sørensen 2023) — often a copula verb — in contrast to requests for information with question words or other cases of declarative word order. However, clausal exclamatives are rare in everyday talk.

5.4 Copula in phonology

This study documents a number of phonological processes or phenomena. Various reduction processes are known to take place in Danish. Brink and Lund (1975) relate copula reduction to schwa-assimilation, while Schachtenhaufen (2012) argues against this and for considering copula reduction a different process.

The prolongation of host words can also be considered a type of clitic or special form. Pronouns are known to cliticize after verbs, especially in Danish dialects (Heltoft 2011). In copula clauses where the pronoun precedes the copula, the copula can be reduced and become cliticized to the pronoun. The prolonged pronouns could be considered "copulative forms" of the pronouns. However, such prolongation is not exclusive to pronouns. It is also worth mentioning that a prolonged host word is not different in form from the same word followed by hesitation in the form of prolongation.

Zero-realization of copula as a highly frequent phenomenon supports the perspective that rather than the phenomenon being the result of a reduction process, it could be considered the standard. From this perspective, the "non-application" could instead be considered the result of an expansion process (cf. Schachtenhaufen 2023), and thus the marked phenomenon to explain. The reduction of the word *har* 'have.PRS' may occur under the same conditions as copula reduction, and complete zero-realization of *har* has been documented (Kristensen, Schachtenhaufen & Boye 2017), which could be a focus for future studies. While an important restriction of this study is the limitation to present tense, some occurrences could also be interpreted as zero realization of the past tense copula *var* 'was'. Various other realizations of *var* were also observed, forming another possible direction for future studies.

5.5 Copula in Samtalegrammatik.dk

In this section, I discuss how to write relevant grammar entries for copula constructions and specifically for Samtalegrammatik.dk, and I reflect on the implications for grammar writing in general. Including zero copula in an accessible description is important, because knowledge about it can be useful for teaching Danish writing and pronunciation, for speech recognition and in evaluating aspects of clear language or assessing language use in relevant applied contexts. This is highlighted by the fact that many Danish speakers are unaware of the copula variation despite its high frequency, a possible case of written language bias. Content in Samtalegrammatik.dk often highlights differences between written and spoken Danish.

Samtalegrammatik.dk is organized with two entrance points containing hierarchical systems of subtypes. The two entrance points start from "social actions" and "the building blocks of talk-in-interaction".[2] The entrance point of social actions contains the action layer of Samtalegrammatik.dk, which has two layers of intermediate categories (e.g., "questioning actions" with the subtype "request for confirmation"). The bottom-level categories then contain entries on specific practices. They can take the form of specific action formats, often based on specific studies, such as questions with turn-final *eller* 'or' (Sørensen 2015), imperative verbs with preceding *bare* 'just' (Heinemann & Steensig 2017), or specific words with specific intonation contours, e.g., *nå* (approx. 'oh') with rising pitch (Steensig et al. 2013).

The entrance point of building blocks presents a subcategorization structure based on linguistic terminology relating to forms (in a broad sense) such as word classes, morphological forms, and syntactic structures. Entries may belong to multiple subtypes through both entrance points. The overall idea is that every entry is connected to its relevant form(s) and action(s).

Samtalegrammatik.dk (2024c) already contains an entry for copula variation (under the name *Kopuladrop* 'copula drop'). The entry contains subsections on the four points on Kragelund's (2015) continuum of realizations of *er* with one example of each. The action descriptions mention assessments and modified repeats used for agreement but do not go into depth. On the building blocks side, the entry is linked to verbs, and on the social action side, the entry is linked to assessment and request for confirmation. With a more detailed action description, each of the four realizations described in that entry could become a separate entry. However, as also stated in the current entry, there are action overlaps between the realizations of *er*.

Based on the analysis in this chapter, two copula entries are suggested: One for copula clauses that are unstressed and may take the form of either reduced copula clauses or zero copula clauses, and one for stressed copula clauses. The entries should form part of the section on assessing actions. It may also be possible to write a third on syntactically conditioned overt copulas, but this could potentially be better handled in an overall description of either turn-taking, stress placement, or word order.

Other specific formats also have the potential to become specific entries, such as *det rigtigt* 'that's right' and *det det* 'that's it', as mentioned here and in the literature. Following Garly (2019) and Forsskåhl (2008), it may also be possible to write an entry for *det er X* 'that's X'. Puggaard (2019) provides evidence that *det* has

---

2. The entrance points were earlier named "function" (and before 2018 just "action") and "form", respectively, which was changed sometime in 2024 during a revision of this chapter.

particular functions that may relate to being in the first slot of the clause, and that could also form the basis for an entry. Some combinations of pronoun and copula (e.g., *der er* 'there is', cf. Garly 2019) may function as fixed constructions and be suitable for an entry, while others, like *jeg er* 'I am' or *hun er* 'she is', will probably not need to be distinct from the entries just proposed, unless future studies are able to offer a description of them as having special characteristics.

The different entries should be connected. Besides the existing categories, a "copula overview" page listing all the copula formats, like the current one, will be useful. It could contain the phonological and syntactic conditions for zero copula clauses. The features of *være* 'be' as an auxiliary verb (potentially together with other auxiliary verbs like *have* 'have') could also be covered and may be worth investigating in futures studies. Some of these also go beyond the current study's limitation to the present tense by needing to include past tense or nonfinite forms and constructions. These properties can be connected through the categories on the building blocks side.

This discussion has also pointed towards other potential overall organizations. The category for assessing actions could contain a description of the role of the semantics of predicate phrases (with links from pages on adjectives and other relevant forms). The syntax section could be expanded with categories for the proposed construction types like verbless or nominal sentences (cf. 5.2) if future studies result in other entries fitting into these categories. It may also be possible to account for the structures that prohibit zero copula clauses in a syntax section on the relevant word order. The section could mention the turn-ending aspect, but a possible organization of turn-taking could also link to the relevant syntax section. The section on "sounds" should ideally describe the reduction phenomena that affect *er*, maybe under a different name like "variation". Stress should also figure somewhere, but it may be distributed across the relevant headings such as syntax, prosody, and others. That all these possible organizations connect to copula in various ways illustrate how different areas of grammar are intertwined with each other — and even more so when interaction is considered.

The website approach of Samtalegrammatik.dk may also be contrasted with grammar writing in the form of books. In a traditional grammar, the main organizing principle is usually the linear structure of a book, divided into sections on different areas of grammar, such as phonology, morphology, and syntax. Phenomena that cut across these divisions can be described by referring from one section to another (potentially distant) part of the work or by repeating the (parts of the) descriptions. Some phenomena may be covered in a fragmented manner due to related descriptions being placed in different sections of the grammar, which can lead to a phenomenon not being recognized or conveyed as a whole.

A non-linear organization like a website makes it possible to have various sections and overall descriptions only one click away from the individual entries (Evans & Dench 2006: 29). For instance, an entry on zero copula clauses could link to a description of the different copula realizations, which could link to Danish phonology or relevant aspects of it (e.g., stress). However, since the reader can approach it from multiple different locations, an entry cannot be written from the context of just one section. As readers consulting a website entry may not necessarily have the knowledge that would have been close by in the same book section, a website entry may need to contain more information than it would have needed if it had been clearly anchored in, e.g., a phonology section. This could mean all entries on different copula realizations need to describe what a copula is. They can link to an article on copula for further information, but some basic information will probably be helpful for certain audiences. While this means that the website approach can require more text, the reader who is specifically interested in the subject of the entry will likely experience it as more concise and to-the-point than having to look through different sections of a book.

In grammar writing, semantics has received different degrees of attention, and there are various issues in working with it (Hellwig 2006). An interactional description may be seen as sidestepping some issues, in that "meaning" is mainly described through the interactional effect of the practices, through the treatment by participants in the interaction. However, the achievements of copula clause assessments often relate to the lexical semantics of the words in the predicate phrase. One issue of interactional description is the need for a corpus (Hellwig 2006: 322), though this study was able to make claims based on a relatively small database (three conversations) because of the high frequency of the phenomenon.

The previous sections and possible connections to Samtalegrammatik.dk point towards different avenues for further research. As an interactional grammar, this area of research could improve the terminology around assessment structures relating to adjacency pairs, tellings, and longer activities. A further issue may relate to the (theoretical) status of the intermediate layers, as some phenomena on the building blocks side relate more clearly to other aspects of form than directly to social action, such as reduction patterns, stress placement, and word order (which together form unit accentuation).

6. Conclusion

In this chapter, I have analyzed some frequent uses of the Danish copula *er* 'is' (including zero copula clauses) to facilitate discussion on relations between various aspects of grammar including interaction.

This study found that copula clauses of different types occur in different practices, and that assessments are a key interactional locus of copula clauses. The practices include zero copula clauses, stressed copula clauses referring to earlier talk, and syntactic patterns requiring overt copula projecting turn-ending. It is possible that Danish in the future could become a language with fully grammaticalized zero copula clauses, one indication being that in many cases there does not seem to be a consistent functional difference between zero copula clauses and other copula clauses.

Based on the analyses, the discussion related the properties of the interactional practices to larger aspects of grammar such as action formation, clause and sentence types, and stress patterns. The discussion formed the basis for proposals for Samtalegrammatik.dk, dealing with how to describe and structure the findings in a grammar. The proposals include specific entries and larger organizations (reduction patterns, sentence types, auxiliaries) that could be part of the grammar. Some of the formal features may not directly connect to interactional properties such as action but should form part of a grammar that aims to be comprehensive and account for interaction. The discussion pointed out possibilities when working with a non-linear website-based grammar, and issues arising from the way the different areas of grammar are intertwined with each other.

The chapter points toward future studies both on specific practices — combinations of formats and interactional function — and theoretical or organizational questions concerning the status of different kinds of structures.

Acknowledgments

This study was supported by the Independent Research Fund Denmark (grant number 9037–00072B), as part of the project *Grammar in Everyday Life*.

References

Aldrup, Marit, Uwe-A. Küttner, Constanze Lechler, and Susanne Reinhardt. 2021. "Suspended Assessments in German Talk-in-Interaction." In *Prosodie und Multimodalität / Prosody and Multimodality*, ed. by Maxi Kupetz, and Friederike Kern, 31–66. Heidelberg: Universitätsverlag Winter.

Antaki, Charles. 2002. "'Lovely': Turn-Initial High-Grade Assessments in Telephone Closings." *Discourse Studies* 4 (1): 5–23.

Bäckström, Linnéa. 2020. *Etableringen av ha-bortfall i svenskan: Från kontaktfenomen till inhemsk konstruktion* [The Rise of *ha*-omission in Swedish: From a Contact Phenomenon to a Language Specific Construction]. Gothenburg: University of Gothenburg. http://hdl.handle.net/2077/62382

Basbøll, Hans. 2005. *The Phonology of Danish*. Oxford: Oxford University Press.

Bergenholtz, Henning. 1992. *Dansk frekvensordbog. Baseret på tekster fra danske romaner, ugeblade og aviser fra 1987-1990* [Danish Frequency Dictionary. Based on Texts from Danish Novels, Periodicals and Newspapers from 1987-1990]. Copenhagen: G.E.C. Gad.

Bondarenko, Antonina. 2021. *Verbless and Zero-Predicate Sentences: An English and Russian Contrastive Corpus Study*. Paris: Université Paris Cité. https://theses.hal.science/tel-03706573

Brink, Lars, and Jørn Lund. 1975. *Dansk rigsmål: lydudviklingen siden 1840 med særligt henblik på sociolekterne i København* [Danish Standard Language: The Sound Changes since 1840 with Special Attention to the Sociolects in Copenhagen]. Copenhagen: Gyldendal.

Brøcker, Karen Kiil, Magnus Glenvad Tind Hamann, Maria Jørgensen, Simon B. Lange, Nicholas Mikkelsen, and Jakob Steensig. 2012. "Samtalesprogets grammatik: fire fænomener og nogle metodiske overvejelser [The Grammar of Language in Interaction: Four Phenomena and some Methodological Considerations]." *NyS* 42: 10–40.

Bruun, Andrea. 2018. "*At* and *og* in Danish Spoken Language: a Description." *Skrifter om Samtalegrammatik* 5 (1): 1–14.

Christensen, Lisa, and Robert Zola Christensen. 2014. *Dansk Grammatik* [Danish Grammar]. 3rd ed. Odense: University Press of Southern Denmark.

Couper-Kuhlen, Elizabeth, and Margret Selting. 2018. *Interactional Linguistics: Studying Language in Social Interaction*. Cambridge: Cambridge University Press.

Den Danske Ordbog. 2024. "være." Copenhagen: Det Danske Sprog- og Litteraturselskab. https://ordnet.dk/ddo/ordbog?query=v%C3%A6re (last visited 01/05-2024).

Dik, Simon C. 1980. *Studies in Functional Grammar*. London: Academic Press.

Evans, Nicholas, and Alan Dench. 2006. "Introduction." In *Catching Language: The Standing Challenge of Grammar Writing*, ed. by Felix K. Ameka, Alan Dench, and Nicholas Evans, 1–40. Berlin: De Gruyter Mouton.

Forsskåhl, Mona. 2008. *Konstruktioner i interaktion*: de e *som resurs i samtal* [Constructions in Interaction: *de e* 'it is' as a Resource in Conversation]. Helsinki: University of Helsinki.

Garly, Katrine. 2019. "*æv bæv* – Et samtaleanalytisk indblik i vurderinger i danske, naturlige samtaler [*æv bæv* 'boo hoo' – A Conversation Analytical Perspective on Assessments in Danish, Natural Conversations]." *Skrifter om Samtalegrammatik* 6 (2): 1–95.

Goodwin, Charles. 1986. "Between and within: Alternative Sequential Treatments of Continuers and Assessments." *Human Studies* 9 (2–3): 205–217.

Goodwin, Charles, and Marjorie Harness Goodwin. 1987. "Concurrent Operations on Talk: Notes on the Interactive Organization of Assessments." *IPrA Papers in Pragmatics* 1 (1): 1–55.

Groot, Casper de. 1989. *Predicate Structure in a Functional Grammar of Hungarian*. Dordrecht: Foris Publications.

Hansen, Erik, and Lars Heltoft. 2011. *Grammatik over det danske sprog* [Grammar of the Danish Language]. Copenhagen: Det Danske Sprog- og Litteraturselskab.

Hansen, Erik, and Jørn Lund. 1983. *Sæt tryk på: syntaktisk tryk i dansk* [Put Stress on: Syntactic Stress in Danish]. Copenhagen: Lærerforeningernes materialeudvalg.

Heinemann, Trine. 2009. "Two Answers to Inapposite Inquiries." In *Conversation Analysis: Comparative Perspectives*, ed. by Jack Sidnell, 159–186. Cambridge: Cambridge University Press.

Heinemann, Trine. 2015. "Negation in Interaction, in Danish Conversation." *Skrifter om Samtalegrammatik* 2 (12): 1–452.

Heinemann, Trine, and Jakob Steensig. 2017. "Three Imperative Action Formats in Danish Talk-in-Interaction." In *Imperative Turns at Talk: The Design of Directives in Action*, ed. by Liisa Raevaara, Marja-Leena Sorjonen, and Elizabeth Couper-Kuhlen, 139–173. Amsterdam: John Benjamins.

Hellwig, Birgit. 2006. "Field Semantics and Grammar-Writing: Stimuli-based Techniques and the Study of Locative Verbs." In *Catching Language: The Standing Challenge of Grammar Writing*, edited by Felix K. Ameka, Alan Dench, and Nicholas Evans, 321–358. Berlin: De Gruyter Mouton.

Heltoft, Lars. 2011. "Lette pronomeners placering: klise og topologisk integritet [The Placement of Light Pronouns: Cliticization and Topological Integrity]." *Ny forskning i grammatik* 18: 61–80.

Hengeveld, Kees. 1992. *Non-Verbal Predication: Theory, Typology, Diachrony*. Berlin/New York: De Gruyter Mouton.

Jefferson, Gail. 2004. "Glossary of Transcript Symbols with an Introduction." In *Conversation Analysis: Studies from the First Generation*, ed. by Gene H. Lerner, 13–23. Philadelphia: John Benjamins.

Jensen, Eva Skafte. 2012. "Trykfordelingens implikaturer: betydningsbærende og meningsbærende tryk [The Implicatures of Stress Distribution in Danish Utterances — on Semantic and Pragmatic Prominence]." *NyS* 42: 116–147.

Jensen, Julie Søndergård. 2021. "At være eller ikke at være: En sprogpsykologisk redegørelse for brugen af kopula i dansk talesprog [To Be or not to Be: A Language Psychology Account of the Use of Copula in Danish Spoken Language]." In *18. Møde om Udforskningen af Dansk Sprog*, ed. by Yonatan Goldshtein, Inger Schoonderbeek Hansen, and Tina Thode Hougaard, 269–292. Aarhus: Nordic — School of Communication and Culture.

Jensen, Per Anker. 2012. "Grænsefladen mellem fonologi og syntaks: evidens fra er-kontraktion og enhedstryk i dansk [The Interface between Phonology and Syntax: Evidence from er-contraction and Unit Accentuation in Danish]." *NyS* 42: 92–115.

Jørgensen, Maria. 2024. "A Question of Embeddedness: On Clausal and Phrasal Responses to Specifying WH-Questions in Danish Talk-in-Interaction." *Research on Language and Social Interaction* 57 (3): 323–44.

Julien, Marit. 2016. "Possessive Predicational Vocatives in Scandinavian." *The Journal of Comparative Germanic Linguistics* 19 (2): 75–108.

Kärkkäinen, Elise. 2003. *Epistemic Stance in English Conversation: A Description of its Interactional Functions, with a Focus on* I think. Amsterdam: John Benjamins.

Kjær, Louise, Signe Brink, and Johanne Kølbæk. 2020. "Hvad *er* det? [What *is* it?]" *Skrifter om Samtalegrammatik* 7 (3): 1–21.

Kjaerbeck, Susanne, and Birte Asmuß. 2005. "Negotiating Meaning in Narratives: An Investigation of the Interactional Construction of the Punchline and the Post Punchline Sequences." *Narrative Inquiry* 15 (1): 1–24.

Kragelund, Mathias Høyer. 2015. "Når 'er' ikke er der: en morfologisk undersøgelse af et dansk talesprogsfænomen [When er 'is' is not There: A Morphological Investigation of a Danish Spoken Language Phenomenon]." *Skrifter om Samtalegrammatik* 2 (5): 1–18.

Kristensen, Line Burholt, Ruben Schachtenhaufen, and Kasper Boye. 2017. "Reduktion i udtalen af grammatiske vs. leksikalske ord [Reduction in the Pronunciation of Grammatical vs. Lexical Words]." In *16. Møde om Udforskningen af Dansk Sprog*, ed. by Inger Schoonderbeek Hansen, Tina Thode Hougaard, and Kathrine Thisted Petersen, 187–208. Aarhus: Nordic — School of Communication and Culture.

Labov, William. 1969. "Contraction, Deletion, and Inherent Variability of the English Copula." *Language* 45 (4): 715–762.

McGregor, William B. 1997. *Semiotic Grammar*. Oxford: Clarendon.

Nguyen, Michael, and Anna Sofie Hartling. 2023. "*Som* som præposition? En reklassificering af *som* og heraf afledte konsekvenser for Dansk Sprognævns sproglige rådgivning og normering [*Som* as Preposition? A Reclassification of *som* 'as' and its Consequences for the Advice and Standardization of the Danish Language Council]." *Ny forskning i grammatik* 30: 150–170.

Ordbog over det Danske Sprog. 1954. "II. være." Copenhagen: Det Danske Sprog- og Litteraturselskab. https://ordnet.dk/ods/ordbog?select=v%C3%A6re,2&query=v%C3%A6re (last visited 31/07-2024).

Park, Innhwa, and Jacob Kline. 2020. "Incomplete Utterances as Critical Assessments." *Discourse Studies* 22 (4): 441–59.

Payne, Thomas E. 1997. *Describing Morphosyntax: A Guide for Field Linguists*. 1st ed. Cambridge: Cambridge University Press.

Petersen, Kathrine Thisted. 2018. *Udviklingen af inkorporation fra gammeldansk til moderne dansk: Fra umarkerede kasusformer til markeret artikelløshed og enhedstryk* [The Development of Incorporation from Middle Danish to Modern Danish: From Unmarked Case Forms to Marked Lack of Articles and Unit Accentuation]. Odense: University Press of Southern Denmark.

Pomerantz, Anita. 1984. "Agreeing and Disagreeing with Assessments: Some Features of Preferred/Dispreferred Turn Shapes." In *Structures of Social Action: Studies in Conversation Analysis*, ed. by J. M. Atkinson, and John Heritage, 57–101. Cambridge: Cambridge University Press.

Puggaard, Rasmus. 2019. "Flexibility of Frequent Clause Openers in Talk-in-Interaction: *Det* 'It, That' and *så* 'Then' in the Prefield in Danish." *Nordic Journal of Linguistics* 42 (3): 291–327.

Puggaard, Rasmus. 2020. "A Semiotic Grammar Account of Copula Clauses in Danish." *Skrifter om Samtalegrammatik* 7 (4): 1–23.

Raymond, Chase Wesley. 2017. "Indexing a Contrast: The *do*-construction in English Conversation." *Journal of Pragmatics* 118: 22–37.

Rijkhoff, Jan. 2014. "Modification as a Propositional Act." In *Theory and Practice in Functional-Cognitive Space*, ed. by María de los Ángeles Gómez González, Francisco José Ruiz de Mendoza Ibáñez, and Francisco Gonzálvez García, 129–150. Amsterdam: John Benjamins.

Rischel, Jørgen. 1982. "On Unit Accentuation in Danish – and the Distinction between Deep and Surface Phonology." *Annual Reports of the Institute of Phonetics, University of Copenhagen* 16: 191–240.

Sacks, Harvey, Emanuel A. Schegloff, and Gail Jefferson. 1974. "A Simplest Systematics for the Organization of Turn-Taking for Conversation." *Language* 50 (4): 696–735.

Samtalegrammatik.dk. 2024a. "Data." https://samtalegrammatik.dk/en/about-samtalegrammatikdk/our-method/data/ (last visited 01/05-2024).

Samtalegrammatik.dk. 2024b. "Transcription Conventions." https://samtalegrammatik.dk/en/about-samtalegrammatikdk/transcription-conventions (last visited 01/05-2024).

Samtalegrammatik.dk. 2024c. "Kopuladrop [Copula-drop]." https://samtalegrammatik.dk/opslag/artikel/kopuladrop (last visited 01/05-2024).

Schachtenhaufen, Ruben. 2012. "Nulrealisering af verbalformer i dansk spontantale [Zero-realization of Verbal Forms in Danish Spontaneous Speech]." *Danske Talesprog* 12: 126–150.

Schachtenhaufen, Ruben. 2023. *Ny dansk fonetik* [New Danish Phonetics]. 2nd ed. Copenhagen: Modersmål-Selskabet.

Schegloff, Emanuel. A. 1996. "Turn Organization: One Intersection of Grammar and Interaction." In *Interaction and Grammar*, ed. by Elinor Ochs, Emanuel A. Schegloff, and Sandra A. Thompson, 52–133. Cambridge: Cambridge University Press.

Sommerlund, Kristina. 2021. "Om danske unges brug af utraditionelle citatmarkører [About the Use of Untraditional Quotation Markers among the Danish Youth]." In *18. Møde om Udforskningen af Dansk Sprog*, ed. by Yonatan Goldshtein, Inger Schoonderbeek Hansen, and Tina Thode Hougaard, 463–78. Aarhus: Nordic – School of Communication and Culture.

Sørensen, Søren Sandager. 2015. "Turfinalt *eller* i spørgsmål i dansk interaktion [Turnfinal *eller* 'or' in Questions in Danish Interaction]." In *15. Møde om Udforskningen af Dansk Sprog*, ed. by Inger Schoonderbeek Hansen, and Tina Thode Hougaard, 377–398. Aarhus: Nordic – School of Communication and Culture.

Sørensen, Søren Sandager. 2023. "Exclamative Clauses with *hvor*, *hvilken* and *sikke* in Danish: Insubordination and Phrasal Discontinuity." *Skrifter om Samtalegrammatik* 9 (1): 1–29.

Steensig, Jakob, Karen Kiil Brøcker, Caroline Grønkjær, Magnus Glenvad Tind Hamann, Rasmus Puggaard, Maria Jørgensen, Mathias Høyer Kragelund, Nicholas Mikkelsen, Tina Mølgaard, Henriette Folkmann Pedersen, Søren Sandager Sørensen, and Emilie Tholstrup. 2013. "The DanTIN Project – Creating a Platform for Describing the Grammar of Danish Talk-in-Interaction." In *New Perspectives on Speech in Action. Proceedings of the 2nd SJUSK Conference on Contemporary Speech Habits*, ed. by Jan Heegård, and Peter Juel Henrichsen, 195–226. Frederiksberg: Samfundslitteratur Press.

Stivers, Tanya. 2005. "Modified Repeats: One Method for Asserting Primary Rights from Second Position." *Research on Language and Social Interaction* 38 (2): 131–158.

Stivers, Tanya. 2008. "Stance, Alignment, and Affiliation During Storytelling: When Nodding Is a Token of Affiliation." *Research on Language and Social Interaction* 41 (1): 31–57.

Tholstrup, Emilie. 2014. "'Ej hvor fint': En undersøgelse af den danske interjektion *ej* [*Ej hvor fint* 'Oh how fine': A Study of the Danish Interjection *ej* 'oh']." *Skrifter om Samtalegrammatik* 1 (3): 2–15.

Thomsen, Olaf. 1972. "Nogle hyppige ord i dansk talesprog [Some Frequent Words in Danish Spoken Language]." *Sprog og Kultur* 27 (3–4): 85–93.

Zewi, Tamar. 1996. "The Definition of the Copula and the Role of the 3rd Independent Personal Pronouns in Nominal Sentences of Semitic Languages." *Folia Linguistica Historica* 30 (17–1–2): 41–55.

CHAPTER 11

An interactional grammar of insubordination
The case of French *si* 'if'-clauses

Simona Pekarek Doehler & Anne-Sylvie Horlacher
University of Neuchâtel

We take French *si* 'if'-clauses as an exemplary case to reflect on how
questions about the structures of a language can be fruitfully addressed by
considering the conversational actions that speakers accomplish by means
of these structures. We demonstrate that an interactional perspective has the
potential (a) to shed light on interactional motivations for the formal
implementation of 'if'-clauses, (b) to deepen our understanding of the
workings of insubordination, and (c) to open a window onto continua of
(in)subordination. Scrutinizing grammatical patterns in relation to
temporality/emergence, to the grammar-body interface, and to social action
has profound implications for understanding core features of grammar —
such as clause-combining and (in)subordination — and for how these
features should be represented in a grammar of language use.

Keywords: insubordination, grammar-in-interaction, emergent grammar,
if-clauses, French

1. Introduction

Is it possible to build a grammar based on descriptions of formats for doing social
actions? This is the challenging question that we are invited to address in the
contributions to this volume. In order to do so, we focus in this chapter on a
grammatical pattern that, in its canonical version, runs as shown in the following
French example, taken from a presidential debate:

Excerpt 1. *délocalisation* 'delocalization' (Sarkozy-Royal 124:00)

```
01 ROY: si l'on veut (.) éviter les délocalisations (.)
        if one wants (.) to prevent delocalization (.)

02      au sein de l'europe .hh alors il faut travailler
        within Europe .hh then one must work

03      à l'élévation des niveaux de vie.
        towards higher standards of living
```

https://doi.org/10.1075/slsi.37.11doe
© 2025 John Benjamins Publishing Company

The format shown in (1) represents a typical case of subordination: The *si* 'if'-clause is an adverbial clause that is subordinate to the subsequent main clause introduced by *alors* 'then'. According to standard grammatical and linguistic descriptions of this type of pattern, a *si*-clause is followed by a main clause with which it forms a conditional ('if-then') construction (e.g., Sweetser 1990); the *si*-clause can also be preceded by the main clause (e.g., Corminboeuf & Jahn 2020). In any case, the *si*-clause represents a dependent clause: It does not have fully independent form and depends syntactically on some other clause (Van Valin 1984 for syntactic subordination in general).[1] In Excerpt (1), a relationship of causality is established between the *si*-clause and the main clause, the latter expressing the so-called 'consequent' of the *si*-clause. The whole construction presents an imagined situation and its possible outcome, and is subsumed under one coherent prosodic contour.

A close look at how speakers use language in naturally occurring talk-in-interaction reveals a much more diversified picture of the formal realizations of *si*-clauses and the clause-combining patterns they are involved in. For instance, in spoken French (just like in English), *si*-clause-combining patterns mostly occur without *alors* 'then' in the main clause (Blanche-Benveniste 2010: 179–180), as shown in Excerpt (2):

Excerpt 2. *dépenses* 'expenses' (Sarkozy-Royal 31:00)
```
01 SAR: si vous AUgmentez les dépenses (.)
        if you augment expenses (.)

02      vous serez obligée d'augmenter les impôts?
        you will be obliged to augment taxes
```

Also, other resources than *alors* 'then' may initiate the consequent clause, such as *eh ben*, roughly glossable as 'well':

Excerpt 3. *le bail* 'the lease' (Corminboeuf & Jahn 2020: 217)
```
01 SPE: si tu contestes eh ben ils te renouvellent pas
        if you dispute well they won't renew

02      le bail
        the lease
```

Furthermore, 'if'-clauses are not always part of a bi-clausal pattern. For instance, we find regular occurrences of a format that has long been either disregarded in linguistic analysis or considered as non-standard: the so-called 'independent' 'if'-clause, as in Excerpt (4), taken from a hairdressing service encounter:

---

1. 'If'-clauses can also work as complement clauses (equivalent to English 'whether'). Such uses were excluded from the present analysis.

Excerpt 4. *un peu plus blond* 'a bit more blonde' (Horlacher 2021)

```
01 CLI: j'aimerais faire mes: mes racines eu:h comme d'hab,
        I would like to have my roots done uh as usual
02      et pis eu::hm ben p't-être un truc un peu plu:s
        and then uh well maybe something a bit more
03      estival?
        summer-like
04      (0.7)
05 CLI: si on pouvait faire un peu plus blond?
        if we could go for a bit more blonde
06      attends j' voulais t' montrer un truc là.
        wait I wanted to show you something there
        ((searches for pictures on mobile phone))
```

Seen from the vantage point of the canonical 'if-then' sentence structure, the *si*-clause in Excerpt (4) appears as 'incomplete'. With regard to prosody, however, it is produced with final rising intonation. Work in interactional linguistics has shown that such independent 'if'-clauses regularly function as directives (Section 3.3 below). Such 'independent' uses of what on formal grounds appear to be dependent structures have come under scrutiny under the label 'insubordination' (Evans 2007: 367).

To summarize, grammars of French are rather reductionist when describing *si*-constructions. Variations on the pattern not only concern the different resources that may introduce the consequent (Excerpt (3)) or other issues such as different verb tense combinations within the pattern, but they also concern the very nature of the *si*-clause as a subordinate clause. Interactional data show *si*-clauses that are to various degrees prosodically and syntactically integrated with another clause, but also fully insubordinate (autonomous) ones; they display co-constructed or incrementally composed 'if-then' types of patterns, as well as patterns in which the *si*-clause combinations are accomplished by a gesture 'in place of' the main clause; and they show different types of pragmatic dependency of the *si*-clause. Such observations provide evidence that interactants rely on patterned practices and syntactic structures as resources for interaction while at the same time adapting — both locally and over time — these resources to suit varying interactional needs. This brings us to the central issue to be addressed here: Such adaptations ensue in locally implemented grammatical formats for accomplishing social actions – and such formats may over time routinize to various degrees.

In this chapter, we take French *si*-clauses as an exemplary case to reflect on how questions about the structures of a language can be fruitfully addressed by considering the conversational actions that these structures accomplish in precise sequential positions within the multimodal ecology of social interaction. Our analysis is based on data taken from a variety of settings: ordinary conversation, service encounters, presidential debates; data were recorded in France and in French-speaking Switzerland. We argue that empirical observations of such naturally occurring language use in interaction have profound implications for our understanding of core features of grammar, such as clause-combining, subordination, or insubordination. An interactional perspective has the potential (a) to shed light on possible interactional motivations for the formal implementation of 'if'-clauses and their combination, (b) to deepen our understanding of the functions of insubordination, and (c) to open a window onto continua of (in)subordination as they are configured along the temporal unfolding of turns and actions. This is so because detailed analysis of language use in interaction reveals that speakers do not simply implement pre-fabricated clausal patterns or combinations thereof, but that these may result from local adaptations in real time (Auer 2009 on on-line syntax; Hopper 1987 on emergent grammar; Mushin & Pekarek Doehler 2021 on the temporality of grammar); such analysis also demonstrates that participants' language use interfaces in complex ways with their bodily conduct (see papers in Pekarek Doehler et al. 2022); most centrally, it evidences that speakers use grammar to accomplish social actions, and for that purpose may routinely resort to structures that have not been inventoried in reference grammars. Scrutinizing grammatical patterns in relation to these features — temporality/emergence, grammar-body-interface, social action — therefore draws our attention to the flexibility, adaptability, and range of formal and functional variation of a given pattern. This in itself is reason enough to reflect in detail on what an interactional grammar of 'if'-clauses, and more generally of (in)subordination, may look like.

In what follows, we first present the structural properties of *si* 'if'-clauses (Section 2.1) and discuss relevant parameters for analysis of their use in social interaction (Section 2.2). We then turn to the analysis of illustrative examples taken from different types of naturally occurring interaction, including both ordinary conversation and institutional interactions (Section 3). We focus on the following: (i) *incrementally composed* patterns (Section 3.1); (ii) *co-constructed* [*si*-clause + main clause] or [main clause + *si*-clause] patterns (Section 3.2); (iii) free-standing *si*-clauses along a *cline of insubordination* (Section 3.3); (iv) *embodied completions* of *si*-clauses (Section 3.4). By doing so, we address two main questions: What functions/actions do *si*-clauses accomplish, and what is their status on the (in)subordinate continuum?

2. Background

2.1 A cline of (in)subordination

The past decade has seen a burgeoning interest in insubordination and related phenomena across a wide range of languages (papers in Beijering et al. 2019; Evans & Watanabe 2016).[2] In his seminal article, Evans (2007: 367) defines insubordination as "the conventionalized main-clause use of what, on prima facie grounds, appear to be formally subordinate clauses". Typical examples are so-called 'free-standing' or 'independent' *because-* or *if*-clauses. Following Evans (2007) and Mithun (2008), existing research associates insubordination with the management of interpersonal relations and speaker-hearer intersubjective alignment, relating it to requests, commands, hints, warnings, and the expression of epistemic, evidential or deontic meanings (papers in Beijering et al. 2019; Evans & Watanabe 2016). Yet, while existing work highlights the dynamic relation between usage and structure, it has typically not dealt with social-interactional data in a systematic way (exceptions are, e.g., Gras & Sansiñena 2015; Sansiñena's 2019 interactional constructional studies on Spanish; see Section 2.2 below on interactional linguistics work on 'free-standing' clauses).

Given the intersubjective workings of insubordination, an interactional perspective can be anticipated to substantially deepen our understanding of the functions of insubordination. This is also highlighted by the fact that some authors have argued that *co-construction* in interaction may be a major factor in the emergence of insubordination (e.g., Evans & Watanabe 2016; Heine et al. 2016; Hilpert 2015). Such observations urge us to go beyond sentence-based analysis, making an interactional approach particularly promising.

Current discussions evolve around the degree of autonomy or independence from adjacent talk or text. This raises issues of *pragmatic dependence* on prior talk by the same or another speaker (Kaltenböck 2019; Mithun 2008), and highlights the importance of prosody for differentiating subordination and insubordination (Couper-Kuhlen & Thompson 2022; Debaisieux et al. 2019; Lombardi Vallauri 2016) and more generally degrees of syntactic integration (Günthner 2020; Lastres-López 2018; Maschler 2020).

Among the burning questions at the current state of research is how different degrees of autonomy are related to different discourse/interactional functions of adverbial clauses, as well as to their formal on-line emergence in interaction, and

---

2. We find these phenomena under a variety of labels: 'independent clause', 'free-standing clause', 'suspended clause', 'de-subordination', etc. Studies on French *si*-clauses include Corminboeuf & Jahn (2020); Debaisieux et al. (2019); Patard (2014).

how they relate to participants' embodied conduct. We address these issues in Section 3.

2.2 Parameters for examining and describing 'if'-clauses as they occur in social interaction

From what we know on grammar-in-interaction (see references below), the use of 'if'-clauses in interaction can fruitfully be examined (in research) and described (in reference grammars) in regard to a range of parameters.

2.2.1 Position of main and subordinate clause

While adverbial clauses can be in principle pre- or post-posed in relation to the main clause, 'if'-clauses have been shown to be massively pre-posed, both in spoken and in written language use, across a range of languages (Corminboeuf & Jahn 2020 for French; Ford & Thompson 1986 for English). The ordering of clauses has been argued to be motivated by principles of language use, such as iconicity (Diessel 2008) and by their pragmatic functions in discourse (Diessel 2001; Ford 1993; Thompson et al. 2007). There is a set of important questions to be addressed in this regard from an interactional perspective. We know from existing research on social interaction that initial elements project trajectories and possible occurrences of next elements. In particular, turn-beginnings are important loci for speakers' achieving joint orientation, displaying uptake, and foreshadowing the action-type and turn-trajectory they initiate (Schegloff 1996); turn-ends, by contrast, are sensitive places for speakers' dealing with issues of recipiency (Pekarek Doehler et al. 2015; Sacks et al. 1974). Accordingly, pre-posed 'if'-clauses can be expected to show substantially different interactional workings and implications than post-posed ones.

However, it is sometimes impossible to determine whether the adverbial clause is post- or pre-posed. In the following example, quoted in Corminboeuf and Jahn (2020), the *si*-clause represents a pivot element (Horlacher & Pekarek Doehler 2014) that can be heard as syntactically and prosodically (no prosodic break; no upgrade or downgrade of pitch) related to either the preceding *non* (line 1) or the following *non* (line 2) – or to both:

Excerpt 5. *non* 'no' (Corminboeuf & Jahn 2020: 209)

```
01 SPE: non si c'est des spécialités locales ou
        no  if these are local specialities or

02      une espèce de:: de patois ou d'argot non
        a kind of of dialect or slang no
```

2.2.2 *Degrees of syntactic integration, co-construction, and incrementation*

As mentioned above, recent research on clause-combining stresses the existence of continua of syntactic integration (following Haiman & Thompson 1984; Lehmann 1988; Van Vallin 1984). Also, paratactic configurations are attested, such as *Tu serais venu, j'aurais fait un gâteau au chocolat* '[If] you had come, I would have made a chocolate cake' (for French: Corminboeuf 2010). Degrees of syntactic integration may materialize in interactional data as co-constructions or incremental composition, which may be functionally motivated by social-interactional factors. As a matter of fact, the 'if-then' pattern represents a classic case of "compound turn-constructional unit" (Lerner 1991), lending itself to co-construction between two speakers: the production of an 'if'-clause makes expectable, or projects, the occurrence of a 'then'-clause as a relevant next.

2.2.3 *Free-standing 'if'-clauses*

Furthermore, independent 'if'-clauses have been treated as a prototypical case of insubordination (Evans 2007). On a functional level, insubordinate 'if'-clauses have been associated with requests and suggestions (Evans 2007:7), though it has been proposed that they may have a broader functional realm (Lombardi Vallauri 2016). In French *si* 'if'-clauses have been studied within the framework of macro-syntax (e.g., Debaisieux et al. 2019; Patard 2014), often referred to as *si-indépendantes* (Corminboeuf & Jahn 2020). Some such clauses have been attested to work as (semi)formulaic insubordinate clauses: e.g., *si tu savais* 'if you knew', *si tu avais vu* 'if you had seen (it)' (Debaisieux et al. 2019), many of these being able to function as pragmatic markers (Debaisieux et al. 2019:370; Sweetser 1990; see also Kaltenböck & Keizer 2022). Overall, existing work on French focuses on the syntactic and morphological realizations of *si*-clauses and questions their micro- vs. macro-syntactic status; systematic investigation into the functional dimension of such clauses is by contrast scarce (but see Horlacher 2021; Horlacher & Pekarek Doehler 2022).

Interactional studies of free-standing 'if'-clauses in other languages have suggested that such clauses function as requests and other types of directives (Ford & Thompson 1986; Laury 2012; Lindström et al. 2016; on French, see Horlacher & Pekarek Doehler 2022), or as warnings and threats (Günthner 2020).

2.2.4 *Grammar and the body*

Lindström et al. (2019) show how 'if'-clauses in Swedish and Finnish used as directives emerge on-line in response to co-participants' verbal and embodied conduct, thereby documenting the key importance of multimodal analysis for understanding the production and function of insubordinate clauses. Based on

French data from service encounters, Horlacher (2021) in turn questions the 'independent' status of *si*-clauses when these are completed by embodied conduct.

2.2.5 *In sum: Parameters for analysis*

The above state of the art points to a range of phenomena and patterns that need to be accounted for — in terms of both form and function — in an interactional grammar of 'if'-clauses, and possibly more generally of (in)subordination. In our analysis, we focus on the following formal realizations:

i. incrementally composed patterns;
ii. co-constructed ['if'-clause + main clause] or [main clause + 'if'-clause] patterns;
iii. free-standing 'if'-clauses and the possible continuum between subordination and insubordination;
iv. embodied completions of 'if'-clauses.[3]

We concentrate on the functions/actions the *si*-clauses accomplish, and what the observed patterns tell us about the (in)subordination continuum.

3. Analysis

3.1 Incremental composition

One of the key characteristics of linguistic structures in use, including clause-combining patterns, is that they emerge step by step in real time (Auer 2009; Hopper 1987; for a recent discussion see Mushin & Pekarek Doehler 2021). One facet of emergence is the observable *incremental* design of turns and related syntactic trajectories (e.g., Ford et al. 2002; Schegloff 1996, 2016). An increment is a grammatical extension that is 'added on' to a turn that has reached possible (syntactic and prosodic, often also pragmatic) completion: That is, the turn extension is heard as a continuation of the syntactic trajectory of the turn-so-far (on French, see Pekarek Doehler et al. 2015, chap. 4).

Consider Excerpt (6), taken from a conversation between co-students. Penny (PEN) and Dana (DAN) are talking about a course schedule while DAN is searching the schedule on her mobile phone:

---

3. We use the term embodied 'completions' as, in the data, we find embodied enactments of the 'main' clause only following the *si*-clause and not preceding it.

Excerpt 6. *cobaye* 'guinea pig' (Pauscaf-9)

```
01 PEN: ah >et pis< du coup j'aurais p'têtre besoin d'toi.
        oh and by the way I would maybe need you
02      (0.2)*#(0.3) ± (1.0) ±
               -------->±licks  spoon±
           --->*gazes at DAN--->
   fig.      #1
03 PEN: ((click)) si tu *veux être mon *cobaye?
        ((click)) if you want to be my guinea pig
                    -------->*closes eyes---*gazes at DAN--->
04      (0.3)*(0.9)±(0.7)#
        ---->*gazes at DAN's phone--->>
                  ±leans twd DAN&continues to inspect
                    phone--->>
   fig.                 #2
05 PEN: >°fais voir.°<
        let me see
06      (1.3)
07 DAN: .hh bon ben ça c'est encore un ancie:n
        .hh so well this one is still an old one
08      que y a pas £la bonne version£.
        whose last version is missing
```

Figure 1. PEN gazes at DAN   **Figure 2.** PEN gazes at DAN's phone

In line 01, PEN operates a topic shift, demarcated by her turn-initial *ah et pis du coup* 'oh and by the way', followed by a syntactically complete unit in the form of a full sentence, ending on final rising intonation with *toi* 'you'. Yet, after a 1.5 second's pause (line 2), PEN extends that unit by adding the syntactically fitted *si*-clause (line 3). The formal trajectory of the turn at talk hence emerges in real time, and so does what is retrospectively a pattern of the [clause + *si*-clause] type: 'I will maybe need you – if you want to be my guinea pig'. Yet, this is not a classic conditional clause-combining pattern. Rather than presenting a condition on the main clause, the *si*-clause implements what Kaltenböck & Keizer (2022: 489) refer to as a 'subsidiary discourse act', somewhat mitigating the request for help implied by the initial clause: the *si*-clause is pragmatically dependent on the preceding clause rather than being syntactically (or prosodically) integrated with it. But what exactly does the speaker achieve interactionally through the post-hoc adding on of the *si*-clause?

Note that PEN's turn in line 01 works as a — somewhat underspecified — request: by declaring the (potential) need for help, it actually requests (potential) help. As such, it normatively projects a recipient's response such as 'ok' or even 'oh sure, how can I help you' as the relevant next. The invitation to respond is here further enhanced by PEN's turning her gaze toward DAN in the transition space (line 2), just after having finished her turn (Figure 1), and maintaining it directed toward DAN as a way of pursuing response (Stivers & Rossano 2010). Yet DAN simply continues tacitly manipulating her phone (Figure 2). It is exactly in reaction to such lack of recipient response that PEN expands her turn, by means of the syntactically fitted *si*-clause (note also the click of the tongue in line 3, one possible feature of turn-(pre)-beginnings). The added-on *si*-clause, produced as a post-gap increment (Schegloff 2016), hence implements one of the well-known workings of increments, namely pursuing response by creating a second sequential opportunity for recipients to respond.

This excerpt illustrates a key property of grammar — and by extension of clause-combining — in social interaction: Grammar in use is an object of continuous and locally contingent 'bricolage' on the part of speakers (Horlacher & Pekarek Doehler 2014; Mushin & Pekarek Doehler 2021). The quoted excerpt should suffice to show that at least some instances of what formally may appear as clause-combining patterns may be usefully understood as situated interactional accomplishments that emerge in real time and are configured to accomplish precise actions in interaction.

In Excerpt (7), the incrementally added *si*-clause is closer to a fully independent structure. DAN and PEN are still talking about course schedules and incompatibilities, while DAN starts consulting her phone so as to provide information to PEN from something (*il* 'it', line 5) she is downloading:

Excerpt 7. *télécharger* 'download' (Pauscaf-9)

```
01 DAN: je vais t'dire ça tout de suite?
        I'm gonna tell you that immediately
        >>looks at her phone, her head lowered over it->>
02      (2.2)
03 DAN: ou pas? .hh
        or not .hh
04      (1.0)
05 DAN: s'il veut bien se télécharger?
        if it wants to download
06      (0.4)
```

```
07 PEN: ((click)) sinon tu peux venir au
         ((click)) otherwise you can come to the
08       cours ragga dance seule avec £moi£ .hh .hh
         ragga dance course alone with me .hh .hh
```

Like in Excerpt (6), the *si*-clause (line 5) does not come off as produced in one unit with the main clause (line 1). Rather, DAN extends her turn, which came to a transition point in line 2, first by a short increment (line 3), and then by the syntactically fitted *si*-clause (line 5). The *si*-clause is hence not a prototypical increment, in that it is not 'glued' onto its host (line 1). The result is like an *insertable* in that the added-on *si*-clause is not where it 'ought' to have been (Vorreiter 2003). This description argues for a syntactically rather autonomous *si*-clause, which is, however, clearly pragmatically dependent on the context where it occurrs. Furthermore, the *si*-clause resembles structures like 'if only X' expressing a wish that have been discussed in the literature as conventionalized insubordinate structures (for French, see Debaisieux et al. 2019).

So far, we have observed instances of the 'if-then' clause-combining pattern that materialize incrementally, 'on the fly', one clause after the other, along the real-time unfolding of turns and actions, and for all practical purposes. A further case of such local emergence of clause-combining patterns is their co-construction, to which we turn in the next subsection.

3.2 Co-construction

As mentioned earlier, the 'if-then' clause-combining pattern is a classic case of "compound turn-constructional unit" (Lerner 1991) in which the production of the 'if'-clause makes expectable (or projects) the occurrence of a 'then'-clause as a relevant next. As such, it lends itself ideally to co-construction between two speakers.

An example is shown in the following service encounter, recorded in a barber shop. Some potential client has shown up without any appointment. Before the excerpt, the hairdresser (HAI) has explained to the current client (CLI) that the team usually does not accept clients without appointment. By co-constructing (line 3) the 'if-then' pattern, CLI possibly displays affiliation with the service-provider's negative stance toward accepting clients without an appointment (line 1).

Excerpt 8. *prendre des gens* 'take people' (Walch corpus)

```
01 HAI: c'est simplement ce n'est pas notre:
         it's simply it's not our
02 CLI: vous n'êtes pas habitués ouais.
         you are not used to that yeah
03 HAI: si on commence à prendre des gens comme ça,
         if we start to take people like that
         [=without appointment]
04       (0.4)
```

Chapter 11. Insubordinate *si* 'if'-clauses in French   343

```
05 CLI: tout l'agenda est perturbé.
        all the agenda is messed-up
06 HAI: on s'occupe pas des autres.
        we are not taking care of the others
07      et nous notre clientèle c'est eu:h une (xxx)
        and to us our customer base is uh one (xxx)
08      et une euh voilà.
        and one uh that's it
09      (0.5)
10 CLI: donc la=
        so the
11 HAI: =la régularité du service.
        the regularity of service
```

The excerpt shows what Lerner has labelled 'reverse-directionality' turn continuations by other: That is, the turn continuation "implement(s) a responding action addressed to the speaker of the prior turn" (Lerner 2004: 161), rather than being directed to the same (third) party as that prior turn (like in co-tellings). Here, CLI (line 5) responds by aligning with HAI's negative stance, and actually produces the syntactically fitted continuation, after a short gap (line 4), right before HAI himself continues his turn (line 6).

Such co-constructed cases of the 'if-then' pattern, and more generally of clause-combining, testify again to the embeddedness of language in the time-course of locally accomplished (and mutually oriented to) courses of action. At the same time, these co-constructions prominently display how speakers orient to the existence of schematic clause-combining patterns in the language.

Excerpt (9), again taken from a hairdressing service encounter, offers an illustration of both co-construction and embodied completion (Section 3.4). Prior to the excerpt, the client (CLI) complained that she expected her highlights to depart from the roots. HAI objects that if one dyes the hair too close to the roots, one can see the roots when the hair grows. In the segment reproduced below, HAI suggests a different service for the follow-up visit (line 1), while warning about a possible negative outcome (lines 5–8).

Excerpt 9. *près de la racine* 'close to the roots' (Horlacher 2021)

```
01 HAI: bah la prochaine fois hein on fait (1.1)
        well next time huh we make it (1.1)
02      on fait partout dès la racine.
        we make it everywhere from the roots
03      (0.4)
04 CLI: non [non pas que ça donne un effet-]
        no no not to have an effect-
05 HAI:     [c'est juste que si-            ]
            it is just that if-
```

```
06      (0.2)
07 HAI: oui c'est +ça, #*si je fais trop #près de la ra*cine
        yes that's it, if I make it too close to the roots
   cli           +raises hands&maintains them frozen--->
   hai                  *pushes CLI's hair backwards-->*
   fig.          #3                    #4
08      [bah après +eu:h c':-]
        well then uh it-
   cli            --->+reaches her head&manipulates hair-->
09 CLI: [(xxx) c'est horrible.]
        (xxx) it's horrible
10 HAI: *#ouais (.) c'est                        *ça.
        yeah (.) that's it
        *shows roots' area on her head w. open palm h.*
   fig. #5
```

Figure 3. HAI grasps CLI's hair

Figure 4. HAI pushes CLI's hair backwards

Figure 5. HAI shows roots' area on her head

HAI produces a *si*-clause in line 7, which CLI completes (line 9) with what appears to be the consequent (*c'est horrible* 'it's horrible') — a negative result of the *si*-clause, produced in overlap with HAI's own turn-continuation. CLI thereby displays understanding of the unfavorable implications of starting the highlights too close to the roots. HAI's simultaneous turn-continuation remains verbally incomplete, but she gesturally displays the negative result on her own head by moving her two hands near the roots (on deictic and iconic gestures at the hairdresser, see Horlacher 2022; on environmentally coupled gestures, see Goodwin 2007). In short, then, the second part to the *si*-pattern, i.e., the consequent, is here initiated by HAI verbally at line 8 but mainly accomplished through embodied resources, and, simultaneously, made explicit by CLI at line 9. Through the co-construction, CLI again displays affiliation with HAI's stance.

So far, we have observed instances of the 'if-then' clause-combing pattern that materializes incrementally (Section 3.1) or based on co-construction (3.2) along the real-time unfolding of turns and actions, and through which speakers get a range of interactional jobs done, such as fishing for recipient response or displaying affiliation. Importantly, the mere fact that a clause-combining pattern spreads across two speakers does not make one of the clauses insubordinate: The subordination pattern is simply co-constructed (see also as Evans & Watanabe 2016: 29; Kaltenböck 2019: 182). At the antipodes of these occurrences lie instances where the *si*-clause is free-standing, in that it is not related to any other clause. Such cases pertain to what has been called free-standing or, in some cases, fully insubordinate 'if'-clauses.

3.3 Free-standing si 'if'-clauses: A continuum of insubordination

Following Couper-Kuhlen and Thompson's (2022) recent discussion of the potential insubordinate status of temporal clauses in English, we operationalize fully insubordinate *si*-clauses as clauses that are syntactically independent, form a free-standing prosodic unit (namely, end on final intonation), implement a discrete action, and are treated as actionable by the recipient in the absence of a consequent clause. In what follows, we specifically relate to recent discussions on a continuum of (in)subordination, as presented in Section 2 above.

3.3.1 Fully insubordinate si 'if'-clauses

A typical case of insubordination is shown in Excerpt (10), where the *si*-clause implements a request. The excerpt is taken from the opening section of a recording among students in a cafeteria. The assistant (ASS) in charge of organizing the recordings is standing behind a table while Joanna (JOA) and Ekta (EKT) are approaching the table. ASS invites JOA to sit at the other side of the table than the side she is approaching (lines 3–4):

Excerpt 10. *te mettre là* 'sit there' (Pauscaf-5)

```
01 ASS: ∞alors vingt  centimes pour toi∞,
        so    twenty cents     for  you
        ∞reaches some  coins  to   EKT∞
02 EKT: merci.
        thank you
03 ASS: et  puis ∞euh(0.4)  ∞ (0.3) si t'arrives  à  te
        and uh       (0.4)    (0.3) if you manage to sit
              ∞points to JOA∞
                        ∞taps 2x on one side of table-->
04      mettre mettre∞ [là    #aussi s'il te plaît?]∞
        sit    sit      there too    please
        ------------>∞holds  still-----------------∞
    fig.                     #6
05 JOA:             [ah ouais excuse        ]
                    oh yeah   sorry
```

```
06 ASS: comme ça vous êtes en ±face.
        so you are face to face
    joa                          ±pushes a cup&then 2 snacks
                                 over to the side of the
                                 table ASS pointed at->>1.08

07 EKT: u(h)u(h)u#
    fig.           #7

08      (2.3)±
            ---->±

09 ASS: et ±voilà?#
        and here we are
    joa      ±moves to side of the table ASS pointed at-->>
    fig.     #8
```

Figure 6. ASS taps on table

Figure 7. JOA pushes cup over to side

Figure 8. JOA walks around table

Simultaneously with his *si*-clause, ASS taps on the table (line 4, Figure 6), thereby indicating the side of the table he is referring to. In response, JOA first pushes her cup and some snacks over to the side indicated (Figure 7), and then moves around the table (Figure 8) and ultimately sits down at the place ASS indicated (not shown). This testifies to her treating his *si*-clause as a request. The sense of the *si*-clause implementing a request is here further enhanced through its ending on the formula *s'il te plaît* 'please'. The *si*-clause is an insubordinate clause: It is syntactically unrelated to another clause, ends on final intonation (on *s'il te plaît*), implements a discrete action, and is treated as actionable by the recipient.

Chapter 11. Insubordinate *si* 'if'-clauses in French   **347**

Even without markers such as 'please', speakers recurrently use the independent *si*-clause for doing a request. Excerpt (11) is again taken from the beginning of a recording at a University cafeteria. The assistant (ASS) is distributing the consent forms to be filled in by the participants:

Excerpt 11. *remplir* 'fill in' (Pauscaf-7)

```
01 ASS: vous vous mettez à l'aise.
         you make yourself comfortable

02       (0.7)

03 ASS: alors voilà,
         so that's it

04       et pis euh::: ben au bout d'un moment,
         and uh well after a while

05       si vous arrivez juste à remplir pour que m:
         if you manage just to fill in [the form] so that

06       enfin pour que vous attestez qu'on puisse
         well so that you confirm that we can

07       utiliser euh les données qu'on va récolter dans
         use uh the data we're gonna collect within

08       le cadre académique,
         the academic framework

         [...]

12 CAM: ça marche.
         ok/will do
```

Here, the *si*-clause itself is followed by an adverbial clause, introduced by *pour que* 'so that'. Yet, there is no main clause related to the *si*-clause. Again, the *si*-clause implements a request, and is treated as such by CAM who responds *ça marche* 'ok/will do' (line 12).

In both excerpts, we observe *si*-clauses that (i) implement an action by themselves, (ii) are treated as such by co-participants, and (iii) form a free-standing prosodic unit by themselves (in Excerpt (11), it does so together with subordinate material). Both instances hence correspond to the operationalization criteria for insubordination proposed by Couper-Kuhlen and Thompson (2022).

While such fully insubordinate *si*-clauses are recurrent in our data (see also Horlacher & Pekarek Doehler 2022 for *si*-requests in emergency calls) and have been attested across a range of languages (Section 2 above), the data also shows a series of cases that are not fully autonomous; they are either structurally and/or pragmatically dependent on environing talk or hinge on contextual inferences. We group the first type, as a heuristics, under the label of 'pseudo-autonomous' *si*-clauses (Section 3.3.2), and then turn to *si*-clauses that are pragmatically dependent on either co(n)text (Section 3.3.3) or formulaic segments (Section 3.3.4).

3.3.2 *Pseudo-autonomous* si *'if'-clauses based on structural latency*

There are cases where the apparently free-standing *si*-clause actually rests on structural latency (Auer 2015). These can be seen as cases where material occurring prior in talk is surface-elided, but still latent, rather than as fully autonomous structures and actions. The following is again taken from a conversation between co-students:

Excerpt 12. *le job de tes rêves* 'your dream job' (Pauscaf-13)

```
01 PAT: mais si on te propose d'aller faire un job à
        but if you are offered a job

02      l'étranger euh: >l'année prochaine< tu pars?
        abroad uh next year you leave

03      (1.3)

04 MAR: °chais pas°.
        dunno

05      (1.2)

06 MAR: franchement j'sais pas.
        honestly dunno

07 PAT: bien sûr [que tu sais. ]
        of course you know

08 MAR:         [si c'est le- ]
                 if it's the-

09 PAT: bien sûr que tu sais.
        of course you know

10 MAR: j' pense plus non que oui a[lors. ]
        I think more in terms of no than yes so

11 PAT:                            [ouai:s] okay.
                                    yeah    okay

12      c'est déjà  pas mal.
        it's already not bad

13 MAR: mais:=
        but

14 PAT: =mais après si c'est le job de tes rêves,
        =but then if it's the job of your dreams

15 MAR: >oui voilà< c'est ça: après quoi [comme   ] job.
        yes there that's it then what kind of job

16 PAT:                                  [qui est?]
                                          which is

17      (1.7)

18 PAT: t'as pas de rêves  (0.2) tu rêves pas?
        you don't have any dreams (0.2) you don't dream

19      ((laughter))
```

The excerpt starts (lines 1–2) with Patrick (PAT) asking Marie (MAR) if she would go abroad if she was offered a job. His question is formatted as a conventional 'if-then' pattern, in which the *si*-clause offers a condition under which the main clause (*tu pars* 'you leave') applies. MAR responds with a hesitant *chais pas* 'dunno' (line 4), and after some further back and forth (lines 7–12), PAT produces a second *si*-clause *mais après si c'est le job de tes rêves* 'but then if it's the job of your dreams' (line 14), thereby re-launching his initial question. This subsequent *si*-clause (note also MAR's aborted turn in line 8) is hearable as resonating with PAT's initial 'if-then'-interrogative, augmenting the initial condition ('if you are offered a job') to 'if it's the job of your life', and thereby re-instituting his initial question as to *tu pars* 'you leave'. Following Auer (2015), the main clause *tu pars* 'you leave' can be heard as structurally latent (some would call this a case of ellipsis), and, by extension, the *si*-clause alone can be heard as redoing the same type of question as the prior one. These features compromise the criterion of both structural and praxeological autonomy of the *si*-clause, which therefore cannot be considered fully autonomous, and hence an insubordinate clause. Note also the continuing intonation on *rêves* 'dreams' at the end of PAT's turn (line 14), as if leaving something in suspense, unsaid. However, as there is no main clause produced by PAT, it is equally inadequate to analyze this *si*-clause as a case of a subordinate clause. We therefore consider this type of occurrence to be placed in the mid-range on a continuum of (in)subordination.

3.3.3 Pragmatically dependent si 'if'-clauses based on contextual inferences

While structural latency puts into question the idea of absolute structural autonomy of the *si*-clause, there are also contextual inferences that appear to provide the grounds for speakers' conferring the consequent of the 'if'-clause (and recipients understanding it) without producing a main clause. This differentiates the cases quoted in what follows from fully insubordinate cases. While fully insubordinate 'if'-clauses have no consequent and alone implement an autonomous structure and action, there is (at least conceptually) a consequent in the following cases. This consequent, however, remains unspoken, as it is highly inferable from preceding talk. We view these as cases of pragmatic dependency — but pragmatic dependency of a different type than what we have observed with the 'subsidiary discourse act' (Kaltenböck & Keizer 2022: 489) in Excerpt (6). While in Excerpt (6) the *si*-clause was pragmatically (though not syntactically) dependent on an adjacent clause, the cases below do not contain any associated clause whatsoever; yet the *si*-clause is not autonomous and does not accomplish an autonomous action. It is, instead, pragmatically dependent on inferences entailed by preceding talk. In the following conversation, Patrick (PAT), a law student, suggests to Marie (MAR) that he might change to studying sports:

Simona Pekarek Doehler & Anne-Sylvie Horlacher

Excerpt 13. *ton stage* 'your internship' (Pauscaf-13)

```
01 PAT: toute ma vie j'ai hésité entre faire du sport
        all my life I've been hesitating between doing sport

02      toute ma vi:e et pis euh: (1.3) .hh le droit,
        all my life and then uh (1.3) .hh law

03      (1.2) pis là j'hésite en fait à
        (1.2) and now I'm actually hesitant to

04      recommencer un bachelor en sport.
        start again a bachelor's degree in sports

05      (0.3)

06 MAR: mais NON:::
        but no

07 PAT: ouai::s
        yeah

08 MAR: mais alors faut te: >décider vite< parce que
        but then you have to decide quickly because

09      si tu commences ton stage et tout=et tout?
        if you start your internship and all and all that

10      (1.0)

11 MAR: mais non patrick tu peux pas être un
        but no Patrick you can't be a

12      [fidèle    étudiant]
         loyal student

13 PAT: [mais pourquoi pas.]
         but why not
```

The *si*-clause ends with *et tout=et tout* 'and all that=and all that' (line 9), which – in French – is typically used as a *generalized list completer* (Jefferson 1990). While MAR ends her clause on final rising intonation, she leaves it up to PAT to draw the relevant inferences about the situation in case he decided to start another bachelor's degree in sports. This hearing is enhanced through the fact that the *si*-clause is presented as an account (see the *parce que* 'because', line 8) for MAR's advice for PAT to change to sports expediently: If you start your internship in law, things become more complicated.

Excerpt (14) shows another case in point. The conversation has been about the fact that Penny (PEN) has a lot of work and little time to exercise her dancing, and that the dance school might be closed when she would have time to practice.

Excerpt 14. *choréographie* 'choreography' (Pauscaf-9)

```
01 DAN: >ah *mais alors c'est fermé.<
        >oh but then it's closed<
   pen     *gazes at DAN--->1.05

02 PEN: ouais mais je vais appeler quand même.=
        yeah but I'm gonna call anyway
```

Chapter 11. Insubordinate *si* 'if'-clauses in French   **351**

```
03 DAN: =ouais mais demande?
        =yeah but ask
04      (0.8)
        ((DAN is gazing at PEN quite continuously))
05 PEN: la *chorégraphie elle est dure alors
        the choreography is difficult so
        -->*gazes down--->
06      *si j' rate un bou(h)t.
         if I miss a part
        >*gazes at DAN, smiling->
07      (0.5)
08 PEN: °*(t'aurais dû/hu hu hu)°
        (you should have/hu hu hu)
        >*shifts gaze to the left--->>
09 DAN: et en fait tu me fais penser et (x)?
        and actually you make me think and (x)
```

The fact that PEN plans to actively check the opening hours of the dance room (line 2) displays her negative stance towards missing classes. Right before producing the *si*-clause, PEN proffers an assessment about the choreography she is currently practicing: It is difficult (line 5). In this context, the undesirable consequences in case she misses part of the choreography are contextually inferable. The smiling and laughter (lines 6–8) accompanying and following the *si*-clause may also be relevant as part of conferring the consequent. Thereafter, DAN turns to another topic (line 9).

The two excerpts cited in this subsection illustrate *si*-clauses that do not by themselves implement an autonomous structure and action, and hence cannot be considered as fully insubordinate. Nor are they fully subordinate clauses, as they are not linked to a main clause — there is, in fact, no associated clause. Rather, there is a consequent which remains unspoken, yet is inferable from preceding talk. Similarly, the cases quoted in Section 3.3.2 are also not fully autonomous, as the apparently free-standing *si*-clause actually rests on structural latency of material occurring prior in talk. Both types of cases testify to a continuum of (in)subordination with various degrees of syntactic and pragmatic autonomy of the 'if'-clause.

3.3.4 *Highly routinized formulaic* si *'if'-clauses akin to particle-like status*

A further element on the cline of insubordination are free-standing *si*-segments that cannot be considered as clauses at all, but rather act as formulaic segments or even discourse markers (for English, see Heine et al. 2016:56–57). Possibly the most wide-spread among these is the politeness formula *s'il vous plaît/s'il te plait* (literally: 'if it pleases you'), meaning 'please' (see Excerpt (10) above). Other instances are *si vous (me le) permettez* (literally: 'if you allow (it to me)') and *si ça (ne) vous gêne pas* (literally: 'if it does not bother you'); both work as politeness formulas similar to English 'if you don't mind'. All of these are formally complete clauses containing a predicate, and can in principle be used in their 'literal' sense as subordinate clauses (combined with a main clause); they can also work as insubordinate clauses (think of a tennis championship referee using *s'il vous plaît* to request silence on the part of the audience). The point however is that they often work as independent parentheticals that can be positioned at various locations within a sentence structure.

Some such formulaic sequences represent only fragments rather than formally complete clauses, and these work as particles (or: discourse markers). An example is *si jamais* (literally: 'if ever', but typically meaning 'just in case'). Consider Excerpt (15). Régis (REG) and Kirian (KIR) are talking about an event to which one has to register; they are worried that their friend, Sam, will forget to do so.

Excerpt 15. *si jamais* 'just in case' (Pauscaf-6)

```
01 REG: mais sam il doit s'inscrire. s'il euh
        but Sam he has to register if he uh

02      (0.2) il va oublier de s'inscrire ce pélo.
        (0.2) he will forget to register this guy

03 KIR: ben=eu:::f on l'inscrit
        well uh we register him

04      (2.0)

05 KIR: je peux envoyer un mail depuis mon adresse
        can I send an email from my address

06      en son nom?
        in his name

07 REG: moi j' connais son mot de passe hein si jamais.
        me  I  know    his password     PTC PTC
        I know his password huh just in case

08      (0.4)

09 KIR: ouai:s ben inscris le alors.
        yeah well register him then
```

Here, *si jamais* is placed in turn-final position — a position where typically discourse markers can occur. It is produced as the last piece in what can be heard as an offer, by REG, to provide or use SAM's password so that either he or KIR can register SAM through his email account. The *si jamais* functions as a post-positioned downgrade of the offer: Given the delicate nature of using another person's email, the offer is made 'just in case', just as a possibility; by that token the preference for KIR to accept the offer is moderated. In the next turn (line 9), it becomes evident that KIR understands the offer as what it is: He treats it as REG offering to register SAM by using SAM's password, which KIR accepts.

Such discourse-marker uses most likely represent a derivate from more conventional uses, as illustrated in the 'if-then' clause-combining pattern in Excerpt (16) below. Penny (PEN) and Dana (DAN) are talking about which person to choose (among Aurélie and a Flemish girl) for their study on speakers of French as a second language.

Excerpt 16. *si jamais ça marche pas* 'if ever it does not work' (Pauscaf-9)

```
01 PEN: ouais ben écoute, (0.2)
        yeah well listen (0.2)

02      ben je- j'ai (vu) à aurélie bon: (.) j'essaie?
        well I- I (saw) to aurélie well (.) I try

03      (.) >et pis si jamais< ça marche pas,
        (.) and then if ever it does not work

04      c'est pas [grave:.]
        that's not a problem

05 DAN:          [ouais  ]
                  yeah
```

Here, the *si jamais* is not only part of a clause ('if ever it does not work'), but that clause itself is part of a bi-clausal pattern in which it has the status of a subordinate clause. This is then a formally and functionally conventional use of the *si*-clause, which stands in stark contrast to the *si jamais* fragment illustrated in (15). The functioning of such formulaic fragments as epistemic or evidential markers remains to be investigated in detail in future research.

3.3.5 Upshot: A cline of (in)subordination

Across the preceding sections, we have seen evidence for a cline of (in)subordination, the free-standing *si*-clauses exhibiting various degrees of autonomy. This continuum ranges from syntactically, prosodically, and praxeologically fully autonomous *si*-clauses, through *si*-clauses that are syntactically (and sometimes prosodically) unrelated to environing talk, but hinge on co- or con-textual elements either structurally (through latency) or pragmatically (through inference), to full subordination in the case of full-fledged 'if-then' types of clause-combining patterns as shown in Section 1. Furthermore, we have seen, at the far end of autonomization, segments that work as highly routinized formulas/parentheticals or particles. While these observations tie into earlier concerns with continua of subordination (Haiman & Thompson 1984; Lehmann 1988; Van Vallin 1984) and some current discussions on insubordination (e.g., Kaltenböck 2019; Kaltenböck & Keizer 2022; Maschler 2020), they have profound implications for the writing of a grammar of spoken language, as they put into question traditional accounts based on categorical and binary features of grammar. This is just one illustration — and one could think of many others — of how an interactional approach based on naturally occurring language use urges us to engage centrally with continua, clines, and degrees (of autonomy, etc.).

One further question that arises for understanding the cline of (in)subordination is the role of bodily conduct: How can we interpret cases in which the 'main' clause is accomplished not verbally, but through gesture or other bodily conduct? And what do such cases tell us about (in)subordination and clause-combining more generally? This is what we turn to in our last analytic section.

3.4 Embodied and other non-lexical completions

In her study on French, Horlacher (2021) challenges the 'independent' status of what may appear as free-standing *si*-clauses in cases when the semantic content of the 'main' clause is enacted through embodied resources (see Excerpt (9) above). In Excerpt (17), a client (CLI) instructs a hairdresser (HAI) about the cut she wants (lines 1–3), and HAI responds with a *si*-clause (line 4) ending on continuative intonation, thereby projecting both syntactically and prosodically a subsequent main clause. Yet the turn is then suspended (possibly due to overlapping talk):

Excerpt 17. *court là* 'short there' (Horlacher 2021)

```
01 CLI: un p'tit peu là au°ssi°.
        a little bit there too
02      (0.2)
03 CLI: pas beaucoup, mais quand même un peu: hein?
        not a lot,   but still a bit huh
04 HAI: #*ben si [j' coupe #court là-]      *
        well if I cut short there-
           *manipulates hair w. comb&fingers*
     fig. #9                  #10
05 CLI:         [et-  et les     o]reilles je veux pas
                 and- and the    ears I don't want
06      trop raser.
        them shaved too much
07 HAI: oui:
        yes
08      (0.4)
```

Figure 9. HAI manipulates CLI's hair   **Figure 10.** HAI manipulates CLI's hair

Chapter 11. Insubordinate *si* 'if'-clauses in French

The consequent of the *si*-clause is here produced in an embodied manner: HAI starts flattening (Figure 9) and lifting (Figure 10) CLI's hair, thereby initiating a demonstration of a negative result. Her facial expression possibly indexes a negative stance. What on a verbal level appears as an 'independent' *si*-clause is actually part of a complex pattern in which the conditional and the consequent are distributed across two different modalities that, here, are deployed simultaneously (Mondada 2018 on multiple temporalities of language and the body).

Excerpt (18) is again taken from a hairdressing service encounter:

Excerpt 18. *cata* 'catastrophe' (Horlacher 2021)

```
01        (17.0)#(2.0) ((HAI is cutting CLI's hair))
   fig.        #11

02 CLI: ah si j' les laisse trop longs+ ((click))+
        oh if I keep them too long      ((click))
                                        +slightly shakes
                                        h.--------+

03 HAI: ah quand i d'viennent longs *les vôtres #euh*
        ah when they become long yours.
                                    *raises eyebrows*
   fig.                                             #12

04 CLI: c'- c'est cata.
        it's a catastrophe

05        (5.0)

06 CLI: mais je s'rais venue un tout p'tit peu avant mais
        but I would have come a little bit earlier but

07        comme j'allais partir, (1.8)
          as I was leaving [on holiday] (1.8)

08        j' me suis dit que: (0.8) j'attendais
          I told myself that (0.8) I was waiting until

09        le dernier moment.
          the last moment
```

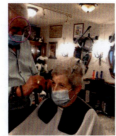

Figure 11. HAI is cutting CLI's hair   **Figure 12.** HAI is raising his eyebrows

CLI's *si*-clause ends on final falling intonation, prosodically not projecting more to come, but is followed by a click of the tongue (line 2) combined with a slight head-shake (line 2), whereby CLI embodies a negative stance (see Ogden 2013) before uttering a negative consequent verbally (line 4). HAI in turn (line 3), instead of completing the projection entailed by the *si*-clause through a main clause (see Section 3.2), joins in choral formulation by producing the first component of another bipartite construction, namely a *quand* 'when'-clause. HAI ends that component with a hesitation. However, his facial expression (see Figure 12) possibly indexes a negative stance (see Excerpt (17)). CLI's subsequent *c'est cata* 'it's a catastrophe' (line 4), given its sequential position after HAI's *quand* 'when'-clause, can be heard as providing the main clause to that clause, ensuing in a co-construction of the bi-clausal pattern. Considering the action it accomplishes, namely a negative consequence of 'if/when the hair is long', it can equally be heard as making explicit the consequent of CLI's own prior *si*-clause (line 2).

In the two cases discussed, what appear to be free-standing *si*-clauses on a verbal level are, in fact, combined with embodied (and vocal) conduct that implements the consequent, i.e., accomplishes what, in the canonical format, would be done by a main clause. A final example shows a similar non-verbal production of the consequent. This time, however, it is implemented through mere non-lexical vocalizations. The excerpt is taken from a conversation between Camille (CAM) and Cedric (CED); CED is inviting some friends over to his parents' house, but needs to check if the parents will indeed be absent.

Excerpt 19. *appeler mes parents* 'call my parents' (Pauscaf-7)

```
01 CED: ben j- je vais appeler mes parents pour bien
        well I- I will call my parents to
02      confirmer qu'ils ne soient pas là, (0.7) bon
        confirm that they are not there (0.7) well
03      [même si ]
        even if
04 CAM: [parce que] s'ils sont là *eu::h
        because if they are there uh hh.
            >>gazes at her apple *gazes at CED --->>
05      e(h) hh. hh. [hh.]
        e(h) hh. hh.  hh.
06 CED:             [ben]
                    well
07      s'ils sont là on peut y aller quand même,
        if they are there we can go there anyway
08      mais c'est pas pareil quoi.
        but it's not the same PTC
```

After CED declares that he will verify with his parents, CAM offers a *parce que* 'because' introduced *si*-clause, followed by mere laughter tokens, the first of which is a very much pushed out, explosive *E(h)*-sound. In the context where it occurs, CAM's exaggerated laughter can be heard as enacting a negative consequence of

Chapter 11. Insubordinate *si* 'if'-clauses in French **357**

the possibility of CED's parents' being around, as well as displaying a kind of complicity with CED as to there being a problem with parental presence when students party (see also CED's downgraded stance-display, line 8). What we learn from this excerpt is that an 'if'-clause can be combined with a consequent that is expressed through mere non-lexical vocalizations.

The bodily and vocal completions shown in this section challenge the insubordinate status of the related *si*-clauses, although these *si*-clauses are not combined with any verbal segment that could be heard as a main clause. The *si*-clauses analyzed do not stand as autonomous actions (Couper-Kuhlen & Thompson 2022); they cannot "'survive' alone as a meaningful event[s]" (Kaltenböck 2019:179). In other words, they are syntactically autonomous but pragmatically dependent on bodily or vocal context. This foregrounds the crucial importance of analyzing language within the multimodal ecology of its occurrence — and of grounding interpretations of language structure in such analysis: It calls for systematic attention to the grammar-body interface (Pekarek Doehler et al. 2022) in future research on (in)subordination.

4.   Discussion and conclusion

In this chapter, we set out to investigate French *si*-clauses as an exemplary case to reflect on how questions about the structures of a language can be fruitfully addressed by considering the conversational actions that speakers accomplish by means of these structures. We have shown that *si*-clauses, as used in social interaction, show a wide range of variation in their syntactic (and prosodic) patterning, and that this variation is functionally motivated: Different formal realizations of the target phenomenon are used by speakers to accomplish a range of different interactional purposes. While our analyses meet current debates on a continuum of (in)subordination, they shed light on different types of pragmatic dependency relations that characterize those cases that are neither fully autonomous (insubordinate) nor fully dependent: In addition to pragmatic dependency with regard to an associated clause, we have identified pragmatic dependencies of 'if'-clauses base on inferences derived from larger contexts. The analyses also document cases in which 'if'-clauses are dependent not on an associated clause, but on meanings that are enacted through vocal or bodily means.

Clearly, the observed formal and functional features go far beyond what has been attested in grammars or classic linguistic analysis of 'if'-clauses. This highlights the fact that empirical observations of language in social interaction have profound implications for our understanding of core features of grammar – which brings us to the driving question motivating this volume: What if the results of such analyses were to be integrated into a comprehensive and systematic grammar of the language?

Based on our analyses, we propose two imperatives for a grammar of interactional language use. (1) An interactional grammar of 'if'-clauses needs to include the following features, in addition to syntactic, semantic, and prosodic considerations: (a) sequential position, (b) the temporality of grammar (namely: projection as well as on-line emergence, as materializing, e.g., in co-construction and incrementation), (c) action accomplishment, and (d) co-occurring bodily and vocal conduct. These features allow us to better understand different degrees of autonomy of the target pattern and how these are related to different discourse/interactional functions. (2) The same features need to be centrally taken into consideration in a grammar's discussion of core features of any lingusitic system, such as subordination, insubordination, and more generally clause-combining. Let us spell this out in some detail.

4.1 A grammar entry for 'if'-clauses

A grammar of interactional language use needs to account for a wide range of formal variation of 'if'-clauses and (related) variation in their functional use:

Formally, this involves:

- Canonical 'if-then' patterns (and variations on these, e.g., absence of 'then', alternative vocal-verbal accomplishments of 'then', pre- vs. post-posing of the 'if'-clause).
- Fully autonomous (insubordinate) 'if'-clauses, based on the criteria of syntactic, prosodic, and praxeological independence.
- 'If'-clauses that formally appear as autonomous, but in which the consequent, instead of being expressed through a main clause, is present based on pragmatic (inference) or structural (latency) relations to co-text or context (what we called 'pseudo-autonomous' 'if'-clauses).
- Incrementally composed and co-constructed 'if'-clauses.
- Embodied and vocal completions, which confer the meaning and action of what, in the canonical form, is expressed by the main clause.

Functionally, the above needs to be related to functional potentials. We speak of 'potentials' as form-function mappings that are highly context sensitive; functions centrally hinge on sequential location and co-occurring embodied conduct. Nevertheless, the analysis presented here points to recurrent functions related to some types of formal patterning of the 'if'-clause(-combinations). As documented earlier, fully insubordinate 'if'-clauses may work as directives, and in particular as requests (Ford & Thompson 1986; Horlacher & Pekarek Doehler 2022;

Chapter 11. Insubordinate *si* 'if'-clauses in French   **359**

Laury 2012; Lindström et al. 2016). In addition, incrementally composed 'if-then' type of patterns may be associated to the pursuit of recipient response when such response is lacking. Co-constructed patterns in turn may reflect the next speaker's alignment with the anticipated stance of a prior speaker. In other words, the functional realm of 'if'-clauses needs to be discussed based on empirical evidence regarding the concrete phenomenon under scrutiny and in relation to what we know from prior research about recurrent interactional patternings such as co-construction and incrementation.

4.2 Beyond the case of 'if'-clauses: Grammar entries for subordination, insubordination, clause-combining

The case of 'if'-clauses allows us to broaden the perspective to address implications for an interaction-grammatical treatment of adverbial clauses, (in)subordination, and clause-combining more generally. An interactional grammar should seek to meet, at least, the following requirements:

– **It should explain the *pre- vs post-posing* of adverbial clauses** with regard to the main clause in terms of speakers dealing with interactional issues such as projection and recipiency. Though space has not allowed us to address this point empirically, we know from the literature (Section 2.2) that initial elements (in a turn, in a TCU) project trajectories and possible occurrences of next elements (Deppermann 2013; Schegloff 1987, 1996), while TCU- and turn-ends are sensitive places for dealing with issues of recipiency (Pekarek Doehler et al. 2015; Sacks et al. 1974). Accordingly, pre-posed adverbial clauses can be expected to show substantially different interactional workings than post-posed ones (De Stefani 2021; Lindström et al. 2020).
– **It should account for how structural properties of clause-combining allow for processes of *incremental composition* and *co-construction* and may be motivated by such processes.** These issues are of crucial importance given recent debates about continua of syntactic integration (Section 2.2). Degrees of syntactic integration may materialize in interactional data as co-constructions or incremental composition, and these may be functionally motivated by social-interactional factors. This point again calls for a discussion of how different degrees of autonomy are related not only to different discourse/interactional functions of adverbial clauses, but also — and concomitantly — to their formal on-line emergence in interaction.
– **It should account for how grammar interfaces with *bodily conduct*.** As we have shown, what formally appears as a free-standing (but morphosyntactically marked as subordinate) clause, may in fact be completed by

gestures or vocalizations that 'stand in place' of the 'main' clause. Such occurrences put into question the praxeological autonomy of the apparently free-standing clause, foregrounding instead its pragmatic dependence (often that clause ends on continuing intonation, which also discards the criterion of its prosodic non-integration).

- **It should account for the role of prosody in clause-combining,** and its key importance for differentiating subordination and insubordination, and more generally degrees of syntactic integration (see Section 2.1). The significance of prosodic factors cannot be underestimated in a grammar of interactional language use.

- **Finally, a grammar of interactional language use should centrally engage with continua, clines, and degrees of autonomy,** which put into question the categorial and binary logic that characterizes much grammatical analysis. Just as the examination of naturally occurring language in interaction urges us to attend to temporality as a core feature of grammar, so it invites us to understand the units and fatures of grammar as characterized by family resemblances (Hopper 1987) and continua.

In a nutshell, based on the empirical evidence provided in this study, we argue that the above issues should be addressed in a grammar section on (conditional) clauses and on clause-combining, respectively. Besides the formal properties of (in)subordinate clauses, such a section would need to identify the ways in which speakers use subordinate and insubordinate clauses to accomplish actions. Furthermore, it would need to relate any entry to the fundamental properties of grammar-in-interaction, namely the temporality of grammar as most prominently evidencing in projection and emergence (Auer 2009; Hopper 1987; Mushin & Pekarek Doehler 2021), the accomplishment of social actions (Ochs et al. 1996), and the grammar-body interface (Pekarek Doehler et al. 2022). Finally, such entries might extend to address issues of grammaticalization or pragmaticization by highlighting how speakers' recurrent dealing with social-interactional needs may in turn shape grammar (Couper-Kuhlen 2011; Pekarek Doehler 2021).

The latter point raises a key issue: Not all insubordinate constructions may have followed the same pathways of emergence (Cristofaro 2016; Kaltenböck & Keizer 2022; Mithun 2008; Sørensen 2023). If that is so, to what extent is it necessary, or even adequate, to think of the bi-clausal 'if-then' pattern as a "canonical" or "primary" form from which insubordinate or pseudo-autonomous constructions are derived? An opposite view would be to consider (some of) the insubordinate patterns and the particle-like fragments (Section 3.3.4) as "primary" with regard to the more conventional forms. Some "canonical" bipartite constructions may have emerged and sedimented from recurrent interactional routines (Hopper

2004) as epiphenomena of frequent combinations of fragments in language use. The lack of extended diachronic data of spontaneous interactional language use puts serious limits on the possibility of addressing these questions empirically — at least for the time being.

Acknowledgments

We thank the editors of this volume for their helpful feedback on a prior version of this paper. The research presented here was conducted with the generous support of the Swiss National Science Foundation, grant no. 10001F_214982.

References

Auer, Peter. 2009. "On-line Syntax: Thoughts on the Temporality of Spoken Language." *Language Sciences* 31 (1): 1–13.

Auer, Peter. 2015. "The Temporality of Language in Interaction: Projection and Latency." In *Temporality in Interaction*, ed. by Arnulf Deppermann, and Susanne Günthner, 27–56. Amsterdam: John Benjamins.

Beijering, Karin, Gunther Kaltenböck, and Maria Sol Sansiñena. 2019. *Insubordination: Theoretical and Empirical Issues*. Berlin/Boston: Mouton De Gruyter.

Blanche-Benveniste, Claire. 2010. *Le français: Usages de la langue parlée*. Leuven: Peeters.

Corminboeuf, Gilles. 2010. "Les structures nominales à interprétation hypothétique. Format syntaxique et constantes sémantiques. In *La Parataxe*, vol. 2, ed. by Marie-José Béguelin, Mathieu Avanzi, and Gilles Corminboeuf, 29–46. Berne: Peter Lang.

Corminboeuf, Gilles, and Timon Jahn. 2020. "Taxinomie des constructions en *si* dans un corpus de français oral. L'exemple d'*OFROM.*" *Studia Linguistica Romanica* 4: 195–220.

Couper-Kuhlen, Elizabeth. 2011. "Grammaticalization and conversation." In *The Oxford Handbook of Grammaticalization*, ed. by Heiko Narrog, and Bernd Heine, 424–437. Oxford: Oxford University Press.

Couper-Kuhlen, Elizabeth, and Sandra A. Thompson. 2022. "Can Temporal Clauses be Insubordinate?: Evidence from English Conversation." *Interactional Linguistics* 2 (2): 165–189.

Cristofaro, Sonia. 2016. "Routes to Insubordination. A Cross-Linguistic Perspective." In *Insubordination*, ed. by Nicholas Evans, and Honoré Watanabe, 393–422. Amsterdam/Philadelphia: John Benjamins.

Debaisieux, Jean-Marie, Philippe Martin, and Henri-José Deulofeu. 2019. "Apparent Insubordination as Discourse Patterns in French." In *Insubordination. Theoretical and Empirical Issues*, ed. by Karin Beijering, Gunthner Kaltenböck, and Maria Sol Sansiñena, 349–383. Berlin/Boston: Mouton De Gruyter.

Deppermann, Arnulf. 2013. "Turn-design at Turn-beginnings: Multimodal Resources to Deal with Tasks of Turn-Construction in German." *Journal of Pragmatics* 46 (1): 91–121.

De Stefani, Elwys. 2021. "*If*-clauses, their Grammatical Consequents, and their Embodied Consequence: Organizing Joint Attention in Guided Tours." *Frontiers in Communication* 6.

Diessel, Holger. 2001. "The Ordering Distribution of Main and Adverbial Clauses: A Typological Study". *Language* 77: 433–55.

Diessel, Holger. 2008. "Iconicity of Sequence: A corpus-based Analysis of the Positioning of Temporal Adverbial Clauses in English." *Cognitive Linguistics* 19 (3): 465–490.

Evans, Nicholas. 2007. "Insubordination and its Uses." In *Finiteness: Theoretical and Empirical Foundations*, ed. by Irina Nikolaeva, 366–431. Oxford: Oxford University Press.

Evans, Nicholas, and Honoré Watanabe. 2016. *Insubordination*. Amsterdam: Benjamins.

Ford, Cecilia E. 1993. *Grammar in Interaction: Adverbial Clauses in American English Conversations*. Cambridge: Cambridge University Press.

Ford, Cecilia E., Barbara A. Fox, and Sandra A. Thompson. 2002. "Constituency and the Grammar of Turn Increments." In *The Language of Turn and Sequence*, ed. by Cecilia E. Ford, Barbara A. Fox, and Sandra A. Thompson, 14–38. Oxford: Oxford University Press.

Ford, Cecilia E., and Sandra A. Thompson. 1986. "Conditionals in Discourse: A Text-based Study from English." In *On Conditionals*, ed. by Elizabeth C. Traugott, 353–372. Cambridge: Cambridge University Press.

Goodwin, Charles. 2007. "Environmentally coupled gestures." In *Gesture and the dynamic dimension of language*, ed. by Susan Duncan, Justine Cassell, and Elena Levy, 195–212. Amsterdam: John Benjamins.

Gras, Pedro, and Maria Sol Sansiñena. 2015. "An Interactional Account of Discourse-Connective Que-Constructions in Spanish." *Text & Talk* 35 (4): 505–529.

Günthner, Susanne. 2020. "Practices of Clause-Combining: From Complex *Wenn*-Constructions to Insubordinate ('stand-alone') Conditionals in Everyday Spoken German." In *Emergent Syntax for Conversation: Clausal patterns and the Organization of Action*, ed. by Yaël Maschler, Simona Pekarek Doehler, Jan Lindström, and Leelo Keevallik, 185–220. Amsterdam: John Benjamins.

Haiman, John, and Sandra A. Thompson. 1984. "Clause Combining in Grammar and Discourse." *Typological Studies in Language* 18: 275–330.

Heine, Bernd, Gunthner Kaltenböck, and Tania Kuteva. 2016. "On Insubordination and Cooptation". In *Insubordination*, ed. by Nicholas Evans, and Honoré Watanabe, 39–64. Amsterdam: John Benjamins.

Hilpert, Martin. 2015. "Kollaborative Insubordination in gesprochenem Englisch: Konstruktion oder Umgang mit Konstruktionen?" In *Konstruktionsgrammatik IV. Konstruktionen als soziale Konventionen und kognitive Routinen*, ed. by Alexander Ziem, and Alexander Lasch, 25–40. Tübingen: Stauffenburg.

Hopper, Paul J. 1987. "Emergent Grammar." *Proceedings of the Thirteenth Annual Meeting of the Berkeley Linguistics Society* 13: 139–157.

Hopper, Paul J. 2004. "The Openness of Grammatical Constructions." *Chicago Linguistic Society* 40: 239–256.

Horlacher, Anne-Sylvie. 2021. "Compound and Independent If-Clauses at the Hairdresser's: Negotiating the Procedures of the Treatment." *17th International Pragmatics Conference* 27 June–2 July 2021, Winterthur, Switzerland.

Horlacher, Anne-Sylvie. 2022. "Negative Requests within Hair Salons: Grammar and Embodiment in Action Formation." *Frontiers in Psychology* 12.

Horlacher, Anne-Sylvie, and Simona Pekarek Doehler. 2014. "Pivotage in French Talk-in-interaction: On the Emergent Nature of [Clause-NP-Clause] Pivots." *Pragmatics* 24 (3): 593–622.

Horlacher, Anne-Sylvie, and Simona Pekarek Doehler. 2022. "'Si vous avez quelqu'un sous la main': les si-indépendantes en tant que format de requête." *Langue française* 216 (4): 47–61.

Jefferson, Gail. 1990. "List-Construction as a Task and a Resource." In *Interaction Competence*, ed. by George Psathas, 63–92. Washington D.C.: University Press of America.

Kaltenböck, Gunthner. 2019. "Delimiting the Class: A Typology of English Insubordination." In *Insubordination: Theoretical and Empirical Issues*, ed. by Karin Beijering, Gunthner Kaltenböck, and Maria Sol Sansiñena, 167–198. Berlin/Boston: Mouton De Gruyter.

Kaltenböck, Gunther, and Evelien Keizer. 2022. "Insubordinate *if*-clauses in FDG: Degrees of independence." *Open Linguistics* 8: 675–698.

Lastres-López, Cristina. 2018. "If-Insubordination in Spoken British English: Syntactic and Pragmatic Properties." *Language Sciences* 66: 42–59.

Laury, Ritva. 2012. "Syntactically Non-integrated Finnish jos 'If'-Conditional Clauses as Directives." *Discourse Processes* 49: 213–242.

Lehmann, Christian. 1988. "Towards a Typology of Clause Linkage." In *Clause combining in grammar and discourse*, ed. by John Haiman, and Sandra A. Thompson, 181–225. Amsterdam: John Benjamins.

Lerner, Gene H. 1991. "On the Syntax of Sentences-in-Progress." *Language in Society* 20: 441–458.

Lerner, Gene H. 2004. "On the Place of Linguistic Resources in the Organization of Talk-in-Interaction: Grammar as Action in Prompting a Speaker to Elaborate." *Research on Language and Social Interaction* 37 (2): 151–185.

Lindström, Jan, Camilla Lindholm, and Ritva Laury. 2016. "The Interactional Emergence of Conditional Clauses as Directives: Constructions, Trajectories and Sequences of Actions." *Language Science* 58: 8–21.

Lindström, Jan, Ritva Laury, and Camilla Lindholm. 2019. "Insubordination and the Contextually Sensitive Emergence of *If*-Requests in Swedish and Finnish Institutional Talk-in-Interaction." In *Insubordination: Theoretical and Empirical Issues*, ed. by Karin Beijering, Gunthner Kaltenböck, and Maria Sol Sansiñena, 55–78. Berlin/Boston: Mouton De Gruyter.

Lindström, Jan, Camilla Lindholm, Inga-Lill Grahn, and Martina Huhtamäki. 2020. "Consecutive Clause Combinations in Instructing Activities. Directives and Accounts in the Context of Physical Training." In *Emergent Syntax for Conversation: Clausal Patterns and the Organization of Action*, ed. by Yaël Maschler, Simona Pekarek Doehler, Jan Lindström, and Leelo Keevallik, 245–274. Amsterdam: John Benjamins.

Lombardi Vallauri, Eduardo. 2016. "Insubordinated Conditionals in Spoken and Non-Spoken Italian." In *Insubordination*, ed. by Nicholas Evans and Honoré Watanabe, 145–170. Amsterdam: John Benjamins.

Maschler, Yaël. 2020. "The Insubordinate — Subordinate Continuum, Prosody, Embodied Action, and the Emergence of Hebrew Complex Syntax." In *Emergent Syntax for Conversation: Clausal Patterns and the Organization of Action*, ed. by Yaël Maschler, Simona Pekarek Doehler, Jan Lindström, and Leelo Keevallik, 87–126. Amsterdam: John Benjamins.

Mithun, Marianne. 2008. "The Extension of Dependency beyond the Sentence." *Language* 84 (1): 69–119.

Mondada, Lorenza. 2018. "Multiple Temporalities of Language and Body in Interaction: Challenges for transcribing multimodality." *Research on Language and Social Interaction* 51 (1): 85–106.

Mushin, Ilana, and Simona Pekarek Doehler. 2021. "Linguistic Structures in Social Interaction: Moving Temporality to the Forefront of a Science of Language." *Interactional Linguistics* 1 (1): 2–32.

Ochs, Elinor, Emanuel Schegloff, and Sandra A. Thompson. 1996. *Interaction and Grammar*. Cambridge: Cambridge University Press.

Ogden, Richard. 2013. "Clicks and Percussives in English Conversation." *Journal of the International Phonetic Association* 43 (3): 299–320.

Patard, Adeline. 2014. "Réflexions sur l'origine de l'insubordination. Le cas de trois insubordonnées hypothétiques du français." *Langages* 196, 109–130. .

Pekarek Doehler, Simona. 2021. "How Grammar Grows out of Social Interaction: From Multi-Unit to Single-Unit Question." *Open Linguistics* 7 (1): 837–864.

Pekarek Doehler, Simona, Elwys De Stefani, and Anne-Sylvie Horlacher. 2015. *Time and Emergence in Grammar. Left-Dislocation, Right-Dislocation, Topicalization and Hanging Topic in French Talk-in-Interaction*. Amsterdam: John Benjamins.

Pekarek Doehler, Simona, Leelo Keevallik, and Xiaoting Li. 2022. "The Grammar-Body Interface in Social Interaction". *Frontiers in Psychology*, 1–3.

Sacks, Harvey, Emanuel Schegloff, and Gail Jefferson. 1974. "A Simplest Systematics for the Organization of Turn-Taking in Conversation." *Language* 50: 696–735.

Sansiñena, Maria Sol. 2019. "Patterns of (In)dependence." In *Insubordination: Theoretical and Empirical Issues*, ed. by Karin Beijering, Gunthner Kaltenböck, and Maria Sol Sansiñena, 199–239. Berlin/Boston: De Gruyter.

Schegloff, Emanuel A. 1987. "Recycled Turn Beginnings: A Precise Repair Mechanism in Conversation's Turn-taking Organization." In *Talk and Social Organisation*, ed. by Graham Button, and John R. E. Lee, 70–85. Clevedon, England: Multilingual Matters.

Schegloff, Emanuel A. 1996. "Turn Organization: One Intersection of Grammar and Interaction." In *Interaction and grammar*, ed. by Elinor Ochs, Emanuel A. Schegloff, and Sandra A. Thompson, 52–133. Cambridge: Cambridge University Press.

Schegloff, Emanuel A. 2016. "Increments." In *Accountability in Social Interaction*, ed. by Jeffrey D. Robinson, 239–263. Oxford: Oxford University Press.

Sørensen, Søren S. 2023. "Exclamative Clauses with *hvor, hvilken* and *sikke* in Danish: Insubordination and Phrasal Discontinuity." *Skrifter om Samtalegrammatik* 9 (1). https://samtalegrammatik.dk/fileadmin/samtalegrammatik/sos/9/Soerensen_2023_Exclamative _clauses_in_Danish_with_hvor_hvilken_and_sikke.pdf.

Stivers, Tanya, and Federico Rossano. 2010. "Mobilizing response." *Research on Language and Social Interaction* 43 (1): 3–31.

Sweetser, Eve. 1990. *From Etymology to Pragmatics: Metaphorical and Cultural Aspects of Semantic Structure*. Cambridge: Cambridge University Press.

Thompson, Sandra A., Robert E. Longacre, and Shin J. Hwang. 2007. "Adverbial Clauses." In *Language Typology and Syntactic Description*, ed. by Timothy Shopen, 237–300. Cambridge: Cambridge University Press.

Van Valin, Robert. 1984. "A Typology of Syntactic Relations in Clause Linkage." *Proceedings of the Tenth Annual Meeting of the Berkeley Linguistics Society*: 542–558.

Vorreiter, Susanne. 2003. "Turn-continuations: Towards a Cross-Linguistic Classification." *Interaction and Linguistic Structures* 39: 1–26. http://www.inlist.uni-bayreuth.de/issues/39/Inlist39.pdf

CHAPTER 12

Action formation, projection, and participation framework
Pseudoclefts in Swedish talk-in-interaction

Sofie Henricson & Jan Lindström
University of Helsinki

This chapter discusses the structural, interactional and situational specifics of the pseudocleft construction in Swedish talk-in-interaction, specifying its use as a resource for turn and action formation but also as a means to regulate discursive trajectories and the participation framework. An analysis of nearly 100 instances of pseudoclefts collected from casual conversations and institutional interactions revealed that this format is a recognizable and conventionally available building block of interaction exhibiting a regular grammatical pattern which can be characterized as a compound turn constructional unit. The pseudocleft is used for discourse organization in marking transitions in the pragmatic course of an interaction. This gives the construction a projecting force on the level of sequence organization. Our analysis illustrates that pseudoclefts are not dedicated to accomplishing one single kind of action but typically contribute to the formation of directive-commissive and evaluative actions. The pseudoclefts in our datasets were often used by participants to claim an expert position. This implies a rather strong link between the grammatical format and the participation framework in which the format casts one of the participants as possibly more knowledgeable and as the one who controls the agenda, has the right to direct others, and to make assessments.

Keywords: action formation, discourse organization, grammar-in-action, participation framework, projection, pseudocleft, Swedish, talk-in-interaction, turn design

1. Introduction

One important aspect of action formation is how speakers design their contributions for their recipients — the selection of linguistic forms for building turns and implementing actions in talk-in-interaction (see Couper-Kuhlen & Selting 2018,

https://doi.org/10.1075/slsi.37.12hen
© 2025 John Benjamins Publishing Company

554). Recipient design is attuned to what the relationship is between interactants, what the recipient knows and what the interactants know in common (Drew 2018; Heritage & Raymond 2005). The scope of recipient design also includes what is projected to be newsworthy in the speaker's contribution and its pragmatic valence, whether it is positive or negative. This chapter deals with these issues by concentrating on one particular type of grammatical resource which is associated with turn projection and stance taking, the pseudocleft construction (see e.g. Hopper & Thompson 2008; Maschler, Lindström & De Stefani 2023; Tao 2022).

The chapter presents pseudoclefts from the perspective of turn and sequence organization, unveiling recurrent links between grammatical form and social action. We also demonstrate that this grammatical format appears noticeably often in social situations that feature a characteristic participation framework and linguistic register (see e.g. Argyle et al. 1981 on social situations), which points to the relevance of this format in establishing speaker identities at the level of activity type.

The data on pseudoclefts for this analysis were excerpted from several corpora of Swedish talk-in-interaction (see Appendix), and the result was a collection of 92 instances of pseudoclefts.[1] The datasets covered three main types of setting: (1) ordinary conversations among friends and family members (23 instances of pseudoclefts), (2) arranged but casual discussions in focus groups (20 instances), and (3) institutional interactions between a novice and expert (49 instances). The distribution of instances across different interactional settings and the size of the datasets is illustrated in Table 1.

Table 1. The distribution of pseudoclefts in three types of interactional setting

Type of setting	Recording time	Occurrences
Ordinary conversation	16 hrs	23
Focus groups	43 hrs	20
Institutional interaction	17 hrs	49
Total	76 hrs	92

The figures in Table 1 suggest that the institutionality of the setting has a certain bearing on the use of pseudoclefts.

We present transcribed excerpts from our datasets, both in short linguistic *examples* culled from the data to make specific grammatical points (in Section 2.1) and in longer interactional *extracts* (referred to as "Examples" or "Extracts" and

---

1. Our actual collection is larger than this, but we report here only instances which were identified through a systematic scanning of datasets.

numbered separately) to display sequential and discursive structure. Our grammatical target phenomenon is indicated with gray highlighting. The speakers have granted their informed consent to participate in the actual recordings to be used for research purposes. However, to assure anonymity, the names of the participants and other similar kinds of details have been pseudonymized.

2. Turn design

Pseudoclefts, which are also referred to as WH-clefts, have attracted considerable interest in grammatical research owing to their structural complexity, which in turn has been related to functional motivations such as information structure (see Maschler et al. 2023). The central structural account in the linguistic tradition is that pseudoclefts constitute a complex sentence, basically a bi-clausal unit, which expresses a single proposition. An example of this is *What I usually notice is the language* ~ 'I usually notice the language' (see Lambrecht 2001). From the perspective of talk-in-interaction, pseudoclefts represent complexity in the domain of turn design because they often result in turn constructional units that are lengthy. The resulting unit could be considered one special type of compound TCUs, that is, consisting of a preliminary TCU component that projects a final TCU component (cf. Lerner 1996 on *if–then* units).

When examining the output in spoken interactions, we can observe certain micro-variation in the syntactic structuring of Swedish pseudoclefts, as not all of them are prototypically bi-clausal (or neatly compound TCUs). Rather, they emerge out of constructional fragments. These ultimately may either resemble pseudoclefts that are canonical, written-language-like, or remain as looser compositions consisting of the initial, contribution-framing TCU component followed by some structurally indeterminate talk (see Hopper & Thompson 2008 for English).

Prosody contributes to the packaging of the constituent parts in structurally compound pseudoclefts: speakers appear to project a constructional and informational continuity until a recognizable syntactic and pragmatic endpoint is reached at the completion of the final component of the format (Lindström, Henricson & Huhtamäki 2022). However, pseudoclefts may contain short pauses, and typically they either follow the format's initial component or occur immediately before the beginning of the final component, thus following the copula verb. Such segmentation phenomena suggest that speakers tend to produce certain prosodic cues to mark the places that constitute the major parts of the turn format, that is, its preliminary and final component; this can make the constituency of the turn unit more transparent for the listener as its construction progresses.

2.1 Grammatical structure

2.1.1 *Standard structure*

Swedish is a typical Germanic V2 language with the basic word order of XVS for declaratives. This means that the order of constituents is rather fixed apart from the initial X position which can include the subject, the object or diverse adverbial constituents to achieve certain textual or focal effects. Various cleft constructions contribute to the variability in the order of the information that is presented in a sentence. The specialty of pseudoclefts is that they place the most important part of information at the end of the sentential unit (see 2.2 below). However, Swedish and Scandinavian grammatical accounts have somewhat overlooked pseudoclefts (for example, see Svenonius 1998). This may be due to pseudoclefts being used less frequently than IT-clefts, which are aptly termed "ordinary" clefts in the Swedish grammatical tradition (Teleman, Hellberg & Andersson 1999).

To illustrate the basic structure of Swedish pseudoclefts, let us turn to Example (1).[2]

Example 1.

va ja inte gillar e hennes nasala röst som e lite för jobbig
what I NEG like.PRS be.PRS her nasal.DEF voice that be.PRS little too disturbing
'what I don't like is her nasal voice that is a bit too disturbing'

Resembling the pseudocleft in English, the Swedish construction is initiated by a nominal relative clause that is introduced by a free (or headless) relative, the pronoun *va(d)* 'what': *va ja inte gillar* 'what I don't like'. This initial clause is what we refer to as Part A of the construction, or a preliminary component of a compound TCU. This part is followed by the copula verb *e* (*är*) 'is', and its tense corresponds to the tense of Part A (in Example (1), the present tense). The final component, Part B, is a noun phrase, *hennes nasala röst* 'her nasal voice', also referred to as the "cleft constituent" in the English tradition (for the terms, see De Cesare 2014).

Although pseudoclefts introduced by the pronoun *vad* 'what' have structural affinity to English, in our data, these are in the minority with only 14 out of 92 instances. The most typical pronominal introducer of Part A is instead a combination of the demonstrative *det* 'it, that' and the relativizer *som* 'that, which' functioning as a headed relative, *de(t) som* 'that (thing) which', as in Example (2). In research on English, these types of variants are identified as TH-clefts belonging to a subset of pseudoclefts (see Collins 1991).

---

2. The examples cited in subsections 2.1.1 and 2.1.2 are culled from our data, but they are taken out of their sequential context and the transcription is simplified.

Example 2.

de som stör   mej mest e   att hon ha   gått å sagt   åt mej
that REL disturb.PRS I.OBJ most be.PRS that she have.PRS go.PRF and say.PRF to I.OBJ
att ja e   helt jätteirriterad
that I be.PRS quite super.irritated
'the thing that (i.e. what) disturbs me most is that she's (curtly) told me that I'm
super irritated'

Here Part B consists of a nominal clause initiated by the complementizer *att* 'that':
att hon ha gått å sagt åt mig... 'that she's told me...'. This latter part of the construction can also contain a clause that is infinitival or even adverbial. The standard structure of Swedish pseudoclefts is illustrated schematically in Table 2.

Table 2. Schematic structure of the Swedish pseudocleft

Pseudocleft construction		
Part A	**Copula verb**	**Part B**
Cleft clause		**Cleft constituent**
vad ja inte gillar		*hennes nasala röst...*
'what I don't like'	*e*	'her nasal voice...'
de som stör mej mest	'is'	*att hon ha gått å sagt åt mej...*
'the thing that disturbs me most'		'that she's told me...'

When the headed relative does not represent the subject of the relative clause in Part A, the relativizer *som* can be understood and left unexpressed (Example (3)). Conversely, if the free relative *va(d)* is the subject of the relative clause, the relativizer *som* must be added as a subject placeholder (Example (4)).

Example 3.

de ja fundera   ännu va   just media
that I wonder.PST still be.PST PRT media
'what I still wondered (about) was the media'

Example 4.

va   som också hände   va   att du faktiskt tog   ifrån Vera tre
what REL also happen.PST be.PST that you actually take.PST from Vera three
poäng
point.PL
'what also happened was that you actually took three points from Vera'

This lack of relativizer as well as the need to insert a subject placeholder in some cases also apply to Swedish relative clauses in general.

2.1.2 Structural variation

The standard pseudocleft construction illustrated in Table 2 can be varied in impromptu speech, either with the addition of some items or omission of others. In one type of expanding, Part A is a syntactically loose element which is followed by a full clause introduced by a pronoun that is co-referential with Part A, as in Example (5):

Example 5.
de som kommer närmast i Finland de e   City
that REL come.PRS close.SUP in Finland it.N be.PRS City
'what gets closest (to it) in Finland, it is City'

This speaker is commenting on the profile of a Helsinki local radio station, *Radio City*. As Part A (*de som kommer närmast i Finland*) stands outside of the following clausal unit *de e City* ('it is City'), the resulting compound unit resembles a left dislocation.

One fairly typical omission concerns the copula verb 'to be', which is a short, unstressed monosyllabic word, with only the vowel *e* [e] in the present-tense form. The tendency to "drop" the copula (cf. Sørensen this volume) may be higher when the pseudocleft is produced in one go and the word completing Part A ends with a vowel and the word initiating Part B begins with a vowel. This is illustrated in Example (6), where Part A ends with the particle *på* 'on' while Part B begins with the complementizer *att* 'that':

Example 6.
de som ja också ha   reagera på att di oftast e   jättetjocka
that REL I also have.PRS react.PRF on that they usually be.PRS very.fat
'what I have also reacted to (is) that they are usually very fat'

At this point, the speaker is commenting on the appearance of a certain category of people. The pseudocleft is produced rapidly in one coherent intonation unit.

More radical types of omission occur when Part A is not followed by a regular Part B but a syntactically loose stretch of talk of some indeterminate length (see also Hopper & Thompson 2008; Koops & Hilpert 2009). One example is provided in Excerpt (1) from a conversation between Leo and Ida, who are planning to video a dance performance. In line 1, Leo's turn begins with something that resembles a typical Part A of a pseudocleft (*va vi sku kunna göra* 'what we could do') followed by the copula *e* and the complementizer *att* 'that', which would project a clausal Part B.

Excerpt 1. *va vi sku kunna göra* 'what we could do' (EGS:EC:2P:02), everyday
conversation

```
01 LEO: .h så (.) dehä va (.) va  vi sku      kunna  göra
            SO    PRT  what  what we shall.PST can.INF do.INF
        .h so (.) um what (.) what we could do
02      e      att .h att ehh hh här e    dehä,
        be.PRS that   that        here be.PRS this
        is that .h that um hh here's this,
03      (1.3)
04      .hh phh dehä mm (0.5)
        .hh phh this mm (0.5)
05      pt .hh okej vi väljer en biisi?
        pt .hh okay we choose a song?
06      (0.6)
07 IDA: ja:
        yes
08      (0.7)
09 LEO: som (0.6) e såhä lång?
        which (0.6) is this long?
10      (0.6)
11      å:, (0.7) sen har den olika delar i sej
        and, (0.7) then it's got different parts
```

Leo is proposing a plan for making the video, launching his suggestion with a
potential Part A of a pseudocleft. In line 2, the progression of this talk halts,
indicated by the repetition of the complementizer *att* 'that', a hesitation sound
(*ehh*) and an out-breath. What follows does not fit the syntactic projection of a
complementizer-initiated Part B. Instead, he produces a fragment of a new clausal
start, *här e dehä* 'here's this', which is nonetheless abandoned after pauses, repetitions, and hesitation sounds. In line 5, Leo uses the particle *okej* 'okay' to resume
his turn, as he begins to lay out his plan with a straight declarative clause: *vi väljer
en biisi* 'we choose a song'.

In our data we also encounter variants that have a potential Part A but have
neither a follow-up with the copula nor complementizer. These cases are related
to those "stranded" A-parts we observed in Excerpt (1) but appear even more
clearly as turn-framing fragments. This lends them a status of a meta-pragmatic
marker, such as *de ja skulle säja* 'what I was going to say' as an introduction to a
continued telling (see Lindström, Henricson & Huhtamäki 2022).

2.2 Information structure and projection

Speakers can construct their turns differently, depending on what they want their recipient to take note of. Swedish resembles English in the general placing of given, thematic information at the beginning of a sentential unit while new information tends to lie at the end. This unmarked structuring of information can be modified through contrastive stress or by changing word order (for example, see Myrberg 2013; Myrberg & Riad 2016; Vallduví & Engdahl 1996). In addition, certain grammatical constructions, like existential sentences or the passive voice, can be understood as a means for dealing with information structure. Various cleft constructions are certainly one further resource to manipulate the information structure (Lambrecht 2001). In fact, the family of cleft constructions itself includes variation in where new or contrasting information is placed: it can occur initially, medially or finally in the complex sentence (De Cesare 2014: 38; Lambrecht 2001: 467). The pseudocleft represents the type where new or contrasting information appears at the end, such as *Vad jag inte gillar är hennes nasala röst* 'What I don't like is her nasal voice', that is, the last constituent "her nasal voice" is highlighted.

From the perspective of talk-in-interaction, the analysis accounting for information structure can be related to the concept of projection. This involves creating expectations for the further development of the emerging utterance (see Auer 2009: 4). As the pseudocleft is basically a bipartite structure, this format has an effective syntactic projection in that once the preliminary component (Part A) has been produced, there is a strong prediction of an upcoming final component (Part B) that fulfills the projection. This is relevant for predicting of a possible turn completion point, which becomes strengthened at the completion of the final TCU component. In addition, pseudoclefts effectively project the pragmatic course of the speaker's contribution. The initial component works somewhat like a pre-announcement, for example of the speaker's stance, and it projects a final component that expresses something noteworthy in relation to the context of speaking. An example of this would be expressing what is wrong with the singing of the artist discussed in Example (1) (revealed in its sequential context in Excerpt (4) below).

Languages differ in their frequency and certain structural details in formatting turns with pseudoclefts (see Maschler et al. 2023). For example, rather than initiating a construction with an interrogative item of the English WH-type, some languages use a demonstrative pronoun in that position (such as *ce que/qui* in French, *quello che* in Italian) or other morpho-syntactic cues (such as in Mandarin; see Tao 2022). As regards frequency, the pseudocleft seems sufficiently common in English and French while it is considered rarer in Swedish and Scandinavian grammatical accounts (for example, see Svenonius 1998), and it is even rarer in Finnic languages (see Ammon & Keevallik 2022 on Estonian). Reasons for these differences may be related to the tendency for languages to using varied word-orders when adjusting information structure. For example, Swedish speakers can deploy the XVS pattern and in this manner have more options than English speakers, who rather consistently prefer the SVO order in declaratives. However, as we will demonstrate in this chapter, a comparatively less frequent use of a construction does not imply unstructured patterns in actual use. Structured patterns arise in turn design, sequential positioning, and in the interactional functions associated with Swedish pseudoclefts.

3. Sequence and action formation

Pseudocleft constructions have the potential to work on both micro and macro syntactic levels of discourse (Auer 2009; Günthner 2011; Hopper & Thompson 2008; Maschler & Fishman 2020; Pekarek Doehler 2011). In other words, this construction is a resource for an *internal syntax*, dealing with the organization of the turn, and an *external syntax* to organize sequences of action and sections of discourse (see Anward & Nordberg 2005:6; Fillmore 1988:36; Jørgensen this volume; Steensig this volume). In relation to this twofold interactional motivation, in the following we will discuss how pseudoclefts are used to launch and implement specific types of actions (Fox 2007, see also Couper-Kuhlen 2014; Steensig et al. 2023). These include advice-giving and making judgements (3.1) as well as to create discursive transitions that change the speaker's perspective or aspects in topic progression during the ongoing interaction (3.2).

3.1 Accomplishing directive-commissive and evaluative social actions

Studies on the uses of pseudoclefts in talk-in-interaction report that they play specific roles in projecting and framing upcoming talk. In other words, they contribute to a certain type of social action, such as expressing speaker stance, highlighting a point, or launching a suggestion (Hopper & Thompson 2008; Maschler et al. 2023; Pekarek Doehler 2011). More specifically, Part A of the construction projects the pragmatic course of the upcoming Part B. An example of this concerns whether the speaker expresses either a positive or a negative stance. An initial framing with a speaker's negative stance was observed in the short Examples (1) and (2) above, and a similarly negative-leaning framing of the speaker's contribution occurs in Excerpt (2) below.

Chapter 12. Action formation, projection, and participation framework **375**

Excerpt (2) is from an undergraduate seminar in which a student assumes the local institutional role as the opponent and consequently comments on a thesis written by a fellow student. The opponent (OPP) leads the discussion and the respondent (RES), the student who has written the thesis under discussion, responds to the opponent's comments and elaborates on them. The excerpt displays a sequence in which the opponent comments on the language, which is generally assessed as *lite knaggligt ibland* 'a little uneven at times' (line 3). The opponent then proceeds to specify which linguistic feature he perceives as particularly disturbing in the text, construing this shift from the prior general evaluation to a description of specifics through the pseudocleft in lines 4–5. The pseudocleft constitutes a prototypical example in our data, that is a syntactically and prosodically coherent unit with the typical Swedish relative introducer *det som* 'that (thing) which'.

Excerpt 2. *de som ja tycker att e svårast* 'what I find most difficult' (IVIP_LFIN-SEM:01), thesis seminar

```
01 RES: [ja h]
         yeah h

02 OPP: [s-  ] språke som du skrev så de e de e (.)
         l- the language as you wrote it's it's (.)

03      lite knaggligt ibland så där å som, (0.4)
         a bit stumbling at times sort of and like, (0.4)

04      de  som ja tycker   att e     svårast
         that REL I  think.PRS that be.PRS difficult.SUP
         what I find most difficult

05      e     de  att du skriver i passivform
         be.PRS that that you write.PRS in passive.form
         is that you write in passive voice

06      å jag vet att de (0.3) att de e tra- tradition
         and I know that it (0.3) that it's tra- tradition

07      att man ska göra så de e de e liksom, (1.1)
         that you're supposed to do so it's it's like (1.1)

08      de e många som säger att, (0.7)
         there are many who say that, (0.7)

09      att att de att de e de enda rätta men
         that that it that it's the only right way but

10      de leder till att texten blir (0.4) jättetung
         it makes the text (0.4) really heavy

11      då på sina ställen att här på sidan sjutton
         then at some parts that here on page seventeen

12      så har du att (0.6) vid intervjun me brukargruppen
         you say (0.6) at the interview with the user group

13      var det ibland tvunget att ge exempel (0.3)
         it was sometimes necessary to give examples (0.3)
```

14   å liksom, (0.9) sånt e (0.6) sånt ger ett (0.4)
       and like, (0.9) these are (0.6) these give a (0.4)
15   sånhänt lite frå- frånvarande intryck å,
       kind of a little abs- absent impression and,
16 RES: m+m

While the first assessment (lines 2–3) is formulated as a general statement of the style of the text reinforced by the respondent's own observations, the assessment launched by the pseudocleft is framed as the opponent's stance on the same topic (lines 4–5). The actual shift from a descriptive account to an assessment framed as the speaker's stance is launched through Part A of the pseudocleft, *de som ja tycker att e svårast* 'what I think is most disturbing' (line 4), which conveys that the speaker is about to express a negative evaluation of an aspect of the text under discussion. Part A thus serves a clear projecting function: the upcoming talk will specify which aspects of the respondent's text are difficult and disturbing. Through its projecting force, Part A reserves the floor until Part B is produced, which in this case occurs directly after Part A. In Part B, then, the opponent points out that he considers the major linguistic challenge of the text to be the passive constructions (line 5), a point that the opponent further elaborates on during the talk that follows in lines 6–15.

This pseudocleft therefore introduces a point that is considered worthy of attention, frames it as the speaker's stance, and establishes the ground for an expansion on the speaker's critique. The social action performed by the pseudocleft is assessment, as it conveys the speaker's critique of a feature of the text under discussion. Simultaneously, the inference of the critique is directive in this specific institutional setting, as the opponent offers the respondent suggestions on how to improve future versions of the text.

Excerpt (3) includes a pseudocleft that constitutes another type of action projection, that of launching a piece of advice. This excerpt is from a tutorial where a counselor (COU) and a student (STU) discuss an academic text that the student is currently working on. The counselor and the student are seated at the same table and the discussion is supported by a printout of the text, which the counselor actively uses while reviewing the comments. The pseudocleft in lines 17–20 marks a transition where the counselor shifts from a positive assessment of the textual structure to offering suggestions on what the student should consider while developing the text further, so that it will be coherent throughout.

Chapter 12. Action formation, projection, and participation framework **377**

Excerpt 3. *de som du kan fundera på* 'what you can think about' (IVIP_LFIN-SHA:03, video), text tutorial

```
01 COU: e- eventuellt om du vill (.) så kan man ju
        p- perhaps if you want to (.) it's possible to

02      ännu också här sen då summera på nåt sätt,
        also like here then summarize in some way,

03      (0.6)

04 STU  [jå+å    ]
        yeah

05 COU  [de här,]
        this,

06      (0.3)

07 STU  jag tror nog att jag kommer att ännu
        I think that I'm still going to

08      lägga till text,
        add some more text,

09 COU  precis,
        exactly,

10 STU  [här] så att [(ännu),]
        here so that (still),

11 COU  [jå ]        [jå    ]
        yeah          yeah

12 COU  men annars de här e ju liksom så här modellexemplet
        but otherwise this is like the model example

13 STU  jå+å,
        yeah,

14 COU  på välstrukturerad,
        of a well-structured (text),

15      (0.5)

16 STU  o[kej]
        okay

17 COU  [e:h] de   som du kan    fundera  på
               that REL you can.PRS think.INF on
        uh what you can think about

18      e    ju sen hur du gör (0.4) mt me   de här (0.3)
        be.PRS PRT then how you do.PRS        with this (0.3)
        is then how you do (0.4) this (0.3)

19      f-få   den här röda    tråden    å  å (0.4)
        get.INF this    red.DEF thread.DEF and and
        keep to the point and and (0.4)
```

```
20      [få    de] här övergångarna     mellan stycken
        get.INF these  transition.PL.DEF between paragraph.PL
        make the transitions between paragraphs
21 STU  [mm     ]
22 COU  då när du (0.5) int har (.) den här färdiga
        when you (0.5) don't have (.) this prepared
23      [ett två] tre strukturen,
        one two three structure,
24 STU  [jå+å    ]
        yeah
25 STU  *jå*
        yeah
```

The pseudocleft in lines 17–20 initiates an expansion of a sequence regarding the structure of the student's text. In this sequence, the counselor and the student discuss different aspects of this topic, a discussion that is summarized by the counselor's exceedingly positive overall evaluation of the text (lines 12 and 14: *modellexemplet på välstrukturerad (text)* 'a model example of a well-structured (text)'. The student expresses acknowledgement by stating *okej* 'okay' in line 16. The counselor uses the pseudocleft to move on from the prior summary evaluation to advise her student on how to continue revising the text. During most of the pseudocleft production, the counselor gazes directly towards the text under discussion. However, towards the end of the long Part B, when the counselor emphasizes the textual context where the advice becomes relevant, *när du int har den här färdiga ett två tre strukturen* 'when you don't have this prepared one-two-three structure' (lines 22–23), she turns her gaze towards her student.

Part A of the pseudocleft is produced as a prosodic unit and is followed by a weak prosodic break (cf. Barth-Weingarten 2016). This occurs before the counselor continues with Part B, in which she mentions the aspects to consider in other types of textual contexts. Part A of the pseudocleft, *de som du kan fundera på* 'what you can think about', projects a discursive transition (see 3.2), from the counselor's preceding praise of the text to something needing critical attention. At the same time, Part A projects the directive-commissive action of advising the student on how to improve the text in the future. The student accepts the advice by uttering short compliance markers (lines 24–25), which she produces while nodding and smiling.

To summarize the analysis of Excerpts (2) and (3), a grammatical description that takes into account different levels of conversational organization can include pseudoclefts as a structural resource for performing certain types of social actions in interaction. In particular, this includes directive-commissive actions (see Couper-Kuhlen 2014) such as suggestions, and evaluative actions, such as assessing and judging. Although suggesting and advice-giving are explicitly directive-

Chapter 12. Action formation, projection, and participation framework 379

commissive, also assessing acts, in particular those involving criticism, can be inferred to be directing in the context of a counseling activity. For these, the overall aim of the interaction is to offer the non-expert suggestions on how to improve their performance or task.

3.2 Initiating discursive transitions

As regards sequence and discourse organization, the pseudocleft format marks points of transition (for example, see Günthner 2006; Henricson & Lindström 2020a; Kim 1995). These types of transitions contribute to a frame shift into something divergent from the preceding talk (cf. Maschler 1997). Typical transitory shifts pertain to expressing speaker stance which often involves a change from a positive stance to a more negative or critical one (Henricson & Lindström 2020a; Lindström et al. 2022; Maschler et al. 2023), as in Excerpt (3) above.

Excerpt (4) illustrates how a speaker uses a pseudocleft in line 6 (previously discussed in Example (1)) for this type of polarity shift. This excerpt is from a group discussion in which the participants are evaluating musical styles, where assessments and expressing speaker stance constitute an overarching thread in the interaction. In this sequence, the assessment regards a song by the Swedish singer-songwriter Lisa Ekdahl.

Excerpt 4. *va ja inte gillar* 'what I don't like' (GSM:01), focus group

```
01 TOM: mm (.) väldigt eh snyggt också=snyggt ljud,
        mm (.) very um nice too=nice sound,

02      många eh (.) duktiga:,
        many um (.) talented,

03      (1.5)

04      >va heter de< musiker.
        >what's it called< musicians.

05      (0.9)

06      å   va  ja inte gillar  e     hennes nasala   röst
        and what I  NEG  like.PRS be.PRS her    nasal.DEF voice
        and what I don't like is her nasal voice

07      som e      lite: >för jobbig<.
        that be.PRS little too  disturbing
        that is a bit too disturbing.

08 DAN: de: håller ja inte me om.
        I don't agree about that.
```

This excerpt begins with a speaker named Tom expressing a positive assessment of the qualities of the song and its production. His assessment includes a somewhat long pause (line 3) and some hesitation (line 1, 4), but he receives no uptake from the other participants. However, Tom's assessment is positioned within a sequence in which a positive stance towards the song has already been established collectively. In line 6, following a gap, Tom moves away from this collective positive position as he adopts a negative stance towards the singer's rather trademark voice and he uses a pseudocleft to make this polarity shift. The predicate in Part A establishes an evaluative frame, *gillar* 'like', in this case negated (*inte*). Tom uses the coordinating conjunction *and* 'å' in the turn beginning (line 6), which signals an elaboration of the ongoing assessing action, while the frame shift is expressed by the pseudocleft and its placement after previous positive assessments. The contrast between positive and negative assessments is emphasized by the stress on the negation *inte* and on the feature disliked by the speaker (line 6), a stance further expanded by the relative clause in line 7: *som är lite för jobbig* 'that is a bit too disturbing'. In this case, Tom's negative assessment is countered by the following speaker, Dan, who expresses strong disagreement (line 8).

Besides performing a transition from a positive to a negative evaluation, the pseudocleft also involves a change from one grammatical format to another. In the positive assessment preceding the pseudocleft (lines 1–4), Tom uses two noun phrases to make his assessment, *snyggt ljud* 'nice sound' and *många eh duktiga: va heter de musiker* 'many um talented what's it called musicians'. He expresses this without explicitly framing this evaluation as the speaker's stance. The following pseudocleft construction (lines 6–7) conveys Tom's negative stance in the first person and a full sentence that expresses the speaker stance, *va ja inte gillar* 'what I don't like' (line 6), followed by a copula and a noun phrase specifying what the speaker does not appreciate in the song, *hennes nasala röst* 'her nasal voice'.

Excerpt (5) illustrates the use of a pseudocleft as another transition type, this time shifting focus from one topic to another. This excerpt stems from a tutorial related to academic writing. During this activity, a writing counselor (COU) and a student (STU) discuss a text written by the student. The counselor read the student's text in advance and the discussion is supported by a printout of the text as well as by the comments that the counselor wrote on it. This excerpt begins after a preceding sequence has just been concluded and shortly after the counselor has begun to erase a comment written on the student's text. The counselor uses the pseudocleft to shift from one topic to another in line 1, turning the focus to why the comment regarding the punctuation is irrelevant and can be erased. The pseudocleft in lines 1–2 is introduced by the pronoun *va(d)* 'what'. After the sequence on punctuation, the counselor uses another pseudocleft in lines 20–21 as a transition to a new topic concerning how publication years need to be listed in the references section.

Chapter 12. Action formation, projection, and participation framework   **381**

Excerpt 5. *va du kan va noga me* 'what you can be careful with' (IVIP_LFIN-SHA:03, video), text tutorial

```
01 COU: va   jag alltså suddar   här e       att (.)
        what I    PRT    erase.PRS here be.PRS that
        what I'm erasing here is that (.)

02      °ja hade°   markera de här kommatecknen
        I  have.PST mark.PRF these comma.token.PL.DEF
        I had marked these commas

03      men vi kolla just att,
        but we just went over that,

04      (0.6)

05 STU: °mm°

06 COU: man får ha kommatecknena,
        it's allowed to keep those commas,

07      (0.4)

08      man får ha hur man vill så då,
        one can choose how one wishes (so in that case),

09      (0.2)

10 STU: aha   [alltså efter just] (.) okej,
        oh you mean after that (.) okay.

11 COU:       [mm+m jå  jå      ]
               mm yeah yeah

12      (0.3)

13 COU: så att,
        so,

14      (0.3)

15 STU: jå för de e jätteolika när jag just har
        yeah because it's really different when I've

16      kollat att vissa har å vissa har [int å] sådär,
        noticed that some have and some don't sort of,

17 COU:                                  [jå: ]
                                          yeah

18      (0.2)

19 COU: jå:
        yeah

20 COU: .h men de   va   du (.) kan   va:   noga   me
        but that what you     can.PRS be.INF careful with
        .h but what you (.) can be careful with

21      e       di här årtalen
        be.PRS these  year.PL.DEF
        is the (publication) years
```

22	de har jag skrivi in här ibland att årtal,
	that's what I've written here sometimes "years",
23	(0.4)
24 STU:	jå+å,
	yeah,

Excerpt (5) illustrates the counselor's use of pseudoclefts to organize topical transitions within a general counseling activity. The first pseudocleft initiated in line 1 constitutes a shift to the topic of punctuation and initiates an account as to why the counselor has erased a comment from the student's text. A short gap arises in the junction between Part A and Part B of this pseudocleft, and Part B is syntactically less integrated, although the pseudocleft constitutes a pragmatically coherent unit, which the student acknowledges in line 10. Using the generic pronoun *man* 'one/you' (lines 6 and 8), the counselor indicates that commas can generally occur precisely as the student used them in the text and that the counselor's comment is therefore superfluous: *man får ha kommatecknena* 'it's allowed to keep those commas'.

The second pseudocleft initiated in line 20 occurs in a junction between a technical detail on commas in referencing, where different variants are allowed, and another detail, which is of greater importance, that is, remembering to always include the publication year in references. This pseudocleft has a gap within Part A but is otherwise a syntactically prototypical example of the structure in our data. The point raised here stands in contrast to the previous point made by the counselor's first pseudocleft in lines 1–2. This contrast is reflected in both content and format. In other words, the pseudocleft in lines 1–2 launches generic guidance concerning how to use commas in references (generic pronoun *man* 'one/you', what is allowed), whereas the point made in lines 20–21 concerns the inclusion of years in references, a detail that this particular student is strongly advised to "be careful with" (note the second person singular *du* 'you', *va du kan va noga me* 'what you can be careful with'). This transition to important advice is further emphasized by the adversative conjunction *men* 'but' that introduces the turn in line 20.

To summarize the discourse-organizing potential of pseudoclefts, we have seen that the construction is a conventionalized resource for introducing transitions. The pseudocleft offers a means for transitioning from one topical aspect or speaker stance to another within an overarching activity, such as making a critical assessment or offering counseling. Pseudoclefts may alert the recipient to topical or aspectual shifts of different types. These include a shift in a speaker's stance from positive to negative, from one topic to another, or from general reasoning regarding a subject matter to a more specific point about it. These types of transitions can also be reflected in other formatting practices of evaluative or directive actions such as the use of adversative conjunctions (*men* 'but'). Hence, we have

Chapter 12. Action formation, projection, and participation framework **383**

shown how the transformative potential of pseudoclefts could be approached from the point of turn and sequence organization, and included in a grammar for talk-in-interaction.

4. Participation framework and epistemic positioning

Our data on Swedish talk-in-interaction suggest a link between the pseudocleft construction, the dynamics of participation framework and recipient design, and the speakers' epistemic positioning. The construction recurs in institutional settings, as suggested by the figures in Table 1 and shown in Excerpts (3) and (5). It can also introduce evaluative or directive actions during instructing activities, such as academic counseling or personal training (Henricson & Lindström 2020a; Lindström et al. 2022). Thus, pseudoclefts are found in environments in which participants position themselves and each other regarding access to knowledge and rights to direct others (see Heritage 2012a, 2012b; Stevanovic & Peräkylä 2012; Stivers, Mondada & Steensig 2011).

Even though the general participation framework of institutional interaction can generally be described as a clear-cut division in expert and non-expert participants, these roles are in reality far more multifaceted and can be locally challenged or altered in the on-going interaction. This is illustrated with a longer transcript divided in Excerpts (6) and (7) below. In the latter excerpt we can see how the pseudocleft is used as a resource to challenge the pre-set institutional participation framework and the expected epistemic positionings.

Excerpt (6) is from the end of a writing tutorial. The student (STU) has expressed to the counselor (COU) feelings of insecurity when dealing with references and avoiding plagiarism. This leads the counselor to launch a long stretch of reasoning talk including general advice which comes to a closure during the first lines of the transcript. The counselor expands the sequence by initiating advice on the management of a specific source text, the curriculum (lines 5–6). She launches this topic with the pseudocleft *de som alltid e svårt e ju att att dehär att referera läroplanen* 'what is always difficult is (of course) to report on the curriculum'. This pseudocleft follows a typical structural patterning, forming a syntactically and prosodically coherent unit, with some indication of a word search at the beginning of Part B. By highlighting reporting on the curriculum as a recurrent challenge in academic texts, the counselor positions herself as knowledgeable in this domain. This pseudocleft serves then as a frame for further specific instructions on how this challenge can be addressed. During this advice-giving sequence, the student adopts the position of someone who is being informed and instructed, using short neutral receipt tokens to acknowledge the counselor's advice.

384 Sofie Henricson & Jan Lindström

Excerpt 6. *de som alltid e svårt* 'what is always difficult', (IVIP:LFINSHA:01), tutorial

```
01 COU: de e nu unjefär de enda jag kan [jag kan säga.   ]
        that's about all I can, I can say.
02 STU:                              [jå (0.3) precis.]
                                     yeah (0.3) exactly.
03      (0.3)
04 STU: [jå,]
        yeah,
05 COU: [.h ] å   de   som alltid e     svårt    e    ju
             and that REL always be.PRS difficult be.PRS PRT
             .h and what is always difficult is (of course)
06      att att dehär att att referera läroplanen?
        to to PRT   to to refer.INF curriculum.DEF
        to to um to to report on the curriculum?
07      (0.4) [de blir ju] lätt tråkigt.
        (0.4) it easily becomes boring.
08 STU:       [jå,      ]
               yeah,
09 STU: jå
        yeah
10 COU: mt så då måst man ju som (0.9) få ner de
        mt so then you must like (0.9) boil it down
11      så mycke som möjligt
        as much as possible
```

The interaction continues 19 lines later in Excerpt (7). When the counselor's advice-formulation approaches the end in line 31, the student initiates her own contrasting perspective concerning the challenges she encountered with the text references in line 32. To achieve this, the student produces a pseudocleft with some hesitation in Part A (possibly because of speaking in overlap), followed by a syntactically rambling Part B.

Excerpt 7. *de som jag tycker e svårt* 'what I find difficult', (IVIP:LFINSHA:01), tutorial

```
31 COU: men de [kan ju nog hända som att (man)         ]
        but it might be like that (you)
32 STU:        [nä för  de (.)de   som (.)de   som jag]
               no because that that REL   that REL I
               no because (.) what (.) what I
33      tycker e    svårt   e    just dedär vettu
        find.PRS be.PRS difficult be.PRS PRT  that PRT
        find difficult is just that you know
```

34	**just om då man (0.8) då man skriver om**
	PRT if when one when one write.PRS about
	just if when one (0.8) when one rewrites
35	(0.3) å å berättar me sina egna ord
	(0.3) and and reports in one's own words
36	å hela den biten så då, (1.4)
	and all that stuff then, (1.4)
37	just dedär om man vetdu syftningsfel
	just like if one you know (has) reference errors
38	[sedan att man] på nå vis, (1.1)
	so that one somehow, (1.1)
39 COU:	[mm]
40 STU:	skriver de så att att man förvränger liks-
	writes it in a way that that distorts like-
41	[eller i-] alltså omedvetet vettu då [förvränger,]
	or I mean unconsciously you know distorts,
42 COU:	[mm] [jå]
	mm *yeah*
43 COU:	mm jå
	mm yeah
44 STU:	deras ande[mening,]
	their essential meaning,
45 COU:	[mm]

This pseudocleft, specifically the Part A, *de som jag tycker e svårt* 'what I find difficult', parallels the one used by the counselor in line 5, *de som alltid e svårt* 'what is always difficult'. The personal pronoun *jag* 'I' is stressed, which adds to the contrast between the contributions by the counselor and student. Thus, a change in perspective occurs from what is "always difficult" in these types of writing, a domain in which the counselor is the more knowledgeable participant, to what the student personally considers to be difficult, that is, what lies within the student's epistemic primacy. This means that the student uses the pseudocleft format to resonate dialogically with the counselor's contribution: she activates a parallelism and difference between the two contributions (see Du Bois 2014). This structural parallelism, then, is a resource for calibrating participants' positions in the domains of knowledge and experience.

Considering our Swedish data and previous research on pseudoclefts (for example, see Henricson & Lindström 2020a, 2020b; Hopper & Thompson 2008; Lindström et al. 2022), we can conclude that this grammatical format serves as a useful means to set the agenda and raise topics in activities that are related to consultative interactional contexts. Pseudoclefts are frequently used to launch or frame either directive or evaluative actions and to construct the speaker as an expert participant in a position to offer advice, instruct, and assess others.

As indicated by some of our examples, expertise is something that can also be claimed in local positionings when the roles are not institutionally pre-set (see Excerpt (4)), or expertise can be negotiated to enhance the epistemic position of the non-institutional participant (Excerpt (7)).

Based on the discussion above and the distribution of instances in our data, an adequate grammar entry on pseudoclefts would need to comment on that this format is suited for certain typical social situations. These often involve directive-commissive or evaluative actions such as giving advice or critical feedback. This coincides with speaker identity given by the (institutional) interactional frame, but these types of identities can also be locally negotiated and pseudoclefts offer a linguistic means for that.

5. Conclusion and outlook

This chapter has examined how speaker turns are constructed, used, and shaped in the pseudocleft format in Swedish talk-in-interaction. This approach has been sensitive to usage in social interaction, including turn and action design, sequence organization, projection, and, in the end, the associations between the use of the construction and the social situation.

Pertaining to turn design, we can note that pseudoclefts exhibit a regular grammatical pattern in Swedish; nonetheless, as in many languages, in actual usage, some microvariation occurs in syntactic detail. The overall structural regularity and recognizability of the pseudocleft qualify this constructional pattern as a conventionally available building block of speaker turns. It can be argued that the pseudocleft, which rests on two major constituent parts (A and B), results in a compound turn constructional unit: this unit consists of a preliminary component (A) which strongly projects a final component (B). This *internal syntactic* feature is an effective turn-holding device until the completion of a final TCU component. When a compound pseudocleft structure occurs, the projection of constructional unity is created by prosody together with syntax.

Furthermore, the construction constitutes not only a building block of turns but of discourse (turn sequences) by marking transitions in the pragmatic trajectory of an interaction. Typical transitions involve a shift to something new or divergent from the prior talk, such as launching a plan, a topic, or an important point in the speaker's argumentation. The latter may concern polarity shifts in a speaker's stance, typically from a positive to a negative one when something is critically evaluated. This transitory functional potential is an *external syntactic* feature of pseudoclefts which results in a projecting force on the level of discourse (see also Berthe et al. 2024). The construction offers a recognizable structural frame which alerts the recipient of a change in what is being talked about and that the upcoming stretch of discourse will, at some unspecified length, address what the pseudocleft brought to the participants' attention.

Pseudoclefts are not used to accomplish one single type of action, but it is clear that this format is used to resolve some recurrent types of communicative problems (cf. Steensig et al. 2023; Thompson & Couper-Kuhlen 2005). From this perspective, pseudoclefts contribute to the formation of at least two types of social action: (1) directive-commissive actions when the speaker launches a suggestion (advice, instruction) as to how another person should act, or a proposal (plan, idea) for a joint future action with another person, and (2) evaluative actions, when the speaker makes assessments or judgements concerning objects, other persons and their work. The projecting force of the compound turn constructional frame is also relevant here: the preliminary component (A) alerts the recipient about the type of action that will follow and about its pragmatic nature, such as expressing an evaluation, a proposal or a suggestion. The core of the action–what the target of the evaluation is or what the suggested action is about–is stated in the final component (B).

The fact that pseudoclefts co-occur with directive-commissive or evaluative actions suggests that the turn format easily lends itself to social situations that involve critical examination. In our datasets, pseudoclefts are used by an expert in academic counseling and personal training or by students who temporarily position themselves as experts during text seminars. But pseudoclefts also appear in mundane contexts to claim superior epistemic or deontic positions, or are used by a non-expert in institutional discourse to negotiate local epistemic positions between participants. Thus, the grammatical description of the pseudocleft construction can point to links between its use as a device for stance taking, speaker identity, and activity type.

Table 3 summarizes the observations we have made above concerning the position of the pseudocleft construction in a grammar for interaction. This includes the relevant levels of grammar description, functional characteristics of speaker (SP) contributions, and their interactional impact.

Traditional grammars have analyzed pseudoclefts under rubrics such as "focus" (for example, see Quirk et al. 1985). However, from a grammar-in-action approach, we need to emphasize the interactional value of such functions and determine what the communicative pay-off is when a speaker uses this complex format as a method for turn construction. We contend that the points concerning action formation, projection, and participation framework contribute to a far fuller understanding of the motivation underlying the use of pseudoclefts in talk-in-interaction.

Table 3. The relevance of pseudoclefts for a grammar-in-action account (SP=speaker, TCU=turn constructional unit)

Level of description	Functional characteristic	Interactional impact
Turn design	SP constructs a compound TCU	Projects a type of TCU
Action formation	SP issues a directive-commissive or evaluative action	Projects a type of action
Discourse organization	SP alerts about a change in orientation	Projects a type of point
Participation framework	SP constructs an expert identity	Projects a type of activity

From an applied perspective, an interactionally sensitive grammatical description of the pseudocleft would be a valuable resource for various professional target groups. This is because the format works in the interface between turn and sequence organization, contributing strongly to the modality of action (deontics), speaker positioning (stance), and the art of discourse (rhetoric). Relevant target groups would be those who work with counseling services or those who participate in institutional interactions as experts or non-experts. More generally, however, the target group would also include those involved in the educational fields of academic discourse, professional training and Swedish as a second or foreign language. A grammatical description based on the features discussed in this chapter would render explicit the linguistic, interactional, discursive and situational specifics of this recognizable turn constructional device. This description would specify how pseudoclefts can be used as a resource to express directives and assessments, but also how it can be utilized as a means to regulate action projection and the participation framework.

Funding

Our research on pseudoclefts was primarily conducted within the project *Emergent Clausal Syntax for Conversation* (EGS) funded by the Academy of Finland in 2018–2022 (project #316865). We are also indebted to the research program *Interaction and Variation in Pluricentric Languages* (IVIP) funded by Riksbankens Jubileumsfond in 2013–2020 (#M12–0137:1) in which we conducted research and collected data; most of the excerpts analyzed in this study stem from the program's datasets.

Acknowledgements

We want to thank our (fellow-)guest editors and the series editors for their insightful comments on earlier versions of this text. Any remaining flaws are our own responsibility.

References

Ammon, Marri, and Leelo Keevallik. 2022. "Ebalohklause eesti keeles: Ühest seni tähelepanuta jäänud lauseliigist." [Pseudo-cleft: On a hitherto undescribed syntactic construction in Estonian.] *The Yearbook of the Estonian Mother Tongue Society* 67 (1): 7–25.

Anward, Jan, and Bengt Nordberg (eds). 2005. *Samtal och grammatik: Studier i svenskt samtalsspråk.* [Interaction and grammar: Studies in Swedish talk-in-interaction.] Lund: Studentlitteratur.

Argyle, Michael, Adrian Furnham, and Jean Ann Graham. 1981. *Social Situations.* Cambridge: Cambridge University Press.

Auer, Peter. 2009. "Projection and Minimalistic Syntax in Interaction." *Discourse Processes* 46 (2–3): 180–205.

Barth-Weingarten, Dagmar. 2016. *Intonation Units Revisited: Cesuras in Talk-in-interaction.* Amsterdam: Benjamins.

Berthe, Florine, Anita Fetzer, and Isabelle Gaudy-Campbell. 2024. "'What we found is': Pseudo-clefts, Cataphora, Projection and Cohesive Chains". *Functions of Language.*

Collins, Peter C. 1991. *Cleft and Pseudo-Cleft Constructions in English.* London: Routledge.

Couper-Kuhlen, Elizabeth. 2014. "What Does Grammar Tell Us about Actions." *Pragmatics* 24 (3): 623–647.

Couper-Kuhlen, Elizabeth, and Margret Selting. 2018. *Interactional Linguistics: Studying Language in Social Interaction.* Cambridge: Cambridge University Press.

De Cesare, Anna-Maria. 2014. "Cleft Constructions in a Contrastive Perspective: Towards an Operational Taxonomy." In *Frequency, Forms and Functions of Cleft Constructions in Romance and Germanic: Contrastive, Corpus-based Studies*, ed. by A.-M. De Cesare, 9–48. Berlin: De Gruyter Mouton.

Drew, Paul. 2018. "Turn Design." In *The Handbook of Conversation Analysis*, ed. by J. Sidnell, and T. Stivers, 131–149. Chichester: Wiley Blackwell.

Du Bois, John W. 2014. "Towards a Dialogic Syntax." *Cognitive Linguistics* 25 (3): 359–410.

Fillmore, Charles J. 1988. "The Mechanisms of 'Construction Grammar'." *Proceedings of the Fourteenth Annual Meeting of the Berkeley Linguistics Society*, 35–55.

Fox, Barbara A. 2007. "Principles Shaping Grammatical Practices: An Exploration." *Discourse Studies* 9 (3): 299–318.

Günthner, Suzanne. 2006. "'Was ihn trieb, war vor allem Wanderlust'. Pseudo-cleft-Konstruktionen im Deutschen." ['What drove him was above all the urge to travel'. Pseudo-cleft constructions in German.] In *Konstruktionen in der Interaktion*, ed. by S. Günthner, and W. Imo, 59–90. Berlin: De Gruyter.

Günthner, Suzanne. 2011. "Between Emergence and Sedimentation: Projecting Constructions in German Interactions." In *Constructions: Emerging and Emergent*, ed. by P. Auer, and S. Pfänder, 156–185. Berlin: de Gruyter.

Henricson, Sofie, and Jan Lindström. 2020a. "La frase pseudoscissa nello svedese parlato e le sue caratteristiche interazionali." [The pseudocleft construction and its interactional characteristics in spoken Swedish.] In *Per una prospettiva funzionale sulle costruzioni sintatticamente marcate / Pour une perspective fonctionnelle sur les constructions syntaxiquement marquees*, ed. by A.-M. De Cesare, and M. Helkkula, 409–427. (*Neuphilologische Mitteilungen* 120.)

Henricson, Sofie, and Jan Lindström. 2020b. "'Va jag inte gillar e hennes nasala röst': Fokusfinala utbrytningar i tal i interaktion." ['What I don't like is her nasal voice': Focus final clefts in talk-in-interaction.] In *Svenskans beskrivning* 37, ed. by Sara Haapamäki, Linda Forsman, and Linda Huldén, 96–110. Åbo: Åbo Akademi University.

Heritage, John. 2012a. "Epistemics in Action: Action Formation and Territories of Knowledge." *Research on Language and Social Interaction* 45 (1): 1–29.

Heritage, John. 2012b. "The Epistemic Engine: Sequence Organization and Territories of Knowledge." *Research on Language and Social Interaction* 45 (1): 30–52.

Heritage, John, and Geoffrey Raymond. 2005. "The Terms of Agreement: Indexing Epistemic Authority and Subordination in Talk-in-interaction." *Social Psychology Quarterly* 68 (1): 15–38.

Hopper, Paul, and Sandra A. Thompson. 2008. "Projectability and Clause Combining." In *Crosslinguistic Studies of Clause Combining: The Multifunctionality of Conjunctions*, ed. by R. Laury, 99–123. Amsterdam: Benjamins.

Kim, Kiy-hyun. 1995. "WH-clefts and Left-dislocations in English Conversation." In *Word Order in Discourse*, ed. by P.A. Downing, and & M. Noonan, 247–296. Amsterdam: Benjamins.

Koops, Christian, and Martin Hilpert. 2009. "The Co-evolution of Syntactic and Pragmatic Complexity: Diachronic and Cross-linguistic Aspects of Pseudo-clefts." In *Syntactic Complexity: Diachrony, Acquisition, Neuro-cognition, Evolution*, ed. by T. Givón, and & M. Shibatani, 215–238. Amsterdam: Benjamins.

Lambrecht, Knud. 2001. "A Framework for the Analysis of Cleft Constructions." *Linguistics* 39: 463–516.

Lerner, Gene. 1996. "On the "Semi-permeable" Character of Grammatical Units in Conversation: Conditional Entry into the Turn Space of Another Speaker." In *Interaction and Grammar*, ed. by E. Ochs, E.A. Schegloff, and S.A. Thompson, 238–276. Cambridge: Cambridge University Press.

Lindström, Jan, Sofie Henricson, and Martina Huhtamäki. 2022. "Pseudo-cleft Constructions in Swedish Talk-in-interaction: Turn Projection and Discourse Organization." *Lingua* 265.

Maschler, Yael. 1997. "Discourse Markers at Frame Shifts in Israeli Hebrew Talk-in-interaction." *Pragmatics* 7 (2): 183–211.

Maschler, Yael, and Stav Fishman. 2020. "From Multi-clausality to Discourse Markerhood: The Hebrew *ma she-* 'what that' Construction in Pseudo-cleft-like Structures." *Journal of Pragmatics* 159: 73–97.

Maschler, Yael, Jan Lindström, and Elwys De Stefani. 2023. "Pseudo-clefts: An Interactional Analysis Across Languages." *Lingua* 291.

Myrberg Sara. 2013. "Sisterhood in Prosodic Branching." *Phonology* 30 (1): 73–124.

Myrberg, Sara, and Tomas Riad. 2016. "On the Expression of Focus in the Metrical Grid and in the Prosodic Hierarchy." In *The Oxford Handbook of Information Structure*, ed. by C. Féry, and S. Ishihara. (Online edition.) Oxford: Oxford University Press.

Pekarek Doehler, Simona. 2011. "Clause-combining and the Sequencing of Actions: Projector Constructions in French Talk-in-interaction." In *Subordination in Conversation: A Cross-linguistic Perspective*, ed. by R. Laury, and R. Suzuki, 103–148. Amsterdam: Benjamins.

Quirk, Randolph, Sidney Greenbaum, Geoffrey Leech, and Jan Svartvik. 1985. *A Comprehensive Grammar of the English Language*. London: Longman.

Skogmyr Marian, Klara, Sofie Henricson, and Marie Nelson. 2020. "Counselors' Claims of Insufficient Knowledge in Academic Writing Consultations." *Scandinavian Journal of Educational Research* 65 (6): 1065–1080.

Steensig, Jakob, Maria Jørgensen, Nicholas Mikkelsen, Karita Suomalainen, and Søren Sandager Sørensen. 2023. "Toward a Grammar of Danish Talk-in-interaction: From Action Formation to Grammatical Description." *Research on Language and Social Interaction* 56 (2): 116–140.

Stevanovic, Melisa, and Anssi Peräkylä. 2012. "Deontic Authority in Interaction: The Right to Announce, Propose, and Decide." *Research on Language and Social Interaction* 45 (3): 297–321.

Stivers, Tanya, Lorenza Mondada, and Jakob Steensig (eds.). 2011. *The Morality of Knowledge in Conversation*. Cambridge: Cambridge University Press.

Svenonius, Peter. 1998. "Clefts in Scandinavian: An Investigation." *ZAS Papers in Linguistics* 10: 163–190.

Tao, Hongyin. 2022. "Scalar Pseudo-cleft Constructions in Mandarin Conversation: A Multimodal Approach." *Lingua* 266.

Teleman, Ulf, Staffan Hellberg, and Erik Andersson. 1999. *Svenska Akademiens grammatik.* [The Swedish Academy grammar.] Stockholm: Svenska Akademien.

Thompson, Sandra A., and Elizabeth Couper-Kuhlen. 2005. "The Clause as a Locus of Grammar and Interaction." *Discourse Studies* 7 (4–5): 481–505.

Vallduví, Enric & Elisabet Engdahl. 1996. "Linguistic Realization of Information Packaging." *Linguistics* 34: 459–519.

Appendix   Data

EGS, everyday conversations collected by the University of Helsinki in 2016; 10 hrs.

GSM, group discussions collected by the University of Gothenburg in 1997–1999; 20 hrs.

HUSA, sociolinguistic interviews collected by the University of Helsinki and the Research Institute for the Languages of Finland in 1994–1995; 12 hrs.

IVIP, academic interactions, e.g. thesis seminars and writing consultations collected by the University of Turku in 2014–2015, 10 hrs; consultations and sessions with personal trainers collected by the University of Helsinki in 2016, 6 hrs.

SAM, everyday conversations and radio interviews collected by the University of Helsinki in 1989–1993; 6 hrs.

SPÖK, youth conversations collected by the University of Helsinki and the Society of Swedish Literature in Finland in the 2000s–2010s; two recordings analyzed.

SVESTRA, everyday conversations collected by the University of Helsinki in 1999–2001; 10 hrs.

CHAPTER 13

Other-extensions in Italian
A case *of* and *for* Collaborative Grammar

Virginia Calabria
Durham University

This chapter focuses on the practice of other-extending a prior speaker's complete turn in Italian. By drawing on the grammatical formatting and/or reusing elements in prior turns to extend them, speakers deploy Collaborative Grammar (Calabria 2022), a set of grammatical formats and resources available in a language to design turns to be heard as grammatically integrated. Using Conversation Analysis and Interactional Linguistics, three actions are identified that speakers achieve by other-extending in Italian multiperson interactions: providing additional information, verifying while demonstrating understanding, and reframing prior talk as laughable. This chapter argues that practices implemented with Collaborative Grammar between multiple speakers should constitute a dedicated section in a comprehensive grammar that aims at describing the competing temporalities of multiperson interactions.

Keywords: Interactional Linguistics, Conversation Analysis, other-extensions, Collaborative Grammar, collaborative turns, shared syntax, multiperson interaction, participation framework, recipiency, Italian talk-in-interaction

1. Introduction

This chapter focuses on a practice at the intersection of grammar and interaction (Couper Kuhlen & Selting 2018): other-extending a prior speaker's potentially complete turn. I aim to position other-extensions within the wider frame of collaborative practices of turn-construction — that is when two or more speakers build a turn, or a turn-constructional unit (TCU) together — among which we find co-constructions (Lerner 1991), collaborative completions (Bolden 2003), other-increments (Schegloff 2016), other-extensions (Calabria 2022), and various types of turn-continuation by other (Sidnell 2012). These collaborative turn-building practices involve sharing syntax (Helasvuo 2004) and an actional project

https://doi.org/10.1075/slsi.37.13cal
© 2025 John Benjamins Publishing Company

Chapter 13. Other-extensions in Italian   393

(or the overall activity, cf. Mazeland 2019) between two or more speakers. As such, they give us an insight into the contingent and recipient-designed emergence of grammar (Hopper 2011), as talk unfolds. Considering the coordination that two or more speakers must achieve to build clauses or more complex sentential structures together, collaborative practices force us to abandon considering verbal productions as monolithic, ready-made items in the mind of one speaker. So far, not a lot of space has been allocated to shared turns and grammatical production in descriptive grammars of spoken languages (cf. Voghera 2017).

In this chapter, while describing the grammatical design of other-extensions, I will focus on the action(s) that other-extending speakers accomplish through this collaborative practice. An other-extension emerges when a speaker A utters a turn that, for all practical purposes, is treated as completed (i.e., it has reached a transition relevance place; TRP), and this turn is extended by a speaker B in grammatically and actionally fitted ways (i.e., ways that show grammatical integration with the prior linguistic unit and continue the action of the prior turn). Speaker B can format the contributing talk as either: (i) a 'canonical' increment (Schegloff 2016), a linguistic unit that from its onset emerges with material that is syntactically dependent on the end of the prior turn (e.g., a relative clause); or (ii) a unit that is built upon a latent grammatical slot (Auer 2014) that remains open in the prior speaker's turn, not necessarily dependent on the prior turn's end. For instance, in Excerpt (1), at line 4 ANG utters a stretch of talk formatted as a complement clause that is dependent on and fits the argument structure of the verb *chiedere* 'to ask' in line 1 of GIO's turn.

Excerpt 1. Mi13PRO2–42 (18:38–18:51), face-to-face, informal interaction

```
01 GIO: >io gli  chiedo< di mettere a posto il tavolo,
         I   ask them    to tidy the table

02       di non sbriciolare per terra, e di non rovesciare
         not to drop crumbs on the floor, and not to spill

03       l'aqua.
         the water

04 ANG: di non buttar via il cibo.
         not to throw the food away

05 GIO: e di non- (.)
         and not to-
```

In order for speaker B to be heard as extending A's turn (and not providing a new turn), B must employ a variety of grammatical interactional resources (e.g., monitoring the grammatical and interactional projection of the other's temporally unfolding turn, cf. Auer 2005, 2015) and bodily resources (e.g., monitoring bodily availability and "catching the eye" of the current speaker just before providing an other-extension).[1] All these resources are part of a "Collaborative Grammar" (Calabria 2022: 5):

> A set of tools available to speakers for achieving a shared and/or combined grammatical unit (be it more or less complex) and displaying this collaboration to each other. Grammar, in this sense, goes beyond syntax to include, lexical, pragmatic, prosodic and multimodal resources.

Collaborative Grammar allows contributing speakers to accomplish actions that are treated not as responsive actions, other-repairs, or part of adjacency pairs, but as extending, reopening, or reframing the prior action, and carrying out the same activity initiated by speaker A.

The aims of this chapter are: (i) to provide a grammatical and interactional description of other-extensions in Italian, expanding the literature on collaborative turns (CTs) as well as the scarce body of studies on Italian talk-in-interaction (hence contributing to studies on Romance languages); (ii) to explore a practice that enables us to reflect on the intersection between grammar and interaction, necessary for descriptions of grammars of talk-in-interaction; (iii) to provide an account of a phenomenon in spoken language that addresses the issue of what people do when they join their voices and collaborate (Luke 2021) — a study that can complement interactive grammatical descriptions that focus on a speaker's production (at a given point in time) and its recipient-designed formats (cf. Henricson & Lindström this volume). Furthermore, this study reflects in conclusion on the place that collaborative practices should have in grammatical descriptions of talk-in-interactions.

The argument and analyses presented will show that phenomena of shared, collaborative practices between two or even more than two speakers that are achieved by means of Collaborative Grammar should constitute a dedicated section in a comprehensive grammar that aims at describing talk-in-interaction (cf. Steensig et al. 2023). Specifically, they should be part of a grammatical description that aims at considering the competing temporalities for turn-taking involved in multiperson interactions (i.e., interaction that involves multiple speakers and voices).[2]

---

1. Grammatical resources refer to the morpho-syntactic inventory available in a given language for speakers to draw on, e.g., for Italian, gender and number agreement for articles, nouns, adjectives, participles, deictic anaphoric and cataphoric pronominal references; as well as specific clausal formats in which the main predicate matches in tense and mood the one in the preceding linguistic unit.

2. The relevance of "voices" for other-extensions, and collaborative turns in general, is that it "opens up an opportunity for us to articulate the 'point' of joint productions above and beyond syntactic or grammatical 'fittedness'. It invites us to address the fundamental issue of what in fact is being built in joint production, and for what purposes" (Luke 2021: 20).

This chapter is organised as follows: Section 2 offers an overview of previous research on other-extensions and other-incrementation. After the data and the methodology that inform this research, and the criteria for establishing the collection are laid out in Section 3, the analysis is presented in Section 4. Section 5 provides a discussion of the analyses. Final remarks are provided in Section 6; they concern the importance of the investigation of these practices for grammars that aim at describing talk-in-interaction.

2. Incrementing talk with other-extensions

This chapter conceptualises "other-extension" as a term that includes and expands on the practice known as "other-increment" or "other-initiated increment" (Schegloff 2016). While the latter labels refer to turns that are grammatically subordinated to a prior host turn and whose action extends the prior one and does not add to it, "extension" includes linguistic combinations such as syntactic coordination and reusing latent grammatical slots in prior talk (Auer 2014), as well as composite actions (Rossi 2018), through which a speaker does more than one action; in this case more than just extending the action in the host turn.

Incrementation has been widely studied in different languages. Different labels have been used to refer to the extending TCU, differing by whether the focus is syntactic, prosodic, or pragmatic: "repairs", "expansions", "retractions" (Auer 2009); "recompletions", "post-completions" (Schegloff 1996), "increments" (Schegloff 1996; Ford, Fox & Thompson 2002; Walker 2004; Ono & Couper-Kuhlen 2007); "add-ons", "glue-ons" (Vorreiter 2003).

"Increments" have been described in prior interactional literature as continuations of a prior possibly complete TCU (see, e.g., Vorreiter 2003; Ono & Couper-Kuhlen 2007; Calabria & De Stefani 2020), thereby occasioning a new possible turn-completion (TRP; cf. Schegloff 1996). This recompletion is shown by grammatically fitting the increment to the prior *host* turn, as Walker (2004: 147) puts it: "An increment is a grammatically fitted continuation of a turn at talk following the reaching of a point of possible syntactic, pragmatic, and prosodic completion". The practice of incrementation involves, then, continuing talk by expanding prior talk after a turn is potentially completed. This can be achieved by the same speaker in the case of *self-increments* or by another speaker in the case of *other-increments*. Incrementing TCUs have to be formatted as grammatically dependent on the prior turn and as continuing the prior action, such that they do not constitute a new TCU. Ford, Fox and Thompson (2002: 16) describe this grammatical requirement as "nonmain-clause continuation after a possible point of turn completion". The possibility of extending the turn of another speaker with syntactically dependent material was already formulated by Sacks in 1967 (Sacks 1992: 647–655). Schegloff (1996: 73), reflecting on the notion of TCU, remarked:

> Recognizing some spate of talk as a TCU is itself an accomplishment. That is, some stretches of talk by a speaker are taken (by us as analysts and by co-participants in the setting) not as TCUs, but, for example, as increments of talk to some other, prior talk — either by that same speaker or by another.

Applying the same logic to other speakers, who extend the prior talk with "spate(s) of talk" which are not new actions, Schegloff established the usage of "other-increment" as in use in the current literature. Specifically, he noticed that stretches of talk produced by different speakers can have the same characteristics as "self-initiated increments", that is: (i) a speaker has reached potential pragmatic, grammatical, and prosodic TCU completeness, (ii) further talk is added to the prior potentially complete turn, (iii) the extending talk is formatted as continuing the preceding TCU and not as a new TCU, and as grammatically fitted to the end of talk-so-far (Schegloff 2016: 241). Schegloff's examples (including one from written language) demonstrate that speakers can achieve a variety of actions through other-incrementing, e.g., displaying alignment or disalignment with the prior speaker, and adjusting/modifying the stance taken by the prior speaker in their turn. Schegloff (2016: 260) adds: "Further, they [the speakers] display an orientation to the possibility of building a collaborative construction by starting in that position in another's just possibly completed turn".[3] However, he also notes that "it remains a matter of ongoing interest what special attraction there is to doing whatever is getting done by doing it as an increment, rather than as a new TCU" (Schegloff 2016: 261).

A grammatically dependent stretch of talk is a linguistic unit which is designed from its onset as depending on previous talk, e.g., by means of "increment initiators" (Lerner 1996) such as 'because'; 'for', 'to', 'if'.[4] Based on both syntactic and semantic criteria, Couper-Kuhlen and Ono (2007) distinguished continuing (or extending) a TCU from starting a new TCU: continuations of TCUs are maximally integrated, while new TCUs are minimally integrated (and speakers implement new actions), with respect to syntactic and semantic criteria. In the middle of the continuum, there are "free constituents", whose degree of grammatical integration can be ambiguous (e.g., some adverbs).

---

3. Cf. *espansioni* ('expansion') in Orletti (2008), defined as one type of *enuciati a più voci* ('multiple-voices utterances').

4. This is the case for stretches of talk that are designed as dependent on a *host* turn, and not as independent new turns, which can be formatted as *insubordinate* clauses and achieve an independent action (cf. Pekarek Doehler & Horlacher this volume).

For other-increments, the relationship between grammatical and actional dependence has been problematised. Extending a prior turn and recognising a bit of talk as an other-increment can be problematic achievements for the interactants. These have been defined as retrospective operations (cf. Luke & Zhang 2007), whose meaning and action is not available to co-participants' understanding from the onset of the practice. Moreover, they can halt the progressivity of the interaction.

Since the emergence of a stretch of talk as an expansion of a prior turn is often unclear from the onset of a speaker's turn, the literature has analysed other elements beyond grammar to identify self-increments. These include voice quality and prosodic contours (e.g., keeping the same pitch or uttering the self-increment with the same prosodic contour of the prior incremented turn, cf. Auer 1996; Ono & Couper-Kuhlen 2007). However, when it comes to turn-extensions done by another speaker (by a different *voice*), the practice can become more "elusive" (Auer 2007) to describe. Lerner (2004:160) tried to disentangle the action from the syntactic criterion:

> When a speaker ties their utterance to a previous speaker's possibly completed turn, the action accomplished through that contribution can constitute one of two types of connections: [...] as an increment to that turn (forwarding the action of that turn for its recipient) or as a distinct turn in response to it but one built off of the prior turn syntactically.

He also introduced the notion of "directionality": an other-incrementing speaker can produce a stretch of speech that is directed to the same recipient of the action accomplished by the prior speaker, "for its current recipient" (Lerner 2004:161). This can be distinguished from a stretch of talk that is uttered in response to or that addresses the prior speaker, which is a new turn, since the speaker thereby "reverses" the directionality of the prior action.

Sidnell (2012), however, invited scholars to use distinctions based on directionality cautiously, since the directionality of an extension is frequently ambiguous for the participants themselves (especially in multiperson interactions). Therefore, he called other-increments "action-elaborating increment-continuations" and considered them a type of "other-continuations", but made a further distinction based on action and grammatical formatting of the TCU continuation. He found cases where a speaker uttering an integrated continuation elaborates on the prior action, and cases where a speaker, uttering a grammatically independent unit, initiates a new action (for example, *and*-prefaced "recipient formulations").

Mazeland (2019), focusing on Dutch *en* 'and'-prefaced continuations by other speakers, provided one of the few accounts of the practice ("position-expansions") in multiperson settings. With position-expansions, speakers carry on the prior action (in contrast to, e.g., other *and*-prefaced formulations), but the continuation is not designed as *dependent* on the prior turn. He also listed some features that are relevant for distinguishing between "same-speaker continuation of the same action-unit and other-continuation of the ongoing activity" (Mazeland 2019: 400–401). However, these features concern mostly a specific format of other-continuation, thus their applicability to a wider scope of formats is not always possible.

Syntactic accounts of turn continuations have been provided by Stoenica (2020) and Stoenica and Pekarek Doehler (2020). In these studies, other-increments formatted as relative clauses in French are investigated both syntactically and multimodally in order to identify specific actions accomplished, e.g., managing specific references by expanding or repairing them. Similarly, Calabria and De Stefani (2020) and Calabria (2022) found that relative clauses in Italian emerge as a useful resource to extend a prior complete turn, providing additional information on the topic at hand or proposing the reopening of a potentially closed activity. Contributing speakers can also utter additional units to multi-unit turns, building them jointly with another speaker (Calabria 2022). They can self-select during a multi-unit turn "big package" (Selting 2000) in a way that is not treated as competitive for the floor, but as collaborative with respect to the ongoing activity.

Some issues arise from formal conceptualizations and descriptions of incremental stretches of talk in the literature. A potentially problematic first element in the conceptualization of other-extensions as expanding the prior "complete" turn is that actions can also be achieved by means of potentially incomplete TCUs (cf. Gubina this volume). Speakers do not orient only to the grammatical design of a TCU to treat it as complete (see, e.g., Ford & Thompson 1996; Selting 2000); they also constantly monitor prosodic and interactional trajectories. Along these lines, Monzoni (2005: 150–151) used the term 'increment' for expansions of potentially completed sentences that are realised with NPs, which, retrospectively, results in right dislocations. For Salzmann (2017), Italian expansions concern only units without inflected verbs ("implicit" in Italian, apparently in contrast with the notion of syntactic and pragmatic utterance-completion). Issues of grammatical "completeness" that could potentially not be actional (or *vice versa*) apply to both A's turn and B's extension. However, accounts of other-extensions that are continuations rather than recompletions of A's turn (i.e., B provides an incomplete unit after a TRP, not occasioning a new TRP) are scarce (cf. Calabria 2022).

Another issue, of syntactic nature, is that speakers also orient to syntactic coordination (in addition to subordinate dependence) when tying their turns to prior talk; syntactic coordination can be achieved through resources such as *and*. Coordination enables speakers to link their TCUs to prior turns more unambiguously than using utterances that have no grammatical open link with prior talk (cf. Rönnqvist & Lindström 2021). Considering *and*-prefaced turns as "independdent" means neglecting the fact they are not uttered in isolation, but are formatted by contributing speakers as being connected to prior talk through the resource *and*. A final, related point is that different languages have different morphosyntactic resources for encoding grammatical dependence. Couper-Kuhlen and Ono (2007) described some of them for English, German and Japanese, but these are not universal. Ultimately, morphosyntactic integration between turns is a locally negotiated accomplishment in the sequential unfolding of turns, beyond grammatical marking and formal descriptions that rely on turn "completion".

Calabria (2022) adopted the term "other-extensions", precisely in order to move beyond definitions of other-increments that only include contributing complete TCUs (that re-occasion a new TRP) whose status as dependent is recognised by speakers from a turn's onset (as shown by Excerpt (4) in the analysis, where the dependent status of the other-extension is not recognisable from the beginning of the turn). In this way, she expanded on the notion of completion, conceptualising it not as structurally given but as a negotiable achievement *in situ*. Other-extensions are not only recompletions that fit the end of the prior talk and through which speakers increment the action achieved by the speaker of the prior's turn. They can be stretches of talk dependent on the ending of the prior turn (cf. *glue-ons* in Couper-Kuhlen & Ono 2007) by means of syntactic markers (e.g., conjunctions) that overtly show their dependence on the grammatical unit that emerges in the extensions to the prior turn; and they can be provided as extending any grammatical item in prior talk, even when the prior unit is not complete (cf. *insertables* in Couper-Kuhlen & Ono 2007). In other words, speakers (at least in Italian) can draw on latent grammatical slots available at any point in the prior speaker's turn which they treat as "reusable" (e.g., the argument structure of a verb, Auer 2014). Moving away from a definition of "other-increments" based on English enables us to consider that the affordances of grammatical integration are broader in highly inflectional languages like Italian (and other Romance languages). This entails broadening the range of what the literature has so far considered jointly built turns.

To sum up, at least three elements emerging in prior literature are relevant for this chapter: (i) the notion of "grammatical dependence", which varies across different (spoken) linguistic systems; (ii) the notion of turn completion (cf. Selting 2000); (iii) the conception of other-incrementation as a collaborative endeavour which involves multiple "achievers".[5] These elements are highlighted in the analyses (Section 4).

---

5. Cf. Ono and Couper-Kuhlen (2007) for a cross-linguistic comparison of self-increments; and Thompson and Couper-Kuhlen (2005) for the importance of considering the resources that speakers have available in each specific language, and the affordances and consequences of this availability for action formation.

3. Data and methods

The data for this study come from the *ALIAS* corpus (*Archivio di LinguA Spontanea*), which contains approximately 60 hours of video recordings in present-day Italian, recorded in Milan (Lombardia) and Tortona (Piemonte) in a variety of settings.[6] For this study, four interactions were selected, totalling 11 hours and 52 minutes. These four settings specifically make up the corpus subsection "conversations around a table" (Calabria 2022) and present three features: they are *multiperson* settings (interactions with three to five participants, including cases where only two are already present in the setting and start interacting), the settings involve *multiactivity* (e.g., cooking, eating, setting up laptops, etc. while conversing), and the participants are stationary, *sitting around a table*. The data include two institutional encounters (business meetings) and two mundane interactions (one table dinner and one aperitif among friends). The total number of participants is fifteen (two of which are present in two events). All of the participants gave their informed consent to the recording and publication of the data in which they are visible; proper names and sensitive information have been pseudonymised. The data were transcribed following CA conventions for talk developed by Jefferson (2004) and for embodied conduct, by Mondada (2018). The original lines in Italian are translated into English, and additional glosses are provided where necessary for the purposes of the analysis (following *The Leipzig Glossing Rules* as explained in Comrie 2015).

Through the lenses of Conversation Analysis (Sacks, Schegloff & Jefferson 1974; Sidnell & Stivers 2012) and Interactional Linguistics (Couper-Kuhlen & Selting 2018) — methods which emphasise a sequential, temporal, and actional analysis of phenomena — other-extensions are considered a locus where grammar can be seen as emerging incrementally, and as an interactional set of practices that enables speakers to carry out socially shared actions. In scrutinising the data, with the aim of identifying instances where multiple speakers jointly achieved a "Collaborative Turn" (Calabria 2022), other-extensions were distinguished from co-constructions (cases where a speaker B contributes a collaborative stretch of talk to an unfolding, incomplete, turn uttered by A). There were 33 other-extensions (16 in the institutional and 17 in the mundane settings) identified in the 185 collaborative turns.

As remarked in Sections 1 and 2, the notion of *completion* is paramount to a definition of other-extensions. Although a detailed discussion of this concept goes beyond the scope of this chapter, a methodological distinction based on it

---

6. The data were collected as part of a project (OWP2012/08) funded by KU Leuven.

is necessary.[7] In providing a co-constructed TCU, speaker B draws on the projections offered by the bit-by-bit unfolding of the grammatical units in A's TCU (cf. Lerner 1991; Auer 2005, 2009), e.g., by uttering a complement clause that is dependent on a complementiser projected in A's incomplete TCU. However, in other-extensions, speaker B does not orient to unfolding grammatical projections, but deploys clausal formats (e.g., relative or adverbial clauses) which emerge as dependent on or integrated with the linguistic units in A's turn. The dependence is achieved by means of adverbs, conjunctions, and complementisers (e.g., *che* 'which, that', *se* 'if', *a* 'to'). Speakers of Italian — a language with a rich morphodeictic system of pronouns and clitics — can also provide extensions that are recognised as such because they reuse "latent slots" that remain open (Auer 2014) in A's turn. This means that B can still be heard as extending A's turn and not providing a new TCU (cf. Sidnell 2012) by formatting a contributing stretch of talk with anaphoric pronouns that re-use prior-mentioned referents in A's turn, or by adapting the gender and number of nouns and adjectives to those of referents in A's turn. In this chapter, all these types of extensions are analysed; in all cases speaker A provides a ratification that displays the treatment of speaker B's talk as a collaboration and brings the parties involved to the interactional achievement of a Collaborative Turn.

4. Analyses

This section presents three excerpts illustrating other-extensions. From the more "canonical" other-extension (a classic other-increment), by which a speaker can add more information while verifying it, described in Section 4.1, the analysis moves to less clearly syntactically dependent extending TCUs, where the overall activity, not only the prior action, is co-built. Specifically, Section 4.2 shows a case of verifying while demonstrating one's own understanding, and Section 4.3 presents a case of an other-extension through which a speaker reframes the prior turn as a laughable (this case is also a dyadic interaction). The analyses of grammatical and embodied resources highlight the shared and collaborative dimension of this practice achieved in everyday conversations by means of Collaborative Grammar.

---

7. Cf. Selting (2000) for a seminal discussion on turn vs. TCU completion; also cf. Ford, Fox, and Thompson (1996), who introduce the concept of "places" (not "points") in which grammatical, pragmatic and prosodic completion is achieved.

402 Virginia Calabria

4.1 Other-incrementing and providing additional information

The first excerpt is taken from the business meeting of a consultancy company; there are four participants. A speaker (Mario) provides an other-extension that emerges as a relative clause (a canonical other-increment), without a precise grammatical antecedent. Through his turn, Mario adds more information to the topic at hand. The vague anaphoric reference is not treated as problematic by his co-participants, and the other-extension is ratified.

Paolo (PAO) and Annina (ANN) communicate to Mario (MAR) and Duilio (DUI) that the company's board has taken new measures, in consequence of not reaching their target budget.

Excerpt 2. Mi13PRO1–49 (31:01–31:20), face-to-face, institutional interaction

```
01 PAO *.hh il       budget
              ART.M.SG budget.M.SG
              the budget
       PAO *....gazes at DUI------------------->

02      Δ>che c'eravamo fissati<   all'inizio*Δ
              that we had set for ourselves at the beginning
       PAO ----------------------------------->*
       DUI Δnods at PAO----------------------->Δ

03      *dell'anno,+(1.5)   non+
              of the year        will not
       PAO *gz. down on his lx side------------->
       PAO             +shakes head+

04      verrà €raggiu*nto.€
              be        met
       PAO ----------->*glances at DUI-->
       ANN       €gz. at PAO-€

05      +Δ(1.2)       Δ +
       PAO +scratches neck+
       DUI Δshakes headΔ

06 ANN *€°°hm°°€ vi ricordo che^era:*
                                 COMP be.PST.IPFV.IND.3SG
              hm     I remind you that it was
       PAO *gz. at ANN----------------->*
       ANN €,,,,,,€gz. at MAR-->1.17

07      *due mi[lioni @novecen[to:^e&
              two million nine hundred and
       PAO *gz. at MAR-->1.10
       MAR             @gz.at  ANN-->1.09

08 DUI      %[s:ì. n::::::°[::::°-   %
              yes  n-
       DUI      %gz. phone in front of him%

09 MAR            [s:ì: @
              yes
       MAR      -->,,,,,@
```

Chapter 13. Other-extensions in Italian   **403**

```
10 ANN &(rotti)* +[mila] euro.
        something thousand euros
   PAO ------->*
11 PAO          +[sì.  ]
                 yes
   PAO           +shakes head-->1.13
12   (0.2)
13 PAO  [no. +
         no
   PAO   ---->+
14 DUI  [(era o-)
         it was o-
15 MAR @$[che^era-              @che era
        REL be.PST.IPFV.IND.3SG REL be.PST.IPFV.IND.3SG
        which was which was
   ANN  $nods slightly--->
   MAR  @gazes ANN--------------@gazes at PAO------------>1.18
16      rispetto          al$
        compare.PST.PTCP.M to.ART.M.SG
        compared to the
   ANN                    --->$
17      ·consuntivo precedente·
        balance.M previous
        previous final balance
   PAO >·moves hands away---->·
18      più::€@ $·quattrocento per    ·ce@nto.$
        plus     four hundred         percent
   ANN ---->€
   ANN         $shakes head----------------->$
   PAO -------->·moves rx hand up-down·
   MAR ---->@gazes at ANN------------->@at PAO->1.23
19   (0.3)
20 MAR #@€$[((sniffles))$      ®
   ANN   €gazes up--------------->
   ANN   $nods-------->$
   MAR   @tilts lx hand lx and rx®
   fig #fig.1
```

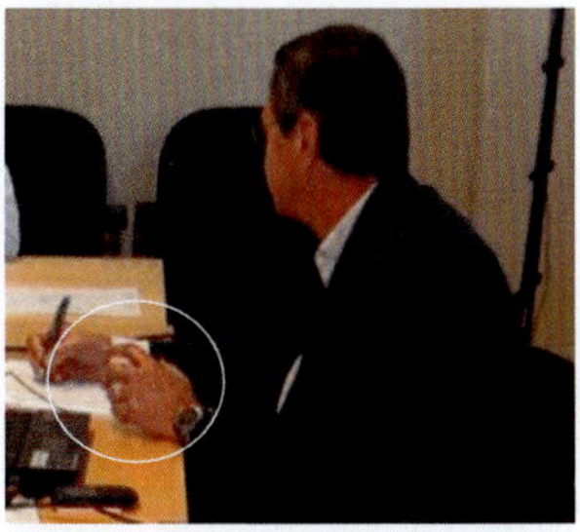

Figure 1. Mario tilts his left hand with open finger left and right

```
21 ANN     [sì.€
            yes
    ANN     ---->€
22   ·+(0.2)                    ·
    PAO  +shakes head-->
    PAO  ·moves rx hand to lx·
23 PAO @$nonə:- (.) no- nonə:-@@non+$
          it will     no-        not
    PAO  ---------------------->+
    ANN  $nods-------------------->$
    MAR  @gazes at ANN-------->@
    MAR                         @writes on sheet in front of him->>
24   verrà raggiunto.
     be    met
```

In lines 1–4, Paolo articulates an informing about the fact that their target budget will not be met, while gazing at Duilio, who is an unknowing participant (K- in Heritage 2011). This is not good news, as shown by Paolo diverting his gaze at the end of line 2 and shaking his head during a long pause at line 5, in co-occurrence with the negative particle *non* (while scratching his neck). Duilio first sustains mutual gaze (line 2), and nods after *budget*, displaying his early acknowledgment of the topic. Then he starts taking notes on papers in front of him and shakes his head (line 5), in alignment with the negative informing. At this point, Annina self-selects while gazing at Mario at line 6. Her turn catches Paolo's gaze, who turns to her. However, Paolo soon turns to Mario as well, who is also a K- participant.

Annina and Paolo select the same recipient(s), forming a party as knowledgeable (K+) participants (they both attended the prior board meeting) who are jointly informing their K- colleagues. Although the piece of information about reaching the budget is new, the budget itself is not new (cf. Duilio's early nodding, at line 2), as shown by the verb *vi ricordo* 'I remind you', which indexes preexisting shared knowledge among all the present participants (Duilio, in line 8, and Mario, in line 9, show early confirmation displays). Annina starts a turn at line 6, which is grammatically formatted as a new unit with the complement-taking predicate *ricordare*. However, the following complement clause, introduced by the complementiser *che*, draws on latent grammar in Paolo's talk, as the verb *era* 'it was' refers directly to *budget* without repeating this lexical item.

At line 15, with some delay compared to either Paolo's (lines 1–4) or Annina's tuns (lines 6 and 10), Mario self-selects and provides an other-extension. His turn is formatted as a relative clause with *budget* as antecedent. Mario recycles (Auer 2014) grammatical material in Annina's turn: the *che* 'which' and the verb at the imperfective *era* 'it was' (in 3rd person singular). But while Annina's turn unfolded as a main verb followed by a complement clause, Mario's turn is a relative clause, subordinated to talk in prior turns. Whether the host turn is Paolo's or Annina's is not an issue for the participants, as shown by Mario shifting his gaze between the two of them (at lines 15–18), thereby treating them as a party who is engaged in the same activity (informing about the budget). Mario's statement is twofold: by uttering a complete clause, he adds more information related to the topic at hand, the *budget,* displaying that he remembers what Annina said; while he also takes the occasion to verify his understanding (as also shown by his gesture at line 20, Figure 1, indexing approximation). Annina treats Mario's turn as both information claiming and checking, as she confirms his extension at line 20 by nodding and vocally at line 21. During a short pause in line 22, Paolo shakes his head, projecting the negative statement which he provides at lines 23–24 and which, in symmetry with line 4, closes the episode.

Mario's other-extension (lines 15–18) allows him to unambiguously build on prior turns without selecting a specific host turn. He designs his contribution as a relative clause introduced by *che* 'which', and, in doing so, overtly ties it to prior talk. In this way, he can be heard as extending the topic at hand, before the conversation progresses further.

This excerpt illustrates participants' contingent flexibility and constant negotiation in every-day interaction, in which people pursue different goals through their practices. Duilio's displays of engagement are embodied, since he is taking notes at the same time, hence managing two courses of action at once: paying attention and writing. Annina self-selects with a new turn that opens a side sequence, but nonetheless builds on Paolo's talk, displaying that she is engaged in a joint endeavour with him. Mario takes the last opportunity with an other-extension to join in before the topic is closed. This also speaks to the choral endeavour (Lerner 2002) of multiperson interactions, where participants have to coordinate and cooperate to jointly build the ongoing activity, not only interactionally but also through grammatical means. Collaborative Grammar emerges *for* and *through* this collaboration of multiple voices.

While this first example shows an other-extension that is more canonically formatted as a grammatical subordinate clause (albeit not produced at the very end of the turn that it extends), the next excerpts show less clearly defined grammatical extensions, which are nonetheless treated as actionally building on prior talk.

4.2 Verifying while demonstrating understanding

The next excerpt is taken from the first minutes of a dinner among friends, when only two of the five participants are present (occasioning a dyadic interaction). It shows a case where a speaker produces an other-extension to check their correct understanding of the original teller's host turn while also demonstrating this understanding.

Before the other friends arrive, Giorgio (GIO) tells Giulio (GIU) that he has reconciled with his girlfriend after a big fight, during which he thought they would break up, but in the end, they worked it out.

Excerpt 3. Mi13DINFULL (00:08:50–00:08:58), face-to-face, informal interaction

```
01 GIO %*#adesso STO RIDENDO perché sono contento+
          now I'm laughing because I'm happy
   GIO %lifts head to gaze at GIU------------>
   GIO >>smiles--------------------------->+
   GIU  *gazes at dishes in front of him---------->>
   fig  #fig.2
```

Figure 2. Giorgio, sitting at the table, looks at Giulio, while Giulio washes the dishes with his back to Giorgio

```
02     ca%pito?
       get it?
   GIO ->%down->1.07

03     (0.3)

04 GIU °m-° per come è fini:ta.
       m-   for the way it ended

05     (0.3)

06 GIO ↑minchia: ma te lo giuro.
       shit     but I swear (to you)

07     (0.2)%
   GIO ---->%

08 GIO %+stavo ma:le di brutto. stavo+ MALE.
       I     felt really bad  I felt bad
   GIO %gz. at GIU-------------------->>
   GIO +shakes head--------------->+
```

While Giorgio tells Giulio about his romantic issues, he sits at the table smoking and drinking. Giulio is washing the dishes and is therefore turned towards the sink with his back to Giorgio (Figure 2). By uttering some of his words with higher volume, Giorgio can be heard as making relevant Giulio's bodily orientation (i.e., lack of mutual gaze) and the noises in the room (i.e., running water and clattering of dishes).

At line 1, Giorgio says, while smiling, that now he can laugh about the big fight he had with his girlfriend, because he is happy. Giorgio contrasts the present situation with the past fight, as shown by the lexical *adesso* 'now' and the present continuous *sto ridendo* 'I'm laughing'. He ends his turn in line 2 with *capito?* 'get it?' (lit. 'understood?'), a "phatic connective" according to Bazzanella (1990).[8] Considering that the participants are not looking at each other and that the setting is noisy, Giorgio deploys *capito* as a device to check his co-participant's understanding, both of the story and of the (positive) stance that he has explicitly expressed (cf. line 1 *perché sono contento* 'because I'm happy'). Indeed, at line 4, Giulio utters a dependent clause *m- per come è finita* 'for the way it ended', which other-extends lines 1–2, and forms: *sono contento m- per come è finita* 'I'm happy m- for the way it ended'. Giulio formats his contribution as an other-extending subordinate final clause, dependent on line 1. Giulio's contribution is uttered with final prosody, statement-like, and it is prefaced by *m-* which could be heard as the adversative conjunction *ma* 'but', used in Italian as turn-entry device without any adversative meaning (Bazzanella 1990). By other-extending Giorgio's turn, Giulio not only demonstrates his understanding to Giorgio, but he is also able to verify that the reason for Giorgio's present happiness, in contrast with his past sadness, is that the story has a happy ending. The conjunction *ma* does not contrast Giorgio's words, but the past and present situations. Indeed, at line 6 Giulio obtains confirmation that his understanding is correct: Giorgio provides a positive ratification by using an emphatic swearword *minchia* 'shit', uttered with high pitch. He then follows this up by providing an even stronger expression of his negative stance towards his past feelings, explicitly stating: 'I felt bad' (line 8) in past tense, as be compared with 'now I'm laughing' (line 1) in present tense. Although with this other-extension, the contributing speaker carries out a *prima facie* new action, not only does the talk emerge as an other-extension (grammatically, a subordinate final clause), but it also builds and extends the argument expressed by the prior speaker, in order to be heard as the correct understanding of this argument.

Speakers are not concerned with the formal status of a turn as grammatically dependent and actionally independent (or *vice versa*), but rather with specific

---

8. Bazzanella describes phatic connectives as resources to monitor an addressee's involvement in the interaction.

action formations and ascriptions which might result in composite actions (Rossi 2018). This excerpt, specifically, shows a contributing participant who is other-extending to verify his own understanding, while also fulfilling a pursuit of response projected by a phatic connective (*capito* 'get it', line 2). This expands on Bolden's (2003:188) remark that "collaborative completions are the most convincing device" that speakers have and use to display understanding of the interlocutor's unfolding turn, by complementing it with other-extensions. Moreover, displaying understanding is a retrospective process as Deppermann (2015:70) points out:

> Collaborative turn-constructions are especially apt for displaying understanding because they create a common cohesive and dependent structure which consists of *ego's* and *alter's* turn. In this way, intersubjectivity is displayed through the production of a shared structure with a collaboratively constructed meaning. Understanding of prior speaker's intention can be displayed by a second speaker through completing the turn in a way he/she assumes the turn to have been intended by the prior speaker (or at least in a way acceptable to him/her), or by formulating its content more explicitly via turn-expansion. In this way, turn-continuations afford first speakers an opportunity to check recipients' understandings.

The other-extension in this excerpt is used to explicitly achieve the action of showing one's own understanding retrospectively, while at the same time verifying or checking this understanding, prospectively, with participants who are treated as the activity-initiators and, therefore, knowledgeable about the narrated facts.

4.3 Reframing prior talk as laughable

The last excerpt, taken from the same dinner as in Excerpt (3), illustrates an other-extension provided as a joke in a constructed dialogue. Calabria and De Stefani (2020) showed that self-increments can be used to reframe a prior turn as a joke. Obana and Haugh (2015) described "transformative continuations" through which speakers extend their own or another speaker's turn with grammatically fitted material, thereby transforming an utterance and the action into something different from the projected trajectory. More specifically, participants can "[take] the words of the other and using them against him or her in a reciprocal action" (C. Goodwin & M.H. Goodwin 1987:218). Before the beginning of Excerpt (4), Rino (RIN) told the others that, on the same day, there was a plainclothes ticket inspection at one of the bus stops, and that although he tried to escape it, he got a fine. At line 1, he explains how it happened.

Chapter 13. Other-extensions in Italian **409**

Excerpt 4. Mi13DINFULL (00:27:23–00:28:01), face-to-face, informal interaction

```
01 RIN @son sce:so: e: questo fa: (.) biglietti:
      I got off and this one goes    tickets
   PIE @gazes at papers in her hands------------->1.08

02 RIN biglietti: siamo:^hm: √l'attiemme[:^in-
      tickets we are hm      the ATM
   RIN                    √gazes at GIO----->1.06

03 PIE                              [me
                                    1SGPRO.OBJ
                                    to me

04    ne    dia        quattro, [grazie.  ]
      of.it give.PRS.IMP.3SG four        please
      give me four of them please

05 GIO                              [in borche]se=
                                    plainclothes

06 RIN =in borghe:se,√ biglitetti.
      plainclothes, tickets
   RIN ------------->√at GIU--->1.09

07 RIN ↑io: (.) [>quando ho visto che  una tipa<
      I          when  I saw   that a  woman

08 GIU      *+[((laughs))£>me ne dia grazie. <£@*
                        give me of them thanks
   PIE ------------------------------------->@GIU->
   GIU     *gz. at PIE----------------------->*
   GIU       +smiles----------------------->>

09 RIN §.h quando@ la  ti- (.) quando una √tipa:-
          when     the ti-     when  a   woman
   RIN ------------------------------->√.....
   PIE §smiles-->>
   PIE -------->@at papers in her hands------->

10 RIN √∞£ah @ah£
      ah    ah
   RIN √gz. at PIE----->1.13
   RIN ∞smiles-------->1.13
   PIE ----->@at RIN--->1.13

11    *(1.3)
   GIU *gz. at RIN-------->>

12 RIN >l'ho capita ades-.< perché §>sembrava
      I got it now        because  it sounded like
   PIE                           §nods----------->

13    biglie-<.§√@∞ +.hh +
      tickets
   RIN --------->√in front->
   RIN ----------->∞
   PIE --------->@hands-->>
   PIE -------->§
   GIU               +nods+

14 GIU ↑BIGLI√∞ETTI:
      tickets
   RIN ----->√at GIU-->>
   RIN         ∞smiles-->>
```

Rino's explanation at line 1 is prompted by a clarification request from Giorgio. According to Rino, after he got off the bus, the ticket inspector (in line 1 referred to as *questo* 'this one', with a singular masculine demonstrative pronoun) started asking for tickets. To continue the story, Rino re-enacts the scene through direct reported speech, introduced by the quotative *fare* 'to do'. He starts mimicking the ticket inspector of the bus company ATM, shouting *biglietti, biglietti siamo l'attieme* 'tickets, tickets, we are ATM.'[9] At this point, Piera self-selects at line 3, orienting to the potential TRP of Rino's turn, and adds a potential response to the request for tickets: *me ne dia quattro grazie* 'give me four of them please'. While doing so, she is still gazing at the consent forms she has in her hands and does not orient her gaze to Rino. She formats her TCU as a quote, using various morpho-deictic resources: the first person singular indirect object pronoun *me*, the partitive object pronoun *ne* referring to *biglietti*, and the verb *dare* 'to give' conjugated in the imperative mood and inflected for the courtesy form of address in Italian *Lei* (which is conjugated in 3rd person singular), directed to the ticket inspector. Her turn is addressed to the same external recipient in the constructed dialogue as for Rino: the ticket inspector. She designs her turn to be unambiguously recognised as an extension of the reported speech (Calabria 2023) started by Rino, as a quote uttered while *doing being* Rino, i.e., voicing him. Overlapping with Piera, at line 5, Giorgio treats the lengthening of the last syllable of *attiemme* in Rino's turn (line 2) as hesitation, and offers a co-constructed completion, *in borchese* 'plainclothes', which Rino ratifies (by repeating it) at line 6 before repeating *biglietti*. At line 6, when Rino is about to go on with his explanation without orienting to Piera's other-extension, Giulio, in overlap (line 8), laughs and turns his gaze to Piera. Contrary to Rino, Giulio partially repeats her quote, rushing, thereby showing he has now come to realise what she said: he treats Piera's turn at lines 3–4 as a funny joke. However, at line 9, Rino is still orienting to the progressivity of his explanation, since he repairs line 6. On the last syllable of *tipa* 'woman', Rino hesitates, orients his gaze to Piera, and finally laughs at line 10. Piera and Rino exchange mutual gaze, and Rino utters a very delayed recognition turn (lines 12–13): he has now understood her joke. Interestingly, even now that Rino has acknowledged the joke, the joke remains inferred and is not spelled out, as the participants have enough shared common knowledge to understand Piera's turn without the need for an explicit explanation. 'Tickets' is ambiguous as it can refer to both the bus ticket that the inspector was after (which Rino did not have and for which he got a fine), and to tickets for a show or movie. Piera's joke lies then in asking the inspector for four tickets (in the latter sense) as Rino could not produce a bus ticket. Piera's joke is then reinforced by Giulio, who shouts *biglietti* 'tickets'.

---

9. ATM stands for Azienda Transporti Milanesi, Milano's public transport company.

Piera's doing being Rino in this constructed dialogue turns the story into a joke, which on the one hand interrupts the story (thus being potentially disaffiliative), but on the other, it enables Piera, Giulio, and Rino to create a jocular mode together. This changes the footing of the story from the telling of a misadventure to a joke, as also shown by the participants' embodied conduct: Giulio and Piera smile when Giulio recognises the joke at line 8, and Rino starts smiling when he recognises the joke at line 10 (and they carry on beyond the end of the excerpt). Piera's turn is an additional action, but she formats it as an other-extension, targeting the lexical item *biglietti*. The turn *me ne dia quattro* 'give me four of them' emerges and is retrospectively recognisable as being in a pragmatic/semantic relationship with the previous turn *e questo fa biglietti biglietti siamo l'attieme* 'and this one goes tickets tickets, we are ATM'. Rino's turn in lines 12–13 shows that he accepts the change of footing and the jocular co-built mode.

Other-extending and, more generally, collaborative practices of turn-construction emerge as collective ways of managing the tones of an episode *in situ*, building it together without the risk of being heard as in competition for the floor (in a multiperson setting) or in overt disaffiliation. These practices allow a reorganization of the participation framework (Goffman 1981) in a choral orientation (or constitution of *parties*) towards the ongoing activity, whose footing and tones are co-shaped and co-built by multiple contributors.

5. Discussion

Participants in multiperson interactions face at least two challenges related to turn-management (cf. Mazeland 2019): the first, to self-select as a candidate next speaker and avoid being heard as in competition for the floor with another or the prior participant; the second, to design a turn from the onset as fitted to the ongoing activity. Participants who aim at achieving collaborative turns face the additional challenge of mobilising grammatical (morpho-syntactic), actional, and embodied resources in order to ensure that their talk is understood as (re)completing or extending prior talk. This chapter analysed a range of activities that are jointly built through the practice of other-extending a prior speaker's potentially completed turn. The aim was to describe a practice that enables us to reflect on the grammar-(inter)action intersection, while also making a case for the necessity of considering shared, collaborative practices in grammars of talk-in-interaction.

By other-extending, contributing speakers can achieve an array of social actions, of which three were presented in this chapter: providing additional information, verifying while displaying one's own understanding, and reframing prior talk as laughable. The data have been presented starting with a more syntactically integrated extension, to arrive at a looser grammatical relationship between turns. Specifically, Excerpt (2) shows an other-extension formatted as a relative clause, while Excerpt (3) presents an adverbial clause and Excerpt (4), a paratactic main clause which has a more pragmatic and semantic relation with the prior linguistic units than a syntactic one. In the last case, re-enactment is involved, whereby the speakers deploy a set of bodily and prosodic resources that more overtly show the interactional link with the host turn that they are extending. Thus, this analysis shows that Collaborative Grammar refers to a set of tools that goes beyond syntactic formats and morphological resources, to include the body-grammar interface (Pekarek Doehler, Keevallik & Li 2022). In this chapter, the claim is not that co-occurring packages of resources accompany the practice of other-extending, but that the emergent verbal units deployed are inextricably intertwined with body orientation, gestures, and gaze, through the logic of maximising co-operative effort, which is necessary in multiperson interactions (cf. Stivers 2021).

Jointly building a turn or a multi-unit turn is, in any case, possible in both dyadic and multiperson interactions. In the latter case, the participation framework can change constantly, involving a different number of speakers and recipients (or hearers), grouped in different parties and sets of addressees throughout the conversation. In other words, extending a prior turn with talk that is designed as (grammatically) building on the prior speaker's turn allows contributing speakers to display that what they are saying is not only related to prior talk, but is also part of it, designed in collaboration with the prior speaker. This changes the participation framework from sequences of cooperative actions (Goodwin 2018) — that is, all actions in conversation implemented in cooperation with other participants to ensure mutual understanding – to jointly built actions between multiple people and voices. In multiperson settings, visibly and audibly self-selecting and aligning with the ongoing activity, thus enhancing the speaker's story, continuing it, merging individual voices into one, or co-explaining a known-in-common topic, are effective practices for demonstrating active involvement, participation, and collaboration. These practices can also be used to show that a story is worth pursuing and to create shared jocular moments.

Other relevant elements for collaborative turns that emerged in the analysis include shared common ground (Clark 2015), knowledge, and experience belonging to all those present and that unite their voices (cf. also Orletti 2008; Luke 2021); this is shown through references to cultural, personal, and specialised domains (Clark 2015:329). Participants' epistemic status (Heritage 2011) is not only available to others based on the shared system of knowledge and experience among the participants (e.g., if they are colleagues working for the same company, or if they have all been students in the same system), it is also displayed when

Chapter 13. Other-extensions in Italian **413**

speakers self-select and complete, continue, or extend another participant's turn. Every turn is an occasion to draw on this common knowledge and use it to join the original teller (cf. Calabria 2022). To paraphrase C. Goodwin (1996:327): every turn offers an "unfolding horizon of future possibilities".

Among these possibilities, other-extensions (and CTs in general) emerge when collaboration is maximised. Specifically, other-extensions are an epiphenomenon of the "narrow" sense of "collaboration" (Luke 2021:13), in the sense that they form a practice that enables participants to build turns and activities together; but they also enable participants to achieve collaboration in the "broader" sense, i.e., reach an intersubjective understanding (Deppermann 2015) in their conversation, which can be challenging when there are more than two participants (cf. Stivers 2021).

Other-extensions expand upon Helasvuo's (2004) description of co-constructions as phenomena of "shared grammar", to incorporate cases of joint construction after potential turn completions.[10] Similar to Helasvuo (2004), this chapter challenges the view of completion as something formally determined and instead conceptualises completion as negotiated locally through the mutual monitoring of each other's unfolding turns and linguistic units.

All excerpts show extensions that result in composite actions, i.e., turns that both continue the prior action, thereby extending the overall activity, and also allow the contributing speaker to introduce new actions. These new actions are not in competition with what the prior speaker was building, but are, rather, additions to it (Excerpt (2)), verifications/demonstrations of understanding (Excerpt (3)), or co-built change of tone to the narrated events (Excerpt (4)). Including these cases in the inventory of collaborative practices allows us to move beyond the formal distinction between incrementing continuations and new TCUs (see Section 2), towards what participants actually achieve when self-selecting and taking the floor. Moreover, it allows us to revise the concept of competition for the turn (cf. Stivers 2021), and advocate for collaborative turn-taking. These actions emerge in specific settings as context-sensitive and activity-bound. When adopting an interactional starting point — i.e., explaining grammatical units with practices and actions (and *vice versa*) — it becomes clear that the grammar of talk-in-interaction is a "syntax-for-conversation" (Schegloff 1979). This means that grammatical resources, beyond their "functions" as described in traditional grammars, allow speakers to design turns through which to carry out a whole spectrum of social actions not exclusively bound to these functions (e.g., *ma* 'but' in Excerpt (3) used as turn-entry device, not as an "adversative" conjunc-

---

10. Helasvuo (2004) focused specifically on collaborative completions accomplished by means of co-constructed clauses in Finish.

tion; cf. Suomalainen this volume).[11] The excerpts in this chapter specifically illustrate how speakers can mobilise a variety of resources to achieve a *collaborative* "syntax-for-conversation".

6. Conclusion

This chapter has provided a grammatical and interactional description of a collaborative practice in spoken language, other-extensions, by addressing the research questions of what people do when they join their voices and collaborate (Luke 2021), with grammar and with their actions; and how collaboration is managed between multiple participants. This study, at the grammar-(inter)action interface, shows what actions can tell us about grammar (Couper-Kuhlen 2014), by highlighting the speakers' need to use situated grammatical resources in order to achieve socially recognisable actions. The incremental emergence of grammatical structures (visible in speakers' orientation to extending already potentially completed turns), which entails tying more syntactic items "on the fly" (Hopper 2011), and complexifying the grammar of clauses and sentences while the turns unfold, proves that it is possible to conceive of a grammatical description of spoken language without starting from a written-language bias (Linell 2005). Moving away from descriptions of languages as static systems allows us to open up the specificities of talk-in-interaction to a non-linguist audience. These specificities include recipient-designed and situated social actions, the unfolding of turns within a specific context and activity, negotiation and collaboration, grammatical and interactional projections, and temporality, intended as both time-unfolding and as the base for turn-sequentiality.

This chapter focused on participants' deployment of Collaborative Grammar, conceptualised as "one key organizational resource in building and recognising TCUs" (Schegloff 2007: 3). Specifically, it is what allows co-participants to display that what they are saying is tied, collaboratively, to what precedes. It is based on the interplay between a cataphoric forward-looking and an anaphoric backward-looking orientation. Through these two processes, collaborative turns, formed by host turns *plus* other-extensions, are achieved.

There are practical applications for grammar writing of this research on a collaborative practice in multiperson interactions. First, to avoid a descriptive (and never exhausted) list of formats and practices, granularity of analysis is paramount when describing talk-in-interaction (cf. Fox & Raymond this volume).

---

11. Specifically, the contrast here is made with traditional grammars that adopt structural approaches to talk and start from written productions (cf. Linell 2005; Voghera 2017).

Granular descriptions of collaborative practices involving shared turns and syntax are basically non-existent when it comes to grammars. Grammars are often based on either monologic data (considering only one speaker's production at a time) or dialogic data (considering one speaker's production and the recipient's reception but not their collaboration). For a long time, the Italian grammatical tradition has been based on a conception of linguistic structures as finite products, without examining how speakers shape language in everyday settings (what Voghera 2017: 20 called "grammar without spoken language").[12] By focusing granularly on the production of the interactive processes that constitute spoken language in real-time, and on the emergence of grammatical units "on the fly", grammars of talk-in-interaction can finally move away from "the written language bias" (Linell 2005), in which grammatical productions are often treated as ready-made chunks. The focus on collaborative productions enables us to observe how paramount it is for speakers to monitor each other's turns, and to coordinate and cooperate in ways that allow them to make sense of each other's actions.

Second, traditional grammatical descriptions, even when using spoken data, often neglect the larger sequential and interactional contexts in which given utterances occur, and instead describe them in isolation. By introducing collaborative turns (co-constructions and other-extensions) in a systematic description of talk-in-interaction, it is possible to show how *situated* grammatical productions are – situated in specific activities and sequences (e.g., an explanation during a business meeting). Their emergence in turns is contextually and contingently linked to the challenges of interactions in which speakers must self-select among several people and coordinate their linguistic behaviour and, hence, their actions with multiple other co-participants. This context-boundedness could be introduced in a special section of a grammar of talk-in-interaction, explaining that there are institutional and mundane settings, that dyadic and multiperson conversations have different participation frameworks (and potentially, bringing in a model of participation framework that expands on Goffman 1981). Serianni et al. (2021) have recently published a grammar of Italian that focuses on "communications and writing", in which the authors present some "communicational contexts" in which specific interactions might occur. If rather than a list of potential contexts, we were to stress the importance of settings, and, in the examples presented, we were to include the larger sequence and activity in which a practice emerges (without analysing them *per se* but using them to inform our explanations), the contingent reasons for the practice would become clearer.

Phenomena of shared, collaborative practices that are achieved grammatically between multiple speakers should be part of any grammatical description that

---

12. "La grammatica senza parlato", in the original Italian.

aims at describing the competing temporalities of multiperson interactions. These phenomena should probably follow, in their own descriptive space, the equivalent action description for one speaker. For instance, reported speech could be followed by collaborative reported speech (Calabria 2023); sequences of explanations or directives (cf. Steensig et al. 2023) could be followed by collaborative instruction giving; suggestions (cf. Couper-Kuhlen & Thompson this volume) could be followed by people constituting parties and providing joint suggestions to the same recipient. In these cases, the grammatical and actional descriptions would be recontextualised and described on the basis of the multiple voices that produce them, allowing us also to discuss the topic of *recipiency* as a less directional (from one speaker to another or others) and a more dynamic concept that involves being at the same time the producer and the recipient of turns.

Other-extensions are just one case *of* and *for* Collaborative Grammar. Talking collaboratively is a pervasive aspect of our everyday interactions, yet descriptions of this achievement are in inverse proportion to its occurrence. This is why in a comprehensive grammar of talk-in-interaction, a description of the practices achieved through Collaborative Grammar would be paramount, and for each of them we would need a dedicated section that follows and integrates sections describing the practices carried out either by the same participant (e.g., practices of self-selection) or in response to prior talk (e.g., answers). Only such a grammar would be able to describe the actual temporal unfolding of talk in naturally occurring conversations, which is bound to the competing temporalities of multiperson interactions, multiactivity settings (Mondada 2018), and their complex participation frameworks.

References

Auer, Peter. 1996. "On the Prosody and Syntax of Turn-Continuations". In *Prosody in Conversation*, ed. by Elizabeth Couper-Kuhlen, and Margret Selting, 57–100. Cambridge: CUP.

Auer, Peter. 2005. "Projection in Interaction and Projection in Grammar". *Text – Interdisciplinary Journal for the Study of Discourse* 25 (1): 7–36.

Auer, Peter. 2007. "Why Are Increments Such Elusive Objects? An Afterthought". *Pragmatics* 17 (4): 647–658.

Auer, Peter. 2009. "On-Line Syntax: Thoughts on the Temporality of Spoken Language". *Language Sciences* 31 (1): 1–13.

Auer, Peter. 2014. "Syntactic Structures and Their Symbiotic Guests: Notes on Analepsis from the Perspective of Online Syntax". *Pragmatics* 24 (3): 533–560.

Auer, Peter. 2015. "The temporality of language in interaction". In *Temporality in interaction*, ed. by Arnulf Deppermann, and Susanne Günthner, 27–56. Amsterdam/Philadelphia: John Benjamins.

Bazzanella, Carla. 1990. "Phatic Connectives as Interactional Cues in Contemporary Spoken Italian". *Journal of Pragmatics* 14 (4): 629–647.

Bolden, Galina B. 2003. "Multiple Modalities in Collaborative Turn Sequences". *Gesture* 3 (2): 187–212.

Calabria, Virginia. 2022. "Collaborative Grammar: The Temporality and Emergence of Clause Combination in Italian Talk-in-Interaction". PhD Thesis, KU Leuven/ Université de Neuchâtel.

Calabria, Virginia. 2023. "Co-Constructing and Other-Extending Collaborative Reported Speech in Italian". *Journal of Pragmatics* 214: 1–17.

Calabria, Virginia, and Elwys De Stefani. 2020. "Per una grammatica situata: Aspetti temporali e multimodali dell'incrementazione sintattica". *Studi Italiani di Linguistica Teorica ed Applicata* 49 (3): 571–601.

Clark, Eve V. 2015. "Common ground". *In The Handbook of Language Emergence*, ed. by Brian MacWhinney, and William O'Grady, 328–353. London: Wiley-Blackwell.

Comrie, Bernard. 2015. "From the Leipzig Glossing Rules to the GE and RX lines." In *Corpus-based Studies of Lesser-described Languages*, ed. by Amina Mettouchi, Dominique Caubet, and Martine Vanhove, 207–219. Amsterdam/Philadelphia: John Benjamins.

Couper-Kuhlen, Elizabeth. 2014. "What Does Grammar Tell Us about Action?". *Pragmatics* 24 (3): 623–647.

Couper-Kuhlen, Elizabeth, and Tsuyoshi Ono. 2007. ""Incrementing" in Conversation. A Comparison of Practices in English, German and Japanese". *Pragmatics* 4: 513–552.

Couper-Kuhlen, Elizabeth, and Margret Selting. 2018. *Interactional linguistics: Studying language in social interaction.* Cambridge: CUP.

Deppermann, Arnulf. 2015. "Retrospection and understanding in interaction". In *Temporality in interaction*, ed. by Arnulf Deppermann, and Susanne Günthner, 57–95, Amsterdam/Philadelphia: John Benjamins.

Ford, Cecilia E., Barbara A. Fox, and Sandra A. Thompson. 1996. "Practices in the Construction of Turns: The "TCU" Revisited". *Pragmatics* 6 (3): 427–454.

Ford, Cecilia E., Barbara A. Fox, and Sandra A. Thompson. 2002. "Constituency and the grammar of turn increments". In *The Language of Turn and Sequence*, ed. by Cecilia E. Ford, Barbara A. Fox, and Sandra A. Thompson, 14–38. New York: Oxford University Press.

Ford, Cecilia E., and Sandra A. Thompson. 1996. "Interactional Units in Conversation: Syntactic, Intonational, and Pragmatic Resources for the Management of Turns". In *Interaction and Grammar*, ed. by Elinor Ochs, and Sandra A. Thompson, 134–184. Cambridge: CUP.

Goffman, Erving. 1981. *Forms of talk.* University of Pennsylvania Press.

Goodwin, Charles. 1996. "Transparent Vision". In *Interaction and Grammar*, ed. by Elinor Ochs, and Sandra A. Thompson, 370–404. Cambridge: CUP.

Goodwin, Charles. 2018. *Co-operative Action.* Cambridge: CUP.

Goodwin, Charles, and Marjorie Harness Goodwin. 1987. "Concurrent Operations on Talk: Notes on the Interactive Organization of Assessments". *IPrA Papers in Pragmatics* 1 (1): 1–54.

Helasvuo, Marja-Liisa. 2004. "Shared Syntax: The Grammar of Co-Constructions". *Journal of Pragmatics* 36 (8): 1315–1336.

Heritage, John. 2011. "Territories of Knowledge, Territories of Experience: Empathic Moments in Interaction". In *The Morality of Knowledge in Conversation*, ed. by Tanya Stivers, Lorenza Mondada, and Jakob Steensig, 159–183. Cambridge: CUP.

Hopper, Paul J. 2011. "Emergent Grammar and Temporality in Interactional Linguistics". In *Constructions: Emerging and Emergent*, ed. by Peter Auer, and Stefan Pfänder, 22–44. Berlin: De Gruyter.

Jefferson, Gail. 2004. "Glossary of Transcript Symbols with an Introduction". In *Conversation Analysis. Studies from the first generation*, ed. by Gene H. Lerner, 13–31. Amsterdam/Philadelphia: John Benjamins.

Lerner, Gene H. 1991. "On the Syntax of Sentences-in-Progress". *Language in Society* 20 (3): 441–458.

Lerner, Gene H. 1996. "On the "Semi-Permeable" Character of Grammatical Units in Conversation: Conditional Entry into the Turn Space of Another Speaker". In *Interaction and Grammar*, ed. by Elinor Ochs, and Sandra A. Thompson, 238–276. Cambridge: CUP.

Lerner, Gene H. 2002. "Turn-Sharing: The Choral Co-Production of Talk-in-Interaction". In *The Language of Turn and Sequence*, ed. by Cecilia E. Ford, Barbara A. Fox, and Sandra A. Thompson, 225–256. New York: Oxford University Press.

Lerner, Gene H. 2004. "On the Place of Linguistic Resources in the Organization of Talk-in-Interaction: Grammar as Action in Prompting a Speaker to Elaborate". *Research on Language and Social Interaction* 37 (2): 151–184.

Linell, Per. 2005. *The written language bias in linguistics: Its nature, origins and transformations*. London: Routledge.

Luke, Kang-Kwong. 2021. "Parties and Voices: On the Joint Construction of Conversational Turns". *Chinese Language and Discourse* 12 (1): 6–34.

Luke, Kang-Kwong, and Wei Zhang. 2007. "Retrospective Turn Continuations in Mandarin Chinese Conversation". *Pragmatics* 17 (4): 605–635.

Mazeland, Harrie. 2019. "Position Expansion in Meeting Talk: An Interaction-Re-Organizing Type of and-Prefaced Other-Continuation". In *Embodied Activities in Face-to-Face and Mediated Settings: Social Encounters in Time and Space*, ed. by Elisabeth Reber, and Cornelia Gerhardt, 397–433. New York: Springer.

Mondada, Lorenza. 2018. "Multiple temporalities of language and body in interaction: challenges for transcribing multimodality". *Research on language and social interaction* 51 (1): 85–106.

Monzoni, Chiara. 2005. "The Use of Marked Syntactic Constructions in Italian Multi-Party Conversation". In *Syntax and Lexis in Conversation*, ed. by Auli Hakulinen, and Margret Selting, 129–157. Amsterdam/Philadelphia: John Benjamins.

Obana, Yasuko, and Michael Haugh. 2015. "Co-Authorship of Joint Utterances in Japanese". *Dialogue & Discourse* 6 (1): 1–25.

Ono, Tsuyoshi, and Elizabeth Couper-Kuhlen. 2007. "Increments in Cross-Linguistic Perspective". *Pragmatics* 17 (4): 505–512.

Orletti, Franca. 2008. "Enunciati a più voci: la conversazione fra grammatica ed interazione". In *La comunicazione parlata. Atti del congresso internazionale (Napoli, 23–25 febbraio 2006)*, ed. by Massimo Pettorino et al., Napoli: Liguori: 1190–1204.

Pekarek Doehler, Simona, Leelo Keevallik, and Xiaoting Li. 2022. "The Grammar-Body Interface in Social Interaction". *Frontiers in Psychology* 13: 875696.

Rönnqvist, Sara, and Jan Lindström. 2021. "Turn Continuations and Gesture: "And Then"-Prefacing in Multi-Party Conversations". *Frontiers in Communication* 6: 670173.

Rossi, Giovanni. 2018. "Composite Social Actions: The Case of Factual Declaratives in Everyday Interaction". *Research on Language and Social Interaction* 51 (4): 379–397.

Sacks, Harvey. 1992. *Lectures on Conversation*. Oxford: Blackwell.

Sacks, Harvey, Emanuel A. Schegloff, and Gail Jefferson. 1974. "A Simplest Systematics for the Organization of Turn-Taking for Conversation". *Language* 50 (4): 696–735.

Salzmann, Katharina. 2017. *Expansionen in der deutschen und italienischen Wissenschaftssprache. Kontrastive Korpusanalyse und sprachdidaktische Überlegungen.* Berlin: Erich Schmidt.

Schegloff, Emanuel A. 1979. "The relevance of repair to syntax-for-conversation". *In Syntax and semantics 12: Discourse and Syntax*, ed. by Talmy Givón, 261–286. Leiden: Brill.

Schegloff, Emanuel A. 1996. "Turn Organization: One Intersection of Grammar and Interaction". In *Interaction and Grammar*, ed. by Elinor Ochs, and Sandra A. Thompson, 52–133. Cambridge: CUP.

Schegloff, Emanuel A. 2007. *Sequence organization in interaction: A primer in conversation analysis*. Cambridge: Cambridge University Press.

Schegloff, Emanuel A. 2016. "Increments". In *Accountability in social interaction*, ed. by Jeffrey D. Robinson, 239–263. Oxford: Oxford University Press.

Selting, Margret. 2000. "The Construction of Units in Conversational Talk". *Language in Society* 29 (4): 477–517.

Serianni, Luca, Valeria Della Valle, and Giuseppe Patota. 2021. *La grammatica italiana. Comunicazione*. Milano: Edizioni Scolastiche Bruno Mondadori.

Sidnell, Jack. 2012. "Turn-Continuation by Self and by Other". *Discourse Processes* 49 (3–4): 314–337.

Sidnell, Jack, and Tanya Stivers (eds). 2012. *The handbook of conversation analysis*. Oxford: Wiley-Blackwell.

Steensig, Jakob, Maria Jørgensen, Nicholas Mikkelsen, Karita Suomalainen, and Søren Sandager Sørensen. 2023. "Toward a Grammar of Danish Talk-in-Interaction: From Action Formation to Grammatical Description". *Research on Language and Social Interaction* 56 (2): 116–140.

Stivers, Tanya. 2021. "Is Conversation Built for Two? The Partitioning of Social Interaction". *Research on Language and Social Interaction* 54 (1): 1–19.

Stoenică, Ioana-Maria. 2020. *Actions et conduites mimo-gestuelles dans l'usage conversationnel des relatives en Français*. Bern: Peter Lang.

Stoenica, Ioana-Maria, and Simona Pekarek Doehler. 2020. "Relative-Clause Increments and the Management of Reference: A Multimodal Analysis of French Talk-in-Interaction". In *Emergent Syntax for Conversation: Clausal patterns and the organization of action*, ed. by Yael Maschler, Simona Pekarek Doehler, Jan Lindström, and Leelo Keevallik, 303–330. Amsterdam/Philadelphia: John Benjamins.

Thompson, Sandra A., and Elizabeth Couper-Kuhlen. 2005. "The Clause as a Locus of Grammar and Interaction". *Discourse Studies* 7 (4–5): 481–505.

Voghera, Miriam. 2017. *Dal parlato alla grammatica*. Roma: Carocci.

Vorreiter, Susanne. 2003. Turn continuations: Towards a cross-linguistic classification. *InLiSt, Interaction and Linguistic Structures* 39: 1–25.

 Walker, Gareth. 2004. "On Some Interactional and Phonetic Properties of Increments to Turns in Talk-in-Interaction". In *Sound Patterns in Interaction*, ed. by Elizabeth Couper-Kuhlen, and Cecilia E. Ford, 147–169. Amsterdam/Philadelphia: John Benjamins.

CHAPTER 14

Discussion

Where are we now and what are the next steps toward an Interactional Grammar?

Jakob Steensig,[1] Maria Jørgensen,[1] Jan Lindström,[2]
Karita Suomalainen[3] & Søren Sandager Sørensen[4]
[1] Aarhus University | [2] University of Helsinki | [3] Åbo Akademi University
| [4] University of Agder

The chapters of this volume have taken important first steps toward the ultimate goal that all contributors to this volume share: The creation of comprehensive grammars of talk-in-interaction in specific languages, which are based on, and true to, how language is used in interaction. In this discussion chapter, we extract the main new findings of the contributions to the volume, discuss how these findings might challenge received notions used in grammars, and make suggestions about the next steps that should be taken toward a truly interactional grammar.

Keywords: grammar, linguistics, language description, clauses, method, applied linguistics, data, action, format

1. Expansion of the grammar

A recurrent motive in the chapters of this volume is that there are aspects of language use that grammars do not usually deal with, which an Interactional Grammar must deal with. Most grammarians would agree that a comprehensive grammar should be able to account for all the kinds of units that can be found in a language, what language users do with these units, how they form larger units (e.g., words), and how speakers combine them to build utterances. Grammarians with a functional outlook would also emphasize the need to link the structural features of linguistic units to their contexts of use. But the interactional perspective laid out in the chapters of this volume calls for important expansions and a revised understanding of these "contexts". In the following, we will extract and discuss the main areas where this perspective adds new knowledge crucial to a grammatical account of a language.

https://doi.org/10.1075/slsi.37.14ste
© 2025 John Benjamins Publishing Company

1.1 Interaction-specific formats and uses of formats

Taking what people actually do in interaction seriously makes it clear that interactants use formats of expression that are not very well accounted for in grammars with a written language bias (Linell 2005). This is the case with, e.g., copula clauses with no audible copula verb (Sørensen), with the different versions of *oh* and *(do) you want* (Fox & Raymond), with *si* 'if'-clauses occurring without main clauses (Pekarek Doehler & Horlacher), and with clauses produced by more than one speaker (Calabria). In other cases, interactants use formats that have been described to some extent in non-interactional grammars, but in underspecified ways, or only cursorily. This is the case for verb constructions used in a particle-like manner, which is shown for Finnish imperatives (Suomalainen), German infinitive constructions used as requests (Gubina), phrasal units used as requests (Steensig), and phrasal units used as responses (Jørgensen). All these phenomena share the feature of deviating from the idealized expectation that a complete utterance should have the form of a complete clause or sentence. Using an Interactional Linguistic perspective, it is possible to describe these phenomena based on their own premises instead of relying on pre-established — and predetermined — categories and concepts. For example, instead of talking about *ellipsis*, which would consider non-clausal formats secondary to a clausal format, the approach of Interactional Linguistics makes it possible to show how these resources are built from the interactional context, and that clausal counterparts may even be considered secondary in meaning in some cases (Deppermann 2020; Thompson, Fox & Couper-Kuhlen 2015: 298–301).

Findings of this type show that these formats and their uses are not exceptional, which has the obvious consequence for grammar writing that such formats must be treated on a par with more canonical forms of expression. This may lead to the recognition and inclusion of "new" types of units in an Interactional Grammar. But, perhaps more importantly, the finding that grammatical formats are flexible and adaptable, and that they must be described as elements in a larger context of use, calls for a different type of comprehensive grammar.

1.2 Context and external syntax

It is a pervasive claim throughout this volume that an Interactional Grammar will have to go beyond the sentence, clause, or individual utterance, as the largest relevant unit for a grammatical description. This is shown to be the case in at least two ways in the volume's chapters. Some authors analyze formats that already go beyond the clause. This is the case especially for Mikkelsen's chapter, where the author shows how parenthetical inserts, which can be larger than clauses, are sensitive to where they are positioned in a storytelling, which is itself a large discourse unit.

The other insight that makes it necessary to go beyond the clause is that all the formats that are analyzed in this volume depend on the context they occur in. Sequential context is a crucial factor in the choice of grammatical format. For this reason, a truly Interactional Grammar needs to describe, in minute detail, the sequential context leading up to a particular format, and also what expectations a specific grammatical format in this context creates for what comes after. Such descriptions are presented in all the chapters, but the authors approach them in different ways.

The perhaps most far-reaching proposal is that the turns in which grammatical formats occur must be described as parts of an "external syntax", sensitive to the turn's position in a sequence of turns. This includes relating the formulation of a turn to (grammatical features of) other, preceding (hence *external*) turns. This is, perhaps, obvious in the case of responsive formats, such as *Oh* (Fox & Raymond) or responses to *wh*-questions (Jørgensen), but the claim also regards formats used for making initiating actions, e.g., requests (Steensig) and suggestions (Couper-Kuhlen & Thompson). Jørgensen and Steensig even present models for describing sequential patterns which look very much like syntactic models for clauses. Other contributions do not formalize the description to the same degree, but all chapters contain accurate descriptions of the sequential contexts and insist on their importance for an adequate structural account in the Grammar.

It is still an open question whether a formal "external syntax", including models of the type mentioned above, should be part of a comprehensive Interactional Grammar. What speaks in favor of its inclusion is that it forces the grammar writer (and reader) to discover and appreciate how grammatical formats are linked to, and even molded by, their sequential context. Such accounts of grammatically relevant sequential relations would allow for new insights into how context matters to the choice of specific grammatical formats, making the concept of "context" — already in use in traditional grammars — more tangible and operational. An argument against the inclusion of a formal "external syntax" would be that formal models might suggest that the choice of grammatical format is an automatic or mechanistic process. Many of the chapters demonstrate that this is not the case. Gubina's as well as Henricson and Lindström's contributions demonstrate how contextual features other than the sequences of actions may be relevant levels of description. Features such as the larger activity (like assessing or planning something) and participants' stances may be crucial too, and it may be difficult to include all these factors in a formal model. Furthermore, many of the described formats are shown to be flexible, adaptable, and emergent in ways that an overly generic structural model might not capture. As Schegloff (1996) argues, a grammar for talk-in-interaction might best be conceived of as a collection of "grammars" concerned with the specifics of sequential location for an action and the positions in a turn-constructional unit forming that action rather than a single, monolithic grammar with maximal generalizations.

1.3 Social action

One main focus of the entire volume is on investigating the relationship between social action and grammatical formats. But does this effort pay off when it comes to creating an Interactional Grammar? What does a social action perspective offer that would go missing if it were not used?

The chapters in the first section, *From Action to Grammar*, take a specific type of social action as their starting point and describe formats for performing this action. These analyses yield insights into why specific formats are chosen, and how the choice of grammatical format matters to action formation. Among the many contributions on directive-commissive actions (such as suggestions, requests, advice-giving, instructions), for instance, we gain insight into how specific verbal and modal constructions are used (Couper-Kuhlen & Thompson; Gubina; Steensig), and how slight modifications of the first part of a request and differences in the object being requested matter for the choice of format (Fox & Raymond). In the chapters by Jørgensen and Mikkelsen, we see how the different actions and their formats influence participants' understanding of the sequence or discourse unit in which they occur.

In the *From Grammar to Action* section, there is often a one-to-many (or sometimes many-to-many) relationship between format and action. This is perhaps especially clear in Fiedler's chapter, in which it is shown that interactants have a choice between two different formats for expressing the past tense of specific verbs in German, and that the choice is linked to different actions. Similarly, Suomalainen shows how imperative forms of specific verbs in Finnish can be part of performing different actions, and Pekarek Doehler and Horlacher take us through more or less free-standing versions of French 'if'-clauses, showing how the choice between these constructions hinges on the actions performed. Sørensen links the use of the copula verb in Danish (in its more or less audible versions) to assessments and to a focus on indexing contrasts. Henricson and Lindström show how pseudocleft constructions in Swedish can do advice-giving, instructing, assessing, and more. Calabria's analyses of other-extensions in Italian show how co-constructed utterances can be used to display understanding and affiliation with prior actions, as well as contribute to advance and modify the action that another participant started. The last two mentioned chapters point to the fact that not all formats perform actions that can be clearly identified on their occurrence, but that they contribute to action-building in more complex, but still describable, ways.

When reviewing all the chapters, we believe we can assert that understanding action in interaction casts a light on how grammatical form is intermeshed with (interactional) meaning, which is a perspective that goes missing in less actional accounts. The question is, of course, which role, and how big a role, action descriptions should play in an Interactional Grammar, and how it can be practically implemented. We return to that in the discussion of practical implications below.

1.4 Prosody and embodied actions

How far should an Interactional Grammar go in describing features of the production of grammatical formats that are sometimes not directly part of building and connecting words and morphemes, such as prosody and embodied actions?

Many reference grammars already have a section on phonetics and phonology, typically focusing on single sounds and the sound inventory of the language. Interactional Linguistics has a great track record of giving attention to prosodic detail and furthering the perspective that prosody plays a role in the creation of grammar for interaction, since prosody is omnipresent when articulating words and units (see Introduction, Section 3.1 this volume). In this volume, prosody and phonetics are not in the foreground, but the chapters by Fox and Raymond, Sørensen, and Henricson and Lindström provide insights into how differences in pronunciation matter to grammatical constructions and their unity. Two chapters review prosodic features and find that they do not matter crucially to the formats they are investigating (Couper-Kuhlen & Thompson; Steensig), but they agree that prosody and phonetics may indeed be an integral part of an Interactional Grammar.

It is perhaps more controversial whether embodied actions should have a place in an Interactional Grammar. At least five of the chapters grant embodied actions a central place in their accounts for the grammatical formats they focus on: Steensig claims that "embodied-only" requests should be part of the "external syntax" of requests in Danish, and Pekarek Doehler and Horlacher describe a type of French 'if'-clause constructions in which part of the syntax (the consequent of the conditional format) is comprised of embodied actions. Mikkelsen describes in detail how gaze and gesture might be treated as systematic resources in a grammar. Gubina describes embodied actions as main factors behind the use of deontic infinitives in German, and Calabria makes extensive use of the embodied orientations of interactants in her explication of other-extensions in Italian.

1.5 Projection, emergence, and Collaborative Grammar

It is a basic insight in Conversation Analysis and Interactional Linguistics that linguistic utterances, and other contributions in interaction, are produced in real time, and that this fact matters crucially to the construction of grammatical formats in interaction (e.g., Auer 2009; Sacks, Schegloff & Jefferson 1974; Schegloff 1996). There is an intricate interplay between the step-by-step construction of an utterance, the projection of where the utterance will go and how it can end, and the linguistic patterns that are available in a given language. This perspective plays a central role in chapters by Mikkelsen, Pekarek Doehler and Horlacher, Henricson and Lindström, and Calabria, who all deal with complex formats and how the projection of their development and completion is an integral part of the description of the format. Sørensen also discusses how the inclusion or non-inclusion of an audible copula verb contributes to projecting when and how a turn can end.

Several authors use the concept of *emergence* (Auer 2009; Hopper 1987) to highlight how formats are not necessarily the result of a generic structural device, but rather figure in ways that are adapted to their real-time context and to the incremental production of utterances and turns-at-talk. This is particularly the case in the chapters by Pekarek Doehler and Horlacher and by Calabria, where the emergence of the second part of an 'if'-clause in French (Pekarek Doehler & Horlacher) or of an other-extension (Calabria) can be seen as emerging out of the local circumstances and needs. Another possible use of *emergence* as a concept has to do with the development of formats, and how more "bleached" or "particle-like" formats have emerged as a result of uses in particular interactional contexts (see Auer & Pfänder 2011). This perspective, of "grammaticalization" or "pragmaticalization", is explicitly mentioned in the chapters by Fiedler, Suomalainen, and Pekarek Doehler and Horlacher as something that ought to be part of an Interactional Grammar.

Grammatical structures may be co-created by several interactants. This collaborative aspect of grammar-in-interaction is in focus in the chapter by Calabria, who explicitly calls for a "Collaborative Grammar" as an important aspect of an Interactional Grammar. This grammar should account for the documented formats that are, perhaps more typically than others, produced collaboratively in the language, and for the resources used in their production. Collaboration in turn construction is also in focus for Mikkelsen and Pekarek Doehler and Horlacher. They show how the question of who says what in their turn is important, and how co-constructed turns achieve something different from producing the "resulting structure" in its entirety in one turn.

In our view, there is no doubt that an Interactional Grammar must spell out the linguistic resources that are used to produce collaborative actions and formats.

How central this should be and which role a Collaborative Grammar might play in a comprehensive Interactional Grammar will be discussed below.

1.6 Identities, settings, larger activities, participation framework, and positioning

In the discussion so far, we have focused on action, sequence, projection, and local resources. But other interactional circumstances may also be central to the construction and understanding of the conditions under which grammatical formats are implemented. Gubina argues explicitly for the inclusion in the grammar of practical activities, agency, epistemic positioning, and embodied involvement. Mikkelsen focuses on the local epistemic positioning of participants and their involvement (the participation framework) as central for the use of parenthetical inserts into storytelling. Pekarek Doehler and Horlacher point to the degree of autonomy (or agency) of participants as central to understanding features of clause-combining. Henricson and Lindström show how the setting, the epistemic positioning of interactants, as well as the participation framework are oriented to when interactants choose pseudoclefts in the service of action construction.

All these things matter. The question, again, is how and where such factors should be included into a comprehensive Interactional Grammar.

2. Methodology, data and grammatical terminology

This section focuses on how the methodologies, data corpora, and terminologies of the authors in this volume add to earlier interactional analyses and grammar writing. The general methodologies of Conversation Analysis and Interactional Linguistics were presented in the introduction to this volume, where we also provided a brief account of the general aims and methods of descriptive linguistic grammar writing. Here, we will examine if, and how, the methodologies used in this volume differ from or align with those traditions.

2.1 Discovery procedures

All chapters in this volume investigate features in well-described languages known by the analysts. This made it possible to single out potentially meaningful actions and grammatical formats for analysis. No testing of hypotheses about sound segmentation, morphemes and allomorphs, or any other procedure that is used in the investigation of lesser described languages, was carried out. However, some degree of distributional analysis is inherent in any Conversation Analytic investigation, which locates elements (here, actions and/or grammatical formats) according to the environment they occur in. This means that examining the distribution of units becomes part of the process of finding out which differences matter to interactants. In the *From Action to Grammar* section of the volume, this is done by comparing different ways of carrying out the same action, or similar types of action, and in the *From Grammar to Action* section, the same grammatical format is examined in its different environments.

Several chapters quantify the number of instances in relation to contexts of use or to formal features. Fiedler's chapter on past tense forms in German talk-in-interaction uses quantification in a more systematic way — as part of the argument for the interactional relevance of particular forms. She claims that "[a]n initial quantitative analysis of grammatical units can be a fruitful procedure to detect units that speakers exploit on a regular basis to implement actions" (Fiedler this volume: 255). However, such detection must still be followed by qualitative analyses of the phenomena in question in order to "build collections that are not based on formal characteristic alone but on praxeological grounds" (Fiedler this volume: 255). Showing that interactional phenomena are frequent is a good argument for why interaction should matter for linguistic description. Fiedler's access to a big, searchable corpus also demonstrates the importance of interactional corpora-building, as it can make the task of counting instances in a systematic way easier and thereby provide useful background information.

Similarly, in Suomalainen's chapter, the data used is collected from an annotated corpus and with the help of a corpus search tool. The Finnish Arkisyn corpus that Suomalainen uses is morphosyntactically annotated, which makes it easy to create collections based on grammatical criteria. However, one potential risk in using grammatically annotated corpora is that, if the annotation is done based on existing grammars with a written language bias, not all relevant cases will show up in search results. This can produce a limited or even biased collection.

Other authors do not limit themselves to investigating formats or actions that are frequent in the language. For instance, "embodied-only" requests (Steensig), pseudoclefts (Henricson & Lindström), and some sub-types of 'if'-clause constructions (Pekarek Doehler & Horlacher) may not be very frequent in the languages studied, but the authors argue that their occurrence, as well as a thorough analysis of them, reveals important findings of specific contexts of use that an Interactional Grammar may benefit from including.

2.2 Interactional setting and grammatical description

Many authors mention that their results reflect the types of settings that occur in their data corpus. Henricson and Lindström claim that pseudoclefts appear in social situations "that feature a characteristic participation framework and linguistic register", typical of counseling discourse or building up speaker identities in accordance with such discourses (this volume: 367). The deontic infinitives described in Gubina's chapter are used for a specific type of instructional activity, and the author encourages future Interactional Grammar writing to consider whether differences in setting, activities, and participation framework influence "the analytical results developed based on the data" (this volume: 123).

The recommendation of the authors in this volume is that such links between formats, settings, and activities should be mentioned and acknowledged in Interactional Grammars, simply because they are part of the social meaning of many grammatical formats. Furthermore, several authors suggest that data corpora could be developed so that they reflect different interactional settings and activities in more systematic ways (for a corpus aiming to do this, see Küttner et al. 2024), which would allow a more systematic detection of genre-related features in the use of grammatical formats.

2.3 Grammatical concepts

In general, the authors of the chapters use well-established grammatical categories without deeply questioning them. This creates a connection to other grammar-writing traditions, which is both practical when it comes to communicating with other grammarians and, probably, inevitable. Throughout the volume, the Leipzig Glossing Rules (Comrie, Haspelmath & Bickel 2015) are used to highlight grammatical features of utterances in focus. This means that morphological categories (which this glossing system lists and abbreviates) are named and used in traditional ways, and that translations are provided in English. Additionally, labels for traditional parts of speech (e.g., nouns, verbs, and adjectives), syntactic constituents (e.g., subject, object) and utterance types (e.g., phrasal, interrogative, declarative, (pseudo)cleft, modal), etc., are used in the same sense as in other grammars of the languages in question. This reflects the fact that the authors have not found much of the established grammatical terminology problematic, which may be due to the volume's language selection, for which the categories provided in the Leipzig Glossing Rules are suitable. It is also a demanding task to revise established concepts, and using them may be a necessary steppingstone toward reconsidering them. As we have seen above, many authors found, however, that some grammatical categories could be used for a wider range of functions than traditionally thought (see Section 1 of this chapter), and that the boundaries between categories, like clauses and phrases (Sørensen), or between particles and verb constructions (Suomalainen; Pekarek Doehler & Horlacher), may be fuzzy.

However, some authors do go further and question otherwise accepted grammatical categories, or the received understanding of them. Pekarek Doehler and Horlacher challenge the idea that French 'if'-clauses are necessarily conditional, providing a more nuanced description of the processes that lead to "insubordination" than accounts that consider bi-clausal structures "primary". Steensig challenges the idea that interrogative formats are by default tied to questioning, showing that their use in requests for action makes a different response relevant than their use in requests for confirmation. Suomalainen challenges the assumption that imperatives are first and foremost used for directive actions and provides us with several cases in which second-person singular imperative forms are used as routinized or fixed expressions in actions that are not primarily directive.

These examples show how interactional descriptions can expand or inform linguistic concepts in ways that should matter not only for an Interactional Grammar, but for any serious account or theory of the phenomena in question.

3. Practicalities of grammar writing and applications of an Interactional Grammar

In this section, we turn to the practical implications of the findings in this volume, and ask how these findings may be structured, and how they may become useful for different target groups.

3.1 The structure of an Interactional Grammar

In the discussion parts of their chapters, the authors consider how their findings could be included in an Interactional Grammar of the language in question, and how such a grammar could be structured.

3.1.1 *Overall organization*

Most authors distinguish more or less explicitly between two sections in a prospective Interactional Grammar, reflecting the organization of the present volume: One section that starts with action descriptions and connects these to different grammatical formats, and one section that goes from grammatical formats to actions, the latter reflecting a traditional organizing principle in grammars, from form to meaning. A division into form and action like this can be found in Couper-Kuhlen and Selting (2018) and on Samtalegrammatik.dk (DanTIN 2024).

The chapter by Couper-Kuhlen and Thompson outlines this possibility in detail, envisioning the Interactional Grammar as an online, digital platform in the style of Samtalegrammatik.dk (DanTIN 2024). Every action description in the Action-to-Grammar section should be on attested actions, containing headings describing them *as* actions (in their case, 'Idea-Suggestions') and explanatory texts including descriptions of their sequential home environments. Following these descriptions, there would be examples of the different attested formats for the actions in question. These formats would have separate entries in the Grammar-to-Action section of the Grammar. From each of these formats there would be hyperlinks to the above-mentioned actions, but also to other actions that make use of the format. More complicated interactional features, such as sequences in sequences or how actions may morph into other actions, may, however, be difficult to capture in the two sections outlined above. To accommodate this, Couper-Kuhlen and Thompson raise the possibility of introducing a third dimension into the Grammar, treating how behavior fits "in a contingent sequence of moves" (this volume: 73; see also Enfield 2013: 31). Mikkelsen's chapter may be seen as an attempt to deal with exactly this dimension, specifically in its treatment of parenthetical inserts into stories that "do not follow neatly along a projected trajectory from beginning to end" (this volume: 217). Mikkelsen's analyses also point to verbal and embodied resources that must be described in the Grammar-to-Action part of the Grammar. This highlights another potential problem: A resource may need to be combined with other resources in complex ways, which makes it difficult to link resources and actions in unambiguous ways.

Fox and Raymond point out that in a digitally available Grammar, an efficient web of hyperlinks between actions and formats, and internally within the action and format parts, may "provide the kind of flexibility we envision being needed to incorporate maximal granularity" (this volume: 41). In order to do this in the way Fox and Raymond suggest, many small entries need to be made with hierarchically ordered levels of detail. This would make it possible for readers with different interests to find the level of description they need, and it would give the grammar writers the possibility to make new links or to link already existing descriptions to show newly found connections.

Sørensen discusses possible differences between a Grammar in book and web form. Readers of a "non-linear" web version, he argues, cannot be expected to read through a hierarchical account of a category or all pages that provide background information to an entry (on, for instance, the copula verb) before reading that entry. Therefore, a web version may need to include basic information about the category, with links to further descriptions. This will demand more (redundant) text than in a book, but, as Fox and Raymond also point out, allow for more flexibility.

3.1.2 *Contents: Action-to-Grammar and Grammar-to-Action*

Both Jørgensen and Steensig exemplify what syntactic models within the Grammar-to-Action part of a Grammar might look like, covering both the unit-internal ones and the external, sequentially based ones. Jørgensen maintains that traditional clause models illustrate grammatical information that is necessary to understand the choices interactants make between clausal and phrasal formats, but she emphasizes that models showing the items used in actual production of questioning and responsive actions should be developed. Similarly, Steensig points to a need for descriptions of syntactic and semantic processes (interrogatives, modal verbs) that are tied to the way they are used for creating different actions. To Jørgensen, information about embeddedness, epistemics, and the indication of social trouble belongs in the Action-to-Grammar section of the Grammar.

Sørensen discusses in detail how the existing description of zero copula in the Danish grammatical account Samtalegrammatik.dk (DanTIN 2024) may be expanded. Descriptions of all four realizations of the copula, and a "copula overview", should be added to the Grammar-to-Action section of the Grammar. In the Action-to-Grammar section, Sørensen suggests adding sections about assessments that use the different types of copula realizations. Sørensen's analyses furthermore demonstrate the need for developing sections on the semantics of predicate phrases, on verbless sentences, on the link between turn-taking and syntax, and on stress.

In line with Couper-Kuhlen and Thompson, Gubina points to the need to include more constraining factors in the entries of a Grammar than just the local sequential context, including the setting. She also emphasizes the need to include less frequent uses of grammatical formats (in her case, infrequent uses of deontic infinitives). It may be important for readers of the Grammar to know that such uses exist, but that they are documented in restricted settings. This, in turn, places demands on the corpus or the corpora used to inform the Grammar (see Section 2.2 above).

The chapters by Fiedler, Suomalainen, and Pekarek Doehler and Horlacher all deal primarily with the Grammar-to-Action section of the Grammar. Fiedler points to the need for a nuanced description of tense forms in the Grammar. It should be explained that the past-tense forms are not just about past time, but specific verbs use the two tense forms in different ways to carry out specific actions. She exemplifies how regularities in the use of specific verbs can be formulated as rules in the Grammar about how the verbs are used in clauses and in clause-combining. She also points to the need to document frequently used formats and to state which formats are not, or are only very rarely, used in talk-in-interaction. Suomalainen suggests that the imperative formats she is studying should be described as a continuum between directive and fixed, particle-like uses. She calls for specific Grammar entries for each format, with examples of their uses and with fact boxes about the semantics of specific verbs under these headings. Both Fiedler's and Suomalainen's descriptions may be entered more or less directly into existing grammars, which would, in turn, make such grammars truer to how grammatical formats are used in talk-in-interaction.

Pekarek Doehler and Horlacher argue that an Interactional Grammar's descriptions of clause-combining need to take both the attested formats (cline of insubordination) and their uses into account. In a similar way to Suomalainen, they suggest changing the Grammar's perspective from that of a taxonomy to, instead, deal with clines and emergent patterns. The different formats should be linked to recurrent actions using the format in question. Pekarek Doehler and Horlacher, furthermore, point to implications of their analyses for the descriptions of larger categories in the Grammar. Pre- versus post-positioning of adverbial clauses, incremental composition, co-construction, and prosody need to be described with a view to how these resources are used in interaction.

3.1.3 *Additional dimensions*

Several authors emphasize the need for considering dimensions that cut across formats, actions, and sequences: Epistemic and deontic stances, participation framework, settings, social problematicity, sequences of sequences, and reiteration. Two chapters make concrete proposals for how such further dimensions could be incorporated into an Interactional Grammar. Henricson and Lindström argue for four levels of description. Besides the levels of "turn design" and "action formation", which are comparable to the Grammar-to-Action and Action-to-Grammar sections described above, they emphasize the need for the levels of "discourse organization" (coherence and contrast) and "participation framework" (roles and activities). Further, Calabria introduces "Collaborative Grammar" as another central dimension in an Interactional Grammar. Calabria outlines a specific section introducing and explaining how collaborative constructions are basic to interaction and containing a list of collaborative practices. When it comes to the actions that are produced collaboratively, Calabria suggests that they can occur in an Action-to-Grammar section, where each such action description may follow "the equivalent action description for one speaker" (this volume: 416). Such follow-up sections would contribute to discussing recipiency and speech production in more dynamic ways.

3.2 The intended users of an Interactional Grammar

An Interactional Grammar is, by nature, a corrective to prescriptive grammars. Many of the attested formats in interaction deviate from conventions about written language. Given that the languages covered in this volume all have long traditions for grammars with a written language bias (Linell 2005), this is something that an Interactional Grammar may need to deal with up front, at least if the Grammar is intended for a wider audience than researchers and students who are already familiar with language as it is used in interaction.

One such audience may be grammarians from other traditions. Several authors mention this group, and some even point to the possibility of having more traditional descriptions on one level and on another level, more "interactionally sensitive" ones that people with an interest in the interactional nature of grammar can find links to. Other authors see the interactional nature of grammar, with its complexity in turn design, its dependence on context, and its fundamental temporal and social nature, as the place where the grammar starts. An Interactional Grammar could, in this view, be understood as a way of teaching, or arguing for, an interactional understanding of language as a reflection of human sociality.

Another user group which is mentioned by several authors are second-language teachers or learners. When the goal is to teach — or learn — a language for interactional purposes, descriptions of how the language is actually used are naturally very useful. This user group (especially the learners) may not know grammatical categories or the structure of grammar books beforehand.

The information contained in an Interactional Grammar would also matter for a range of other contexts where language and/or interaction takes place. Conversation Analysis has already contributed significantly to Applied Linguistics in various areas, including medical interaction, and other institutional interaction in many different types of settings (Kasper & Wagner 2014). Structuring an Interactional Grammar in a way where the use of different formats in various settings could be systematically represented may be a difficult task (see Section 3.1 above), but practitioners in various fields would benefit from having an Interactional Grammar available, even if their particular work setting is not directly represented.

Communicating to different audiences makes demands on how concepts should be used in an Interactional Grammar, and on how complex the descriptions and explanations can be. This points to the need to develop different layers or different versions of the Grammar, aimed at user groups with different backgrounds.

4. Possible next steps

The final question remains — how are we to proceed with the findings of the contributions in this volume? The obvious next steps will be to implement the descriptions in this volume into existing grammars, or, for languages where no attempts at constructing Interactional Grammars have been made as yet, to start building such grammars.

The physical format of a grammar matters. Several authors suggest online platforms with the possibilities of hypertext linking between different parts of the Grammar, rather than a more linear format, as in grammar books. The argument for a web-based format is that several approaches can exist side by side. It would be possible to access grammatical formats, with links to the actions they perform, and it would be possible to access social actions, with links to the different formats that can be used to perform these actions. This may also solve other issues by allowing for connections to different dimensions that authors of the volume emphasize as central to language use in interaction. Epistemics, participation framework, larger organizations (beyond sequences), the relation between specific actions or formats and settings, and Collaborative Grammar are all factors that influence grammar but may not be ascribable uniquely to specific actions or grammatical formats. It may be possible to link more general descriptions of such features to different actions and formats.

There is a further practical motivation to build a grammar as a network rather than as one linear account. The present volume is full of in-depth insights and proposals for how different actions and formats may fit into a comprehensive grammar. But no one seems to have a full overview of an entire, comprehensive grammar. Building the Grammar incrementally may be a solution to this lack of total overview. As pointed out in several chapters, a web-based Grammar may make it possible to both incorporate new findings and link to different levels, or granularities, of description, which may cater to different audiences. Some authors also question the notion of "comprehensive": the grammar of talk-in-interaction, as well as our understanding of it, develops all the time. It is a moving target, so there cannot be a final result. But the Grammar's incremental construction, based on the idea of networks of "grammars in a grammar" that complement one another, is perhaps compatible with the view that the nature of a Grammar for talk-in-interaction is non-finite. Hence, the goal is not completeness as such, but instead continued work towards the goal. This presupposes a new kind of conceptualization of "comprehensiveness", sensitive to detail in real language use. In the pursuit of our goal, we can only aim for a description of as much as we know at a certain point in time, and this will have to be updated and changed continuously. Not surprisingly, some formats and actions described in this volume occur only, or primarily, in specific contexts or settings. There may also be dialectal or sociolectal differences in grammar and action formation within what is normally understood as the same language. Does this mean that there are different grammars for the "same" language?

This leads us to another concern which is mentioned in several chapters (and above). What kind of data is needed as a basis for a comprehensive grammar as envisioned in this volume? The practical solution for the authors has been to use what they have. And this has worked; it has been possible to find grammatical formats and social actions that are recurrent and which the authors argue should be described in a comprehensive Interactional Grammar. On the other hand, what kind of data we use dictates what we can find. So, as mentioned above, there is a need for a more systematic organization of data to reflect different settings, activities, and language varieties. This might seem self-evident, but the new perspective here is that such data collection is intricately linked to efforts at constructing Interactional Grammars.

The authors use formalization of their findings to different degrees in their respective chapters, and we have discussed the pros and cons of such formalizations in the sections of this present chapter. Looking to the future, we argue that researchers trying to construct Interactional Grammars should experiment with models and formalizations of the patterns that they find. This is both a way of testing the generalizability of findings and of reaching out to — or starting discussions with — grammarians from other traditions.

In this discussion, other issues that may have to be clarified when writing Interactional Grammars have also emerged. The first issue has to do with the productivity of formats. Several formats described in this volume have a more literal usage on the one hand, and, on the other, a "bleached" or formulaic (particle-like) usage. All authors who describe such formats agree that an Interactional Grammar must contain and describe also the more formulaic usages; several chapters propose that the different usages can be put on a cline or continuum regarding their productivity or fixity. Exactly how this should be reflected in the Grammar is, however, still an open question. Are the more literal usages basic and the others derived, or are they just cases of differentiated formats linked to different actions? If an Interactional Grammar is to be used to say something about grammaticalization or pragmaticalization, this Grammar will have to take a stance on, and/or investigate, such questions.

The second issue is perhaps even more basic. Do the dimensions of prosody and embodied, nonverbal expression belong as integral parts in an Interactional Grammar? We believe that all authors agree that these dimensions are part of the research agenda of Interactional Linguistics. But, when writing grammars, we can either include different prosodic realizations and actions carried out with embodied means (partly or fully) as integrated elements in the grammar, or we can leave them out of the grammar while still acknowledging that they are part of meaning-making in social interaction. Grammar writers will have to either take on the challenge of integrating them and hope that it will contribute to a fuller picture of what is grammatical in interaction, or aim at building an Interactional Grammar that is less complex, with the risk of leaving out potentially important communicative resources.

There are, thus, many next steps and decisions that must be taken in order to construct Interactional Grammars of languages. We hope that this volume may inspire researchers to try it out, on larger or smaller scales, and that such attempts may bring about new perspectives to Interactional Linguistics and bring interactional perspectives into grammar writing.

References

Auer, Peter. 2009. "On-Line Syntax: Thoughts on the Temporality of Spoken Language." *Language Sciences* 31 (1): 1–13.

Auer, Peter, and Stefan Pfänder. 2011. "Constructions: Emergent or emerging?" In *Constructions: Emerging and Emergent*, ed. by Peter Auer and Stefan Pfänder, 1–21. Berlin: De Gruyter.

Comrie, Bernard, Martin Haspelmath, and Balthasar Bickel. 2015. "The Leipzig Glossing Rules: Conventions for Interlinear Morpheme-by-Morpheme Glosses." https://www.eva .mpg.de/lingua/pdf/Glossing-Rules.pdf (last visited 23/02-2025).

Couper-Kuhlen, Elizabeth, and Margret Selting. 2018. *Interactional Linguistics: Studying Language in Social Interaction*. Cambridge: Cambridge University Press.

DanTIN. 2024. "Samtalegrammatik.dk." 2024. https://samtalegrammatik.dk/.

Deppermann, Arnulf. 2020. "Lean Syntax: How Argument Structure Is Adapted to Its Interactive, Material, and Temporal Ecology." *Linguistische Berichte* 263: 255–294.

Hakulinen, Auli, Maria Vilkuna, Riitta Korhonen, Vesa Koivisto, Tarja Riitta Heinonen, and Irja Alho (eds). 2004. *Iso suomen kielioppi*. Suomalaisen Kirjallisuuden Seuran toimituksia 950. Helsinki: Suomalaisen Kirjallisuuden Seura.

Hopper, Paul J. 1987. "Emergent Grammar." *Proceedings of the Thirteenth Annual Meeting of the Berkeley Linguistics Society* 13: 139–57.

Kasper, Gabriele, and Johannes Wagner. 2014. "Conversation Analysis in Applied Linguistics." *Annual Review of Applied Linguistics* 34: 171–212.

Küttner, Uwe-A., Laurenz Kornfeld, Christina Mack, Lorenza Mondada, Jowita Rogowska, Giovanni Rossi, Marja-Leena Sorjonen, Matylda Weidner, and Jörg Zinken. 2024. "Introducing the 'Parallel European Corpus of Informal Interaction' (PECII): A Novel Resource for Exploring Cross-Situational and Cross-Linguistic Variability in Social Interaction." In *New Perspectives in Interactional Linguistic Research*, ed. by Margret Selting and Dagmar Barth-Weingarten, 132–60. Studies in Language and Social Interaction. Amsterdam: John Benjamins.

Linell, Per. 2005. *The Written Language Bias in Linguistics: Its Nature, Origins, and Transformations*. New York: Routledge.

Sacks, Harvey, Emanuel A. Schegloff, and Gail Jefferson. 1974. "A Simplest Systematics for the Organization of Turn-Taking for Conversation." *Language* 50 (4): 696–735.

Schegloff, Emanuel A. 1996. "Turn Organization: One Intersection of Grammar and Interaction." In *Interaction and Grammar*, ed. by Emanuel A. Schegloff, Elinor Ochs, and Sandra Thompson, 52–133. Cambridge: Cambridge University Press.

Thompson, Sandra A., Barbara A. Fox, and Elizabeth Couper-Kuhlen. 2015. *Grammar in Everyday Talk: Building Responsive Actions*. Cambridge: Cambridge University Press.

Index

A

acceptance, 32–34, 120
Acholi, 6
account, 52, 168, 250–251, 376
acknowledge, 64–66, 101, 382
action format, action formation, 11–14, 79, 127, 179–181, 230, 233–234, 247, 256–258, 323, 374, 387, 424, 433, 436 *see also* social action format
advice, 48–49, 66–68, 70–71, 374, 376–378, 385–387, 424
affiliation, 197, 207–209, 218, 282, 293, 344–345, 424
agency, 16, 47, 119, 131, 145, 166, 186, 427
alignment, 282, 287, 293, 336, 359, 396
Alto Perené, 6
American English, 10, 15, 49, 51, 66, 69, 185
assessment, 28–29, 198–199, 206, 215–218, 236–237, 242, 255, 282, 291–293, 305–306, 308–315, 319–320, 323–325, 376, 379–382

B

benefaction, beneficiary, 47, 81

C

change-of-state token, 27–30, 38, 125
clause, clausal, 9, 31–35, 96–99, 108–111, 157–160, 165–168, 201–203, 401, 422–424
compound TCU/turn-constructional unit, 338, 342, 368–369, 386–388
conditional, 56–57, 340, 355, 360, 425
construction grammar, 12
conversation analysis, 1, 7–8, 26, 426, 434
copula, 170, 369–372, 424, 426
corpus analysis, 6

D

Danish, 78–79, 156, 192, 301
deontic, 67, 143–146, 433
descriptive grammar, 3, 6, 68, 82, 393
discourse
act, 340, 349
identities, 92
marker, 235, 254, 265, 351–353
organization, 379, 388, 433
particle, 99, 284, 293
pattern, 12
structure, 229
unit, 193, 218, 422, 424

E

ellipsis, 97, 349, 422
embodied, embodiment, 4, 7, 39, 74, 78, 83–89, 92, 95, 111, 145, 176, 181, 193–194, 199, 218–219, 272, 335–339, 343–344, 354–356, 358, 411, 425, 436
emergence, emergent, 9, 12–13, 234, 266, 335–336, 339, 358–360, 414–415, 426
entitlement, 81
epistemic, epistemics, 10, 28, 81, 119, 132–133, 136, 145, 164, 166, 185, 253, 321, 383–386, 387, 412, 432–433
Ewe, 6

F

Finnish, 6–7, 96, 233, 266, 294–296
Finno-Ugric, 14
fixed expression(s), 9, 13, 70, 126, 269, 284, 293–296
formulaic, formulaicity 9, 18, 52, 233, 284, 287–288, 295–296, 338, 347, 351–353, 436
French, 18, 332–335, 373

G

German, 117, 228
glossing, 4, 429
grammar-in-action, 387
grammatical format(s), 3, 11–13, 48, 73, 169, 252, 254, 266, 294–295, 334, 385, 422–430

I

imperative, 5, 67, 73, 130, 139, 266, 410
increment(s), incremental, 9, 120, 339, 341–342, 393, 395–399, 402, 426
Indo-European, 14
insert sequence, 167, 174, 178–179
instruction, 81, 94, 129–133, 387, 416
insubordination, 334–336, 338–339, 351, 358–360, 430
interactional linguistics, 8–12, 74, 146, 193, 231, 400, 422, 425–427
interrogative 32, 41, 52, 61, 89, 99, 103, 109–112, 158, 184, 304, 349, 429–430
Italian, 4–5, 373, 394, 415

L

language learners, 74, 145, 234, 254, 257–258, 296, 434
Leipzig glossing, 4, 159, 429

M

Mandarin, 9
methodology, methodological, 7–8, 193–194, 255, 427–428
modal verbs, 52, 54–56, 58, 71, 83, 98–104, 118, 143
morphological, morphology, 2, 4, 79, 228, 266, 294, 323
morphosyntactic, morphosyntax, 34, 38, 268, 338, 399
multimodal conversation analysis, 124

Grammar in Action

multimodal, 220, 338, 357, 394
multiperson interaction, 394, 397, 405, 411–416

N
nexus, 158, 170
non-verbal 6, 84, 87, 120, 145, 436
noun phrase, 92, 96, 98, 170, 202, 232, 236–243, 257, 369

O
online syntax, 13
offers, 31–34, 47–49, 167–168, 352

P
participation framework, 293, 383, 388, 412, 415, 427, 429, 433
particles, 99, 106–107, 266, 295, 352, 422, 430
parts of speech, 79, 193, 429
phonological, phonology, 2, 303–304, 322
phrase, phrasal 4–6, 16, 32–34, 78, 89–98, 108, 111–112, 145, 155–158, 161–162, 166–177
    predicate phrase, 302–306, 311–314, 316–320 see also *noun phrase*
pre-announcement, 289–290
pre-sequence, 50, 87, 289–290, 293
project, 81, 86, 95, 105, 107–108, 129, 144, 202, 276

projection, projectability, 13, 109, 173, 194–196, 206, 359–360, 368, 373–376, 386–388, 426
prosody, 30, 38–39, 41, 73–74, 112, 185, 334, 336, 360, 368, 425

Q
question, 28, 155–158, 184, 187, 323, 349

R
recipiency, 293, 337, 359, 416
recruitment, 27, 40, 81–82, rejecting, 63–64
request, requests, 35–37, 80–82, 129–130, 138–141, 265, 267, 340–341
    action-guiding, 92–98
    corrective, 131–132, 136
    embodied only, 84–89
    for permission, 103, 124
    "item-only", 89–92, 95–98
reported speech, 195, 227, 230, 243–247, 251, 257, 416

S
samtalegrammatik.dk, 7, 79–80, 156–157, 161–162, 306–308, 322–326, 430–432
sequence, 173–174
    closure, 310
    expansion 36, 162
    of sequences, 73
    organization, 367, 379, 386, 388

sequential embeddedness, 159–160, 162, 164, 186
second language, 145–146, 234, 296
side sequence, 194–195, 212
social action format, 7, 11–12, 48, 79–80, 83–84, 88–89, 107, 110–112, 145–147, 172–175, 179–185, 193–194, 230, 256, 266
    see also action format
suggestion, 48, 50, 338
Swedish, 18, 373–375
syntax, 13, 169, 172–176, 182–183, 304
    external, 422–423
    inter-unit and intra-unit, 79, 84, 88–89, 94–95, 107–108, 111, 174–176, 180, 187

T
transcription conventions, 4, 124, 159, 232
turn design, 368, 388

W
written language bias, 3

X
X, the problem with, 35–37

Z
Zapotec, 6